THE COURSE OF LIFE

Volume VI

THE COURSE OF LIFE

Volume VI

Late Adulthood

Edited by
George H. Pollock, M.D., Ph.D.
Stanley I. Greenspan, M.D.

INTERNATIONAL UNIVERSITIES PRESS, INC.
Madison   Connecticut

This is a revised and expanded version of *The Course of Life: Psychoanalytic Contributions Toward Understanding Personality Development*, edited by Stanley I. Greenspan and George H. Pollock, published by the U.S. Government Printing Office, Washington, D.C., 1980.

Library of Congress Cataloging in Publication Data

The Course of life.

  "Revised and expanded version"—T.p. verso.
  Includes bibliographies and indexes.
  Contents: v. 1. Infancy — — v. 6
Late adulthood.
  1. Personality development. 2. Psychoanalysis.
3. Development psychology. I. Greenspan,
Stanley I. II. Pollock, George H.
[DNLM: 1. Human Development. 2. Personality
Development. 3. Psychoanalytic Theory.
WM 460.5.P3 C861]
BF698.C68 1993   155   88-28465
ISBN 0-8236-1123-X (v. 1)
ISBN 0-8236-1128-0 (v. 6)

Manufactured in the United States of America

Contents

List of Contributors

E. James Anthony, M.D., is Clinical Professor of Psychiatry and Human Behavior, George Washington University Medical School; Training and Supervising Analyst, Washington Psychoanalytic Institute, and Director, Child and Adolescent Psychotherapy, Chestnut Lodge, Rockville, Maryland.

Jean K. Carney, Ph.D., Instructor of Clinical Psychiatry and Behavioral Sciences, Northwestern University Medical School; Associate Attending, Scientific Staff, Humana Hospital–Michael Reese; private practice of psychoanalytic psychology, Chicago.

Bertram J. Cohler, Ph.D., William Rainey Harper Professor of Social Sciences, Professor, Departments of Psychology (Human Development), Education and Psychiatry, University of Chicago.

Paul A. Dewald, M.D., Clinical Professor of Psychiatry, St. Louis University School of Medicine; Training (Emeritus) and Supervising Analyst, St. Louis Psychoanalytic Institute.

John Frosch, M.D., Director Emeritus, Department of Psychiatry, Brookdale Hospital Medical Center; Editor Emeritus, *Journal of the American Psychoanalytic Association*.

Louis A. Gottschalk, M.D., Ph.D., Professor of Psychiatry, Social Science, and Social Ecology, University of California, Irvine, California; Training Analyst and Supervising Adult and Child Psychoanalyst, Southern California Psychoanalytic Institute, Los Angeles, California.

Roger L. Gould, M.D., Associate Clinical Professor of Psychiatry, UCLA.

Kalman J. Kaplan, Ph.D., Professor of Psychology, Wayne State University, Detroit; Research Associate, Department of Psychiatry, Humana Hospital–Michael Reese; private practice.

Helen Q. Kivnick, Ph.D., Associate Professor of Social Work, University of Minnesota, Minneapolis; Research Associate, Long-term Care Decisions Resources Center, School of Public Health, University of Minnesota.

Sara H. Koury, M.S.W., Department of Psychiatry, Dartmouth Medical School.

Morton A. Lieberman, Ph.D., Professor and Director, Aging and Mental Health Program, University of California, San Francisco.

Arnold H. Modell, M.D., Clinical Professor of Psychiatry, Harvard Medical School at the Beth Israel Hospital; Training and Supervising Analyst, Boston Psychoanalytic Institute.

Nancy A. O'Connor, Assistant Professor, School of Nursing, Oakland University, Rochester, Michigan.

Stanley R. Palombo, M.D., Teaching and Supervising Analyst, New York Freudian Society; Clinical Associate Professor of Psychiatry, George Washington University Medical School.

Herbert J. Schlesinger, Ph.D., Alfred J. and Monette C. Marrow Professor of Psychology, Emeritus, New School for Social Research, New York; Adjunct Professor of Psychology in Psychiatry, Cornell Medical College; Training and Supervising Analyst, Columbia Center for Psychoanalytic Training and Research; Lecturer in Psychiatry, Columbia University College of Physicians and Surgeons; Editor, Psychological Issues Monograph Series.

Clarence G. Schulz, M.D., Training and Supervising Analyst, Washington Psychoanalytic Institute; Assistant Professor of Psychiatry, The Johns Hopkins University School of Medicine; Teaching and Supervising Faculty, The Sheppard and Enoch Pratt Hospital, Baltimore.

Rebecca Shahmoon Shanok, M.S.W., Ph.D., Director, Early Childhood Group Therapy Program, Child Development Center, New York.

George E. Vaillant, M.D., Professor of Psychiatry, Harvard Medical School; Director, Study of Adult Development, Harvard University Health Services.

Edward A. Wolpert, M.D., Ph.D., Professor of Psychiatry, Rush Medical College; Senior Research Scholar, Rush Institute for Mental Well-Being; Consultant, Sonia Shanicman Orthogenic School, University of Chicago.

Preface

The transition from adolescence has occurred. The boundaries are as yet not fixed, and there are evidences of earlier psychological, emotional, and behavioral states that can make their appearance in a variety of contexts ranging from the negotiation of more stable patterns of intimacy to patterns stirred up by the development of one's own children. Biologically both genders have achieved what is considered to be completeness. Career, work, occupation, and role are identifiable. There is movement toward or establishment and further development of adult dyadic relationships.

Adult bio-psycho-social organization has taken place. Parenthood and significant and positive intimate relationships may be established. Work trajectories can be identified and responsible social roles may be assumed. There is movement toward psychological maturity, and the resolution of earlier developmental conflicts and possible psychological deficits. The personality organization expressing what is traditionally known as adult life—work, play and pleasure, sexual competency, a fairly clear definition of self—biologically, psychologically, and morally is in operation. Toward the middle to later phases of this stage of development, we begin to see evidences of the transition to the next life course.

In the phase known as middle age, we find significant transitions occurring: i.e., biologically we find the onset of menopause; we find changing attitudes toward self, significant others, and children who may be leaving home; parental responsibilities are less; and we find role shifts in the genders. Many women, freer in time and care of offspring, may seek to achieve new (or redefine earlier) goals. Socially we find variations in different economic, ethnic, and religious groups, although much research is needed to fill our knowledge gaps in this life course phase. There are concerns regarding financial planning, health care, relations with older parents, children who themselves now are married and have their own families, leisure activities, and health and longevity issues.

Research into the last phase of the life course, old age, is very active: geriatrics, geropsychology, geropsychiatry, and gerontology. This period is now by some investigators and clinicians divided into subphases, based on observations and studies that indicate important changes occur in different parts of the older-adult period: body shape, appearance, energy levels, memory functions, sleep patterns, sexual capacities, wisdom and world views, and abilities to use leisure or freed time. The distinctions between the young elderly, the older adult, and very aged individuals are more clearly evident. Relations with children, grandchildren, siblings, and friends evolve, reflecting the passage of a lifetime's knowledge on to others.

Authors from the first edition of *The Course of Life* have been given the opportunity to update their original papers. In addition, new contributions by outstanding investigators have been added for this revised and expanded edition.

1

Late Midlife Development

GEORGE E. VAILLANT, M.D.

SARA H. KOURY, M.S.W.

During adult life people change, but they do not change. On the one hand, part of the cultural history of the 1970s may be remembered as the discovery of "adult development," as dramatized by Gail Sheehy in *Passages.* On the other hand, science depends upon replication, and neither the retrospective work of Levinson (1978) nor the cross-sectional study of Gould (1978), upon which Sheehy's book was based, have been definitively replicated by prospective studies. Instead, as summarized by McCrae and Costa (1984), there is an impressive body of replicated data suggesting that the personalities of adults (at least as measured by trait psychologists) do *not* change. McCrae and Costa suggest that adult behavioral change will be more in accord with culturally determined age-graded expectancies.

We believe that the truth about adult development lies somewhere between the views of Sheehy and those of McCrae and Costa. If mankind does not truly experience a life cycle in the caterpillar-to-butterfly sense, we believe that adult personality is changed from within as well as from without. We doubt that the history of science will remember Erikson as a mere chronicler of contemporary, age-graded social mores. We doubt that the ages of man that Erikson—and Shakespeare before him—described are merely what history and culture allow the individual during a given life span. However, the evidence for uniform inner changes is less than perfect. Nevertheless, novelists, biographers, psychoanalysts, and historians "know" what the trait psychologists cannot prove, namely, that adults change during their adult life span.

1

Thus, in this chapter, we explore the utility of a modified version of Erikson's stages model (1950) to organize the process of psychosocial maturation in late middle age. To do this, since the sequential ordering of the earlier stages has already been documented for an inner city subsample (Vaillant and Milofsky, 1980), we focused on the later Eriksonian tasks: Generativity; Keeper of the Meaning, a subset of Generativity; and Integrity. We rated case records for age of completion of Eriksonian stages of development. The records rated are from the highly educated subsample of the Study of Adult Development, begun at the Harvard University Health Services in 1938 (Heath, 1945). During their sophomore year in college, the men of this group were selected for emotional and physical health. These men have been followed with questionnaires, phone calls, and interviews for half a century.

The Eriksonian Model

From the memories and associations of his adult patients, Sigmund Freud gave the developmental process of childhood a theoretical frame. In contrast, Erik Erikson studied childhood empirically. Erikson spent time, first as a student and then as an analysand, with Freud's daughter, Anna, an analyst who also studied real children. Then Erikson, as an investigator at Berkeley's Institute of Human Development, engaged in the empirical—not the theoretical or retrospective—study of childhood development. With this as a foundation, Erikson gave the developmental process of adulthood a theoretical frame—a frame which now informs our own empirical observations on adult development.

In this chapter, on the basis of a prospective empirical study of adult lives from ages 18 to 65 (Heath, 1945; Vaillant, 1977), we reexplore Erikson's theory as diagrammed in Figure 1. The individual stages of adult development have been described in detail elsewhere. Erikson (1959) has himself provided the best and most detailed account of the developmental sequences involved in the mastery of Identity. Goethals and Klos (1976) have best explicated the sequences involved in Intimacy, as has Levinson (1978) for Career Consolidation. Kotre (1984) has examined Generativity in detail, and Clayton (1975) has tried to explicate Erikson's final stage of Wisdom or Integrity. This chapter will add to a preliminary effort (Vaillant, 1977) to provide an empirical basis for Keeper of the Meaning.

It should be noted that in the life span model depicted in Figure 1, stages are functional, not structural. Eriksonian stages are enormously vulnerable to social and intrapsychic influences. Preordered biological development plays only a facilitative role at best. Erikson's stages reflect affective more than cognitive integration, and depend on identification and commitment rather than perception and cognition. Although our figure captures adult development as an ascending spiral, Carol Gilligan's metaphor of a pond with expanding ripples, each emanating from the last (personal communication, 1980), is an equally vivid and less goal-directed—less "masculine"—model of adult development.

It occurs to us, in considering our modified scheme, that Erikson's earlier stages—Industry, Identity, Intimacy, and Career Consolidation (see Figure 1)—are collecting processes, whereas the later stages appear to be giving-away processes. What do we mean by "collecting processes"? First, a sense of self is collected as the adolescent or young adult achieves Identity. Second, interpersonal skills and further sense of self obtain from the tasks of Intimacy—an ability to live with, depend on, care for, and yet *be* oneself with another human being. Third, during Career Consolidation (which appears to be a more extensive collecting process), people are gathering technical skills, role definitions, awards, achievements, and work-centered relationships, and are cementing them by commitment. The major task of Career Consolidation, then, must be to achieve an integrated state from which one can speak with authority, a phrase which must evolve in turn into a less patriarchal form: giving oneself away.

What allows the giving-away process, by which the career or autonomy of another becomes more important than one's own, to begin? By what developmental alchemy can Snow White's stepmother willingly participate in a generative process by which mirror-mirror-on-the-wall proclaims her daughter

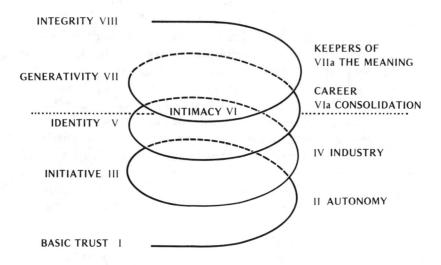

FIGURE 1. Schematic diagram of the "stages" in the modified Eriksonian model. Stage 5, *Identity,* included men who had mastered the subordinate task of adolescence—social, residential, and economic independence from the family of origin—for at least a decade. Identity involves who one cares to be. Stage 6, *Intimacy,* included men who had achieved tasks associated with stage 5 and had lived with another person in an interdependent and intimate fashion for ten years or more. Stage 6a, *Career Consolidation* (versus self-absorption), reflects a facet of Eriksonian identity that empirically is not usually achieved until after Stage 6 (Vaillant and Milofsky, 1980). This task includes making a clear, specialized career identification as measured by occupational satisfaction, commitment, and skill. Over the years Erikson puzzled about the placement of this facet of development (Erikson, 1959, 1974). In describing identity, he (1974) wrote, "In youth you find out what you *care to do* and who you *care to be*" (p. 124). Yet a moment's reflection on oneself or on the lives of young people today reminds us that discovery of what one cares *to do* is often not discovered until age 30. Stage 7. *Generativity,* included men who demonstrated a clear capacity for "care," "productivity," and "establishing and guiding the next generation." Stage 7a, *Keeper of the Meaning* (versus rigidity), removes from Erikson's concept of generativity the development of those characteristics that have less to do with "care" and more to do with "wisdom" and the preservation of culture. Stage 8, *Integrity,* is epitomized by accepting one's life as it has been lived and letting it go with equanimity. Erikson appeared uncertain whether the virtue of wisdom belonged to stage 7 or stage 8.

fairer than herself? By what maturational legerdemain can Ibsen's master builder willingly step aside so that his apprentice can take his place? To refuse is to risk stagnation—Erikson's antonym for generativity.

What triggers the giving away? We would suggest that the so-called crisis of midlife is a catalyst for reassessment. Such developmental unrest, really more a midlife task than a crisis, forces us to look with wonder again at where we are and how we came to be here. In this reassessment the individual takes stock, noting what he has and wondering why he does not have other things. It is this dangerous doubt, this reorienting opportunity, that makes a person get out the old lists, the old life-achievement criteria, and decide that the painfully won partnership, the parental authority, mirror-mirror's approval, the master builder's license all lose their savor unless shared, unless spiced with the new task of becoming mentor to the next generation, unless each is somehow given away.

Other traumatic life events—an untimely death, a historical catastrophe, a serious illness—may trigger the same process. "Off-time" events can lead to a nonsequential order of reviewing what has been accomplished, what has been collected, how one has succeeded or failed. Being forced to reflect—observing oneself from a different vantage point—a person begins to take pause and wonder again. This self-reflection can never be decreed by society or culture. It comes from within, as does looking where one is going.

The Method of Study

If they are to be taken seriously, theoretical constructs require empirical documentation. The empirical methodology of our study was as follows. A rater read through the dossier assembled on each man; chronologically sequential, these dossiers ran to several hundred pages. All of the subjects responded to an identical series of questionnaires, each of which was administered to the men when they were roughly the same age. The interview protocols were semistructured. Thus, unlike biographies, the data sets on which the men could be compared were very similar. Each time the rater found an item or quotation that illustrated a stage or task depicted in Figure 1, this evidence was recorded. When enough evidence was gathered so that the rater felt certain that a given task was completed, the process of collecting evidence was stopped. A mean age of "task completion" was estimated from averaging the ages at which each item, quote or vignette was recorded.

The process of adult development, we observe, is not nearly as tidy as it is for "Piagetian" cognitive development in children. For example, Gilligan (1982) and others have suggested that women's and perhaps men's lives do not unfold in strict sequence as the spiral of Figure 1 suggests, but rather can unfold with several of the tasks being addressed in parallel. Certainly in the lives of the men in our sample the next stage was begun long before the present one was complete. In individual cases items in the sequence could even be reversed. In our sample 31 percent of men were involved in Career Consolidation and 10 percent in Generativity before Intimacy was achieved. Nevertheless, Figure 2 illustrates that for the majority of our sample, and in a previous study of inner city men (Vaillant and Milofsky, 1980), a pattern of sequential maturation emerges and in no case was Generativity observed to precede Career Consolidation.

By way of example, Table 1 gives an idea of the range in age of task completion that was observed for the illustrative cases to be presented here. These three men—Carey, Mason, and Young—varied greatly in character, in interests, in professional lives, and in life course. One, Mr. Mason, was a solitary if not lonely youth who had rich fantasies and developed creative interests which provided him comfort, but which were seen as potential sources of trouble by the professionals who evaluated him in college. Through his adult life Mr. Mason, a sculptor both in reality and in metaphor, used his self-soothing abilities as a base on which to build his marriage, his family life, his artistic career, and two successful businesses.

The second man, Dr. Carey, was a far more gregarious member of a close family; both of his parents were social workers in the spirit if not the letter of the phrase. As a 13-year-old, Dr. Carey made a commitment to a life of good works. All

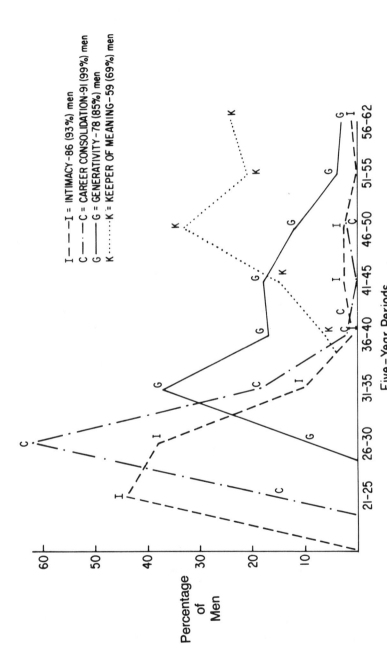

I — — — I = INTIMACY–86 (93%) men
C — · — C = CAREER CONSOLIDATION–91 (99%) men
G ———— G = GENERATIVITY – 78 (85%) men
K ·········· K = KEEPER OF MEANING–59 (69%) men

FIGURE 2. The distribution of ages at which 92 men appeared to master four principal developmental tasks of adulthood.

TABLE 1
Contrasting Ages of Task Completion for the Three Illustrative Cases

Life Task	Age at Estimated Task Completion		
	Carey	Mason	Young
Intimacy	23/35*	27/33*	53
Career Consolidation	28/26	30/37	not yet
Generativity	34/42	36/58	not yet
Keeper of the Meaning	?/44	57	60
Integrity	45	60	not yet

*Alternate ages reflect the choice of different raters.

life events—and there were severe setbacks for this man—were moderated by his relationship to people, on both a personal and a professional level.

But both Mason and Carey collected a sense of themselves, consolidated it, and shared it with discretion throughout the forty-five years they have revealed themselves to the study. In contrast, Mr. Young collected little and had little to give away. (His case will be used to illustrate how biographical vignettes can be used to document that a man has failed to complete a given life task.)

Generativity

Assuming that the reassessment and wondering have begun, let us look at the first giving away: Generativity. The emphasis at this stage is upon the harvesting of Intimacy and Career Consolidation—the ability to be in an individual relationship where one "cares" for the other's needs and simultaneously respects the other's autonomy. When in Ibsen's *A Doll's House* Nora slams the door, moving herself on from a cloying intimacy to finding herself again in a career, her behavior is *just* but no longer *caring*. As Erikson stresses, however, with Generativity care again comes to the fore. Kotre (1984), in his illuminating book on generativity, sums the task up succinctly. It is "to invest one's substance in forms of life and work that will outlive the self" (p. 10).

In trying to settle this matter of relationship, there must be wonder at what has been attained and at what has been produced—the children, the careers, the marriages. These productions can no longer be seen as extensions of the self, or as belonging to the self, but rather as something autonomous to which there is connection and for which one must be somehow responsible.

At this point the reader may argue that most mothers of young children are generative. Our reply would be that young children are viewed partially as possessions and that there is a critical difference, after all, between caretaking and caregiving. Generativity is not changing one's daughter's diapers but, as it were, giving her away in marriage. As the "child's" separateness is recognized and as the relationship with the child is reexamined, one begins to wonder at what has been derived from the relationship. To quote Erikson (1950) again, "The fashionable insistence on dramatizing the dependence of children on adults often blinds us to the dependence of the older generation on the younger one. Mature man [and woman] needs to be needed, and maturity needs guidance as well as encouragement from what has been produced and must be taken care of" (pp. 266–267).

As Erikson suggests, the capacity to accept such guidance requires intrapsychic maturation. In Alcoholics Anonymous, a "pigeon"—a newly recovering alcoholic—is defined as "someone who came along just in time to keep his sponsor sober," yet a "sponsor" is generative and a "pigeon" is not. By accepting the proferred assistance, the pigeon, like any person in need of a caregiving relationship, is providing a reason and a way for new behaviors to be experienced by the giver. The pigeon in need stimulates fresh growth in the sponsor. Thus, by beginning to share, by allowing the younger generation to see what it is that can be offered, the mature individual becomes needed in a fresh way, and through such relationships begins to give the self away.

Let us look at generativity through the lives of the three subjects mentioned above. In his forties, besides beginning the process of launching his adolescent children, Mr. Mason was the chief executive officer of a company he had created. (Despite his capitalist stigma, the entrepreneur who creates jobs and meets a payroll is nonetheless often appreciated, by city fathers and workers alike.) Generativity for Mr. Mason was also documented by his questionnaire responses: At age 49 (1968), when asked how he felt about campus demonstrators, this arch-Republican wrote, "I find many of the protesting young people very interesting and potentially constructive members of society." In contrast, at the same age Mr. Young (without children and himself a salaried employee unpromoted for twenty years), when asked the same question, wrote with muted despair, "I feel that we truly have a lost generation. Some of today's youth have already impaired their health, lost their minds, and seemingly destroyed their future. What bothers me most is the fact that every complaint and protest strives to destroy anything and everything and build nothing in its place." In short, Mr. Mason was enriched and Mr. Young impoverished by the next generation.

At age 59, when asked which of his career accomplishments he believed offered others the most, Mr. Mason wrote, "Teaching others the advantages of relaxing and enjoying life and getting something done at the same time." At that point his life consisted of running two companies part time, while also maintaining both a farm and an artistic career. These four jobs were balanced by Mason's capacity to pause to take adventurous vacations. At age 63, Mr. Mason's interviewer wrote that he was planning "to help some young friends of his start a business. He thought he would just leave it [the running of the business] up to them, and would provide, apparently, a good deal of the capital." In short, he planned in retirement to continue to give himself away.

Dr. Carey illustrates a life that violates our general experience that the Eriksonian tasks must be completed in a set sequential order, but then there was no one else in our study quite like him. At age 23, when asked about his "fitness for his present work" (at that time it was medical school), Carey wrote, "children fascinate me; I enjoy playing and working with them. . . . I get along well with children, enjoy taking the time to amuse them or circumvent their distrust of doctors; . . . I'm patient enough to do with children what many other people do not have time nor patience to do." When challenged that this was just Career Consolidation, the rater argued for Generativity by observing, "this is more than Career Consolidation . . . . it is what a pediatrician does, but there is such a sense of self-content in his words. It is not the career, but the relationship and the skill in the relationship that comes through." Later, at age 26, when Dr. Carey was asked what was stimulating or interesting about his career, he replied, "the opportunity for aid to children through increasing parental understanding"; for him the meaning of work was "to make a contribution to the community."

Perhaps because of contracting polio just as he finished his residency, and perhaps in spite of it, what Dr. Carey liked most about work by age 32 was not just the care of young children but the teaching of medical students. Despite being confined to a wheelchair, he did not use teaching as an excuse to withdraw from being a full-time clinician. Nor did his pleasure in teaching come from didactic instruction, from self-aggrandizing *telling*. It came instead from enabling, from, as it were, giving the self away. Dr. Carey wrote that the nurses and the medical students he taught "seem to respond to increased participation and responsibility, in contrast to the passive roles they often play in our clinics." Later in the same questionnaire he wrote, "the fact that I work from a wheelchair means that others can get not only professional help but some measure of comfort from my carrying on as if nothing had happened." Mentorship means to show and to share, not simply to tell.

In contrast, Mr. Young illustrated Self-absorption, not Career Consolidation; Stagnation, not Generativity. Further, he did not achieve Intimacy until late in his life. This inhibited growth occurred despite a socially privileged mother, a private boarding school education, and intellectual gifts superior to those of most of his college classmates. Indeed, the study staff had given Mr. Mason at age 23 a "C" and Mr. Young at age 21 an "A" for psychological stability. But psychological instability does not preclude Generativity, nor does mental health guarantee it. Perhaps the reader can find sense in the paradox that Young's mother had described her son as "a grown man when he was two years old," whereas Mason's adolescence extended through college. Maturation takes time and often surprises us.

In college Young had wanted to become an automotive engineer. Instead, in thirty years this man had never risen beyond a $15,000-a-year position (1978 dollars) in a White Plains heating and plumbing firm, and his occupational responsibility never changed. Nevertheless, he took pleasure from his job because, as in childhood, he could build things. He told his interviewer in detail and with real enthusiasm about furnaces; but he could not share a sense of responsibility for other people or show pride or commitment regarding his work role.

The study anthropologist noticed that Mr. Young at age 29 was still "closely tied to his mother, unwilling to make new associations." At 49 he was still unmarried and living only a few blocks from where his parents had lived. His life revolved around his pets, not his relationships. He was too busy for the latter. "Catering to six cats," he assured me, "can be a big affair."

Evidence that Mr. Young had not dealt with Career Consolidation is illustrated by his writing, at age 29, "The brevity of my answers leads me to believe that my life must have been pretty substandard. It still may be . . . my fondness for my current work has grown less. I seem to be stuck in a rut." At age 50 Young, unpromoted, still worked twelve hours a day and often on Saturdays; but he complained that his work involved the "same old rat race." At 58, when asked what contribution he had made that would benefit others, he wrote, "If there is one, I can't imagine what it would be."

Nor did Mr. Young ever come to grips with Generativity. He felt perpetually out of control of his life. At 46, when far less socially privileged and less intellectually gifted classmates were firmly established in the upper middle class, Young still worked for his plumbing firm and wrote, "I feel deeply inadequate . . . . I have always felt that I could never sell myself." At age 60, after thirty-five years of work, what he liked best about his job were "the good benefits and the lack of stress."

At 50 Mr. Young's philosophy over rough spots was, "I know I can't be my brother's keeper." But he tried to be a good citizen and care for his Westchester neighbors who, like him, commuted to work on the Merritt Parkway. "We try to look out for each other," he told the interviewer, but then added that in his twenty years of commuting he had never actually seen anyone on the parkway except strangers. Gratuitously, he added that one day a drunk had wandered out on the parkway and twenty cars had run over him before anybody stopped.

Keeper of the Meaning

Consider the second giving away: Keeper of the Meaning. As with Generativity, this stage is characterized by a combination of Intimacy and Career Consolidation, but here the emphasis is on the skills acquired in Career Consolidation: organizational skills and informational skills. It seems that the wonder in this stage is with the collective products of mankind (the culture in which one lives and its institutions rather than in the development of its children). Generativity and its virtue, care, require taking care of one rather than another. Keeper of the Meaning and its virtue, wisdom, involve a more nonpartisan and less personal approach to others. Wisdom, unlike care, means not taking sides. As in the passage from Intimacy to Career Consolidation, care is supplanted once more by justice. Although in his writing Erikson often fuses care and wisdom, Kotre (1984) separates the two components by observing that the targets of Eriksonian Generativity must be *both* "the culture and the disciple, and the mentor must hold the two in balance" (p. 14). If he puts too much into his disciples, "he neglects and dilutes the culture's central symbols. But if the preservation of culture is paramount he makes anonymous receptacles of disciples" (p. 14). What differentiates the stage of Keeper of the Meaning from that of Generativity is that the individual, rather than caring for a younger person in a direct, future-oriented relationship, is speaking for past cultural achievements and is guiding groups, organizations, and bodies of people toward their preservation. As one study subject said at age 55, " 'Passing on the torch' and exposure of civilized values to children has always been of importance to me but it has increased with each ensuing year." The organizers and preservers of the Olympic Games traditions must play a very different role from that of the "generative" coaches and trainers.

The work of Keeper of the Meaning lies in resolving what one has that can be returned to the cultural trust. As an illustration, Henry Ford, having ripped small-town America asunder by his generative creation of the Ford Motor Company, tried to preserve America's past in his wistful construction of Greenfield Village. Charles Lindbergh in midlife was a pathfinder, a creative architect of global air routes to the far corners of the Pacific; in late life he devoted his efforts to global conservation movements in order to protect the very Shangri-las he had helped to endanger.

At 57 Mr. Mason—a man of few words—was asked if he viewed the world fit for grandchildren. "Yes—Awareness of problems of food—population—ecology will bring solutions." Two years later, at age 59, Mr. Mason reported his new duties: "Chairman of Rhode Island Chapter of the Nature Conservancy, Member of the Board and Chairman of the Planning Committee of the Mystic Seaport Maritime Museum, a Trustee of the Rhode Island Environmental Trust." Stodgy, perhaps, for a man who had once built and navigated a Phoenician trireme through Newport Harbor and had shot lions in Africa—but adults do change, in that they can attempt to repay the world for their personal pleasure by preserving their pleasure in the form of a cultural trust.

At 19 Dr. Carey, our model of precocious development, had already so impressed the college psychiatrist that the latter wrote, "[Carey] dislikes intolerance in either an intellectual or moral form, and it is distinctly part of his manner of thought to hold problems away from himself and to judge them in a rather intellectual manner. One could not say that he was coldly objective, but certainly he has an ability to relegate his emotional attitude to a secondary role . . . . One never has the impression that he is merely saying words and one would always attend to what he was saying because of the strength of the thought." In other words, in college Dr. Carey could already speak with the dispassionate yet plausible authority that we associate with wisdom. At age 32 Dr. Carey wrote of his work motivations: "to add an iota to pediatric knowledge, the sum totals of which may ultimately aid more than the patients I see personally." In using this statement as evidence for stage achievement, the rater was not scoring pious words but tangible behavior. When Dr. Carey died, an endowment for a professorship was raised to perpetuate his lifelong contribution to pediatrics.

Of course, it is not just the change in ourselves that drives us to play new roles; the roles that others play in our lives also transform us. But this transformation often takes place from within, through internalization, rather than from without, through simple socialization or instruction. If internalization fails to take place, we fail to grow. It was hard to tell what had stunted the growth of Mr. Young. In his adolescence, both of his parents had let him down; five years apart, they had had severe depressions. At 11, when his father had been hospitalized for the first time, Young had stopped believing in God. In midlife, at the death of a friend, Mr. Young wrote, "Do not ask for whom the Bell tolls; it tolls for thee"; every time a friend died, he wrote, he felt he had lost a piece of himself. At age 49 he could still say, like a 10-year-old boy, "My main interest is in things mechanical." Our guess—and it is no more than a guess—is that his parents' weakness left him guilty and ambivalent, unable to take leave of them and unable to take in much that was new. We stop growing when our human losses are no longer replaced. Parenthetically, in forty years of follow-up there was no evidence that Mr. Young ever met the criteria for an inherited major depressive disorder.

But how, over the latter course of the adult life span, are losses replaced? The difficulty with internalized people and values is that they are analogous to buried geological strata. Thus, the relationship can be laid down in one era, covered up for years, and then decades later exposed—a variant of what Pollock (1977) has called "the mourning-liberation process." In Young's adolescence, his parents had been profoundly disappointing; any earlier contribution they had made to his sense of self remained buried during the first three decades of his adulthood. But then, in late midlife, he was able to use them as a source of identification, a turn perhaps facilitated by their death. In his early fifties, Young's mother died and shortly after, he married. For him, intimacy was a developmental task postponed but not abandoned. He also gave up his agnosticism, maintained since the age of 11, and returned to the Episcopal Church. Young returned to his parents' church not just as a regular church member, but as a deacon and an active trustee of an Episcopalian retirement home (a responsibility that required twenty hours a week of volunteer service). Now asked if he saw the world as a fit place for grandchildren, Mr. Young wrote, "America is essentially a Christian country; and, here, at least, I believe grandchildren will have as much chance as my generation did." This man who for thirty-five years had seen his job as "humdrum," valuable only for its pension plan not for its use to others, this man who had concerned himself with cats and pipes and heating plants rather than with people, was now happily married for over a decade and was finally playing a sustaining role in passing on a religious heritage that for forty years had meant nothing to him.

Dr. Carey illustrated the metaphorical, if catalytic and inspirational, process of internalization more concretely. When asked to "give a character sketch of the person whom you most admire," he wrote, "The person whom I most admire is dead. Before I had polio he was in that category; since then, he is even more firmly entrenched. He is Franklin D. Roosevelt. A character sketch by me would be superfluous. But imbibing what he left behind at Warm Springs, Georgia has given me additional impetus to do, in a small way, as much for others as that great Harvard man with polio did in his time." Modern psychology needs to learn more about how people "imbibe" other people.

Integrity

Finally, let us attend to the last giving away: Erikson's final life stage, Integrity, or letting go. If one has given one's collected skills and authority to people directly and indirectly, what is left to give, then, is simply the self. The load has been lightened. The "possessions" are given away. The voice that once spoke with authority is now muted. Letting go and giving one-self away is not just to serve immortality but is also a means of accepting with understanding the small deaths that make up aging.

Examining the process of dying is like the inspection of an old, old tree; one can mourn the branches that no longer are, or one can admire and accept the craggy simplicity that remains. Such developmental simplicity is different from poverty, and this is important to understand. Aging is change—development and decay simultaneously. The widower has willed his mansion to the church and lives now in a single room. The bedridden widow has given away the perennials from her formal garden and now tends only the potted plants in the nursing home sunroom. The image should bring to mind not the derelict's residential hotel room but the dignified, if spartan, cubicle of Thomas Merton, Mother Theresa, or Francis of Assisi. As one study subject wrote, "It's a brand new marvelous life for us and we love it. We no longer own a car or a lawnmower or a hedgeclipper or a dog." Gender is gone, and one is celibate not just because the body ceases to arouse and be aroused, not just from renunciation, but because the self is no longer "sticky." Androgynous Tiresias does not fall in love, nor does anyone fall in love with him.

Before one can consider the self as something that can be given up, before one can let go, one needs first to have been impressed by the *wonder* of the self. There needs to be a sense of it, a full sense of it. Thus, Erikson (1950) defines Integrity as "the ego's accrued assurance of its proclivity for order and meaning. . . . It is the acceptance of one's one and only life cycle as something that had to be and that, by necessity, is permitted of no substitutions" (p. 268). A Shaker song puts this all into rhyme:

'Tis a gift to be simple, 'tis a gift to be free
'Tis a gift to come down where we ought to be. . . .
To turn, turn will be a delight
'Til by turning, turning we come round right."

Most simply, that is what Integrity is—realizing that right here, right now, this life and this lifetime, is exactly where one ought to be. Of course, there is too much wonder in life for anything to be merely right or wrong.

A study subject described this task well when he asked, "What's the difference between a guy who at his final conscious moment before death has a nostalgic grin on his face as if to say, 'Boy, I sure squeezed that lemon,' and the other man who fights for every last breath in an effort to turn time back to some nagging unfinished business? Damned if I know, but I sure think it's worth thinking about."

In response to the question of had he developed a sense of mortality, Mr. Mason wrote at age 59: "I believe in a continuation of the life of the soul or perhaps self but I don't know how it will happen. I also realize that my present life has a limit of probably fifteen to twenty years more at most. I accept this." At 61 he perceived that his legacy to the world would be "some accomplishments in conservation and three very satisfactory children and one grandchild." Thus, in twelve words this laconic sculptor conveyed that he would go on by having given himself away both to the cultural, natural trust and to the personal, human chain. Together, there is a feeling of continuity, of being one part of a progression.

Dr. Carey began the work of Integrity early. By age 26 the not yet crippled physician had already told the study "that no matter what personal difficulty I struggle with, others have survived worse; and that, fundamentally, there is a force of events which will carry us through, even though at personal sacrifices." At age 32, newly liberated from six months in an iron lung and knowing that he would never walk again, Dr. Carey responded as follows to the TAT card of a youth with a violin:

> Here is a young boy who . . . started out in college with brilliant prospects, a bright future but becomes disillusioned with life, morose, despondent . . . and decides to end his life. He is apprehended in the process of jumping from a tall building. As he does so, he closes his eyes. Before them flashes a panorama of his past life, hopes, aspirations, sadness of . . . failure, realizing then the agony of being cornered . . . the despondency to end his own life.
>
> He'll be examined by a psychiatrist and placed in a hospital for therapy. After months, his goals will be altered. After being in therapy

a little longer, he'll get what he wants. He'll be able to be of use to society again, to go on to achieve that which . . . in later years will be satisfying.

Again, at age 52, the progressively crippled Dr. Carey set forth the challenge of old age: "The frustration of seeing what needs to be done and how to do it but being unable to carry it out because of physical limitations imposed by bedsores on top of paraplegia has been one of the daily pervading problems of my life in the last four years." But at 55 Dr. Carey answered his own challenge. "I have coped . . . by limiting my activities (occupational and social) to the essential ones and the ones that [are] within the scope of my abilities." At 57, although he was slowly dying from pulmonary failure, he wrote that the last five years had been the happiest of his life. "I came to a new sense of fruition and peace with self, wife and children." He speaks of peace, and his actions portray it. During this time he had "let go" his stamp collection that had absorbed him for half a century and given it to his son. A year before his death, in describing to an interviewer his "risky anesthesia" and recent operation, Dr. Carey said, "Every group gives percentages for people who will die: one out of three will get cancer, one out of five will get heart disease—but in reality 'one out of one will die'—everybody is mortal."

Conclusion

If the stages through Career Consolidation are an accumulative process, then it seems that the development included in Generativity through Integrity is a stripping-away process, allowing one to leave life as it was entered—simple, free, right. In *War and Peace,* Tolstoy allows Pierre Bezukhov to express this crescendo and decrescendo: "there is an inner freedom that is not controlled by circumstance . . . . wealth, power, life, all the things men organize and protect with such care, are valueless except for the joy with which one is able to abandon them" (quoted in Troyat, 1967, p. 327). Erikson (1950) also brings it back to the beginning again—to childhood: "And it seems possible to further paraphrase the relation of adult integrity and infantile trust by saying that healthy children will not fear life if their elders have integrity enough not to fear death" (p. 269).

Since certain tasks of adult development—for example, setting adolescent children free and burrying the dead—must be repeated from generation to generation, it is possible to hypothesize a compliant nervous system. It is possible to wonder, as does Margaret Mead (1972), about the reasons that humankind is unique among mammals in living beyond the age of effective reproduction: is it to provide for the survival of children and grandchildren through social instead of biological mechanisms? If so, it is possible to imagine a brain whose evolution as well as experience changes with adulthood; but we do not know this for a fact. It is worth reflecting, however, that although the Neanderthal and the Cro-Magnon had the same cranial capacity, Neanderthals died before the age of 40, while Cro-Magnons lived often into the sixth decade. Was this prolonged life span related in any way to their development of art and human culture? We do not know, but we think it is certainly worth thinking about.

Bernice Neugarten (1979) cautions us that "the themes of adulthood . . . do not in truth emerge at only given moments in life, each to be resolved and then put behind as if they were beads on a chain" and that we oversimplify if we try "to describe adulthood as a series of discrete and neatly bounded stages, as if adult life were a staircase" (p. 891). Nevertheless, we hope that we have shown the value of using a modified Eriksonian model of development as a scaffold, a stage on which to imagine the life span. Indeed, the theater is a particularly useful metaphor for conceptualizing adult development, because it stresses both capacity and commitment, both role and biology. On the one hand, we are no more than good repertory actors, who become the roles in which we are rehearsed by life and society. For the metaphor of the stage stresses plasticity, an ability to enact; in this sense, much of adult development is an illusion. In part the task of becoming a Keeper of the Meaning is just a role offered by life. The death of our parents rehearses us in the role of executor; our grandchildren's questions drive us to attend to genealogies, and the growth of cataracts compels us to replace the task of duck shooting with that of conservation. Actors and artists often have the ability to play many roles, and CPA's and engineers often do not. Thus, it is no accident that Mr. Young was an engineer and an accountant and seemed never to change, at least not until rather late in life, while Mr. Mason was an artist with a flair for the dramatic—and for adult development.

On the other hand, some roles require change from within. Actors must evolve into certain roles; and these roles once played may change them forever. Lawrence Olivier's MMPI probably did not change after he played Hamlet, and yet one wonders if afterward he could ever be the same again. It is no accident that a study subject had to wait until after retirement, until he was established in his community as a very model Keeper of the Meaning, to play the leading roles in *King Lear* and *On Golden Pond*. But these enactments only rehearsed him in what he had to become. "All the world's a stage," wrote Shakespeare, " . . . and one man in his time plays many parts, his acts being seven ages" (*As You Like It*, act 1, scene 7).

Lawrence Kohlberg (1973) and Jane Loevinger (1976) take the most extreme position, and suggest that young adults develop in a single direction and that previous roles must be mastered before we can play new ones. In this view, until one has played Holden Caulfield one cannot play Hamlet; until one has played Hamlet, not Polonius; and Lear can be played only after one has mastered Polonius. If true, then we belong to more than a repertory theater and Shakespeare's cross-cultural life span psychology may yet be established. We may one day discover the neurobiological underpinnings for why living past the age of reproduction gave Cro-Magnons an evolutionary advantage.

In any case, good biography always finds change and development. So do great novels and convincing drama. And yet the trait psychologists offer numbers to prove that people do not change. We believe that something has been lost in their data reduction. We are impressed that the wisest course has been that taken by Erikson and by Kegan (1982). Both have steered a middle course between the presumably neurologically wired, universal developmental model of Kohlberg and Loevinger and the static view that nothing of interest happens to adult personality after 18 that is not dictated by the external environment.

References

Clayton, P. V. (1975), Erikson's theory of human development as it applies to the aged: Wisdom as contradictive cognition. *Human Devel.*, 18:119–128.

Erikson, E. (1950), *Childhood and Society.* Rev. ed. New York: Norton, 1963.

——— (1959), Identity and the Life Cycle. *Psychological Issues*, Monograph 1. New York: International Universities Press.

——— (1974), *Dimensions of a New Identity: The 1973 Jefferson Lectures.* New York: Norton.

Gilligan, C. (1982), *In a Different Voice.* Cambridge: Harvard University Press.

Goethals, G. W., & Klös, D. S. (1976), *Experiencing Youth.* Boston: Little, Brown.

Gould, R. (1978), *Transformations.* New York: Simon & Schuster.

Heath, C. (1945), *What People Are.* Cambridge: Harvard University Press.

Kegan, R. (1982), *The Evolving Self.* Cambridge: Harvard University Press.

Kohlberg, L. (1973), Continuities in childhood and adult moral development revisited. In: *Life-Span Developmental Psychology: Personality and Socialization*, ed. P. B. Baltes & K. W. Schaie. New York: Academic Press, pp. 180–204.

Kotre, J. (1984), *Outliving the Self.* Baltimore: Johns Hopkins University Press.

Levinson, D. J. (1978), *The Seasons of a Man's Life.* New York: Knopf.

Loevinger, J. (1976), *Ego Development.* San Francisco: Jossey-Bass.

McCrae, R. R., & Costa, P. T. (1984), *Emerging Lives, Enduring Dispositions.* Boston: Little, Brown.

Mead, M. (1972), Long living in cross-cultural perspective. Paper presented at the Gerontological Society, San Juan, Puerto Rico.

Neugarten, B. (1979), Time, age and the life cycle. *Amer. Psychiat.*, 136:887–894.

Pollock, G. H. (1977), The mourning process and creative organizational change. *J. Amer. Psychoanal. Assn.*, 25:3–34.

Sheehy, G. (1977), *Passages.* New York: Dutton.

Troyat, H. (1967), *Tolstoy.* Garden City, N.J.: Doubleday.

Vaillant, G. E. (1977), *Adaptation to Life.* Boston: Little, Brown.

——— Milofsky, E. S. (1980), Natural history of male psychological health: IX. Empirical evidence for Erikson's model of the life cycle. *Amer. J. Psychiat.*, 137:1348–1359.

2

Transformational Tasks in Adulthood

ROGER L. GOULD, M.D.

Adult Development and the Sense of Time

In childhood, separation anxiety is a basic fact and hence a fundamental concept of developmental theory. It underlies self-object theory and the psychoanalytic understanding of defenses, structure formation, and the oedipal constellation. It is during childhood that we are formed, largely by our parents, with separation anxiety mediating every step of that formation.

During adulthood we transform ourselves. No one else carries the task of our change or bears responsibility for it, though many continue to affect us and unfortunately many continue to try to change or control us. It is that lonely transformational process I speak to in this chapter. Although separation anxiety remains a powerful controlling dynamic during adulthood, I index my ideas about adult development with a related but different phenomenon and concept—the sense of time. It is the changing sense of time that characterizes epochs of the adult cycle in a manner homologous to the epochs in childhood that are characterized by different expressions and responses to separation anxiety.

The changing sense of time between ages 16 and 50 is easy to describe from the aerial view of a life cycle perspective. Before leaving the family around the age of 18, we feel protected from life but surrounded by restrictions in payment for that protection. We never quite believe we'll ever get out of the family world, and in that sense we live in a timeless capsule. The future is a fantasy space that possibly may not exist.

23

Upon leaving home, we break out into that space and begin to believe emotionally that we are really starting a trip with an endless amount of time ahead of us, if in fact we aren't being tricked—that is, if we aren't going to be snatched back unexpectedly but inevitably into old family time and the restrictive codes and world view that are part of that time.

By the time we're in our twenties, we've established that we have made it out of the family but have not yet made it into a solid form of adult life. Because of all the new decisions and novel experiences that come with setting up new adult enterprises, our time sense, when we're being successful, is one of movement along a chosen path that leads linearly to some obscure prize decades into the future. There is plenty of time, but we're still in a hurry once we've developed a clearer, often socially stereotyped, picture of where we want to be then.

By the end of our twenties we have a past as adults, as well as a future. The prize is a decade closer, but the pathway, no longer linear, branches out in all directions. Choices are becoming more complex, and it is clear that there is not enough time to take all of the pathways. That becomes frustrating because we can still see the many forks in the road, as the vision of the linear pathway is lost forever. Between our midthirties and midforties we experience a sense of urgency in conjunction with an emotional awareness of our own mortality. Time to get the prize is running out. There is an urgency to act, while at the same time there is a fundamental question about the prize. What is it? Is it an illusion? Is the prize a Zen riddle—to become aware that there is no prize, to let go of something in order to be reborn into a new order?

From roughly the midforties on, there is an awareness of death somewhere in the future, and this thought is never again far off the screen of consciousness. How time is spent becomes a matter of great importance.

Time, illusion, death, prize—these are the colors necessary to paint the aerial view of adulthood. We'll just finish that picture before we come down to earth. Death, an ugly word and an ugly prospect, is the organizing principle. As young children we were protected from the idea of death by staying physically close to our omnipotent parents. Later we were able to be physically separate as long as we internalized their values, regulations, and world view. When we followed these codes, we were safe. When we transgressed we felt endangered—superego anxiety. The strict adherence to the codes and regulations that was demanded by our parents allowed us to participate in the *illusion of absolute safety*. In the aerial view, we see that that illusion is finally destroyed in the midlife period, when we become emotionally (rather than just intellectually) aware of our mortality.

The prize, I believe, is final liberation from strict adherence to the remaining codes and regulations enforced by the people who formed us—in other words, a full ranging mind to know inner and outer experience without fear of encountering sacrosanct preconceptions that can't be questioned. Preconceptions, habits, routines, patterns, old object images, old self-images, and unquestioned values are the structures supporting and composing the illusion of absolute safety. They act as constrictions on learning from experience. They are the closed doors to split-off parts of the self, and they release anxiety when forcibly or even voluntarily breached.

From the aerial view we have composed a picture half from observation and half from imagination. The imagination contributes the idealized portion—a full-ranging mind free to know inner and outer experience. This implies liberation from blind adherence to all past codes and the abandonment of the illusion of absolute safety. Probably none of us ever gets there—certainly not by 45. But observations also contribute to the portrait, and what I see is that we are striving toward that ideal and that in fact we are driven toward the ideal. We are driven to live off our own experience and impose a view of reality that fits that current experience in order to expunge a view of reality infected by past imperatives. It is freedom we are struggling toward; internal freedom to have a full experience of life and to connect all the affects with all the split-off ideas—these are the terms of Freud's earliest formulation (1893)—or, in the modern vernacular, to reach a "higher consciousness."

Now back to earth. How does this happen in everyday life, while we are busy making a living, raising children, and figuring out how to keep a love relationship working? When not trying to do it directly via therapy or consciousness-raising activities such as est or the range of activities collected under the rubric of holistic medicine, we do it automatically, in response to a set of signals that sets a transformational process into motion. First we'll look at the transformational process in general, and then, in the section following that, we'll look more specifically at a transformation in the case of Nicole.

Transformational Process: General Remarks

For me it is axiomatic that we never reach our full potential as humans and that we never stop pushing in that direction. While moving along at a steady pace, we take the sense of movement for granted and feel pretty good about life, subject of course to daily fluctuations and periodic tragedies. When blocked and at war with ourselves, we recognize that growth is a conflict; one part of us is ready to move, while another part threatens disaster if we dare grasp for a little more life. When blocked for too long we become negative, sour joy killers dwelling on our inadequacies, consumed with envy, and blaming others because we can't admit the powerful split within us. When about to move out of the stuck position or, ironically, when in the midst of a large or accelerated move, we experience anxiety and often other baffling psychosomatic symptoms that warn us to remain within the constricted, safe self, the self as others have known us.

As we expand into our potential, we disturb the patterns within ourselves (our defensive system) and our relationship to those close to us (we're part of their defenses; if we stay the same, that part of their world *feels* safe). That is why growth is a conflict—the disturbance of safety patterns; and that is why growth is more than learning and practicing new activities or changing by willpower. It is a transformation of self in which we enlarge the license to be, but only after going through mythical dangers in order to arrive at a new secure place that will in turn be left when feelings of stagnation and claustrophobia initiate still another cycle.

It is easy to dismiss the concept of growth toward full potential as an idealistic and simple-minded notion or to misidentify growth with its degraded forms—an activity for the weekend (the fastest growth occurs without clothes) or the "hip" rationale for an insensitive and hostile divorce action. Growth is too valuable a concept to be forfeited to these misinterpretations.

What unseen thing inside our heads changes when we grow—a chemical balance, a neuronal pattern, a new patch of cross-connections? Nobody knows! But what we do know is that we feel and behave differently as we come to believe differently. If we believe we are a bad person, we'll act accordingly, brusque and insensitive to others, overdefensive when anyone gets close, and exquisitely sensitive to intimations that our "badness" is showing. If we believe we are good and loving, we act accordingly. Our habits and patterns, those behaviors that others call our personality, are organized by what we believe to be true. Similarly, if we believe the world is hostile we act and feel differently about life than if we conceive of the world as benign or at least neutral. Our subjective experience of life and our behaviors are governed by literally thousands of beliefs and ideas that compose the map used for interpreting the events of our life (including our own mental events). When we grow, we correct a belief that has restricted and restrained us unnecessarily. For example, when we learn as young people that there is no universal law requiring us to be what our parents want us to be, we are released to explore and experiment. A door to a new level of consciousness is opened once we've discovered we were wrong about our interpretation of life. We can learn from our current experience and current reading and no longer have to ward off contradictions to that idea.

In short, in order to grow we have to discover we were wrong about something we took for granted or modify some rule or regulation we imposed upon ourselves too rigidly. These ideas are sometimes the values we were taught as children, or stereotypes reinforced by a particular subculture, or impressions from childhood transmuted into commandments by an immature mind. They all add up to what life is supposed to be and what we are supposed to be. They are sturdy structures that resist the wear of contradictory experience because, like any habit, we feel safe when living within them and feel endangered and awkward when modifying them—just like learning a new tennis stroke.

Transformational Process: The Case of Nicole

The following involves a two-year period in the life of Nicole. At 37 she had been married for fifteen years and had four boys ranging in age from 5 to 13. Vivacious, bright, and charming, she excuded warmth and vitality within an overall sense of solid settledness. Her love of life included the telling of embroidered stories of her children's mishaps and discoveries—"No, Jay, jellyfish are not like grape jelly"—and an unusually strong pleasure in her husband's company. Not only were they the best of friends, who talked about everything and shared their inner lives, but they were great lovers on their frequent trips, when spontaneity and zaniness ruled the day. He was a successful, hard-working professional, and they had abundant material goods which they saw as toys to play with. Up until the time Nicole was 36, she had been very happy to be a full-time mother and wife. That way of life afforded her enough time for her own activities, which included photography, reading several books a week, and being on the board of an experimental school. Quite literate, she appreciated the witty remarks of others as well as her own, as when referring to her life with four small boys she joked, "My life is one long interrupted conversation."

Around 36, she found herself wanting more out of life, partly in response to her youngest child's entering school and partly in order to use and develop certain talents that she regards as vital parts of herself. She wanted to add something to her established life. She didn't want to leave home or give up what she enjoyed and was not offended by the work of motherhood and wifehood, though she was, like most educated women, uncomfortable when at cocktail parties she was asked what she does in life only to find herself summarily labeled "just a housewife." On a conscious level, there was a rather simple and easy solution in sight; since she enjoyed photography and had been doing quite a bit for the school, she thought she might develop a part-time photography business. She could do it on her own time and still be at home during crucial hours. She had a darkroom constructed in the guest room. One thing led to another, and soon an acting agency wanted to give her steady work as a portrait photographer.

At this point, on the verge of commercial success, she put aside her photography. She bumped into her first internal obstacle! Working and selling herself commercially contradicted her unrecognized dream of continuing to be the special loved child who displayed and was stroked for being talented but never really had to discipline herself or compromise her talents in order to earn an income. Her mother's labeling her photographic interest as "only a phase" strengthened, but did not cause, the internal obstacle—the unconscious self-definition. While she was in the midst of working through this internal struggle, her parents moved in. They took over the room that was her studio and darkroom, and just as the sink and plumbing were being ripped out she developed a pain in her stomach. Within a day she was in bed with a full-blown peptic ulcer that required medication and care for over two weeks. During the next year she didn't touch her photographic equipment (which had been moved to an outside darkroom) nor unsheathe her camera. Several months later her father developed symptoms of brain cancer and died within six months. His illness occupied all of her life, and his loss was grieved painfully. He was not only a father, but also a very special intellectual companion steeped in opera, who had the same love of life that she herself has, and that her mother has never been able to join. She was left with her own grief, the absence of a buffer between herself and her mother, and the grief of her four children, who dearly loved their grandfather.

Her mother's grief seemed to overpower her. She was unable to express her own feelings when her mother was around. Her mother intimated that only she, who had lost her husband, had the right to express her loss, while Nicole, who had a loving husband and a young family, had no such right. It was partly because of the burden of her mother's presence six months after the death of her father that she came to see me, and partly because she felt stuck in life. She was constantly on the verge of ulcer symptoms that were unresponsive to special diet and medication.

At this point, being stuck meant that the self-initiated expansion of her self-definition allowing her to exercise her talent in photography in a way recognized by the world had felt the impact of a conjunction of inner and outer forces—her wish to remain the pure, admired, talented, untested little girl—and the lack of support by her mother, who perceived her as a mere dilettante. The symbolic ripping out of her right to be a photographer, together with the ripping out of the plumbing, translated into a visceral ripping peptic ulcer.

Underlying the first rather benign articulated version of the internal obstacle—her unwillingness to relinquish the ideal of the special child—were a series of more basic ideas. The first mythic fear Nicole encountered was that her desire to have things for herself would erupt uncontrollably as she took the first step into the life of a worker-mother. Since she had been "too good" as a girl and gave "too much" to her children and husband in return for their praise, she feared that she would totally and suddenly abandon the role of mother and wife that she was beginning to feel as obligatory. On the other hand, she recognized that she enjoyed her home and family. Only after articulating her fear of having a greedy, impulsive child inside of her that would act contrary to her conscious wishes to integrate a work life with her role as mother and wife was she able to emotionally credit the intellectual awareness that she had options along the way and that she was not really in an either/or position. With that, she began to process the greedy child images as archaic parts of herself that, once acknowledged, were controllable. The internal dialogue helped her understand how much she had worked for her mother's love. Following this insight, she had a burst of fury at her mother, who continues to subvert her efforts at individuation by rewarding her only when she's a sweet little girl-woman.

Following this episode, she found she could no longer read the two or three books a week she had been used to. Out of a fuzzy-headed inability to concentrate, she began to see images of Lady Macbeth and a knife plunging into a body. She came in touch with her second mythic fear—that in order to grow, she'd have to fight her mother to the death. With this access to the demonic fury within her came the realization that the killer imagery belonged to an archaic battle displaced onto a rather vacuous current battle with her mother, who indeed stood against her change but was in no position to stop her. The greedy child image was transmogrified to the killer-child or killer-mother image, but once held up to the light of day that imagery could no longer endure or control so absolutely.

Next Nicole discovered that she believed she could change only if she could get her mother to change. Though she resented having to perform for affection and praise, she also felt she was hooked on it. When she went against her mother, and her mother was cold in response, she first felt a pain in her stomach, then felt very angry, and then felt a tremendous urge to retreat and do what her mother wanted. Since her mother's withdrawal of love was translated so viscerally to Nicole's belly, she believed she could go forward only if she could get her mother to admire, understand, and endorse her quest for individuality. If she could convince her mother to praise her for becoming a worker-mother, then she could avoid a primitive, unconscious kill-or-be-killed battle and silence the pain in her stomach, which made her feel her mother must ultimately win any such contest.

When Nicole asked herself why she didn't explore and proceed along various career lines experimentally, she discovered the next myth blocking her path. The first reason that came to her was the somewhat cliched notion of the fear of rejection; i.e., she might ask for a job and not get it. Imagining what that might feel like, she saw how much she wanted to preserve her own self-image as the special child who is loved and adored and gets whatever she wants because she is so vivacious and bright. A deeper understanding followed—being accepted, not rejected, was what really kept her from experimenting. Going to work in *any* real job was a step down from the position of the special child. Being accepted on the job was a loss both of the special child image of the past and of the future ideal career. Since she was so good with words, she had reason to believe that she could write better than many contemporary authors. Someday she hoped to use that talent. Any beginning job in photography would be interpreted as a relinquishment of that talent, as if once entering the work world she wasn't free to move from her initial entry position.

She next challenged the myth that her children and husband could not survive without her and that she couldn't survive without them. She went on a trip to New York with a friend. On the way to the airport she had a strange worry that a killer earthquake might occur in Los Angeles while she was away.

Having worked her way through these first five mythic obstacles, she encountered a powerful ulcer attack. It left her in bed for two days with stomach pains. The strength of her marriage rested in part on total openness with her husband. She had been discussing with him her conflicts and desires about work, and, as she became more firm in her resolve, she felt him to be irritated with her and rejecting sexually. She was no longer able to turn him on in the way she had before. At first she thought that she was doing something terribly wrong; then she thought there was something terribly wrong with him. He must hate women, since he had such a hateful mother! Her ulcer began to act up as she came to the conclusion that her husband's reaction faced her with a choice. He was saying indirectly that she must be a caretaker and mother to him or he would be angry and punish her. She was not allowed to be a competent working woman in this marriage. To have her new self was to lose her man. To be sick in bed with stomach pains was both the result of a conflict that seemed unresolvable and at the same time an attempt to resolve the conflict by instituting a relationship with her husband in which she was the taken-care-of child and no longer the threatening, competent woman. At the same time, it got her out of the resentful role of having to be a mother to him while not being allowed to be a self to herself. She responded to his transitory shift as if it were an absolute statement that he did not give her permission to change. He temporarily became the absolute authority, replacing the original absolute authority over her growth—i.e., her mother. At the moment she went to bed she thoroughly believed the myth that some other person could continue to have veto power over her path of growth and development and that she had encountered that person in the husband she totally trusted. Her best friend had become her worst enemy.

The corollary is that men, the generic, will not allow women to leave home. She unraveled that overgeneralization. In response to her stress and ambivalence about being on the school's executive board, her husband suggested she resign. Her first interpretation was that her enemy wanted to return her to the confines of the home—barefoot and pregnant, as it were. As she probed the matter more deeply, she discovered that she wanted to resign from the board because sitting on it was tied to the identity of mother-volunteer rather than mother-worker. After that insight she remembered the conversation with her husband differently and saw how she selectively fed him information and almost demanded that he suggest she resign from the board in order to displace the responsibility for the decision onto him, and to battle with him rather than with her own separation-depression fears about leaving the major role of her adult life. She was pleasantly surprised to find that when she admitted to herself that she wanted money and power in her own right, she was able to resign from the board in a diplomatic and timely way; as a surprise bonus the surging sense of power that resulted made her feel more sexual and lustful. She engaged in some pattern-breaking sexual activities with her husband that previously had been fantasies, and after an initial period of wish-fulfilling fear that she become hypersexual and go crazy with lust, she settled into a new, more open and uninhibited sexual life with her husband—the kind she had been able to have on trips with him but had never been able to carry off at home, while surrounded by children's bedrooms.

Following this, she began to believe that she was too strong for her husband and that in fact she must sacrifice her capacities to his ego. This was the reverse of her earlier belief that he was a strong, potentially destructive enemy who refused her permission to grow. Now he was viewed as really a little boy, and the sacrifice she resented most was sacrificing the joyous, fun-loving part of herself, her frivolous and zany side, to his solid, sometimes too serious view of life and pleasure. This seemed too much the reverse of what went on between her joyous father and her drab mother. Nicole's belief that her strength was overpowering alternated with its opposite—the belief that she was really a little girl. If she showed her strength clearly, she would lose her husband as the promised protector if her strength waned. It was after dealing with this complicated set of barrier images that she once again took up photography.

This brought to the surface the next false belief; that now that she had everything—a direction, internal permission to work, and a family that loved her—it was too much! She was too lucky; some evil must befall her. The evil eye must be there, watching and waiting for the time to strike.

After challenging this superstition by taking a fun trip with her husband, a rather intellectualized barrier surfaced. Was she becoming her mother? Was she voluntarily leaving her children just as her mother had voluntarily worked? Did she really want a career outside the home, or was she doing unto her children what was done unto her, in some kind of primitive retaliation?

Several weeks later her career interest took a twist, and she found herself with a whole series of creative ideas about travel agencies that might better customize service. Ideas were coming to her fast and furiously out of the blue. She might become a travel agent, work part-time, still be around for the children, and at the same time participate in a great love of hers—traveling. A very exciting integration was taking place. She knew she was ready to act and called several travel agencies to find out how to get trained. While talking to one agency owner, who was about to get rid of her, she said, "You really ought to interview me, I'm quite special!" This took him by surprise, and he listened to her account of why she would be a good travel agent. He interviewed her, and within two weeks she was working happily and with a great deal of energy and vitality.

Interestingly, on the way home from work the first day, she felt compelled to buy perfume she didn't need. Then she encountered the last false belief standing in her way. She believed that her mode of selling and servicing clients would have to be like her saleswoman mother, who survived the Great Depression by exploiting every opportunity to make a little more.

She came to recognize how different she was from her mother. Her own style and ethics and life circumstances were different. She would service all of her clients the way she would service her friends and family.

After beginning to work, she still had members of her family to deal with. Her mother's belittling, nonsupportive attempt to return her to a little-girl role failed. Nicole dealt with it firmly and understandingly, though she resented her mother's envy. Her husband had some minor trouble adjusting, complained of her being unavailable around dinnertime, and had a mild hypochondriacal attack. These responses by the important people in her life were seen clearly because she was not hampered by the false belief that she was not entitled to do what she found herself doing. She had gone through an odyssey of mythic barriers and arrived at a self-definition that included her right to work; from this perspective the reverberations in her family were seen for what they were: temporary responses to change—not evidence that what she was doing was wrong, dangerous, or destructive. She had truly undergone a transformation of self.

The transformation of Nicole was large and dramatic. We encounter such transformations when we make career changes or major substitutions in our love life. But we also undergo transformations on an everyday basis that are not as dramatic, but just as compelling as we strive for higher levels of intimacy, greater freedom of sensuality, of increased license to use talents heretofore underutilized, to reach a greater confidence in our own authority, and to overcome internal prohibitions which unnecessarily restrict our fullest humanity. All of this is done in equilibrium with our family and others we are close to at home and work. All this is done within a definite historical period, within a culture and a subculture. And while responding to this drive toward fuller realization of ourselves, we necessarily encounter the false ideas, self- and object images, beliefs, values, habits, regulations, and "shoulds" that comprise our current restrictive self-definition. As we push the boundary to gain internal freedom, we automatically destroy pieces of the illusion of absolute safety. That is the transformational process.

The Illusion of Absolute Safety: 18–35

We have now covered the full range. We started with the aerial view, life cycle perspective indexed by the sense of time that showed us the extent of the cloud covering our consciousness—the illusion of absolute safety—and where that cloud breaks off—somewhere in the midlife period. Then we went down to earth to everyday life struggles and into the head of one person, Nicole. There we saw the illusion of absolute safety at work as a series of barriers to a driven redefinition of the self in the form of false ideas that were temporarily believed to be correct ideas or correct experiences. These are ideas that confuse the past and the present and are projected into the future—ideas taken from the deep well of early unintegrated experiences of childhood rage, greed, emptiness and fear, and the questions about being out of control.

Now that we have the overview of the illusion of absolute safety as well as an intimate detailed view, we can try to chart a middle view. In that middle view, we will look at a set of ideas that comprise the illusion of absolute safety and ask what subset of these ideas surface for challenging at what ages. In other words, what is the changing structure of the illusion of absolute safety that leads up to the climactic midlife period?

Each life is a unique drama played against the compelling past family that inheres in the boundaries of our current superego-supported self-definition and is played out against the backdrop of a current subculture.

But there are also similarities among people. Culture produces some homogenization; genes produce a limited number of phenotypes; there are a limited number of viable defenses and coping styles to choose from, so valid categories can be used to divide the population into various descriptive types. We each have distinct faces, fingerprints, and voiceprints, but we also have similar faces, fingers, and voices. In discussing age-related change in the structure of the illusion of absolute safety, I am trying to highlight and understand the age homogenization that complements, but does not contradict, the unique evolutionary drama of an individual life.

It is a simple thesis: at each age we have a different posture toward life. This posture makes up the background tone of living for each phase of life, in which the central evolutionary issues are embedded. The posture dictates a strategy upon the evolutionary center. It affects the pace of change, the depth of the psyche available to change, the surfacing of issues and perspective, and the urgency of engagement with issues ranked by priority.

The illusion of absolute safety is a fixture of childhood encompassing the belief in omnipotent thought, omnipotent protective parents, the absoluteness of parental rules and world view, and a whole system of defenses as controlling structures against a rage reaction to separation. Just as the infant can hallucinate the feeding mother, real internal dangers can be soothed by images of the all-giving, all-protective, omnipresent parents by children of all ages—including adults.

The illusion of absolute safety is in compensatory equilibrium with the demonic pole of childhood consciousness. The ghosts, monsters, and robbers of childhood phobias are transmogrifications of dangerous rage in reaction to imperfect parenting, or against the sturdy pieces of reality that fail to bend to the wish-produced version of reality. The illusion of absolute safety becomes a compensatory device for these gothic childhood fears; thereby the acceptance of parental absoluteness is institutionalized.

The illusion of absolute safety is fixed in childhood by four major false assumptions that remain the silent underpinning of our adult assumptive world until they are challenged by powerful realities that force a deeply felt contradiction requiring psychological work. It is the meeting of a social context linked to place in the life cycle that forces psychological work on these deep idea structures that long before had been intellectually mastered. It is this work that causes the posture shift, for as the idea structure, deriving its effectiveness from an illusory wish-fulfillment base, is modified, a warping influence is removed, the impact of direct experience is changed, and different constructions of reality are formed. The locus of power and the nature of the feared inner reality of infantile memory are two major reality constructions that undergo radical transformation over the thirty-year span from 20 to 50. The four major false assumptions are:

1. I will always belong to my parents and believe in their version of reality.

2. Doing it their way with willpower and perseverance will bring results, but when I am frustrated, confused, tired, or unable to cope, they will step in and show me the way.

3. Life is simple and controllable. There are no significant unknown inner forces within me; there are no contradictory realities present in my life.

4. There is no evil in me or death in the world; the demonic has been expelled.

In this section I will cover in outline form the surfacing and challenging of the first three of these. The reader interested in greater detail can find it in my book *Transformations* (Gould, 1978). In the section following I go into more detail about the midlife period and cover the fourth and last false assumption.

Assumption I: I Will Always Belong to My Parents and Believe in Their Version of Reality (Late Teens, Early Twenties)

This assumption is emotionally challenged by the deep contradiction of experience when we "leave home," as to go to college or work. "Leaving home" becomes an emotional reality as that time approaches and the expectation of the culture is perceived. This includes the approximate age range of 16–22 in our culture. According to some longitudinal studies, about 10 percent of the population breeze through this period without an apparent ripple; yet it is also the period of the highest rate of first admissions for psychosis. For most of us in between these two poles, it is a period of intense feelings: vulnerable, painful, sensitive, controlled feelings at one moment and supercharged euphoric activism and freedom the next. Many of these descriptive characteristics can be understood as responses to the first major challenge of the monolithic illusion of absolute safety—the first crack that releases the demonic powers to become psychosis for some, an intermittent infusion of muted demonic consciousness for most, and a source of energy for all to be molded and channeled by talents and opportunities into the fuel of selfhood.

The first false assumption can be broken down into five components, which are the easily recognizable conflicts characteristic of the late adolescent period.

1. If I get any more independent, it'll be a disaster. The disaster can take one of three forms. A more independent position will expose some latent inadequacy; or parents will fall apart without the glue of a special child to take care of; or an unacceptable strain of uniqueness or competency will cause a forfeiture of love from misunderstanding parents and envious friends. The dialectic of becoming as independent as capacity warrants is played out with parents and is a preoccupying content of anxious periods.

2. I can see the world only through my parents' assumptions. The myth of family one-mindedness is a powerful and confining dynamic. There are punishments for divergence in every group process, and differences are the focus of hate, attack, and warfare. It is dangerous to be different from a reference group and doubly dangerous to be different from the primary reference group, the family. Nevertheless, the push for individuation requires differentiation from the family symbiosis. It is within this ambivalence that differences are expressed and negotiated. Any topic can be a subject of differences; but the true target is the basic assumptive pillars of the parents' world, since it is the period of creating a world view upon which to organize an adult life. The Marxist radical son of a wealthy, liberal lawyer is doing more than rebelling to express his power and his difference. He's plumbing the assumptions of society which are his father's world and need not necessarily be his world.

3. Only they can guarantee my safety. Accepting responsibility for our own safety is prerequisite for independence. It is often confused with having to have the same magical, safety-providing capacity parents are supposed to possess. Taking excessive risks to prove absolute invulnerability is a spurious challenge to this component assumption, for it displaces parental omnipotence onto fate and does not diminish the illusion of absolute safety. If this assumption is not modified, we accept that only they know what a safe career, marriage, or lifestyle would be for us. Even if we rebel against their advice, the belief remains intact.

4. They must be my only family. We suffer great loyalty conflicts when we choose friends and lovers to become as important to us as our parents. Friends become support for our newly emerging beliefs about ourselves in the world and, in a sense, become a new family. Yet groups of friends can be as coercive as parents, requiring agreement with a core set of ideas. Going back and forth between family and friends is the rhythm of emancipation and growth. Friends also teach us a new mode of functioning, since they refuse to treat us as special or to sacrifice for our welfare. When they become the important new family, a new relationship to social reality is forced.

5. I don't own my own body. The main experience that forces a contradiction with this false assumption is sexual. Deciding to have intercourse, or allowing a greater degree of pleasure to occur, is a statement of ownership that defies the internalized lifelong rule that intercourse is for adults only. The connection with oedipal restrictions is obvious, and the confusion for many, of intercourse as an inherent biological and human right with intercourse as an oedipal crime, is a clinical commonplace in this age period as well as beyond. The connection with the demonic rage reaction is more directly apparent in the challenge of this component assumption when we remember that being left out of the parents' life and bedroom is essentially a separation situation.

Assumption II: Doing It Their Way with Willpower and
Perseverance Will Bring Results, but When I Am Frustrated,
Confused, Tired, or Unable to Cope, They Will Step in and Show
Me the Way (the Twenties)

During our twenties we're confronted with decisions that only we can make about the major adult enterprises of work, family, and marriage. Though others may give advice, no one knows exactly what is right for us. It is while confronted with the subtle and profoundly important choices required to set up an initial life structure that an experience powerful enough to challenge this second major false assumption is met. But while the assumption is being challenged, it is being endorsed and reinforced by the social tasks of the twenties. For to become economically independent and competent as an adult requires us to learn how to do, in a socially accepted way, what it is we've chosen to commit ourselves to. Whatever it is, others have done it before, and many subscribe to a "right way" theory that they are willing to teach us or measure us by. And many times we have to learn their ways, even if we don't agree, during this apprenticeship period in life.

The second major assumption can be broken down into four subassumptions, each causing a specific warp in our thinking and relating:

1. Rewards will come automatically if we do what we are supposed to do. We are willing to sacrifice for the future because we believe in an automatic payoff system. If we do our part, people will respond to us as loving and decent people ought to respond. There will be just compensation for our work. Our dreams of life will come true. Often a rigid idealized dream of life formed in the oedipal period becomes an obsessive guide for life that overwhelms all contrary experience. This assumption fosters excessive expectations when the idealized dream is realized. Women who expect marriage to be the key to an automatic payoff system are very disappointed with life. Men who expect that planned career success will erase their vulnerability or ambivalence toward women are painfully disillusioned when their denial system is penetrated. Insistence on living out the promised dream life is really a failure to live off of current experience. Current experience calls for a continuous processing of intuition rather than living off a static concept of what *has to be,* thinly disguised as a rational life plan. The processing of intuition includes sorting out talents in order to find or create a confirming structure, struggling over disparate identifications, and daring to transcend parental identifications. This false assumption is particularly difficult to challenge if reality seems to confirm the false message. Those who are particularly attractive, or have been raised as special, or have been overconforming in order to receive rewards are easy victims of this particular false assumption.

2. There is only one right way to do things. The childhood idea that there is one right way, and that it is entrusted to our parents, is on one hand a prison and on the other a cherished hope. For if there is one right way, then we've found a magic key to the complex processes of reality and can guarantee our future against the terror of the unknown. This idea is resurgent and challenged during our twenties, as we adapt to the host culture as "adults" and become unreasonably hard on ourselves and intolerant of others. We hold ourselves responsible for the child's view of the adult. Adults know all the right answers automatically; adults aren't greedy like children; adults handle misfortune with a stiff upper lip; adults don't have doubts or fuzzy thinking or ambivalences, etc. Parents continue to monitor us during our twenties. When we do it their way, we're afraid we're capitulating. When we violate their rules and are successful, we feel free but also triumphant and somewhat guilty. When we're faced by a failure, we wonder if they weren't right all along. We feel betrayed when we do it their way and find we're still not happy. These are all responses to our continuing belief that there is only one right way.

   This false assumption affects our reaction to new roles in life, since each new social role is by definition a set of rules about how to behave and think that is reinforced by the reference group. Bankers wear ties, and their priority is money; artists don't wear ties, and their priority is expression. When bankers and artists each think their lifestyle is the only right way, they are hostile to the others' rules, but at the same time they are equally confined by their own set of rigidities. This is equally true for the roles of masculinity and femininity, for being husband and wife, or for being father or mother, while this false assumption is operative. The current social expectations to be a different kind of a person are as coercive as the internal imperative to be exactly like our parents. Squeezed out between those two grinding wheels there has to be a self-definition that is nobody else's "only right way." With the birth of a child a powerful conservative surge is born, and this false assumption is energized and in turn energizes both current social expectations and the internal imperative to be more like the parents. The battle to be expansively self-defined is temporarily unbalanced, and young parents in their twenties find themselves narrowly and rigidly defined. Through a complicated set of dynamics, women tend to undervalue themselves outside the realm of motherhood, and men tend to see their realm of competence confined to their work. Male and female internal prohibitions are formulated along these lines, splitting the androgynous potential and at the same time splitting the parental couple.

3. *My loved ones are able to do for me what I haven't been able to do for myself.* Essentially, what we can't do for ourselves is instantly rid ourselves of our internal prohibitions—the conflict boundaries of our self-definition. When we believe in this assumption, we expect a "cure" by love. We form a conspiracy with a loved one who magically makes us whole and temporarily cures us of the painful feeling of inadequacy which is the signal of an internal prohibition. The painful feeling of inadequacy is usually not about some objective limitation, but is the result of a strong urge to be what we're capable of, but won't let ourselves be. The cure by love "warehouses" future growth movement. At some future time, individual growth can occur only by disrupting the pattern of the marriage to weed out the conspiratorial cures. In the meantime the rhythm of intimate feelings corresponds to the success of the partner in overcoming feelings of inadequacy. When these feelings break through, the partner is held responsible as not loving enough—to the degree we continue to believe in this assumption. Only when this false accountability is suspended on a particular internal prohibition is growth through the dialects route open to the individual and the particular issue taken out of the warehouse of the marriage. To the degree that we are dependent on someone else to erase our feelings of inadequacy, that person is seen as superior. In each intimate relationship there are a number of such mutual conspiracies; we feel superior to our partners (who confirm it) on some issues (those internally prohibited to them but not to us) and inferior on others (those internally prohibited to us but not to them). This leads to conspiracies like "I can be sexually free, but you can't unless I help you" or "You can't be competent intellectually unless I support your intellect," etc. The feeling of being controlled and at the mercy of the other reproduces the parent-child relationship and sets up the victim-tyrant polarity and the attendant revenge, withholding, and competition. Vulnerability to this complicated dynamic is the cost of the "cure" by love. The shift toward the

cure by love, away from the cure by the dialects of growth, is enhanced by the belief in this component false assumption. It is an inevitable concomitant of the twenties, and no intimacy is free of this contaminant, since we are far from being free of the mass of internal prohibitions laced into the latticework of our self-definition during childhood. But this assumption is affected also by outer forms. The more "special" the form of the intimacy, the more this false assumption is energized. The more the form of the relationship is like the family structure, the more "special" expectations are taken for granted. So the hazard of forming a cure by love increases as we go from single coupling, through living together, to marriage, and then to marriage with children. Through the "rule" of selflessness, young parents are often drawn into a particularly malignant conspiracy of this social era. It is the conspiracy of male superiority and female inferiority, reinforced by a social value system based on earnings, but originating in the conditions of mothering measured by the criterion of complete and selfless devotion to others. The mother can't fulfill her own impossible criterion and so feels inadequate and unappreciated for her efforts, while her husband is fulfilling the relatively simple criterion of beoming more competent in a defined and structured world. The power of the rule of selflessness comes from the child's unrelenting desire to own a need-satisfying object and the mother's memory of her own unfulfilled desires as a child.

4. *Rationality, commitment, and effort will always prevail over other forces.* This last component assumption is a cherished belief, for if it were true, we'd be totally in control of our destiny. It also closes the door to the unconscious. As long as we continue to focus on the partial truth that rationality, commitment, and effort go a long way toward solving problems and are absolutely necessary ingredients to any control we have over our lives, we can ignore the whole truth that requires us to look also toward what is unconscious, dynamically operative, and outside our immediate rational reach. The great contradiction of this false assumption is met in the experiences of intimacy and other close personal relationships related to power, such as employer-employee or parent-child. Conspiracies based on "cure" of an internal prohibition are constantly being entered

and exited from, setting off currents of unrest, victimization, defense, tyranny, competition, etc. These currents are unrelated to the rationally committed partnership tasks of the relationship and can't be totally understood on a conscious level. They are negotiated on some other channel, and only when this assumption is modified can that channel be opened for a deeper and more comprehensive dialogue. Some of the conspiracies of our twenties that must remain unavailable to inspection are based on the overall task of this period—to become independent of the parents long enough to set up a self-determined life structure. Certain identifications must be suppressed, while others are sustaining. The suppressed identifications threaten to undermine the coupling, until a new platform of strength is reached at the threshold of the thirties.

Assumption III: Life Is Simple and Controllable. There Are No Significant Contradictory Forces Within Me (Late Twenties, Early Thirties)

Focusing away from the inner contradictions of life gives us a false sense of clarity and at the same time serves as a defense against the feared and unmastered demonic responses of childhood. The global strategy of becoming independent of parental authority by achieving high levels of role competence during the twenties forces a focus outward. At the end of the twenties, when a first-level sufficiency is reached in the novel tasks of adulthood, we can afford to return to unlived inner selves that were suppressed or shelved during the twenties and which prove to be the vital centers of future unfolding. Along with this discovery comes a new, less magical mode of dealing with complex reality. We attack problems more directly and realign our expectations of results so they correspond to our effort.

Often this transition is ushered in with disillusionment, confusion about what life is all about, or a depression. Surprising and unexpected feelings and insights break through that force a contradiction with the life structure we've set up, even if we're living the life we've always wanted. We are not sure if our discontent is a sign of our immaturity or the beginning of a new vision.

1. What I know intellectually, I know emotionally. Half knowing, and half not wanting to know, is a state we all find ourselves
in from time to time. It is a state of self-deception that dictates
anxiety and depressive equivalents as long as we don't complete
the process to some satisfactory state of knowing. Committing
ourselves to a fuller emotional knowledge of half-known truths
becomes an issue of the early thirties, as we challenge the assumption that our intellectual knowledge is the same as our
emotional knowledge. We develop new methods for dealing
with information about ourselves. We selectively suspend techniques that keep our emotions suppressed, such as changing
directions of an uncomfortable conversation or buying off a
depression. To the degree that we allow emotions to rise to the
surface, we detoxify the dangerous interior and come to see
that a bit of sadness today is not the same as the endless pool
of childhood sadness. Past and present diverge. Cliches about
life come alive. Life is a struggle. You are responsible for yourself. A stitch in time saves nine. Life isn't fair. As we get in
touch with the complexities of our own inner life, we become
more self-tolerant and tolerant of others; we no longer require
perfection along some arbitrary social definition of adultness.
We find as we know others more deeply, they share a similar
inner life. We come to know directly what work life is really
like and what it costs us to pursue the American dream. Work-
ing-class men realize their hourly wage income won't go up
much, and the fragile economy of their household can't continuously be supplemented by overtime or second jobs. Middle-
class men still push ahead toward the promise of escalating
wages and rank, yet realize they don't have the time or energy
to invest in their families; they still aren't "there," even if they're
making plenty, and they have to sacrifice much of their intellectual and emotional integrity in order to be the "company man"
who gets promoted. Women have to struggle with the choices
between children and career, no matter what their situation has
been. The opening-up period lets them know what they have
been missing so far, as well as what within them prohibits them
from going where they individually need to go. Very few
women have achieved the perfect balance.

2. *I am not like my parents in ways I don't want to be.* Part of the opening up of this era relates to warded-off identifications with parents. During our twenties, our knowledge of these identifications had to be suppressed so we could believe in the illusion of our complete independence from parental influence. Now, in order to avoid blind repetition of their patterns and in order not to forfeit the piece of self underlying the parental identification, we must first acknowledge the presence of this mysterious, slightly foreign inner self. "I found myself talking just like my father (mother) to my child. It just came out of me, exactly what I didn't like in them." It is this ubiquitous experience that has to be admitted and worked with, if the identification with parents is going to proceed to higher levels of self. The cost of the ignored, acted-out parental identifications is to pass on the problem to our children, who have to live with our conscious repudiation and our unconscious repetition. It leads to internal prohibitions in our children over the specific issues with our parents. Unadmitted parental identifications are also the subject of unresolved controversy between husband and wife, particularly expressed as arguments over child rearing. The final solution to a successful processing of identifications comes when we find we have a *similarity* to a parent but are *not identical.* We may share the stem of a value but not the ramifications. We may share a temperament characteristic but use it for different purposes. Hostility might be spunk; niggardliness may be prudence. But only after the similarity is admitted can the necessary discriminations be made and the self attached to that characteristic be allowed to live.

3. *I can see the reality of those close to me quite clearly.* The opening up to the marital conspiracies formed in our twenties is essential if a significant change in self-definition is to occur and be confirmed. That means a great deal of confusion between lifelike, inner demonic misinterpretations and real other people. In addition, what we are sure we know about the other person is no longer true, just as what was true about us ceases to be the whole new truth. In addition to the sets of unique conspiracies we each set up in a relationship, the three fundamental conspiracies set up in our twenties by most of us must be opened: (a) our partner has a temperamental characteristic

like a parent we had conflict with; (b) we set up aspects of our parents' marriage in our own; (c) we insist on one-mindedness.

During the course of breaking up these conspiracies in order to release ourselves from the hold of our partner's induced negative image of us, marriage can be hell. Only our acceptance of ourselves as we are becoming and our partner's equal acceptance can end this hell. In the meantime, the battles are fueled by the overestimation of our partner's power over us and the underestimation of our power over the partner.

4. *Threats to my security aren't real.* All of the opening up described under the first three subassumptions are threats to the pattern of life already formed and to the security inherent in living an unchanged life. At first we disavow those intrusive thoughts and urges and insights, half hoping they'll go away. Nevertheless, there is an insistence to these urges that is stronger than in our twenties but not yet as pressured as in our forties. To the degree we modify these false assumptions, we'll be able to deal with our emerging selves early and avoid charging the marriage with our delay later on, when layers of bitterness may make reconciliation problematic if not impossible. The urges that threaten our security come in the following forms: career change; seeking either more intimacy or more space; returning to school; seeking more fun or bodily pleasure; settling down; having a baby; ceasing to be a baby; ceasing to fight parents when you need not; or starting to fight parents when you must. The greatest threat to security patterns is thinking about breaking up a marriage, particularly one with children. The critical issue to decide is whether the apparent enemy, the spouse, is really an enemy to our growth or a projection of our internal prohibitor. It is easy enough to maneuver a spouse into behavior that convinces us that he or she is the internal prohibitor incarnate. Some marriages are unnecessarily dissolved because this discrimination is not made along with an equally easy error to make—that when we feel powerless and mistreated it is necessarily because the other is mistreating us. It may only be that the other is growing more rapidly at the time. All of these considerations must be processed completely if important judgments about the future are

to be reached at the highest possible level. This can be done only if the urges and confusions are given the status of reality.

The End of the Illusion of Absolute Safety: 35–50

Much has been made of the midlife period by journalists in the last several years. It is quite popular to have a midlife crisis, and in fact a humorist once suggested that men who have not yet had one should go directly to a special camp in the Catskills where it can be properly induced. Why this phenomenon is so popular is still a mystery, although eventually we may see it in the perspective of a century of life stage discoveries beginning with childhood by Freud (1905), adolescence by Anna Freud (1958), youth by Erikson (1956), and gerontology in response to a growing social need. On a less lofty plane, "midlife" was probably discovered by American journalism because those who write and select articles were having troubles and looking for an explanation that didn't brand them as defective neurotics.

The Surface

Despite the subject's popularity which might make it suspect, we can start from solid ground. We know by common sense alone that midlife is a unique period of life, just as any other period in the life cycle. The multitude of studies that have been produced so far mainly codify what most of us between the ages of 35 and 50 already know. We know that we are at the height of certain powers in the world and have reached positions which only ten years previous we were sure would satisfy us and make us feel mature and complete. Along with the power come responsibilities, and those of us in management positions know that responsibilities are both opportunities and drains on our time and energy. Something is happening in our relationship with our parents. For those of us fortunate enough to have parents who are alive and healthy, we witness a subtle reversal of roles. Our parents come to us for advice and help, recognizing that we're more acquainted with the details of business and life than they are, since they have been cropping their interests in response to their own position in the life cycle. Others of us have experienced the death or illness of our parents, which happens more frequently during this period life than any other. We suffer not only the pain of loss but also a severely wounded sense of invulnerability. We are next in line to go!

Our children range from their teens to their twenties and are like messengers of time as they emancipate themselves from our protection and control in order to enunciate their own world view and starting position in adult life. Both our children and our parents are receding from their fixed positions in the constellation of our lives, and by undergoing their necessary transitions they leave us standing quite alone and separate. We find we not only want more private time for ourselves, but we require it, for when we don't get it we feel irritable and pushed and can no longer easily override those sensations and get on with our "duty." Only a complicated time trade-off calculus can save the day, and often that breaks down. Other wories emerge at this time of life that were background considerations prior to this. Planning for retirement becomes an issue along with the fear that our strength may dwindle with the years or be stolen from us by unexpected or unavoidable illness. All the future imponderables complicate the daily struggle over monthly bills, the current job market, and decisions about whether or not the work we are doing is right for us. Commitments to marriages, careers, and roles are all intimately tied to a self-definition that is the only self we have known but may not be the only self that is still possible.

It is during this period of life that our emotions catch up with our intellect on the issue of our existence. We now know with our whole being what it means to be mortal and finite; to be of the culture but apart from it; and to be separate and alone even when closely connected. How we respond to this frighteningly solid state of knowledge is crucial. If we accept it, we make our life course decisions from a sturdy base and are likely to have a life open to surprise. On the other hand, if this knowledge is too much for us, we'll spend our energies fortifying some island of safety, hoping the feeling of safety built into unchanging patterns turns out to be real safety. We are at a crossroads deciding whether our future will be ordered by a modern preconception of adulthood—joyless, dutiful, fat, sexless creatures who just dry up—or whether adults are whatever we happen to be. Many of us discover during the midlife period a sense of internal freedom never before tasted or even imagined, and we tell everybody we actually feel younger than ever before.

Central Subjective Shifts

This is the midlife situation in a nutshell. There are three cardinal subjective shifts that characterize the midlife period and begin to organize the psychology of the midlife situation. First of all, we discover that we are no longer "young." Although the everyday experience of becoming older is gradual and unavoidably reflected in many mirrors, it seems as if we have been becoming older on a "young-self foundation," and in the midlife period we have come to the end of that basis of self-definition. "This is me, I can't believe it. I'm 40 years old—impossible, I'm just out of college. How could all those years have gone by so soon? How can I have almost grown children soon to go off to college?"

Questioning is the second cardinal subjective shift of the midlife period. "What have I done with my life? Where is it going?" Values, lifestyles, and life structures that were pursued with full commitment come under the scrutiny of a ripe and mature mind once more asking fundamental questions about life—questions that were asked and answered first in the late adolescent period, at the very beginning of the young adult foundation of self-definition. These questions now arise again to be reanswered.

This questioning takes many forms, and there seems to be no immunity from it—not even success. Successful professionals question the value of their work, just as successful mothers question the value of life spent as a mother. For some of us it is an articulate, self-conscious questioning process, while for others the questioning process is expressed in a reborn curiosity about other ways of life or a new openness to ideas.

The third cardinal shift is time urgency. There is a vague but implacable sense that it is becoming time to act in some definitive, important, and therefore dangerous way. What action is required is not exactly clear in the beginning but eventually comes into focus; and when in focus, a decision to act or not, or to what degree to act definitively, must be made with enormous implications for life to follow.

For those now in the midlife period, I have chosen to discuss four false assumptions that collectively compose the fourth major false assumptive pillar of the illusion of absolute safety, that "There is no evil in me or death in the world; the demonic has been expelled." When the next cohort reaches midlife, this set of characteristic issues may change. Only time will tell.

These are observations about people generally, not just the special category called patients. Though I've chosen to highlight my conviction that growth takes place by the correction of false ideas (and the correction of negative self-images), I hope I won't be misunderstood. All people, not just patients, harbor false assumptions and negative self-images, though obviously some more than others, making life harder for some than for others. Release from the *disguised* rigid application of these false ideas is what allows proactive activity and the flowering of life, while the work on these ideas is part of the heaviness of life.

Death Can't Happen to Me (Men)

The awareness of personal mortality seems to weaken the immunity pact men make with work. That is, if we are successful we will never feel like small, helpless little boys again, and the prospect of our death is banished. The next round of success should clean up all of the problems.

We pay dearly for this spurious immunity pact. We behave as if we still have to please angry fathers, or we have to be in control all of the time (including being protective and in control of our women), or we have to fill roles rather than be true to ourselves. These are all constrictions of our full humanity. These are all violations of our authenticity and interfere with an empathic caretaking of the next generation.

As the immunity pact with work weakens, we become aware of the costs we've paid for the illusion of immunity. We can deny the awareness of costs by working twice as hard, or we can accept the insight and undergo a transformation process which may leave us bored or discontent with our work for a while before we reach a new balance of self and workplace. That is, work effort must be derived from a closer fit between our talents and daily activities so that meaning comes out of the pleasure of work rather than the hope for magical immunity from the hazards of the human condition. The breakdown of the immunity pact can come at the height of triumphant success, when we again find there is no magic payoff or when our career plateaus and we're depressed because our achievements haven't met our aspirations. Through despair can come a self that hasn't yet lived.

Matters of discretion keep me from sharing with you a fully developed case history, but let me offer instead the presenting symptoms and dynamics of four physicians who suffered such a crisis of success. The great danger of being a doctor is being seduced from the dialectical pathway of personal growth by approbation, respect, and attribution of omnipotence—by the cure of "love." It is an occupational hazard and leads to the disease of psychic rigidification. The crisis of success at midlife for doctors occurs when we have professional maturity, the trappings of rank, and the prequisites of status, yet feel "deadened" inside. We feel confined, our work ceases to be a labor of love, our love seems to be all labor, and we continue to act as if we're still involved because the rewards are too great to let slip away.

Physician A was successful beyond his wildest dreams, and though he enjoyed performing surgery and was charming during the day, office hours and the constant demands on him turned him into a tired, hypercritical ogre the moment he hit home. He drove his beautiful, accommodating wife away from him by constant criticism and then stopped sleeping with her altogether. He fell in love and took weekday time off for the first time in years. He left his wife; his girlfriend either left him or he let her go; and he returned to his wife, still angry at her for not livening up his life.

Physician B until the last six months was absolutely dedicated to medicine. Then about the time he was sure he had cancer of the colon, he lost interest. After repeated G.I. series, he gave up the idea of cancer and became obsessed by subtle signs of a muscle-wasting disease which never developed. Dissatisfaction with his life, his children, his wife, his practice, and his past performance paraded before him before he got back in touch with his vital passions.

Physician C found love notes in his wife's purse and went wild with fury, for days threatening to kill the lover. During a moment of despondence, he almost drove off a cliff. Years of a polite, distant, asexual relationship had preceded the discovery. The early passion of their marriage had given way to an agreed-upon definition of him as an aggressive man she feared, which was something he felt guilty about. He worked twice as hard at the office to prove he was a good man and was polite to the point of obsequiousness at home to prove he was caring, not cruel.

Physician D was ready to quit his surgical practice at the height of the malpractice crisis. He had had enough abuse, ingratitude, and blame to last a lifetime. He was already feeling burdened with guilt and was unable to sleep since he had confessed to his wife a very brief affair he had had, so brief it could hardly be called an affair at all; actually it was more a touching of two lonely souls than either a threat to her or an act of aggression against her.

Each of these physicians confounded their work, which was originally a labor of love, by adding to their work the load of banishing all feelings of personal inadequacy. Work had become both a love cure and an affirmation of their talents and interests. They managed to keep the system balanced until the midlife period, appearing to all the world and to themselves just as men pursuing a demanding career, growing professionally, and producing a family—but underneath this truth was another truth; psychic rigidification was taking place just as surely as arteriosclerosis takes place before the thrombosis.

Each of these physicians failed to relabel his processes. Each accepted the 4-year-old's label and then tried to deny it was present. Dr. A mislabeled his deep love for his wife as a weakness that would put him in bondage to her, as if she were his mother, so he cut her down mercilessly to distance himself.

He finally stopped sleeping with her altogether before his attempt to get away from his fear forced him to face it through the crisis of separation.

Dr. B's muscle weakness was the final defense against what his 4-year-old mind labeled as unbridled destructiveness. As he was called on to exercise more power as an administrator, he became more aware of his dread of hurting anyone, and of feelings of cowardice that followed when he didn't confront a sensitive issue because of that fear. The passion to use his power for good causes without feeling guilty broke through, first preceded by the defensive symptom.

Dr. C's wife was afraid of men and convinced him that the intensity of his attachment to her and his personality in general were really an indication of male cruelty. He agreed to this label because he feared she was right, though he'd never willfully hurt anybody.

Dr. D was afraid that the loneliness and sensitivity he felt were a sign he was the sissy his brothers said he was. He was a tough surgeon in a field with high mortality rates until this vital, passionate part of his being broke through in this brief affair.

It is during midlife that the imperative of authenticity touches us all. The dams we've erected against the feared reentry of a vital passion come crumbling down, not because there's a new biological surge of instinct, but because the deterred imperative of wholeness and deep self-knowledge can wait no longer. Dr. A must no longer be afraid of his love, if he is to live with love. Dr. B must no longer be afraid of his firmness, if he is to be effective in the area of life he's decided is meaningful. Dr. C must accept his intensity as his biological heritage, not a sign of inherent evil, if he's going to live as a free citizen rather than as a criminal who has to prove himself worthy. Dr. D must harvest the lonely, sensitive parts of himself that can lead him into deeper and richer excursions into the life processes.

It is in this sense that the crisis of success in midlife is a critical turning point; what starts out as disaster in any ordinary view of the subject may end up to be either a worse disaster or the beginning of a new aliveness. These four men were risking divorce, murder, suicide, or chronic hypochondriasis in order

to gain sensitivity, effectiveness, and decriminalization of the
self. The issue is deadness versus aliveness. There is more about
the process of change under the false assumption, "I am an
innocent."

In industrial culture there is a premium on being able to
control things and people in order to wield executive power in
response to large corporate plans. To carry out these functions
successfully, feelings and intuitions often have to be ignored or
compartmentalized. In addition, men often form a conspiracy
with their wives early in marriage to let their wives be the feeling
person of the pair. As the magical immunity pact with work
breaks down, feelings associated with the fear of death break
through, the absolute value of the corporate world diminishes
in favor of complex life values, and men have an opportunity
to learn, accept, and integrate a previously sacrificed part of
themselves. Initially their fear of feelings is associated with the
false idea that they will lose their rational thinking capacity and
can have only one mode of operating at a time. Eventually, if
successful, they learn that feelings and thoughts are interdependent, and that in feelings the content is not yet articulated.
The content can be retrieved through the operation of intelligence on the feeling states.

As an example, one day in the middle of a patient hour, I
had an inexplicable sudden surge of depression which colored
most of the remainder of the day. It followed a statement by
my patient that there is an economic recession and that during
the recession he thought my profession would be the first to
suffer. Out of that diffuse depressive feeling the first content
statement retrieved was, "Roger, soon you'll be selling apples
on the street corner." That idea made me laugh; my depression
began to lift, and I was able to trace that idea back to a dream
the night before in which I was going to be punished for daring
to publish some of my ideas. That is, before I rescued the initial
thought content from the depressive feeling, my depressive
world view was that soon I would be a helpless victim of the
failing local economy. My view of reality was warped. If at
that time I were making career decisions involving income or
position, my judgment would have been influenced by that
warped view. Rescuing the content from the depressed feelings

allowed the correction of the reality view of my economic future and at the same time led me to the processes going on in my own head about the internal consequences of moving ahead in my scientific career. Similarly, other feelings, including anxiety, terror, misery, exhilaration, are information sources for processes going on in us. As men get in touch with these processes and coordinate them with their rational thinking, they acquire new and important powers over their own unfolding life. They feel themselves to be wider and deeper and wiser than ever before.

Another consequence of the processing of feelings is that men begin to make contact with the visceral self. Knowledge of themselves in the world takes place on the level of sensations rather than abstractions. That is, they know what is real because there is a familiar sensation in their chest or in their belly or coursing through their arms rather than knowing what is right in the worded sense. This reunion with the visceral source of knowledge that dominates childhood often occurs traumatically after episodes of emotional pain, including the recognition of not feeling loved enough, recognizing a real love gap, or letting go of a wished-for but illusory version of important others.

The processes described above take place slowly and episodically over a period of years, during which most of us don't know quite what's happening to us except for the awareness that what is happening seems inexorable and quite different from anything we've previously experienced.

It's Impossible to Live Without a Protector in Life (Women)

Women have babies and menstrual periods and worry about children crossing the street. Because of this basic biological groundedness, their own mortality comes as no surprise, but the awareness becomes a spur to act on their own behalf. The greatest inhibition to this mandated action is belief in the false assumption that it is impossible to live without a protector. The immunity pact that is breaking down is not with work but with their relationship to men.

For as long as life is believed to be so dangerous that only a man can guide you through the hazards, then you owe that man your life and must give him what he wants. You must either surrender to a man, or in the dichotomized thinking organized by this false assumption, you must become your own protector and give up all intimate relationships with men. As long as this false assumption is believed, married women can't expand themselves or enter careers without their husband's explicit permission, and unmarried career women dare not marry, for then they'll automatically lose their autonomy. Though our culture, through the women's movement, declares this assumption false, each woman must carry out her own transformation on the deeply embedded and often cleverly disguised version of this false idea. The case of Nicole, presented earlier, illustrates most of this.

Only after this false assumption is transcended can intimacy and softness and firmness and assertiveness become situationally appropriate qualities without relevance to sacrifice or abandonment. The process is simple, yet difficult. Power that was given away must be taken back. But to redefine oneself as powerful means to abandon all claim on the illusion of safety and to meet squarely the existential question. Because this transformation is momentous, it is often confused and agonizingly prolonged. Often the battle is fought in the wrong arena.

The basic question is who, or what set of forces, is not letting me be as powerful as I am capable of being? Is it the prejudice of the workplace? Is it the husband who fights against the loss of his protectee? Or is it the internal prohibition manifested in the continuing belief in this false assumption?

Often the husband is made into the enemy to avoid the deeper, elusive, and devastatingly powerful images of a primitive jealous mother (the original protector) who won't let her daughter grow beyond the program of the mother's life. At other times, the feared demonic images occupying the transition zone from one self-definition to the next expanded self-definition take the form of an angry maleness that threatens to come out of the first crevice of official assertive action and wipe away all previous femininity. As with Nicole, I've observed two other women moving into careers, buying lipstick or perfume they didn't need just after a decisive confirmation of their career—almost always on the way home.

Taking back the power is usually objectified at some higher level of commitment and risk. This may include returning to work, in which case real obstacles are intertwined with fantasy obstacles. Difficulty in finding the right job, beginning at 40 in entry jobs, and comparing one's status to that of one's husband are real problems that interact with the fantasy elaborations (angry maleness and jealous mother images) just discussed.

Some women go the other way, from exclusive career concerns to family and career. They are also taking back their powers, since before risking the combination of career with family they had been operating on the equation that being with a man meant sacrificing to a protector who could grant an immunity pact against the hazards of living. The experimentation that leads to the challenge of this false assumption is usually pushed by the sense that youthful good looks are wearing out and time for having a child is running out. Women, like men in the midlife period, are looking for the authenticity and wholeness that their life has been missing so far.

On a visceral everyday level, traditional women are working with a distinctly different set of feelings than men in their attempt to reunite themselves with their powerful-in-the-world selves. Being intuitive and rescuing information from feelings, as well as being loving and giving and caring, have been, for most traditional women, the psychological work of the period preceding midlife. But while confronting the false idea of needing a protector, a whole new set of feelings has to be mastered for the reunion to take place. These are feelings centering around anger, of having been imprisoned by what was a life choice of a different era, of unfairness and inequity, fears of fantasy revenge, and unlived-out sexual fantasies. The definition of female as everything nice, sugar and spice, must be destroyed if access to executive power and control over one's destiny is ever to be achieved. This often leads to distancing one's self from intimacy with men because men are sometimes experienced as jailers. On a deeper level, women fear that their husbands are really little boys who will fall apart when the woman becomes independent. Her fear of hurting him, and his hurt, become imprisoning forces. Confusion and pain in this transformation process are often compensated for by bursts of new strengths felt on a visceral level.

Women are afraid that as they learn and exercise the more executive, linear mode of thinking, they will lose the breadth and depth of feeling/thinking that are at the foundation of their sense of feminine selves. Like men, eventually they learn to integrate the two, but not without going through the processes of transformation and doubt. Often, distancing themselves from warm, loving feelings is required to protect their boundaries and to give a new distinctiveness and focus to their lives. Usually this is a temporary strategy.

There Is No Life Beyond This Family

As children, we felt safe as long as we believed we'd always remain with our parents. Likewise we feel safe as adults as long as we believe there is no life beyond our current husband or wife, i.e., that separation or divorce is not possible. As long as we believe this false idea, our partners must bear whatever we deliver to them, and we must, as partners to the same set of regulations, accept the same. There is no room for negotiation in response to the rapid changes taking place as we break out of the stereotypes of maleness and femaleness, often one marital partner leading the way and dragging the other.

When this assumption is challenged, the renegotiation of the rapidly changing midlife marriage is impassioned, while the risk of separation or divorce is heightened in exchange for the possibility of ending up with a renewed and vital relationship that incorporates the growth of both partners.

Some categories to be renegotiated are sex; unstated contracts that restrict both partners; and the degree of difference and aloneness that is compatible with a love relationship. Sex becomes an issue because of the general demand for more intrinsic satisfaction before it's too late, the weakening of early guilt patterns, the absence of small children in the house (adult parental inhibition is reflexive of a child's wishful view of the asexual parental couple), and the sex brought into the house by older sexual children. The rule of fidelity is questioned along with all other internalized rules, and it is either strengthened because it becomes a self-generated, ethical-practical value, or

it is violated. Being exposed to the infidelity of a spouse traumatically reminds us of the remaining powerful object-posses-
sion drive that underlies a monogamous marriage.

Being different from what our partner wants us to be becomes a critical issue. Experimentation in those arenas the other
is critical of, threatened by, or thinks are silly is an essential
vital activity. Wondering what it would be like to be alone or
married to someone else is part of the exploration of individual
and marital boundaries. For example, when a 40-year-old professor began to jog, he was growing by challenging the false
restrictive idea about himself that he was not "physical." Jogging made him feel vital and alive. His wife had two reactions—"It's good for you" and "It irritates me, don't do it." The
second reaction was based on her feeling of inadequacy—he
suddenly became the one with the quality of self-determination,
and she was still procrastinating about her music. She felt relatively inadequate. If her irritation had been strong enough to
stop his jogging, she would have been the enemy to his growth
that returned him to his previous restrictive self-definition and
deprived him of his new sense of vitality. Instead she challenged
her feeling of inadequacy, returned to her music, and ceased
to be irritated. He jogged, and she felt alive with her music.
Soon she got a bonus in life—she felt more sexual. At this
next level of sexuality, her husband initially felt inadequate. He
literally ran away from the problem by running longer and
going to bed earlier. The contemporary man's version of the
wife's headache! When he dealt with his feeling of inadequacy
as a growth issue by challenging the false idea restricting him
from full enjoyment, the story had a happy ending. At any
point, these marital partners could have become enemies to the
other's new growth and started a slide into divorce or chronic
hostility.

Whether this assumption is challenged or not, there are
consequences to pay. No challenge yields no change; growth is
sacrificed to marital stability. The cost is resentment. Challenging the assumption may lead to divorce as a casualty of the
process, divorce because there is nothing there anymore, or a
renewed relationship with two vital centers and no rank, no
leader, no victor, and no victim.

I Am an Innocent

If we continue to believe in this false assumption because we are still afraid of our deep demonic childhood badness, we won't have the opportunity to relabel these primitive, biological cognitive processes of infancy through the perspective of adult consciousness. The psychological work on this false assumption is often mediated through feelings of inadequacy. These unwelcome feelings do not reflect inadequacy per se, but a moral judgment we place on ourselves when a vital passion is trying to find a place in our lives—that we are adequate to be at that moment what we know we're capable of being. It is information about our attempt to correct the judgment our 4-year-old mind once made about our vital passions.

We must review the overly moral labels we put on our inner processes so we no longer interpret dissatisfaction as greed, self-concern as selfishness, sensuality as lasciviousness, pleasure as irresponsibility, curiosity as something forbidden, anger as destructiveness, love as weakness, imperfection as a fault, change as danger, or wicked thoughts as the equivalent of wicked actions. The moral misinterpretation of our core selves can be reinterpreted only after a period of reflective thinking from the perspective of adult consciousness. Then our impulses become guides to our constant unfolding. Only through that activity can we have a full inner chamber of feeling. Only then can we be vital and alive. Our aliveness doesn't come from the things we do; our aliveness comes from the spirit in which we do things—either freely, flexibly, and joyfully, or joylessly, as if we're criminals who have to be watched and guarded. The reward of reworking the self-labeling of earliest childhood passions is to keep our work as a labor of love and do the work of our love freely.

The correction of previously denied negative self-images can take place at this time of life because we are adults at the apogee of our real power in the world and of our real power over ourselves and the ideas inside our heads. The following are five common negative self-images exposed by midlife questioning.

1. I have had to work too hard, and when I try to slow

down I find that I am uncomfortable with fun and feel small and unimportant. If I'm not moving ahead quickly, I am vulnerable to feeling envious and hostile and become extremely sensitive to criticism.

2. I've been too passive and too afraid of taking risks. I'm too fearful and too controlled. Because of these flaws I have not lived up to my potential, and other people have had an undue influence over my life course.

3. I am too aggressive, greedy, and bold and not responsive or respectful enough of other people's reality. I am afraid of periods of doubt and uncertainty because they lead directly to intolerable feelings of helplessness. I am really quite hypocritical about the abuses of power. On one hand, I'm indignant when slighted in the least; on the other hand, I abuse those below me whenever I feel slighted.

4. I don't really like or know people. I manipulate them instead of supporting them. Privately I am quite intolerant of their ideas and mannerisms. I hardly know my children, and I am not sure I really know my spouse.

5. I don't really enjoy sex the way I should. It's a performance or part of the power battle between the sexes.

Negative self-images are acknowledged and worked with during the midlife period because they are more than vague blemishes; they are severe restraints. Though we can cover over and rationalize our actions, we discover that we *can't* act any other way. And if we can't respond to sex as anything but warfare, we can't enjoy tenderness and love. If we can't stop being controlling, we can't participate in life outside our control. If we can't stop being big, we can't enjoy the growth of our family or know life without incessant inner pressure. If we're too fearful and passive, we can't claim our rights or optimize our talents. If we abuse power, we can't ever trust ourselves to be close or to trust that anyone else can love us.

Since cover-ups and rationalizations for these negative self-images are often interwoven into the fabric of the life structure we've produced, we often abandon temporarily our identification with that life structure, its values, and the roles we have previously accepted. Often our behavior is seen as self-destructive, as we heighten the dialogue with the negative self-image by destroying the rationalized image of ourself in the eyes of others. Being a responsible worker and serious dedicated adult can cover up "having to work too hard." Disappointing colleagues and spouses who mirror and share that valued "me" is a powerful way of shattering the encasing armor. In a similar vein, being too passive and controlled is commingled with the popular positive images of being steady, reliable, dutiful, or professional; being too aggressive is commingled with being a doer, shaker, or mover; being intolerant of others' complexity can be covered by being a loner, an independent, or a highly principled superior boss; and not enjoying sex can be reversed by being a sober, serious, moral, paternal, or maternal person—a family person to whom sensuality is unimportant.

The imperative to act against one's valued roles and postures in life then can be understood in terms of a change of strategy in life that is characteristic of the midlife period. In the words of the once popular song, the prior strategy can be epitomized as "Accentuate the positive and eliminate the negative, don't mess with Mister Inbetween." Building up a confirming mirroring relationship with spouse or workplace (being sober and serious) so that truly positive abilities hide self-critical partially accurate self-accusations (that one is unable to enjoy the sensual aspects of life) is a strategy that works for quite a while. It is based on the belief that there is nothing that can be done about the self-accusation except to cover it up and hope for the best. It is a belief that most of us harbor about our deep negative self-images because they are rooted in early childhood. It is a belief that is questioned naturally during the midlife period under the press of time urgency to free ourselves from intolerable internal constrictions caused by the deep negative self-images. There is now a "Mister Inbetween," i.e., a mature self and ego willing to attempt a synthesis of mental contents where no synthesis was thought possible. The midlife period is a time when the adult self no longer wishes to alternate between the judgments of the surface and the judgments of the mysterious deep but feels an imperative to act on behalf of exposing and correcting and coming to terms with self on a new basis of authenticity and coherence.

Once we have tracked, captured, and successfully contained or modified our original, insatiable passions, the mysteries and complexities of the human mind and life on this planet between human beings become awe-inspiringly open to us.

Life After 50

From 16 to 50 we are working to dismantle gradually the four major false assumptions built up in response to our childhood demons. By about 50, we complete the work of dismantling the last false assumption. *There is no evil in me or death in the world. The demonic has been expelled.* This is helped along because events are forcing us to accept that there never will be any magical powers by which we can bend the world to our will; with that, we make the final passage from *I am theirs* to *I own myself.* With that momentous awareness, we are finally able to step out of the familiar world of struggle for status into a yet-to-be-developed frame of reference. For the next few months or for years, we're in a fog of awe. Nothing is the same any more. We are nowhere despite being surrounded by the familiar. If we will allow it room, our new perception will force us to transcend the pettiness inspired by our former feelings of possessiveness and battles over control and competition—though the change is not completed easily. It does not happen immediately. But the life of inner directedness finally prevails.

Some see this new noncompetitive frame of mind as a religious experience. Others put their new philosophy into effect by settling into the overlooked details of their everyday lives; they find new riches right at home. Others become teachers, benefactors, or world citizens.

This major transition in life does not occur sharply at age 45. Cycles of work, family, and marriage extend in varying degrees into the fifties. For some men, the work plateau may not be reached in the early forties but later on, so the disillusionment with the "magical" payoff from work is delayed to the late forties or early fifties. For some, having a family of children who are still young, or parents who remain healthy and active, continues throughout the forties, supporting the illusion of safety in life despite contrary messages. For some women, the excitement of a new career or the luxury of having only a career and not also a home and children to worry about can lend a temporary new sense of power just as the old power of youthful attractiveness fades.

But sometime in our forties—for most people, it is the mid-forties—we step from the intense heat of the midlife period to a cooled-down, post-midlife attitude. We live with a sense of having completed something, a sense that we are whoever we are going to be—and we accept that—not with resignation to the negative feeling that we could have been more and have failed, but with a more positive acceptance: "That's the way it is, world: Here I am! This *is* me." And this mysterious, indelible "me" becomes our acknowledged core, around which we center the rest of our lives.

That doesn't mean we'll be immune from the hazards of life after we hit 45 or 50 or that we'll ever again be able to ignore the specter of death or how limited our time is. Sickness, divorce, physical deterioration, reduced circumstances, forced retirement, ingratitude of those we love, tragedies, and disappointments—all the events that begin to pile up after 50—whittle away at all of us. Those of us who have made contact with our inner core face these inevitable hazards of later life with greater strength; we are able to bounce back because we don't get lost in how bitter the reversal is. We can't be reduced to nothing by any ordinary quota of misery; neither our present nor our past can become a source for despair or make us believe our life is meaningless. Our sense of meaning resides within us; it does not inhere in any extension of us that can be amputated by the wheel of fortune. There are giants among us that live through the muck of life with an unimpeachable dignity.

But there are also mean and crotchery old folks. They've not made contact with their inner core, and they cling to the childhood view that power and status are an index of human worth. As reversals occur to such people with increasing frequency as they age, they perceive themselves as losing the battle of life. They begin to attack life itself as meaningless as they slide downhill. Their envies and jealousies become larger, like warts on the nose, as their humanity shrinks.

Some of us awaken from this nightmare slide downhill and, through a flash of insight and a tremendous commitment of will, initiate changes leading back to our true inner self—to Jung's center (1963), "the self that is the principle and archetype of orientation and meaning." Sometimes this occurs only after a severe loss, followed by a deep mourning reaction. The loss then becomes the source of an unintended and unexpected miracle: the man or woman who came alive only at the end of life.

At any age we can make the discoveries described in the midlife section and find a new burst of vitality. At any age we can challenge and conquer the last false assumption and touch the incandescent stream within us that turns life inside out and causes a light of meaning to shine on our lives from within.

Summary

I have tried to deal with the illusion of absolute safety as a set of interlocked ideas that channel, color, warp, and create the world we experience. The evolution and modification of these ideas form the ever changing "posture" toward the world that could only be loosely and vaguely formulated earlier in this chapter.

These ideas are not at the forefront of our consciousness. They exist by implication; they are part of our silent organizational framework and slip out only occasionally in "My God, that's the irrational way I've been relating to the world." But nevertheless, work on the illusion of absolute safety takes place in the forefront of our consciousness anyway. It plays itself out in our favorite drama.

Each of us can recognize a life theme or a drama being played out. For some it is patently oedipal; for others it is the abandoned child or the special child or the superman or superwoman or the rescuer or the one to be rescued. Every time we *re-create* the drama, we live off of and continue our current belief in the illusion of absolute safety. But at times we have choices. We catch ourselves in the act of re-creation. Then we can decide to live out the old drama or create a new drama out of the stuff of current reality. When we choose the latter, we've abandoned a piece of the illusion of absolute safety and inadvertently modified one of the organizational ideas constituting that illusion.

It is these choices that lead to transformations, both the personal idiosyncratic transformations, as illustrated by Nicole, and the shared transformations linked to age and the illusion of absolute safety. The timetable of the shared transformations may be an artifact of this culture or truly a rhythm inherent in the nature of man.

As concepts, the personal and shared transformational tasks deserve to be discriminated because they point to different aspects of a complicated process; they are inextricably intermixed in the life we experience.

The study of adulthood in social context is in its infancy. To my mind we would do well to study adulthood with the concept of the transformational task as a valued tool, for, as I see it, it is more than a concept. It is the organizing unit and vital center of adult experience.

References

Erikson, E. (1956), The problem of ego identity. *J. Amer. Psychoanal. Assn.*, 4:56–121.

Freud, A. (1958), Adolescence. *The Psychoanalytic Study of the Child*, 13:255–278. New York: International Universities Press.

Freud, S. (1893), On the psychical mechanism of hysterical phenomena (preliminary communication). *Standard Edition*, 2:3–17. London: Hogarth Press, 1955.

———— (1905), Three essays on the theory of sexuality. *Standard Edition*, 7:123–234. London: Hogarth Press, 1953.

Gould, R. (1978), *Transformations*. New York: Simon & Schuster.

Jung, C. (1963), *Memories, Dreams, Reflections*. New York: Pantheon.

3

A Reexamination of Adult Life Crises: Spousal Loss in Mid- and Late Life

MORTON A. LIEBERMAN, Ph.D.

The study of adult life crises does not represent a coherent intellectual discipline but rather is a vast and varied collection of empirical studies and/or conceptual perspectives stemming from a variety of academic disciplines: epidemiology, sociology and psychology, psychiatry, psychoanalysis, and adult developmental studies. The purpose of this chapter is to examine how the study of such crises illuminates our understanding of adult development.

How do we determine what external life events or inner manifestations are appropriately seen as "adult life crises?" By definition, life crises are normatively defined by each society. Crises otherwise ignored by society are relegated to, and become the province of certain institutions that deal with the marginal, the ill, and the disabled. Thus psychiatry and its allied professions has become the repository for those individuals whose disrupted emotional lives receive no other succorance or aid. One approach, then, for defining the current arena of adult life crises is to examine the array of institutions that society has made available to ameliorate the psychological consequences of life stresses. This definition of adult crises based on community response has changed historically and, of course, does not produce a fixed and eternal list.

The usual academic definition of adult life crises involves discrete changes in life conditions that are consensually recognized as entailing some degree of distress, challenge, and/or hazard by the individual and member of his or her social group.

69

The commonsense meaning is contained in the list of major life events, both normative (marriage, birth of a child, retirement) as well as those nonscheduled but all too common life events such as divorce, widowhood, and illness. Interest for many investigators is in the particular event (widowhood, retirement, marriage, divorce, and so forth) or a class of events (losses). Numerous modifiers are evoked to explain the linkages between life crises and responses. Often the major point of departure is not the event, but the modifier.

Other investigators have focused on the accumulation of life events (life stress). Still others examine life events from a phenomenological perspective. Although they begin with real external events that have an objective definition in time and place, interest is in the processing of these events rather than the events themselves (Lazarus and Folkman, 1984).

Life crisis research is also represented by a distinct developmental position. The work of Buhler (1935), Jung (1933), Erikson (1982), Levinson, Darrow, Klein, Levinson, and McKee (1978), and Gutmann (1987) articulate this tradition. Adult life crises are seen as representing or inaugurating distinct psychological stages which require energy and effort for "successful" adaptation. Although "developmentalists" link crises to external events, these events are not at the forefront of their theory.

I have chosen one life crisis to illustrate the issues confronting investigators who study adult life crises from an adaptational perspective. Moreover, the loss of a spouse exemplifies the conceptual and methodological promise and problems inherent in the study of adult life crises. Spousal-loss research is of interest to the mental health disciplines, sociology and epidemiology. The history of such research also demonstrates development in changing methods, and respecifications of the relevant questions and the conceptual frames to explicate this singular adult life crisis.

Five studies of spousal bereavement will be presented. They draw on two nonclinical populations; a seven-year follow-up study of 600 widows and a smaller sample recruited for a brief preventive group therapy experiment randomized into treatment and controls who were followed for 1 year. Study 1, using the large sample survey, reexamines the classical view of mourning; Study 2 provides for a replication of the first study using data from the intensive clinical sample; Study 3 examines factors that contribute to the resolution–nonresolution of mourning; Study 4 examines the contribution to mourning resolution of the prior marital relationship; Study 5 provides evidence about the limitations of examining spousal bereavement solely in a loss framework. Collectively these studies address the question of how best to conceptualize a common adult crisis.

The Studies

Core Sample

The sample of 596 widows/widowers was generated from a list of recently bereaved people provided by two self-help organizations, THEOS, a national self-help group (SHG) for widows and widowers; and NAIM, based in the Chicago metropolitan area. Since the sampling procedures differed, each will be described.

The THEOS sample was recruited from mailing lists provided by 71 chapters who identified bereaved persons from obituaries, and referral sources, primarily funeral directors and clergy. One thousand four hundred seventy-eight questionnaires were mailed to THEOS members and to nonmembers (those who declined an invitation to participate), 721 completed and returned the time 1 questionnaire (49%). A year later a second questionnaire was sent to the 721 and was completed by 502 subjects (70%).

NAIM, based in the Chicago metropolitan area, was sponsored by the Catholic Archdiocese. Recent widows/widowers are invited to an informational conference. Our research team attended each of seven conferences, described the research, and subsequently mailed a questionnaire to each of those conference attendees. A total of 145 people responded to the time 1 (T1) questionnaire (48%) and 96 of them returned the time 2 (T2) questionnaire (56%).

A total of 866 of them completed and returned the initial questionnaires, 596 at T2 and 190 at time 3 (T3). The sample was assessed at three points in time; baseline was typically during the first 2 years of widowhood/widowerhood, the second a year later, and the last was 6.5 years after the initial assessment.

Sample Description. Of the 596 respondents who returned their questionnaire at T2, 517 were women; 16 percent of the respondents were under age 40, 24 percent were in their forties, 40 percent were in their fifties, and 20 percent were 60 or over. Four hundred and thirty-seven were or became members of the SHG, 159 did not. With regard to educational background, 8 percent had not completed high school, 53 percent were high-school graduates, 16 percent had some college, 17 percent were college graduates, and 6 percent had gone beyond college to either graduate school or professional schools. Ninety-three percent of the sample had children, of whom slightly more than half (54%) were still living in the house.

Approximately three-quarters of the men and half of the women were working prior to the spouse's death. After the spouse's death, employment status increased for the women by 14 percent so that 63 percent of them were working within the first year of widowhood.

Those who returned the T2 questionnaire were compared with those who did not on demographic and status variables as well as several psychological indices. Included in this analysis were comparisons of returners and nonreturners at baseline on work and socioeconomic status, length of SHG membership, educational level, economic distress, marital status, whether they lived alone or not, religious affiliation, number of years married, their ages, and length of bereavement. No significant differences were found (based on chi square analysis) on any of these demographic and status characteristics. They were also compared (using two-tailed *t*-tests) on several mental health indices: depression, anxiety, somatic symptoms, and substance abuse. No significant differences were found.

An analysis comparing SHG members ($N = 437$) to nonmembers ($N = 159$) indicated that for age, sex, education, work status, religious affiliation, living arrangements, current standards of living, and self-reported level of grief, members were similar to those who chose not to affiliate themselves.

How representative was the sample of the widowed/widowered population in the United States as a whole? We know that they were younger, of a higher socioeconomic class, and more likely to be women when compared to the spousally bereaved population shown by the 1980 census. The sample is also skewed in its greater participation in psychotherapy for problems associated with bereavements: 24 percent sought professional psychotherapeutic assistance compared to an estimated 4 percent of the widowed in a national probability sample (Veroff, Kulka, and Dowan, 1981).

The characteristics of this sample can be further documented by comparing it to longitudinal study based on a large ($N = 3000$, age 18–65) probability sample (Pearlin and Lieberman, 1979) in which many of the outcome measures used in this study were employed. The two samples were compared on symptoms of depression, anxiety, and somatization, level of self-esteem, and coping mastery. The study sample were younger, better educated, more likely to be Protestant, more recently widowed/widowered, more likely to be female, and less likely to be remarried than the normative spousal loss sample.

The spousally bereaved in the study sample were significantly more distressed than were those in the normative population. They showed higher levels of anxiety, depression, and somatic symptoms; they also showed lower self-esteem and lower mastery scores. Neither demographically nor in terms of psychosocial functioning did the study sample resemble a probability sample of the spousally bereaved.

How poorly was the study sample functioning? To provide a context for looking at the scores used to index adaptation, the study sample was compared with a demographically matched nonspousally bereaved sample from the Lieberman and Pearlin study. As anticipated, death of a spouse has profound effects on the social–psychological functioning of the survivor. On all measures (symptoms of depression, anxiety, and somatization, level of self-esteem, and coping mastery) the *nonbereaved normative sample* was functioning significantly better (using the *t* statistic, $p < 0.05$) than the widows/widowers sample.

Intervention Sample

The spousally bereaved were recruited to test brief group therapy compared to matched nonintervention controls. The study targeted a consecutive sample of all surviving spouses of individuals who had died of cancer four to ten months before at two Palo Alto, California medical centers. To maximize the chances of recruiting a total sample of bereaved subjects we enlisted the cooperation and sponsorship of the deceased spouses' oncologist who contacted each surviving spouse by mail to introduce and support the research project and principal investigators. We followed the oncologist's letter first with a letter announcing the project and then a phone call in which we described the project in detail and urged each to participate.

Fifty-eight subjects were assigned to the experimental condition,[1] forty-seven agreed to be seen in two to three in-depth interviews, at which time they were invited to participate in a bereavement therapy group. (Eleven subjects could not be interviewed: of these, only five were outright uncooperative; the other seven could not participate for health or logistical reasons—two were critically ill, two were in their late eighties and extremely frail, and three had no available transportation.)

Of the forty-seven interviewed, thirty-six agreed to start the group and eleven refused. Three of these eleven had scheduling conflicts which made attendance in the group impossible, two had serious psychiatric problems, two were Hispanic, spoke limited English, and declined the group. The remaining four, all male, were overtly resistive and declined because they felt that a group would be irrelevant, or that they were too busy, or that they were coping well and did not need support.

The thirty-six subjects who agreed to participate in the eight session support group constitute the study/sample. The mean age of the sample was 56.7, twenty-seven were women

---

[1]Seventy-eight subjects were contacted. Of these, twenty were randomly selected as controls and asked to complete an interview and a battery of questionnaires twice: within the next week and again a year later. All twenty agreed. (They served as controls for the effects of the support group intervention.) The data for the present study, however, are based only on the support group participants because we had far more data on these subjects: intensive interviews as well as information derived from their group participation.

and nine were men. They were middle to upper economic level, all were Caucasian. When they were first interviewed their length of bereavement was from 4 to 11 months.

At T1 each was seen two to six times in an intensive clinical interview conducted by one of the authors, completed a battery of questionnaires, and was given a self-sort interview to assess the self-concept. The entire procedure was repeated at T2, one year later. The interview was semistructured and designed to investigate a broad range of areas pertaining to bereavement: past and current life situation, events surrounding spouse's death, adjustment to widowhood, history and texture of the marriage, personal autonomy, coping modes, symptoms, social adaptation, dreams, death awareness, regrets, isolation, loneliness, and meaning in life. The interviews were audiotaped and later rated by trained judges.

Study 1: Patterns of Grief

The first study to be discussed set out to examine, using the core sample, the effects various patterns of grieving have on adaptation indexed at three points in time after the loss (baseline, one year, and six years later) by measure of mental health, social adaptation, and positive emotional states.

Methods

Measures of Adaptation. Three conceptually relevant areas for quantifying adaptation were chosen: *mental health, positive states,* and *role functioning* (Table 1). Mental health measures reflect indices typically used to assess the effects of spousal bereavement. For some investigators they are synonymous with the definition of grieving. Measured were depression, anxiety, and somatic symptoms, a self-report measure of health (based on the degree to which the respondent perceives health as interfering with his or her normal life tasks), and the frequency and amount that the respondent utilizes alcohol, and/or psychotropic medication to alleviate negative emotional states.

Positive states measures, although frequently used in studies of adaptation, are less common in spousal bereavement studies. Measures of self-esteem, coping mastery (a variant of locus

TABLE 1
Adaptation Measures

A. *Mental Health*
   Depression, Anxiety, and Somatization. Three Hopkins Symptom Checklist scales drawn from a random sample of 2300 adults (Pearlin, Lieberman, Mennaghan, and Mullan, 1981). Further evidence for these scales was developed from a subsequent study of 600 widows and widowers (Lieberman and Videka-Sherman, 1986). The reliabilities were high (alpha: Depression [0.87], Anxiety [0.82], Somatization [0.74]).

   Frequency of Using Psychotropic Medication and Alcohol for Tension Reduction. We used a five-item scale assessing the frequency of using psychotropic medication and alcohol for tension reduction and mood improvement. Previous studies of the spousally bereaved using this scale report a significant abuse of medication and alcohol (soon after the loss) compared to a demographically matched control group of nonbereaved. The scale's sensitivity is further demonstrated in longitudinal studies of the spousally bereaved where used of drugs and alcohol markedly decreases over six years (Lieberman and Videka-Sherman, 1986).

   Health: 2 (5 pt. scales), health interferes and compared to other people your age.

B. *Positive Psychological States*
   Psychological Well-Being. The Bradburn Affect Balance Scale (Bradburn, 1969), a widely used measure, provides two independent dimensions of affective state—positive and negative well-being. Reliability is high; alphas of 0.91 and 0.92.

   Coping Mastery. To measure this we used a coping mastery scale (Pearlin, Lieberman, Mennaghan, and Mullan, 1981)—a 7-item scale based upon confirmatory factor analysis of a random sample of 2300 adults. However we found low reliability among the spousally bereaved (alpha = 0.53).

   Self-Esteem. We used the Rosenberg scale (1965), a well-established eleven item, Gutmann scaled questionnaire.

   Life Satisfaction: 4 pt. scale, very satisfied to not at all.

TABLE 1 (*continued*)

C.	*Role Functioning* *Single Role Strain.* A 14-item scale assessing the amount of strain experienced in occupying this role. Alpha = 0.82 (Pearlin et al., 1981). *Parenting:* Quality of parenting. The scale is based upon confirmatory factor analyses of the Pearlin–Lieberman normative study (Mullan, 1981) (alpha = 0.84) Parental Strain; two general dimensions—worries and problems. Parental Strain; amount of perceived stress, a 9-item Likert scale, confirmatory factor analysis T1, T2 (alpha, 0.89).

of control), positive and negative well-being and life satisfaction were used to index this area. Positive states are not mirror images of distress measured by the mental health scales. The same person can demonstrate high levels of mental distress and high positive states scores. Empirically it is more common to observe both levels of mental distress and low levels of well-being, coping mastery, life satisfaction, and self-esteem. Positive states represent another frame for looking at the effects of the grief pattern that is conceptually independent of mental health.

Role functioning provides a behaviorally linked assessment of adaptation. It asks, based on self-reports, how well the person is performing in the major role areas—economic, parental, and in the newly acquired "single" role. Single strain indexes the respondent's perceptions of how the widow or widower is treated within their extended social world. Malfunctioning in the parental role may represent a combination of both the widow's or widower's own internal state, particularly depression, as well as, of course, the reactions of his or her children who are obviously independently affected by the deaths of their father or mother.

It is quite possible that the three domains reflect "recovery" at different points following the loss. Depression, anxiety, and the use of alcohol and psychotropic medication to affect mood may be the earliest to rebound as grief diminishes. Positive states, particularly measures of well-being and self-esteem, may require a somewhat longer period to return to a level more characteristic of the person prior to the loss. Role measures may be the most resistant to "recovery" because the social context they are imbedded in may be permanently skewed after the loss of the spouse. Although the present study did access the spousally bereaved at three separate periods, much of the information needed to fully understand the progression of adaptation is lacking. Most critical, we do not have a realistic assessment of how the person was functioning prior to the loss. Nor do we have enough points in time to closely follow the progression of adaptive–maladaptive responses as they are reflected in the three domains. Nor can we finely track how changes in one domain may impinge on changes in another. Finally, we do not have external independent information about the social context's effect on particular roles; nor independent information on the impact of the loss on the children and how this may impinge on the parent response manifested in measures of the strain and stress of parental roles. Nevertheless, the assessment of these domains goes beyond the usual symptom evaluation of spousal bereavement and does provide an increment in knowledge about the vicissitudes of reactions to spousal loss.

Measures of Grief. Most bereavement studies use reactions for evidence that a person is grieving (e.g., depression, distress, physical symptoms). This study relied on phenomenological measures for indexing levels and intensity of grieving. Each respondent was asked to indicate how much grief they were experiencing (3 pt. scale) and the frequency of intrusive thoughts about the lost spouse (4 pt. scale). Respondents who reported that they experienced no grief and did not think about their dead spouse were classified as a low grief group; those reporting they experienced some grief and occasionally thought about their dead spouse were classified as a mild grief group; those who experienced some grief and reported that they frequently thought about their dead spouse were classified as a moderate grief group; and those who indicated a great deal of grief and were frequently preoccupied with thoughts of the dead spouse were classified as showing intense grief. At baseline, 12 percent reported little or no grief, 30 percent reported mild grief, 43 percent moderate grief, and 15 percent intense grief.

How well did this phenomenological measure mirror grief assessed by more typical reaction measures? Zero order correlations showed that for mental health, grief intensity was correlated with depression $r = 0.52$, anxiety $r = 0.34$, somatic symptoms $r = 0.23$, and abuse of alcohol and drugs $r = 0.27$. It was not correlated with health. For positive states grief intensity was negatively related to coping mastery $r = -0.23$, self-esteem $r = -0.17$, well-being $r = -0.42$, and life satisfaction $r = -0.44$. In the role area, grief intensity was correlated with single strain, $r = 0.35$, parental strain $r = 0.20$. Grief intensity was not associated with economic distress. Nor was there a significant relationship between grief intensity and age or social class.

Grief Patterns. Scores on grief intensity at baseline and one year later (T2) were used to develop four grief types.[2] *Typical* or normative grief was defined as those widows/widowers who at baseline showed high levels of grief (moderate to intense) but at T2 demonstrated little or very mild grief (N = 66). These widows and widowers show the prototypical "healthy" pattern of grief described in the loss literature. Three nontypical grief patterns were defined. Widows/widowers who showed little or no grief both at T1 and T2—the *limited-grievers* (N = 79); *delayed grievers* reported little or no grief at baseline but one year later demonstrated moderate to intense grief (N = 33); and lastly, a group of widows/widowers who showed moderate to intense grief both at T1 and T2 were designated as *prolonged grievers* (N = 134).

"Validity" of these Phenomenologically Defined Grief Patterns. Grief in this study was defined by the person's own judgment of grief intensity and reports of intrusive thoughts about the dead spouse. Grief types were based upon changes in grief

---

[2]Of the T1 and T2 cases, sixty had missing data and were deleted from further analysis. Clear-cut grief patterns could be found for 392 of the complete cases. Most of the remainder showed mild grief levels at both T1 and T2 and thus did not fit into any of the four theoretically relevant grief patterns. They were excluded from further analysis.

intensity over one year's time. How well did this phenomenological measure of grief patterns mirror reaction measures typically used to index grief? Analysis of variances compared base-
line adaptation scores; all were statistically significant $P < = 0.05$. For all scales widows/widowers who showed limited grief
at T1 had the most positive values on measures of coping,
mastery, self-esteem, and well-being, and the lowest scores on
various measures of distress. The typical and prolonged grief
types showed the most symptoms, the lowest coping mastery
and substantially lower well-being. Those classified as a delayed
grief group, widows/widowers who early on in bereavement did
not show patterns of grieving but did a year or two after the
death of their spouse, demonstrated baseline score similar to
the nongrief group.

These analyses suggest that the clustering of widows into
categories based upon phenomenological measures of grief are
commensurate with the more traditional measures of grief consequences. The subsequent analyses address the studies' central
question; the examination, over time, of the adaptive consequences of these grief patterns.

Method of Analyses

To answer the study's central question, the relationship
of the four different grief patterns to adaptation over time,
multivariate analysis of covariance is the method of choice.
Baseline scores on the dependent variables were entered in as
covariants for the T1, T2 analysis; for the long-term (T3) analysis both the T1 and T2 dependent measures were entered in as
covariants. Because of the serious sample attrition that occurred
over the seven years of study, analyses were computed independently for the T1, T2 panel and the smaller panel T1, T2,
T3. The strategy is based on the expectation that widows and
widowers designated as showing a *typical* grief pattern would at
baseline show high levels of depression and other measures of
distress, comparable to those designated as prolonged grievers.
Differences between these two groups would be expected only
after the passage of time. Those classified as the *delayed* grievers
should, at baseline, show little evidence of distress. The adaptational consequences of this grief pattern would manifest itself

later. We had no theoretical expectation for those individuals who are classified as *limited* grievers. *Chronic* grievers should show high initial distress with little recovery over time.

Results

The results of the study will be shown first for the T1, T2 panel, and then for the long-term follow-up. Three multivariate analyses of covariance were computed: the first was for mental health measures (depression, anxiety, somatic symptoms, self-reports of health and amount and frequency of drug and alcohol abuse). Time 1 scores on these measures were used as covariants. The second analyses examined positive emotional states indexed by self-esteem, the Bradburn well-being index (separate scores for positive and negative dimensions were entered into the equation), coping mastery and life satisfaction. The third analyses used measures of role performance indexed by levels of economic distress, the stresses and strains of parenthood and of being single. Table 2 shows the results of these analyses. In two of the three domains, mental health and positive emotional states, significant differences were found among the grief patterns. Table 2 shows the overall levels of significance, the univariate test for each measure and the mean scores.

An examination of the five mental health components indicates, in order of significance levels, that the grief groups are maximally differentiated on depression, anxiety, and substance abuse. Examination of the mean scores indicates in all instances, the limited grief patterns are the least anxious, depressed, and utilize less psychotropic medication or alcohol for mood change. And in all cases, those classified as extended or protracted grievers show the highest level of anxiety, depression and next to the highest level on substance abuse. The typical grief pattern shows the next best level of adaptation while the delayed generally show poorer performance, particularly in the use of alcohol and psychotropic medication.

For positive states, most of the univariant tests approach significance. An examination of the mean scores for the four grief types indicates that the highest positive effect is again

TABLE 2
Grief Patterns and Adaptation

	Limited			Typical			Delayed			Prolonged			T1-T2 T1-T2-T3 Univariate F's	
	T1	T2	T3	T1	T2	T3	T1	T2	T3	T1	T2	T3		
Mental Health														
Anxiety	1.41	1.40	1.33	1.78	1.52	1.38	1.55	1.56	1.33	1.82	1.69	1.53	1.89	0.06
Depression	1.59	1.53	1.60	2.21	1.84	1.70	2.02	1.95	1.54	2.48	2.19	1.97	3.06**	0.71
Somatic	1.51	1.47	1.55	1.83	1.69	1.53	1.73	1.72	1.38	1.85	1.80	1.69	1.32	1.38
Drug Abuse	0.81	0.76	1.07	2.47	1.20	0.10	1.82	2.48	1.25	2.48	2.07	0.77	3.62*	3.19**
Health	4.0	3.91	4.51	3.72	3.74	4.57	4.25	4.0	4.44	3.82	3.82	4.77	0.05	0.84
Positive States														
Coping Mastery	5.18	5.42	NA	4.03	4.44	NA	5.03	4.48	NA	3.75	4.14	NA	3.22**	
Negative Feelings	1.46	1.29	0.87	2.73	2.30	1.53	1.97	2.57	1.94	2.87	2.58	2.28	0.63	0.58
Positive Feelings	4.08	3.92	4.20	2.98	3.41	3.53	3.38	3.60	3.60	2.67	2.70	3.19	2.95**	0.53
Self Esteem	5.28	5.41	5.33	4.62	5.12	5.44	4.93	5.0	5.47	4.45	4.75	5.14	1.93	0.82
Life Satisfaction	3.09	3.16	NA	2.39	2.71	NA	2.61	2.69	NA	2.08	2.42	NA	1.60	
Role Functions														
Economic	1.60	1.69	1.87	1.69	1.72	1.34	1.69	1.76	1.38	1.62	1.79	1.70	0.47	2.79**
Single Strain	13.85	13.51	15.57	16.05	14.86	15.27	14.57	14.78	16.60	17.42	16.49	17.66	0.37	2.08***
Parental Strain	2.05	2.85	NA	2.44	2.66	NA	1.96	2.74	NA	2.37	2.69	NA	0.40	NA
Parental Strain	1.89	1.98	NA	1.99	2.33	NA	1.80	1.98	NA	1.96	2.18	NA	0.19	NA

*P < 0.001   **P < 0.05   ***P < 0.10

demonstrated by the limited grieving group, the lowest the chronic. This pattern is similar for negative effects, self-esteem, coping mastery, and life satisfaction. The patterns among the remaining groups (the typical and the delayed) are somewhat more complex: on positive feelings, the delayed group is somewhat higher than the typical; their positions are reversed on negative emotional states; they are about equal on self-esteem and life satisfaction. On coping mastery the delayed group shows better scores.

The role measures failed to reveal consistent significant differences among the grief patterns. We could find no evidence that grief patterns affected economic distress, problems encountered in being a single parent, or single role strain.

Long Term Follow-Up

Of the 190 subjects, 38 percent could not be classified into one of the four grief patterns, 118 subjects were available for the analysis of grief patterns and long-term adaptation 6.5 to 10 years after the death of the spouse (limited, 13; typical, 29; prolonged, 60; and delayed, 16). To evaluate the long-term effects of the grief patterns, the same three domains were used. However, some of the measures in each of the three domains were not available at T3 (see Table 1). Multivariate analysis of covariance with the dependent variables at both baseline and T2 as well as the subjects' age and their length of bereavement as covariates were calculated. For mental health, the overall F was 1.37, $P = 0.18$. None of the univariate tests was statistically significant. For positive states, the overall F was 0.73, $P = 0.69$ and again, none of the univariates approached statistical significance. Role measures, however, did reveal an overall F of 2.16, $P = 0.05$. The univariate test indicated that economic distress was significant, $F = 2.79$, $P = 0.05$. The findings that the linkage between different patterns of grieving and adaptation are manifested during the first several years of bereavement and that seven to ten years after the loss of a spouse, the effects are small, is not surprising. The mean scores for each of the grief types, however, does suggest that the relative position of the groups were similar at all three measurement times. The limited grief group was functioning best in comparison to all the other grief types; the prolonged grievers remained the least adequately functioning of the four typologies. The analyses based upon covarying the T1, T2 scores, however, as indicated did not reach statistical significance. A multivariate analysis of covariance, based only on T3 scores, controlling for age and length of widowhood, supports the observations on the mean scores for the various grief patterns. These analyses reveal that, at T3, there was an overall $F = 3.5, P = 0.001$ for mental health, $F = 2.35, P = 0.02$ for positive states, and for role, $F = 2.33, P = 0.03$. To locate the source of the significant differences between grief patterns, a series of one-way analyses of variances were computed on those measures that showed univariate significance in the multivariant analysis of covariance. The Duncan Procedure to compare means revealed that for depression, the prolonged grievers were significantly different; for positive affect states, the prolonged and delayed grievers were significantly different; on positive emotions, the prolonged grievers were significantly different, while on economic distress, it was the no grief group that was significantly different. Overall, the prolonged grievers were the outlayers at T3, a period long after the death of their spouse.

The observations that the prolonged grievers are characterized soon after the death of their spouse and again seven to ten years later by a pattern of psychiatric symptoms and negative affects may indicate that the source of such malfunctioning could represent a preexistent or characterological pattern. Of course, this pattern was probably enhanced by the loss of their spouse but the long-term findings suggest that, in part, this is a pattern that may have existed prior to their loss. The data available in this study, unfortunately, do not permit an examination of this speculation. Overall, it is probably reasonable to conclude, however, that different reactions to the loss of the spouse in the first several years is shaped by the way the widow or widower grieves; the long-term adaptation, seven to ten years after the loss, is less influenced by these initial patterns of grief.

Study 2: A Replication

The intervention study (Yalom and Lieberman, 1991; Lieberman and Yalom, 1992) provided a sample to test the previous findings. Although a much smaller sample, the methods of recruitment and the brief time since the loss of the spouse made this an ideal population for replication.

Grief was assessed by identical scales to those described previously. Of the 65 subjects, 48 were classifiable into grief types: 18 limited, 8 typical, and 22 prolonged. No examples of the delayed grief pattern was observed. No differences were found in grief type distributions between the intervention and control samples ($X2 = 1.63$, N.S.).

Outcome measures consisted of the mental health domain as previously described; positive states by three of the five measures utilized in the first study (self-esteem, coping mastery, and positive affect). Roles were assessed by single strain and a new measure, perceived stigma of the widow/widower role. The restricted range of time since the loss of the spouse (4–11 months) simplified the analyses. Mutivariate analysis of covariance for the three domains was utilized with the baseline scores as covariates.

As shown in Table 3, the findings in this replication sample were similar to those reported in the larger sample. The best adapted were the limited grievers. At baseline both the typical and prolonged are similar. However, one year later, the typical grievers demonstrate recovery while the prolonged remain symptomatic.

Implications: Studies 1 and 2

The most unexpected finding was the uniformity in which those respondents who demonstrated little or no grief (limited grief) were, over the seven years studied, the best adapted. Interpretation of this finding is unfortunately complex. Theoretically, the usual dynamic theories of loss would not have anticipated this finding. Empirically, an examination of the intensive case

TABLE 3
Replication Sample
Grief Patterns and Adaptation

Mental Health	Non		Grief Pattern Typical		Prolonged		Overall F = 2.50 P = 0.02 Univariate F	P
Anxiety	1.28	1.22	1.67	1.50	1.68	1.53	0.81	0.46
Depression	1.55	1.43	2.64	1.69	2.20	2.10	7.60	0.003
Somatic	1.42	1.46	2.00	1.55	1.71	1.64	0.37	0.70
Substance Abuse	1.47	0.78	2.00	1.88	2.60	1.68	2.64	0.10
Health Interferes	1.83	1.67	2.50	2.75	2.27	2.18	0.07	0.93
Positive							Overall F = 2.31 P = 0.04 Univariate	
Coping Mastery	4.94	5.00	3.38	4.75	4.10	4.14	1.65	0.21
Well-Being	4.00	4.12	3.00	4.00	3.33	3.57	0.89	0.42
Self Esteem	4.72	5.00	3.63	4.50	4.63	4.46	4.61	0.02
Role							Overall F = 1.87 P = 0.13 Univariate	
Single Strain	1.91	1.76	2.27	1.94	2.05	2.08	3.92	0.03
Stigma	2.07	2.86	2.31	2.76	2.03	2.95	0.02	0.98

studies available in the Intervention Study suggests that the limited grief pattern is a heterogeneous group of bereavement reactors. Some of the widows and widowers show *no grief* after the loss. Others could more appropriately be viewed as showing an "interrupted" grief pattern. Still others manifested intense but very short-lived grief, a few weeks or at most two months. For some limited-grievers, new relationships "took over." Whatever the process, this group of people were well adapted early in widowhood and maintained the successful adaptation over a seven-year period. Clearly, the conceptual linkage ordinarily made between grief and resolution is not borne out by our findings.

To gain some perspective on the loss effects on the limited grief pattern, Figure 1 provides a comparison of the four grief patterns with the matched sample of nonbereaved drawn from the random sample discussed earlier. The limited overlap of measures from the random sample was addressed by creating two composite measures using identical measures, symptoms, and positive emotions. As shown in Figure 1, at the baseline, the limited grievers are not identical to the nonbereaved; some, albeit small, effect can be imputed. Another indicator that the limited grievers were affected by the loss can be found in their seeking out mental health services soon after the loss; 22 percent did so, compared to 24 percent for the typical, 28 percent delayed, and 20 percent of the prolonged grievers. However, their evaluation of the helpfulness of these contacts was distinct, for the four grief patterns: limited 26 percent, typical 36 percent, delayed 50 percent, and prolonged 36 percent, reported the therapy as very helpful. Clearly then, the limited grievers did not find psychotherapy as helpful as the other grief types.

Among the other patterns of grieving, responses to the loss of a spouse also had significant consequences for the adequacy of adaptation assessed within the first several years of bereavement. Expectations based on clinical studies about prolonged grieving are fulfilled. So are the conceptual expectations about the resolution of grief; those who show intense grieving early on in widowhood/widowerhood with significantly decreased grief intensity within a year, exhibit the expected "recovery" and their level of functioning approaches the normative range. For the small group of widows and widowers who exhibited a delayed grief pattern, some of the conceptual expectations about this pattern are fulfilled. They do slightly poorer over time, although the expected catastrophe as measured by our assessment of adaptation is certainly not borne out. They, by and large, never reach the level of malfunctioning of the prolonged grievers.

It is worth noting, in examining all the groups, including the chronic, that over time the negative effects, whether measured by mental health indices, positive states or role, show "improvement" for all. To what extent is it appropriate to look at reactions to spousal loss as intrinsically self-limiting? What

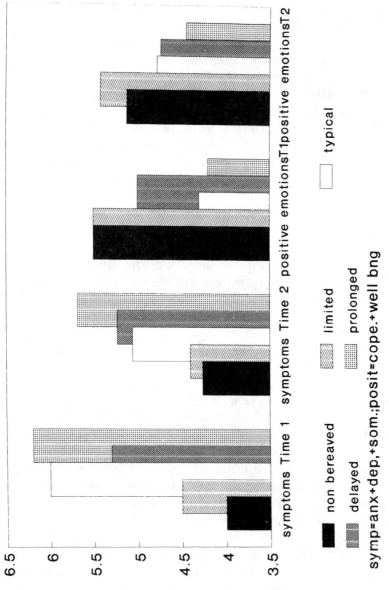

FIGURE 1. Comparisons: Grief patterns to nonwidow.

differs, obviously, is the rate at which the return to "homeosta-sis" occurs. There are differences between, on the one hand, the group we have designated the limited grief group con-trasted with those that we have described as protracted.

Plaguing our research, as well as most if not all studies of spousal loss, is the fact that we do not have a zero point. We know our respondents, sometimes very well but only after the fact. It is difficult, if not wellnigh impossible, to fully appreciate how they were functioning prior to the loss of the spouse. The bereaved sampling frames used in both the studies reported are clearly superior to sampling frames that rely on populations suffering from grief reactions sufficient to bring them into a mental health setting. This is not uniformly a sample of individ-uals who were in trouble, if trouble is defined in the presenta-tion of self to psychiatric services. On the other hand they are not representative of a random sample of widows. Obviously to fully appreciate the complexity of reaction to spousal bereave-ment, information is desperately needed on the persons prior to the loss, conceptually a simple solution but logistically an enormously complicated one.

Study 3: Predictors of Grief Patterns

The third study asks, using the sample developed in the first study, whether the vicissitudes of grief over the course of study (baseline, soon after the loss; one year later; and then again, 6.5 to 7 years after T1) are linked to the widow's current social context and/or characteristics of her past life.

The hypotheses to be tested are based upon the empirical consensus in spousal bereavement "risk factors" research. Be-ginning with Freud's (1917) seminal insight about the role of ambivalence in mourning and melancholia, investigators have identified the nature and quality of the lost relationship as play-ing a key role in the vicissitudes of grief and mourning. Particu-larly highlighted has been the role of ambivalence and depen-dency in the marriage (Raphael, 1977; Parks and Weiss, 1983). The absence or presence of adequate social supports, as well ıs characteristics of the widow's social network, play a role in mitigating and/or exacerbating adaptation to spousal loss. Madison and Walker (1967), Madison, Viola, and Walker (1969), and Raphael (1977) among others have pointed to the role of social supports and social network characteristics in adaptation. Other factors associated with risk include the age at which spousal loss occurs (younger widows, those under 40, are most likely to suffer negative consequences), and the effects of socioeconomic class. There is some evidence that how the death occurred, sudden versus lingering, may be associated with the speed of recovery. Some investigators have pointed to the role that other contemporaneous stresses play in adaptation, and a few have pointed to prior adaptational patterns and "personality" as contributors to the success or failure of adaptation.

Five hypotheses will be explored:

1. Do certain psychological characteristics of the widow's relationship to the dead spouse affect grief patterns?
2. What is the effect of concurrent stress on grieving?
3. Can differences in social context, such as the presence of children in the household, social class, and age, influence grieving?
4. Does the structure of the widow's social network influence these grief patterns?
5. How do the sources and types of support mitigate or increase grief?

Methods

Predictor Variables

Relationship to the Spouse. Three scales were used to assess this domain, level of dependency on the husband prior to his death, and feelings of guilt and anger toward the spouse. All three of these measures were assessed at baseline. *Dependency* was indexed by asking the widows to rate themselves on how much they relied on the deceased spouse (completely, quite a bit, somewhat, not at all) in raising children, companionship, day-to-day household decisions, transportation, managing money, arranging social get togethers with friends and family, and discussing personal problems (alpha = 0.71). *Guilt* was assessed by a seven-item scale which asked subjects to respond (not at all, somewhat, very much) to questions: You felt God was punishing you by taking your spouse; the way you treated your spouse when your spouse was alive; feelings of responsibility for the death; incomplete relationship; God had abandoned you; things you said or didn't say to your spouse (alpha = 0.70). *Anger* was indexed by eight items: the unfairness of it all; your spouse for dying; doctors and nurses who cared for your spouse; the funeral home; someone connected with the death; your spouse because of the financial situation the death brought about; God for allowing the death; God for abandoning you (alpha = 0.72).

The present study shares with most, if not all, studies of spousal bereavement, the problem that the assessment of the relationship with the dead spouse is only available through the eyes of the widow after the death and is obviously open to problems of retrospective distortion. The independence of measures commonly used to assess grief, and the assessment of a widow's perception of her prior relationship to the spouse is complex, and potential confounds are not easily resolved. We have no independent way of separating these two theoretically distinct but contemporaneous empirical measures.

Social Supports. A variety of indices were used to characterize the social support available to and utilized by the widow. Social supports measures provided information on who provides support, how much, and the type of support provided. Type of social support was assessed by measures of *intimacy*, talking about important personal problems; *emotional*, being able to depend on various people for support and comfort when they were feeling down; *guidance and information*, availability of others to talk about issues they were experiencing as widows; *dependability*, being able to count on people for help in emergency situations; and *sanction*, support for their life-style and behavior as a widow. In each area, the widow was asked to indicate how much each of the following people provided support: *parents, in-laws, children, relatives, married friends*, and *single widowed friends*. A five-point scale was used for each source, with zero being used to indicate a source was not available, with four indicating frequent availability. Thus, for each respondent we had a 6 × 6 matrix, six types of support, and six sources of support. Twelve scores were generated to reflect this matrix, the six types of support and the six sources of support.

To obtain an overall single score for how much support was available for the widow, a somewhat different approach was used. Subjects were asked to indicate the most important or compelling problem they experienced as a widow, and then they were asked to rate the amount of stress the problem was causing them (1 to 10). They were then asked to indicate who they would turn to for help with this problem. The response of what people they turn to for help was used to create a score, *number of helpers*, and index the size of the widow's perceived helping network.

To assess possible changes in relationships to people since the death of the spouse, each widow was asked whether they preceived *changes in the amount of contact* they had with family and friends: more, about the same, less.

Network Characteristics. Here the interest was in certain formal characteristics of the widow's network. Examined were the *density* of the network (the number of people defined as close friends who knew one another); the *heterogeneity–homogeneity* of the network (the proportion of widows among their close friends); *network stability*; the ratio of new friends made since the death of the spouse to old friends; and the *size* of network, the number of close friends.

Social Context. The widow's current social context, characteristics describing the social envelope currently occupied, were indexed by *socioeconomic status, occupational status, number of children*, and the *number of children living at home, social class, education*, and *age*.

Concurrent Stress. This domain was indexed by measures of role strain and role stress reported by the widow in the major role areas, economic, parenting, and the newly acquired role of singleness. *Economic distress* was assessed by two items, perceived difficulty in living on present income and comparison of current living standard to status prior to the death of the spouse.

Single role strain was measured by a 7-item scale (from zero, never, to 7, very often) on feeling out of place, having fun, fear of going out, having people to talk to, sharing experiences, fear of not being interesting, and not having the kind of sex life they would prefer (alpha = 0.86). *Parenting strain* was indexed by 9 items that asked about how much they felt tied down, worried about their children, and feelings that they must hide grief from children (alpha = 0.89).

Method of Analysis

Five hypotheses will be tested: the influence of the relationship to the dead spouse on grieving; the type and quality of social supports currently available to the widow; network characteristics; the widow's social context; and her concurrent stress indexed by role strains. The hypotheses were explored using a multivariate analysis of variance for each of the domains representing the hypotheses.

To aid in the analyses of the differences among the five grief patterns, four planned contrast analyses were computed based upon the multivariate analysis of variance. Selection of contrasts was based on the patterns of grieving. At baseline, those described as typical grievers were similar in grief patterns to the chronic and prolonged grievers; the first contrast compared the typical to the chronic plus prolonged grief groups. The second contrast examined the limited grievers in comparison to those described as delayed grievers. At baseline both were similar in grief pattern; the third contrast examined the comparison between the prolonged and chronic grievers, two groups that at baseline and at T2 were similar but differed on grief pattern at T3. The last contrast compared the limited grief group with the typical grievers, groups that were dissimilar at baseline but increased in similarity over time. Table 4 shows the results of these analyses.

Results

Overall, the three measures used to index the relationship to the deceased spouse are significantly associated with patterns

TABLE 4
Predictors of Grief Patterns

	Limited	Typical	Delay	Prolonged	Chronic	Sign
OVERALL $F = 3.92$ $P = 0.001$						
A. Relationship to Spouse						
Dependency	2.48	2.68	2.69	2.93	2.98	0.97*
Guilt	1.40	1.63	1.44	1.63	1.62	3.19*
Anger	1.73	2.0	1.83	2.08	2.11	8.44*
OVERALL $F = 1.66$ $P = 0.02$						
B. Type of Social Support						
Intimacy	9.26	9.69	12.70	4.37	5.92	3.59*
Sanctioning	14.44	13.81	10.90	7.48	4.56	3.11**
Guidance	4.13	10.95	7.77	3.31	4.39	4.13*
Depend	7.96	7.34	8.32	4.77	5.05	0.74 NS
Contact	12.04	14.03	12.39	8.66	10.72	1.73 NS
Emotional	12.53	12.96	12.88	9.16	5.36	1.87***
See Family More	1.92	1.98	2.04	1.96	2.09	0.41 NS
See Friends More	1.41	1.53	1.59	1.44	1.61	0.73 NS
Number of Helpers	2.00	2.31	2.85	2.23	2.82	0.99 NS
Sanctioning	3.22	3.05	3.36	3.04	2.89	3.10*
OVERALL $F = 1.80$ $P = 0.01$						
Source of Support[a]						
Parents	7.80	9.80	6.07	7.17	7.18	1.23 NS
In-Laws	7.23	6.78	9.20	7.70	7.11	1.41 NS
Children	15.96	15.43	18.15	17.04	18.50	2.74**
Relatives	13.78	13.66	16.82	13.76	14.26	1.95***
Married Friends	14.45	14.61	16.33	14.3	15.14	1.21 NS
Single Widowed Friends	18.01	16.49	15.96	16.18	14.54	2.23***
OVERALL $F = 1.64$ $P = 0.05$						
C. Network Characteristics						
Number of Friends	5.27	5.54	6.23	5.30	5.60	1.45 NS
New Friends	3.51	2.97	3.45	2.89	2.29	2.99*
Homogeneity	2.11	1.88	1.80	1.93	1.85	1.23 NS
Density	2.17	2.13	2.39	2.13	2.17	0.49 NS
OVERALL $F = 2.81$ $P = 0.001$						
D. Current Stress						
Economic Distress	1.64	1.67	1.70	1.60	1.72	0.67 NS
Single Strain	14.00	16.50	14.10	17.24	17.97	6.87*
Parent Strain	1.92	1.46	1.79	1.91	1.97	0.08 NS
Parental Distress	2.08	2.42	1.96	2.38	2.27	2.78**

TABLE 4 (*continued*)

	Limited	Typical	Delay	Prolonged	Chronic	Sign
OVERALL $F = 0.94$ P = NS						
Social Characteristics						
Age	50.85	51.08	53.89	53.73	56.89	1.94***
SES	45.20	48.00	47.60	49.50	49.00	0.61 NS
Percent Working	64%	68%	73%	65%	61%	1.78 NS
Number of Children	2.97	2.37	2.77	2.58	2.61	0.68 NS
Education	2.52	2.67	2.51	2.56	2.30	0.81 NS
Percent Living Alone	44%	54%	48%	58%	53%	1.10 NS
Number of Children Home	1.27	0.83	1.28	1.04	0.76	1.48 NS

[a]Separate analyses were computed for type and source of support. Number of widows whose parents were decreased reduced sample size for support source.
*$P < 0.001$ **$P < 0.05$ ***$P < 0.10$

of grieving. The limited grief pattern widows showed the lowest dependency, guilt, and anger; in sharp contrast, the prolonged and chronic grievers demonstrated the highest dependency, guilt, and anger toward the deceased spouse. The other grief patterns showed less consistent characteristics. The delayed grief group was most similar to the limited grievers, excepting their reported higher dependency during the marriage, while the typical group (those widows who had intense grief at T1 but who significantly recovered one year later) were similar to the prolonged and chronic and delayed grievers at baseline, demonstrating relatively high anger and guilt but in contrast to the prolonged grievers, they were lower in dependency during the marriage.

An examination of Table 4 reveals that all three domains assessing social supports (type and amount of social support, the source of such support, and certain structural characteristics of the social network) significantly differentiated among patterns of grieving. Clear differences were found in type and amount of social support; those classified as limited, typical, and delayed grievers reported more intimacy, sanctioning, guidance, and emotional support than did the prolonged and chronic grievers. The contrast analyses did not reveal significant differences among the limited, typical, or delayed grievers;

nor did it suggest differences in amount and source of social support between the prolonged versus the chronic.

Sources of support were similarly significantly different among the grief types: generally, the chronic, prolonged, and delayed received more overall support from the children than did the limited or typical. In contrast, the limited grievers were highest in receipt of support from single widowed friends, and the chronic group, the lowest in this area. Contrast analyses revealed that there were significant differences between the limited grievers and delayed grievers on sources of social support, as well as significant differences between the typical grievers and the chronic/prolonged. This analysis suggests that it is not only the amount and type of social support received but the source of the support that appears to make a difference in the pattern of grieving.

Network characteristics were overall significant, the univariate analyses suggest that the major contribution to the difference was the number of new friends made since the loss. The limited and delayed grievers show the highest number of new friends, the chronic the lowest. None of the other network characteristics shows univariate significance. The contrast analyses in this area revealed that the typical made significantly more new friends and had social networks characterized by heterogeneity compared to the chronic grievers. Comparisons between the prolonged and chronic revealed that the prolonged made more new friends early on in widowhood compared to the chronic. Comparisons between the limited and delayed found that the delayed had a larger social network of close friends compared to the limited and, in fact, to all other grief patterns.

Thus, the hypothesis testing the relationship between social support characteristics and grief patterns is supported by our analysis, the patterns of social support established during the first year or two of widowhood appear to influence grieving patterns over time.

As Table 4 indicates, there was a substantial relationship between concurrent stress and grief patterns. The prolonged and chronic experienced considerably more single strain and parental distress than did the other three grief patterns, limited, typical, and delayed. Of particular interest is that early on in widowhood, single strain was higher for the typical, compared to the limited and delayed. Of note is that economic distress did not distinguish among the groups. Thus, the hypothesis that concurrent stress in the life of the widow influences the patterns of grieving and consequently adaptation is supported.

The last hypothesis, that the social context indexed by the widow's age, social class, work status, education, and living arrangements, as well as children in the home, did not show overall significant differences among the five grief patterns. It should be pointed out that the variations, particularly with regard to age and social class, were not high compared to epidemiological studies of widowhood. This is primarily a relatively well-educated and middle-class population.

Study 4: The Role of the Past Marital Relationship for Grief

This study, relying on the sample described in Study 2, permits a clinical view of the past marriage on current grief. At T1 each was seen two to six times in intensive clinical interviews conducted by one of the authors (I.Y.), completed a battery of questionnaires, and were given a self-sort interview to assess the self-concept. The entire procedure was repeated at T2—one year later. The interview was semistructured and designed to investigate a broad range of areas pertaining to bereavement: past and current life situation, events surrounding spouse's death, adjustment to widowhood, history and texture of the marriage, personal autonomy, coping modes, symptoms, social adaptation, dreams, death awareness, regrets, isolation, loneliness, and meaning in life. The interviews were audiotaped and later rated by trained judges.

Grief was assessed by identical scales to those described previously. Of the 65 subjects, 48 were classifiable into grief types: 18 limited, 8 typical, and 22 prolonged. No examples of the delayed grief pattern were observed. No differences were found in grief type distributions between the intervention and control samples ($X2 = 1.63$, NS).

Characteristics of the Marital Relationship

Raters, upon listening to the recordings of the clinical interviews, were asked to make five judgments about the marital relationship: the degree, on a three-point scale, to which the bereaved person *idealized* their spouse; whether evidence was presented in the interview that the respondent believed himself/herself *stunted* by the marriage; and to make an overall judgment about the *quality of the marital relationship*, a five-point scale from most positive to most unsatisfactory. (At T1, 42 percent of the respondents had idealized their dead spouse, 30 percent were stunted by their marriages, and 66 percent were rated as having positive marriages. Idealization was correlated 0.27 with quality of marriage and -0.34 with stunting, quality of marriage and stunting correlated at a -0.44 level.)

Ratings of *autonomy* during the tenure of the marriage were based upon a variety of areas including work, independent friends, and the like as well as a judgment about the overall level of psychological autonomy. Approximately half of the respondents (48%) were rated as showing overall psychological autonomy. The intercorrelations between the individual items in the autonomy scale, for example, between work identity and separate sets of friends, were low and nonsignificant; we decided for the purposes of the analysis presented in this paper to utilize the overall ratings of autonomy which correlate an average of 0.30 with the various subscales of autonomy ranging from 0.06 to 0.63. The last area were ratings based on assessment of whether the person was *lonely prior* to the death of the spouse.

In addition to these ratings based on intensive clinical interviews, the identical measures used in the previous study of guilt and anger were available.

Method of Analysis

The small sample size precluded multivariate statistics, so one-way analyses of variance were used to test the seven indices

TABLE 5
Replication Sample:
Marital Relations and Grief Patterns

	Grief Type			F	P
	Non	Typical	Prolonged		
Guilt	1.22	1.77	1.47	5.88	*
Anger	1.41	2.04	1.68	4.96	*
Communications about death	1.40	1.60	1.43	0.26	NS
Quality of Marriage	1.45	1.20	1.36	0.45	NS
Stunted by Marriage	1.45	1.60	1.86	2.45	*
Autonomy	1.50	1.40	1.43	0.08	NS
Loneliness	1.64	1.60	1.69	0.07	NS

$*P < 0.001$ $**P < 0.10$

measuring the prior marital relationship. Table 5 shows the results of these analysis.

Three of the seven measures used to assess the prior marital relationship were significantly associated with grief patterns. Similar to findings in the first study, guilt and anger were found to differentiate the grief patterns. One of the ratings, the degree to which the prior marital relationship had stunted the remaining spouse, showed a consistent trend, the least stunted were the limited grievers, the most stunted, the prolonged. The typical (those who experience intense grief initially but by the end of one year show considerably less intense grief) were at midpoint. Of equal interest is the absence of statistically significant findings on the quality of the marriage. It would be an oversimplification to view the findings about marriage, both in the initial study and this one, to conclude that the quality of the marriage in general terms is linked to patterns of grieving. It appears to be particular aspects of the marriage, the sense of anger and guilt, and reflection that the marriage has prevented the remaining spouse to fully "be their own woman."

However, as we indicated in the discussion of the previous study, findings about the marriage are speculative at best since our information is contingent upon the reports of the remaining spouse. The availability of intensive clinical interviews in this replication sample provided a closer examination of reports on the prior marital relationship and the raters were asked to make "clinical" judgments. However, we are still left with a portrayal of a relationship in the past under the complex emotional life of a recently bereaved person.

Summary: Studies 3 and 4

Five hypotheses were tested to examine "risk" factors associated with the course of grief over an extended time after the death of the spouse. These hypotheses were embedded in the accumulation of evidence developed by a number of investigators. Asked were the contribution to the course of bereavement of ambivalence to the spouse, the amount and type of social support, social network characteristics, current stress and the location of the widow in the social structure.

Positive findings were obtained for four of the five hypotheses; only the location in the social structure failed to reach an acceptable level of statistical significance. We have not as yet asked if each of the areas explored independently contributes to risk. To explore this question the large number of dependent variables used to explore the five hypotheses needed simplification. Data reduction of the dependent variables was achieved by computing principal components for each of the areas. The first principal component was extracted from the three spousal relationship measures (53% of the variance); the four role stress measures (48% of the variance); the four social network characteristics (43% of the variance). The twelve measures representing type and source of social support required four principal components to adequately reflect these scores (66% of the variance). The first rotated factor reflected types of support, the remaining three primarily sources—second, inlaw and parents; third, single and married friends, and the fourth, children.

These seven summary indices were entered in a regression with grief types as the dependent variable. (Simple ANOVAS using the seven summary measures yielded the expected statistical significance distinguishing among the grief patterns.) A simple regression equation revealed that two of the seven composite scores contributed to the significant F ($F = 6.01$, $p = 0.000$; Multiple $R = 0.26$), the relationship to the spouse ($\beta = 0.18$, $t = 4.1$, $p = 0.000$) and the fourth principal component of social supports, children ($\beta = 0.18$, $t = 4.1$, $p = 0.000$). The results of the regression equation do point to the importance of two characteristics that appear to independently contribute to risk. In a finding that echoes classical loss theory, ambivalence toward the deceased spouse increases risk. The reliance for support on children and relatives with less attention to friends appears also to *increase* risk (all the other support dimensions operate in the opposite direction, the more support the less the risk). Another regression equation using the original twelve support variables, six types, and six sources provided confirmation; the more support received from children the higher the risk. A useful comparison is to examine the mean support amounts for children versus single friends for each of the grief patterns: limited, children 15.9; single friends 18.1; typical, 15.4, 16.5; delayed 18.2, 15.9; prolonged 17.1, 16.2; chronic 18.5, 14.5.

The complexity of social supports is the topic of another study; suffice to say here that although overall amount of social support is a "risk" reduction factor, such a conclusion seriously oversimplifies the role such supports play in helping widows over the course of bereavement.

Study 5: "Growth" as a Response to Spousal Loss

Study 5 was based on an exploration of the consequences of engaging in existential explorations for the course of bereavement (Yalom and Lieberman, 1991). The portion of that study to be examined in this chapter focuses on a new way of looking at "outcomes" associated with spousal loss in mid- and late life. The final study began, stimulated by our clinical interviews that many of the widows in the intervention study had undergone some form of personal growth; many had reintegrated themselves and had changed their relationships and their self-concept in ways that were new to them and represented marked improvements from their prior functioning during their marriage.

First, a measure of personal growth was developed based upon the intensive T1, T2 clinical interviews. Two independent raters who had no information regarding the existential ratings or any other data on the subjects listened to audiotapes of the T1 interviews and rated each subject on a four-point scale (1 = no growth; 2 = slight; 3 = some; 4 = much growth—categories 3 and 4 were subsequently combined for analytic purposes). The raters were also asked to listen to both T1 and T2 interviews and rate whether the subjects had changed on growth during the time between the interviews.

The growth scale was anchored by category 4 Much, i.e., definite signs of personal growth. The person is obviously stretching (doing new things, taking educational courses, struggling to find her or his own identity and own roots). Such people may be more aware of being an "I" rather than a "we," have developed new interests, visited new places, are willing to explore new relationships. They may be more self-sufficient, taking care of their own finances, their own cars, house maintenance; they may be taking better care of their physical health (for example, exercise regimens, walking more, or taking swimming lessons). They may be engaged in new or renewed forms of creative expression like painting or writing.

Category 1 people, i.e., those showing no signs of personal growth. The person is very much the same or there may be evidence of regression of behavior. The person may be stuck, not progressing in any way. There may be evidence of the person clinging to sameness, i.e., engaged in the same life routine and activities. Some cling to their spouse's clothes and possessions, others leave all effects in place untouched.

Case Illustration of a Woman with "Much" Personal Growth
(Category 4)

Mrs. D., a 62-year-old woman, underwent a number of changes after the death of her husband. She felt she first needed to rediscover her own identity—she had been a "we" and had long lost touch with her "I." Hence, she took a pilgrim-age back to the country of her birth, searched for the house in which she had been born, spoke to old townspeople and rela-tives in order to reconstruct her family and her early life. She began a number of new activities—some had been interrupted during her earlier life, some she had long yearned to do: she had braces put on her crooked teeth, took swimming and piano lessons, attended poetry writing workshops, sold a house she had never liked and designed a new one, and enrolled in the freshman class of a nearby university's intergenerational program.

Growth and Existential Awareness

Eleven of the thirty spousally bereaved (37%) showed clear-cut evidence of growth (T1 growth rating of 3 or 4 and main-tained or increased this pattern of growth when assessed one year later). Was there a relationship between heightened exis-tential awareness and growth? We found that it was positive and significant, $X2 = 9.80$, $df = 3$, $P = 0.02$. In contrast to our findings of no differences between the existentially aware and nonaware in the course of bereavement (i.e., symptoms of grief, intensity of mourning, role, stresses and strain), here we find a substantial relationship between engagement in the existential process and personal growth.

An examination of the correlates associated with engaging in existential exploration that were linked to growth (Yalom and Lieberman, 1991) suggested that these were people who look *into*, rather than *away from*, death. They were able or willing to bear and experience their aloneness. They were more willing to examine the limitations of their marriages and to view their spouse in more realistic, nonidealized terms. They grasped the idea that their loss offered an opportunity for psychological freedom and recognized and acknowledged the fact that they had been stunted by their marital relationship. This recognition does not necessarily imply that the overall quality of such mar-riages was poor; in fact, they were rated higher in overall of marital quality.

We would suggest that these individuals were upset about the right thing, about the real situation they faced in life. Often, individuals mired in chronic grief tend to be fixated on their loss, fixated in anger, fixated on their spouse. Not so the existentially aware individuals in our study: they showed less grief, and less guilt and anger toward their spouse. They *did* have more anxiety and depression but their dysphoria may be linked not to grief, but to death, their own death, to questions about life meaning, and to the opportunity and challenge of freedom.

Another cluster of findings centered around aspects of the self. Existentially aware individuals had higher self-esteem and were more prone to change their self-image by taking in new elements into the self. Our data are consistent with the view that existentially aware individuals possess a certain type of internal strength—a sureness about oneself, a relative freedom from neurotic or distorting defenses that enables them to fix their gaze on their existential situation.

The profile also indicates that the existentially aware Ss, generally females, are engaged in a psychosocial moratorium. They experience more loneliness and are less prone to use heterosexual pairing to avoid it. Apparently, most of the males in our sample could not tolerate aloneness: rather than engage in a psychosocial moratorium, they leaped into a new heterosexual relationship. At T1 several men struggled with existential issues, but after engaging in a new relationship were, at T2, not perceived to be continuing their existential explorations.

Summary 5

The findings of this inquiry raise some important questions about how we in this field have investigated the impact of bereavement on both men and women. The traditional measures that have always been studied in bereavement research (symptoms, vicissitudes of grief, and social adjustment) represent a homeostatic model in which the underlying assumption is that spousal bereavement is a stressor which upsets the equilibrium of the person. This perspective assumes that the most appropriate way to assess the consequences of spousal bereavement is to examine whether or not the bereaved individual returns to equilibrium. It further assumes that, after an "appropriate passage of time," following spousal loss, the optimal and only meaningful outcome should consist of the resolution of depression and grief and a return to the previous adaptive pattern of social adjustment.

But the homeostatic model has limitations; it is not sensitive to some important phenomena, for example, the fact that loss has such powerful and highly individualized meaning to bereaved individuals and that there is within each individual a deep capacity for self-exploration and personal change. Bereaved individuals are challenged in many areas but, perhaps most importantly, they are confronted with major and mortal questions about existence—about finitude, freedom and responsibility, isolation and meaning in life.

These existential challenges always confront widows and widowers, but not all choose to attend to the challenge or respond to it. Our data suggest that those who do respond ultimately have a meaningful payoff—they are very likely to undergo personal growth. Obviously not all such individuals experience the same degree of growth but our data indicate that all of the widows who engaged in the existential task underwent some growth.

Implications

We are now ready to return to the questions posed at the outset of this chapter. What kind of adult life crises does spousal loss pose? What are the appropriate frameworks to view widowhood/widowerhood? In the language of the research on modifiers of life crises, spousal bereavement represents a negative event. It is both a role exit and a loss that is not controllable; yet is, especially for women, part of the expectable life cycle. Studies of spousal bereavement are imbedded in a homeostatic model. Loss is seen as creating a disturbance, while the mourning processes are seen as the mechanism by which the organism returns to prior levels of adaptation. The factors affecting the successful working through of grief and mourning emphasize individual differences in prior losses, the relationship with the deceased spouse, and current or past "other" psychological problems. It has been shown that timing (in the sense of on or off time) influences the consequence of widowhood/widower-hood. Available evidence also suggests that the consequences of this life event have changed dramatically over large periods of historical time. In these senses, then, the loss of a spouse is an ideal surrogate for many other adult life crises.

Classical spousal-loss research (Freud, 1917; Bowlby, 1980) lays emphasis on the loss consequences for psychological health through a focus on the vicissitudes of mourning and grief. Much of the early work in the classical view was based on small opportunistic samples, skewed to the mentally distressed who sought help. The early interest was in determining processes that led to restoring the person to previous levels of function-ing. Particularly important in Freud's thinking was an emphasis on reattachment; mourning was a gradual surrender of psycho-logical attachment to the deceased in order to liberate the be-reaved for new attachments. He believed that relinquishment of the love object involves an internal struggle between intense yearning for the lost loved one and the reality of the loved one's absence. It was Freud who advanced the idea that many psychiatric illnesses are expressions of pathological mourning. Such pathology includes not only excessive grief but failure to grieve and suppression or denial of emotional feelings. Con-versely, psychological health after spousal loss is said to depend on capacity to grieve as reflected in depressive reactions.

Fundamental to all dynamic theories of grief, despite varia-tions of the underlying process (Freud, 1917; Bowlby, 1980), is a time-line of progressions in grief intensity. Some believe that there are formal stages through which the prototypical be-reaved person must pass. This time-line is frequently used to provide a guideline to the bereaved person's successful adapta-tion. Departures from the "expected" time-line, rather than intensity alone, are the theoretical underpinnings for ex-plaining variations in outcomes associated with the loss of a spouse. Thus, the failure to grieve or the brevity of grief are used to suggest failures in appropriate processing of the loss; similarly, protracted grieving beyond some arbitrary point in time is seen equally as pathological.

In addition to the findings presented in this chapter, other studies have raised questions about the model of adaptation outlined by Freud and other dynamic theories which imply that absence of grieving is linked to negative outcomes as a delay, suppression or denial of affect. (See Osterweis, Solomon, and Green [1984]; Wortman and Silver [1987] for excellent views of the empirical literature.) Many widows and widowers who show no evidence of grieving have been found to be well adapted subsequent to the loss of their spouse. Little evidence is available to document the hypothesis that manifestly undistressed or undepressed widows/widowers are at high risk for subsequent maladaptation because of not managing the process of grieving. The evidence reported here on the consequences of different grief patterns and long-term adaptation certainly questions the ubiquitousness of a simple loss theory. I believe that to fully appreciate the complexity of spousal loss as an adult crisis in mid- and late life, our view must expand on both what the task or challenges of spousal loss are and what the possible consequences are for the widow or widower traversing such dilemmas can be.

Beyond grieving and loss of the partner, the spousally bereaved are faced with a set of challenges and alternative paths. It disrupts plans, hopes, and dreams for the future (Silver and Wortman, 1980). The loss also challenges individuals' beliefs and assumptions about their world. Social supports and social network must be renegotiated. The spousally bereaved must reexamine their self-image which has been embedded in a long-term relationship, and move to a self based on an "I" rather than a "we." Many of the spousally bereaved are faced with inner psychological tasks that can be described by the label "existential dilemmas"; confrontations of their regrets not only in regard to the deficits of their past marital relationship but to undeveloped aspects of their own life. Such confrontations lead some from a sense of aloneness to the "closeness" of their own death, and then to seeking new meanings in life (Yalom and Lieberman, 1991). Such challenges can be a source of distress for many; for others, however, it can provide a sense of accomplishment.

Studies on the transforming characteristics of spousal bereavement are not numerous, yet their findings are evocative.

They depart from the predominantly homeostatic model specifying restoration to initial (preloss) levels. Yalom and Lieberman (1991) found that 37 percent of the spousally bereaved showed clear-cut evidence of growth. The development of new behaviors and perspectives was not related to the typical measures of recovery, such as depression levels, social functioning, and grief resolution. Lieberman (1991) replicated the growth findings in a panel study of nonclinical widows followed for seven years. Fifty-three percent of the widows showed some evidence of growth, i.e., new patterns of behavior and/or ways of thinking. Clearly, loss of a spouse in mid- and late life is a complex event that can lead not only to adaptive failures and illness, but to enhanced functioning. The narrow confines of a homeostatic framework for understanding the impact of adult crises need expansion.

The perspective developed in this chapter echoes the historical changes in spousal bereavement inquiry. As attention turned toward nonclinical samples and different researchable hypotheses about spousal loss, evidence began to accumulate that: (1) grief reactions to spousal loss are not universal; (2) adaptation is not highly predictable, in a normative sample, from the dynamics of mourning; (3) classical risk factors (other losses and an ambivalent relationship to the deceased) do not account for most of the variations in successful–unsuccessful adaptation. Increasingly concern has been with the modifiers rather than affective reactions to spousal bereavement. Attention has moved from an internal dynamic to external conditions; social supports, social contexts, as well as internal processes, cognitive characteristics such as coping strategies and adaptive skills. Although such newer studies represent a shift in both method and paradigm, most still share a common homeostatic framework for indexing consequences; that of restoring the widow/widower to their initial adaptive level.

One clear implication of our findings is that the study of spousal bereavement must be broadened and individualized; it must go beyond loss and recovery therefrom. It must be sensitive to the fact that spousal loss in mid- and late life is highly complex; it impinges both on the inner life of the spousally bereaved as well as on external tasks and adjustments. The called for expansion and reconceptualization of one critical adult life crisis, spousal loss, is not a call for abandoning the rich legacy of loss theory. The findings reported in this chapter provide ample support for the insights and concepts previously provided. For example, we did find that chronic grief, lasting upwards of seven years, does occur for a substantial minority; we also found that a central dynamic, ambivalence toward the lost object, played an important role in grief resolution. It is equally clear that most do not follow this pattern and extensive grieving *is not* a prerequisite for successful adaptation. A theory based on clinical cases, those who seek professional help, cannot adequately describe the phenomena, after all only 4 percent of the spousally bereaved seek such help (Veroff, Kulka, and Dowan, 1981). Nor can a framework that assumes that crises simply potentiate adaptive failures capture the rich texture of people's potential for development in the face of adversity.

References

Bowlby, J. (1980), *Attachment and Loss: Vol 3. Loss: Sadness and Depression.* London: Hogarth Press.

Bradburn, N. (1969), *Structure of Psychological Well-Being.* Chicago: Aldine.

Buhler, C. (1935), The curve of life as studied in biographies. *J. Appl. Psychol.,* 19:405–409 (138).

Erikson, E. H. (1982), *The Life Cycle Completed.* New York: Norton.

Freud, S. (1917), Mourning and melancholia. *Standard Edition,* 14:152–170. London: Hogarth Press, 1957.

Gutmann, D. (1987), *Reclaimed Powers: Towards a Psychology of Men and Women in Later Life.* New York: Basic Books.

Jung, C. (1933), *Modern Man in Search of a Soul.* New York: Harcourt, Brace, & World.

Lazarus, R. S., & Folkman, S. (1984), *Stress, Appraisal and Coping.* New York: Springer.

Levinson, D., Darrow, G., Klein, E., Levinson, M., & McKee, B. (1978), *The Seasons of a Man's Life.* New York: Knopf.

Lieberman, M. A. (1991), Bereavement self-help groups: A review of conceptual and methodological issues. In: *Bereavement: A Sourcebook of Research and Intervention,* ed. M. S. Strobe & R. O. Hanson. Oxford: Cambridge University Press.

———— Videka-Sherman, L. (1986), The impact of self-help group therapy on the mental health of widows and widowers. *Amer. J. Orthopsychiat.,* 56:435–449.

———— Yalom, I. D. (1992), Brief psychotherapy for the spousally bereaved; A controlled study. *Internat. J. Group Psychother.,* 42/No. 1.

Madison, D. C., Viola, A., & Walker, W. L. (1969), Further studies in bereavement. *Austral. & N.Z. J. Psychiat.*, 3:63–66.

———— Walker, W. L. (1967), Factors affecting the outcome of conjugal bereavement. *Brit. J. Psychiat.*, 113:1057–1067.

Mullan, J. (1981), Parental Distress and Marital Happiness: The Transition to the Empty Nest. Unpublished doctoral dissertation, University of Chicago.

Osterweis, M., Solomon, F., & Green, M., eds. (1984), *Bereavement: Reactions, Consequences, Care*. Washington, DC: National Academy Press.

Parkes, C. M., & Weiss, R. S. (1983), *Recovery from Bereavement*. New York: Basic Books.

Pearlin, L. I., & Lieberman, M. A. (1979), Social sources of emotional and distress research. *Community and Mental Health*, 1:217–248.

———— Mennaghan, B., & Mullan, J. (1981), The stress process. *J. Health and Social Behavior*, 22:337–356.

Raphael, B. (1977), Preventative intervention with the recently bereaved. *Arch. Gen. Psychiat.*, 34:1450–1454.

———— (1983), *The Anatomy of Bereavement*. New York: Basic Books.

Rosenberg, M. (1965), *Society and the Adolescent Self-Image*. Princeton: Princeton University Press.

Silver, R. L., & Wortman, C. B. (1980), Coping with undesirable life events. In: *Human Helplessness: Theory and Applications*, ed. J. Garber & M. E. P. Seligman. New York: Academic Press, pp. 279–375.

Vachon, M. L. S. (1976), Grief and bereavement following the death of a spouse. *Canadian Psychiat. J.*, 21:35–44.

Veroff, J., Kulka, R. A., & Dowan, E. (1981), *The Inner American: A Self Portrait from 1957–1976*. New York: Basic Books.

Wortman, C. B., & Silver, R. L. (1987), Coping with irrevocable loss. In: *Cataclysms, Crises, and Catastrophes: Psychology in Action*, ed. G. L. Vanden Bos & B. K. Bryant. Washington, D.C.: American Psychiatric Association, pp. 198–233.

Yalom, I. D., & Lieberman, M. A. (1991), Bereavement and heightened existential awareness. *Psychiat.*, 54:334–345.

4

The Archaic Adaptive Ego

STANLEY R. PALOMBO, M.D.

Psychoanalytic ego psychology came into its own with the publication in 1936 of Anna Freud's *The Ego and the Mechanisms of Defense*. This epoch-making work clearly demonstrated that the discoveries of psychoanalysis extended beyond the hidden world of unconscious wishes to the hitherto unrecognized defensive functions of the ego. The establishment of the principle that important aspects of ego functioning may themselves be unconscious opened the way for the study of unconscious adaptive mechanisms which might be identified for the first time only from the perspective of psychoanalysis.

The contributions of Hartmann and his co-workers, beginning in 1939 with Hartmann's *Ego Psychology and the Problem of Adaptation*, developed a broad theoretical foundation for further progress in the psychoanalytic study of the ego (Hartmann, Kris, and Loewenstein, 1964). Hartmann's work brought much of what was already known about the ego, from psychoanalytic sources and from the behavioral sciences generally, into relationship with the earlier psychoanalytic explorations of unconscious impulses and their conflicts with the mechanisms of defense. The stage was set for new discoveries about the as yet poorly understood integrative mechanisms of the ego.

Important advances came through the psychoanalytic study of ego development in early childhood. The work of Erikson (1950), Spitz (1959), A. Freud (1965), and others demonstrated that adaptive ego functioning is present from the very beginning of life. This finding was confirmed by the developmental psychology of Piaget, introduced to American psychoanalysts by Wolff (1960). Later contributors, including White (1963), Jacobson (1964), Mahler (1968), and Bowlby (1969), have diverged in their detailed views of the process of ego development. But all have agreed that it takes place in accordance with an autonomous maturational ground plan which begins to unfold as soon as the baby is born.

As a result of these important studies, we now have a clear idea that the primitive cognitive and affective structures we observe in children are the direct precursors of the more familiar conscious and rational problem-solving mechanisms we associate with the adult ego (Holt, 1967). It is well understood that these primitive structures never disappear and that they may reassume control of the psychic apparatus under unusual circumstances, as in the various forms of psychopathology. It is not generally understood, however, how much and to what extent the more primitive structures of the adaptive ego may play a continuing part in the nonconscious (as distinct from preconscious) adaptive functioning of the mature adult ego.

Our current state of knowledge is most deficient regarding the synthetic or integrative functions of the ego. These are the functions that evaluate the vast quantity of new information continually impinging on us, select from it what is important enough to retain, and then connect this new information, wherever appropriate, with preexisting psychic structures. This integrative work is carried on outside our normal awareness as a prelude to conscious problem solving.

Much of our successful responsiveness to the ordinary demands of everyday life is due to the nonconscious integrative functions of the ego. These functions have a special importance for psychoanalysis, in addition, since the therapeutic benefits of analytic treatment go far beyond anything that can be accounted for by the patient's conscious insight into his neurotic difficulties. We speak of "regression in the service of the ego," but this useful formulation by Kris (1932) suggests an occasional excursion from the conscious norm, rather than the massive infrastructure that supports the specialized capabilities of conscious verbalization.

Since then, important developments have occurred in the biological sciences. Success in adaptation is now closely linked with the capacity of an organism to extract information from its environment and store it internally in meaningful configurations. This principle, dramatically established by the breaking of the genetic code, is currently being elaborated at the higher levels of psychological integration (Lindsay and Norman, 1972).

Many of the theoretical problems yet to be resolved in psychoanalytic ego psychology were formulated in the important collection of essays edited by Holt (1967). Peterfreund's pioneering work (1971) states the premises for an information processing approach to psychoanalytic theory. Rosenblatt and Thickstun (1977, 1978) have given us an exceptionally clear and convincing statement of the issues at stake for the further development of a psychoanalytic science.

My focus in this chapter is on those primitive mental processes which Freud (1923) assigned to the structure he called the id. At first glance, they appear to represent the persistence of infantile mental operations into adult life. *Operations* may be too strong a word here, for the traditional psychoanalytic view pictures these primary processes as unorganized.

Nevertheless, all psychoanalysts since Freud have recognized that the primary processes are meaningful, that they appear to result from the action of consistently identifiable mechanisms (e.g., condensation and displacement), and that they have a decisive influence on the mental life of human beings at all levels of development, including the highest. Beres (1965) and Arlow (1975) have each suggested that many of the characteristics traditionally ascribed to the id may also be viewed as unconscious ego functions.

Applegarth (1973) has pointed out that psychoanalytic theory has suffered from its inability to sort out these inconsistencies in the concept of the id, most graphically represented in this famous passage from Freud's *New Introductory Lectures on Psychoanalysis* (1933): "We approach the id with analogies: we call it a chaos, a cauldron full of seething excitations. . . . It is filled with energy reaching it from the instincts, but it has no organization, produces no collective will, but only a striving to bring about the satisfaction of the instinctual needs subject to the observance of the pleasure principle" (p. 73). Here the id is characterized by the disconnectedness and instability of its contents, the "seething excitations." Yet in the same paragraph he remarks: "Wishful impulses which have never passed beyond the id, but impressions, too, which have been sunk into the id by repression, are virtually immortal; after the passage of decades they behave as though they had just occurred" (p. 74).

We know that these sunken impressions are not isolated or disconnected. They are embedded in an associative network of almost unlimited complexity which also remains intact over the span of decades. Freud says: "Again and again I have had the impression that we have made too little theoretical use of this fact, established beyond any doubt, of the unalterability by time of the repressed. This seems to offer an approach to the most profound discoveries. Nor, unfortunately, have I myself made any progress here" (p. 74).

I suggest here that the id derivatives Freud actually observed are themselves compound events, the product of at least three distinct psychic structures working in conjunction.

Although Freud repeatedly disavowed the spatial imagery of his models, his usage continually points to the id as a region with well-defined boundaries, an interior and an exterior. This region is a repository in which affectively charged mental contents are stored and restrained. One could readily interpret the image of a container as merely metaphorical, if it were not made to bear semantic weight in the theoretical structure. The problem here is that the image of the container is the only element of the theory that establishes a relationship between two kinds of mental content whose properties are essentially dissimilar.

The first of these are "excitations," mental contents which have observable physiological concomitants, which exist for a limited duration in real time, and which reflect the current state of need of the organism independently of environmental conditions. The second are "memories," which are purely intrapsychic constructions, existing indefinitely in the virtual time (or timelessness) of the permanent memory structure, and which record the completed interaction of the organism with its environment in the (often remote) past. In what sense can these disparate elements be "contained" by a single structure?

What Freud observed was that when defense mechanisms are successfully circumvented in psychoanalytic treatment, currently experienced excitations are derepressed simultaneously with memories of events in which closely similar excitations were expressed or acted upon (either in reality or in fantasy formation). From this observation Freud correctly inferred that the mechanisms of defense react to these two varieties of mental content as if they were equivalent. If the mechanisms of defense are thought of as defining the boundary of the unconscious, then all mental contents excluded by them from consciousness can be considered to be contained by that boundary.

Freud himself was not satisfied with this clinical definition. For him the unconscious was not merely the repository of repressed excitations and memories; it was also the source of all fresh excitations arising within the psychic apparatus. By identifying the source of fresh excitations with the repository of repressed memories, Freud hoped to give repressed memories the power to initiate excitations on their own. This would serve to explain the unconscious acting out of repressed wishes from the distant past.

Freud's topographic model, which divides the psychic apparatus into the systems preconscious and unconscious, is based primarily on the clinical data (Gill, 1963). The assignment of new excitations to the unconscious is a step that can be retracted without endangering Freud's basic discoveries in the analytic situation. If we simply assume that it is not the excitation itself that is repressed, but rather a newly formed mental representation of it, then we can consider the unconscious to contain nothing but mental representations. The "repressed excitation" is the memory of an event in the immediate past. In order to make this adjustment, of course, we would have to postulate a source of excitations in some region of the psychic apparatus other than the unconscious.

The structural model, whose major components are the ego, the id, and the superego, does not allow us this choice. Here the id, which takes over the relevant functions of the unconscious, is defined as the source of excitations. Memories enter the id only secondarily, as "impressions which have sunk into the id by repression" (Freud, 1933, p. 74).

It should be remarked that Freud's consignment of repressed memories to the id runs counter to the logic of the structural theory as a whole. The topographic model makes accessibility to consciousness the criterion for Freud's partitioning of the psychic apparatus. In the structural model, it is the presence of structure itself which defines the boundary between the id and the other agencies of the mind. Freud is here emphasizing his view that excitation is without structure and that structure evolves in the ego in order to contain the excitations rampant in the id. Hence, the mechanisms of defense, which are inaccessible to consciousness, must belong to the ego (Freud, 1923). But repressed memories, which are also structured, are located within the structureless id.

This inconsistency at the very heart of his theoretical model was tolerated by Freud for only one reason. The clinical data show that current excitations and childhood memories of similar excitations are derepressed together. Therefore, according to Freud's conceptualization, they had to be located together within the psychic apparatus.

Among those who have struggled with this issue in recent years, a consensus appears to have developed that the id is in reality not a chaos without organization, but rather a structure which is organized in a very primitive way. For example, Holt (1967) suggests that the primitive cognitive structures of infants, which Piaget has demonstrated to be coherent and systematic in their own terms, can mistakenly appear to be lacking in structure when compared with examples of rational adult thinking. He appears to believe that the "seething cauldron" metaphor grew out of an observational error based on adultomorphic preconceptions.

Gill (1963, 1967) and Schur (1966) agree that observation fails to confirm the existence of an unstructured id. However, they suggest that the "seething cauldron" image was never meant to be a description of observed phenomena, but rather a statement at the metapsychological or theoretical level of scientific discourse.

Freud's critics are responding to the extension of developmental observations back to the very beginning of postuterine life. They suggest a theory which places id and ego at the ends of a developmental continuum, proceeding from simple and primitive "id" structures to complex and elaborate "ego" structures.

The record of excitations experienced in the past must be structured. To the extent that the contents of the id include such a record, the id too must be structured. When they conclude that the id is structured in its entirety, however, the more recent writers appear to be attributing the structure of remembered events to the currently experienced excitations which Freud included among the contents of the id. This is the reverse of Freud's procedure, which was to transfer the structurelessness of current excitations to the repressed memories said to be contained in or by the id.

To see the id entirely in developmental terms is to ignore the double nature of id contents revealed when derepression takes place in the clinical situation. I suggest that the way out of this dilemma, which appears to pit clinical data against developmental observations in a contest for the dominant position in the id, is to embrace the duplicity. The contents of the id are not isolated excitations and memories randomly mixed within the confines of a single structure. The unit of observation is a currently experienced excitation paired with a related past memory for a particular purpose.

The particular purpose I wish to suggest is the formation of a new associative link between the mental representation of the current excitation, in its relation to internal and external opportunities for gratification, and the memory of a past event in which a similar excitation was acted upon. This associative link permits a comparison between present and past situations which determines whether the current excitation may be answered with the program of action already generated and stored during the related past event. The stored program may involve active pursuit of gratification, flight from the current external situation, repression of the excitation, fantasy formation, or any combination of these factors. Alternatively, the comparison may fail and the conclusion be reached that the current situation is unique and in need of an entirely new program of action to be constructed de novo.

This purpose is, of course, an adaptive one. The sequence I have described constitutes what I would imagine to be the lowest level of activity mediated by the psychic apparatus (as distinct from the pure reflex arc). For the most part it takes place outside consciousness, apparently without the use of the sensory projection mechanisms. When these more primitive procedures fail to operate smoothly, however, we find that more deliberate techniques for locating matching experiences from the past are brought into play.

These techniques involve a replay or simulation of past experiences in which a similar excitation was followed by a successful program of action to achieve gratification. Occasionally the replay becomes conscious and organized, as in daydreams and reveries. More often it is a kind of stream of consciousness, though not quite conscious, which frequently accompanies the problem-solving activity of waking thought. The dreamlike states which often occur during the entry into sleep are prolongations of this stream of semiconscious replay beyond the cessation of more organized problem-solving activity.

Elements of current experience are worked into the replay from the past in order to test the degree to which they fit these previously established patterns. In daydreaming we see a narrative structure which is more naturalistic and subtle than the interweaving we observe in the superimpositions of the nocturnal dream (Palombo, 1976, 1977). In the more usual case, when the replay is not fully conscious, the mechanism of condensation or superimposition is frequently, if not generally, employed. Freud's early work on puns and parapraxes (1901) brought this layer of everyday information processing to our attention.

We cannot specify as yet the precise sequences and mechanisms involved in this continuous processing effort, but we know enough by now to establish a very powerful generalization. The basic procedure, applied repeatedly and in a variety of ways, which converts reflex automatism to intelligent biological activity, is *the comparison of the relatively unstructured experience of the present moment to the more highly structured experience of the past.*

As mentioned earlier, during this process of repeated comparison there are occasional moments when a level of complexity is reached which requires that the sensory projection mechanisms and the scanning mechanisms of waking consciousness be brought into play. It is at these moments that we observe the excitation-memory pairs which Freud referred to as "the contents of the id." The clinical evidence suggests that these are moments in which the present and past elements of the pair are brought together in the psychic apparatus for the first time. (Later, the paired elements may be jointly retrieved from memory for comparison with a still newer excitation.) We have no evidence of a single structure which "contains" both elements before the association is achieved. In reality, three distinct adaptive structures or substructures must be operating in this situation:

1. *A mechanism which converts the physiological (biochemical, hormonal, etc.) indications of stress or need into "mental representations."* These signal representations may have a primitive perceptual quality localized in a particular body zone, as in the case of hunger, thirst, or sexual arousal, but they may also consist of more generalized affective states like anxiety or grief.

2. *A store of memory representations of past events in which similar excitations were experienced and acted upon.* Memory representations are not mere traces of perceptual processes. They are programs that can be activated to reconstruct the cognitive imagery, affective sensation, and behavioral activity which characterized the organism's participation in the event. We include here a mechanism for retrieving particular memories or classes of memory. The task performed by this mechanism is far from trivial (Palombo, 1973, 1976).

3. *A mechanism which compares the current physiological signal with the memories of relevant past events.* This mechanism must also receive a report on the current situation of the organism, in order to evaluate the opportunities for gratification at the present time in relation to those previously experienced and

acted upon. I believe that this mechanism is most efficient when it uses the sensory projection mechanisms for a simultaneous display of the current situation and the relevant memories. The degree of coherence possessed by the composite image, formed when the two mental representations are superimposed, may then determine whether the present situation can be regarded as another instance of something already familiar and the current excitation acted upon in a manner already known to be successful.

Repression and other defensive operations prevent the current excitation and the relevant memories from being brought together in the third of these mechanisms, the comparator. When repression is overcome during psychoanalytic treatment, the comparison is achieved, and the two component representations can be observed, usually in the form of the composite image or "condensation" which is displayed in the sensory projection mechanisms.

We may wish to refer to these three structures taken together as "the id." But there are other possibilities open to us if we try to redefine Freud's term in relation to them. We may reserve the term *id* for the mechanism that converts physiological changes into signal affects. Or we may confine it to the output of that mechanism, the sequence of representations it continuously throws up. If we take these options, the "id" we define will be the "source" of fresh excitations but will exclude the paired excitations and memories observed in the clinical situation. If we base our definition on the pairs observable in the comparator display, the id loses its status as the source of excitations and the repository of repressed memories. But in this case we would have a rational interpretation of the notion that the id "contains" these two varieties of mental content.

Further, we must decide whether to include in our definition of "the id" every element of past and present experience which may be linked in the process of comparison, or only those that require the overcoming of repression or other forms of defensive interference before the comparison can be effected. By far the greater number of comparisons are successfully achieved without the very costly use of the sensory projection mechanisms and the recruitment of waking consciousness in the scanning of the resulting displays.

I have suggested (Palombo, 1977) that dreams which awaken the dreamer and are likely to be remembered and reported in analysis constitute a relatively small subset of dreams in which the censorship mechanisms have prevented a successful matching between an element of current experience (the day residue) and the possibly relevant representations stored in the permanent memory structure. I believe that the same relation holds for the subset of excitation–memory pairs which are displayed in such a way that they become observable during waking consciousness.

In the light of these considerations, it seems highly probable that Freud's conception of the id confounds a number of distinct adaptive structures, the equally distinct varieties of mental content associated with these structures, and the defensive operations that interfere with their normal functioning. In particular, it appears that Freud attributed the unstructured quality of currently experienced excitations to the structured elements of the psychic apparatus responsible for evaluating and processing these excitations.

The alternative model suggested here preserves the facts observed in the clinical examination of the patient's chaotic subjective states by dropping the unnecessary assumption that these appearances reflect the underlying structure of the psychic apparatus itself. The subjective chaos is the effect of defensive interference with the orderly information-processing activity of the (largely unconscious) adaptive ego.

The developmental theorists are certainly correct in pointing out to us that the adaptive ego functions at a variety of structure-building levels beginning with the most primitive coordinating operations observable in the first weeks of life. However, the primitive quality of mental operations at these early levels of ego activity is by itself insufficient to produce the subjective disorder observed by the psychoanalyst. Here the critical factor is the failure to incorporate unstructured excitations arising at the present moment into adaptive programs developed and stored at all levels of past experience. The role of the defenses in bringing about this failure cannot be overestimated.

The activity that produces the "id derivatives" described by Freud does two things at once. It facilitates the gratification of physiological and emotional needs by bringing the accumulated experience of the past to bear on the present situation, supplying already existing structure to newly arising excitations. By determining when existing structures are inadequate for the gratification of a new excitation, however, it also initiates the creation of new structure by the higher level mechanisms more suited to that purpose.

The mechanisms of defense interfere with the latter of these functions by preventing the higher level adaptive mechanisms from responding to the new excitation. The result is that the new excitation is acted upon as if it were merely the repetition of an older excitation which, in some essential characteristic, it no longer resembles. The continuous updating of the memory store, which takes place when the mechanisms of the id are functioning normally, is interrupted. If this happens often enough in a particular area of experience, further developmental progress is brought to a standstill.

To put this in terms of the structural model: Under normal circumstances the pleasure-seeking aims of the id are directly coupled with the adaptive mechanisms of the ego that accommodate these aims to changing internal and external opportunities for gratification. Only when the mechanisms of defense intervene in this process of accommodation do the pleasure-seeking aims appear to be isolated from the adaptive purposes of the psychic apparatus as a whole.

What Freud referred to as "the id" would be more accurately described as an archaic portion of the adaptive ego. When free of defensive interference, this *archaic adaptive ego* plays a critical role in normal development. It promotes the efficient, unconscious use of existing structure in dealing with repetitive experiential situations and focuses the activity of higher level adaptive mechanisms, including those which ordinarily require conscious attention, on the new tasks brought into prominence by the unfolding of the maturational sequence.

When we speak of the id as an archaic portion of the adaptive ego, we are faced once again with the ambiguity of the concept of the ego in Freud's structural theory. There are two clear and distinct meanings of this term which must be separated. The first of these, which I have been using throughout this chapter, designates the ego as the system of adaptive structures within the psychic apparatus which functions to advance the interests of the individual organism of which it forms a part. The id may be thought of as a portion of the adaptive ego defined in this sense. From this point of view, Freud's suggestion that the ego evolves from the id is not only reasonable but almost certainly correct.

The second distinct meaning of the term *ego*, which I shall refer to with capitalization as the Ego, is the region of the mind and its contents that is ordinarily accessible to consciousness and identified by the subject as an essential part of himself. This Ego is the counterpart of the Id as the Id is defined by the repressive powers of the mechanisms of defense. This is the defense-determined definition of the Ego. In this sense of the terms, the Ego and Id must be created simultaneously by the boundaries set up between them through the operation of the defense mechanisms.

We have seen that the adaptive ego is not coextensive with the defense-determined Ego. The defense-determined Id, also with capitalization, cannot be identical to the archaic adaptive ego, much of which remains outside normal consciousness for reasons other than the repressive influence of the defense mechanisms. The ambiguities can be resolved if we adopt a two-layered terminology based on the distinction between adaptive structure and accessibility to consciousness.

In this new system, we reserve the term *structure* for the adaptive ego and its various components. These structures are biologically given and develop through a relatively constant maturational sequence (subject, of course, to the necessary feedback from the environment). The divisions of the psychic apparatus established by the mechanisms of defense are not structures but *superstructures*. Here we follow Freud's usage with regard to the Superego, which in its clearest meaning is another portion of the adaptive ego rendered inaccessible to consciousness by the mechanisms of defense. But we go further than

Freud to include the defense-determined Ego and Id as super-structures along with the Superego.

From the psychoanalytic point of view, the most interesting and important major component of the adaptive ego is the archaic adaptive ego which underlies the superstructure Id. The archaic adaptive ego includes the series of mechanisms that evaluate and assimilate new affective experience by comparing it with the body of information stored in memory throughout the past life of the organism. These mechanisms are designed for rapid processing of large amounts of information, as exemplified by the mechanism of comparison by superimposition in dreaming, rather than for the reflective problem solving typical of the mature adaptive ego.

The rapidity of processing and the lack of reflection at this primitive level of ego functioning leave the organism vulnerable to serious dangers in the evaluation of new experience. An emergency system for interrupting the flow of information when these dangers threaten is needed. This system must also act quickly and without reflection. It must deflect the flow of information without stopping it, however, since continuity in the associative flow is critical to the operation of the adaptive mechanisms. This emergency system comprises the mechanisms of defense, of which the substitutive activity of the dream censor may be taken as typical.

The antagonism between the adaptive mechanisms of the archaic ego and the mechanisms of defense is an intimate one. There are many critical points in the sequence of decisions which follow from the registration of a physiological feedback signal. The perceptual elements of the defense mechanisms must be in position to monitor these decisions continuously, for the level of danger attaching to a given wish-program must be subject to sudden alterations as it makes contact first with one and then with another related wish-program which has been recovered from storage in order to be compared with it. We cannot reasonably picture the defense mechanisms observing the processing of wish-programs from across the gulf which is said to separate the Ego and the Id in Freud's structural model.

The most striking characteristic of the archaic adaptive ego is that it is involuntary. Decisions are made by the application of various generalized procedures to particular cases. These procedures are sufficiently flexible, in the case of the adaptive mechanisms, to permit some degree of growth and creative innovation, but they are quite different from the problem-solving methods of conscious thought. In the archaic ego, decisions are computed rather than willed, automatic rather than thought through.

These primitive structures of the archaic adaptive ego provided the evolutionary foundation on which the more familiar structures of the mature adaptive ego developed. The "cauldron of seething excitations" described by Freud cannot have been the ancestor of the problem-solving structures which have made possible the dominant position of our biologically vulnerable species.

An organism survives through its accumulation of patterned information. It imposes a structure of unimaginable complexity on a domain of inanimate material small enough to be isolated in space and time from the destructive forces at large in the physical universe. It proceeds through the storage and retrieval of coded information, through countless comparisons, transformations, and elaborations of that coded information. The psychic apparatus stands at the summit of a gigantic pyramid. From its base in the discrete chemical processes of the nucleic acids and proteins to its apex in the problem-solving activity of waking consciousness, the pyramid is structured hierarchically and in minute detail.

Today any reasonable biological theory must find the sources of vital activity within this pyramid. The domain of living things falls entirely within the class of ordered information-processing mechanisms (Miller, Galanter, and Pribram, 1960; Simon, 1969; Lindsay and Norman, 1972; Pattee, 1973). The developmental sequence observed by psychoanalytic investigators and developmental psychologists records the building up of a hierarchical pyramid of mental structures. When development is arrested at any level of the hierarchy by either a lack of appropriate stimulation or by the operation of the defense mechanisms, the consequence is psychopathology.

The subjective sense of disorder observed in the psychoanalytic patient can be localized to a particular set of malfunctioning adaptive structures. These are the structures which relate current needs and constraints to the record of relevant past experience at all levels of psychological development. When development has been arrested early, current needs must be related, if at all, to memories having a primitive cognitive structure and a highly charged affective value. This circumstance reinforces the subjective feeling of disorder initiated by the failure to find a satisfactory match between current needs and experiences earlier in life.

Psychoanalysis can fulfill its aspirations as a general psychology only if it allows room for the massive substrate of primitive adaptive processes which support the psychic superstructures revealed by the clinical investigation of neurotic illness. It is my belief that this broadening of the adaptive point of view in psychoanalytic theory will facilitate the assimilation of developmental data into the therapeutic procedures of the practicing psychoanalyst.

References

Applegarth, A. (1973), The structure of psychoanalytic theory. *J. Amer. Psychoanal. Assn.*, 21:193–237.

Arlow, J. (1975), The structural hypothesis—Theoretical considerations. *Psychoanal. Quart.*, 44:509–525.

Beres, D. (1965), Structure and function in psychoanalysis. *Internat. J. Psycho-Anal.*, 46:53–63.

Bowlby, J. (1969), *Attachment and Loss, Vol. I, Attachment*. New York: Basic Books.

Erikson, E. (1950), *Childhood and Society*. New York: Norton.

Freud, A. (1936), *The Ego and the Mechanisms of Defense*. New York: International Universities Press, 1965.

——— (1965), Normality and pathology in childhood assessments of development. *The Writings of Anna Freud, Vol. 6*. New York: International Universities Press, 1965.

Freud, S. (1901), The psychopathology of everyday life. *Standard Edition*, 6:1–31. London: Hogarth Press, 1960.

——— (1923), The ego and the id. *Standard Edition*, 19:3–66. London: Hogarth Press, 1961.

——— (1933), New introductory lectures on psychoanalysis. *Standard Edition*, 22:3–182. London: Hogarth Press, 1964.

Gill, M. (1963), Topography and Systems in Psychoanalytic Theory. *Psychological Issues*, Monograph 10. New York: International Universities Press.
——— (1967), The primary process. In: Motives and Thoughts: Psychoanalytic Essays in Honor of David Rapaport. *Psychological Issues*, Monograph 18/19. New York: International Universities Press, pp. 259–298.
Hartmann, H. (1939), *Ego Psychology and the Problem of Adaptation*. New York: International Universities Press, 1958.
——— (1964), *Essays on Ego Psychology: Selected Problems in Psychoanalytic Theory*. New York: International Universities Press.
——— Kris, E., & Lowenstein, R. (1964), Papers on Psychoanalytic Psychology. *Psychological Issues*, Monograph 14. New York: International Universities Press.
Holt, R. (1967), The development of the primary process: A structural view. In: Motives and Thought: Psychoanalytic Essays in Honor of David Rapaport. *Psychological Issues*, Monograph 18/19. New York: International Universities Press, pp. 345–383.
Jacobson, E. (1964), *The Self and the Object World*. New York: International Universities Press.
Kris, E. (1932), *Psychoanalytic Explorations in Art*. New York: International Universities Press, 1952.
Lindsay, P., & Norman, D. (1972), *Human Information Processing*. New York: Academic Press.
Mahler, M. (1968), *On Human Symbiosis and the Vicissitudes of Individuation*. New York: International Universities Press.
Miller, G., Galanter, E., & Pribram, K. (1960), *Plans and the Structure of Behavior*. New York: Henry Holt.
Palombo, S. (1973), The associative memory tree. In: *Psychoanalysis and Contemporary Science*, Vol. 2, ed. B. Rubinstein. New York: Macmillan, pp. 205–219.
——— (1976), The dream and the memory cycle. *Internat. Rev. Psycho-Anal.*, 3:65–83.
——— (1977), Dreams, memory and the origin of thought. In: *Thought, Consciousness and Reality: Psychiatry and the Humanities*, Vol. 2, ed. J. Smith. New Haven: Yale University Press, pp. 49–83.
Pattee, H., ed. (1973), *Hierarchy Theory: The Challenge of Complex Systems*. New York: George Braziller.
Peterfreund, E. (1971), Information, Systems and Psychoanalysis. *Psychological Issues*, Monograph 25/26. New York: International Universities Press.
Rosenblatt, A., & Thickstun, J. (1977), Energy, information and motivation: A revision of psychoanalytic theory. *J. Amer. Psychoanal. Assn.*, 25:537–558.
——— (1978), Modern Psychoanalytic Concepts in a General Psychology. *Psychological Issues*, Monograph 42/43. New York: International Universities Press.
Schur, M. (1966), *The Id and the Regulatory Principles of Mental Functioning*. New York: International Universities Press.
Simon, H. (1969), *The Sciences of the Artificial*. Cambridge: M.I.T. Press.
Spitz, R. (1959), *A Genetic Field Theory of Ego Formation*. New York: International Universities Press.

White, R. (1963), Ego and Reality in Psychoanalytic Theory: A Proposal Regarding Independent Ego Energies. *Psychological Issues*. Monograph 11. New York: International Universities Press.

Wolff, P. (1960), The Developmental Psychologies of Jean Piaget and Psychoanalysis. *Psychological Issues*, Monograph 5. New York: International Universities Press.

5

Adult Phases of the Life Cycle

PAUL A. DEWALD, M.D.

The phase of adulthood covers the timespan between the emergence of the individual from adolescence to the onset of senescence and the advanced aging process. Chronologically, this phase varies considerably among different cultures, but in the highly complex structure of Western civilization it usually covers the era between ages 21 and 70.

The data base for psychoanalytic conceptualizations of adult mental life is obtained primarily from the clinical situation of the therapeutic analysis of adult patients. Once the analytic situation has been established and the patient has begun to experience a full-blown regressive transference neurosis and has learned verbally to report on the flow of his psychic and mental experience, he provides a source of information not obtainable by any other method. From the subjective reports and relatively objective observations of a patient experiencing such a regressive transference neurosis, the analyst is able to observe the interplay of psychic functions as they are reenacted and experienced by the patient. Being simultaneously able to observe himself and his participation within the psychoanalytic situation, the analyst is able, at least with some degree of objectivity, also to take account of his own role in the patient's situations of stress and conflict and their resolution. Simultaneously, the analyst has available the patient's reports of interactions, behavior patterns, and relationships with key individuals and situations outside the analysis itself, stemming from the patient's current life as well as his past history.

By grouping multiple sets of observations of individual patients, a variety of generally demonstrable and identifiable issues can be described (Rapaport, 1960). However, as a general psychology, psychoanalysis then depends on the extrapolation from certain clinical experiences to other clinical, therapeutic, or observational settings, as well as to nonclinical situations, in the development of the general principles for understanding adult behavior.

Psychoanalytic understanding of the multidetermined complexities of adult behavior requires an appreciation of the interplay of intrapsychic as well as interpersonal and external conflicts and motivations, and an appreciation of the varying levels of consciousness in regard to the forces and factors that determine behavior.

In recent years there has emerged an active debate regarding the limitations and inconsistencies in the metapsychological concepts of psychoanalytic theory (Klein, 1976; Gill and Holzman, 1976; Schafer, 1976; Kohut, 1977). However, most psychoanalysts continue to systematize observational data through consideration of their structural, dynamic, genetic, economic, and adaptational aspects.

The central core of the personality has been established during infancy and early childhood as a result of the multiple interactions between the child's constitutional endowment, its internal psychic experiences and developing capacities, and the responses to the child from the environment. These core elements in the personality tend to be organized in the primary process mode of thought and continue to influence the individual at a deeply unconscious level.

Evolving from and influenced by the core functions are a large number of derivative personality elements resulting from the later experiences, maturational sequences and relationships, and their internal psychological elaboration. These derivative psychological functions and personality elements simultaneously reflect the persistent unconscious effects of the core functions and the more conscious current internal and external psychological forces impinging on the individual. The derivative psychic functions (structures) provide the form, conscious manifestations, and patterns of personality organization which characterize the observable behavior of the adult and through which the persistent effects of the infantile and early childhood core of the personality are expressed.

Psychoanalysis has always stressed the importance of the multiple inherited and constitutionally determined variations among individuals. Such differences and predispositions will modify the effects of the individual's intrapsychic experience and capacities, as well as the impact of experience and interaction with the environment. Some constitutional factors may become manifest early in the individual's development, while others may exert their effects only during later phases of the individual's life.

The chronologically and psychologically adult individual thus evolves from and is the product of the multiple developmental and maturational processes previously active during his phases of infancy, childhood, latency, and adolescence. He enters adult life and status influenced by the various developmental distortions or arrests that may produce deviations of varying degree from the optimal maturational sequence and progression. By the time the individual has become an adult, he has adopted particular characteristic modes and methods of adaptation and integration, and his character and personality form and style have evolved into a generally stable and consistent organization.

During adulthood the overall rate of psychological maturation, development, and change is usually slower and less abrupt or dramatic in intensity than occurs in the previous phases of development. However, phase-specific developmental experiences and stages occur during adult life, and adulthood is not a static state but rather a continuing unfolding of the processes of change. But although psychological maturation and development continue, the psychological equipment with which the adult now confronts both intrapsychic and external environmental needs, stresses, and conflicts has basically been established.

Early in the development of psychoanalysis, the emphasis for understanding was placed primarily on unconscious intrapsychic components of adult functioning. Even Hartmann's emphasis on adaptation to reality (1939) postulated "an average expectable environment." However, more recent observation and conceptualization have demonstrated that environmental factors have a far more varied, idiosyncratic, and less routinely expectable influence on behavior. In order to become a general psychology, psychoanalysis has had to take account of the many sociocultural variables and recognize that the previously over-simplified concepts did not account for many aspects of normality and pathology (Wallerstein, 1973).

Normality in the Adult

From a psychoanalytic perspective, the concept of normality or mental health usually involves an evaluation of how closely an individual approaches a theoretical ideal of mental functioning. Ideal mental health is seen as an evolving process inasmuch as health is not a static and fixed set of functions. The ideally healthy individual continues to develop, mature, and evolve as life progresses, and is capable of effective adaptation to the inevitable changing vicissitudes of intrapsychic experience, a constantly changing external environment, and constitutionally determined biological evolution and processes.

Ideal mental health is thus seen as one end of a spectrum from pathology to normality, and although major variations along this spectrum may be easily identifiable, there are no sharp points of demarcation. There are no perfectly healthy individuals (in an ideal sense), and the differences between pathology and health tend to be more quantitative than qualitative.

Within this conceptual framework the healthy adult individual is capable of an effective balance between satisfying his own personal needs and gratifications and the needs and gratifications of important love objects within the environment. He is capable of direct and fulfilling instinctual derivative drive discharge toward age-appropriate objects, but is capable also of tolerating the frustration of such drive derivatives when appropriate. He is capable of sublimation of his aggressive impulses into effective and pleasurably fulfilling performance of work in his chosen line of endeavor and of achieving the full utilization of innate talents and abilities without intrapsychic inhibition. He has a cohesive sense of self and is capable of tolerating and accepting his liabilities and limitations as well as enjoying his assets and capacities. He has a capacity for internal psychological awareness and a recognition of his own mental processes. This allows him stable capacity to perceive, test, and relate to external reality and makes him capable of recognizing distortions which emanate from his own intrapsychic mental processes and residual conflicts. He is relatively free of neurotic symptoms, restrictions, or inhibitions and is capable of tolerating unpleasurable affects without recourse to neurotic symptom formation.

Freud (1916–1917) expressed this succinctly by saying that the normal individual has the full capacity to love (in all its various forms and intensities) and to work. Anna Freud (1962, 1965) developed a diagnostic profile for children in which observations of the individual are compared with the conceptualizations of ideal function at the particular level of maturation and development, subsequently extending it to a similar diagnostic profile in adults (Freud, Nagera, and Freud, 1965).

Potentials for Adult Psychopathology

The potentials for the development or manifestation of psychopathology in the adult include the following:

1. Previous arrests, partial arrests, or distortions in any or several of the intrapsychic functions during prior development and maturation. Such fixations of development or deviations from optimal maturation are particularly characteristic of individuals with various forms of personality disorder.

2. Although the various individual functions may have developed adequately, there may be significant continuing intrapsychic conflicts from infantile, childhood, and later phases of development. These remain unconscious and thus are unresolved in spite of growth and maturation in other areas of personality and function. They thus are susceptible to reactivation under particular circumstances, characteristically in situations of neurotic or psychotic symptom formation.

3. Given the relative nature of psychological health, all individuals may become subject to psychopathological disturbances as adults in the face of overwhelming current stress or

psychic trauma beyond the expectable capacity for adaptation. These individuals tend to exhibit more transient and less chronically disabling forms of psychopathology, and their decompensations tend to be more amenable to relief of environmental stresses.

4. Biological, constitutional, toxic, or physical traumatic factors which interfere with previously established integrative, synthetic, defensive, or adaptive functions, particularly those relating to the ego, may also produce manifestations of psychopathology. If a specific adaptive or defensive function is interfered with by such phenomena, and if as a result the previous capacity for adaptation to preexisting conflict can no longer be maintained, the underlying difficulty previously effectively controlled may now be "released" and become more overtly manifest. This is particularly likely if the individual does not have the capacity for utilization of other compensatory synthetic, adaptive, or defensive functions.

The individual's intrapsychic organization and capacity for adaptation to inevitable psychic conflicts and their vicissitudes or exaggerations during the usual developmental phases serve as a background to the individual's capacity for function in adulthood. They form a *psychological internal template* by which an individual perceives and organizes, processes and then carries to execution the previously described multiple interactions between internal and external psychological environments and relationships.

The *repetition compulsion* is more a descriptive than an explanatory concept. It is used to conceptualize the observation that an individual tends to repeat earlier levels of unconscious developmental arrest or conflict in his current adult life situations, object choices, emotional reactions, motivations, and behavior patterns. Several factors contribute to this observable tendency to repeat the past in the present. There may be a continuing search for gratification and fulfillment of outmoded infantile and childhood wishes, object choices or defenses, and adaptive patterns; there may be repeated attempts at mastery of a previously unresolved traumatic, dangerous, or conflictual situation; there may be a continuing search for fulfillment of unconscious wishes which served initially as a regressive defense from conflict at more advanced stages of development; or the tendency may represent an escape from perceived danger situations which maturation, change, or new psychological development would entail.

In keeping with the concept of unconscious intrapsychic levels of development and organization serving as a template for later forms of behavior, this tendency represents an unconscious attempt by the individual to validate and confirm his preexisting unconscious core fantasies, wishes, defenses, superego expectations, etc. He seeks in current adult life those objects, situations, or environmental responses which are in keeping with preexisting compromise formations, unconscious fantasies, and other psychic experiences. At the same time, the individual tends to ignore, avoid, or misinterpret current situations or relationships that would be incompatible with the preexisting organizing fantasy or conflict solving systems.

This tendency to react in stereotyped ways toward situations or objects unconsciously chosen from those available in the current constellation is particularly typical of individuals in whom various forms of characterological deviation have occurred. In other words, the concept of an intrapsychic template describes the clinically observable phenomenon of an individual selecting from among available internal or external objects or situations those which will most closely approximate his preexisting unconscious wishes, defenses, fantasies, demands, or expectations.

For example, a 35-year-old man had been repeatedly neglected and abandoned as a young child by his mother, who died unexpectedly when he was 10 years old. Throughout his adolescence and adult life he remained emotionally aloof and self-contained, consciously mistrustful, and expectant of abandonment or withdrawal by anyone to whom he might feel tempted to be close. He maintained this emotional position with his wife and children, in spite of multiple realistic experiences and reassurances to the contrary.

A 31-year-old woman described a long series of unhappy and painful relationships with men, in which she was repeatedly humiliated, abused, neglected, and at times physically harmed.

However, whenever a new man showed himself to be kind, warm, or lovingly supportive, she reacted with contempt and could not feel sexual or emotional interest in him.

An attractive 26-year-old woman complained that there were no appropriately eligible and appealing men available to her and that the only attractive men she met were already married. After a series of such affairs, she persuaded a 40-year-old man to divorce his wife and marry her, only to find herself no longer responsive or interested in him following the wedding ceremony.

This tendency unconsciously to repeat the past in the present is also strikingly demonstrated in the adult by the observation of patients' behavior and reactions during the regressive therapeutic transference neurosis, where distortions of the analyst and the analytic situation, as well as interpretations of the analyst's behavior and motivations, tend to conform to the patient's preexisting unconscious organization.

In an opposite fashion, current adult conflicts, object relationships, experiences, or the vicissitudes of life which in one way or another are similar to relatively dormant preexisting intrapsychic configurations of conflict or levels of organization tend to reactivate the previously latent psychic organizations, particularly when the current conflict, reaction, or relationship appears to the individual to be relatively insoluble.

For example, a 34-year-old university assistant professor had been capable of successful and fulfilling sexual function with a number of earlier girlfriends as well as with his wife. He was expecting to be granted tenure by his university and was deeply hurt and surprised when given a negative decision. He developed complete sexual impotence which persisted for five years, even though he quickly obtained tenure at a university of comparable reputation.

Symptom Formation in the Adult

These concepts allow for an understanding of the specificity of response among different individuals to similar current psychic stresses or conflicts. If the current conflict is relatively unrelated to previous levels of unconscious conflict, and if the individual can effectively cope with the current stress, his behavior and responses tend to be appropriate to the nature and intensity of the current conflict. In such a situation the adult may experience a variety of distressing or gratifying affective or behavioral responses, but his reactions to them tend to remain within relatively effective levels of psychic adaptation and function.

For example, a 45-year-old professional man was told that his adolescent son had developed a malignant tumor. He experienced acute anxiety and depressive symptoms, insomnia, difficulty concentrating on his work, preoccupation with the son's illness, and brief episodes of quiet crying. He made arrangements for the son's medical and surgical treatment, and following these procedures his symptoms rapidly subsided and he resumed his previous level of function and feeling.

The onset of neurotic decompensation or symptom formation in the adult occurs when a person is confronted by a current form or level of psychic conflict for which his usual adaptive capacities and mechanisms are not effective in bringing about conflict resolution or tolerance. If the current conflict is associated in its form, content, or intensity to a preexisting unconscious conflict (even though that preexisting conflict may previously have been successfully contained psychologically), the associations between the current conflict and the internal one tend to evoke an exacerbation of the latter. The adult then tends psychologically to regress to the level of the preexisting intrapsychic disturbances, partly as a means of escape from the current form and level of conflict, and partly as an unconscious attempt to achieve gratification of the continuing earlier and now unacceptable wishes and impulses reactivated in the current situation.

As a result of such regression, the unconscious conflict is reactivated, with reexperiencing in the present situation of the previously unresolved elements of psychic conflict, experienced now at the level of regression that has occurred in the id, ego, and superego functions. The more intense and more widespread the form and nature of the previously dormant intrapsychic unconscious conflict, the greater is the potential for its reactivation when the vicissitudes of adult life present situations of conflict similar to or associated with the earlier ones. The less intense and more circumscribed the preexisting intrapsychic conficts or developmental arrests, the less will be the tendency toward their reactivation by the vicissitudes of adult behavior and stress situations, and the greater will be the specificity of the adult situation necessary to induce the reactivation of the earlier levels of conflict.

For example, I reported in considerable detail (Dewald, 1972) on a patient whose acute neurosis was precipitated when she was told that her first pregnancy would require delivery by cesarean section. This procedure had specific unconscious associations to an unresolved childhood core neurotic fantasy and conflict, the regressive reactivation of which resulted in a severe, mixed neurosis for which she underwent successful psychoanalysis. Following the analysis and resolution of the conflict in question, the patient successfully underwent a hysterectomy, with only the realistically appropriate amount of concern and psychic distress, and without any recurrence of neurotic symptoms or decompensation.

In returning to earlier levels of psychic conflict, previously perceived situations of danger or threat are unconsciously reexperienced as current perceptions. The fantasies of these dangerous situations remain unconscious, and their effects are perceived and felt as real. This evokes the affective response appropriate to the nature of the original real or fantasized danger situation (usually one or another form of anxiety or guilt and shame). But because of the unconscious regression that has occurred, the individual is now incapable of effective adaptation or conscious control of the currently experienced unpleasurable affects.

As a result, the individual attempts a solution to the current as well as to the regressively reactivated previously unconscious conflicts through the institution of a compromise which simultaneously expresses the various elements of the original conflict. The particular form of this attempted compromise solution depends on the nature and effectiveness of the adaptive and defensive methods available for use by the individual, the specific neurotic symptoms and manifestations being a function of the psychological defense mechanisms employed.

In cases of neurotic personality and character disorders, the same complex variables which were described for neuroses are also active. The chief difference is that as a result of the intensity of the psychic conflicts, or of more manifest and intense degrees of developmental arrest, the manifestations of pathological deviation and distortion are continuously present and are observable from childhood onward. The specific subjective or objective signs of difficulty may change with chronological maturation, but the individual has developed a persistent and idiosyncratically typical pattern of behavioral responses. These are the final common pathways for the expression of id, superego, and ego processes, with compromised and disguised expression of all intrapsychic component groups of functions. The more intense the character disorder, the more rigidly does the individual use stereotyped responses and patterns of adaptation, increasingly independent of the specific variation in the nature of the external stimulus or stress.

Of particular importance in the personality disorders is the personality of the emotionally significant objects in the child's early environment, since they serve as models for positive or negative identification in the formation of character traits. Individuals with personality disorders tend to have a limited repertoire of defensive and adaptive responses, and thus their adult behavior tends to be repetitive and relatively unmodifiable through conscious experience or learning. Their behavior and subjective responses tend to be perceived by them as ego-syntonic and familiar, in contrast to the classically neurotic individual, who perceives his symptoms as new, different, and ego-alien.

The individual with a personality or character disorder tends to "act out" in his manifest behavior various elements of his unconscious early conflicts, and these elements tend to distort significantly his perceptions of reality in keeping with the peremptory nature of unconscious fantasies.

In recent years, particular interest has been focused on the borderline character disorder. The definition of this group of adult patients has been varied, with some observers seeing them as representing an essentially stable syndrome of severe psycho-pathology, while other observers conceptualize them as inter-mittently oscillating between severe neurosis and acute psycho-sis. All observers agree that the etiologically significant disturbances have occurred at primitive preoedipal levels of development, with major arrests or distortions in ego develop-ment. Kernberg (1975) emphasizes the importance of distur-bances in object relations, with the persistent use of splitting as a mechanism of self- and object representation. Kohut (1977) stresses the distortions and arrests in the psychology of the self and its unfolding as the major pathogenic factor.

In regard to the psychoses, there is general agreement among analysts studying such patients that the manifestations of the psychotic disorder reflect major psychopathology in re-gard to the synthetic, defensive, and adaptive functions of the ego. Some observers (e.g., Arlow and Brenner, 1964) see this in terms of overwhelming and intense structural conflict. Oth-ers see psychosis as qualitatively different from the usual intra-psychic structural conflicts, and emphasize a constitutional fac-tor as well (e.g., Arieti, 1974). Others (e.g., Lidz, Fleck, and Cornelison, 1965) emphasize familial and social patterns of be-havior, communication, and interaction as the major patho-genic influence. But all observers agree that there are major prephallic disturbances and that during the psychosis there is profound psychic regression to primitive levels of function and object relationship, with utilization by the patient of primitive adaptive and defensive mechanisms. Regardless of the etiology of the psychosis, its behavioral effects are mediated and ex-pressed through mental processes.

Manifestations of Psychopathology

At one time in the evolution of psychoanalytic observation and theory formation it was anticipated that manifestations of psychopathology in the adult could be directly correlated to the nature of the unconscious conflict and the level of psychosexual fixation that occurred in the individual's childhood. For exam-ple, it was believed that hysterical phenomena and phobic reac-tions result from conflict and fixation at the phallic-oedipal phase of development; obsessive-compulsive neuroses were said to be caused by regression to the anal phase from a conflict at the phallic-oedipal level; and depression was thought to be etiologically related to oral fixation and the turning of aggression inward against the self.

More detailed and sophisticated observations have indicated that these formulations were only partially correct and that the choice of psychiatric disturbance in the adult is significantly influenced by a much larger number of factors. Among these are such things as the individual's constitutional endowment, in terms both of specific vulnerabilities in organ systems or biological processes, and of creative talents and other adaptive ego capacities; the pathology or health of the early objects for identification in the child's life; the nature, intensity, and level of preexisting unconscious developmental conflicts; the modes of defense or adaptation to conflict encouraged or discouraged by the social and family environment; the facilitating or disruptive vicissitudes of life experience; the social and cultural setting in which the individual developed; the specific positive or negative attitudes manifest in that culture regarding typical developmental conflicts; the nature and effectiveness of environmental objects and support systems in helping the developing child cope with specific psychically traumatic events or conflicts; the forms and effectiveness of the defensive or adaptive functions the individual has developed; the adaptive or defensive opportunities offered by the environment; the individual's susceptibility to uncontrolled regression; and the nature of the current adult stress situation.

The results of these more sophisticated observations indicate that, dependent on these factors, the same unconscious psychic conflict or fixation may produce in different individuals a wide variety of adult psychopathology. For example, depending on the relative intensity of the factors listed above, a man with significant unconscious phallic-oedipal conflicts might manifest any or several of the following: phobic symptoms, obsessive-compulsive neurosis, sexual potency problems ranging from a madonna-prostitute dichotomy to complete impotence; exhibitionism; feelings of inferiority; work inhibition;

exaggerated fears of competition or of bodily injury; a count-erphobic attitude toward physical danger; etc. Conversely, the same psychopathological outcome may arise from various forms or levels of unconscious conflict.

For example, a neurotic symptom such as agoraphobia or bulimia may be traceable to a variety of developmental conflicts: fears of aggression at various developmental levels; fears of sexuality; separation anxiety; conflict over passivity and dependency; etc.

Pollock (1970) studied the impact of significant object loss in childhood. He demonstrated that its effects in the adult may range from creative and adaptive sublimation through artistic production, to mild and transient neurotic reactions on the occasion of specific anniversaries of the particular loss, to profound and severe reactions on such anniversaries, to severe and chronic pathological character traits or psychic decompensations traceable to the original loss. Fleming and Altschul (1963) demonstrated that the effects of object loss in childhood are inversely related to success or failure in the completion of the mourning process at the time of the loss. Engel (1975), in an autobiographical study, noted the continuing manifestations and effects of such losses and the need for repetitive psychological work in coping with them.

Studies of conflict specificity in psychosomatic syndromes (Alexander, French, and Pollock, 1968) indicate that the same forms of intrapsychic conflict may occur in a variety of syndromes and that the specific form of pathology is determined by the presence of specific and constitutional organ system vulnerability; in the absence of such genetically determined vulnerability, a different form of disorder may be manifest. The same concept holds for such illnesses as schizophrenia or manic depressive psychosis. Certain forms of intrapsychic conflict have been frequently associated with these conditions, but they are not specific; in the absence of constitutional predisposition or vulnerability, a different clinical syndrome will emerge.

However, some syndromes observable in adults have regularly been traced to developmental arrests at specific levels of psychic development, particularly in cases of personality or character disorder. For example, Kohut (1977) describes the self pathology particular to certain narcissistic personality disorders stemming from a partial fixation at the level of the child's fusion with the maternal object. Kernberg (1975) describes developmental arrests at primitive levels of ego function in borderline conditions where the pathogenic feature is the persistence of primitive splitting mechanisms. Stoller (1975) describes specific early constellations of psychic conflict in patients with severe gender disturbances, and Socarides (1968) describes similarly specific conflicts in cases of obligatory homosexuality.

In summary, individuals who have passed through earlier developmental phases with minimal intensity of psychic conflict, or who have through their own devices or through the assistance of the objects in their environment been able to resolve those conflicts reasonably well, tend as adults to be relatively immune to significant psychopathology. They tend to be able to respond to the inevitable conflicts and stresses induced by the vicissitudes of adult life in appropriate, effective, and nonregressive ways. By contrast, individuals with major active unresolved conflicts and developmental arrests or distortions from earlier phases tend selectively to reenact such conflicts in response to the multiple opportunities presented by the vicissitudes of their adult lives, activities, and object relationships. And those individuals with significant but relatively dormant unconscious conflicts from earlier phases of development tend to be susceptible to a reactivation of these conflicts if the vicissitudes of adult life present them with situations beyond their capacity for adaptation, or situations which in one or another element are unconsciously associated with those conflicts.

These conceptualizations permit an understanding of why different individuals may respond to the same adult conflict or stress with significantly different reactions and responses. They permit as well an understanding of why a given individual may respond with appropriate and nonneurotic reactions to one form of stress while responding inappropriately and maladaptively to another.

Typical Adult Developmental Tasks

As mentioned above, the phase of adulthood is not a static or fixed one, and although normally the rate of change is slower and less dramatic than in earlier phases of development, effective adaptation requires of the individual a capacity for progressive change and psychological maturation.

In Western society and culture there are a number of typical developmental and maturational tasks and crises to which the adult must adapt by using the psychological capacities and organizations which have evolved as the result of his previous life and experience.

Occupation or Profession

The choice of an occupation or profession is an important developmental challenge. It requires preparation for the career that is chosen, as well as the capacity for achieving the various individual goals which may be set, and involves a variety of issues in regard to status, role in the society, economic and social opportunities and satisfactions, and enhancement or restriction with regard to self-esteem and the capacity for social adaptation.

Observations in the clinical situation show that such conscious adult decisions are significantly influenced by a variety of unconscious factors and forces. Such issues as positive or negative identification with important childhood objects, fears of or needs for competitive struggle, narcissistic needs, expression of otherwise unacceptable instinctual drive derivatives, parental or internalized superego values and demands, reversals from passive to active roles, unconscious guilt or shame, etc., may all represent significant unconscious influences on these choices.

The greater the intensity of such unconscious forces, the greater is the likelihood of disillusionment, dissatisfaction, or eventual symptom formation in relation to issues activated in the occupational situation. The less the impact of unconscious forces, and the more that such choices are based on a realistic appraisal of innate talents, motivations, and interests, the more stable and satisfying such choices tend to be.

In an optimally adaptive situation, occupational choice permits the expression of sublimated instinctual strivings compatible with ego ideal value systems, unencumbered by unconscious inhibition or conflict. The work role and situation thus provide pleasurable fulfillment and narcissistic self-esteem over and beyond immediate social or economic rewards. However, for large numbers of people the work role does not fulfill these needs, and such satisfactions must be achieved through other forms of activity.

For some individuals the work role may serve to express unconscious conflict (neurotic inhibitions, success neuroses, difficulties in interpersonal relationships, problems in frustration tolerance, etc.), while for others it may serve as a defense against more difficult intrapsychic disturbances (e.g., the individual who uses work to avoid relating to his family). Other individuals may find that specific occupational requirements intensify preexisting intrapsychic conflicts and thus promote manifestations of psychopathology.

Whatever choice has been made in this regard, the individual remains vulnerable to the possibility that changing internal or external factors may subsequently alter the perception and experience of one's chosen life's work and role in society.

Marriage

Another developmental milestone involves issues of marriage, the selection and development of a relationship with the marital partner, and the establishment of a new and autonomous independent family unit. The sustained, intense, intimate, and exclusive nature of the marital relationship makes it particularly subject to unconscious influences from one or both of the partners. The choice of marital partner is often significantly influenced by unconscious transference reactions from past important objects, often additionally accompanied by various degrees of idealization of the object. If, in addition, there are reality-oriented perceptions, interests, and emotionally satisfying elements in the relationship, the inevitable disillusionments that accompany prolonged interaction between partners will not prove overly disruptive.

The evolution of the marital relationship involves the simultaneous interplay of conscious and unconscious forces within each of the participants, leading to the establishment of a dynamic interactional relationship. Optimally, each partner is capable of maintaining a sense of personal identity, a capacity for balance between satisfaction of one's own needs and those of the spouse, a commitment to the relationship, a capacity to tolerate temporary disappointment and frustration, and a sense of mutual participation in a new and autonomous family unit. Both partners may use their own family of origin as a model for marital interaction, through either positive or negative identifications. Optimally, the spouses share a sense of basic mutual trust and a capacity to fuse erotic and nonerotic elements into a love relationship with a single object.

However, each spouse may bring to the relationship a variety of unresolved unconscious conflicts or neurotic symptoms or character traits which may significantly influence the marital interaction. In some instances, the unconscious wishes or defenses of the two partners may be complementary to each other, thus leading to unconsciously satisfying and stable interactions, even though an outside observer might recognize neurotic interactional patterns. For example, one spouse may tend to be passive and dependent, while the other is active and seeks the nurturing role; or one spouse may have masochistic needs while the other tends to be aggressively sadistic; or both spouses may fear intimacy and have a need for remoteness from each other; or both spouses may have similar degrees of sexual or aggressive inhibition.

However, the neurotic or character traits of the spouses may be in various degrees noncomplementary. For example, both may have deep passive needs for nurturance, and neither may be capable of fulfilling such needs in the other; or one may seek intimacy and sharing, while the other seeks to avoid it; or one may have intense and persistent sexual needs while the other manifests severe sexual inhibition; or one may be seductively provocative toward other people, while the other is pathologically jealous; etc. In such instances the marital interaction may provide little or no satisfaction for one or both partners, and this may lead to a variety of stress situations within the marriage, or to separation or divorce.

The individual who from choice or necessity remains single faces a different but equally important set of intrapsychic, interpersonal, social, and cultural forces to which adaptation is required. For such individuals, preexisting conflicts and patterns of adaptation may allow ego-syntonic responses to these forces; others, however, may find the bachelor or spinster life adjustment to be ego-alien and a source of further conflict and stress.

Parenthood

Becoming a parent is another important maturational crisis in the life of the adult, requiring a variety of new forms of adaptation and experiences, and at times involving a considerable reorganization in regard to previous patterns and levels of function. Not only are marital, social, economic, and personal lifestyle changes required, but the role of being a parent carries intrapsychic associations to the individual's own childhood and parents.

For example, the infant and young child's helplessness may activate fears of aggression in the parent; the necessity of providing for the child's needs may activate feelings of envy in parents whose own needs were not satisfactorily met in childhood; parents may reverse passive experiences from their own childhood to active ones and repeat toward their children what they experienced from their own parents; parents may unconsciously identify with their child and vicariously enjoy giving it satisfactions the parent did not receive as a child; parents may perceive the child as a threat and experience various competitive feelings toward the child; the sibling position, sex, appearance, and innate talents of the child may have specific associational meanings in relation to the parent's own childhood experiences; etc. These are but a sample of the types of conflict that may be activated in the parent by the birth of a child.

The more intense the residual psychopathology in the parent, the greater is the likelihood of significant conscious or unconscious disturbance in relation to the child; the less the residual psychopathology in the parent, the more likely is it that the parental role and functions will be fulfilled effectively and appropriately.

During subsequent growth and development, children may at times evoke specific forms and degrees of conflict and reorganization for the adult, depending on the parent's previous adaptational capacities and the ways in which the developing child's maturational stages and problems reverberate with the intrapsychic conflicts and their organization within the parent. There may be specific phases in the life of the child (e.g., adolescence) which evoke particular difficulty, turmoil, or conflict in the parent, but optimally the healthy adult remains capable of effective maturation and adaptive response to the changing status, needs, and demands of the developing child.

These issues tend to be particularly highlighted for parents in middle age, when both parents must cope with the crisis induced by the separation of the children from the nuclear family as the result of their own maturation, and the changes that this provokes in the parents' lives and status and in their relationship with each other.

This is a particularly stressful period for the mother who has devoted a major portion of her activity and energy to child rearing. Unless suitably equipped to participate in other forms of activity and interest, she may feel useless and unneeded and may require additional support and need satisfaction from the environment. Not infrequently, the children in a family unit may have served as a focus of mutual interaction between the parents, and their absence through maturation and emancipation may force the parents to reassess their relationship.

Adult Limitations and Disappointments

Another midlife crisis is occasioned by the adult's progressive awareness of limitations in reaching whatever goals had been set earlier in life, particularly in terms of marriage, interpersonal relationships, work, achievement, and economic and social status. Often the adult must cope with a sense of disappointment in these areas. A similar sense of disappointment or disillusionment may become manifest in regard to loss of physical vigor and attractiveness, decline in the intensity of sexual drives and function, and the increasing recognition of progressive passage through the life cycle.

These issues are particularly highlighted at the time of menopause in women and at the time of the typical midlife crisis in men. The various forms and methods of response to these typical stages are determined by the effectiveness of adaptation and the degree of fulfillment occurring in the prior stages of maturation and development. The greater the satisfaction of internal needs earlier on, the more effectively the individual can tolerate and adapt to the changes occurring during this phase; lost capacities are replaced by new ways of functioning, fulfilling needs, and maintaining a dynamic equilibrium. The more the individual has experienced frustration or postponement in regard to conscious and unconscious needs, the greater the narcissistic injury from advancing age, and the more intense the pressures to achieve fulfillment "before it is too late." In the latter circumstance the individual may experience increasing pressures to "act out" inappropriately or maladaptively, not infrequently resulting in disruptive or idiosyncratic new behavior patterns. Many such individuals may experience intensified conflict over such impulses, leading at times to the onset of significant psychopathological symptoms.

Illness and Disability

Throughout the life cycle of the adult, major illness, injury, or other acute or chronic disability may significantly induce new and additional stress to which adaptation is required. Chronic illness or disability may, in vulnerable individuals, represent serious narcissistic injury, increase their dependency on others, thus activating previously dormant unconscious conflict, and make impossible certain activities which previously had served a defensive or adaptive function. Sometimes specific illnesses or medical procedures (mastectomy, colostomy, amputation, etc.) have idiosyncratic associations to unconscious conflicts (Castelnuovo-Tedesco, 1973), thus significantly reactivating them. These issues may also influence the intrapsychic and interpersonal dynamic equilibrium of the afflicted's spouse, with subsequent secondary effects on the individual suffering the disability.

Retirement

Another major phase, particularly in the life of the working adult, is the issue of retirement, with its various repercussions in regard to role, status, economic security, and sense of purpose. This may require major psychological adaptation and the reworking of previously integrative personality patterns, not only for the individual but also for the spouse whose patterns of life may also be significantly disrupted.

This is a particularly stressful phase for individuals whose work role has been highly cathected and for whom it has served significantly narcissistic or sublimatory functions. The psychologically healthier the individual, the more likely the possibility of finding substitute activities to fulfill these psychic functions. But the more rigid or limited the individual's capacities, the greater the disruptive psychological effects.

Retirement may involve narcissistic injury to the individual, but it also involves symbolic or actual object loss related to the work activity itself and also to the loss of contacts with colleagues. Such losses require appropriate grief and mourning if they are not to serve as possible foci for conflict and symptom formation. There are more frequent losses through illness or death of one's spouse, friends, and neighbors, as well as new living arrangements such as in a child's home or retirement or nursing home. This may result in loneliness or depression, and the need to develop new adaptations at a time of diminished resources.

Aging

Aging, with its progression toward senescence with loss of physical and mental capacities, is another life crisis. It intensifies narcissistic injury, the recognition of mortality, and the inevitable approach of the end of life, with consequent stress and demands for adaptation to this ever more imminent threat. It also shifts the balance toward dependency on others, loss of independence, and decrease in available outlets for need satisfaction.

Death

Finally, there is the issue of death itself, both for the individual approaching it and for the survivor, for whom it may involve a major shift in intrapsychic, interpersonal, social, economic, or other factors and the need for adaptation to these new circumstances.

Concluding Remarks

The intrapsychic and interpersonal behavior of the adult is the result of the simultaneous interaction of many factors. Some of these are constitutionally and biologically determined; some are psychologically and experientially determined. Some exert their effects at conscious levels of awareness, while others operate at deeply unconscious levels of experience. Some arise primarily from environmental influences, others arise primarily from intrapsychic forces; and still others are the result of various forms of complex interplay between external and intrapsychic factors.

The adult phase of the life cycle requires a continuing (if less rapid and dramatic) maturation if optimal adaptation and function are to be maintained. Inevitably, conflicts and the vicissitudes of life vary widely among different individuals, but no one is immune to them. Emotional health vs. psychopathology is less significantly related to the existence of conflict than to the individual's capacities for conflict resolution or containment. And these functions are the result of the multiplicity of factors considered earlier in this chapter.

References

Alexander, F., French, T. M., & Pollock, G. H. (1968), *Psychosomatic Specificity*. Vol. 1. Chicago: University of Chicago Press.

Arieti, S. (1974), *Interpretation of Schizophrenia*. New York: Basic Books.

Arlow, J. A., & Brenner, C. (1964), *Psychoanalytic Concepts and the Structural Theory*. New York: International Universities Press.

Castelnuovo-Tedesco, P. (1973), Organ transplant, body image, and psychosis. *Psychoanal. Quart.*, 42:349–363.

Dewald, P. (1972), *The Psychoanalytic Process*. New York: Basic Books.

Engel, G. L. (1975), The death of a twin: Mourning and anniversary reactions. Fragments of 10 years of self-analysis. *Internat. J. Psycho-Anal.*, 56:23–40.

Fleming, J., & Altschul, S. (1963), Activation of mourning and growth by psychoanalysis. *Internat. J. Psycho-Anal.*, 44:419–431.

Freud, A. (1962), Assessment of childhood disturbances. *The Psychoanalytic Study of the Child*, 17:149–158. New York: International Universities Press.

——— (1965), *Normality and Pathology in Childhood*. New York: International Universities Press.

———— Nagera, H., & Freud, W. E. (1965), Metapsychological assessment of the adult personality. *The Psychoanalytic Study of the Child*, 20:9–41. New York: International Universities Press.

Freud, S. (1916–1917), Introductory lectures on psycho-analysis. *Standard Edition*, 15/16. London: Hogarth Press, 1963.

Gill, M. M., & Holzman, P. S., eds. (1976), Psychology versus Metapsychology. Psychoanalytic Essays in Memory of George S. Klein. *Psychological Issues*, Monograph 36. New York: International Universities Press.

Hartmann, H. (1939), *Ego Psychology and the Problem of Adaptation*. New York: International Universities Press, 1958.

Kernberg, O. (1975), *Borderline Conditions and Pathological Narcissism*. New York: Aronson.

Klein, G. S. (1976), *Psychoanalytic Theory: An Exploration of Essentials*. New York: International Universities Press.

Kohut, H. (1977), *The Restoration of the Self*. New York: International Universities Press.

Lidz, T., Fleck, S., & Cornelison, A. R. (1965), *Schizophrenia and the Family*. New York: International Universities Press.

Pollock, G. H. (1970), Anniversary reactions, trauma, and mourning. *Psychoanal. Quart.*, 39:347–371.

Rapaport, D. (1960), *The Structure of Psychoanalytic Theory*. New York: International Universities Press.

Schafer, R. (1976), *A New Language for Psychoanalysis*. New Haven: Yale University Press.

Socarides, C. W. (1968), *The Overt Homosexual*. New York and London: Grune & Stratton.

Stoller, R. J. (1975), *Sex and Gender. Vol. 2, The Transsexual Experiment*. New York: Aronson.

Wallerstein, R. (1973), Psychoanalytic perspectives on the problem of reality. *J. Amer. Psychoanal. Assn.*, 21:5–33.

6

From Mistrust to Trust: Through a Stage Vertically

KALMAN J. KAPLAN, Ph.D.

NANCY A. O'CONNOR

> Therefore, it is our duty to thank and to praise in song and prayer, to glorify and extol Him who performed all these wonders for our forefathers and us. He brought us out from slavery to freedom, from anguish to joy, from sorrow to festivity, from darkness to great light. Let us therefore sing before Him a new song. Praise the Eternal [*Passover Haggadah*, 1966, p. 24].

In his seminal work, Erik Erikson (1950, 1968, 1980, 1982) has described stages in ego development at eight different stages of life. Each stage presents its own psychosocial crisis. If the crisis is satisfactorily resolved, a positive quality is added to the ego. If it is unsatisfactorily resolved, a negative factor is added. For example, the crisis at infancy is between the infant's physiological needs such as hunger, need for contact, and alleviation of discomfort and the ways in which caregivers respond

An initial version of this paper was presented at the Ninety-seventh Meetings of the American Psychological Association, New Orleans, Louisiana, August, 1989.

The authors would like to thank Dr. John Meacham, then editor of *Human Development*, for his encouragement and advice in the initial conceptualization of this paper in 1983; Dr. David Gutmann, Director of NIMH Training Grant #0600-370-T3334 in Clinical Geropsychology at Northwestern Memorial Hospital for teaching and supervision furthering development of this work; Dr. Rhonda Montgomery, former Director of the Institute of Gerontology at Wayne State University; and Dr. Martin Harrow, Director of Psychology at Humana Hospital–Michael Reese and of the Chicago Followup Study (NIMH Grant #MH-26341) for making available the time and resources to complete this project. Acknowledgments are also due Drs. Renee Lawrence and Marlene DeVoe for help in aspects of this paper. Any distortions in the treatment of their ideas are, of course, those of the present authors.

to such needs. Satisfactory resolution of this crisis leads to the acquisition of the positive ego quality of basic trust. Unsatisfactory resolution of this crisis leads to the negative quality of basic mistrust. A similar analysis can be made at the next stage, toddlerhood, beginning at 18 months and continuing until 36 months. Improved neuromuscular coordination facilitates the potential for many new areas of conflict with the environment. The toddler may soil himself, eat in a messy fashion, or destroy the property of others. The child may thus encounter societal prohibitions or discipline to keep his or her behavior in line. Satisfactory resolution of this crisis will add the positive ego trait of autonomy, whereas unsatisfactory resolution will lead to shame. A comparable analysis can be made for each of Erikson's other six stages. Satisfactory resolution of the psychosocial crisis at play age will lead to initiative and unsatisfactory resolution to guilt. Resolution of the school age crisis leads to addition of the positive ego quality of industry; unsatisfactory resolution leads to addition of the negative ego quality inferiority. Satisfactory resolution of the psychosocial crisis at adolescence leads to the positive ego quality identity; unsatisfactory resolution leads to the negative ego quality identity confusion. At young adulthood for Erikson, the issue becomes intimacy versus isolation. Satisfactory resolution of this life stage leads to the acquisition of intimacy; unsatisfactory resolution leads to isolation. Satisfactory navigation of middle adulthood leads to the positive ego quality of generativity; unsatisfactory resolution leads to stagnation. Finally, old age must be satisfactorily navigated to add the final positive ego quality of integrity; unsatisfactory resolution leads to the negative quality of despair.

Although progression through these stages represents the very dynamic of human development, it is often seen in a somewhat flattened horizontal manner and does not reflect ontogenetic within-stage development. Typical interpretations of Erikson suggest healthy development is achieved by resolving each stage crisis in favor of the syntonic as opposed to the dystonic ego quality. Thus, for example, the psychosocial crisis of infancy is resolved by achieving a balance between trust and mistrust in the direction of trust. The underlying developmental process seems to be one of *horizontal* oscillation on a continuum where both aspects of trust and mistrust are necessary for successful navigation of the infant stage.

Our view, in contrast, suggests an often obscured ontogenetic view of the developmental process within a stage. Further, it suggests a between-stage conception, of *forward regression* or what Anna Freud (1936) referred to as regression in the service of development. A life event forwardly regresses an organism into the negative or dystonic quality at the beginning of the next life stage. Successful *vertical* navigation through this stage involves passing from the negative to the positive quality and the attaining of a stage-specific syntonic equilibrium. However, that very syntonic quality interacts with the subsequent life event or stressor to promote dystonicity with regard to the now broader social radius (i.e., to upset that now inadequate equilibrium). For example, the life event of weaning invariably forwardly regresses the infant into the dystonic position of mistrust toward the mother and the self. It must be worked through vertically to attain the syntonic position of trust. Trust toward the mother (and self) then interacts with the next life event, fecal embarrassment, to forwardly regress the infant into shame, a negative ego quality—albeit at the next advanced stage and with the broader social radius, parental persons, and the within-stage process must be once more worked through. Thus the trusting infant now experiences toilet training, which plunges the now-toddler into the dystonic position of shame with regard to parental persons. This, in turn, must be worked through vertically to attain the syntonic quality of autonomy. In other words, what we are suggesting is that successful development involves not the avoidance of the negative or dystonic ego qualities at each stage but the very plunging into each of them as the natural sequela of the preceding life event. Successful development involves working through a stage vertically to attain the respective stage-specific positive or syntonic ego position.

Our method of analysis evolves from a multistage, multilevel conception of human development proposed by Kaplan ([1988]; see also Kaplan, Schwartz, and Markus-Kaplan [1984], Markus-Kaplan and Kaplan [1984]) entitled TILT: Teaching Individuals to Live Together. The logic of this model suggests that the underlying developmental process across the life-span involves the integration of individuation and attachment in a one step backward/two steps forward fashion. This is why we have referred to this journey as a "forward regression" to successively more advanced life stages. We now delineate a template emerging from the TILT model that we apply consecutively to each of Erikson's life stages. We will thus attempt to demonstrate the continuities in personality patterning from early infancy to later adulthood, albeit expressed in forms revolving around the stage-specific life issues.[1]

TILT: Teaching Individuals to Live Together

TILT is a multistage–multilevel model that has been developed in an attempt to differentiate clinical oscillation between individuation and attachment from healthy integrated ontogenetic development. The essence of this work is to divide interpersonal distance into two subdimensions: attachment–detachment and individuation–deindividuation. Attachment–detachment is designated by external square icons or *walls* and defined as the capacity to bond (▢), semibond (▢), or not bond (▢) to external objects. Individuation–deindividuation is designated by internal circle icons or *boundaries* and defined as the capacity to differentiate (○), semi-differentiate (○) or not differentiate (○) from these same external objects.

Two axes can be differentiated in Figure 1: a developmental BED axis (Figure 1a) and a clinical AC axis. (Figure 1b). Let us consider the developmental BED axis first (Figure 1a). Cell B represents an immature individual who is deindividuated but detached. Deindividuation (○) represents a low state of individual organization and definition and detachment (▢) can be thought of as defensive in structure. An impermeable wall is necessary to shield the inarticulately defined individual from external engulfment (▢). In Cell E, the individual is

---

[1]See related work by Rank (1936), Bakan (1966), Kohut (1966, 1971), Loevinger and Wessler (1970), Gutmann (1980b), Levinger (1980), Kegan (1982) and McAdams (1985).

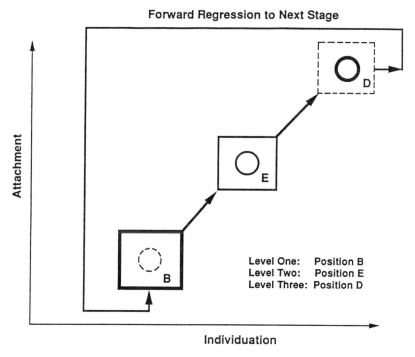

FIGURE 1a. The developmental axis.

slowly maturing. He is semi-individuated and semiattached. He has achieved a modicum of self definition, a semiarticulated boundary (◯). Some defensive structure is necessary, a semi-permeable wall (▢). The E individual can be described as semi-individuated and semiattached (▣). In Cell D, the individual is individuated and attached (▣). He has matured to the point where he has achieved a high degree of self-defini-tion, an articulated boundary (◯). Here the defensive struc-ture can be quite minimal, a permeable wall (▢) as there is little danger of external engulfment. The logic of this develop-mental axis is simply that the loosening of one's defenses (i.e., greater permeability of walls) should occur in conjunction with the strengthening of one's ego (i.e., greater definition of bound-aries).

In contrast to healthy congruency between individuation and attachment is clinical incongruent resolution of the individ-uation–attachment dilemma reflected in pathological spiraling

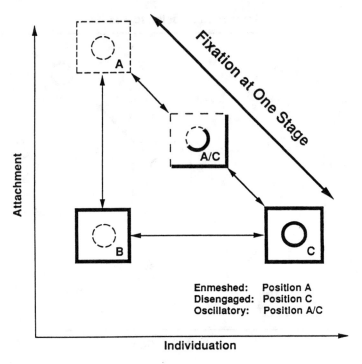

Enmeshed: Position A
Disengaged: Position C
Oscillatory: Position A/C

FIGURE 1b. The clinical axis.

or oscillation between these two forces (i.e., Positions A and C).[2] What makes this AC axis clinical (Figure 1b) is the bad fit and lack of coordination between walls and boundaries. The A individual attempts to become attached to the external world before he is individuated (🔲). In other words, he loosens his defenses (permeable walls: 🔲) while his ego is still ill-defined (inarticulated boundaries: ◌). The C individual, in contrast, remains detached even after he has become sufficiently individuated (🔲). In other words, he holds onto his defenses (impermeable walls: □) even after his ego has become sharply defined (articulated boundaries: ◯). The A/C individual oscillates horizontally between these styles (🔲), first favoring attachment and then individuation. A and C individuals thus

―――――――――――

[2]Kegan (1982, p. 108), in contrast, seems to see this spiraling as essential to healthy development.

represent polarities on this clinical axis, the A individual manifesting a tendency toward enmeshment (deindividuated attachment) and the C individual a tendency toward disengagement (detached individuation). These pathologies, we suggest, may have long-term effects in the absence of corrective intervention by which the individual may reenter (through the initial B position) the developmental BED axis. Further, life demands might prompt an individual to attempt to "pseudo-resolve" imbalances on the AC axis through rapid oscillation between enmeshment and disengagement (A/C). Such a pseudo-resolution may serve to mask pathology, both to self and to others. However, it does not represent any true integration between individuation and attachment and may even deepen and disguise the disintegrative process.

It should be emphasized at this point that this model is stage-specific. A new life event $(i + 1)$ represents the stressor precipitating movement to the next stage whether the individual is on the developmental or clinical axis. A person at the D_i level of Stage i on the developmental BED axis is forwardly regressed to B_{i+1} at the next stage, $i + 1$.[3] A person on the AC axis at Stage i may be prompted to achieve an A/C pseudo-resolution to enter stage $i + 1$. However, such a pseudo-resolution represents a dangerous, disguised, and disintegrated oscillation between the pathological polarities of enmeshment and disengagement and does not offer any hope of true integration of individuation and attachment.[4]

---

[3]Forward regression states simply that "progression in stage" is achieved through "regression in level." In other words, the developmental progression from Level One (B) to Level Two (E) to Level Three (D) occurs within a specific stage. Each successive stage must be entered at Level One (B). This concept is long overdue in developmental psychology. It reflects both the traditional psychoanalytic view that regression represents a return under stress to an earlier stage of development (Noam, O'Connell-Higgins, and Goethals, 1982) and the specific insight of Anna Freud (1936) that in some circumstances regression is the way by which, paradoxically, the individual moves forward in development.

[4]The reader is referred to Dabrowski's distinction between "negative integration" and "positive disintegration" (Dabrowski, 1973, pp. 37–47).

TILTing Erikson: Through a Stage Vertically

We are now ready to apply TILT to an expansion and reconceptualization of the Eriksonian life stages. The template presented previously is applied sequentially in Figures 2a and 2b
to the eight Eriksonian life stages as well as three additional
ones to complete the journey from womb to tomb. This analysis
is aimed at demonstrating a consistency in functioning from
early infancy to later adulthood, albeit expressed in the forms
emergent in the particular life stage. A stage in our model
is initiated by a life event (LE) which forwardly regresses the
organism into Level B, a dystonic position. The core strength
propels the organism forward to a syntonic D level. The core
pathology veers the individual off of this developmental BED
axis and onto the clinical AC axis.

An organism is confronted with a particular life event
which thrusts the individual into Level B at that life stage.
Healthy navigation of the issues paramount at that life stage
represents successful developmental change along the BED
axis. This we see as corresponding to Erikson's concept of the
basic strength at that life stage. Unhealthy navigation of these
life issues represents a veering onto the clinical AC axis. This
fixation and oscillation between polarities corresponds, in our
mind, to Erikson's conception of core pathology.[5] In either case
the organism confronts the next advanced life event, which
regresses the individual forward into Level B at the next advanced stage. It should be noted, however, that individuals who
enter B from the developmental axis are more prone to continue on this axis than those who enter from the A or C positions. This is because the unresolved incongruencies between
individuation and attachment from the previous stage leave an
individual with insufficiently developed ego strength (boundaries) or inappropriate defenses (walls) with which to cope with
this new life event. Once again, the individual must work his
way forward to Level D and once again we will be confronted
with another life event, perhaps the continuous refrain of the

---

[5]Note that the TILTed view of Erikson verticalizes his conception of ego
strength and bidimensionalizes his understanding of core pathology.

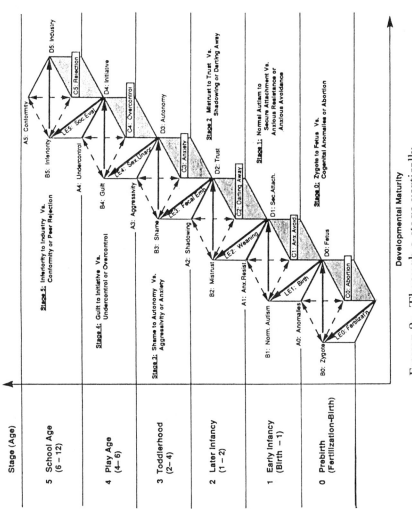

FIGURE 2a. Through a stage vertically.

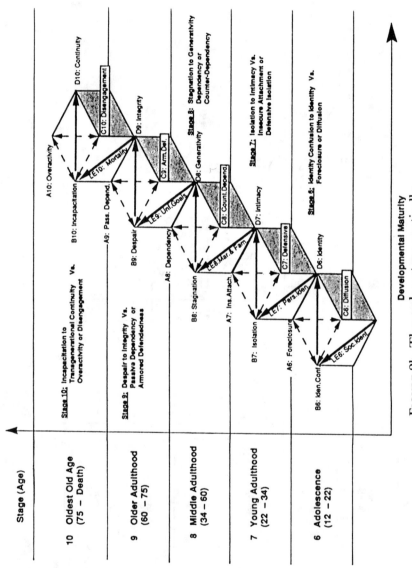

FIGURE 2b. Through a stage vertically.

entire life journey. Table 1 summarizes all of Erikson's negative or dystonic ego qualities as Level B structures at each respective stage; all of his positive or syntonic ego resolutions are described as Level D structures. Incongruous and unhealthy solutions are described as A and C structures.

Stage 0 to Prebirth—From Zygote to Fetus

Stage 0 in our model is an addition to Erikson and describes the prebirth period. The social radius of prebirth (SR_0) is the mother's uterus. The logic for extending TILT into prebirth is threefold. First, the model proposes that the integration of individuation and attachment represents a basic ontogenetic process. Thus it posits the beginnings of this process to be visible at all stages of life, including "life in utero," albeit in concrete physiological terms. Perhaps it is the very early kinesthetic imprinting of the individuation–attachment process that enables its further recognition, development and refinement across the life span. Second, the prebirth period is one of increasing importance in preventive health care, from both a physiological and psychosocial viewpoint. Thus, it must be included in any complete life stage theory in the 1990s. Third, the area of object relations so critical to a verticalized individuation–attachment view of Erikson has its roots in mother–child interaction. It can only deepen our understanding to extend it to the prenatal period. Nonetheless, our treatment of the prebirth period differs from the tradition of psychological research during this period which focuses on maternal–fetal attachment from the maternal perspective. Leifer (1977) and Cranley (1981) have studied the phenomenon extensively and seem to be continuing the line of inquiry into the psychological processes of pregnancy as experienced by the mother. This body of knowledge focuses on maternal incorporation of the fetus (Deutsch, 1948), the developmental tasks of pregnancy (Clark, 1976), maternal tasks of pregnancy (Rubin, 1975), maternal affect behaviors during pregnancy (Leifer, 1977), the extent of maternal affiliation and interaction with the fetus (Cranley, 1981) and the importance of these events to postbirth mother–child interaction. Our emphasis here, in contrast, is

TABLE 1
Developmental versus Clinical Axes at Each Life Stage

#	Precipitating Life Event	Stage	Social Radius	Core Strength	Developmental Axis		Core Pathology	Clinical Axis	
					B Level	D Level		A Expression	C Expression
0	Fertilization	Prenatal (Fertilization–Birth)	Mother's Uterus	Survival	Zygote	Fetus	Genetic–Environmental Inadequacy	Birth Defects/ Some Congenital Anomalies	Ectopic Pregnancies/ Some Spontaneous Abortions
1	Birth	Early Infancy (Birth–1)	Physical Presence of Mother	Reciprocity	Normal Autism	Secure Attachment	Noncontingency	Anxious Resistance	Anxious Avoidance
2	Weaning	Later Infancy (1–2)	Psychological Presence of Mother	Hope	Mistrust	Trust	Withdrawal	Shadowing	Darting Away
3	Fecal Embarrassment	Toddlerhood (2–4)	Parental Persons	Will	Shame	Autonomy	Compulsion	Aggressivity	Anxiety
4	Sexual Impulse Unacceptability	Play-Age Childhood (4–6)	Nuclear Family	Purpose	Guilt	Initiative	Inhibition	Undercontrol	Overcontrol

TABLE 1 (*continued*)

#	Precipitating Life Event	Stage	Social Radius	Core Strength	Developmental Axis		Core Pathology	Clinical Axis	
					B Level	D Level		A Expression	C Expression
5	Social Evaluation	School-Age Childhood (6–12)	School/Neighborhood Peers	Competence	Inferiority	Industry	Inertia	Conformity	Peer Rejection
6	Social Identity Demands	Adolescence (12–22)	Peer Group/Outgroups	Fidelity	Identity Confusion	Identity	Repudiation	Foreclosure	Diffusion
7	Personal Identity Demands	Young Adulthood (22–34)	Intimate Partners	Love	Isolation	Intimacy	Exclusivity	Insecure Attachment	Defensive Isolation
8	Marriage and Family Demands	Middle Adulthood (34–60)	Household and Children	Care	Stagnation	Generativity	Rejectivity	Dependency	Counter-dependency
9	Unfulfilled and Fulfilled Goals	Older Adulthood (60–75)	Mankind/My Kind	Wisdom	Despair	Integrity	Disdain	Passive-Dependency	Armored-Defendedness
10	Mortality Physical Decline (Life Cycle Shock)	Oldest Old (75–Death)	Present/Future	Faith	Incapacitation	Trans-generational Continuity	Doubt	Overactivity	Disengagement

on the developmental position of the developing fetus as a precursor to later development of the organism.

The prebirth period is initiated by the very first stressor or life event, *fertilization* (LE_0), which results in the dystonic position of an undifferentiated cell mass (B_0) known as a zygote or blastocyst. This zygote is neither individuated nor attached. The core strength is survival, which is manifested physiologically in this primal stage. Critical life processes of differentiation (individuation) are crucial during the first two weeks of zygote life, known as the germinal stage (Papalia and Olds, 1982). Yet the zygote is also preparing for implantation into the uterus (attachment). Early in development, the blastocyst separates its cells into outer and inner layers. The outer trophoblastic layer (walls, in TILT terms) is mainly concerned with the process of attachment to the uterine lining via chorionic villi whereas the inner layer (boundaries) individuates into the fetus. Once implantation has occurred, the zygote becomes known as the embryo (E_0) and undergoes further processes of differentiation and attachment (further progression along the developmental BED axis). Major organ systems are formed (individuated-more articulated boundaries), and the placenta grows to become the organ of attachment between the embryo and the mother. By the end of the embryonic stage (8 weeks) all major structures and organs that will be found in the full-term infant are present (Olds, London, and Ladewig, 1988). A gradually increasing social radius accompanies the early fetal period as the fetus begins to respond to mild stimulation and then becomes increasingly more responsive (attached-more permeable walls) to extrauterine sensations such as touch and light (Newman and Newman, 1987). Given healthy development via the core strength of survival, the fetus further individuates and becomes more securely attached. The fetal period (8 weeks to full term) then ensues with continuing refinement of fetal structures and physiological function. For example, the development of fingerprints occurs by 24 weeks (Moore, 1982) and signs of fetal temperament such as feeding, sleeping and activity patterns occur after 5 months (Olds et al., 1988). This process culminates in a firmly individuated full term fetus (articulated boundaries) which is temporally associated with a degenerating placenta and a thinning-out cervix (loosening of walls). Thus the fully developed fetus in the ninth month (D_0) displays the familiar syntonic TILT template of a more articulated intrapersonal boundary enabling a more permeable interpersonal wall.

The core pathology within this prenatal period can be viewed as genetic and/or environmental inadequacy. It can be expressed either in A or C forms, both positions on this clinical AC axis reflecting incongruencies between individuation and attachment. The prenatal A_0 structure (deindividuated attachment) is expressed in congenital anomalies which are carried to term. These fetuses display pathological inadequacy in differentiation but remain firmly attached. Conversely, the prenatal C_0 expression (detached individuation) can be seen in ectopic pregnancies, some spontaneous abortions, in placenta previa and abruptio placentae. In all these conditions, the problem is primarily one of inadequate attachment rather than individuation–differentiation. At the same time, 50 percent of commonly occurring spontaneous abortions are thought to result from extreme congenital inadequacy (Carr and Gedeon, 1977). Thus, survival and healthy development from zygote (B_0) to full-term fetus (D_0) depend upon an integrated and synchronous dovetailing of the processes of individuation and attachment (i.e., the loosening of the interpersonal wall in conjunction with the strengthening of the intrapersonal boundary).

Stage 1—Early Infancy: From Normal Autism to Secure Attachment

The division of infancy into its earlier and later stages is necessitated by distinct life events, an expanding social radius and an enlarging developmental capacity of the human infant. The great preponderance of research has concentrated on attachment in the period of early infancy and its ability to predict later developmental outcomes (Bowlby, 1969; Ainsworth, 1973; Sroufe and Waters, 1977). One of the few researchers into later infancy is Sroufe (cf. Joffe and Vaughn, 1982) and he has focused primarily on individuation within this later infancy phase (Sroufe, 1979). Both Mahler, Pine, and Bergman (1975) and Stern (1977), in contrast, reflect the present model's rejection of an oscillatory view of individuation and attachment and a call for the recognition of their reciprocal intertwining at each stage. With this in mind, we now turn to a description of these stages.

Stage 1 in the present model refers to the earliest infancy stage (birth to approximately age 1). It corresponds to the first part of Erikson's infancy stage and Freud's oral stage (Freud, 1905). The activating stressor is Life Event 1, the *birth process* itself which forwardly regresses the syntonically secure fetus (D_0) out of its now restrictive social radius, the uterus, into the more expanded radius (SR_1) of the mother's arms and body. This new radius is a prime example of what Winnicott (1965) calls the "holding environment." According to Mahler (1968), the stage of early infancy is characterized by the development of a "social symbiosis" analogous to the physiological symbiosis of intrauterine life. This continuing physiological and now so-cial-emotional dependency of the early infant on the mothering agency is absolutely necessary for the infant's ego development.

Normal development along the BED axis at this stage is promoted by the core strength of reciprocity between moth-ering agency and infant. Ainsworth (1973) has described this process as an "attachment–exploration" balance proceding from a "secure base," Mahler describes it as "mutual cueing" while Stern (1977) and Brazelton, Koslowski and Main (1974) describe it as a reciprocal dance or cycle that occurs simultane-ously between mother and infant. Various metaphors have been used to describe the B_1 (deindividuated and detached) infant. Khan (1964) describes the "protective shield" of the mother while Mahler refers to the mother serving as an auxil-iary ego for the infant. The mother acts as an impermeable wall protecting the infant's still inarticulated boundary. Mahler further describes this stage as one of absolute primary narcis-sism and of normal autism in which the infant does not distin-guish between his own tension-reduction efforts and those of his mother. By the end of the second month, this normal autistic period gives way to the "symbiotic stage proper," an E_1 struc-ture in the TILT model. Here the infant "behaves and func-tions as though he and his mother were an omnipotent sys-tem—a dual unity within one common boundary" (Mahler, 1968, p. 8). The infant begins to perceive that need satisfaction comes from a part object (i.e., breast or bottle) which is still within the dual unity system. Given optimal symbiosis or "good enough mothering" (Winnicott, 1971), the infant is ready to "hatch" (Mahler) from the symbiotic orbit. The caretaker may also gradually "deadapt," a process which allows the beginning of differentiation between self representations and the heretofore fixed self-plus-object representations (D_1). At this syntonic level, termed the "practicing period" by Mahler, the infant has achieved the beginning sense of I as distinct from not I and can sustain this sense given the presence and emotional availability of the mothering agency. This syntonic D_1 structure can also be recognized in the behavior of the securely attached infants described by Ainsworth (1979). These infants can actively explore their environment in the presence of the mother. Furthermore, upon reunion with the mother after brief periods of separation they are comforted by her and then return to their environmental explorations.

Without optimal symbiosis (Mahler) or given any missteps in the dance (Stern), safe developmental passage along the BED axis is blocked, primarily by the core pathology which we label noncontingency of mother or caregiver response. Prototypical A and C expressions can be discerned in Ainsworth's (1972) anxious–resistant (A_1) and anxious–avoidant (C_1) behaviors upon reunion after a mother's absence. In subsequent data, Main (1973) reported that mothers of avoidant (C_1) infants differed from those of resistant infants (A_1) in that they expressed dislike of establishing physical contact with their infants. The former A_1 (deindividuated attachment) infants display anger at the mother and also resist her efforts to comfort them, while ambivalently wanting to be held. The latter C_1 (detached individuation) infants avoid or ignore the mother upon her return, displaying a high tolerance for being alone. Significantly, mothers of infants changing from an insecure $(A_1$ and C_1 structures) to a secure (D_1) attachment relationship reported a significantly greater reduction in stressful life events than did mothers of infants changing in the opposite direction (Vaughn, Egeland, Sroufe, and Waters, 1979). Longitudinal studies demonstrate that mental representations of attachment are shown by the end of the first year of life (Main et al., 1985).

Stage 2—Later Infancy: From Mistrust to Trust

Stage 2 (approximately ages 1 to 2) denotes the period of later infancy corresponding to the latter part of Erikson's infancy stage and Freud's oral stage (Freud, 1905). The precipitating stressor is the life event of *weaning* (LE_2), which forwardly regresses the previous securely attached D_1 infant into a dystonic state of profound mistrust (B_2). The infant is shockingly reminded once again of his separateness from his mother, albeit at a more representational stage than that experienced through birth trauma. The social radius thus expands from the physical to the representational presence of the mother (SR_2) and begins to include the father as well (Mahler, Pine, and Bergman, 1975). Mahler (1968) puts it this way,

> at the very height of mastery, toward the end of the practicing period, it already had begun to dawn on the junior toddler that the world is not his oyster, that he must cope with it more or less on his own, very often as a relatively helpless (deindividuated) small and separate (detached) individual unable to command relief or assistance merely by feeling the need for it or even giving voice to that need [p. 78].

This sense of separateness is only enhanced by the later infant's increasing locomotor ability to move physically away from the mother (further individuate). The accompanying increments in cognition and language make possible a more representational (rather than primarily physical) sense of attachment.

This new process is reflected in Erikson's core strength of hope which Mahler has described as "confident expectation." At about 15 months, the weaned infant becomes more aware of his physical separateness yet seems to have an increased need to share with his mother each new skill he has experienced (Mahler, Pine, and Bergman, 1975). The source of the child's pleasure shifts from independent locomotion to social interaction, such as peek-a-boo games (Kleeman, 1967). The father, too, is becoming included into the infant's psychological world (Greenacre, 1966; Mahler, 1968; Abelin, 1971). From 16 to 17 months on, Mahler, Pine, and Bergman (1975) and Feldman and Ingham (1975) observe that early toddlers like to spend increasing amounts of time away from their mothers (individuation) and begin to form close attachments to substitute adults.

They often engage in symbolic play (Galenson, 1971). For most children, this period of early "rapprochement" culminates at age 17 to 18 months in a seeming acknowledgment and acceptance of separateness. However, the fragility of this equilibrium is indicated by the high occurrence of temper tantrums for young toddlers at this age. By 18 months, the late infants seem quite willing to express their rapidly emerging autonomy and conflicts emerge between their desire to push their mother away (individuate) and to cling to her (attach). During the 18- to 21-month period, the infant develops the capacity to realize that his physically absent mother has not permanently disappeared. The attainment of "object permanence" (Piaget, 1937) in conjunction with increased verbal skills makes possible increasingly representational forms of attachment which enable ever further environmental exploration (individuation). Indeed by the age of 2 years some (in our mind, D_2) infants can attach to photographs of their mother in her absence (Passman and Longeway, 1982). This representational attachment demonstrates both the infants' trust (D_2) in her return and in their own capacity to function in her absence.

The syntonic D_2 state of trust also involves an overcoming of the pathological splitting of the object world into "good" and "bad" objects (Kernberg, 1967) and the beginning of libidinal "object constancy" (Hartmann, 1964) through which a constant relationship with the mother can be maintained throughout normal ambivalences. Mahler (1968), however, has pointed to the time lag between the attainment of object permanence and that of object constancy which may, given inconsistent mothering, lead to oscillation on the clinical AC axis. This is reflected in Erikson's core pathology of withdrawal from navigating the life issue of representational attachment. Stability has been demonstrated in both Ainsworth's secure (D) and insecure (A or C) attachment styles in the period of 12 to 20 months and beyond (Main et al., 1985). Bowlby (1969, 1973, 1977) has suggested that in the absence of security, infants may become anxious or insecure (A) while Parkes (1972) has pointed to the opposite (C) pole of compulsive self-reliance. Though there is a paucity of empirical research at this later stage of infancy (Joffe and Vaughn, 1982), Mahler et al. (1975) has pointed to two patterns of infant–mother attachment which, in exaggerated form, may represent stage-specific forms of these A–C pathologies. The first (A_2) pattern can be discerned in a pretoddler's prolonged and excessive shadowing of his mother whereby he does not want to let her out of his sight. The opposite (C_2) pattern is displayed by a pretoddler who incessantly darts away from his mother, perhaps in an attempt to induce her to chase him. Both of these patterns, unresolved, may represent a failure to attain object permanence and/or constancy and inadequacies in the achievement of individuation and attachment.

Stage 3—Toddlerhood: From Shame to Autonomy

Stage 3 (approximately ages 2 to 4) denotes Erikson's toddlerhood and Freud's anal stage (Freud, 1905). The initiating life event is *fecal embarrassment* (LE_3) which is brought on by the necessary stressor of toilet training—the toddler learns to his dismay that "his feces are not golden." This shock forwardly regresses the syntonically trusting later infant (D_2) into a profoundly dystonic state of shame (B_3) that he has done something wrong. The social radius has expanded too, from a warm maternal figure with whom the later infant has painfully achieved rapprochement to impassive parental persons (SR_3) who insist that the toddler deposit his feces in a toilet (White, 1960). Classic psychoanalytic thinking (Freud, 1905, 1913) has considered this anal stage to lie at the source of many obsessive–compulsive characteristics. This is perfectly understandable from the point of view of the present model. Obsessions are persistent ritualized thoughts; compulsions, repetitive ritualized actions. Both serve a protective function—to bind the anxiety the suddenly vulnerable toddler must feel. Toddlers seem to assert a pseudo-independence (setting up impermeable walls to protect inarticulated boundaries) through bed, dress and other well-ordered rituals (Albert, Amgott, Krakow, and Marcus, 1977) and a generally unreasonable negativity (Erikson, 1951/1953). Alternatively, shameful toddlers may attempt to shield a lack of confidence (deindividuation) through refraining from all kinds of new activities (detachment). If the child does not try new things, he will not be further embarrassed for violating social norms.

Shame is the signal that prompts the 2-year-old toddler to withdraw.

Although the B_3 level may be effective temporarily in protecting the toddler, it will not suffice in this period of rapidly expanding environments. The toddler is becoming proficient in walking and is rapidly developing in thought and language (Anglin, 1977; Molfese, Molfese, and Carrell, 1982). Erikson's core strength at this stage is will, which works to propel the toddler ahead on the BED developmental axis toward the new syntonic equilibrium of autonomy (D_3). This D_3 structure is reflected in the toddler's sense that he can control his own impulses (Freud, 1953) and thus safely reengage with his environment in a more masterful and less defensive way (White, 1960). Erikson (1951/1953) describes the journey of toddlerhood as proceeding from "naysaying" and ritualization (B_3) to independence and persistence (D_3). Newman and Newman (1987) characterize it as proceeding from doing things "one's own way" to doing them "on one's own." Murphy and Moriarty (1976) have noted that between the ages of 2 and 4, children come both to experience less frustration than they did previously and to manage better whatever amount still exists. Toddlers may learn to control their environment through symbolic imagery and fantasy play (Singer, 1973, 1975) and through imitation (Parton, 1976; Bandura, 1977; Grusec and Abramovitch, 1982). Learning through imitation has the advantage of bypassing the child's anxiety regarding the violation of social norms (the shame signal) and allowing the attainment of autonomy and efficacy (D_3).

Hoffman (1977) has discovered that parental discipline techniques based on "inductions" (i.e., explanations to the toddler as to why behavior was wrong and appeals to his sense of mastery and fairness) may be more effective in producing a D_3 "autonomously concerned" child (Baumrind, 1971; Odom, Seeman, and Newbrough, 1971; Leizer and Rogers, 1974) than are two other discipline techniques, "power assertion" and "love withdrawal," each of which seem to trigger Erikson's core pathology compulsion, albeit in opposite forms. Power assertion involves physical punishment, shouting and inhibitions of the child's behavior (an intrusive A parenting style) while love with-drawal reflects parental disapproval, refusal to communicate, and a general turning away (a disengaged C parenting style). It is not surprising that research has shown that the power-assertion style tends to produce aggressive (A_3) children (Anthony, 1970; Chwast, 1972) who lose control of their anger and moral prohibitions in interactions with others (deindividuated attachment). Love withdrawal, in contrast, tends to produce anxious (C_3) toddlers who remain overly controlled in their emotions and interact in a compliant (Forehand, Roberts, Doleus, Hobbs, and Resuick, 1976) or conformist (Hoffman, 1980) way with adult authorities (detached individuation). Both of these toddler types fall on the clinical AC axis and must be distinguished from autonomous (D_3) children who in Bandura's (1977) terms, can express anger while not losing control (individuated attachment). Significantly, this autonomous toddler may represent a developmental bridge between the securely attached (D_1) infant (Matas, Arend, and Sroufe, 1978) and the confident, skilled, and initiating (D_4) preschooler (Arend, Gove, and Sroufe, 1979; Sroufe, 1979).

Stage 4—Play-Age Childhood: From Guilt to Initiative

Stage 4 (approximately ages 4 to 6) denotes Erikson's play age and Freud's classic oedipal period (Freud, 1933). The environmental stressor is Life Event 4—*sexual impulse unacceptability* which interacts with the previous social radius, parental persons, to forwardly regress a syntonically autonomous toddler (D_3) into a dystonic position of guilt (B_4) with regard to the expanded social radius, the nuclear family (SR_4). From an orthodox psychoanalytic point of view, the oedipal or phallic stage is the period in which the oedipal and Electra conflicts emerge. Both of these conflicts (Oedipus for the son, Electra for the daughter) involve the giving up of the opposite-sex parent as a sexual object and the identification with the same-sex parent. A result of this outcome is the emergence of a well-differentiated superego (thus, the psychoanalytic axiom "the superego is heir to the Oedipus complex"), guilt and a repression of the sexual and aggressive tendencies on the part of the child toward the parents (see the review by Greenspan and Pollock [1980] on

current psychoanalytic thinking on this period). The Eriksonian view of this stage is somewhat looser, but the outcome is the
same. The play-age child is faced with a heightened awareness
of his sexual organs and often becomes involved with exploration of his own body and that of his friends. Embarrassment
on the part of adults as to the sexual implications of this frank
exposure of body parts may create guilt and withdrawal in the
child. This guilt may extend beyond sexual issues per se to all
areas of open conflict between the social norms of the culture
as represented by adults and the child's age-appropriate tendencies to actively question and investigate his universe. Newman
and Newman (1987) suggest that "guilt is the internal psychological mechanism that signals when a violation of a forbidden
area is about to occur" (p. 263), for example, the incest taboo
(Gagnon, 1977, McCary, 1978). We suggest that guilt becomes
the signal for social withdrawal (detachment) to protect the
particularly vulnerable (deindividuated) school-age child from
adult criticism and resultant fluctuation in self-esteem (Long,
Henderson, and Ziller, 1967; Cicirelli, 1976; Wells and Marwell, 1976; Kegan, 1982). Thus we have the guilty (B_4) child
who erects impermeable walls around himself (detaches) to protect his suddenly inarticulated boundaries (deindividuation).

The core strength for Erikson at this stage is purpose which
nudges the B_4 guilty child ahead on the developmental BED
axis. Psychoanalytic thinkers suggest that the process of moral
development (i.e., the internalization of values that sustain impulse control under conditions of temptation) is achieved
through identification with the parents (Bronfenbrenner,
1960). They view the superego emerging from the resolution
of the Oedipus complex as the structure for internalization of
parental and societal standards. Jacobson (1964) has viewed
identification more broadly as the process by which a child gains
independence from his parents (individuates) and at the same
time internalizes many of their (and society's) values (attaches).
This process is facilitated by a warm and democratic parenting
style (Baumrind, 1975; Hoffman, 1979). This syntonic D_4 (individuated attachment) state of initiative (D_4) has been described
as "ego resilient" by Arend et al. (1979) and allows for a healthy
blend of control and spontaneity.

The core pathology at this stage is inhibition which tends to fixate a play-age child on the clinical AC axis. Harsh parental discipline techniques tend to produce children who are physically aggressive and who do not control their behavior well when they are away from home (Anthony, 1970; Chwast, 1972). Other children develop strong phobias toward surrounding objects (whether school, the dark, strangers, or certain animals), sharply curtailing their ability to explore their environment. For example, Davison and Neale (1982) estimate 17 per 1000 schoolchildren experience school phobia each year. This polarized structure is indicative of an inability to integrate successfully the child's need for individuation and attachment. Arend et al. (1979) define this axis by the endpoints of overcontrol (C_4) and undercontrol (A_4). Overcontrol leads to rigidity and lack of spontaneity (detached individuation) while undercontrol relates to the inability to delay gratification (deindividuated attachment). This research also demonstrates striking continuity in distancing positions across the life span. Using the Blocks' Q-sort measure (Block and Block, 1980), Arend et al. (1979) demonstrated that children who had been classified as securely attached (Ainsworth, 1979) at 18 months of age (D_1) were independently described by their teachers at ages 4 to 5 as highly ego-resilient (D_4). They were also described as being moderate on control, neither over- nor undercontrolled. Similar results have been reported by Vaughn et al. (1979) showing that securely attached infants display increased resiliency, self-control and curiosity as preschoolers. In contrast, infants classified at 18 months as anxiously attached (either A_1 or C_1) were found by Arend et al. (1979) to be significantly lower on resiliency. Furthermore, those in the anxious–avoidant infant group (C_1) were described as overcontrolled (C_4) at ages 4 to 5 and those in the anxious–resistant infant group (A_1), undercontrolled (A_4). Unresolved A–C pathology at one stage seems then to bias an individual in that same direction at later stages while healthy BED development seems to further subsequent healthy development.

Stage 5—School-Age Childhood: From Inferiority to Industry

Stage 5 denotes Erikson's school age (approximately ages 6 to 12). It is initiated by Life Event 5, *social evaluation* with the new social radius of the school-age child being school and neighborhood peers (SR_5) rather than the nuclear family. According to Barker and Wright (1955) about 50 percent of the school-age child's interactions are with other children as opposed to only 10 percent in this regard for 2-year-olds. Social evaluation forwardly regresses the syntonically initiating (D_4) play-age child into a dystonic state of inferiority (B_5). The B_5 child has been studied by Dweck and Licht (1980), Ruble (1983), and Phillips (1984) among others. Criticism from peers and negative social comparison can lead to a pessimistic self definition with regard to future success and even a sense of "learned helplessness" and depression (Seligman, 1975). Withdrawal from social interaction (detachment) accompanies the self-doubt (deindividuation) for the B_5 child and may well provide a protective shield until the child begins to feel better about exposing (permeable wall) his abilities (articulated boundary).

The core strength behind this BED journey is Erikson's competence and the major process is education (Newman and Newman, 1987). The child is exposed to a range of disciplines and to the language of concepts that allow him both to organize his experiences and acquire new skills (Rubin, 1980; Cole and D'Andrade, 1982). Children can be helped to set realistic goals for themselves so they can experience success. Each child is different in response to critical evaluation. For some it may be devastating, for others it may be quite helpful in this developmental journey (Crandall, 1963). When tasks are difficult, a child's concentration and persistence may be adversely affected by external evaluation (Maehr and Stallings, 1972). Under more relaxed conditions, however, outside evaluation can improve the child's performance (Hill and Sarason, 1966). In any case, individuation and attachment are inextricably linked in healthy development. Pellegrini (1985), for example, has shown that children who display maturity in their social reasoning (individuation) are likely to be more positively evaluated by their peers (attachment). The strength of a healthy child's (D_5) need for success is well established by the end of the school-age stage (Atkinson and Birch, 1978). These are also the years when children can have "best friends" (Berndt, 1981), a process Sullivan (1949) argued is crucial for later heterosexual relations.

There are many pitfalls along this developmental journey, however. Calhoun and Morse (1977), for example, have shown that failure in school and the experience of public ridicule can interact with an initially negative self-concept to cause long-lasting damage to a child's self-esteem. The core pathology for Erikson at this stage is inertia, which can be expressed either in A or C pathologies. One type of A_5 pathology may be labeled hyperactivity (Sainz, 1966; Werry, 1968), the hyperactive child unable to control his impulses (insufficiently articulated boundaries). Stewart (1967) estimated that hyperactive children represented some 4 percent of the grade school population in the United States. Another form of the A_5 (deindividuated attachment) structure can be labeled conformity (Pepitone, Loeb, and Murdock, 1977). Children learn to dress, talk, and joke in ways that gain peer approval, in extreme cases showing willingness to go along with antisocial peer behavior. Indeed Costanzo (1970) has shown that late childhood/early adolescence represents a peak period of conformity. The A_5 child is quite simply afraid to be different lest he receive a negative social evaluation. Thus he blends in (deindividuates) to avoid the evaluation process. The child may accomplish the same goal through going to the opposite pole, a C_5 (detached individuation) structure. This can be labeled peer rejection with associated feelings of loneliness. The direction of this process is not always clear. Sometimes the C_5 child may reject (detach) to avoid being rejected. However, the result is the same—loneliness and feelings of social dissatisfaction (Asher, Hymel, and Renshaw, 1984). A significant proportion of children in this study felt left out, had trouble making friends and felt that they were alone. Furthermore, children who are rejected tend to be disruptive and aggressive with peers and often require psychiatric treatment in adolescence or adulthood (Robins, 1966; Coie and Krehbiel, 1984; Sroufe and Rutter, 1984). Though Robins (1978, p. 611) cautions us that "most antisocial children do not become antisocial adults," there is no question that the clinical conformity–peer rejection axis is more problematic for the school-age child than is the developmental inferiority–competence one.

Stage 6—Adolescence: From Identity Confusion to Identity

Stage 6 in our model describes Erikson's very important adolescent stage (approximately ages 12 to 22). It is initiated by the life event of *social identity* demands (LE_6) which forwardly regresses the syntonically industrious (D_5) school-age child into an initial dystonic position of identity confusion (B_6). The social radius at this stage is peer groups and outgroups (SR_6). The life task is to find what groups one belongs to and what groups to avoid. The adolescent may experience a sense of omnipotentiality with the resultant lack of ability to commit to any particular group. This stage has been studied at length by Marcia (1966, 1980) and by Bourne (1978a,b) among others and refers to the process by which an adolescent matures to the point of achieving a social identity which allows him to make a realistic social commitment. According to Marcia, this journey involves the process of both exploration (what we mean by individuation) and commitment (what we mean by attachment). This dystonic first level (B_6) represents neither individuation nor attachment and seems to correspond quite well to what Marcia has labeled moratorium. Individuals in this moratorium or identity-confusion state have not proceeded very far into exploration (deindividuation) nor have they made any commitment (detachment).

Erikson has labeled the core strength at Stage 6 as fidelity which is realized through the integrated achievement of both individuation (Marcia's exploration) and attachment (Marcia's commitment). A successful integrated progression along the developmental BED axis with regard to both of these life issues leads to a syntonic position of identity achievement (D_6) which for Marcia involves an individual who has both undergone exploration and made commitments. A number of studies have shown that such individuals do well on a number of achievement and interpersonal indicators (cf. Cross and Allen, 1970; Marcia and Friedman, 1970; Jordan, 1971; Josselson, 1973; Donovan, 1975; Orlovsky, 1978).

The core pathology at this stage has been described by Erikson as repudiation which can lead to fixation and oscillation on the clinical AC axis expressed either in what Stierlin (1974) has called "expelling" (adolescents pushed by their families into premature autonomy) or "binding" (adolescents infantilized by their families). Marcia has labeled these polarities diffusion (an adolescent who engages in pseudo-exploration without social commitment) and foreclosure (an adolescent who prematurely commits to a group without sufficient exploration). Diffusion represents then our C_6 (detached individuation) structure and foreclosure our A_6 (deindividuated attachment) position.[6] Bourne (1978b) has described the diffusion state as one of withdrawal while Donovan (1975) has described individuals in this state as feeling out of place and socially isolated from the world. Maccoby and Jacklin (1974) evaluated the results of over 1600 studies comparing individuation (agency) and attachment (communion) responses between males and females. Lerner and Shea (1982) conclude that most of these reviewed studies show no sex differences but when they do occur, females score higher on attachment–communion (foreclosure) behaviors such as dependency, social desirability, compliance, general anxiety and staying in the proximity of friends (Block, 1976) while males tend to score higher on individuation-agency (diffusion) behaviors such as aggression, confidence in task performance, dominance and activity level (Block, 1976). Other studies have documented a strong relationship for both males and females, between foreclosure status and authoritarianism (Marcia, 1966, 1980; Marcia and Friedman, 1970; Schenkel and Marcia, 1972) and conformity (Podd, 1972). Significantly, still other studies have shown that both foreclosures and diffusions have tended to score at lower moral stages (Podd, 1972; Poppen, 1974; Rowe, 1978) and are less ethical, empathic or socialized (Hayes, 1977) than are identity achievers or moratoriums. In other words, adolescents on the developmental moratorium/ identity achievement axis tend to do better in a variety of personal, social, and moral indicators than do individuals on the clinical diffusion/foreclosure axis.

---

[6]The placement of Marcia's moratorium and diffusion categories requires a brief comment. Moratorium might be rigidly labeled a C structure (exploration without commitment) and diffusion a B (neither exploration nor commitment). Fuller descriptions of what Marcia meant by these positions led us to reverse the above placement.

Stage 7—Early Adulthood: From Isolation to Intimacy

Stage 7 in our model describes Erikson's younger adulthood (approximately ages 22 to 34) with a social radius of partners in friendship and sex (SR_7). It is initiated by Life Event 7, *personal identity demands* which forwardly regresses a previously syntonic identity-achieving adolescent (D_6) into a dystonic state of isolation (B_7). The hard-won social identity emerging from group commitment and membership is no longer enough. The young adult requires a more developed personal identity, but must first free himself from the intense peer pressures emerging from his preceding social radius (deindividuation). This confusion in his personal identity (deindividuation) leads to a sense of loneliness and isolation (detachment). Marcia's previously discussed moratorium position also applies here. Young adults in this moratorium or isolation level have only begun the personal exploration (individuation) necessary for any intimate interpersonal commitment (attachment).

Erikson has labeled the core strength at this stage love, which in Buber's (1970) sense allows the formation of one's own identity and respect for that of the other (in other words, an I–thou relationship) essential to any genuine syntonic intimacy (D_7). Central to this journey is the establishment of a self separate from one's parents on which one can base one's own life. Peers have served the adolescent well in facilitating this separation process. But now the young adult must turn to more intimate dyadic encounters to further develop this separation. This process has been studied by a number of researchers, some (Silber, Hamburg, Coelho, Murphey, Rosenberg and Pearlin, 1961; Offer and Offer, 1975) focusing on the movement from high school to college, others looking at the development from childhood to adulthood (Kagan and Moss, 1962; MacFarlane, 1964). With regard to healthy development on the BED axis, Korn (1968) discovered that healthy young adults learned to make decisions without seeking permission from their parents and moved toward closer relationships and assumption of the marital role. Vaillant (1977) found that the "best outcome" younger adults tended to be well integrated and practical in late adolescence and early adulthood and the "worst outcome" young adults were asocial. Vaillant argues that the "best outcome" individuals shifted to more mature defenses and adaptation modes (in our terms more permeable walls with more articulated boundaries). In a cross-sectional study of young adult clinic outpatients, Gould (1972) found two distinct periods: 18 to 22 (in our model, late adolescence) and 22 to 28. In the former period, the individuals were in the process of taking steps to implement separation from parents. In the latter, the subjects felt established and secure in this separation. They were engaged in the work of being adults.

The core pathology in Stage 7 is for Erikson exclusivity which blocks this healthy developmental journey. It can be expressed either in what Minuchin (1974) calls enmeshment (A_7) or disengagement (C_7). Enmeshment refers to a diffuse set of self–other boundaries (in our sense, a premature removal of walls); disengagement refers to rigid self–other boundaries (a delayed removal of walls). Marcia has called these same structures foreclosure (A_7) and diffusion (C_7) and Stierlin has described them in family terms: either as bound (infantilized) by the family (A_7) or expelled by it (C_7). Work by Bell, Billington, and Becker (1986) points to longitudinal consistency across the life span in these positions. Ainsworth's pathological early infant attachment styles (A_1 and C_1) are reflected in high insecure attachment (A_7) and defensive isolation (C_7) scores on the Bell Object Relations Inventory as administered to young adults. Hawkins, Weisberg, and Ray (1980) contrast different interaction styles for these young adults, the pathological polarities represented by speculation (exploring the other's point of view without revealing one's own), an A_7 structure and control (expressing one's own view without taking the other's into account), a C_7 structure. These AC polarities are clearly not as healthy as is their D_7 "contactful" communication style which reflects openness to the other while expressing one's own opinion. This contactful style must be achieved developmentally and is essential to the attainment of syntonic intimacy at Stage 7.

Stage 8—Middle Adulthood: From Stagnation to Generativity

Stage 8 in the present model corresponds to Erikson's middle adulthood (approximately ages 34 to 60) with a social radius of household and children (SR_8). It is initiated by Life Event 8, *marital and family demands* which forwardly regresses a syntonic intimacy-achieving younger adult (D_7) into the dystonic stage of stagnation (B_8). Here a middle adult feels overwhelmed by the demands of marriage and family (deindividuated) and finds himself in a state of confused withdrawal. Indeed the very intimacy he has achieved with a particular partner in Stage 7 must make room for the expanded social radius of household and children in Stage 8. Neugarten (1968, 1973) has focused on the middle adult's increased preoccupation with his inner life, his "interiority," which enables him to look backward for the first time rather than forward. The dynamic of withdrawal to inner space is necessitated by the overwhelming demands of marriage and family life and may be associated with a sense of "burnout," of just going through the motions. This has been associated empirically with personal feelings of worthlessness (Pines and Aronson, 1981).

Erikson defines the core strength at this stage as care which propels the stagnating middle adult forward along the developmental BED axis into a syntonic state of generativity (D_8). Withdrawal to his own resources has freed the generative middle adult to get in touch with his individual sense of creativity (individuation), enabling him to enter the role of a mentor for the next generation (attachment) whether in a home or work environment in a way that integrates care for self and care for others. Shanan (1985) has labeled this midlife personality structure the "active integrated coper"—investment at work is not at the expense of family relationships. A number of studies have explored the difficulties women have had with this transition with regard to role-strain, overload, and generally lowered morale, problems that increase with the births of subsequent children (LeMasters, 1957; Dyer, 1963; Meyerowitz and Feldman, 1966; Rossi, 1968; Russell, 1974; Yalom, Lunde, Moos, and Hamburg, 1968). Levinson and his colleagues have conducted similar research on men (Levinson, 1977, 1978). They suggest that the demands of the career mentor role raise the same basic generativity issues as those associated with family parenting.

The core pathology for Erikson at this stage is rejectivity, which can be expressed either in what Gutmann, Griffin, and Grunes (1982) have called dependency (an A_8 structure) or counterdependency (a C_8 structure). Stewart and Salt (1981) have reported that single "agentic" (C_8) working women exhibited ill health in response to stress. In contrast, homemakers with a traditional communal (A_8) orientation responded to stress with depression. However, working wives combining agentic and communal (D_8) orientations experienced no negative effects in response to stress. Similar benefits of combining agency and communion have been reported by Stewart and Malley (1987) and Malley (1989) with regard to both the physical and emotional health of divorcing mothers. Much of the research on this AC clinical axis emerges from the work of Gutmann and his colleagues on the "parental imperative." Gutmann's basic idea that the demands of parenting itself produce traditional sex-role differentiation has found considerable empirical support, even among nontraditional couples (cf. Shereshefky, Liebenberg, and Lockman, 1973; Belsky, 1981; Cowan, Cowan, Coie, and Coie, 1978; Hoffman, 1978; Hoffman and Manis, 1978; Lamb, 1978; Belsky, 1981). Gutmann goes even further to suggest associated personality structures, both men and women repressing contrasexual tendencies in the service of parenting. Thus fathers adapt an "active mastery style" (in exaggerated form, a C_8 detached individuation structure) and mothers a "passive-nurturant style" (an A_8 deindividuated attachment structure). When the nest is emptied, the psychologically repressed returns with a vengeance (Stein, 1979), women often shifting from passive to active styles and men in the opposite direction, i.e., the famous "midlife crossover" effect (Neugarten and Gutmann, 1958; Gutmann, 1975, 1980a,b, 1987; Fiske, 1980). This journey, sadly, often represents oscillation along the AC clinical axis (an exchange of symptoms if you will) rather than any true BED development. Such confusion represents one of the great dangers of this particular life stage producing what Shanan (1985) has labeled "dependent passive copers" (an A_8 structure) or "failing overcopers" (a C_8 structure). Neither of these groups is as happy with his life as is

Shanan's D_8 "active integrated" coper group described previously.

Stage 9—Older Adulthood: From Despair to Integrity

Stage 9 in our model refers to Erikson's older adulthood (approximately ages 60 to 75). The social radius (SR_9) for the older adult has become mankind/my kind,[7] a differentiation of universalistic and particularistic affiliations. It is initiated by the life event (LE_9) of *unfulfilled goals* (or perhaps *now meaningless fulfilled goals)*, a stressor which forwardly regresses the previously syntonic generative (D_8) middle adult into a profound dystonic state of despair (B_9). All of one's previous achievements have proved meaningless and many of one's dreams are now out of grasp. The B_9 individual has lost his meaning in life (deindividuation) and as such withdraws from social involvements (detachment). Life has lost its taste. The classic work by Neugarten, Havighurst, and Tobin (1968) has labeled adults in this position as unintegrated. Such people have defects in psychological functioning (deindividuation) as well as low levels of role activity and life satisfaction (detachment).

Erikson defines the core strength at this stage as wisdom which guides the older adult forward along the developmental BED axis to a position where he is both individuated and attached. Such a syntonic D_9 individual finds a self-integrity (articulated self–other boundary) based on something more profound than simple fulfilled personal goals and is thus able to reintegrate into mankind (permeable interpersonal walls) with a particularistic affirmation of his own kind. Neugarten et al. (1968) refer to this position as integrated, characterized by a well-functioning ego and a flexible openness with regard to environmental stimuli.

Erikson describes the core pathology at this stage as disdain, which can lead to fixation and oscillation on the clinical AC axis. This can be expressed either in what Neugarten et al. have labeled armored-defended (personalities which are striving, achievement-oriented, and ambitious, with high defenses

---

[7]The term "mankind" reflects Erikson's choice of language. Less sexist language would suggest usage of "humankind."

against anxiety and with the need to maintain strict controls over impulse life). Or this can be expressed in what they have labeled passive-dependent (individuals who have strong dependency needs and who seek responsiveness from others). The armored-defended position represents a C_9 structure in our terms (detached individuation), in Erikson's view a jingoistic individual who sacrifices mankind for his own kind. The passive-dependent personality, in contrast, represents an A_9 structure (deindividuated attachment), an individual who in an all-too-embracing universalism sacrifices his own kind for mankind. Indeed, Neugarten (1979) points specifically to the adaptive role of some paranoia for older adults—the self must be fought for against an often increasingly indifferent mankind.

Several more recent studies speak to these same points. Klemmack and Roff (1984) report that older adults with high fear of loneliness (an A_9 structure) are least satisfied with the quality of their lives. Ryff and Heincke (1983) found that healthy older adults perceived themselves to be higher in integrity (D_9) than they had been at previous life stages. Finally, Shanan (1985) points to the greater life satisfaction reported by the aging active coper (D_9) as compared to the aging passive coper (A_9) or the overcoper (C_9) even though he acknowledges the difficulty in maintaining the D structure at more advanced age. Once again, individuals, this time older adults, on the developmental BED axis seem to do better than those on the clinical AC axis.

Stage 10—The Oldest Old: From Incapacitation to Generational Continuity

Stage 10 in our model, the oldest old, has not been covered specifically by Erikson nor has it been studied as extensively as some of the earlier adult stages. Peck (1968) represents a classic attempt to extend Erikson's thinking to the oldest old, offering finer distinctions in the second half of life than he felt were made by Erikson. Issues of old age, as distinct from those of middle age, which have been offered by Peck, are ego-differentiation versus work-role preoccupation, body transcendence versus body preoccupation and ego transcendence versus ego preoccupation. Newman and Newman (1987) have tried more recently to extend Erikson's thinking to the oldest old, suggesting the life issue here is "immortality versus extinction." In other papers, Levin (1963) has emphasized depression among the aged, Berger and Zarit (1978) have studied later life paranoid states, and Cath (1966) has differentiated depression and depletion among the elderly.

Our model sees the oldest old stage as initiated by the staggering life event or stressor of *physical decline* and *awareness of mortality and life-finiteness* (LE_{10}). Guttman et al. (1982) have labeled it "life cycle shock" or "existential stress," which upsets the syntonic equilibrium (D_9) achieved by the integrity-achieving older adult (Birren, Butler, Greenhouse, Sokoloff, and Yarrow, 1971) and forwardly regresses the now oldest old into the helpless dystonic position of incapacitation (B_{10}). A previously healthy older adult may now need a cane or a walker—or even a wheel chair. Memory may fail—as may kidneys. Previously reliable social supports may themselves have died and the individual may become aware of his own limited time. In short, the now oldest old individual may find himself both enfeebled (deindividuated) and isolated (detached). What is critical here is how the individual manages to transcend the present-centered integrity of mankind/my kind to deal with his once again expanded social radius (SR_{10}) of present versus future generations. Does the incapacitated or terminal oldest old behave like dying King Berenger the First in Ionesco's (1963) brilliant satire *Exit the King*, losing all interest in the present and future world? "I am only present in the past," says the king (p. 50) in response to his second wife Marie's attempts to console him. When she later (p. 67) points to the expanding future, "the younger generation's expanding the universe, . . . conquering new constellations, . . . boldly battering at the gates of Heaven," Berenger again cuts himself off, "I'm dying, . . . I'm dying, . . . they can knock them flat for all I care." Or does the incapacitated oldest old adult utilize his core strength at this stage, faith, to carve out a historical self (individuation) which allows the individual to connect in a genuine way (attachment) with future generations (D_{10})? Lifton (1973) has called this a "sense of immortality," which overcomes a preoccupation with one's own ego, body, and generation through a faith, a vested interest if you will, in future generations. Indeed Augustine and Kalish (1975) propose that older people and dying people of all ages need to establish some kind of attachment that will be ongoing after the death of the body, whether it be through a divine being, being remembered by others, through accomplishments, through progeny or through association with a cause or ideology. This sense of a transgenerational continuity is deepened by the oldest old taking on the role of transmitter of history to the next generation and helps to prepare the individual for his own death—the final life event (LE_{11}).

The core pathology at this stage is what Newman and Newman have labeled doubt, a profound uncertainty that there is anything beyond the present ego, body and life-finiteness. It tends to truncate the individual's sense of time in the present and may be expressed in one of two forms. One expression is what Cumming and Henry (1961) have labeled disengagement (a C_{10} structure), which is indicated by increased preoccupation with the self and decreasing emotional investments in persons and objects in the environment. When such social withdrawal is voluntary and mutual, it may represent a normal reconsolidation of older adulthood (Lowenthal, 1975). However, when it is not so mutual or voluntary, it may represent a more pathological structure. This structure may also have a paranoiac aspect to it (Berger and Zarit, 1978) which may involve suspicions and accusations of others. The second expression is paraphrased from the work of Havighurst, Neugarten, and Tobin (1968) and may be labeled overactivity (an A_{10} structure) where the individual trivializes himself through mindless activities designed to numb him to his terminal position in the life cycle. While Lawton (1980) has reported that residents of institutions for the aged seek out areas of high activity, Lemon, Bangston, and Peterson (1972) find that activity per se was not found to be significantly related to life satisfaction among new residents of a retirement community. In extreme form, an obsession with overactivity may block the private time necessary to achieve the syntonic D_{10} state of transgenerational continuity and reflect aspects of the depressed state discussed by Levin (1963) and by Cath (1966) with an attendant loss of self-esteem. One recent study (Sonnenberg and Jacobowitz, 1989) points to the greater preponderance of these pathological A and C structures among clinical (depression, personality disorders, paranoia, and anxiety disorders) as opposed to normal older adults. Two other studies (Windle and Sinnott, 1985; Kaplan, Linky, and Jacobowitz, 1987) suggest that a major developmental component of normal older adults (including the oldest old) is the dissipation for both men and women of the rigid gender differentiation evoked at earlier life stages. Here, finally, similar life experiences enable the oldest old to integrate individuation and attachment (the developmental BED axis) in a way not totally determined by rigid gender stereotypes.

References

Abelin, E. L. (1971), The role of the father in the separation–individuation process. In: *Separation–Individuation: Essays in Honor of Margaret S. Mahler*, ed. J. B. McDevitt & C. F. Settlage. New York: International Universities Press, pp. 229–253.

Ainsworth, M. D. S. (1972), Attachment and dependency: A comparison. In: *Attachment and Dependency*, ed. J. Gerwitz. Washington, D.C.: V. H. Winston & Sons, pp. 97–137.

——— (1973), The development of infant-mother attachment. In: *Review of Child Development Research*, Vol. 3, ed. B. M. Caldwell & H. N. Ricciuti. Chicago: University of Chicago Press.

——— (1979), Infant–mother attachment. *Amer. Psychol.*, 34:932–937.

Albert, S., Amgott, T., Krakow, M., & Marcus, H. (1977), Children's bedtime rituals as a prototype rite of safe passage. Paper presented at the annual convention of the American Psychological Association, San Francisco.

Anglin, J. M. (1977), *Word, Object and Conceptual Development*. New York: Norton.

Anthony, E. J. (1970), The behavior disorders of children. In: *Carmichael's Manual of Child Psychology*, 3rd ed., Vol. 2, ed. P. H. Mussen. New York: Wiley.

Arend, D., Gove, F., & Sroufe, L. A. (1979), Continuity of individual adaptation from infancy to kindergarten; A predictive study of ego resiliency and curiosity in preschoolers. *Child Develop.*, 50:950–959.

Asher, S. R., Hymel, S., & Renshaw, P. D. (1984), Loneliness in children. *Child Develop.*, 35:1456–1464.

Atkinson, J. W., & Birch, D. (1978), *Introduction to Motivation*, 2nd ed. New York: Van Nostrand Reinhold.

Augustine, W., & Kalish, R. A. (1975), Religion, transcendence and appropriate death. *J. Transact. Psychol.*, 7:1–13.

Bakan, D. (1966), *The Duality of Human Existence*. Boston: Beacon Press.

Bandura, A. (1977), *Social Learning Theory*. Englewood Cliffs, N.J.: Prentice-Hall.

Barker, R. G., & Wright, H. F. (1955), *Midwest and Its Children*. New York: Harper & Row.

Baumrind, D. (1971), Current patterns of parental authority. *Developmental Psychology Monographs*, 4:99–103.

———— (1975), *Early Socialization and the Discipline Controversy*. Morristown, N.J.: General Learning Press.

Bell, M., Billington, R., & Becker, B. (1986), A scale for the assessment of reality testing—Reliability, validity and factorial invariance. *J. Clin. Psychol.*, 42:733–741.

Belsky, J. (1981), Early human experience: A family perspective. *Develop. Psychol.*, 17:3–23.

Berger, K., & Zarit, S. (1978), Late-life paranoid states: Assessment and treatment. *Amer. J. Orthopsychiat.*, 48(3):528–536.

Berndt, T. J. (1981), Relations between social cognition, nonsocial cognition, and social behavior: The case of friendship. In: *Social Cognitive Development: Frontiers and Possible Futures*, ed. J. H. Flavell & L. D. Ross. Cambridge, U.K.: Cambridge University Press.

Birren, J. E., Butler, R. N., Greenhouse, S. W., Sokoloff, L., & Yarrow, M. R. (1971), *Human Aging I: A Biological and Behavior Study*. (DHEW Publication No. ADM77-123). Washington, D.C.: U.S. Government Printing Office.

Block, J. H. (1976), Issues, problems and pitfalls in assessing sex differences: A critical review of *The Psychology of Sex Differences*. *Merrill-Palmer Quart.*, 22:283–308.

Block, S. M., & Block, J. (1980), The role of ego control and ego-resiliency in the organization of behavior. In: *Minnesota Symposium on Child Psychology*, Vol. 2, ed. W. A. Collins. Hillsdale, N.J.: Lawrence Erlbaum Associates.

Bourne, E. (1978a), The state of research and ego identity: A review and appraisal (Part 1). *J. Youth & Adol.*, 7:223–251.

———— (1978b), The state of research on ego identity: A review and appraisal (Part 2). *J. Youth & Adol.*, 7:371–392.

Bowlby, J. (1969), *Attachment and Loss*, Vol. 1, *Attachment*. New York: Basic Books.

———— (1973), *Attachment and Loss*, Vol. 2, *Separation, Anxiety and Anger*. New York: Basic Books.

———— (1977), The making and breaking of affectional bonds: Etiology and psychopathology in the light of attachment theory. *Brit. J. Psychiat.*, 130:201–210.

Brazelton, T. B., Koslowski, B., & Main, M. (1974), The origins of reciprocity: The early mother–infant interaction. In: *The Effects of the Infant on Its Caregiver*, ed. M. Lewis & L. A. Rosenblum. New York: Wiley.

Bronfenbrenner, U. (1960), Freudian theories of identification and their derivatives. *Child Develop.*, 31:15–40.

Buber, M. (1970), *I and Thou*. New York: Charles Scribner's Sons.

Calhoun, G., Jr., & Morse, W. C. (1977), Self-concept and self-esteem: Another perspective. *Psychol. in Schools*, 14:318–322.

Carr, D. H., & Gedeon, M. (1977), Population cytogenetics of human abortuses. In: *Population Cytogenetics: Studies in Humans*, ed. E. G. Hook & I. M. Porter. New York: Academic Press.

Cath, S. (1966), Beyond depression—The depleted state: A study in ego psychology in the aged. *Can. Psychiatric Assn. J.*, 11(Supplement): 329–339.

Chwast, J. (1972), Sociopathic behavior in children. In: *Manual of Child Psychopathology*, ed. B. B. Wolman. New York: McGraw-Hill.

Cicirelli, V. G. (1976), Effects of evaluating task competence on the self-concept of children from different socioeconomic status levels. *J. Psychol.*, 94:217–223.

Clark, A. L. (1976), Application of psychological concepts. In: *Childbearing: A Nursing Perspective*, ed. A. L. Clark & D. D. Alfonso. Philadelphia: F. A. Davis, pp. 239–262.

Coie, J. D., & Krehbiel, G. (1984), Effects of academic tutoring on the social status of low-achieving socially rejected children. *Child Develop.*, 55:1465–1478.

Cole, M., & D'Andrade, R. (1982), The influence of schooling on concept formation: Some preliminary conclusions. *Quart. Newsletter Lab. Compar. Cognit.*, 4:19–26.

Costanzo, P. R. (1970), Conformity development as a function of self-blame. *J. Personal. & Soc. Psychol.*, 14:366–374.

Cowan, C. P., Cowan, P. A., Coie, L., & Coie, J. D. (1978), Becoming a family: The impact of a first child's birth on the couple's relationship. In: *The First Child and Family Formation*, ed. W. Miller & L. Newman. Chapel Hill, N.C.: Carolina Population Center and University of North Carolina, pp. 296–324.

Crandall, V. C. (1963), Reinforcement effects of adults' reactions and nonreactions of children's achievement expectations. *Child Develop.*, 34:335–354.

Cranley, M. S. (1981), Development of a tool for the measurement of maternal attachment during pregnancy. *Nurs. Res.*, 30:281–284.

Cross, H., & Allen, J. (1970), Ego identity status, adjustment and academic achievement. *J. Consult. & Clin. Psychol.*, 34:288.

Cumming, E., & Henry, W. E. (1961), *Growing Old.* New York: Basic Books.

Dabrowski, K. (1973), *The Dynamics of Concepts.* London: GRYF Publications.

Davison, G. C., & Neale, J. M. (1982), *Abnormal Psychology: An Experimental Clinical Approach*, 3rd ed. New York: Wiley.

Deutsch, H. (1948), *Psychology of Women*, Vol. 11. New York: Grune & Stratton.

Donovan, J. M. (1975), Identity status and interpersonal style. *J. Youth & Adol.*, 4:37–55.

Dweck, C. S., & Licht, G. G. (1980), Learned helplessness and intellectual achievement. In: *Human Helplessness: Theory and Applications*, ed. J. Gerber & M. E. P. Seligman. New York: Academic Press.

Dyer, E. (1963), Parenthood as crisis: A restudy. *J. Marr. & Fam. Living*, 25:196–201.

Erikson, E. (1950), *Childhood and Society.* New York: Norton.

——— (1951/1953), *Childhood and Society*, rev. ed. New York: Norton.

——— (1968), *Identity: Youth and Crisis.* New York: Norton.

——— (1980), *Identity and the Life Cycle.* New York: Norton.

——— (1982), *The Life Cycle Completed.* New York: Norton.

Feldman, S., & Ingham, M. (1975), Attachment behavior: A validation study in two age groups. *Child Develop.*, 46:319–330.

Fiske, M. (1980), Tasks and crisis of the second half of life. The interrelationship of commitment, coping and adaption. In: *Handbook of Mental Health and Aging*, ed. J. E. Birren & R. B. Sloan. Englewood Cliffs, N.J.: Prentice-Hall.

Forehand, R., Roberts, M. W., Doleus, D. M., Hobbs, S. A., & Resick, P. A. (1976), An examination of disciplinary procedures with children. *J. Experiment. Child Psychol.*, 21:109–120.

Freud, A. (1936), *The Ego and the Mechanisms of Defense*. New York: International Universities Press, 1966.

Freud, S. (1905), Three essays on the theory of sexuality. *Standard Edition*, 7:130–243. London: Hogarth Press, 1953.

—— (1913), The disposition to obsessional neurosis: A contribution to the problem of choice of neurosis. *Standard Edition*, 12:313–326. London: Hogarth Press, 1958.

—— (1933), New introductory lectures in psychoanalysis. *Standard Edition*, 22:3–182. London: Hogarth Press, 1964.

Gagnon, J. H. (1977), *Human Sexualities*. Glenview, Ill.: Scott-Foresman.

Galenson, E. (1971), A consideration of the nature of thought in childhood play. In: *Separation–Individuation: Essays in Honor of Margaret S. Mahler*, ed. J. B. McDevitt & C. F. Settlage. New York: International Universities Press, pp. 41–60.

Gould, R. L. (1972), The phases of adult life: A study in developmental psychology. *Amer. J. Psychiatry*, 129:521–532.

Greenacre, P. (1966), Problems of overidealization of the analyst and of analysis: Their manifestations in the transference and countertransference relationships. *The Psychoanalytic Study of the Child*, 22:193–212. New York: International Universities Press.

Greenspan, S. I., & Pollock, G. H., eds. (1980), *The Course of Life: Psychoanalytic Contributions Toward Understanding Personality Development, Vol. 2, Latency, Adolescence and Youth*. Washington, D.C.: U.S. Government Printing Office.

Grusec, J. E., & Abramovitch, R. (1982), Imitation of peers and adults in a national setting: A functional analysis. *Child Develop.*, 53:636–642.

Gutmann, D. (1975), Parenthood: A key to the comparative psychology of the lifecycle. In: *Life Span Developmental Psychology: Normative Life Crises*, ed. N. Datan & L. Ginsberg. New York: Academic Press.

—— (1980a), The post-parental years: Clinical problems and developmental possibilities. In: *Midlife: Developmental and Clinical Issues*, ed. W. Norman & T. Scaramella. New York: Brunner/Mazel, pp. 38–52.

—— (1980b), Psychoanalysis and aging: A developmental view. In: *The Course of Life: Psychoanalytic Contributions Toward Understanding Personality and Development, Vol. 3, Adult Years and the Aging Process*, ed. S. I. Greenspan & G. H. Pollock. Washington, D.C.: U.S. Government Printing Office, pp. 489–517.

—— (1987), *Reclaimed Powers: Toward a New Psychology of Men and Women in Later Life*. New York: Basic Books.

—— Griffin, B., & Grunes, J. (1982), Developmental contributions to the late onset affective disorders. *Life Span Develop. & Behav.*, 4:244–261.

Hartmann, H. (1964), *Essays on Ego Psychology: Selected Problems in Psychoanalytic Theory*. New York: International Universities Press.

Havighurst, R. J., Neugarten, B., & Tobin, S. (1968), Disengagement and patterns of aging. In: *Middle Age and Aging*, ed. B. Neugarten. Chicago: University of Chicago Press, pp. 161–172.

Hawkins, J. L., Weisberg, C., & Ray, D. W. (1980), Spouse differences in communication style preference, perception, behavior. *J. Marr. & Fam.*, 42:585–593.

Hayes, S. M. (1977), *Ego Identity and Moral Educational Development in Male College Students*. Unpublished doctoral dissertation. The Catholic University of America, Washington, D.C.

Hill, K. T., & Sarason, S. B. (1966), The relation of test anxiety and defensiveness to tests and school performance over the elementary school years: A further longitudinal study. *Monographs of the Society for Research in Child Development*, 31:1–76.

Hoffman, L. W. (1978), Effects of the first child on the woman role. In: *The First Child and Family Formation*, ed. W. Miller & L. Newman. Chapel Hill, N.C.: Carolina Population Center and University of North Carolina, pp. 340–367.

——— Manis, J. D. (1978), Influences of children on marital interaction and parental satisfactions and dissatisfactions. In: *Child Influences on Marital and Family Interaction*, ed. R. W. Lerner & G. B. Spanier. New York: Academic Press.

Hoffman, M. L. (1977), Moral internalization: Current theory and research. In: *Advances in Experimental Social Psychology*, Vol. 10, ed. L. Berkowitz. New York: Academic Press.

——— (1979), Development of moral thought, feeling and behavior. *Amer. Psychol.*, 34:958–966.

——— (1980), Moral development in adolescence. In: *Handbook of Adolescent Psychology*, ed. J. Adelson. New York: John Wiley.

Ionesco, E. (1963), *Exit the King*, trans. D. Watson. London: John Calder.

Jacobson, E. (1964), *The Self and the Object World*. New York: International Universities Press.

Joffe, L. S., & Vaughn, B. E. (1982), Infant–mother attachment: Theory, assessment, and implications for development. In: *Handbook of Development Psychology*, ed. B. B. Wolman & A. G. Stricker. Englewood Cliffs, N.J.: Prentice-Hall, pp. 190–207.

Jordan, D. (1971), *Parental Antecedents and Personality Characteristics of Ego Identity Statuses*. Unpublished doctoral dissertation, State University of New York, Binghamton, N.Y.

Jordan, W. D. (1978), Searching for adulthood in America. In: *Adulthood*, ed. E. H. Erikson. New York: Norton, pp. 187–200.

Josselson, R. L. (1973), Psychodynamic aspects of identity formation in college women. *J. Youth & Adol.*, 2:3–52.

Kagan, J., & Moss, H. A. (1962), *Birth to Maturity*. New York: John Wiley.

Kaplan, K. J. (1988), TILT: Teaching individuals to live together. *Transact. Anal. J.*, 18:220–230.

——— Linky, H. B., & Jacobowitz, J. (1987), Patterns of individuation and attachment for nonclinical men and women across the adult years. Presented at the Third Congress of the International Psychogeriatric Association, Chicago.

——— Schwartz, M. W., & Markus-Kaplan, M. (1984), *The Family: Biblical and Psychological Foundations*. New York: Human Sciences Press.

Kegan, R. (1982), *The Evolving Self: Problems and Process in Human Development.* Cambridge: Harvard University Press.

Kernberg, O. (1967), Borderline personality organization. *J. Amer. Psychoanal. Assn.*, 15:641–685.

Khan, M. M. R. (1964), Ego distortion, cumulative trauma, and the role of reconstruction in the analytic situation. *Internat. J. Psycho-Anal.*, 45:272–279.

Kleeman, J. A. (1967), The peek-a-boo game. Part I: Its origins, meanings and related phenomena in the first year. *The Psychoanalytic Study of the Child*, 22:239–273. New York: International Universities Press.

Klemmack, D. L., & Roff, L. L. (1984), Fear of personal aging and subjective well-being in later life. *J. Gerontol.*, 39:756–758.

Kohut, H. (1966), Forms and transforms of narcissism. *J. Amer. Psychoanal. Assn.*, 9:567–586.

——— (1971), *The Analysis of the Self.* New York: International Universities Press.

Korn, H. A. (1968), *No Time for Youth: Growth and Constraint in College Students.* San Francisco: Jossey-Bass.

Lamb, M. E. (1978), Influence of the child on marital quality and family interaction during the prenatal, perinatal and infancy periods. In: *Child Influences on Marital and Family Interaction: A Life-Span Perspective*, ed. R. Lefner & G. Spanier. New York: Academic Press, pp. 137–164.

Lawton, M. P. (1980), *Environment and Aging.* Monterey, Calif.: Brooks Cole.

Leifer, M. (1977), Psychological changes accompanying pregnancy and motherhood. *Gen. Psychol. Monographs*, 95:55–96.

Leizer, J. I., & Rogers, R. W. (1974), Effects of method of discipline, timing of punishment, and timing of test on resistance to temptation. *Child Develop.*, 45:790–793.

LeMasters, E. E. (1957), Parenthood as crisis. *Marr. & Fam. Living*, 19:352–355.

Lemon, B. W., Bangston, V. L., & Peterson, J. A. (1972), Activity theory and life satisfaction in a retirement community: An exploration of the activity theory of aging. *J. Gerontol.*, 27:511–523.

Lerner, R. M., & Shea, J. A. (1982), Social behavior in adolescence. In: *Handbook of Developmental Psychology*, ed. B. B. Wolman. Englewood Cliffs, N.J.: Prentice-Hall, pp. 503–526.

Levin, S. (1963), Depression in the aged. In: *Normal Psychology of the Aging Process*, ed. N. E. Zinberg & I. Kaufman. New York: International Universities Press.

Levinger, G. (1980), Toward the analysis of close relationships. *J. Experiment. Soc. Psychol.*, 16:510–544.

Levinson, D. (1977), The mid-life transition: A period in adult psychosocial development. *Psychiatry*, 40:99–112.

——— (1978), *The Seasons of a Man's Life.* New York: Knopf.

Lifton, R. J. (1973), The sense of immortality: On death and the continuity of life. *Amer. J. Psychoanal.*, 33:3–15.

Loevinger, J., & Wessler, R. (1970), *Measuring Ego Development*, Vol. 1. San Francisco: Jossey-Bass.

Long, B. H., Henderson, E. H., & Ziller, R. C. (1967), Developmental changes in the self-concept during middle childhood. *Merrill-Palmer Quart.*, 13:210–215.

Lowenthal, M. F. (1975), Psychosocial variations across the adult life course: Frontiers for research and policy. *Gerontol.*, 15:6–12.

Maccoby, E. E., & Jacklin, C. N. (1974), *The Psychology of Sex Difference.* Stanford, Calif.: Stanford University Press.

MacFarlane, J. W. (1964), Perspectives on personality consistency and changes from the guidance study. *Vita Humana*, 7:115–126.

Maehr, M. C., & Stallings, W. M. (1972), Freedom from external evaluation. *Child Develop.*, 43:177–185.

Mahler, M. S. (1968), *On Human Symbiosis and the Vicissitudes of Individuation.* New York: International Universities Press.

—— Pine, F., & Bergman, A. (1975), *The Psychological Birth of the Human Infant.* New York: Basic Books.

Main, M. (1973), Analysis of a peculiar form of reunion behavior seen in some day-care children who are home reared. In: *Social Development in Daycare*, ed. R. Webb. Baltimore, Md.: Johns Hopkins University Press.

—— Kaplan, N., & Cassidy, J. (1985), Security in infancy, childhood, and adulthood: A move to the level of representation. In: Growing points of attachment theory and research. *Monographs of the Society for Research in Child Development*, ed. I. Bretherton & E. Everett. 50 (1–2, serial no. 209):66–104.

Malley, J. (1989), The importance of aging and communication for well-being—Individual difference in needs and experiences. In: *Individuation (Agency) and Attachment (Communion) Across the Life Span*, chair, K. Kaplan. Symposium presented at the meetings of the American Psychological Association, New Orleans, Louisiana.

Marcia, J. E. (1966), Development and validation of ego identity states. *J. Personal. & Soc. Psychol.*, 31:551–558.

—— (1980), Identity in adolescence. In: *Handbook of Adolescent Psychology*, ed. J. Adelson. New York: Wiley, pp. 145–161.

—— Friedman, M. L. (1970), Ego identity status in college women. *J. Personal.*, 38:249–263.

Markus-Kaplan, M., & Kaplan, K. J. (1984), A bidimensional view of distancing: Reciprocity versus compensation, intimacy versus social control. *J. Nonverbal Behav.*, 8:315–326.

Matas, L., Arend, R. A., & Sroufe, L. A. (1978), Continuity of adaptation in the second year: The relationship between quality of attachment and later competence. *Child Develop.*, 49:547–556.

McAdams, D. P. (1985), *Power, Intimacy and the Life Story.* Homewood, Ill: The Dorsey Press.

McCary, J. L. (1978), *McCary's Human Sexuality*, 3rd ed. New York: Van Nostrand Reinhold.

Meyerowitz, J., & Feldman, H. (1966), Transition to parenthood. *Psychiat. Res. Reports*, 20:78–84.

Minuchin, S. (1974), *Families and Family Therapy.* Cambridge, Mass.: Harvard University Press.

Molfese, D. L., Molfese, V. J., & Carrell, P. L. (1982), Early language development. In: *Handbook of Developmental Psychology*, ed. B. B. Wolman. Englewood Cliffs, N.J.: Prentice-Hall, pp. 302–322.

Moore, K. L. (1982), *The Developing Human: Clinically Oriented Embryology.* Philadelphia: Saunders.

Murphy, L. B., & Moriarty, A. E. (1976), *Vulnerability, Coping and Growth*. New Haven, Conn.: Yale University Press.

Neugarten, B. (1968), The awareness of middle age. In: *Middle Age and Aging*, ed. B. Neugarten. Chicago: University of Chicago Press.

—— (1973), Personality change in late life: A development perspective. In: *The Psychology of Adult Development*, ed. C. Eisdorfer & M. P. Lawton. Washington, D.C.: American Psychological Association, pp. 311–338.

—— (1979), Time, age and the life cycle. *American J. Psychiat.*, 136:887–894.

—— Gutmann, D. L. (1958), Age–sex roles and personality in middle age: A thematic appreciation study. *Psychol. Monographs*, 72(whole no. 470).

—— Harvighurst, R. L., & Tobin, S. S. (1968), Personality and patterns of aging. In: *Middle Age and Aging*, ed. B. Neugarten. Chicago: University of Chicago Press, pp. 173–179.

Newman, B. M., & Newman, P. R. (1987), *Development through Life—A Psychosocial Approach*, 4th ed. Chicago: The Dorsey Press.

Noam, G. G., O'Connell-Higgins, R., & Goethals, G. W. (1982), Psychoanalytic approaches to developmental psychology. In: *Handbook of Developmental Psychology*, ed. B. B. Wolman & G. Stricker. Englewood Cliffs, N.J.: Prentice-Hall.

Odom, L., Seeman, J., & Newbrough, J. R. (1971), A study of family communication patterns and personality integration in children. *Child Psychiatry & Hum. Develop.*, 1:275–285.

Offer, D., & Offer, J. B. (1975), *From Teenage to Young Manhood. A Psychological Study*. New York: Basic Books.

Olds, S. B., London, M. L., & Ladewig, P. A. (1988), *Maternal Newborn Nursing*, 3rd ed. New York: Addison-Wesley.

Orlovsky, J. L. (1976), Intimacy status: Relationship to interpersonal perception. *J. Youth & Adol.*, 5:73–89.

—— (1978), Identity formation, achievement and fear of success in college men and women. *J. Youth & Adol.*, 7:49–62.

Papalia, D. E., & Olds, S. W. (1982), *A Child's World: Infancy through Adolescence*, 3rd ed. New York: McGraw-Hill.

Parkes, C. M. (1972), *Bereavement: Studies of Grief in Adult Life*. London: Tavistock.

Parton, D. A. (1976), Learning to imitate in infancy. *Child Develop.*, 47:14–31.

Passman, R. H., & Longeway, K. P. (1982), The role of vision in maternal attachment: Giving 2 year olds a photograph of their mother during separation. *Develop. Psychol.*, 18:530–533.

Passover Haggadah (1966), ed N. Goldberg. New York: KTAV Publishing.

Peck, R. C. (1968), Psychological developments in the second half of life. In: *Middle Age and Aging*, ed. B. Neugarten. Chicago: University of Chicago Press, pp. 88–92.

Pellegrini, D. S. (1985), Social cognition and competence in middle childhood. *Child Develop.*, 56:253–264.

Pepitone, E. A., Loeb, H. W., & Murdock, E. M. (1977), Social comparison and similarity of children's performance in competitive situations. Paper presented at the annual meeting of the American Psychological Association, San Francisco, Calif.

Phillips, D. (1984), The illusion of incompetence among academically competent children. *Child Develop.*, 55:2000–2016.

Piaget, J. (1937), *The Construction of Reality in the Child*. New York: Basic Books, 1954.

Pines, A., & Aronson, E. (1981), *Burnout: From Tedium to Personal Growth*. New York: Free Press.

Podd, M. M. (1972), Ego identity status and morality: The relationship between two developmental constructs. *Develop. Psychol.*, 6:497–527.

Poppen, P. S. (1974), *The Development of Sex Differences in Moral Judgement for College Males and Females*. Unpublished doctoral dissertation. Cornell University, Syracuse, New York.

Rank, O. (1936), *Will Therapy*. New York: Knopf.

Robins, L. N. (1966), *Deviant Children Grown Up*. Baltimore, Md.: Williams & Wilkins.

——— (1978), Childhood predictors of adult antisocial behavior: Replications from longitudinal studies. *Psychol. Med.*, 8:611–622.

Rossi, A. (1968), Transition to parenthood. *J. Marr. & Fam.*, 30:26–39.

Rowe, I. (1978), *Ego Identity Status, Cognitive Development and Levels of Moral Reasoning*. Unpublished master's thesis. Simon Fraser University.

Rubin, R. (1975), Maternal tasks in pregnancy. *Maternal–Child Nurs. J.*, 4:143–153.

Rubin, Z. (1980), *Children's Friendships*. Cambridge: Harvard University Press.

Ruble, D. N. (1983), The development of social comparison processes and their role in achievement-related self-socialization. In: *Social Cognition and Social Behavior: Developmental Issues*, ed. E. T. Higgins, D. N. Ruble, & W. W. Hartup. New York: Cambridge University Press.

Russell, C. (1974), Transition to parenthood: Problems and gratifications. *J. Marr. & Fam.*, 36:294–303.

Ryff, C. D., & Heincke, S. G. (1983), Subjective organization of personality in adulthood and aging. *J. Personal. & Soc. Psychol.*, 44:807–816.

Sainz, A. (1966), Hyperkinetic disease of children: Diagnosis and therapy. *Dis. Nerv. Syst.*, 27:48–50.

Schenkel, S., & Marcia, J. E. (1972), Attitudes toward premarital intercourse in determining ego identity status in college women. *J. Personal.*, 3:472–482.

Seligman, M. E. P. (1975), *Helplessness: On Depression, Development and Death*. San Francisco: W. H. Freeman.

Shanan, J. (1985), Personality types and culture in later adulthood. In: *Contributions to Human Development*, Vol. 12, ed. J. Meacham. Basel, Switzerland: Karger.

Shereshefsky, P. (1972), *Psychological Aspects of a First Pregnancy and Post Natal Adaptation*. New York: Raven Press.

——— Liebenberg, B., & Lockman, R. F. (1973), Maternal adaptation. In: *Psychological Aspects of a First Pregnancy and Post Natal Adaptation*, ed. P. M. Shereshovsky & L. J. Yarrow. New York: Raven Press.

Silber, E., Hamburg, D. A., Coelho, G. V., Murphey, E. B., Rosenberg, M., & Pearlin, L. I. (1961), Adaptive behavior in competent adolescents. Coping with the anticipation of college. *Arch. Gen. Psychiat.*, 5:354–365.

Singer, J. L. (1973), *The Child's World of Make-Believe: Experimental Studies of Imaginative Play*. New York: Academic Press.

——— (1975), *The Inner World of Daydreaming*. New York: Colophon Books.

Sonnenberg, J., & Jacobowitz, J. (1989), Psychological attachment to the family and adaptation during the later years of the life span. In: *Individuation*

(Agency) and Attachment (Communion) Across the Life Span, Chair, K. Kaplan. Symposium presented at the meetings of the American Psychological Association, New Orleans, Louisiana.

Sroufe, L. A. (1979), The coherence of individual development: Early care, attachment, and subsequent development issues. *Amer. Psychol.*, 34:834–841.

———— Rutter, M. (1984), The domain of developmental psychopathology. *Child Develop.*, 55:17–29.

———— Waters, E. (1977), Attachment as an organizational construct. *Child Develop.*, 48:1184–1199.

Stein, J. (1979), Gender and midlife developmental processes: Commonalities and differences. In: *Midlife Development Influences of Gender Personality and Social System*, Chair S. Cytrynbaum. Symposium presented at the meeting of the American Psychological Association, New York.

Stern, D. (1977), *The First Relationship: Mother and Infant*. Cambridge: Harvard University Press.

Stewart, A. J., & Malley, J. E. (1987), Role combination in women: Mitigating agency and communion. In: *Spouse, Parent, Worker: On Gender and Multiple Roles*, ed. F. S. Crosby. New Haven: Yale University Press.

———— Salt, P. (1981), Life stress, life-styles, depression and illness in adult women. *J. Personal. & Soc. Psychol.*, 210:1063–1069.

Stewart, M. A. (1967), Hyperactive child syndrome recognized 100 years ago. *JAMA*, 202:28–29.

Stierlin, H. (1974), *Separating Parents and Adolescents: A Perspective on Running Away, Schizophrenia, and Waywardness*. New York: Quadrangle.

Sullivan, H. S. (1949), *The Collected Works of Harry Stack Sullivan*, Vols. 1 & 2. New York: Norton.

Vaillant, G. E. (1977), *Adaptation to Life*. Boston: Little, Brown.

Vaughn, B., Egeland, B., Sroufe, L. A., & Waters, E. (1979), Individual differences in infant–mother attachment at 12 and 18 months: Stability and change in families under stress. *Child Develop.*, 50:971–975.

Wells, L. E., & Marwell, G. (1976), *Self-esteem: Its Conceptualization and Measurement*. Beverly Hills, Calif.: Sage.

Werry, S. S. (1968), Developmental hyperactivity. *Ped. Clin. N.A.*, 15:581–599.

White, R. W. (1960), Competence and the psychological stages of development. In: *Nebraska Symposium on Motivation*, Vol. 8, ed. M. R. Jones. Lincoln: University of Nebraska Press.

Windle, M., & Sinnott, J. D. (1985), A psychometric study of the Bem Sex Role Inventory with an older adult sample. *J. Gerontol.*, 40:336–343.

Winnicott, D. W. (1965), *The Maturational Processes and the Facilitating Environment*. New York: International Universities Press.

———— (1971), *Playing and Reality*. New York: Basic Books.

Yalom, I., Lunde, D. T., Moos, R. H., & Hamburg, D. A. (1968), Post-partum "blues" syndrome: A description and related variables. *Arch. Gen. Psychiat.*, 18:16–27.

7

Developmental Continuities and Adjustment in Adulthood: Social Relations, Morale, and the Transformation from Middle to Late Life

JEAN K. CARNEY, Ph.D.
BERTRAM J. COHLER, Ph.D.

Study of the lives of older adults is a relatively recent invest-igative development within both the social sciences and psycho-analysis. This work builds on the extensive study of childhood and adolescence during the past half-century, but requires the construction of concepts especially fitted for an understanding of the course of the second half of life. During the childhood years, developmental processes are determined largely by mat-urational forces, although social context is important even dur-ing the preschool years (Farnham-Diggory, 1966). In adult-hood, social context largely replaces maturation as the determining factor in development. The self experiences change across a life course that is defined and experienced socially. Across the second half of life, as a consequence of increasing awareness of personal mortality and of the finitude of life, older people experience a marked change in the ways in which social interactions facilitate feelings of personal well-being. Sources of life satisfaction that were particularly salient across the first half of life, such as continuing investment in a wide network of kindred and friends, may not be as satisfying for persons after midlife. The present chapter considers the significance of this changing experience of social relations

199

across the second half of life for maintaining personal adjustment and morale, in an effort to relate normative findings regarding the transition from middle to late life to psychodynamic issues in the study of the mental health of older persons.

Development and Aging

The study of lives over time, from earliest childhood to oldest age, makes particular assumptions regarding issues of development and change. While change refers to any alteration of structure or process over time, maturation refers to those largely biologically determined characteristics that emerge in the course of an orderly, natural growth process (Birren and Renner, 1977). Psychodynamic perspectives on development generally have made three assumptions about the course of development: (1) Development proceeds in a hierarchical, orthogenetic, or epigenetic manner from relatively global and undifferentiated to differentiated states; (2) social–cognitive development during early childhood provides a representative template for development across the course of life from earliest childhood to oldest age; and (3) development necessarily proceeds in an orderly and predictable manner in which understanding of earlier transitions in the course of life makes possible prediction of the manner in which successive transitions will be negotiated (Freud, 1905; Abraham, 1921, 1924; Erikson, 1950; Clausen, 1972). This third assumption is particularly important in studying personality and aging, since findings from empirical studies of adjustment across the second half of life have questioned the more traditional view of orderly continuity across life transitions (Neugarten, 1969, 1979; Gergen, 1977, 1980; Kagan, 1980).

Orthogenesis and Development

Within psychoanalysis, development has most often been understood in terms of the increasing differentiation and hierarchically organized integration of function over time. Witness Freud's initial interest in developmental neuroanatomy (Sulloway, 1979) and later clinical applications of the concepts of differentiation and integration (Hartmann and Kris, 1945; Rappaport and Gill, 1959) which built on Abraham's (1921, 1924) elaboration of Freud's views, Glover's (1930, 1932) emphasis upon grades of ego differentiation, and Spitz's (1959) emphasis on the concept of cumulative development.

It is interesting to note that Erikson (1950, 1980) in his discussion of epigenesis, relies quite explicitly upon embryology as the intellectual foundation for the study of psychological development (1950, p. 65). Contributions in the area of social–cognitive development have also relied upon the orthogenetic perspective represented by the work of Piaget and others. Piaget's own earliest research was biologically based and, in a manner parallel with Freud's interest in developmental neurobiology, later studies on genetic epistemology were founded on biological assumptions. The epigenetic view of development, based on a biological model, has been the dominant approach underlying the relatively small body of psychoanalytic literature on middle and old age (Liptzin, 1985; Oldham and Liebert, 1989; Hildebrand, 1990).

Whatever the extent to which an epigenetic or orthogenetic perspective may provide an adequate basis for understanding developmental processes across the childhood years, it clearly is not adequate to the task of understanding adulthood development and aging. The epigenetic model does not take into account the complex and often unpredictable impact of social context, or the dramatic changes in personality and adjustment that may be observed as a result of normatively inspired transformations in the subjective understanding of the self and others across middle and late life.

Continuity and Change in Adult Lives

In contrast with the biological perspective so important in epigenetic formulations of development, other studies have noted the significance of the social surround in understanding development across the course of life. The field of life course social science (Clausen, 1972; Neugarten and Hagestad, 1976; Riegel, 1979; Cohler, 1982; Cohler and Boxer, 1984) offers an understanding of lives—including the expression of personality characteristics believed to be salient for a particular place in the life course—in the context of a socially shared understanding of the life course itself. Indeed, it is precisely the recognition that the culture provides expected transition points and defines even the expected duration of life, that makes it important to differentiate life cycle from life course. What has been too narrowly seen as progression through hierarchical differentiation intrinsic to personality can be better appreciated as progression through a series of culturally provided, shared understandings of what behavior is expected and when. Personal meanings, based on the totality of life experience, interact with larger, socially determined expectations of the course of life. It is not that biology is not important in the second half of life. Physical decline and eventual deterioration that come with age clearly are biological processes. The point being made is that the individual's experience of bodily change is socially created and shared.

At least from middle childhood through old age, people continually contrast their present place in the expected course of life with that expected. They have a sense of being "on" or "off" schedule for particular roles and for transitions into and out of these roles according to the social timetable. Aging is experienced in the context of what individuals have been socialized to expect as normative. For that reason, the psychodynamics of individual lives can best be understood within the social context of experience which becomes the basis of particular subjective interpretations or personal narratives (Cohler, 1982) regarding the purpose and direction of the life as a whole (Buhler, 1935).

Recently, there has been increased appreciation of the impact of unanticipated events across the life course, including those occurring among significant others or consociates (Plath, 1980) and sociohistorical events such as international conflicts and adverse economic conditions which may affect an entire generation or cohort (Elder, 1974; Caspi and Elder, 1986). Findings from a number of reports have supported the idea that the course of personality development is not necessarily continuous across adulthood (Elder and Rockwell, 1979; Kagan, 1980). Reporting on findings from a study of persons involved from early infancy through middle age in studies by the Institute of Human Development at Berkeley, Maas and Kuypers (1974) note that the greatest stability of personality across a forty-year period was characteristic of those older men viewed as least well adjusted both in young adulthood and, once again, in later life. This finding is consistent with Moss and Sussman's (1980) observation that stability over time may be most clearly observed in the study of personal adjustment and distress.

Other reports from the Berkeley studies (Block with Haan, 1971; Mussen, Eichorn, Honzik, Bieber, and Meredith, 1980), as well as the study at the Fels Institute of persons from birth to young adulthood (Kagan and Moss, 1962), and even the continuing studies of middle aged and older persons in the NIA Baltimore collaborative study (Costa and McRae, 1980; Costa, McRae, and Arenberg, 1980) provide evidence of some stability in personality over time, though these findings of continuity are confined largely to those aspects thought to reflect innate disposition or temperament such as introversion and emotional instability. However, as Emmerich (1968) has cautioned, it is important to differentiate between consistency in the relative rank order or position of persons with particular attributes, reflected in these studies of temperamental factors, and consistency in personality structure over time, such as is reflected in the study of the impact of early experience upon later personality and adjustment.

Focus on demonstration of stability and order, rather than discontinuity across the course of life, may have led investigators to miss the most interesting question about lives: not how they stay the same over time, but, rather, how they change (Neugarten, 1977). Instead of either a linear or an orthogenetic perspective, the most appropriate view of personal development may be one stressing dramatic, discontinuous transformations of personality over time (Emmerich, 1968; Cohler, 1982; Cohler and Galatzer-Levy, 1990). Reviewing Freud's (1905, 1910) formulation of the "nuclear conflict," or the so-called oedipal phase of ages 5 to 7, Cohler (1980, 1982), following Shapiro (1977) and Abrams (1977, 1978), has suggested that Freud's portrayal of this prototypic conflict may reflect a view of development based not on epigenetic, but rather transformational processes.

Just as the resolution of this first nuclear conflict leads to the reordering of memory, as well as a changed sense of time, with the past subjugated to infantile amnesia, subsequent changes in perception of self and place in the life course also take place in adolescence, permitting integration of a presently remembered past, experienced present, and anticipated future in a narrative of the course of life which is experienced as more or less effectively integrated and consistent with perceived self. A third transformation may be observed at midlife, with realization of the finitude of life, reflected in increased concern with a foreshortened future. A fourth transformation may be observed among those very old persons who view themselves as "survivors" of their generation and for whom a life review (Butler, 1963) once more reorders a sense of time and memory.

Reorganization of personality may accompany each such personal transformation over the course of life, permitting a continued sense of congruence, of self-consistency, which may not necessarily appear to observers as coherent. Vaillant (1977) notes how differently middle-aged men remember adolescence from the way they reported events at the time. Peskin and Livson (1981) have docu.nented the changing meanings of recollections across the course of adulthood. What is of great interest is the study of the ability shown by most adults to remain open to new experiences in their lives and to tolerate degrees of uncertainty, changing their subjective interpretations or narratives in the service of maintaining personal integrity over time.

Social Relations Across the Second Half of Life

Awareness of Finitude and the Midlife Transformation

Sometime in their fifties, people begin to realize in a new way that their lives are finite. This transformation of personality, marking the change into late middle age, is largely a consequence of social context; this is in contrast with earlier transformations, including the shifts accompanying the resolution of the childhood nuclear conflict portrayed by Freud or resolution of identity issues occurring with the capacity for logical thought in adolescence (Erikson, 1959; Piaget, 1975). The socially shared understanding of the expectable length of life forces middle-aged persons to confront the reality that they have already lived more years than are left to be lived. This realization is further personalized by the experience of the death of friends and loved ones (Jaques, 1965, 1980; Neugarten and Datan, 1974), the departure of adult children from home (Gutmann, 1975, 1977), and an increased need to mourn unfulfilled dreams and aspirations (Pollock, 1961, 1981).

This awareness of one's own mortality, portrayed by Munnichs (1966) as increased "awareness of the finitude of life," and elaborated by Marshall (1975, 1980), Neugarten (1979), and Sill (1980), results in a transformation of the experience of time and memory (Cohler and Galatzer-Levy, 1990). Time shifts from an emphasis on time already lived to time left to be lived before death. Memory shifts to increased reminiscence or preoccupation with the past. At first, this reminiscence is used actively in the service of resolving issues involving career and family (Lieberman and Falk, 1981; Lieberman and Tobin, 1983), but with advancing age, reminiscence activity becomes increasingly important in taking stock of one's own life. The self uses memory in mourning dreams never attained, taking stock of the past, and proceeding with a life review (Butler, 1963).

As a consequence of the personalization of death, persons begin to develop a more inward orientation toward life, termed *introversion* by Jung (1933) or *interiority* by Neugarten (1973, 1979). Interiority includes: increased preoccupation with the inner world; lessened time and effort devoted to social relations, particularly obligatory rather than voluntary relationships; and lessened interest in assuming new challenges. Attention is shifted from family and community to an interior process of making sense of one's own life.

The transformation of middle life refers to psychological activity, and does not necessarily lead to a change in the external appearance of social relationships. However, George, Okun, and Landerman (1985), using a large national sample, found that the social supports of family, friends, and confidants were significantly less important to life satisfaction in middle age, when persons are highly structured by occupational and institutional roles, than either in youth or old age. Just as in the study of other transformations of self, memory, and the experience of time across the life course, a key issue is the particular way in which the interior transformation is associated with changes in social relationships.

Findings reported by Back (1974), Gutmann (1975, 1977, 1986, 1987), and Sinnott (1982) suggest that there may be sex differences in the expression of increased interiority. At midlife, men may move away from active mastery in solving problems at home and in the workplace and increasingly seek comfort, while women move away from their previous emphasis on taking care of others (Cohler and Grunebaum, 1981). Findings from Back's study suggest that women in middle age may begin to experience themselves more directly, rather than in terms of relationships with others.

The transformation of midlife involves for both men and women an increased absorption with the self and decreased patience with demands on limited time and energy (Back, 1974; Lowenthal, Thurner, and Chiriboga, 1975; Cohler and Lieberman, 1980; Erikson, 1980; Kernberg, 1980; Cohler and Galatzer-Levy, 1990). The middle aged find that reworking the presently understood story of the past into a story of a life of some significance and coherence becomes a primary task, leaving less time and energy available for other activities. A relatively successful resolution of conflicts associated with the midlife transformation is marked by the ability to mourn goals not attained and increased acceptance of the finitude of life.

Social Relations and Morale across the Second Half of Life

For decades social scientists have been studying life satisfaction among older people. It has been suggested that the vigor with which this study proceeds reflects the personal preoccupation of younger researchers who may fear aging and look for clues as to the fate of their own morale in late life (Kaufman, 1986) and who seek to allay fear of the unknown (Coleman, 1986). By now an impressive body of literature addresses the link between relationships with other people and morale. Many of these studies present problems of measurement and method which limit conclusions regarding the changing significance of social relations for morale and adjustment across the second half of life. It is difficult to measure morale (Lawton, 1982; Hoyt and Creech, 1983; Stock, Okun, and Benin, 1986), and most studies have been cross sectional, which cannot distinguish cohort from age differences. Furthermore, in defining social relations, researchers have tended simply to count the frequency of social contacts. This statistical approach to aging research reflects traditional methods of social science, of course, but the great reliance on numbers at the expense of understanding the experience of aging is consonant with a defensive attempt on the part of younger researchers to stay distant from death (Cohler, 1977; Poggi and Berland, 1985). Nonetheless, more recently a number of large empirical studies (Baldassare, Rosenfield, and Rook, 1984; Deimling and Harel, 1984; Chappell and Badger, 1989) have more productively considered the subjectively perceived experience of relationships between elders and those whom they feel are important to them. Other smaller studies have collected life stories as reported by elders (Kaufman, 1986; Coleman, 1986) and attempted to integrate descriptive interview data with statistical findings (Wood, 1989). This relatively small body of literature, which examines the significance of relationships, is one to which psychoanalytic case studies are uniquely fitted to contribute. It is useful to examine research on the link between social relations and morale in older people as a step toward relating this literature to a complementary approach that continues to emerge in psychoanalytic understandings of old age.

First, it should be noted that these studies consistently find health not social relations to be the most important predictor of feelings of well-being in later life (Palmore and Luikart, 1972; Edwards and Klemmack, 1973; Spreitzer and Snyder, 1974; Palmore and Kivett, 1977; Larson, 1978; Deimling and Harel, 1984; Doyle and Forehand, 1984; George, Okun, and Landerman, 1985; Chappell and Badger, 1989). Second, there is a striking number of studies that find little or no link between morale in old age and amount of interaction with other people

(Pihlblad and Adams, 1972; Edwards and Klemmack, 1973; Martin, 1973; Conner, Powers and Bultena, 1979; Liang, Dvorkin, Kahana, and Mazian, 1980; Deimling and Harel, 1984; Larson, Zuzanek and Mannell, 1985; Chappell and Badger, 1989). It is now well established that frequency of contact with other people does not, by itself, enhance elders' morale. This has opened the way for further questions: Do certain relationships promote morale more than others? If amount of time spent with others is not significant, are there other aspects of human relationships that do enhance morale in old age?

It is generally accepted that elders interact regularly with relatives and that the notion of the isolated elder is largely a myth (Arling, 1976; Peters and Kaiser, 1985; Chappell and Badger, 1989). About 80 percent of people over 65 have living children, most of them middle aged, whom they generally see or talk with by telephone about once a week (Cicirelli, 1983). Elders and their adult children often avoid sharing intimate thoughts, so as to minimize conflict and enhance feelings of warmth and affection (Cicirelli, 1983). As Cohler and Boxer (1984) have suggested, young adults, married and beginning their families, look to their parents for emotional support and financial assistance. Concerned with enhancing family traditions, and expecting understanding and assistance, young persons seek to maintain interdependent ties. However, their requests for help and support may be acknowledged less positively by middle-aged and older grandparents (Cohler and Grunebaum, 1981). Middle-aged children report "filial anxiety" (Cicirelli, 1981), apprehension about the burden their parents may become, even when they are not providing any help and little help is needed. When parents actually do require assistance, children feel less positively toward them (Johnson and Bursk, 1977). Most children experience some frustration, impatience, guilt, and feelings of helplessness in dealing with elder parents (Cicirelli, 1983).

Given the strain reported in these relationships, perhaps it should not be surprising that researchers have found that elders' morale is not enhanced by interaction with their children (Pihlblad and Adams, 1972; Edwards and Klemmack, 1973;

Martin, 1973; Spreitzer and Snyder, 1974; Arling, 1976; Campbell, Converse, and Rodgers, 1976; Conner, Powers, and Bultena, 1979; Mancini, 1979; Lee and Ishii-Kuntz, 1988). In a ten-year longitudinal study of people over 65, Britton and Britton (1972) found that both men and women reported seeing family less frequently over the years, but with no stated increase in feelings of neglect. Findings from a continuing longitudinal study of older persons first seen when their offspring were young children as a part of the intergenerational studies carried out through the Institute of Human Development at Berkeley (Maas and Kuypers, 1974) indicate that the greatest satisfaction in old age was found among those older mothers and fathers who spent relatively less time within the family circle. Among older fathers, increased morale was associated with increased involvement in hobbies and lowered levels of visiting and other forms of sociability while, among older mothers, higher morale was associated with club attendance and lowered levels of visiting. More family centered older parents reported less satisfaction with their present life than these more remotely involved older adults.

Furthermore, in contrast to what younger people might expect, the experience of having had children is not crucial to life satisfaction in old age. For example, Chappell and Badger (1989) found that never having had children is not related to lower morale in late life. In interviews with elders, Kaufman (1986) was surprised to find little spontaneous mention of memories about child rearing, motherhood, or fatherhood (in contrast with many references to childhood within the family of origin). She concluded that having reared a child may not be a particularly salient aspect of the identity of the aged. In a related vein, having children has been found to be unrelated to the self-esteem of older persons (Lee and Shehan, 1989).

According to popular stereotypes, among older family members, the grandparental role is perhaps the one that provides the greatest satisfaction, serving to reduce the otherwise stressful impact of growing old. Ironically, and particularly among women, the grandparental role appears either to contribute to lowered morale, or to be independent of morale (Hess and Waring, 1978; Troll, Miller, and Atchley, 1979; Lee and Ishii-Kuntz, 1987). In the first place, as Rosow (1967) has noted, the advent of grandparenthood is not a role individuals select for themselves. Becoming a grandparent often reminds older people of the fact of their own aging. Further, the grand-parental role is, of necessity, somewhat strained and formal. Grandparents cannot have access to younger grandchildren ex-cept with parental consent; often requests by parents for grand-parental help are made at times convenient for the parents, but not necessarily convenient for the grandparents (Rosow, 1976). Troll (1983) describes grandparents as "family watchdogs," maintaining frequent, but nonintimate, contact with children and grandchildren. If all is well, grandparents prefer to keep some distance to pursue their own lives; only if trouble ensues, particularly divorce, do they feel compelled to forego nonfam-ily activities in order to help out (Troll, 1983).

Nor does frequency of interaction with siblings—the other close kin—relate to morale in old age (Lee and Ihinger-Tall-man, 1980). Scott (1983) reports that aged siblings tend to maintain a high degree of closeness, but with limited contacts that serve to revive the good memories and warm feelings of early life.

Kin relationships may be felt as obligatory rather than vol-untary, reducing their power to enhance morale. In contrast, there is an indication that relationships with friends—who mu-tually select each other—promote life satisfaction (Wood and Robertson, 1978; Mancini, 1979; Mancini, Quinn, Gavigan, and Franklin, 1980; Lee and Ishii-Kuntz, 1987) and better function-ing (Thomae, 1990) among the aged. Kaufman (1986), how-ever, drawing on interviews, reported that those elders who mentioned friendship indicated that new friendships made in old age tended to be "on the surface" and that "you don't make close friends in old age." Nevertheless, as Palmore and Luikart (1972) suggest, friendship ties are particularly important for older men, an observation which is consonant with the shift in sex roles observed in midlife (Gutmann, 1975, 1977, 1986; Sinnott, 1982). Women, who characteristically rely upon social relations as a major source of satisfaction before midlife, may become somewhat less sociable and more introspective, while men, for whom work achievements had been a major source of satisfaction prior to midlife, become somewhat more sociable, seeking greater contact with friends.

Strain and Chappell (1982) found that the quantity of interaction with friends is no more important to morale than is the quantity of interaction with kin. Their study of the confidant relationship is part of the relatively small body of research that attempts to examine the significance of interpersonal relationships for elders. This literature shows quite clearly that older persons do not feel socially isolated or necessarily less satisfied with opportunities available for continuing social relations than earlier in the course of life (Medley, 1976, 1980). Defining confidant as someone in whom an individual confides about the self and personal problems, Strain and Chappell (1982) found the existence of at least one confidant—whether family or friend and whether contacted more or less often—significantly predicted life satisfaction among the elderly. Likewise, Deimling and Harel (1984), using a large probability sample of well elderly, found that, although perceptions of the adequacy of the social relations are virtually unrelated to objective measures of the social networks, it was important to the morale of elders that they had some social relations which they perceived as adequate. Chappell and Badger (1989), controlling for health and sociodemographic factors, found that of ten indicators of social isolation, only the lack of a companion and confidant diminished subjective well-being. They further found that having another in the household who is not considered a companion contributed most to feelings of unhappiness. It is better to be alone than to live with someone with whom one does not have an intimate relationship. Noting that many older persons who have numerous family and friends choose to spend much of their time alone, Larson, Zuzanek, and Mannell (1985) found that older people positively value time alone as an opportunity for thought and reflection. Coleman (1986), in his interviews, found that those who felt most lonely were no more objectively isolated than the others, but were less able to be content in their own company and more likely to experience worrisome thoughts about the past. What seems to be important for the elders' morale is not the quantity of interpersonal contact, but rather the subjective experience that someone is there for them (Lowenthal and Haven, 1968; Lowenthal and Robinson, 1976; Baldassare, Rosenfield, and Rook, 1984; Chappell and Badger, 1989; Wood, 1989). Older people consistently prefer modes of relating to others that are characterized by greater formality, closer ties with fewer significant others, and lessened investment of time and effort in social relations than has been found in studies of social ties and morale among young adults.

It may be useful to expand the understanding of social ties that sustain the elderly. The internal meaning of connections that provide emotional sustenance may change throughout life (Pollock, 1987). Coleman reports a moving description by an elderly woman of how she has been supported by a sense of personal connection and communication with her dead husband. Kaufman's (1986) interpretation of her case histories includes the suggestion that elders need a modicum of social interaction, but of the kind that supports their idea of connectedness, rather than too much genuine human communication which can disrupt the idea of themselves that they are working to maintain in order to sustain morale.

Implications for Psychodynamic Theories of Aging

Psychoanalysis and social science represent complementary methods for the study of lives. The structure of personality is the internalization of particular role relationships, as Parsons (1952, 1958) has noted. Furthermore, lives are shaped by the social surround, especially by the sense of being more or less on time in terms of socially expected points in the course of life. Since individuals continually compare their attainments with what the culture has defined for them as normative, such benchmark events have the capacity to provide individuals with a continuing sense of well-being (Kohut, 1977).

In understanding the second half of life, social science can be particularly useful because the inner transformation sparked by the increasing sense of awareness of finitude (Jaques, 1965, 1980; Munnichs, 1966; Neugarten, 1973, 1979) seems to be largely socially determined. The timing of this transformation, which leads to increased concern with psychological processes and less interest in maintenance of obligatory ties such as those with family, is not primarily maturational. For example, while much of what Levinson (1985) and his colleagues observe about the midlife transition appears to be an accurate portrayal of the psychological world of contemporary American men, it is the social structure, not chronological age, which seems to be determinant. For both sexes, as Neugarten and Hagestad (1976) have noted, chronological age is an empty category. The timing of transformations depends on particular perceptions of the appropriateness and significance of pending role transitions, together with unanticipated life events and particular role strains. These are experienced in a particular way because of shared experience of sociohistorical events, such as the Great Depression, the World Wars, the Vietnam era, and the like. In specific cohorts, the age at which evidence of a midlife transformation may be realized will be closer to 50, while for others it may be closer to 60. Characteristically, this shift does not occur until some time during the fifth decade of life.

Psychoanalysis can contribute to an understanding of older persons through the study of the enactments of the older analysand toward the analyst in the psychoanalytic process. This can be the case within the classic conflict model of psychoanalysis, as well as within self psychology and other approaches.

Within psychoanalysis, it is well accepted that frequent contact with a benign person not directly involved in daily life helps the analysand make explicit feelings and attitudes otherwise not within the awareness of everyday life. Within the classic conflict approach, the most representative of these reenactments stems from unresolved and unacknowledged wishes associated with what Freud (1910) termed the "nuclear complex" or conflict. Freud viewed the jealousy of the father's special access to the mother as a universal event of early childhood. It is this conflict which is portrayed in Oedipus, and which is unacceptable and subsequently repudiated, both in culture, where Oedipus becomes Hamlet, and in personality, where infantile amnesia successfully prevents awareness of this infantile mental wish. Wishes associated with mental life remain potentially active in later life, unacknowledged and inaccessible in daily life, but capable of at least partial satisfaction through dreams, symptoms, slips of the tongue, and, in appropriate instances, disguised satisfaction in relations with others. The unconscious (Freud, 1900, 1915) is a term used to describe this phenomenon of unacknowledged wishes capable of stimulating dreams and symptoms.

As the significance of these wishes is experienced, observed, appreciated, and interpreted in analysis, these wishes lose some of their power to motivate actions. This results in increased self-understanding. In classic theory, analysis of wishes based on the nuclear conflict of early childhood has been understood as the realm of mental distress in which psychoanalysis is most effective. Indeed, this nuclear conflict is virtualy identical with the term *conflict* as used in psychoanalysis. However, it is possible that, associated with each of the transformations across the course of life, there are additional conflicts which may be similarly observed and interpreted. Concerns with issues of identity (the conflict unique to the transformation of adolescence) and finitude (the conflict unique to the transformation of middle life) may also be represented in the analytic setting and may be observed and understood in ways similar to the infantile mental conflict itself.

This life course perspective suggests that there are a variety of reenactments in addition to the infantile mental conflict of early childhood. Furthermore, the nuclear conflict may not necessarily be the most useful model for expression of later conflicts, any more than other aspects of childhood are adequate models for understanding adult development in general. The infantile conflict can coexist with the conflicts of adolescence and middle life as sources of enactments which inspire distress. In midlife, it may be possible to observe in the transference an enactment of the experience of finitude (Cohen, 1982; Loch, 1982; Pollock, 1982; Sandler, 1982; Mann, 1985), particularly as it is associated with changing satisfaction in interpersonal relationships. The analysand may experience the analyst as making interpersonal demands, as intrusive, and as interfering with the privacy so important to older persons. Issues of solitude and engagement, of self-engrossment and extension of the self to others may also be included in this analytic enactment of the crisis of finitude.

If aging is understood as a series of potentially discontinu-ous reorganizations of understanding of the self—woven into a consistent life narrative by the experiencing individual—then it is possible to ask how aging individuals use other people in their own intrapsychic reorganization as they move through life toward death. Based on Kohut's (1971, 1977) self psychology, this understanding posits that adults are able to use attributes of other people as functions of the self as they resolve current tensions throughout life. It is possible that the specific ways in which they use other people in the service of tension regulation and the maintenance of self-esteem change across the life course. Given the increasing self-preoccupation with age and the changing ways in which interaction with others is needed for morale, the question arises as to how others are needed for the preservation of the self. This may be of special interest in the study of old, old age when the developmental task, as Grif-fin and Grunes (1990) and Tobin (1991) describe, is to preserve the experience of self-continuity in the face of extinction. Tobin describes how the aged use memory, including distortion, to keep alive and vivid an experience of the self as it was. This is consonant with Kaufman's (1986) description of how the very old seem to use stories of interaction with other people, includ-ing memories (regardless of their verisimilitude) to confirm and validate themselves as they have always been. There is a way in which the very old seem to prefer the memories and reports of social interactions in the past to a quantity of new social interactions in the present. This suggests that the reminiscence associated with aging may be understood as having a special self–object function in old age. The analyst may be aware of an aspect of mirroring that seems peculiarly effective in old age, the reflection back to the patient of a picture of the self as it once was.

Implications for Psychoanalytic Psychotherapeutic Treatment

Clearly, psychoanalytic study of older persons is more com-plex than of younger persons, for there is a much larger set of enactments to be observed and interpreted (Nemiroff and Colarusso, 1985). Memories of the past also have a changed role in the patient's present life and adjustment; the concept of "screen memory" does not sufficiently encompass the psychological significance of memory and reminiscence with the advent of midlife (Cohler, 1980). Further, Gill (1990) notes the particular problem faced by the middle-aged analyst who may find it hard to allow middle-aged patients to fully experience the depth of grief at losses both patient and analyst are experiencing.

A more difficult issue is that while all analytic observers have been children, and are able to employ an understanding of past life in attempting to understand the patients' experience, empathy with one's own future is not available in the same fashion. It may be much easier to recognize the patient's efforts at making the therapist into the critical, seductive, or apparently rejecting parent of childhood, than to recognize efforts at making the therapist into a grandchild or a lost spouse or friend (Cohen, 1985; Levinson, 1985; Nemiroff and Colarusso, 1988). Since the very significance of death and of awareness of finitude changes across the second half of life, it may be particularly difficult for younger analytic observers to understand the significance attached to issues of finitude and mortality by older persons. There may even be a tendency to interpret these issues in terms more relevant to the place of the therapist in the life course than that of the patient. For example, a younger therapist may mistake normal increases of time spent alone as evidence of psychopathology, including depression, in the aging. A middle-aged therapist struggling with the loss of children leaving the home may find it hard to imagine that an older person's seeming acceptance of distance between the self and children is a comfortable adaptation, rather than a defense. Similarly, the younger therapist may feel differently than the older patient when the patient does not offer to take care of children and grandchildren, and, in the transference, the therapist. Myers (1986) suggests that the younger analyst's responses to older patients may be a function of unresolved conflicts about the analyst's parents, but also about the analyst's training analyst.

In a related vein, it may be difficult for both patients and therapists in their thirties and forties, to imagine that older people can be satisfied with their lives if they have not raised children, and to understand the younger person's longing for a child within the current context, rather than as a requisite for morale in old age. Likewise, young therapists of both sexes may find themselves threatened and confused by a patient's grappling with moves toward the normal androgyny of the second half of life. Also, young and middle-aged therapists may mistakenly consider as defensive those dramatically staged, relatively fixed, mythicizing presentations of memory that have been described (Revere and Tobin, 1980; Tobin, 1991) as needed by the normal elderly to keep their identities vivid in their own self-views. Finally, younger therapists may underestimate the importance of their function in the role of confidant. As the social science literature on the relationship between morale and social interaction suggests, a quantity of contact with family is less important than the subjective experience that someone, whether kin or not, maintains abiding interest in the older person.

The findings reviewed in the present chapter suggest that middle age brings increased reminiscence and introspection. As the second half of life begins, people need time and effort to sort out hopes, goals, and disappointments and to successfully make peace with a new vision of the period of life left to live. While social ties, including considerable obligations, continue, what changes is the manner in which these continuing social relations are experienced. What may have brought satisfaction in younger life may no longer do so in older age.

Younger persons, including empathic analytic observers working with older patients, are at a different point in the course of life, and may find it difficult to appreciate both increased preoccupation with self and changing priorities regarding important sources of life satisfaction. For example, the effects of loneliness, so much a concern in the lives of young adults, appear to have quite different significance in the lives of older persons. Even when there have been significant role losses, if these losses, such as widowhood, are relatively expectable or on time according to the social timetable (Neugarten and Hagestad, 1976), loneliness may be somewhat less of a problem than it is among younger persons. Overall, there is little evidence to suggest that loneliness has the same poignancy among older persons as observed among the young. While older people may feel sad about role losses, the meaning and manner in which they use other people for consolation and support may change over the course of life. However, to date, relatively little detailed study has been given to the means used by older persons for consolation and support. This represents an area where continued analytic observation would make important contributions.

In order to be most effective in studies of the second half of life, psychoanalysis must not assume that questions relevant to the first half of life, and particularly those related to early childhood, are necessarily questions most relevant in the study of older persons. Indeed, one of the essential questions to be answered by psychoanalytic inquiry concerns the extent to which present understandings of childhood, adolescence, and young adulthood influence present life and adjustment in middle age and beyond. Psychoanalytic investigation is uniquely suited to the task of studying the changing significance of others for present adjustment across the second half of life and, more generally, for exploring the changing role of the remembered past and experienced present for maintaining the continuity and integrity of the self.

References

Abraham, K. (1921), Contributions to a discussion on tic. In: *Selected Papers on Psychoanalysis*. New York: Basic Books, 1953, pp. 323–325.
——— (1924), A short study on the development of the libido, viewed in the light of mental disorders. In: *Selected Papers on Psychoanalysis*. New York: Basic Books, 1953, pp. 418–501.
Abrams, S. (1977), The genetic point of view: Antecedents and transformations. *J. Amer. Psychoanal. Assn.*, 25:417–425.
——— (1978), The teaching and learning of psychoanalytic developmental psychology. *J. Amer. Psychoanal. Assn.*, 26:387–406.
Arling, G. (1976), The elderly widow and her family, neighbors, and friends. *J. Marr. & Fam.*, 38:757–768.
Back, K. W. (1974), Transition to aging and the self-image. In: *Normal Aging*, Vol. 2, ed. E. Palmore. Durham, N.C.: Duke University Press, pp. 207–216.

Baldassare, M., Rosenfield, S., & Rook, K. (1984), The types of social relations predicting elderly well-being. *Res. Aging*, 6:549–559.

Birren, J., & Renner, V. (1977), Research on the psychology of aging: Principles and experimentation. In: *Handbook of the Psychology of Aging*, ed. J. Birren & K. W. Schaie. New York: Van Nostrand Reinhold, pp. 3–39.

Block, J., with Haan, N. (1971), *Lives Through Time*. Berkeley, Calif.: Bancroft Books.

Britton, J. H., & Britton, J. O. (1972), *Personality Changes in Aging: A Longitudinal Study of Community Residents*. New York: Springer.

Buhler, C. (1935), The curve of life as studied in biographies. *J. Appl. Psychol.*, 19:405–409.

Butler, R. (1963), The life-review: An interpretation of reminiscence in the aged. *Psychiatry*, 26:65–76.

Campbell, A., Converse, P. E., & Rodgers, W. L. (1976), *The Quality of American Life: Perceptions, Evaluations and Satisfactions*. New York: Russell Sage.

Caspi, A., & Elder, G. H. (1986), Life satisfaction in old age: Linking social psychology and history. *J. Psychol. & Aging*, 1:18–26.

Chappell, N. L., & Badger, M. (1989), Social isolation and well-being. *J. Gerontol.*, 44:169–176.

Cicirelli, V. G. (1981), *Helping Elderly Parents: The Role of Adult Children*. Boston: Auburn House.

———— (1983), Adult children and their elderly parents. In: *Family Relationships in Later Life*, ed. T. H. Brubaker. Beverly Hills: Sage Publications, pp. 31–46.

Clausen, J. (1972), The life course of individuals. In: *Aging and Society*, Vol. 3, ed. M. Riley, M. Johnson, & A. Foner. New York: Russell Sage Foundation, pp. 457–514.

Cohen, G. D. (1985), Psychotherapy with an eighty-year-old patient. In: *The Race Against Time: Psychotherapy and Psychoanalysis in the Second Half of Life*, ed. R. A. Nemiroff & C. A. Colarusso. New York: Plenum, pp. 195–204.

Cohen, N. (1982), On loneliness and the aging process. *Internat. J. Psycho-Anal.*, 63:149–155.

Cohler, B. J. (1977), The life cycle, aging and death: Dialectical perspectives. *Internat. J. Aging & Hum. Develop.*, 20:210–226.

———— (1980), Adult developmental psychology and reconstruction in psychoanalysis. In: *The Course of Life: Psychoanalytic Contributions Toward Understanding Personality Development, Vol. 3, Adulthood and the Aging Process*, ed. S. Greenspan & G. Pollock. Bethesda, Md.: National Institute of Mental Health, pp. 149–199.

———— (1982), Personal narrative and life course. In: *Life-Span Development and Behavior*, Vol. 4, ed. P. Baltes & O. G. Brim, Jr. New York: Academic Press, pp. 206–241.

———— Boxer, A. (1984), Settling into the world: Person and family during the middle years. In: *Normality and the Life Course*, ed. D. Offer & M. Sabshin. New York: Basic Books, pp. 145–203.

———— Galatzer-Levy, R. M. (1990), Self, meaning, and morale across the second half of life. In: *New Dimensions in Adult Development*, ed. R. A. Nemiroff & C. A. Colarusso. New York: Basic Books.

———— Grunebaum, H. (1981), *Mothers, Grandmothers, and Daughters*. New York: Wiley-Interscience.

―――― Lieberman, M. (1980), Social relations and mental health. *Res. Aging,* 2:445–469.

Coleman, P. G. (1986), *Ageing and Reminiscence Process: Social and Clinical Implications.* Chichester, U.K.: John Wiley.

Conner, K., Powers, E., & Bultena, G. (1979), Social interaction and life satisfaction: An empirical assessment of late-life patterns. *J. Gerontol.,* 34:116–121.

Costa, P., & McCrae, R. (1980), Still stable after all these years: Personality as a key to some issues in adulthood and old age. In: *Life-Span Development and Behavior,* Vol. 3, ed. P. Baltes & O. G. Brim, Jr. New York: Academic Press, pp. 65–102.

―――― ―――― Arenberg, D. (1980), Enduring dispositions in adult males. *J. Personal. & Soc. Psychol.,* 38:793–800.

Deimling, G. T., & Harel, Z. (1984), Social integration and mental health of the aged. *Res. Aging,* 6:515–527.

Doyle, D., & Forehand, M. J. (1984), Life satisfaction and old age. *Res. Aging,* 6:432–448.

Edwards, J., & Klemmack, D. (1973), Correlates of life satisfaction: A re-examination. *J. Gerontol.,* 28:497–502.

Elder, G. (1974), *Children of the Great Depression.* Chicago: University of Chicago Press.

―――― Rockwell, R. (1979), The life-course and human development: An ecological perspective. *Internat. J. Behav. Develop.,* 2:1–21.

Emmerich, W. (1968), Personality development and concepts of structure. *Child Develop.,* 39:671–690.

Erikson, E. (1950), *Childhood and Society,* rev. ed. New York: Norton, 1963.

―――― (1959), *Young Man Luther.* New York: Norton.

―――― (1980), Elements of a psychoanalytic theory of psychosocial development. In: *The Course of Life: Psychoanalytic Contributions toward Understanding Personality Development,* Vol. 1, *Infancy and Early Childhood,* ed. S. Greenspan & G. Pollock. Bethesda, Md.: National Institute of Mental Health, pp. 11–61.

Farnham-Diggory, S. (1966), Self, future and time: A developmental study of the concepts of psychotic, brain-injured and normal children. *Monographs of the Society for Research in Child Development,* 33 (Whole Number 103).

Fiske, M. (1980), Tasks and crises of the second half of life: The interrelationship of commitment, coping and adaptation. In: *Handbook of Mental Health and Aging,* ed. J. Birren & R. B. Sloane. Englewood Cliffs, N.J.: Prentice-Hall, pp. 337–373.

Freud, S. (1900), The Interpretation of Dreams. *Standard Edition,* 4/5. London: Hogarth Press, 1953.

―――― (1905), Three essays on the theory of sexuality. *Standard Edition,* 7:130–243. London: Hogarth Press, 1953.

―――― (1910), Five lectures on psychoanalysis. *Standard Edition,* 11:9–55. London: Hogarth Press, 1953.

―――― (1915), The unconscious. *Standard Edition,* 14:159–216. London: Hogarth Press, 1957.

George, L. K., Okun, M. A., & Landerman, R. (1985), Age as a moderator of the determinants of life satisfaction. *Res. Aging,* 7:209–233.

Gergen, K. (1977), Stability, change and chance in understanding human development. In: *Life-Span Developmental Psychology: Dialectical Perspectives on Experimental Research*, ed. N. Datan & H. Reese. New York: Academic Press, pp. 136–158.

—— (1980), The emerging crisis in life-span developmental theory. In: *Life-Span Development and Behavior*, Vol. 3, ed. P. Baltes & O. G. Brim, Jr. New York: Academic Press, pp. 32–65.

Gill, H. S. (1990), Analysis of patients in their fifties: Some aspects of technique. *J. Geriat. Psychiatry*, 23:129–145.

Glover, E. (1930), Grades of ego differentiation. In: *On the Early Development of the Mind*. New York: International Universities Press, 1956, pp. 112–122.

—— (1932), A psychoanalytical approach to the classification of mental disorders. In: *On the Early Development of the Mind*. New York: International Universities Press, 1956, pp. 161–186.

Graney, M. (1975), Happiness and social participation in aging. *J. Gerontol.*, 30:701–706.

Griffin, B. P., & Grunes, J. M. (1990), A developmental approach to psychoanalytic psychotherapy with the aged. In: *New Dimensions in Adult Development*, ed. R. A. Nemiroff & C. A. Colarusso. New York: Basic Books.

Grunes, J. M. (1981), Reminiscences, regression, and empathy—A psychotherapeutic approach to the impaired elderly. In: *The Course of Life: Psychoanalytic Contributions Toward Understanding Personality Development*, Vol. 3, *Adulthood and the Aging Process*, ed. S. Greenspan & G. Pollock. Bethesda, Md.: National Institute of Mental Health, pp. 545–548.

Gutmann, D. (1975), Parenthood: Key to the comparative study of the life cycle. In: *Life-Span Developmental Psychology: Normative Life-Crises*, ed. N. Datan & L. Ginsberg. New York: Academic Press, pp. 167–184.

—— (1977), The cross-cultural perspective: Notes toward a comparative psychology of aging. In: *Handbook of the Psychology of Aging*, ed. J. Birren & K. W. Schaie. New York: Van Nostrand Reinhold, pp. 302–326.

—— (1986), Oedipus and the aging male: A comparative perspective. *Psychoanal. Rev.*, 73:541–552.

—— (1987), *Reclaimed Powers: Towards a Psychology of Men and Women in Later Life*. New York: Basic Books.

Hartmann, H., & Kris, E. (1945), The genetic approach in psychoanalysis. *The Psychoanalytic Study of the Child*, 1:11–30. New York: International Universities Press.

Hess, B., & Waring, J. (1978), Changing patterns of aging and family bonds in later life. *Fam. Coordinator*, 27:303–314.

Hildebrand, H. P. (1990), Toward a psychodynamic understanding of later life. In: *Clinical and Scientific Psychogeriatrics, Vol. 1, The Holistic Approaches*, ed. M. Bergener & S. I. Finkel. New York: Springer, pp. 66–75.

Hoyt, D. R., & Creech, J. C. (1983), The life-satisfaction index: A methodological and theoretical critique. *J. Gerontol.*, 38:111–116.

Jaques, E. (1965), Death and the mid-life crisis. *Internat. J. Psycho-Anal.*, 46:502–514.

—— (1980), The midlife crisis. In: *The Course of Life: Psychoanalytic Contributions toward Understanding the Aging Process, Vol. 3, Adulthood and the Aging Process*, ed. S. Greenspan & G. Pollock. Bethesda, Md.: National Institute of Mental Health, pp. 1–23.

Johnson, E. S., & Bursk, B. J. (1977), Relationship between the elderly and their adult children. *Gerontol.*, 17:90–96.

Jung, C. G. (1933), *Modern Man in Search of a Soul*. New York: Harcourt, Brace & World.

Kagan, J. (1980), Perspectives on continuity. In: *Constancy and Change in Human Development*, ed. O. G. Brim, Jr. & J. Kagan. Cambridge: Harvard University Press, pp. 26–74.

——— Moss, H. (1962), *From Birth to Maturity*. New York: John Wiley.

Kahn, R. (1979), Aging and social support. In: *Aging from Birth to Death: Interdisciplinary Perspectives*, ed. M. H. Riley. Boulder, Col.: Westview Press, pp. 77–91.

——— Antonucci, T. (1981), Convoys of social support: A life-course approach. In: *Aging: Social Change*, ed. S. Kiesler, J. Morgan, & V. Oppenheimer. New York: Academic Press, pp. 383–405.

Kaufman, S. R. (1986), *The Ageless Self: Sources of Meaning in Late Life*. Madison: University of Wisconsin Press.

Kernberg, O. (1980), Normal narcissism in middle age. In: *Internal World and External Reality: Object Relations Theory Applied*. New York: Jason Aronson, pp. 173–192.

Kohut, H. (1971), *The Analysis of the Self*. New York: International Universities Press.

——— (1977), *The Restoration of the Self*. New York: International Universities Press.

Larson, R. (1978), Thirty years of research on the subjective well being of older Americans. *J. Gerontol.*, 33:109–125.

——— Zuzanek, J., & Mannell, R. (1985), Being alone versus being with people: Disengagement in the daily experience of older adults. *J. Gerontol.*, 40:375–381.

Lawton, M. P. (1982), The well-being and mental health of the aged. In: *Review of Human Development*, ed. T. Field, A. Huston, H. Quay, L. Troll, & G. Finley. New York: Wiley-Interscience, pp. 614–628.

Lee, G. R., & Ihinger-Tallman, M. (1980), Sibling interaction and morale: The effects of family relations on older people. *Res. Aging*, 2:367–391.

——— Ishii-Kuntz, M. (1987), Social interaction, loneliness and emotional well-being among the elderly. *Res. Aging*, 9:459–482.

——— Shehan, C. L. (1989), Social relations and the self-esteem of older persons. *Res. Aging*, 11:427–442.

Levin, D., Darrow, C., Klein, E., Levinson, M., & McKee, B. (1978), *The Seasons of a Man's Life*. New York: Alfred A. Knopf.

Levinson, G. A. (1985), New beginnings at seventy: A decade of psychotherapy in late adulthood. In: *The Race Against Time: Psychotherapy and Psychoanalysis in the Second Half of Life*, ed. R. A. Nemiroff & C. A. Colarusso. New York: Plenum, pp. 171–188.

Liang, J., Dvorkin, L., Kahana, E., & Mazian, F. (1980), Social integration and morale: A re-examination. *J. Gerontol.*, 35:746–757.

Lieberman, M., & Falk, J. (1981), The remembered past as a source of data for research on the life-cycle. *Hum. Develop.*, 14:132–141.

——— Tobin, S. (1983), *The Experience of Old Age: Stress, Coping, and Survival*. New York: Basic Books.

Liptzin, B. (1985), Psychotherapy with the elderly: An Eriksonian perspective. *J. Geriat. Psychiat.*, 18:183–202.

Loch, W. (1982), Comments on Cohen's paper—Loneliness and the aging process. *Internat. J. Psycho-Anal.*, 63:267–273.
Lowenthal, M. F. (1964), Social isolation and mental illness in old age. *Amer. Sociol. Rev.*, 29:54–70.
—— Haven, C. (1968), Interaction and adaptation: Intimacy as a crucial variable. *Amer. Sociol. Rev.*, 33:20–30.
—— Robinson, B. (1976), Social networks and isolation. In: *Handbook on Aging and the Social Sciences*, ed. R. Binstock & E. Shanas. New York: Van Nostrand, pp. 432–456.
—— Thurner, M., & Chiriboga, D. (1975), *Four Stages of Life*. San Francisco: Jossey-Bass.
Maas, H., & Kuypers, J. (1974), *From Thirty to Seventy*. San Francisco: Jossey-Bass.
Mancini, J. (1979), Family relationships and morale among people 65 years of age and older. *Amer. J. Orthopsychiatry*, 49:292–300.
—— Quinn, W., Gavigan, M., & Franklin, H. (1980), Social network interaction among older adults: Implications for life satisfaction. *Hum. Rel.*, 33:543–554.
Mann, C. H. (1985), Adult development: Individuation, separation and the role of reality. *Contemp. Psychoanal.*, 21:284–296.
Marshall, V. (1975), Age and awareness of finitude in developmental gerontology. *Omega*, 6:113–129.
—— (1980), *Last Chapters: A Sociology of Death and Dying*. Monterey, Cal.: Brooks/Cole.
Martin, W. (1973), Activity and disengagement: Life satisfaction of in-movers into a retirement community. *Gerontol.*, 13:224–227.
Medley, M. (1976), Satisfaction with life among persons sixty-five years and older: A causal model. *J. Gerontol.*, 31:448–455.
—— (1980), Life satisfaction across four stages of adult life. *Internat. J. Aging & Hum. Develop.*, 11:193–209.
Montepare, J. M., & Lachman, M. E. (1989), "You're only as old as you feel": Self-perceptions of age, fears of aging and life satisfaction from adolescence to old age. *Psychol. & Aging*, 4:73–78.
Moss, H., & Sussmann, E. (1980), Longitudinal study of personality development. In: *Constancy and Change in Human Development*, ed. O. G. Brim, Jr. & J. Kagan. Cambridge: Harvard University Press, pp. 530–595.
Munnichs, J. (1966), *Old Age and Finitude: A Contribution to Psychogerontology*. New York: Karger.
Mussen, P., Eichorn, D., Honzik, M., Bieber, S., & Meredith, W. (1980), Continuity and change in women's characteristics over four decades. *Internat. J. Behav. Develop.*, 3:333–347.
Myers, W. A. (1986), Transference and countertransference issues in treatments involving older patients and younger therapists. *J. Geriat. Psychiatry*, 19:221–239.
Nemiroff, R. A., & Colarusso, C. A. (1988), Frontiers of adult development in theory and practice. *J. Geriat. Psychiat.*, 21:7–27.
—— —— (1985), The literature on psychotherapy and psychoanalysis in the second half of life. In: *The Race Against Time: Psychotherapy and Psychoanalysis in the Second Half of Life*, ed. R. A. Nemiroff & C. A. Colarusso. New York: Plenum, pp. 25–43.

Neugarten, B. (1969), Continuities and discontinuities of psychological issues into adult life. *Hum. Develop.*, 12:121–130.

────── (1973), Personality change in late life: A developmental perspective. In: *The Psychology of Adult Development and Aging*, ed. C. Eisdorfer & M. P. Lawton. Washington, D.C.: The American Psychological Association, pp. 311–338.

────── (1977), Personality and aging. In: *Handbook of the Psychology of Aging*, ed. J. Birren & K. W. Schaie. New York: Van Nostrand Reinhold, pp. 626–649.

────── (1979), Time, age and the life cycle. *Amer. J. Psychiat.*, 136:887–894.

────── Datan, N. (1974), The middle years. In: *American Handbook of Psychiatry. I: The Foundations of Psychiatry*, ed. S. Arieti. New York: Basic Books, pp. 592–606.

────── Hagestad, G. (1976), Age and the life course. In: *Handbook of Aging and the Social Sciences*, ed. R. Binstock & E. Shanas. New York: Van Nostrand Reinhold, pp. 35–55.

Okun, M. A., Stock, W. A., Haring, M. J., & Witter, R. A. (1984), The social activity/subjective well-being relation: A quantitative analysis. *Res. Aging*, 6:45–65.

Oldham, J. M., & Liebert, R. S. (1989), New psychoanalytic perspectives. In: *The Middle Years: New Psychoanalytic Perspectives*, ed. J. M. Oldham & R. S. Liebert. New Haven: Yale University Press, pp. 1–3.

Olrich, I., & Lehr, U. (1976), Social roles and contracts in old age; Consistency and patterns of change. In: *Patterns of Aging: Findings from the Bonn Longitudinal Study of Aging*, ed. H. Thomae. Bonn, Germany: Karger.

Ortega, S. T., Crutchfield, R. D., & Rushing, W. A. (1983), Race differences in elderly personal well-being. *Res. Aging*, 5:101–118.

Palmore, E., ed. (1974), *Normal Aging*, Vol. 2. Durham, N.C.: Duke University Press, 1974.

────── (1978), When can age, period and cohort be separated? *Soc. Forces*, 57:282–295.

────── (1981), *Social Patterns in Normal Aging: Findings from the Duke Longitudinal Study*. Durham, N.C.: Duke University Press.

────── Kivett, V. (1977), Change in life satisfaction: A longitudinal study of persons aged 46–70. *J. Gerontol.*, 32:311–316.

────── Luikart, C. (1972), Health and social factors related to life satisfaction. *J. Health & Soc. Behav.*, 13:68–80.

Parsons, T. (1952), The superego and the theory of social system. *Psychiat.*, 15:15–26.

────── (1958), Social structure and the development of personality. *Psychiat.*, 21:332–340.

Peskin, H., & Livson, N. (1981), Uses of the past in adult psychological health. In: *Present and Past in Middle Life*, ed. D. Eichorn, J. Clausen, N. Haan, M. Honzik, & P. Mussen. New York: Academic Press, pp. 154–183.

Peters, G. R., & Kaiser, M. A. (1985), The role of friends and neighbors in providing social support. In: *Social Support Networks and the Care of the Elderly*, ed. W. J. Sauer & R. T. Coward. New York: Springer.

Piaget, J. (1975), *The Equilibration of Thought: Equilibration of Cognitive Structures*, trans. M. Cook. New York: International Universities Press, 1977.

Pihlblad, C., & Adams, D. (1972), Widowhood, social participation, and life satisfaction. *Aging & Hum. Develop.*, 3:323–330.

Plath, D. (1980), Contours of consociation: Adult development as discourse. In: *Life-Span Development and Behavior*, Vol. 3, ed. P. Baltes & O. G. Brim, Jr. New York: Academic Press.

Poggi, R. G., & Berland, D. I. (1985), The therapists' reactions to the elderly. *Gerontol.*, 25:508–513.

Pollock, G. H. (1961), Mourning and adaptation. *Internat. J. Psycho-Anal.*, 42:341–361.

—— (1981), Aging or aged: Development or pathology. In: *The Course of Life: Psychoanalytic Contributions Toward Understanding Personality Development, Vol. 3, Adulthood and the Aging Process*, ed. S. Greenspan & G. Pollock. Bethesda, Md.: National Institute of Mental Health, pp. 549–585.

—— (1982), On ageing and psychopathology: Discussion of Dr. Norman A. Cohen's paper "On loneliness and the ageing process." *Internat. J. Psycho-Anal.*, 63:275–281.

—— (1987), The mourning-liberation process: Ideas on the inner life of the older adult. In: *Treating the Elderly with Psychotherapy: The Scope for Change in Later Life*, ed. J. Sadavoy & M. Leszcz. Madison, Ct.: International Universities Press, pp. 3–29.

Quinn, W. H. (1983), Personal and family adjustment in later life. *J. Marr. & Fam.*, 45:57–73.

Rapaport, D., & Gill, M. (1959), The points of view and assumptions of metapsychology. *Internat. J. Psycho-Anal.*, 40:153–162.

Revere, V., & Tobin, S. S. (1980), Myth and reality: The older person's relationship to his past. *Internat. J. Aging & Hum. Develop.*, 12:15–26.

Riegel, K. (1979), *Foundations of Dialectical Psychology*. New York: Academic Press.

Rosow, I. (1967), *Social Integration of the Aged*. New York: Macmillan.

—— (1976), Status and role change through the life-span. In: *Handbook of Aging and the Social Sciences*, ed. R. Binstock & E. Shanas. New York: Van Nostrand Reinhold, pp. 457–482.

Sandler, A. (1982), Psychoanalysis and psychoanalytic psychotherapy of the older patient: A developmental crisis in an aging patient: Comments on development and adaptation. *J. Geriat. Psychiat.*, 15:11–42.

Schaie, K. W. (1981), Psychological changes from midlife to early old age: Implications for the maintenance of mental health. *Amer. J. Orthopsychiatry*, 51:199–218.

Scott, J. P. (1983), Siblings and other kin. In: *Family Relationships in Later Life*, ed. T. H. Brubaker. Beverly Hills: Sage Publications, pp. 47–62.

Sears, P., & Barbee, A. (1977), Career and life satisfactions among Terman's gifted women. In: *The Gifted and the Creative: A Fifty Year Perspective*, ed. J. C. Stanley, W. George, & C. Solano. Baltimore, Md.: Johns Hopkins University Press, pp. 27–65.

Sears, R. R. (1977), Sources of life satisfactions of the Terman gifted men. *Amer. Psychol.*, 32:119–128.

Shapiro, T. (1977), Oedipal distortions in severe character pathologies: Developmental and theoretical considerations. *Psychoanal. Quart.*, 46:559–579.

Sill, J. (1980), Disengagement reconsidered: Awareness of finitude. *Gerontol.*, 20:457–462.

Sinnott, J. (1982), Correlates of sex roles of older adults. *J. Gerontol.*, 37:587–594.

Snow, R., & Crapo, L. (1982), Emotional bondedness, subjective well-being and health in elderly medical patients. *J. Gerontol.*, 37:608–615.

Spitz, R. (1959), *A Genetic Field Theory of Ego Formation*. New York: International Universities Press.

Spreitzer, E., & Snyder, E. (1974), Correlates of life satisfaction among the aged. *J. Gerontol.*, 29:454–458.

Stock, W. A., Okun, M. A., & Benin, M. (1986), Structure of subjective well-being among the elderly. *Psychol. & Aging*, 1:91–102.

Strain, L. A., & Chappell, N. L. (1982), Confidants: Do they make a difference in quality of life? *Res. Aging*, 4:479–502.

Sulloway, F. (1979), *Freud: Biologist of the Mind*. New York: Basic Books.

Thomae, H. (1990), Stress, satisfaction, competence—Findings from the Bonn Longitudinal Study on Aging. In: *Clinical and Scientific Psychogeriatrics, Vol. I, The Holistic Approaches*, ed. M. Bergener & S. I. Finkel. New York: Springer, pp. 117–134.

Tobin, S. S. (1991), *Personhood in Advanced Old Age*. New York: Springer.

Troll, L. E. (1983), Grandparents: The family watchdogs. In: *Family Relationships in Later Life*, ed. T. H. Brubaker. Beverly Hills, Calif.: Sage Publications, pp. 63–74.

——— Miller, S. J., & Atchley, R. C. (1979), *Families in Later Life*. Belmont, Ca.: Wadsworth.

Vaillant, G. (1977), *Adaptation to Life*. Boston: Little, Brown.

Wood, L. A. (1989), Social relationships among the rural elderly: A multimethod approach. In: *Research on Adulthood and Aging: The Human Sciences Approach*, ed. L. E. Thomas. Albany: State University of New York Press, pp. 204–225.

Wood, V., & Robertson, J. (1978), Friendship and kinship interaction: Differential effect on the morale of the elderly. *J. Marr. & Family*, 40:367–375.

8

Intimacy and Isolation Under Apartheid: A Psychosocial Consideration

HELEN Q. KIVNICK, Ph.D.

Background: Psychosocial Theory

Dynamic Balance of Opposites

As elaborated by Erikson, Erikson, and Kivnick (1986) and further explained by Kivnick (in press), life-cycle theory recognizes a series of successive developmental stages through which the individual moves from birth to death. Each stage is dominated by a tension between two opposite psychosocial senses. For example, the stage of young adulthood is characterized by a tension between the sense of intimacy and the opposing sense of isolation. Successful development is most frequently described as the adequate resolution of each dominant tension, in turn, achieved by a victory of the syntonic tendency over the dystonic. More accurate, however, is the notion that at each stage the individual must work through the focal psychosocial theme by means of a dynamic process of balancing the two opposite tendencies.

Research supported by a Fellowship from the W. K. Kellogg Foundation.

This paper was originally written before recent repeals of longstanding apartheid legislation went into effect. Current South African developments notwithstanding (and changes in day-to-day life in no way keep pace with changes on the statute books), today's black young adults in South Africa have lived most of their lives under the circumstances described in this paper.

227

For example, healthy young adult development does not constitute the "achievement" of a capacity for intimacy to the exclusion of isolation. Rather, the task of young adulthood is to consolidate a robust sense of intimacy in balance with an appropriate measure of isolation. No person can realistically hope to be consistently intimate and loving—even with the closest of partners. Comprehensive, mutual intimacy requires intermittent experiences of isolation that continue to clarify and consolidate the self that is involved with an other. That self has personal needs, fears, and capabilities; that self also has boundaries. Together, personal capacities and boundaries interact to determine individual limits to possible closeness. Thus an essential sense of intimacy exists only in the presence of appropriate, also essential isolation, and the love that is consolidated during young adulthood represents both of these tendencies, each in appropriate measure. There is no ultimately "successful" equilibrium between the two opposite tendencies. Rather, their balance is dynamic, and the individual's involvement in maintaining it is perpetual.

Vital Involvement

The process of balancing each focal psychosocial tension depends on the individual's involvement in all life experiences that are appropriate to a given period of life. The actual psychodynamic work of balancing takes place largely on an unconscious level. However, vital involvement with life's relationships, materials, activities, ideas, and institutions provides an essential medium outside of which these psychodynamics cannot meaningfully proceed.

For example, a young adult's interactions with friends, lovers, family, neighbors, peers, and significant figures of all generations are of primary importance to consolidating a robust sense of intimacy in balance with appropriate isolation. Commonly cited sexual love, on the one hand, and introspection about one's true feelings, on the other, are clearly important in meeting the psychosocial challenge of young adulthood. But the essence of balancing a capacity for mutual intimacy with the need to be alone is embedded in the young adult's diverse interpersonal relationships in love, in work, and in play.

Anticipating and Renewing

All too often life-cycle theory is misinterpreted to imply that at any given stage a person is simply struggling with the dominant psychosocial theme, and that current success depends on the success of earlier development. Current success, in turn, is said to determine the success of development yet to come. In fact, the individual is never *only* struggling with a focal tension. At every stage he or she is also engaged in anticipating or previewing those themes which have yet to become focal, and in reviewing or renewing those themes which were focal in earlier life. Reviewing takes place not only for themes which were inadequately balanced when they were focal, but also for those whose age-appropriate balancing was adequate.

Young adulthood's struggle to balance intimacy with isolation is an example. Clearly, early-life closeness as experienced with siblings, age-mates, and relatives (Figure 1, Boxes 6, 14, 22) is different from young adulthood's intimacy in terms of more comprehensive mutuality and more consciously determined commitment (Figure 1, Box 46). Young adult intimacy, in turn, differs from middle age's struggle to balance love, friendship, and time alone with conflicting demands in the arenas of work and community (Figure 1, Box 54). And later life's inevitable losses of lifelong friends and loves turn this same old theme in directions that are still new (Figure 1, Box 62). As the balance between intimacy and isolation is previewed and renewed throughout the life cycle, this general theme expresses itself in specific terms that are constantly changing. At each stage this tension, like all others, is either anticipated or reequilibrated in terms of current life issues. At each stage it is integrated into the developmental theme that is currently focal. As represented by the column of Boxes 6–62 in Figure 1, the theme of intimacy and isolation is in effect a *part* of every stage of the life cycle. In fact, it is almost a misnomer to separate the notion of balancing a dominant psychosocial tension from that of reworking earlier themes or anticipating subsequent ones. The very process of seeking a dynamic balance between two opposites *includes* the process of renewing earlier themes and previewing later ones.

	1	2	3	4	5	6	7	8
Older Adulthood	57	58	59	60	61	62	63	64 Integrity & Despair. WISDOM
Middle Adulthood	49	50	51	52	53	54	55 Generativity & Self-Absorption. CARE	56
Young Adulthood	41	42	43	44	45	46 Intimacy & Isolation. LOVE	47	48
Adolescence	33	34	35	36	37 Identity & Confusion. FIDELITY	38	39	40
School Age	25	26	27	28 Industry & Inferiority. COMPETENCE	29	30	31	32
Play Age	17	18	19 Initiative & Guilt. PURPOSE	20	21	22	23	24
Toddlerhood	9	10 Autonomy & Shame/Doubt. WILL	11	12	13	14	15	16
Infancy	1 Basic Trust & Basic Mistrust. HOPE	2	3	4	5	6	7	8

Adapted from Vital Involvement in Old Age; used with permission from W. W. Norton & Co.

FIGURE 1. Psychosocial stages of life.

Black Psychosocial Development Under Apartheid

According to life-cycle theory we must expect that South Africa's meticulously choreographed laws of apartheid not only influence the *lives* that country's black citizens are able to live. We must also expect that at a basic psychosocial level, apartheid influences the *kinds of people* these black South Africans become—who then live the lives dictated by apartheid. In the body of this discussion, I shall use psychosocial, life-cycle theory to understand development in this unique setting. I shall consider young adulthood's focal psychosocial theme of intimacy and isolation, as it would seem to develop in black South Africans under apartheid. I shall review the essential tension and the involvements through which it is balanced during its time of ascendancy. I shall then explore the ways apartheid's oppressive legislation constrains black South Africans' experiences of intimacy and isolation throughout the life cycle. These constraints may be expected to constitute a detrimental, lifelong influence on this essential psychosocial theme. In addition, I shall consider the importance of elements of traditional African culture, exemplified by singing, in developing unique capacities for intimacy and for isolation. Descriptions of black life under apartheid supplement media accounts with observations made during my three months of fieldwork in South Africa in 1984 and with frequent trans-Atlantic telephone conversations since then.

As noted above, it is the individual's task in young adulthood to balance a capacity for intimacy with a need for some isolation. By exploring these opposing social tendencies in friendships and cooperations with people of both sexes and of all ages, the young adult seeks to engage with others that he or she can love and be loved by, with true mutuality. Throughout life, the individual must reconcile the senses of closeness and compromise with the experiences of being alone and interpersonally unfettered, consolidating, again and again, the capacity for mutual love—in all of its diversity (Erikson, Erikson, and Kivnick, 1986). This exploration clearly invokes nonfocal capacities for trust and mistrust of others, for independence and self-doubt, for initiative and self-restraint, and for hard work

catalyzed by perceived inadequacy. Just as clearly, it involves
ongoing effort to consolidate a sense of self as enhanced or
challenged by others, to provide loving care for others while
securing necessary care for oneself, and to understand oneself
in relationships across time, in perspective.

Paradoxically, both interpersonal intimacy and individual
isolation are strangled in the tightly regulated environment of
apartheid. Overcrowding in the black townships, along with
capricious police behavior toward blacks on the streets, makes
it difficult for black people of any age to find the privacy in
which intimacy can flourish. Sexual intimacy, nonsexual closeness, personal aloneness—all these require a privacy that gov-
ernment-orchestrated black overcrowding makes, physically,
nearly impossible. In standard urban matchbox houses, rooms
may sleep as many people each night as the floors will accommodate mattresses. Resettlement shacks are even worse. Black
mass transportation carries people from the locations where
they are forced to live, to the urban centers where their jobs
are to be found. Primarily buses and trains, these vehicles keep
people packed like sardines for as long as six or eight hours'
commuting time, each day. As described by Joseph Lelyveld
(1985), many of these black commuters are forced, quite literally, to sleep *on top of* one another—on strangers—day after
day, year after year, in order to hold the jobs and live in the
places apartheid has reserved for them. These people are
forced to spend far more time in intimate physical contact with
strangers than they are permitted to enjoy with those they love.

In the absence of adequate community facilities such as
libraries, recreational buildings, cafés, or social halls, township
houses constitute the only places that urban blacks are relatively
free to *be*. As such, these tiny structures force people of all ages,
with widely varying needs and agendas, into perpetual physical
proximity. During the wintertime, for example, evening may
find a family's schoolchildren studying, young children playing
and whining, adolescents listening to battery-powered radios,
youths debating political strategy, one granny sick in bed, another granny cooking dinner, an uncle sleeping in preparation
for working the night shift, Mother and Father returning home
from work with parcels to sort out and bills to pay, and friends

stopping by to socialize—all in three tiny rooms heated by kerosene, lit by candles, and perpetually filled with smoke and noise. And not all township homes have even three rooms.

Where do adults go, to renew the private, mutual intimacy that sustains family life? Where is the room for moments of private closeness between adult and child? Where do children create their own private worlds, apart from grown-ups? Where do elders find the quiet to put life's chaos into perspective? Where do young adults explore the exciting, private promise only they can offer one another?

With houses so crowded, people overflow into township streets in an attempt simply to breathe. But the streets are the province of the *tsotsis*, the legendary township brigands who live fast and high on violent crimes devised against others in the community. The streets are also the province of the police and, with Official States of Emergency and unofficial states of unrest, the military. Far from offering protection against crime, these agents of governmental authority represent alternative forms of danger. Police have long patrolled the townships, conducting late-night pass raids and vandalizing property, ostensibly in search of unauthorized residents and illegal home brew. Contemporary raids add journalists, trade unionists, community activists, and black leaders of any sort to the list of official quarry. Black people are detained at will, homes broken into, sleep shattered, and family privacy violated as one member is dragged, literally, from its bosom.

With the 1986 State of Emergency, the government imposed curfews in various areas, making it illegal for people to be on the streets at all except insofar as they are going to or from work (Iams, 1986)—and people who were accosted under such restrictions had to prove their legitimacy to authorities who were not predisposed to be convinced. In addition, military and police patrols were alleged, under the State of Emergency, to have taken to firing teargas, buckshot, and rubber bullets at random or, worse, at will. Even before formal legislation of immunity for these personnel, successful legal prosecution was extremely rare. Finally, recent escalation of political tension has promoted suspicious, often violent polarization of the black community, into those people seen as loyal to the struggle for liberation and those seen as selling out to the government or to its black agents. It is in this environment of physical density, ubiquitous danger, and emotional urgency that South Africa's urban black people must struggle for both intimacy and isolation.

Apartheid conspires against robust intimacy and healthy isolation outside the urban townships, as well. Migrant workers, for example, must live away from their rural wives and families for eleven months of each year. For perhaps thirty years of working life, these predominantly male workers are housed in single-sex hostels that, depending on quality, resemble prisons, army barracks, or dormitories. Sixteen men may share a single unventilated room in which individual kerosene appliances support heating, cooking, and lighting, and in which little or no provision is made for the locked or protected storage of personal belongings. Meaningful intimacy and ongoing companionship with wife and children are all but impossible. A man may impregnate his wife each Christmas and return home, annually, to view the progeny who can never be more than symbols to him. From the filthy crush of work and hostel, these men escape to the relative privacy and comfort of township mistresses whose children they father, and whose intimacy they must leave abruptly when work contracts are peremptorily terminated.

Rural women find themselves deposited amidst their husband's families and then, if their men are lucky enough to find employment, abandoned for the lion's share of every year. Daily closeness and mutual cooperation are developed with those who remain in the rural villages—the old, the sick, the very young, and the other lonely wives. For South Africa's migrants and those whose love they share, apartheid spins and unravels the webs of family and friendship, unconcerned for the human beings whose lives are ensnared.

Domestic workers, mostly women, are often housed in white areas, in accommodations provided by their white employers. But the law stipulates both that after infancy their children must live in black areas, and also that their husbands may not live with them or, in some cases, even visit them in their "white" homes. For these women, ongoing, daily closeness may develop with their counterparts in neighboring houses. And daily contact with white employers often nourishes relationships that the white madams (the women who employ black domestic workers) describe as intimate, and black maids view as guarded and superficial. With husbands, children, and other relatives these domestic workers have little opportunity for the regular contact and sharing of experience that are taken for granted around the world as a basis for family intimacy and mutuality. In its various manifestations, apartheid requires that black people demonstrate love for one another by abandonment. With few lucky exceptions, blacks who choose to love and live together do so at the risk of breaking the law and endangering their survival, both economic and physical.

In addition to problems of contact, friendship and closeness in South Africa must surmount the very real problem of trust. The government pays informers to report on the activities of people it regards as dangerous. In addition, the government offers financial incentives to black people at various levels, for cooperating with government-sponsored economic and administration schemes in the black community. Bantustan officials, for example, are viewed throughout the country as having sold out to Pretoria's interests. Realistic black economic opportunity is all but nonexistent in South Africa, and in exchange for a license to operate one of the few shops in a crowded township, a man may well be persuaded to agree to support the government's self-serving proposals in the township Community Administrative Council. Black people are starving in South Africa, and in exchange for feeding her children for another week a woman may well find herself agreeing to inform on someone who is, to her, nothing more than a stranger. People know that such treachery is commonplace, and they recognize, at some level, that they may someday find themselves betrayed by the friend with whom they have worshipped every Sunday for years. Still, they must live with one another and share what they can, simply in order to survive from day to day.

Throughout all of this twisted intimacy and violated self-reliance run the themes of outside control and constraint. The lives and relationships of black South Africans are controlled and constrained, from minute detail to overall contour, by

apartheid legislation. Where a capacity for mutual love and
cooperation is said to develop between partners who choose
intimacy with one another in balance with isolation alone, apartheid denies black people the opportunity for choice. Perpetual
contact with others is forced by environmental crowding at
work, at school, at home, and at play, but the individual has
little choice about the specific others with whom contact is
forced. Young people may try to love one another, but the laws
of apartheid limit the kinds of intimacy they can share, the
kinds of cooperation they can demonstrate, the kinds of mutuality they can count on, and the kinds of plans they can realistically expect to fulfill. Marriage partners may commit themselves
to a lifetime of love and caring, but the laws governing daily
life seriously constrain the expression of marital affection and
encourage the abrogation of mutual responsibilities. This dissolution of intimate family ties in the black community is consistent with a freely shared white view of blacks, that, "They don't
have family ties as we have. For us family is everything. But
they're not like that. One time it's one person, and one time
another, and that's just the way they are" (Klopper, 1984 personal communication).

However, as they have around other psychosocial themes,
black South Africans have managed to develop new forms of
intimacy and love, while sustaining the psychosocial injuries
inflicted by apartheid. The marriage between Winnie and Nel-
son Mandela illustrates both apartheid's destructiveness toward
intimacy, and the alternative kinds of intimate strength that
can be forged under apartheid's relentless hammering. Due to
legislation that makes de facto criminals of effective opposition
leaders, these two people were physically apart and often out
of contact, as well, for most of their married life. Nonetheless,
their love survived for roughly three decades, and their marriage has become a symbol of the endurance and tenacity of
the black people's will to be free, decent, and self-determined.

In her autobiography Winnie Mandela observes, "I had so
little time to love him, and that love has survived all these years
of separation" (1985, p. 72). I suggest that rather than simply
"surviving," as she says, their love deepened and intensified
throughout much of their time apart, in ways that were directly

related to apartheid. Over their long, cruelly manipulated separation, each of these people developed meaningful closeness and mutuality with available friends and comrades, while struggling to maintain the unique, paramount mutuality of their support and caring for one another. For many years they were able to use the apartheid that kept them apart as a catalyst for the spirit and commitment that brought them ever closer together. Ultimately, as we now know, these apartheid-instigated commitments to other people and to conflicting courses of action irreparably broke down their intimacy. The Mandelas are extraordinary people, and their circumstances are unusual, even by South African standards. That their love survived as much of their ordeal as it did is testament to their individual strength, and to the creative resilience of their intimacy. Their relationship exemplifies ways that apartheid's duress can spark alternative forms of love and mutuality, even as it destroys more conventional forms of intimacy. It also highlights the brutal strains to which apartheid subjects human connections that are, under any circumstances, fragile and difficult to maintain.

Given the importance of the social group in traditional African life, we should not be surprised at the intensity of the bonds of group support and cooperation that have flourished under apartheid's oppression. Every indigenous South African people has a saying that translates, roughly, "A person is most fully human when interacting with others." This ethos pervades rural traditional life, and, at least partially in response to over a century of foreclosed Westernized urban aspirations, it pervades more recent, urban life, as well. Traditional ceremonies abound. Around life themes as diverse as religion, harvest, and puberty, they involve participants in age- and sex-segregated activities of which musical performance is one of the most important. And musical performance is grounded in a lively style of part-singing that relies on every voice, individually, to make the whole song larger and more powerful than a simple aggregation of singers.

In black South Africa singing is such an integral part of everyday life that its role in psychosocial development must be taken seriously. For these people, singing is a lifelong activity, a part of the social environment, an expression of cultural tradition. As such, it seems to serve as a source of psychosocial strength throughout the life cycle. At each stage and for each theme, singing would seem to promote essential health and resilience in the face of apartheid's overwhelming pressure toward psychosocial ruin.

Singing is part of cohort-based ceremony and celebration. Singing is part of daily family life, casual socialization, and work activity. Although city life is far removed from rural, agrarian-based traditions, group singing has developed as integral to urban life, expressing the ever-shifting relationships among blacks as whites control their land and their lives. Singing pervades activity in the black townships and reminds residents, with every note, of the diverse group solidarities that are a cornerstone of contemporary urban survival. In the absence of liberty and self-determination, traditional group bonds and feelings of unity take on new importance. Within church groups, extended families, neighborhood self-help groups, school-based cohorts, work-related unions, ideology- or issue-based community organizations, there is a spirit of mutuality and support expressed, powerfully, directly, and immediately, in the singing without which group gatherings simply do not take place.

Although individual relationships may be torn apart by government legislation, underlying feelings of group closeness and responsibility may be strengthened in their stead. For children who move from perpetual physical contact with mother's body into spaces that are, quite literally, filled with the sounds, movements, and bodies of other people, the developing sense of self is quite likely to include the presence of others, and the sound of their singing. For these children, mutuality and cooperation are integral to daily life and survival. As they grow through life, the ways they balance the psychosocial capacities for being close and being alone must take such enforced togetherness into account.

Migrant workers are torn from their families and packed into compounds. Under conditions of impersonal crowding and rigid behavioral control, they organize to protect one another from treachery at the hands of the authorities' intrusive

informers, guards, and "bossmen." These men organize themselves into home-based religious groups and funeral societies.
Most familiar to contemporary Westerners, these men also organize themselves into singing groups that compete, every Sat-
urday night, in the *mbube* or *isicathamiya* musical genre popular-
ized by Ladysmith Black Mambazo. This performance style is
based on a close harmony and mutual responsiveness of voice
and body that reflect high levels of sensitivity and cooperation.
Separated from their families and infantalized by the authorities, these men effectively rely on one another for sustenance
of the spirit.

In rural villages women live without their men, but they
live together with one another. Together they raise their children, working among themselves to provide at least the essentials of food, clothing, shelter, and education. Like their husbands in urban compounds, women in rural villages sing
together. Their words are of historical glory now past, and of
daily struggles to be endured. But the sound is the sound of
solidarity and support among women who know they need one
another to survive.

Women's self-help organizations characterize black urban
life, as well. For decades township women have sponsored rotat-
ing parties, concerts, and home-brew sales to generate the income they need to buy food, and to pay rent and school fees
as authorities capriciously manipulate male employment and
residence eligibility. In the urban churches, Mothers' Unions
or Mothers' Guilds organize local women into active, effective
support groups. And these groups sing out in lively defiance
of apartheid's efforts to destroy the bonds that have always
been so much a part of who they are.

South Africa's blacks may have little opportunity for the
ongoing, dependable, private, sexualized mutuality that is said
to characterize intimacy in Western industrialized society. They
have far more experience than the industrialized West with
enduring mutuality in groups. Private intimacy between two
lovers or friends may be difficult to come by, but group intimacy
is part of everyday black life. Group intimacy is encouraged in
black tradition; it is enforced by apartheid regulation. So when
township children see one another tear gassed on the street,

taken away by the military, or, as in the 1976 Soweto uprising, shot dead while peacefully marching in their own community, they must experience these injuries—even to those who may be strangers—as *personal.* The authorities do not shoot at blacks as individuals. By and large, they shoot at anonymous, interchangeable black bodies. In response to indiscriminate violence from outside, these people experience themselves as inseparable, as *part of* one another, from the inside. This unique sense of intimacy endures, from earliest childhood until oldest age. The much-repeated trade union slogan "An injury to one is an injury to all" is rooted at least as deeply in African tradition as in Western politics.

Feelings of love and support permeate community activities, religious services, and political gatherings. And singing is part of these gatherings that are so large and, at the same time, so intimate. Increasingly important as the government continues to abet repression and directed violence, political gatherings focus on true liberation. With that commitment in common, people promise to work and die for one another and for their future. Promises for the future are difficult to make in pairs; promises of liberation are dangerous to voice in individual speeches. But these promises underlie the freedom songs that ring from church halls, to sports arenas, to the township graveyards of martyrs.

Black South Africans do not sing together by repeating the same melodic line, five hundredfold, in a crowded hall. Their call-and-response musical style, and their intricate harmonies and rhythms demonstrate active cooperation and mutuality. When an American baseball audience sings our national anthem, we sing, each voice weak and alone, in bland unison. When black South Africans sing "Nkosi Sikelel'i Afrika" they are actively engaging one another, each voice interacting with all the others. No song sounds the same twice, as voices sing new variations to reflect subtle changes in the interpersonal feelings and relationships of the moment. For black South Africans, singing together *en masse* represents creating something together, all together, and using that mass-intimate creation as a source of the strength they know they will all need to survive.

Conclusion

The laws of apartheid exert a unique, lifelong developmental destructiveness on the black people of South Africa. With respect to intimacy and isolation, apartheid interferes with the involvements that permit the robust psychosocial balancing of this theme at every stage throughout the life cycle. In the face of apartheid's destructiveness, however, it seems that South Africa's black people rely on elements of traditional culture as compensatory or counterbalancing sources of strength. That is, traditional culture—and singing is an important part of this culture—would seem to serve as an ongoing source of psychosocial strength throughout the life cycle, contributing to essential health and resilience in the face of overall pressure toward psychosocial destruction. Intimacy in balance with isolation, for blacks under South African apartheid, certainly develops differently from the way this theme emerges for whites in the West, but it *does* develop. Integral to black South Africans' cultural history, singing exemplifies the inspiring use of indigenous culture to defend psychologically against political outrages, in the service of survival with integrity.

References

Erikson, E. H., Erikson, J. M., & Kivnick, H. Q. (1986), *Vital Involvement in Old Age*. New York: Norton.

Iams, J. (1986), Emergency rule bans playing in the streets. UPI newswire, June 26.

Kivnick, H. Q. (in press), Through the life cycle: Psychosocial thoughts on old age. In: *The Course of Life*, ed. G. H. Pollock & S. I. Greenspan. Madison, Conn.: International Universities Press.

Lelyveld, J. (1985), *Move Your Shadow*. New York: Times Books.

Mandela, W. (1985), *Part of My Soul*. Harmondsworth, U.K.: Penguin Books.

9

Towards an Inclusive Adult Developmental Theory: Epigenesis Reconsidered

REBECCA SHAHMOON SHANOK, M.S.W., Ph.D.

As intellectual and historical heir to Freud and to Jung, Erik Erikson has had unparalleled influence on current understandings of adulthood. Specifically, Erikson expanded the psychoanalytic conceptualization of children's libidinal phase development to include maturational, ego and social psychological components into what he termed epigenetic stages. Further, Erikson defined and labeled epigenetic stages encompassing the entire life course from birth to death (Erikson, 1950, pp. 247–269). It must be emphasized, however, that in his original epigenetic scheme the descriptions of adulthood are sketchy compared with the rich descriptions of childhood; Erikson's model was derived primarily from the study of children.

The foundation of Erikson's scheme is epigenetic. This model was implemented to describe psychological development in analogy to embryonal development whereby the differentiation of each part progresses from the simpler to the more complex, each part having its time of ascendance, while all parts grow simultaneously (Katchadourian, 1980, p. 51); proper rate and proper sequence are the critical guiding and limiting factors (Erikson, 1950). The emphasis on rate and especially on

The author acknowledges with deep appreciation the comments and suggestions made by John A. Meacham, Ph.D. on an earlier draft and the assistance of librarian Susan Weiland.

This paper is based, in part, on my doctoral dissertation in clinical psychology completed at Teachers College, Columbia University in May, 1987.

sequencing led to a model that is primarily hierarchical. In describing his chart of the "Eight Ages of Man," Erikson wrote, "(1) . . . each critical item of psychosocial strength discussed here is systematically related to all others, and . . . *they all depend on the proper development in the proper sequence of each item*; and (2) . . . each item exists in some form before its critical time normally arrives" (p. 271; emphasis added).

The sequential aspect of Erikson's epigenetic stage model lies at the heart of all prominent psychiatric–psychoanalytic investigations of adult development (Gould, 1972; Levinson, 1977; Vaillant, 1977; Levinson, Darrow, Klein, Levinson, and McKee, 1978), in the sense that each of them assumes an unfolding in adulthood parallel to that of childhood. Yet a close reading of Erikson's work reveals that a greater complexity, which is not fully explained, exists. For one thing, Erikson (1968, pp. 261–294) wrote a special chapter about women which reveals his implicit recognition that the "Eight Ages of Man" does not adequately account for adult female development. Several writers (Douvan and Adelson, 1966; Josselson, 1973; Stewart, 1976; Boynton, 1980; Gilligan, 1979, 1982; Fischer, 1980; Morgan and Farber, 1982) have raised questions about *the sequence* of Erikson's adult stages of identity, intimacy, generativity, and ego integrity as they apply to women. If these questions are valid, and Erikson's special chapter contributes to the sense that they are, then they may point to a problem in the sequencing aspect of epigenesis as it relates to *all* adulthood, male and female.

Social psychology and sociology researchers have also raised questions about the epigenetic model. They believe that change in adulthood occurs in response to particular personal or environmental events (Kohn and Schooler, 1978; Fiske, 1980; Pearlin, 1980). Bernice Neugarten has also written about the "oversimplification" of stage theories of adult life (1979, p. 887); her emphasis is on people's sense of timing. "Whether the life cycle is perceived as consisting of 3, 6, or 10 periods, individuals develop a concept of the 'normal expectable life cycle', a set of anticipations that certain life events will occur at certain times and a mental clock telling them . . . whether they are on time or off time . . . being on time or off time is a compelling basis for self-assessment" (1979, p. 888).

Developmental psychologists debate the usefulness of the biologically based concept of epigenesis being applied to questions of psychological unfolding (Kitchener, 1978, 1980; Lerner, 1980). If taken from biology without modification, epigenesis suggests that nature variables alone have explanatory power. Lerner has proposed the term *probalatistic* epigenesis to encompass "strong interactive notions . . . [which] emphasize the causal role of both nature and nurture variables" (p. 69; emphasis added). Clearly, Erikson, with his emphasis on "society's" influence, had such a transactional model (Sameroff, 1975) in mind when he drew on the epigenetic concept.

In Erikson's scheme, once the stage of identity has been reached toward the end of adolescence, there are three remaining stages: intimacy, generativity, and ego integrity. It need hardly be argued that the identity issues classically pertaining to adolescence are, in contemporary middle-class society at least, pushing their way past the teens and way into the twenties (cf. Goleman, 1980). Unemployment, the extension of college to graduate school, availability of contraception, and increased life expectancies account for this shift since Erikson first described identity. But the fact that identity issues now push on later than Erikson described merely suggests that identity should be studied not only as a transition from adolescence but as an adult stage proper; it does not in itself incriminate the sequential element as a straw man in the effort to understand adulthood.

The other, and perhaps most critical issue embedded in Erikson's work, which raises questions about the sequential aspect of epigenesis as it is applied to adulthood, rests deep in his descriptions of the adult stages themselves. Consider, for example, his effort to define ego integrity:

> *Lacking a clear definition,* I shall point to a few constituents of this state of mind. It is the ego's accrued assurance of its proclivity for order and meaning. . . . It is the *acceptance of one's one and only life cycle* as something that had to be and that, by necessity, permitted of no substitutions: it thus means *a new, a different love* of one's parents [Erikson, 1950, p. 268; emphases added].

I believe that Erikson lacked a clear definition because, in trying to define ego integrity, he was, in fact, defining a renewed sense of identity *and* a broadened capacity for intimacy. This holds true for both of the last two "stages" of his schema. Indeed, *both generativity and ego integrity include reintegration of identity and intimacy issues, and both identity and intimacy development thus occur concurrently.* The use of the term *reintegration* should be read to imply psychic revival of aspects of previous stage development in relation to the negotiation of current adaptation.

A look at the adult developmental literature coming from both the psychiatric and the social psychological schools confirms this perspective: Neugarten's (1968) middle-agers, and Gould's (1972), Levinson's (1977; Levinson et al., 1978), and Vaillant's (1977) men are all struggling with issues of identity and intimacy, as those issues relate to shifting internal and external factors. And Sullivan's interpersonal theory of psychiatry is an approach to understanding psychic development through the lens of the individual's need for others (1953).

Identity implies a sense of confidence in continuity of the self matched by consistency of one's meaning to others (Erikson, 1950, p. 261). Intimacy is the ability to face the fear of ego loss in situations of close, sexual affiliation and the capacity to commit to and abide by concrete affiliations (Erikson, 1950, p. 263). Identity and intimacy, together, combine dialectically to form the essence of human experience, inner and the relationship to outer, the discrete self in relation to community.

The capacities for identity and intimacy are what all previous stages have been leading toward and what all later stages are continuing to evolve, modify, and refine. Everything that comes afterwards is a variation on these twin themes. The twins compete and are complementary; there is an inherent tension between them but it is inconceivable to live one without the other.

Support for this integrated view is embedded in object relations theory. For example, Kernberg closely followed Erikson's conceptualization in his elaboration of ego identity. Implicit in his formulation of identity are concurrent identity–intimacy processes, as well as the aspect of ongoing reintegration. Ego identity is seen as the overall organization of identifications and introjections, composed of (1) an organization of self representations, with an accompanying "sense of continuity of the self"; and (2) an organization of object representations with an accompanying "sense of consistency in *one's interpersonal interactions*" (Kernberg, 1966, p. 242; emphasis added).

Coupe (1982) noted that "Kernberg's addition of the organization of *object* representation seems to have implications for intimacy; as one's ego identity is formed it may be expressed not only in occupation and ideology [as Erikson (1950) has stated and Marcia (1966) has operationalized], but *also in intimate relationships*" (emphasis added) (see also Orlofsky, Marcia, and Lesser [1973]). Indeed, by definition, identity includes the intrapsychic outcomes of object relations. And just as identity formation is rooted in evolving object relationships, so, too, does intimacy flower with lifelong roots in introjections and identifications, the processes which are subordinate, and contribute, to identity. Individuation and the capacity for intimacy are achieved simultaneously.

Kernberg (1966) considers "ego identity . . . the highest level organization of the world of object relations in the broadest sense, and also of the self" (p. 243). This view corresponds with the perspective advanced above that identity and intimacy are together the apex of the epigenetic stage model, a model which works relatively well for childhood; all succeeding development in adulthood includes modifications and refinements of them. For readers familiar with the psychoanalytic concept of object constancy (Mahler, Pine, and Bergman, 1975), "that state of object relations in which the child has the capability to retain the memory of and emotional tie to parents, his primary love objects, and to feel their nurturing, guiding presence even when they are a source of frustration or disappointment or when they are absent" (Solnit, 1982, p. 202), the intertwining of identity and intimacy suggested here seems familiar. Object constancy depends on internalization of soothing experiences with one's caregiver early in life, becomes the bedrock of an expanding ego (identity-related), and enables confidence in relationships (intimacy-related).

It is precisely this reciprocity between identity and intimacy which the family literature has highlighted (Rhodes, 1977; Carter and McGoldrick, 1980; Mallouk, 1982; Combrinck-Graham,

1985); individuation takes place in the context of the family, or to put it in these terms, in the context of intimate relations. Coincidentally, intimate family relations are affected by each developing individual.

This alteration away from the sequential emphasis of epigenesis in adulthood is crucial to apprehending its complexity. When physical maturation no longer leads as it did in childhood, the predominance of unfolding growth recedes from its position as a central sequential organizer. By making this modification in the theory, discussion about interstage relationships (i.e., about transitions between one crisis and the next) (Meacham and Santilli, 1982, pp. 1461, 1465) may be recast with a richer, more accurately inclusive base. Indeed, in adulthood, identity–intimacy modifications and refinements succeed to the central organizing function. Looking at these areas together, rather than one after the other, permits elaboration of the variegated fabric of real lives over time (and not coincidentally, pulls together the worlds of psychoanalytic and family clinical practice, developmental psychology, and object relations theory).

The critical principle here is that, while there are substantial enough continuities that they previously masked the area, the character of development during childhood and adolescence is different from that in adulthood. In debating the usefulness of the epigenetic model for developmental psychology, Kitchener anticipated this idea: "How legitimate is it to use a model originally developed in the context of embryology and imbued with genetic variables and then extended to cover the entire life span, *an extension in which biological variables become increasingly less important*" (1980, p. 75; emphasis added)? In fact, the point at which biological variables cease to exert an organizing developmental function can be pinpointed to the late teens, when biologically determined physical growth stops. It is at this juncture that the sequential emphasis in Erikson's model yields confusions.

Listening to adults describe their lives crystallizes the concurrence of identity–intimacy issues. Summing up her sense of the shifts she had made in psychotherapy, a 33-year-old divorcee and mother said:

I always felt I needed a man and would impulsively leap into relationships. But I didn't know who I was. You can only find (that) out by struggling within yourself. I had always questioned my judgment, but (for the first time) I was successful in choosing the right person for myself in you. . . . So I felt less alone in my struggle and you were a good model, always showing me that I didn't have to be so quick to judge and so black and white. . . . In the past, with Peter (her 8-year-old son), I became either so wrapped up in his demands and then resented it, OR I would have barked, 'Don't bother me!' Now, I can deal with him and not let the situation take me over; I have more flexibility in human relationships . . . I can handle ups and downs. I feel like a strong woman. I didn't plan it this way, but (being single) is a precious freedom and since I'm here I want to make the most of it. . . . I always resented having to make choices, but today I'm resigned; each (choice) has its price but each is a challenge I can choose. . . . It's not totally wonderful; I'm lonely. But I think that the way I am (now) will let me be closer to someone really.

It is evident that this patient feels that her sense of self has been deeply affected through her relationship with her therapist. Equally important in exemplifying the concurrence of identity and intimacy is the way that this woman moves back and forth between describing her sense of self and her relationships; indeed, she is not truly *shifting* between identity and intimacy descriptions because, in fact, the two are inextricably related, two perspectives of the same whole.

Barring debilitating accident or serious illness, the years from young adulthood through mid or even late adulthood are relatively free of either the maturationally linked growth impetus of childhood and adolescence or the physical decline of later years. Without biologically based maturation or decline to lead, the years from young adulthood through the end of mid-adulthood are freer of an age-related timetable, relative to childhood, adolescence, and late life. Instead, greater age and sequence variability among healthy young, mid and late life adults regarding the prominence and intersection of the issues of identity and intimacy, and secondarily of generativity and integrity, would be expected given variations in the occurrence of various events, situations, and relationships in a given individual's life (Shanok, 1981, 1987).

On the other hand, the range of variation is limited by the individual's inner (and the actual) clock, and by the fact that the same issues must be approached by everyone; society shares the schedule of expectations (Neugarten, 1979; Shanok, 1981). Furthermore, "the changes that take place in one's parents and in one's children would suggest that time-mediated object changes are of the utmost importance during the adult years and the necessity for change is as imperative as in the period before age 21" (Gould, 1972, p. 522). But for adults, these time-mediated shifts in the areas of identity and intimacy take a central, ascendant position relative to physical maturation as an organizer of change in children.

It is important to note that the concepts of concurrent and reintegrating adult development around the twin issues of identity and intimacy do not supplant the epigenetic nature of Erikson's model in childhood nor even fully so in adulthood. Rather, the concurrence and reintegration concepts as applied to adulthood magnify a previously underemphasized aspect of the principle itself: that salient issues may exist and develop together. The stage issues of identity and intimacy emerge to prominence, recede, and then reemerge in new contexts, always informing and affecting each other (Erikson, 1968). In an often brilliant analysis, Franz and White (1985) reworked each stage of Erikson's theory from the perspective of its relational components, suggesting that throughout the model autonomous (male) elements have been emphasized at the expense of relational (female) constituents.

There is ample evidence that Erikson himself agrees, at least with the idea that identity is remolded throughout adulthood. For example, "the return of some forms of identity crisis [occurs] in the later stages of the life cycle" (Erikson, 1968, p. 135). And also, "identity *formation* [as distinct from identity crisis] neither begins nor ends with adolescence: it is a lifelong development largely unconscious to the individual and to his society" (Erikson, 1980, p. 122). Erikson never meant to establish a simple linear framework. But because the contrast between child and adult development was not noted, thinkers in the Erikson tradition (Gould, 1972; Orlovsky et al., 1973; Levinson, 1977; Vaillant, 1977) have produced linear models. In fact, transformations in adulthood are characterized less by a stage-to-stage unfolding, and more by the interpenetration between identity, intimacy, and the inner and outer worlds.

Thus, the broad outline of Erikson's model is retained, with this essential modification: concurrent reintegration of identity and intimacy concerns are twin themes *throughout* adulthood. With this perspective, generativity comes into sharp focus as a broadening of one's sense of self and one's capacity for intimacy, to include creativity, production, and care within one's community. Ego integrity is a life review process (Butler, 1975, pp. 1–21) dealing with identity and intimacy issues, once again. In its achievement, ego integrity is a sense *of integration*, both of the self and with the human community and its continuity through generations past and future. But in what contexts do the twin stage issues of identity and intimacy evolve, once attained?

The stage issues of identity and intimacy unfold in relation to normal life challenges, turning points around which adaptation is organized (Erikson, 1950; Bibring, 1959; Bibring, Dwyer, Huntington, and Valenstein, 1961). In adulthood, these normal life challenges almost always evoke the past on a continuum from conscious review to unconscious regression. Experientially, the individual goes backward in time even while moving forward in actuality. For example, during pregnancy and early parenting, women usually experience evocation of thoughts, fantasies, memories, and feeling states from their own childhoods. In most women this process eventually enhances the capacity for empathy both with their offspring as well as with their own mothers. Not only do normal life challenges evoke the past, but they consist of events and processes which are temporally intrinsic on a continuum to those which are temporally extrinsic to the individual. (Consider, for example, the temporal dimensions of menstruation, a planned pregnancy, or a rape in terms of the individual's experience.) These intersecting time-related continua, generated as they are both by factors within and outside the individual, account for the theoretical elusiveness of adult development. From this vantage point, it is possible to glimpse the view that the stage perspective and the timing perspective are both aspects of the same developmental terrain.

Recognizing these time-related variables facilitates classification of normal life challenges into the following categories. "Marker events" (such as the death of a parent) signify those events that challenge and change an individual's life situation to which adaptation must occur. The individual's current developmental period does not influence the timing of this event, but it does shape both the type of adaptation and the influence that adaptation has on the individual's subsequent life. Conversely, the timing and character of the event have influence over the outcome of the individual's adaptation in relation to the particular developmental period (Levinson, Darrow, Klein, Levinson, and McKee, 1978, pp. 54–56). A "marker process" (such as parenthood) distinguishes those relationships and situations which have ongoing influence upon the individual over months or years (Shanok, 1981, 1987). Marker events and marker processes may occur in concert with an individual's choices and unfolding life (e.g., job selection, marriage), or they may impinge upon that individual's choices (e.g., rape, war), that is, they may be normative or catastrophic, occurring in sequence or out of sequence with the expected. The events or situations defined as either "marker event" or "marker process" may differ from individual to individual, depending on the duration of the impactful event. Which situations attain marker status for a particular individual will, of course, depend on context: unemployment will affect a family breadwinner, a wealthy playboy, or a contented homemaker quite differently.

Finally, the "inner clock" also acts as a normal life challenge, calling as it does for periodic appraisal. The inner clock (Gould, 1972; Jaques, 1965, 1981; Neugarten, 1968, 1979; Shanok, 1981) is defined as transitions in the self view imposed by the passage of time linked to felt accomplishments relative to the image of length of time left to live. What is felt to be accomplished is connected both to goals and to the ego ideal. Similarly, one's conscious or unconscious image of time left to live is related to one's state of health, exposure to serious illness, and to deaths of contemporaries, to one's conception of ancestors' health, and their ages at and causes of death (especially the same-sex parent), and to self and object representations.

In his paper on "Self and Object Constancy," Albert Solnit recognized the relationship between identity and object constancy, and he anticipated the categories of normal life challenges just described: "there is mounting evidence that object constancy continues to unfold and change throughout the life cycle, especially under the marked influence of sudden object loss, traumatic experiences, and aging" (1982, p. 213). He adds, "Object constancy is a developmental capacity that provides the child with a sense of himself and his parents and enables him to become increasingly independent in forming new personal relationships, which in turn increasingly enable him significantly to shape his own social environment" (p. 217). Indeed, with a developmental perspective as guide, we can see that identity and intimacy in adulthood are both aspects of the process and structure which object constancy represents.

Greenberg and Mitchell (1983) presented an inclusive and cogent overview of the major psychoanalytic theorists, delineating each of their perspectives in terms of what the authors call the drive/structure or relational/structure models. They wrote:

> The human condition embraces a fundamental paradox . . . man is an essentially individual animal; man is an essentially social animal . . . the drive/structure model [originated by Freud] and the relational/structure model [originated by Sullivan, Fromm, Horney, Thompson, and Fromm-Reichmann] embody these two major traditions within Western philosophy. . . . Psychoanalytic theorists, like political philosophers, have built models on one or another side of this paradox [pp. 400–403].

One model emphasizes separation, autonomy, and objectivity, the other integration, connection, and subjectivity. In feminist terms, one model derives from male experience, the other from female experience. Using the terms employed here, the fundament of one is identity and of the other is intimacy. In describing and clarifying the drive/structure and relational/structure models the authors put in relief a fundamental controversy intrinsic to the humanities (Bakan, 1966) and particularly to psychology and psychoanalysis.

Greenberg and Mitchell (1983) take the position that each model "rests on different visions . . . each is a complete account,

[and] *each makes absolute claims"* (p. 403; emphasis added). Attempts to mix models result in internal inconsistencies at best. Neither model is "right" or "wrong." Rather, according to Greenberg and Mitchell,

> each is complex, elegant, and resilient enough to account for all phenomena. The drive model establishes individual pleasure seeking and drive discharges as the bedrock of human existence . . . the relational model establishes relational configurations as the bedrock [p. 404].

Greenberg and Mitchell insist on separate models, as have numerous other investigations, both wittingly and completely (as above) and unwittingly and incompletely (as Franz and White [1985] and Shanok [1981, 1987] argue that Erikson did). Yet the value of separating the models may be seen as analogous to the value placed on objectivity and autonomy, which until recently drove straight through Western thought and culture. Contrary to their view, the perspective of this effort and of others (Fairbairn, 1941; Fromm, 1941; Kohut, 1977; Franz and White, 1985; Bach, 1987) consolidates the autonomous and the relational perspectives. To do otherwise entails a fallacious choice from the vantage point established here, a choice analogous to the folly of coming down fully on one or the other side of the old nature–nurture controversy (of which this one is a distant variant). Even while there may be internal inconsistencies and clarifications left to be made, state of the art considerations nevertheless require that development be understood in context.

Family therapists (Carter and McGoldrick, 1980; Mallouk, 1982; Combrinck-Graham, 1985) and infant researchers and practitioners (Sameroff, 1975; Stern, 1977; Greenspan, 1981; Provence, 1983; Field and Fox, 1985) are demonstrating that a fundamental unit of study is the person-in-relationship. Where paradigms are concerned, one or the other model may be self-sufficient. But in terms of the complexity of human lifetimes, each has something essential to contribute. As Greenberg and Mitchell themselves noted, "the human condition embraces a fundamental paradox" (1983, p. 400).

Identity and intimacy together are the twin adult achievements toward which all of child development leads. All succeeding development includes modifications and refinements of them. This view accepts context, relationship, and interrelationships (both actual and intrapsychic) as necessary to the understanding of adulthood and, indeed, insists that both paradigms are essential. Inherent in the "fundamental paradox" is lifelong tension as well as lifelong opportunity.

Erikson's formulation of development took Freud's drive/structure model and placed it in its social context. In terms of adults, however, he remained tied to the autonomous constituents of the drive/structure perspective; he was unable to fully integrate the relational into his schema, which he left with women in a separate chapter (1968, pp. 261–294). The present effort retains Erikson's basic conception of identity but modifies his work to allow the relational its full measure.

The essential pivot around which the two perspectives (or models, according to Greenberg and Mitchell) come together is how identity—the sense of self—gets formed, that is, in relationship through a myriad of interactions between the infant and then growing child with caregivers. Embedded in this process are attachment (Bowlby, 1969) and identification. Once the centrality of attachment and internalization in developmental process are noted, as increasing numbers of even drive/structure adherents have delineated (Hartmann, 1939; Jacobson, 1964, 1967; Kernberg, 1966; 1976; Mahler, Pine, and Bergman, 1975; Sandler and Sandler, 1978), the concept of identity must include relational components. And once the relational components of identity are incorporated, a mixed model results, and the expanded view of adult development explored here becomes not only possible but necessary.

Thus, we gather a versatile and inclusive framework through which to organize and understand the vicissitudes of normal adult development. As adult stage issues, identity and intimacy form a summit of ascendant development begun in infancy and continued through adolescence. Because the processes of identity and intimacy formation are so intricately connected in their development, they approach, attain, and maintain this acme together, although the relative weight between them differs from culture to culture, individual to individual, and within each individual over time. Kegan commented:

"What is most striking about these two great human yearn-ings . . . one . . . the yearning to be included, to be part of, joined with . . . ; the other, . . . the yearning to be independent or autonomous, to experience one's distinctness . . . is that they seem to be in conflict, and it is, in fact, their *relation*—this ten-sion—that is of more interest . . ." (1982, p. 107). Indeed, it is the interpenetration of identity and intimacy issues which form the core of adult experience.

While normal adults "demonstrate an internally consistent capacity to experience self and other in characteristic ways that reflect the developmental level of underlying psychic structure" (Urist, 1977, p. 3), that structure will be challenged and modi-fied over time (Benedek, 1959) through adaptation to marker events, marker processes, and the inner clock. These variations are "time-dominated but not age-specific" (Gould, 1972).

With these modifications of the adult developmental model, it becomes possible to understand more clearly why several investigators (Douvan and Adelson, 1966; Josselson, 1973; Gilligan, 1979; Stewart, 1976; Boynton, 1980; Fischer, 1980; Morgan and Farber, 1982) found that women did not conform to the sequencing aspect of Erikson's stage model. Because women in our society tend to be relationship-oriented, it was thought that perhaps the sequence for women's develop-ment differed from men's, with intimacy coming first. What is emphasized here is that for *both* men and women, identity and intimacy are concurrent processes, each of whose unfolding leads to further delineation of the other. They are self and other, masculine and feminine, agency and communion, figure and ground, I and thou, each impossible to exist one without the other.

References

Bach, S. (1987), The development and pathology of the self. Paper presented at conference "Drive and Object Relations in Psychoanalytic Theory" sponsored by Albert Einstein College of Medicine/Montefiore Medical Center, Department of Psychiatry and Gralnick Foundation/Highpoint Hospital.

Bakan, D. (1966), *The Duality of Human Existence: An Essay on Psychology and Religion.* Chicago: Rand McNally.

Benedek, T. (1959), Parenthood as a developmental phase. In: *Psychoanalytic Investigations: Selected Papers*. New York: Quadrangle Books/The New York Times, 1973.

Bibring, G. L. (1959), Some considerations of the psychological processes in pregnancy. *The Psychoanalytic Study of the Child*, 14:113–121. New York: International Universities Press.

——— Dwyer, T. F., Huntington, D. S., & Valenstein, A. F. (1961), A study of the psychological processes in pregnancy and of the earliest mother–child relationship. *The Psychoanalytic Study of the Child*, 16:9–72. New York: International Universities Press.

Bowlby, J. (1969), *Attachment and Loss*, Vol. 1. New York: Basic Books.

Boynton, G. M. (1980), *The Relationship Between Identity Development and Attitudes Toward Motherhood in Young Married Professional Women*. Unpublished Ph.D. dissertation. Columbia University, New York.

Butler, R. (1975), *Why Survive? Being Old in America*. New York: Harper & Row.

Carter, E. A., & McGoldrick, M. (1980), *The Family Life Cycle: A Framework for Family Therapy*. New York: Gardner Press.

Combrinck-Graham, L. (1985), A developmental model for family systems. *Fam. Proc.*, 24(2):139–180.

Coupe, P. (1982), Unpublished notes. Clinical Psychology Program, Columbia University, Teachers College. Typescript.

Douvan, E., & Adelson, J. (1966), *The Adolescent Experience*. New York: John Wiley.

Erikson, E. H. (1950), *Childhood and Society*, 2nd ed. New York: Norton, 1963.

——— (1968), *Identity, Youth and Crisis*. New York: Norton.

——— (1980), *Identity and the Life Cycle*. New York: Norton.

Fairbairn, W. R. D. (1941), A revised psychopathology of the psychoses and psychoneuroses. In: *An Object Relations Theory of Personality*. New York: Basic Books.

Field, T., & Fox, N. (1985), *Social Perception in Infants*. Norwood, N.J.: Ablex Publishing Corp.

Fischer, J. L. (1980), Transitions in relationship style from adolescence to young adulthood. *J. Youth & Adol.*, 10:11–24.

Fiske, M. (1980), Changing hierarchies of commitment in adulthood. In: *Themes of Work and Love in Adulthood*, ed. N. J. Smelser & E. H. Erikson. Cambridge: Harvard University Press.

Franz, C. E., & White, K. M. (1985), Individuation and attachment in personality development: Extending Erikson's theory. *J. Personal.*, 53(2):224–256.

Fromm, E. (1941), *Escape from Freedom*. New York: Avon Books.

Gilligan, C. (1979), Woman's place in man's life cycle. *Harvard Ed. Rev.*, 49:431–446.

——— (1982), *In a Different Voice: Psychological Theory and Women's Development*. Cambridge: Harvard University Press.

Goleman, D. (1980), Leaving home: Is there a right time to go? *Psychol. Today*, 14(3):52–61.

Gould, R. (1972), The phases in adult life: A study in developmental psychology. *Amer. J. Psychiat.*, 129(5):33–43.

Greenberg, J. R., & Mitchell, S. A. (1983), *Object Relations in Psychoanalytic Theory*. Cambridge: Harvard University Press.

Greenspan, S. I. (1981), *Psychopathology and Adaptation in Infancy and Early Childhood: Principles of Clinical Diagnosis and Preventive Intervention.* New York: International Universities Press.

Hartmann, H. (1939), *Ego Psychology and the Problem of Adaptation.* New York: International Universities Press.

Jacobson, E. (1964), *The Self and Object World.* New York: International Universities Press.

———— (1967), *Psychotic Conflict and Reality.* New York: International Universities Press.

Jaques, E. (1965), Death and the mid-life crisis. *Internat. J. Psycho-Anal.,* 46:502–514.

———— (1981), The mid-life crisis. In: *The Course of Life,* ed. S. Greenspan & G. Pollock, Vol. 5. Madison, Conn.: International Universities Press, 1993, pp. 201–231.

Josselson, R. (1973), Psychodynamic aspects of identity formation in college women. *J. Youth & Adol.,* 2:3–52.

Katchadourian, H. A. (1980), Medical perspectives on adulthood. In: *Adulthood,* ed. E. H. Erikson. New York: Norton.

Kegan, R. (1982), *The Evolving Self: Problem and Process in Human Development.* Cambridge: Harvard University Press.

Kernberg, O. (1966), Structural derivatives of object relationships. *Internat. J. Psycho-Anal.,* 47:236–253.

———— (1976), *Object Relations Theory and Clinical Psychoanalysis.* New York: Jason Aronson.

Kitchener, R. F. (1978), Epigenesis: The role of biological models in developmental psychology. *Hum. Develop.,* 21:141–160.

———— (1980), Predetermined versus probabilistic epigenesis—A reply to Lerner. *Hum. Develop.,* 23:73–76.

Kohn, M. L., & Schooler, C. (1978), The reciprocal effects of the substantive complexity of work and intellectual flexibility: A longitudinal assessment. *Amer. J. Sociol.,* 84:24–52.

Kohut, H. (1977), *The Analysis of the Self.* New York: International Universities Press.

Lerner, R. M. (1980), Concepts of epigenesis: Descriptive and explanatory issues—A critique of Kitchener's comments. *Hum. Develop.,* 23:63–72.

Levinson, D. J. (1977), The mid-life transition: A period in adult psychological development. *Psychiatry,* 40:90–112.

———— Darrow, C. N., Klein, E. B., Levinson, M. H., & McKee, B. (1978), *The Seasons of a Man's Life.* New York: Alfred Knopf.

Mahler, M., Pine, F., & Bergman, A. (1975), *The Psychological Birth of the Human Infant.* New York: Basic Books.

Mallouk, T. (1982), The interpersonal context of object relations: Implications for family therapy. *J. Marit. & Fam. Ther.,* 10:429–441.

Marcia, J. E. (1966), Development and validation of ego identity status. *J. Person. & Soc. Psychol.,* 3:551–558.

Meacham, J. A., & Santilli, N. R. (1982), Interstage relationships in Erikson's theory: Identity and intimacy. *Child Develop.,* 53:1461–1467.

Morgan, E., & Farber, B. (1982), Toward a reformulation of the Eriksonian model of female identity development. *Adolescence,* 17:199–211.

Neugarten, B. (1968), Adult personality: Toward a psychology of the life cycle. In: *Middle Age and Aging: A Reader in Social Psychology*, ed. B. L. Neugarten. Chicago: University of Chicago Press.

—— (1979), Time, age and the life cycle. *Amer. J. Psychiat.*, 136:88–94.

Orlofsky, J. L., Marcia, J. E., & Lesser, I. M. (1973), Ego identity status and intimacy versus isolation crisis of young adulthood. *J. Person. & Soc. Psychol.*, 27:211–219.

Pearlin, L. I. (1980), The life cycle and life strains. In: *Sociological Theory and Research: A Critical Appraisal*, ed. H. M. Blalock, Jr. New York: Free Press.

Provence, S. (1989), Some relationships between education and psychotherapy in the treatment of developmentally delayed infants and toddlers. In: *Learning and Education: Psychoanalytic Perspectives*, ed. K. Field, B. Cohler, & G. Wood. New York: International Universities Press, pp. 517–537.

Rhodes, S. L. (1977), A developmental approach to the life cycle of the family. *Soc. Casework*, 58:301–311.

Sameroff, A. (1975), Transactional models in early social relations. *Hum. Develop.*, 18:65–79.

Sandler, J., & Sandler, A. (1978), On the development of object relationships and affects. *Internat. J. Psycho-Anal.*, 59:285–296.

Shanok, R. S. (1981), *Motherhood, Womanhood and the Life Cycle: Fresh Perspectives on the Psychoanalytic and Adult Developmental Literature*. Unpublished M.A. thesis. Columbia University, Teachers College, New York.

—— (1987), *Identity and Intimacy Issues in Middle Class Married Women During the Marker Processes of Pregnancy, Adoption, and Ph.D. Work*. Unpublished doctoral dissertation. Columbia University, Teachers College, New York.

Solnit, A. J. (1982), Self and object constancy. *The Psychoanalytic Study of the Child*, 37:201–218. New Haven: Yale University Press.

Stern, D. (1977), *The First Relationship: Infant and Mother*. Cambridge: Harvard University Press.

Stewart, W. A. (1976), *A Psychosocial Study of the Formation of the Early Adult Life Structure in Women*. Unpublished Ph.D. dissertation. Columbia University, Teachers College, New York.

Sullivan, H. S. (1953), *The Interpersonal Theory of Psychiatry*. New York: Norton.

Urist, J. (1977), The Rorschach test and the assessment of object relations. *J. Person. Assess.*, 41:3–9.

Vaillant, G. E. (1977), *Adaptation to Life*. Boston: Little, Brown.

10

Psychoanalysis and Environment

E. JAMES ANTHONY, M.D.

Until I was about forty, I got the sort of satisfaction that Plato says you can get out of mathematics. It was an eternal world, a timeless world, a world where there was a possibility of a certain kind of perfection, and I certainly got something analogous to religious satisfaction out of it . . . the first World War made me think "it just won't do to live in an ivory tower. *This world is too bad. We must notice it.*"

—Bertrand Russell (1959)

One gets the impression that in recent years, psychoanalysts have undergone a type of "agonizing reappraisal" similar to Russell's; but they have begun to question the gratification to be derived from the eternal and timeless world of the psychoanalytic situation and the cognitive–emotional measures induced by daily life in an ivory office. It is as if they were concluding that the world must be getting worse because their patients seem to be worse than they used to be and that, if the world was as bad as this, they ought to notice it. They have begun to notice it, for the most part, not systematically, but sporadically and episodically. In this chapter, we trace the thrust of analytic interests into this expanding environment and record some of the problems it has raised for psychoanalytic theory.

It is difficult for the child analyst to remain as encapsulated, since work with the child is constantly impinged upon by his family, his school, or his community; and the external parents currently functioning in the child's life make much more impact on the ivoried seclusion than the internal parents of the adult patient, who are more in the nature of disturbing ghosts. "Ghosts" do not inhabit and shape an environment in a tangible way, whatever effect they might have on the "psychic reality" of the patient.

261

As if to underline these preoccupations with the actual environment, a young boy in analysis wrote to me, giving at the same time his own address on the back of the envelope. It ran as follows:

John G. Junior, Patient
15 Mildred Lane
 St. Louis County
  Missouri
   United States
    North America
     The Western Hemisphere
      The World
       The Solar System
        The Milky Way
         The Universe

We had been in the process, before he went on vacation, of exploring, somewhat intensively, his inner environment and the psychic paraphernalia of fantasies, feelings, fears, and fictions that populated it. His grandiose address was a hint that not only intended to remind the analyst that he was a special kind of patient, unique in the universe, but also perhaps that he inhabited another world, adjacent to his inner one, that also had infinite possibilities and potentialities for the shaping of his life and person. In brief, he wished me to know who he was, what he was, and where he was, in addition to the psyche-in-vacuo upon which I had been focused. He was conceptualizing his total environment, both inner and outer.

It is no accident of history that both philosophy and psychology have struggled with the problem of environment, since for centuries they occupied the same academic bed. There were philosophers for whom the internal environment was the only environment (the idealists),[1] and others for whom nothing existed outside the material universe and for whom the mind was

---

[1]The dilemma of students confronted by idealism has been pithily summed up in a limerick depicting the reactions of an Oxford undergraduate, to which I have appended my version depicting the modern psychological dilemma being considered in this article:

nothing more than a figment of the imagination that was itself only a peculiar reverberation of matter. Between the two lay the commonsense notion that mind and matter, the intrapsychic and the extrapsychic, lived in peaceful coexistence. The philosophical dilemma may be summarized as follows:

> The idealists have sometimes carried subjectivism to a point that seemed to common sense almost psychotic, implying, as it did, that the world existed only because it was posited by the self and consequently had a subordinate reality. It was nothing more than a wonderful mirage, a figment of thought. On the opposite side, the empiricists found this grandiosity not only repugnant but devious; Locke referred to it contemptuously as a "kind of fiddling." A mind was a product of things operating upon it "in a natural way," and, in the words of Hume, there could be "no idea without an antecedent impression." An intermediate approach, the philosophy of naturalism, postulated that the environment was indeed "out there" but that it consisted, as Russell put it, "of events, short, small, and haphazard." If there were order, unity, and continuity, these were human inventions just as truly as were catalogues and encyclopedias [Anthony, 1975, p. 279].

If the "order, unity and continuity" of the environment were human inventions, it could be as reasonably said that the mental apparatus that brought order, unity, and continuity to the inner environment was also a human invention, an explanatory model rather than an actuality.

Psychoanalysis, like many other disciplines, is undergoing change, and the occurrence of change, as always, brings with it the equal necessity of staying the same, of preserving one's basic identity while making progress. One would therefore expect scientific history to be discontinuous, recurrent crises punctuating the course of relationship or fit between theory and practice. Kuhn (1962) sees four distinct steps in the evolution of scientific thinking in any discipline, and psychoanalysis would be a case in point: (1) if the fit is good enough, problems or puzzles are solved within the framework of existing theory, and practitioners continue to practice traditionally with optimism and

---

There was a young man who said "*God!*"
I think it is extremely odd
  That the sycamore tree
  Just ceases to be
When I'm not out there in the quad.

A very young analyst said "Freud!"
The thought gets me much annoyed
  That the whole personality
  And "psychic reality"
Have nothing beyond them but void!

confidence; (2) if the fit is not good enough, qualifications of existing theory are attempted; if minor revisions meet the needs of the situation, confidence and optimism are again restored; (3) if minor revisions fail to reestablish the fit, discontinuity results, and an interim period of crisis ensues in which the prevailing mood is one of discomfort associated with pessimism, loss of confidence, and at times cynicism; (4) if this situation continues, it gradually becomes clear to the majority of practitioners, against a great deal of traditional resistance, that a major revision in theory is necessary. This revision is hard for established practitioners to accept, since it invariably entails the need for a new language to reflect the new theory. Observations that cannot be expressed in the new language begin to seem archaic and anachronistic and may therefore be rejected.

During the interim period, from the onset of crisis to its resolution, a feeling of commotion, not unlike an identity crisis, pervades the individual, and questions such as, Where are we now? Where are we going? What is our future? And should we forget our roots and start afresh? become the hidden agenda of many professional meetings. Judged by these criteria, psychoanalysis seems to be passing through a time of crisis, with maladjustment appearing between ideas and observations. Two instances of lack of fit that are causing this discomfort relate to the significance of environment in psychoanalytic theory and the usefulness of environment in psychoanalytic practice. Both are controversial and both have stimulated innovations.

At the annual meeting of the American Psychoanalytic Association in Denver, May 1974, one of the panels focused its attention on a critical assessment of the future of psychoanalysis as viewed by some if its senior practitioners. The environment was introduced by one of the speakers as an integral part of this future perspective, and his viewpoint was reported as follows:

> Turning his attention to our need to re-evaluate our concept of "the average expectable environment," Gaskill said that the psychoanalytic theory has assumed that the individual's conflict is intrapsychic. The recognition that the conflict may relate to outer reality introduces a new variable that makes our theory more inclusive. Moreover, the recognition that reality is fashioned by man, often unwisely or to the disadvantage of segments of our population, is not a fact new to analysis, but

one to which we may have been less sensitive than was an earlier generation. We are, therefore, vulnerable to attack in certain quarters and need to recognize these omissions with appropriate correction in therapy and practice [Miller, 1975, p. 141].

One should add that none of the remaining speakers shared a similar concern about the need to include environment within the ambiance of psychoanalysis. For the most part, they restricted their remarks to the possibility of a logical psychoanalytic theory of the mind that could coordinate experience with explanatory construction, but apparently they did not perceive any need to coordinate the mind with the environment. From a theoretical point of view, one can sympathize with this exclusion. Mind is hard enough to deal with, without adding the endless dimensions of matter. Psychoanalysts, in fact, are dealing with environment in ways reminiscent of the idealist philosophers: they live in it, work in it, play in it, and die in it, but they keep it out of their theory. Times, however, are changing, and so are psychoanalysts, who find the environment, in various ways, knocking on their office doors and asking to be let in with the patient. As Russell would say, they are being compelled to notice it.

Before acquiescing to the admission of environment into our conclaves, four very pertinent questions need to be answered: (1) What factors led to the virtual exclusion of environment from developing psychoanalytic theory and the turning inward of interest? (2) What new developments have occurred to warrant a fresh appraisal of the role of environment in a comprehensive psychoanalytic psychology? (3) To what extent can environment become a regular nutriment for the intrapsychic apparatus with a modulating influence on its structure and function? (4) How is environment related at successive developmental stages to the psychic apparatus?

The Great Turning-In Process in the Development of Psychoanalysis

It is often alleged that the evolution of psychoanalysis took a decisive turn when its founder and major contributor turned his back on environment. The history of this disavowal is an interesting but murky one, and there are parts of it that remain unclear. We have learned that science reflects not only the mind of the scientist but also his personality and that the personal factor of experience may become an inseparable part of the style of inquiry, the facts obtained, and the theories elaborated. Let us review the parallel procedures of theory making and self-analysis that took place in Freud toward the end of the last century.

In 1896 Freud postulated his first general theory of neurosis, and it was an environmental one. In this so-called seduction hypothesis, he postulated a traumatic sexual experience before puberty based on the actual stimulation of the genital organs. He was convinced that "appalling" and "disgusting" pedophilic practices had occurred in each of a sample of eighteen subjects and offered six bits of data as conclusive evidence: The descriptions were uniform, the effects were generally considered harmless by the victims, the neurosis appeared to be logically and consistently connected with the preceding trauma, the disturbance was relieved when the matter was uncovered, confirmation from other sources was obtained in a few cases, and, most convincing of all, neurosis followed inevitably in the wake of every seduction (Freud, 1896).

However, a few months later, Freud underwent an abrupt and revolutionary change of mind. First of all, he began to question his evidence. He experienced repeated disappointments at bringing treatment to a successful conclusion. The patients, even those who had been most favorably inclined at the beginning, dropped out of therapy. He felt wounded and spoke with some bitterness of his "present uselessness as a therapist." It also seemed to him less credible, as time went on, that perverted acts against children should be so general, and there seemed to be no definite way to confirm the actual reality of the alleged seduction. He considered several possibilities: that the traumata had been inflicted in adult life but had been projected back into childhood; that the neuroses had nothing to do with environmental experience but were genetically determined; and, finally, that the seductions occurred not in fact but in fantasy (Freud, 1887–1902).

At this point he was ready to abandon his basic and cherished notion that not only were neuroses completely resolvable, but their etiology lay somewhere in childhood. He was on the fourth step of Kuhn's schema of scientific revolution, and a major revision of theory had become clearly necessary. He had sustained a loss of confidence, and one might have expected, in view of the complete turnabout, a sense of shame; but, on the contrary. "I feel not in the least disgraced," he said, somewhat surprisingly, and there was good reason. He was on the wave of another discovery and had more or less completed a major revision of theory. He not only abandoned the seduction theory but threw the environment out with it at the same time. This recantation was based not on external but on internal evidence, and it was this evidence inside himself that overthrew the hypothesis of an actual external environmental event.

In 1897, in a letter to Fliess (Freud, 1887–1902), he wrote that a "great secret . . . has been slowly dawning on me in recent months" (p. 215). What was happening, under conditions of great anguish, was the discovery in himself of the internal cause of neurosis—the Oedipus complex. There was no doubt that this lonely self-analysis was proving harder than any other analysis. Stone (1961) has referred to this undertaking as "one of the most stupendous achievements of human scientific genius." Objectivity demanded a self-alienating condition—the treatment of the self as a stranger. By an intense act of introspection, Freud attempted the impossible, since he himself clearly recognized that, if it were really feasible, there would be no illness. This entailed great suffering, and he developed peculiar symptomatic states that he was far from understanding. He was drawing daily closer to the "terrible formulation" that recognized both the sexual and aggressive impulses of small children toward their parents. He had no further use for seduction. "When this error was overcome, the door was open to an insight into the spontaneous manifestations of infantile sexuality" (Freud, 1887–1902). He had no further use for environment.

As he turned inward, psychoanalysis followed behind him into the intrapsychic regions and stayed there with him. It is often alleged that this so-called "downgrading" of the environment by Freud persisted until the years 1922–1923 and formed a watershed between his endogenous and exogenous thinking. While it is true that his major preoccupation was internally directed, Freud was too astute, too much in touch with the everyday world in which he lived, to ignore or neglect it completely. For instance, he took detailed family histories from his patients and remained alert to familial contributions to illness, both physical and psychological. In the case of Dora (Freud, 1905), he had this to say:

> It follows from the nature of the facts which form the material of psychoanalysis that we are obliged to pay as much attention in our case histories to the purely human and social circumstances of our patients as to the somatic data and the symptoms of the disorder. Above all, our interests will be directed towards their family circumstances [p. 18].

Hartmann (1944) reviewed Freud's contributions to the environmental sciences, such as anthropology, sociology, and group psychology. In Freud's paper on "civilized" sexual morality and nervous illness (1908), he systematically and explicitly presented his views on the relation of psychoanalysis to a sociological problem as reflected in the influence of cultural factors on instinctual life, neurosis, and perversion. Several years later, in *Totem and Taboo* (1913–1914), he made a most stimulating and provocative attempt to apply psychoanalytic results to anthropology, linking primitive man's fear of incest, ambivalence, the psychopathology of the obsessive–compulsive state, animal phobias in children, and the Oedipus complex in general. His primal horde hypothesis has been much challenged, but it represented a wonderful imaginative flight from the parricide of primitive times to the unconscious struggles of modern man. His second decisive contribution to social psychology was made in "Group Psychology and the Analysis of the Ego" (1921), in which he showed himself to be highly aware of the conflicts that beset the human environment. His notion of group dynamics, the problems of leadership, the predicament of the leaderless group, the "group of two," and the way in which members of a group replace the ego ideal with the leader and can thus identify their own egos with those of the other members, demonstrates his extrapsychic sensitivity—his intuitive appreciation of interpersonal events. From this same seminal source came ego psychology and a new appreciation of the subtle interface between ego and environment. Finally, in his great exposition *Civilization and Its Discontents* (1930), he relates not sexuality but aggression to the civilizing process.

In a review of this material, it is obvious that real life and intrapsychic life were closely interwoven in Freud's mind and that the leadership struggles in his young psychoanalytic group were closely connected with his understanding of the unconscious factors involved. The three main works, *Totem and Taboo*, "Group Psychology and the Analysis of the Ego," and *Moses and Monotheism*, seem to represent the three stages in the emergence of the primal leader as an irreplaceable hero who is ultimately responsible for the group's cultural development. All three throw an interesting light on the mechanism of maintaining leadership following the death of a leader, and the account can be viewed as an intriguing allegorical description of the early history of the psychoanalytic movement and as an expression of Freud's fears and fantasies regarding its future (Ostow, 1977).

> At the age of 56 he had to deal with the defection of his most promising disciples, and so he wrote of the death wishes underlying the rebelliousness. At 65 he appeared more concerned with the problem of finding a suitable though necessarily lesser replacement for the leader after his death. The new leader would hold the group together, purging internal threats, cultivating a loyal cadre and exploiting the libidinal needs of the group members. (At this point, he had Otto Rank in his mind as his successor.) Shortly before his death, he once more returned to developments following the death of the older leader and the fate of the group is now separated from the fate of its doctrine [Anthony, 1979].

We know that a radically different group structure now makes its appearance in Freud's thinking. Leadership is now delegated to a trained elite whose function would be to conserve the valuable core of the system by setting up institutions for the purpose. His deep understanding of human nature and group dynamics led him to see that this evolution would be punctuated by periodic splitting, since there would always be bad sons and daughters who would want to go their separate ways. Given his holistic grasp of the environmental factors operating within his movement, he would not, were he alive today, "be in the least surprised at the regularity with which psycho-analytic societies have found it necessary and even imperative to break away or break off from time to time" (Anthony, 1979).

The ego was crystallizing out as a considerable entity in itself, carrying a host of adaptive functions in relation to the outside world. Freud saw it as acting as an intermediary between inner and outer environment, with one of its primary roles being to alert the individual to what was going on about him (Freud, 1923), yet the environment as he perceived it was still hardly more than a nebulous background of the mind. As Benjamin (1966) has pointed out, Freud's new ego psychological thinking from 1923 onward did not by any means make him a complete ego psychologist. He only very gradually overcame the tendency to neglect what was on the outside.[2] For years he had seen the world mirrored in his patients, and psychic reality had come to have precedence over actual reality in his frame of reference.

The watershed year of 1923 signified another important shift in his therapeutic perspective. Before that, he was mainly concerned with problems of repression, what lay behind this opaque defensive barrier, and the internal pain associated with it. After 1923, the concept of denial and disavowal became salient, together with the phenomenon of external pain (Freud, 1924).

One should emphasize that Freud was in no way, philosophically speaking, an idealist. As mentioned previously, outside his analytic work he was very much in touch with the world and realistically oriented toward it. His letters indicate the intensity of his interests in social and political forces. If he chose to neglect the environment, it was for much the same reason that he, a neurologist by training, paid scant attention to somatic factors. It was not that soma and environment did not exist but that psyche was where his interests lay and what he wanted to explore. He not infrequently apologized for the fact

---

[2]There is an apocryphal story in which Freud was asked to write a letter of recommendation for an ex-patient and demurred on the grounds that he only knew him "from the inside"!

that he did to some extent neglect extrapsychic matters simply on the grounds of time; to create an intrapsychic system was a lifetime occupation.

Some Premature Migrations from the Psyche: The Culturalists

The culturalists became aware that something was missing from psychoanalytic theory, and they went through the Kuhn steps (1962) in an attempt to deal with this hiatus within the confines of classical theory. Horney (1939), for example, was an orthodox Freudian psychoanalyst for over fifteen years, and it was her coming to the United States that led her to challenge Freud's formulations and his comparative neglect of culture:

> The greater freedom from dogmatic beliefs which I found in this country alleviated the obligation of taking psychoanalytical theories for granted, and gave me the courage to proceed along the lines which I considered right. Furthermore, acquaintance with a culture which in many ways is different from the European taught me to realize that many neurotic conflicts are ultimately determined by cultural conditions.

The terms "normal" and "neurotic" were not universal but comparative terms that varied with class and culture. She could not agree with Freud's emphasis on the infantile sexual roots or the contents of the nuclear complex that was essentially similar in all neuroses. For her, the conflicts referred to specific life conditions in a given culture and not to problems common to human nature, since the motivating forces in other cultures were different.

According to Horney, the childhood experiences of individuals with a character neurosis showed that their environment had certain typical characteristics, such as a lack of genuine warmth and affection, unjust reproachfulness, unpredictable changes between indulgence and rejection, unfulfilled promises, and often a complete lack of consideration of the child as a person. In essence, she agreed with Fromm that the understanding of personality and personality difficulties did not require the knowledge of instinctual life but of the entirety of the conditions of living. The Oedipus complex was not a given of early life but an outcome of too much stimulation or too much prohibition of the children sexually. This was in some respects a return to Freud's original seduction theory. Environment was prepotent. Specific cultural conditions engendered specific characteristics in both men and women. If a culture designates as masculine the characteristics of strength, courage, independence, success, freedom, and the right to choose a partner, then the women in that culture might well wish to have a penis.

Kardiner (1939), Fromm (1947), and Sullivan (1947) also applied contemporary knowledge of sociology and anthropology to psychoanalysis, but most threw the basic tenets of psychoanalysis out with the libidinal bathwater. Fromm stressed that the key problem for the individual was his relatedness, not only to himself, but toward the world. Primitive religions and myths, he said, bore testimony to man's original "primary ties" to nature—to the soil he lived on, the sun, moon, and stars, the trees and flowers, the animals, and the people with whom he was related through kinship. He was rooted in an organized, structuralized totality in which he had an unquestionable place. Thus, he had a complete sense of belonging and was protected against aloneness and tormenting uncertainty and doubt. Similarly, the modern child gradually develops his capacities within the limits ordained by his family, his constitution, and his culture. Like Kardiner, Fromm believed that, by adjusting himself to these primary and secondary institutions, the child acquired a personality whose core was common to most members of his class and culture. On this common core were superimposed all the variations of the individualized character. The sexual aspect of the Oedipus myth was only a secondary element to the primacy of the rebellion of the son against the father's authority. In a matriarchal culture, democracy would flourish, since all men are equal because they are all the children of mothers, loved alike and without limiting conditions. Autocracies and social and political hierarchies grow out of patriarchal systems.

Sullivan has also been charged with being a culturalist, although he has been criticized by the culturalists as paying little attention to the qualitative differences in acculturation. He used the term "interpersonal" to refer not only to real people existing in space and time but also to fantasied "personifications" who were once significant in the individual's past life, not in the sense of an Oedipus complex but simply in the general way that parents tend to treat their children in the primary interpersonal situation of the family. The extent to which satisfaction and security are met within these situations helps to integrate and otherwise mold the personality. Sullivan's concept of "not-me" does not seem, however, to go beyond the immediate familiar environment, although it stresses its personalization during the early stages of development.

The Rise of the New Environmentalists within the Fold

As a result of the work of the culturalists and the revolutionary revisions in theory they introduced, the terms "culture" and "environment" became bad words in the lexicon of classical psychoanalysis and put the orthodox on the defensive: the extrapsychic had become heretical. It is symptomatic of the situation that "environment" is not listed in the index of any of the standard psychoanalytic compendiums. Indirect allusions may be discerned, for example, in sections dealing with object choice, object relations, and object loss, presupposing that something out there could be chosen, related to, or lost that was not part of the self. Thus, there appeared to be a latent if not a manifest theory of object relations within the system. The problem was to find the niche for self and object within the metatheory.

Why did the culturalists fail, and why have the new environmentalists succeeded in adding the dimension of environment without splitting from the parent body? The answer lies somewhere along the schema constructed by Kuhn (1962). First of all, a major revision was attempted before the groundwork had been prepared and before minor revisions had been given a chance to solve the problem; second, the major revision involved the elimination of a sizable chunk of classical theory and so mobilized a good deal of traditional resistance; and, third, practitioners were required to unlearn the old language and learn a new one. Further, each major revisionist created a new system of theory and language so that culturalist forces were scattered while the orthodox troops closed ranks and consolidated their position. Besides, not one of the culturalists had anything approaching the stature of Freud, and on close inspection the major revisions began to look very minor indeed and hardly worth the effort of revolution. Psychoanalysis at this time was not looking for a massive individual contribution but rather a more collective set of convergent operations. The timing was all wrong, and the strategy was self-defeating. The ego had still to be elaborated by Hartmann, and the self needed much more work than the little provided by Sullivan. In addition, the new environmentalists were more scholarly than charismatic and more inclined to consolidate than to innovate. We will deal with their contributions in turn.

Hartmann's Theory of Environment

Hartmann opened the way to new considerations of the environment when he put forward the idea of an "average expectable environment" to which the human infant was pre-adapted at birth. By sharpening the psychology of the ego and self, he prepared the way for others to explore a possible psychoanalytic universe of the nonself. Hartmann was conscious of the "developmental environment" (Anthony, 1975), beginning with the world of mother and infant, in which both seemed endowed with the basic capacity to transmit and receive signals from each other, the mother guiding the infant and the infant guiding the mother in a mutual relationship.

Hartmann was positive in his approach to the environmental scientists, and in the areas of nonconflictual development and nonconflictual spheres of the ego he was able to make scientific contact with them. He pointed out that sociologists and psychoanalysts could collaborate in a common investigation, studying the same phenomena from different angles and gradually evolving a common scientific language. He also pointed to the fact that anthropologists who were analytically trained had begun to concern themselves in their fieldwork with aspects of primitive behavior that previously would have escaped their notice. The same was true of historians. He denied that psychoanalysis had ever been a purely internal discipline.

Psychoanalysis, in contradistinction to some other schools of psychology, has never been confined exclusively to the consideration of "innerpsychic" processes; *it has always, and by no means accidentally, included the consideration of the individual's interactions with the environment.* At any rate, the study of object relations in human development has more recently become one of the most fruitful centers of analytic interest ("new environmentalism," Kris, 1950). Ego psychology represents a more balanced view of the biological and the social and cultural aspects of human behavior. We may say that in analysis cultural phenomena are often studied in their biological context and significance, and biological phenomena in relation to the sociocultural environment [Hartmann, 1959, pp. 329, 330].

Hartmann also described two concepts of "our real world." This differed from the world of objective science. It was a personal, meaningful world that developed over time and formed the basis of our relations with reality. In the presence of normal ego functioning, it was shaped by the nature of our mental apparatus and by our history. As a further complement to our development, a workable equilibrium is normally established between "our world" and the world of science. Using this subtle distinction, Hartmann has categorized environment and the ego's manipulation of environment into two organized systems of orientation—the world of science and the world of immediate experience. The individual needs to bring together his objective and subjective environments and reach some compromise between the two ways of dealing with reality, each of which is in itself adaptive. Inner and outer, subjective and objective, intrapsychic and extrapsychic environments are synthesized by the ego and rendered coherent. What Hartmann is saying here is that the environment is not simply something into which one projects one's inner reality, but a complicated world of its own that has its own externality, its own reality, its own objective scientific life, and its own subjective, personal side with its own meanings and values.

Perhaps Hartmann's most valuable contribution is the distinction he made between inner and outer reality, between inner and outer reality testing, between inner reality and psychic reality and between real and realistic. Fantasy activity can be real although not realistic (Hartmann, 1956).

Here he is dealing with environment, not in the simplistic way of the culturalists, but in the sophisticated way of metapsychology. The individual relates to environment in three different ways: autoplastically, in which he effects a change in himself; alloplastically, in which he effects a change in the outside world; and by a third mode, in which he does not effect changes in himself or in the world outside but instead changes the relationship between himself and the outside world by searching for and finding a more appropriate environment. The main instrument in all this is the ego as the "representative of reality." Hartmann went on to isolate three groups of factors that formed man "from the outside": nonhuman elements of the environment, such as air, water, and food; the human environment, such as relatives, friends, enemies, inferiors, superiors, teachers, and pupils; and the cultural environment, such as government, law, art, science, and commerce. The processes that go into making man "from the outside" are as complicated as those that go into forming him "from the inside." The environment "from the outside" is never identical for any two people, even identical twins (Hartmann, 1931–1935). Relations between ego and environment are therefore central to the ego psychology propounded by Hartmann—according to him, in direct continuity with the thinking of Freud. He always vigorously denied that the founder of "depth" psychology disregarded the causal role of experiential–environmental factors, reminding us that as early as 1905 Freud had insisted on the model of "complemental series" in which constitution and environment worked cooperatively together. The predominance of one or the other in the psychoanalytic approach was largely a function of theory or practice. In theory, one was always inclined to overestimate the former; in practice, the latter. At no time, said Hartmann, did Freud observe the individual "in splendid isolation," but always as part of the world. The alternation in emphasis was a feature of all scientific development that dealt with theories and their applications. There was no great inward turning in the history of the movement, no time in which environment was ignored or repudiated. The "complemental series" always provided a stable background to the foreground of evolving ideas that needed to be worked on at a particular time: "Psychoanalysis does not claim to explain human behavior only as a result of drives and fantasies; human behavior is directed toward a world of men and things. The approach of psychoanalysis in many cases includes the structure of this world in its scope; and in this sense psychoanalysis is applied Social Science" (Hartmann, 1944, p. 30).

Environment was always with us, but its impingement was especially marked during childhood. It was for this reason that the child analyst was more constant in his appreciation of environmental forces. "For the small child the external world is a strong ally against his instinctual drives," and, in the psychoanalytic treatment of the child, the child's progression is viewed both in relation to his biological growth and to the world around him (Hartmann, 1939). In the process of adaptation, the "environmental compliances" of society interrelate constantly with the ego as the organ of adaptation. A patient's picture of his environment may be real or fanciful, but even if it is real he may have made it what it is.

This brings us to consider the adaptation of psychoanalysis to its environment. To what degree is it influenced in its development by the pressures around it and by the demands made on it to be more medically oriented, more socially oriented, or more intrapsychically oriented, depending on whether the analysts in question work in academia, in agencies, or in "ivory offices"? It also brings up the question as to whether neighboring theoretical systems help to modify the theory. Finally, it may well be that changes in the patient population seen by analysts exert their own subtle influence on psychoanalytic thought, simply because the conditions seen today fail to fit earlier theories. In relation to Hartmann and his concerns with the reciprocal relation between organism and environment, one cannot help but notice similarities to the work of Piaget.

Hartmann's fascination with outer reality led him to Piaget. It is surprising how the two of them, approaching the environment in quite different ways, have come up with many ideas in common. That Hartmann borrowed from Piaget is evident in his references, but the reverse is not so obvious. Both theorists assume that the outside world is reconstructed by the individual within the individual in the course of development and, at the same time, is gradually separated from the individual. Hartmann's world is more personal and more cathected than Piaget's. For Piaget, the environment is like a good mother providing unlimited *aliment*—translated by Rapaport (1958) as "stimulus nutriment"—that creates structures (or schemas) within the mind. As time goes on, more and more of the environment is assimilated through the internal structures, which are thereby modified. This in turn is followed by accommodation so that the organism is once again restored to an adaptive equilibrium. When this happens, the new structure is confirmed. On exposure to new environmental stimuli to which the schema is not yet adapted, the equilibrium is disturbed and generates "desirability" and further alternations of assimilation and accommodation. A new differentiation within the schema is brought about, and the cycle continues. Piaget's structural theory, like that of psychoanalysis, assumes a hierarchic layering of structures that are progressively differentiated. According to this system, the child sequentially constructs a series of environments appropriate to his capacities and both "average" and "expectable" in Hartmann's sense. Thus, this internal representation of the external environment grows with the child until, at adolescence, it more or less resembles the environment perceived by the adult. The process of accommodation is at first superficial and touches only the surface of external reality, but later, as it penetrates more deeply, inner and outer experiences become more congruent. Piaget raises the interesting and intriguing question as to why the developing individual begins to construct the representational world and why he does not remain satisfied with the immediate experience or activity. His answer to this, and it is an interesting one for the psychoanalyst, is that there is a growing need to satisfy the collective consciousness and the demands of others. Without a representational world, not only would thought remain undeveloped, but it would not be possible to communicate with others or learn from them. A model of the environment has to be internalized before relationships can be fully established. It was difficult for Piaget to understand how psychoanalytic theory could do without the notion of environment and its corresponding influence on development. He criticized the early Freudian description of development for being too endogenous, and he approved, without really understanding its implications, the culturalist attempt to interweave instinct and environment along developmental lines (Piaget, 1971).

The affinity of Hartmann's autonomous ego psychology to Piaget's ego psychology is particularly evident in their approach to the construction of reality. The comparison can be summarized as follows:

The Construction of the Outer Environment

Hartmann (1956)
1. Speaks of "building the outer environment as a primary developmental task."
2. Speaks of "a constant process of assimilation coupled with normal projection" as a constructional device.
3. Speaks of achieving "a workable equilibrium between the knowledge of personal and objective environments."
4. Speaks of the "gradual differentiation of perception and idea through reality testing, and what is external and what is externalized."
5. Speaks of the need of "a good synthetic ego to carry out the work of constructing our real world."

6. Speaks of the ego's activity in manipulating reality so that the environment becomes a product of the mental apparatus and the developmental history.

Piaget (1954)
1. Speaks of "constructing reality from the earliest stage of development."
2. Speaks of "the process of assimilation coupled with accommodation as a concomitant process" in the construction of environment.
3. Speaks of achieving "equilibrium between assimilation and accommodation in the knowledge of the real environment."
4. Speaks of "the gradual differentiation of thought from things, of internal from external, of subjective from objective in the resolution of egocentrism."
5. Speaks of "the parallel development of the cognitive and affective apparatus leading to the conceptualization of the outer world."
6. Speaks of the activity of the infant reaching constantly into its environment and manipulating it in the service of the construction of reality.

Erikson's Theory of Environment

Although Piaget apparently knew nothing of Hartmann's writing, he was familiar with Erikson's contributions and approved of their general trends. In relation to his understanding of the epigenetic sequence, he brought up the general problem of transition from one stage to another: How was it possible for a baby, who begins by reducing everything to himself and is seemingly unaware, except dimly, of the environment, to succeed eventually in looking outward, in understanding events and their external causes, and in relating to objects independent of himself? In other words, how was a radical solipsism transformed into a complete and objective consciousness of the world outside? In Piaget's view, two processes, operating simultaneously, were involved in this profoundly important metamorphosis: the gradual differentiation of the self coupled with a consciousness of self and a gradual differentiation of environment coupled with the construction of an object world objectively perceived. In psychoanalytic terms, how did autoplasty shift to alloplasty? In Piaget's terms, how did egocentrism give place to decentration, or subjectivity to objectivity, so that the baby is able to "place himself" in a world of external objects and activities? Was it because of something inherent or something learned? Was the infant object-seeking from the moment of birth (if not before), or did object relations emerge at a specific time out of primary narcissism? In his earlier and more dynamically oriented work, Piaget had made use of the concept of "participation" borrowed from the anthropologist Levy-Bruhl (1926), who had described it to account for certain magical beliefs among primitives. It was essentially a bipolar mechanism, one root of which originated inside the individual and connected with another root on the outside. Piaget (1929), in turn, discovered that many early notions in childhood had this bipolar structure that linked inner and outer environments but expressly excluded any reality testing, so that external phenomena were readily infused with internal dynamisms.

Freud explained the occurrence of primitive animism in much the same way—the projection of inner thoughts and feelings onto the outside. It is not clear, either in Piaget's theory or in Freud's, whether it is the internal that influences the external or the other way around: The environment may be invaded by consciousness, brought to life, and made to act in a magical, omnipotent way, or the magic may be "imitative" or "homeopathic." To use an analogy from Freud (1913–1914):

If I wish it to rain, I have only to do something that looks like rain or is reminiscent of rain [mystic system]. At a later stage of civilization, instead of this rain-magic, processions will be made to a temple and prayers for rain will be addressed to the deity living in it [religious system]. Finally, this religious technique will in its turn be given up and attempts will be made to produce effects in the atmosphere which will lead to rain [scientific system] [p. 81].

Hartmann, as already noted, includes this observation in his bifurcation of the environment into a subjectively perceived world ("our real world") and an objectively perceived one ("the scientific world"). Freud would doubtless agree that animistic, religious, and scientific conceptions can exist compatibly side by side, not only in the same society but in the same individual.

Although Hartmann's world view was somewhat limited in its horizons and empty of content, he prepared for others to venture further afield and correlate the wider environment systematically and developmentally with the progression of stages within the individual. Erikson (1950) attempted to do just this in his sequence of the psychosocial stages, and his effort has been both welcomed and repudiated. For some it brought the environment in all its diversity into touch with the vicissitudes of instinctual development, while for others it was little better than a sociological description that lacked depth and understanding of psychoanalytic metapsychology.

According to Erikson, Hartmann's theory of adaptation based on inborn preparedness applied not only to neonatal or infantile stages but also to the entire human life cycle, which he conceived of as an evolving series of "average expectable environments." Each developmental step created and solved problems in relation to the external environment, which meant that human beings, like other organisms on the evolutionary scale, are fitted in a dynamic balance to an ecological niche. Erikson's concept of organ modes can be regarded as inclusions within Hartmann's concept of the primary and secondary autonomous apparatuses, while Hartmann's ego developmental approach is implicit in Erikson's epigenetic view. Together they have provided a theoretical framework in which the environment interacts with the instinctual drives to determine behavior. The theories are complementary and even at times congruent, the one overlapping the other. It was Erikson's view (1968), however (if one can presume to interpret him), that the psychoanalytic approach to environment prior to his work had been "fixated" at the mother–infant stage of development and had not evolved along with the expanded ego and the newer self-concept:

> In psychoanalytic writings the terms "outer world" or "environment" are often used to designate an uncharted area which is said to be outside merely because it fails to be inside. . . . such a vague yet omnipresent "outerness" by necessity assumes a number of ideological and certainly unbiological connotations, such as an antagonism between organism and environment. Sometimes "the outer world" is conceived of as "reality's conspiracy" against the infantile organism's instinctual wish world and sometimes as the indifferent or annoying fact of the existence of other people. But even in the recent admission of the at least partially benevolent presence of maternal care, a stubborn tendency persists to treat the "mother-child relationship" as a "biological" entity more or less isolated from its cultural surroundings which then again become an "environment" of vague supports or of blind pressures and mere "conventions."

There is therefore not one basic environment but a whole wide range of environments and a long sequence of environments; as the child adapts to one expectable environment, he is preparing the way for his next environment, so that the generations are joined together in an organizational effort providing an integrated series of "average expectable environments."

What Erikson has to say about the first "upgrading" of environment in psychoanalysis was true. It relates, in fact, to a very small area of space around the infant that contains only his mother and focuses exclusively on the psychobiological transaction. In every way it is restricted, "unfurnished," and cut off from the rest of the world so that hardly any social or emotional traffic passes between this inner orbit and its ambiance. It represented, as he points out, the first tentative steps of psychoanalysis outside the psyche. But the world was more than a mother's breast and belly; it was more than just Bowlby's attachment behavior (1969), Spitz's "anaclitic union" (1946), Benedek's "depressive constellation" (1956), or Mahler's "separation-individuation" from the mother (Mahler, Pine, and

Bergman, 1975). Psychoanalytic thinking had become so accustomed to dyads and triads that anything beyond, even group psychology, sanctioned by Freud's interest, seemed not only impractical but unthinkable.

Erikson was able, unlike the culturalists, to extend the notion of environment without breaking his tie to the core principles of psychoanalysis. Critics suggested that his version of psychoanalysis is attenuated and diluted, but it can be said in response to this that he was faithful to Freud not only in the preservation of his metapsychology but also of his anthropological and social interests, referred to earlier. Even a cursory glance through the *Standard Edition* reveals the fact that Freud's genius had many more sides to it than some of his followers are prepared to recognize.

Rapaport's Theory of Environment

Rapaport's definition of "dynamic psychology" (1947) is indicative of his total approach. He sees it as "the most advanced stage of the psychology that investigates the interrelationships of the individual and his environment, attempting to do justice both to the forces that impinge upon the individual and to the physiological and psychological (conscious and unconscious) forces and regulative mechanisms that determine the individual's functioning within this environment" (p. 290). Throughout his psychoanalytic career, he emphasized this interdependence of organism and environment and the many ways in which they are coordinated. The world shapes the individual, but the individual also shapes his world according to his perceptions, history, and life situation, or, to put it in Rapaport's words, "the world of the individual is organized according to the organizing principles of the individual" (p. 296). There are three components of human functioning, according to him, that must be considered in every situation, since they all stem from human nature—environment, psyche, and soma. Admittedly, one of these, because it is more accessible, may receive more attention in certain situations, but one should never give up the hope that sooner or later the other components may be included in a more comprehensive picture. Here he is articulating, clearly and concisely, what was always implicit in Freud.

Although it seems that Rapaport for the most part underscored the views of Hartmann and Erikson with regard to environment, he added one aspect that is of crucial importance to
any psychoanalytic theory of environment—the ego's relative
autonomy from the environment. It is a commonplace in life
that strong beneficent ego interests or urgent instinctual drives
may divorce us temporarily from the environment so that we
can go about our intrapsychic business more or less unham-
pered. Rapaport wanted to stress the fact that, while the impingement of environment was important for the individual's
development, it was equally important for his development that
at times he could be relatively immune from its influence. For
healthy development, ego and environment must sometimes be
associated and sometimes dissociated.

Rapaport, like Hartmann, was captivated by the wealth of
Piaget's ideas, two of which he felt should be incorporated in
some way into psychoanalysis. The first of these is the idea of
stimulus nutriment from the environment (both internal and
external) that Piaget postulated as necessary for the creation of
both cognitive and affective structures within the mind; this
could be applied as easily to psychoanalytic structures, since
they too could be considered undergoing development as a
result of stimuli from inside and outside, rather than as emerging fully formed at a particular point of development. This
concept of nutriment bears a certain similarity to Hartmann's
use of cathexis for the assimilation of certain selected portions
of the environment. With further development, learning enters
the situation as the needed nutriment for the formation of
structure.

Second, Rapaport espoused the concept of a representational world deriving again from external objects, internal
drives, etc. Sandler and Roseblatt (1962) have since made an
attempt to incorporate Piaget's theory of representation into a
psychoanalytic framework.

In addition to these two important theoretical offerings
regarding the developing individual, Rapaport (1960) offered
a view of the environment from the perspective of the patient
being treated. He felt that the psychoanalyst should keep a

constantly vigilant eye on the effects of environment on the patient:

> The very defenses which the work of the patient and therapist would have to weaken and penetrate are continuously maintained and strengthened by the environment. In fact the vicious circle of neurosis crucially involves the fact that the patient persistently exposes himself to situations which tend to elicit his defensive behavior and to reenforce his defenses, and avoids other situations which would tend to elicit alternative behaviors and thus would facilitate giving up his defenses [p. 892].

It would seem that the modern-day analyst would have his hands full if he responds to these advances and allows his free-floating attention to hover over the psyche, the soma, and the environment of his patients. Some will no doubt feel that he has his hands full enough simply coping in the traditional fashion with the psyche.

Winnicott's Theory of Environment

Winnicott has provided perhaps the most logically conceived and most fully worked-out theory of environment in psychoanalysis. His pediatric background brought him constantly into contact with the mother-infant dyad, and, although this limited his concept of environment, it also provided him the basis of his theory. Subsequently, his experience of borderline cases led to a further elaboration of his notion of environment, together with an expansion of its horizon.

To fully comprehend this rich and complex theory, one needs to divide it into its different parts before examining it in its totality. These are as follows: (1) the environment-individual setup; (2) the need for a perfect environment and a good-enough mother; (3) the transitional environment and its relation to the internal and external environments; (4) the diagnostic assessment of environment; (5) the failure of environment and the resulting psychopathology; (6) the classification of patient groups in relation to different environmental experiences requiring different therapeutic approaches.

The environment–individual setup (1952, 1954a). Winnicott (1952) begins his theoretical approach in his usual paradoxical way by stating categorically that "there is no such thing as a baby"; there is always the nursing couple (p. 99). The primary unit, therefore, is not the individual but the environment-individual setup. When development proceeds normally, the infant's being evolves from the center of the setup, the soma, and spreads outward, so that he begins to construct an external world at the same time as he acquires the limiting membrane that demarcates his inside world. A personal environment gradually emerges out of the environment-individual setup, and, if all goes well, this personal creation approximates the actual environment. At first the individual is isolated within this environment, and then, as motility develops, he starts to explore its boundaries; when it "impinges" on him, he accepts it. When the environment is able to adapt to the baby's needs, he can remain in undisturbed isolation, thus becoming aware of his environment without losing his sense of self. In order to develop healthily as a psyche-soma, the infant very much needs to experience this undisturbed continuity of being (1949b).

The need for a perfect environment and a good-enough mother (1948, 1949b). The perfect environment is the womb. When the baby leaves this at birth to enter his first environment, the mother compensates for any deficiency in it by means of her "primary maternal preoccupation," thus maintaining the perfect environment. Winnicott seems to regard the mother's preoccupation during this neonatal phase as some sort of normal illness that increases her sensitivity to the needs of her baby. As the latter develops, he can take over some of the mother's compensating capacity for transforming a good-enough environment into a perfect environment or, to put it another way, the relative failure of adaptation into adaptive success. This involves two elements: the infant's understanding of his environment and the mother's ability to keep this environment as simple and uncomplicated as she can. As the child develops further, the mother can reduce her preoccupation and allow the growing ability of the infant to take up the slack and so preserve the level of adaptation. Winnicott summarizes this part to his theory as follows: "in the development of every individual, the mind has a root, perhaps its most important root, in the need of the individual, at the core of the self, for a perfect environment" (1949b, p. 246).

The transitional environment and its relation to internal and external environments (1951). Winnicott adopted and expanded the concept of transitional phenomena first put forward by Fairbairn (1944). Between the experience of internal and external reality, an intermediate area of experiencing is postulated in which both the internal and the external environment make contributions. It comes into being mainly because at this time the infant is unable to distinguish events that occur within him or within his body from those that occur in the outside world. The potential space is populated with objects, thoughts, ideas, and memories. With perfect or good-enough mothering, the infant's needs are generally met as soon as they arise, and this leads to the illusion that he himself creates what he needs. Even in the absence of need satisfaction, he can still create a satisfying agent by hallucinating it. Winnicott refers to this as "primary creativity." As the reality sense develops, acceptance of contemporary frustration gradually replaces illusions and hallucinations; when this happens, the infant begins to "acknowledge his indebtedness" to benign, predictable, and giving objects that must exist in the outer world. This reality acceptance is never quite completed, so that human beings of all ages must constantly struggle with the task of reconciling the inner world of wish fulfillment and the outer world of stern reality. This produces from time to time considerable strain, from which the individual obtains some measure of relief by retreating to an intermediate environment where he can indulge himself in play, in creativity, and in recreational activities. It is in this intermediate environment that inner tensions, wishes, or subjective states can be mixed in optimal proportion with relatively undistorted percepts from the external world. The psychoanalytic situation provides a good example of this intermediate environment, and the analyst himself may at certain times play the role of transitional object. In both primitives and children, internal and external environments "participate" in the genesis of the transitional environment, which often seems to be the whole environment, highly animated and magical. All relationships become imbued with these qualities, so that mothers and witches are easily interchangeable. Winnicott believes that a different kind of mother resides in each of the separate environments and is treated in a different way. The external mother has the job of correcting some of the exaggerations of "good" and "bad" and "loving" and "hating" that accrue through the internal mother. The transitional mother is there to furnish a source of constancy, consistency, and reliability, and there is much greater control over "her" and over "her" activities.

The diagnostic assessment of environment (1954b). The individual, from infancy to childhood, enters a series of environments that have different "holding" and "facilitating" potentialities. The analytic diagnostician must be perpetually on the alert for environmental factors in the etiology of disorder; in order to do this, he needs to recognize and assess the type of environment that allows for normal development. In sequence, there is the intrauterine environment, the birth environment, the neonatal environment when the mother's preoccupation and devotion come into play, the infant's environment when the parental team takes on joint responsibility for helping the infant become a little child, the child's environment that brings in the social setting to facilitate the cooperative parental efforts, and finally the individual's environment that allows him to play a part in the creation and maintenance of the social setting (1949a).

The failure of environment and the resulting psychopathology (1954b). The environment can fail in several different ways. One example is when it makes a faulty adaptation to the infant at a time when the personal environment is beginning to emerge from the environment-individual setup and the infant reacts to the impingement and loses the sense of self that can be regained only by a return to isolation. This requires an increasing defense organization, and, as a result, a basic split in the environment-individual setup occurs so that the inner life gets shut off from the outside and derives very little from external reality. The individual is now easily seduced by the environment into a false life. Second, the environment may fail because "primary maternal preoccupation" is missing, as a result of which the baby's needs are soon exaggerated. To deal with this, the mother resorts to "treating" or "spoiling" to make up for her past incapacity. Third, if the baby is not adequately endowed, he may not be able to convert a not-so-good environment to a good-enough one, and adaptive failure results.

When the environment fails from being insufficient, inadequate, or erratic, various types of "environmental deficiencies syndromes" may result. When it is completely inadequate, psychosis may result. When it is marginally adequate, the infant may have to take over prematurely from the environment and organize self-care; from this situation, psychosomatic disorders ensue. Finally, when it is erratic, as in the case of the tantalizing mother, the psyche takes over the mother's role completely, becoming sufficient in itself and rendering her unnecessary. This leads to the emergence of a false, "as if" personality that appears to function in relation to the environment but actually makes only a minimal emotional contact with it. Interactions are extremely brittle, and breakdowns are constantly threatening.

Another serious failure of environment conduces to the development of a borderline disturbance involving failures in the formation of the self, in object relations, in object constancy, in the capacity to test reality, and in the ability to generate a normal rather than a delusional transference neurosis during psychoanalysis. Yet another failure may arise from the experience of some trauma, the effect of which on the psyche-soma depends on its stressfulness, the developmental phase at which it occurred, its phase-specificity, the degree to which it was prepared for, the amount of support offered by the environment at the time, and the child's understanding of what it means. Within this same developmental–environmental context, Winnicott came up with a concept of regression to good and bad fixation points within the instinctual experience of the individual and of his particular environment. The idea he was suggesting was that a particular early environmental failure could lead to a fixation point to which the individual would regress when a similar failure of environment later occurred.

The classification of patient groups in relation to different environmental experiences requiring different therapeutic approaches (1949b, 1954b). On the basis of this environmental theory, Winnicott produced a diagnostic and treatment classification that attempted to correlate different kinds of environmental failure with different kinds of environmental experience and different kinds of technical intervention. The classification was simple but clinically meaningful. Three groups were described. In the first, the patient is able to operate as a whole person whose difficulties are almost exclusively confined to the intrapsychic sphere, and he is best treated by classical analysis. In the second, the patient has barely achieved wholeness, but, having brought his love and hate together within an ambivalent dependency, he is beginning to show concern and is best treated by the analysis of mood and the occasional management of environmental problems when they arise. In the third group, the patient is fixated at the earliest stage of emotional development as a result of a serious failure of environment; he is best treated by management, with short periods of analytic work.

The environment may fail at different times during the child's development and to different degrees. Early failure sets up a fixation point to which regression takes place when the individual experiences failure in his later environment. In the case of minor failure, a personal defense system is organized by the individual; but when the failure is more serious, it may result in the development of a false self or an antisocial tendency that "compels the environment to become important." This also implies that the individual has reached the level where he can perceive that the cause of his predicament lies in an environmental failure, and he can thus look to the environment to provide the necessary assistance. Borderline patients often try to create the illusion that they are self-sufficient and unneedful of others, and they then encapsulate their own environments within the general environment and ignore the latter (Modell, 1968).

From his long experience in the field, Winnicott was sure that psychoanalysis could not do without a close consideration of the environment. As he put it: "We can build theories of *instinct* development and agree to leave out the environment, but there is no possibility of doing this in regard to formulation of *early ego* development" (1954b, p. 283).

The Concept of the Developmental Environment

The concept of a "developmental environment," then, is implicit in the work of Hartmann, Erikson, Rapaport, and Winnicott. It takes into account Hartmann's "average expectable environment," Erikson's "epigenetic steps of successive psychosocial crises," Rapaport's "epigenetic-maturational matrix," and Winnicott's "environment-individual setup," as well as Lewin's (1936) topological conception of "life space" and "hodological space." The term "developmental environment" attempts to summarize all the dynamic features that contribute to any particular stage of development. Thus, it would comprise internal, transitional, and external environments; near and distant environments depending on the "horizons" achieved by the individual; past, present, and anticipatory experiences incorporated into the stage; and dynamic, structural, and economic aspects of intrapsychic life and ongoing interpersonal and nonpersonal events. It might be objected that this compendium of intrapsychic and extrapsychic factors may be theoretically illuminating but too complicated and unwieldy to manage within the analytic situation. It attempts to add a developmental and adaptive point of view to the metapsychological one, and at present the summation may seem somewhat indigestible, as we have no comprehensive theory to encompass it all and blend it into a coherent mix. Further, in moving in this direction, one is always confronted by danger signals in the form of various deviant psychoanalytic groups who, to quote Rapaport (1947), "employ their enthusiastic discovery of environmental relationships for the purpose of defensive denial of drive and intrapsychic conflict."

This is certainly not what I had in mind (Anthony, 1970a,b) when I emphasized the constant interaction between the development of the child and the development of the parents as parents, and the mutuality that existed between the developmental problems of the child and parental psychopathology. Erikson has referred to this as a "cogwheeling" of the needs of the child and of the caretaking people at each point of development. The work done so far that has been summarized in this presentation provides a possibly solid base for what Rapaport

(1960) has referred to as "the psychological equivalent of biological ecology," and that has more recently been termed "human ecology" or the science of "ekistics," which takes into account the complex interplay between the developing child and the human and nonhuman environment. This adaptive point of view considers that the psychoanalytic explanation of any psychological phenomenon must include propositions concerning the relationship of individual to environment, the processes of adaptation at different points of life, the autoplastic or alloplastic modes of adaptation, the significance of internal and external, human and nonhuman environments, and the extent to which individual and environment adapt reciprocally to each other.

Thus, at every stage in the life cycle, the accounting must involve the inborn factors, the maturational factors, and the factor of environment expanding in conjunction with ego expansion. We have called this the "developmental environment" (Anthony, 1975) to remind us *that each stage of development in a sense creates its own environment and that each environment helps to generate its own type of development.*

The Relationship of Environment to the Psychic Apparatus through Successive Developmental Stages

As the child develops, so do his self-awareness and his awareness of the environment. The animate and inanimate worlds through which he moves are gradually but incompletely internalized and thus become part of inner reality. This representational compartment of the mind is in juxtaposition to the Freudian mental apparatus and has its own postulated sequences of development. It is, in many respects, a Piagetian construct that has been taken over by psychoanalysis, but it has been modified to meet not cognitive but affective needs. For Piaget (1929), the child's conception of the world is interwoven with his consciousness of self, but his grasp of consciousness is such that it leads him to confuse self and nonself and results in a degree of egocentrism. As long as the child believes in parental omniscience, his own self remains nonexistent, and the contents of his mind are common knowledge or, at any rate, known to his parents in the smallest detail. The discovery of the subjective self is not therefore a primitive intuition but is made relatively late and is apparently brought about by a dissociation of reality due to social experience. Piaget offers data that suggest that the moment of self-realization is frequently associated with the first deception of the parent with which the child gets away. This informs him for the first time that he possesses a secret inner world containing thoughts, dreams, and fantasies that are quite unknown to those around him. With the gradual resolution of egocentrism, the outside world gains an increasingly less distorted representation within the child's mind. He gets to know, for example, that dreams and thoughts come from inside him and that sticks and stones belong to the outside and are not endowed with life in the way that he is.

Piagetian representations may thus be said to form a stage for the dynamic representations—self and object relations—conceptualized by psychoanalysts such as Hartmann (1950), Sandler and Rosenblatt (1962), Jacobson (1964), and Mahler, Pine, and Bergman (1975). In place of egocentrism one now deals with narcissism with, as Hartmann says, two different sets of opposites: self in antithesis to the object and ego in antithesis to other substructures of the personality. In the resolution of narcissism, one can speak either of ego cathexis being replaced by object cathexis or of self-love giving way to object relation. The kind of development postulated by Piaget with respect to egocentrism has also been construed by Kohut (1966) with respect to narcissism.

The constancy of objects in the environment was also originally a Piagetian construct and was incorporated into psychoanalysis by Hartmann (1952), who libidinized the cognitive concept. This idea was given its classical sanction by Anna Freud (1960), who used the term "object constancy" to represent the libidinal attachment to the mother. If both libidinal and cognitive representations are subsumed under the rubric of "mental representation," some degree of parallelism between the two may be assumed to exist. An attempt to bring together Piaget's empirical studies of cognitive development and psychoanalytic libidinal development was made by Fraiberg (1969), who suggested that the bridge might lie in making the distinction between cognitive and evocative memory. The critical point in development would be when the infant is capable of evoking the image of the mother in her absence. For Piaget (1971), true "mental representation" is evocative memory and cannot be demonstrated until about 18 months of age. Jacobson (1964), whose insights into self- and object representations have helped to clarify this conceptual field, warned us to distinguish more carefully than we commonly do between the self and real objects and their respective mental representations, and between ego attitudes and actions in the outside world and changes in the cathexes of self- and object representations. To some extent, these confusions between inner and outer environment have been created by analysts themselves because of a built-in ambivalence toward outer reality. The analyst, like Piaget's infant, must conceive of the outer environment and its objects in a way that will help him to better reconstruct the inner environment. To do this, he must enduringly invest the outer environment with libidinal, aggressive, and neutralized psychic energy so that he comes to regard it as a field of action that has intimate intrapsychic implications. Thus, he must understand the external environment in order to understand the internal environment, or else he will be less successful in his analytic work. Unless he himself has an ongoing "love affair" with the outside world and has discovered its rich potentials for himself, his analytic posture may reinforce the unrealistic and wishful strivings of his patient. Further, unless the analyst is able to distinguish for himself the operational uses of Freud's structural propositions, the later psychoanalytic propositions regarding self- and object representations, and the realities of the self and the object world, he will consistently confuse himself in his work, both terminologically and analytically.

The interplay between inner and outer worlds is so mutually productive that it is difficult to give one or the other primacy. One might be tempted to conclude that the outside world creates the inside world by imprinting itself passively, like a rubber stamp, on the impressionable mind of the small child. Piaget has demonstrated to us the falsity of this view: From the beginning, the infant reaches out actively, seizing the world and making it his own to suit the idiosyncratic needs of each developmental stage. Winnicott (1950) has pointed to the forces within the infantile mind that help to shape the inner and outer worlds:

> It is the destructive drive that creates the quality of externality.
>
> it is this impulsiveness, and the aggression that develops out of it, that makes the infant need an external object . . . [p. 217].
>
> the enironment is constantly discovered and rediscovered because of motility [p. 211].
>
> This quality of "always being destroyed" makes the reality of the surviving object felt as such, strengthens the feeling tone, and contributes to object constancy.

This destruction of the object in unconscious fantasy has been likened to a "cleansing process" that permits one to rediscover and renew one's objects constantly.

In the next phase, the junior toddler conducts his "love affair" with the world by practicing newfound skills. His environment requires exploring. This is not to say that the child has not been observing and exploring the environment through his five senses before this, but at this stage he is able to mobilize himself in the service of his curiosity and in his hunger for external reality. He becomes intensely object seeking, and the objects may be both animate and inanimate, human and nonhuman, and he may seek and find and lose and then seek, find, and lose over and over again. Having satiated himself with the environment, he spends the next phase retreating from it to some extent and reconnecting to his primary object love. The cognitive and libidinal balance is once again upset in favor of the libidinal, and he now appears to need his mother almost more than ever. Even though he can now evoke her image in her absence, she is still not libidinally constant within him, and so his insecurity and dependence persist and may even become exaggerated if she rejects his overtures. As the world outside assumes more cognitive constancy and the world within more libidinal constancy, he becomes prepared, as it were, for more complex relationships.

The environmental setting of the Oedipus complex may be critical for its resolution. The environment now contains an essential three-body structure of father, mother, and child, in which the parents are not only internally represented but are also outwardly transacting persons, both with each other and with the child. The relationship of extrapsychic and intrapsychic phenomena is not easy to disentangle, since both feed into each other in complex ways that are not yet sufficiently understood. It has been pointed out (Anthony, 1970b) that in the great majority of cases the oedipal period represents a silent revolution in which highly significant intrapsychic shifts occur without the participants becoming consciously aware of their involvement. Parents, however, may respond to the child's oedipal provocations and pressure, especially when they have sexual hangups of their own. For instance, a mother will frequently take a son into bed with her even against the wishes of her husband, or into the toilet with her because she is unable to resist his importunities. In other cases, an impotent or frigid parent may react to the child's erotic overtures with repugnance, reproachfulness, and condemnation of his "bad" behavior. The oedipal wishes of the parent are often reactivated by these oedipal manifestations in the child, but, curiously enough, these parental reactions may be overlooked by the child analyst during his treatment of the child. Unconscious erotic wishes and guilt reactions on the part of the parent may cause a fluctuation in parental behavior between seductiveness and severity that both mystifies the child and intensifies his ongoing intrapsychic conflict.

> Sandra was an attractive 5-year-old child with a happy, outgoing personality. She fell in love with her father in a rather dramatic way. She had been somewhat naughty on a particular day and had been scolded several times by him until he eventually lost his patience and gave her a spanking. He was so upset by this that he bought her a chocolate Santa Claus. She was overwhelmed by the gift, could not bring herself to eat it, slept with it at night and took it with her wherever she went. A little later, she carried Santa inside her underpants. The chocolate gradually softened with the heat and the figure became distorted in an

unpleasant-looking mess. When the father heard about this, he became curiously excited and insisted on them having what he termed a "love feast," in which they solemnly divested Father Christmas of his silver paper covering and then ate him up together [Anthony, 1970b, pp. 286–287].

Then internal things began to happen. On the night after the "love feast," the mother had had a pregnancy dream in which she was about to give birth to a monster. Following this, the father's behavior changed toward Sandra. He was aloof and strict, even contemptuous. He distressed her with demeaning remarks, and when she would try to get onto his lap, he would mock her for being babyish. His wife would champion Sandra's cause against these cruel attacks, but when this happened, the daughter would scream at her angrily to leave them alone, causing her mother to withdraw sadly.

During latency, especially in its latter part, the child once again turns his attention to the outside environment, becoming involved in work, in developing intellectual and practical skills, and in making scholastic progress. Parents learn to rely on the relative peace and quiet of this period and do their best to ignore signs of impending adolescent changes. School absorbs much of the child's life and creates the reality platform from which he can explore new areas of knowledge. Home, on the other hand, remains for him the symbol of his past dependency and the setting of many painful and best-to-be-forgotten regressive episodes.

Adolescents are even more in touch with "the world outside," not only outside themselves but outside their homes and families, their schools, and even their cities and countries. They begin to read the front pages of the newspaper for the first time and are more likely to watch news on television relating to events in distant places. Inwardly, it is a reactivation period—a reactivation of preoedipal and oedipal developments, of the individuation process, so that the psychosexual aims of early life are now almost incongruously harnessed to biological development. To escape this new set of quandaries, the adolescent turns more and more to peers and to the excitements created and cultivated by them. As Erikson (1968) puts it, he enters a tribal situation and becomes part of a pseudospecies. The regressive pull, together with the new biological urgencies and the rapidly expanding environment, may have severe repercussions on intrapsychic life and the adolescent then struggles not to be submerged under the welter of new emotions. To counteract these turbulences, he develops self-therapeutic proclivities that lead him to complete his development, consummate the pressures generated by his drives, repeat past emotional experiences, assimilate and integrate new experiences from the outside, attempt to master stresses generated by the immediate surroundings, and externalize parts of his personality onto a variety of new objects.

The balance between internal and external forces, from infancy onward, helps to structure the developing personality, and it is difficult for the child analyst, with his specialized knowledge of early development, not to remain intensely aware of the influence of environment. As Anna Freud (1966) has remarked, "The analyst of adults, due to the impression which he receives in his daily work, is in no danger of becoming an environmentalist" (p. 49). Immersed as he is in his analytic practice, he is constantly reminded of the predominance of the internal over the external. He can observe the mood swings affecting the daily lives of his patients; he can observe ways in which they manipulate the environment to feed their unconscious fantasies, and the tendencies they have to transfer irrational and false feelings from early life inappropriately onto current individuals. "The analyst of adults," she continued, "is a firm believer in psychic as opposed to external reality; if anything, he is too eager to see during his therapeutic work all current happenings in terms of resistance and transference and thereby to discount their value in reality. For the analyst of children, on the other hand, all the indications point in the opposite direction, bearing witness to the powerful influence of the environment" (p. 50).

In the treatment situation, children give evidence of the way in which their normal and abnormal behavior is environmentally influenced and the degree to which they are sensitive to every position and negative interchange their parents have with them or with each other. In his play the child reveals not only his inner world of fantasy, but also his outer world of everyday life, especially anxiety-arousing activities having to do with sex or aggression. Anna Freud concludes her commentary on child analysis and environment with this remark: "This child analyst who interprets exclusively in terms of the inner world is in danger of missing out on his patient's reporting activity concerning his—and at the same time equally important —environmental circumstances" (p. 50).

There is, however, a warning attached to these comments. There is accumulating evidence that environment may both harm and cure, but there is an intervening variable that must not be forgotten—the mental apparatus. The environment can work only through this, once the structure is established. Whereas the adult analyst may be blind to the outer environment, the child analyst may become blind to the fact that adverse environments can achieve their pathological significance only through the medium of inherent disposition and acquired libidinal and aggressive developments and associated ego activities.

The Influence of Abnormal Environments on Development

The interrelation of ego and environment for some reason appears to pose less of a problem than the interaction of ego and bad environment. The question is whether a bad environment can create an intrapsychic disorder, whether it can only amplify it, or whether it merely covers it over with an outer layer of interactional, interpersonal disturbance. It is by no means an easy question to answer, and some of the attempts made at answering it have added further to the confusion. Let us try and summarize these points of view as they have been reported.

1. At a meeting of the British Psycho-Analytic Society in the 1930s, a speaker suggested that the mother of his adult patient had exerted a baneful influence on her son's development and hence on the formation of his symptoms. This was challenged by some of his listeners, who maintained that the mother's "badness," as recalled by the patient, could itself be

a product of his neurosis and therefore subject to defensive distortions. Such mother hatreds, they maintained, became salient at different stages of an analysis and were frequently covers for deeper love attitudes that were intolerable to consciousness at that time. They concluded that the patient's need to portray a "bad" maternal image was related to his own ineffectiveness to love and to preserve a good internal representation. Glover (1964), who happened to know the mother in question, reported that the analyst and his patient were both correct in their estimates that she was, judged by any criteria, in every sense a dreadful woman! However, he reminded his audience that the proof of an actual detrimental environment did not exclude the analytic necessity for exploring the part played by the patient's own impulses in generating his pathological anxiety, even though these endogenous reactions were heavily reinforced by external factors.

2. Waelder (1964) reported on a case in which analysis was able to disentangle an "endogenous" neurotic development in a woman from the effects of a severe traumatic experience that occurred during middle childhood. The work of analysis was facilitated by the fact that the ongoing psychoneurosis continued into adult life whereas the superimposed traumatic neurosis reverberated for a while in the form of persistent nightmares, anxiety attacks, general apprehensiveness, etc., but then abated and became more of a disturbing memory than a disturbing cause. The environmental disturbance, therefore, was situational and transient and did not seem to penetrate the structural system and become part of a character response.

3. Meers (1970) reported on two cases of ghetto first graders in analysis in an interesting attempt at differentiating between environmental and psychological determinants of intellectual dysfunction and deviant behaviors. He found that the deviant behavior induced by the bad environment obscured the broad range of intrapsychic psychopathology, including psychoneurotic disorders (from which ghetto children were supposed not to suffer), and that these latter would be considered as much responsible for intellectual dysfunctioning as the cultural factors. The message here is not to overlook the presence of intrapsychic disorders and conclude too easily that a bad

environment is responsible for bad performance or bad behavior.

4. The borderline case had certainly helped the psychoanalyst to become more aware of the outer environment and the realities of its impingement on his patient. As we have seen, Winnicott believed that in such cases there was always an early failure of the maternal environment. This early failure in "management" may lead to one of two directions: as the individuals grow up, they may learn to compensate for any deficiencies in environmental resources, or they may constantly force others, including analysts, into acts of management that an analyst would hesitate to use with his more neurotic clients. The failure of environment is therefore considered to be responsible for profound intrapsychic disturbances that distort personality development in the form of borderline, narcissistic, and "as if" developments. On the other hand, speaking of the effect produced by the mentally ill mother, Winnicott (1965) has this to say: "it must be remembered, however, that the child's illness belongs to the child. . . . the child may find some means of healthy growth in spite of environmental factors, or may be ill in spite of good care." What he seems to be saying here is that the mother's disturbance or disturbing influence is incorporated into the intrapsychic systems of the child and then becomes his own disturbance, in the same way as food from the outside environment is taken in, digested, assimilated into the structure of the individual, and thereby becomes part of him. The process is still far from clear and needs more analytic work.

5. Several years ago I studied, as an example of a bad environment, the influence on the developing child of manic-depressive psychosis in the parent (Anthony, 1975). In carrying out this investigation, it was soon brought home to us that the knowledge of environment was indispensable to the understanding of both intrapsychic and interpersonal development of the offspring. Before analyzing the children, we needed to analyze the ingredients of this type of psychotic environment that fed so directly into the "developmental environment" of the child. The manic-depressive parent generates an environment in which his narcissistic, infantile hunger leads him to search desperately and constantly for any available supplies, to

the detriment of the needs of the children. As the manic phase
sets in, there is an enormous increase in self-esteem concomitant with a diminution in superego activity and the hunger for
objects, not for themselves, but for their potential for absorbing
uninhibited impulses. The exaggerated "mental metabolism"
not only intensifies insatiable orality but leads to exaggerations
of omnipotence, grandiosity, elation, the need to be loved by
everyone, and a huge output of energy, all of which help to
create the veritable "festival of the ego." The depressive part
of the cycle produces the same ingredients in reverse—despon-
dency, despair, guilt, impotence, and apathy. The effect on the
developing child is of two kinds: psychosexual development
may become variously impaired, and from time to time traumatic psychotic events may impose an additional strain on development; second, as a result of the ingredients of manic-
depressive environment, there may be a failure in the resolution of certain lines of development, inducing a persistence of
infantile narcissism, a poor regulation of self-esteem, an inability to control affects, the maintenance of omnipotence, and
exaggerated displays of optimism or pessimism. The children
from this extraordinary setting become accustomed to "playing
god," symbolically creating new worlds and unconsciously controlling and manipulating people in their environment. In turn,
they tend to feel controlled and manipulated by the sick parent
in the service of his private and personal gratification. Two
types of disturbance have been observed in the children: a preoedipal megalomanic disorder in the case of manic-depressive
mothers and an oedipal megalomania in the case of manic-
depressive fathers. The former is characterized by marked anaclitic tendencies, proneness to depression, orality, and the display of free and defused aggression; the manic-depressive father appears to affect the oedipal configuration and its
resolution in a powerful and troubling way, so that narcissistic
and omnipotent fantasies of a primal nature—the killing of the
father, the carrying off of the mother, and the control of parental intimacies—are rampant in such children (Anthony, 1975).

The Threatening Outer Environment and Its Inner Consequences

Freud's original etiological formulation (1916–1917) of a sliding scale of internal and external influences—the so-called "complemental series"—provides us the balanced outlook required to assess the mysterious interplay between endogenous and exogenous factors. In reference to this "sliding scale," Anna Freud (1966) asks us to select, for research, patients from the two extreme ends of the scale: those in whom innate damage (blindness, deafness, and deformities) may afflict the child from the beginning of life, and patients who have been severely traumatized by the loss of parents or gross parental abnormalities. Psychoanalysts have known for some time that maternal depression during the infancy of the child may predispose it to depression many years later, because its only means of achieving any sense of unity with its mother may be by reproducing her mood in itself. Psychoanalysts have also known for some time that component drives may be intensified by the interaction of external seductions with a weak ego or superego, or that parents can pass on their symptoms to their children and subsequently act them out together in the form of a folie à deux (Burlingham, Goldberger, and Lussier, 1955; Anthony, 1970a). In general, the more a parent expresses his abnormal relationship in action as distinct from fantasy, the more pathological the consequences for the child; and the more the child's pathology fits with that of the parents, the more likely is it to be maintained. When the environment is grossly threatening, the child may identify so closely with the parental psychopathology that his personality becomes patterned on that of the parent, with the neglect of his own innate potentiality. This shaping effect may take various forms. The parents may assign the child a role in their own psychopathology and relate to the child on this basis rather than on the basis of his real needs, or they may pass on their symptoms to their younger children and subsequently act them out together in the form of a folie à deux. By developing a similar psychopathology, the child may be able to preserve some semblance of unity with the mother;

and, finally, the mother's inability to effectively mirror functions during early infancy, as described by Mahler (1961), may lead to a marked degree of unresponsiveness to the outer environment coupled with inwardly directed aggression.

In response to such parental psychopathology, the innate givens, such as hypersensitivity, may lead to extreme vulnerability and failure of adaptation, while a strong push toward individuation may help to counteract the most adverse environmental influences.

Sudden changes in the expectable environment for which there is no previous preparation may set the child at risk. In such instances, the home no longer helps to maintain and develop the sense of safety and security; it no longer fulfills its primary holding and facilitating functions; it no longer provides the steady background against which the child can grow and develop. The disturbing environment generated by psychosis in a parent is especially prone to interfere with these crucial functions. The lack of predictability and the degree of chaos and disorganization may induce a crisis mentality in the child so that it subsequently provokes any environment in which it is placed to become inconsistent, inconsiderate, and inconsequential. Environment and child then collaborate to his extreme disadvantage.

The "invulnerable" child, on the other hand, develops a kind of self-immunizing capacity against harsh and threatening environments. It was often surprising how such children would extract narcissistic supplies necessary for their survival from the most desolate and ungiving caretakers. The heightened narcissism made its own pressing demands on the environment; a precocious ego learned early to conceptualize danger from any source, a self-reliant self cultivated its independence and autonomy while sharpening its coping skills and competences; a good sense of humor frequently helped to maintain a sense of proportion; and a creative energy was often able to turn misery into artistic or literary achievement. Such individuals seemed to thrive on adversity and to come out best in the face of misfortune. It is not easy to understand such resilience in psychoanalytic terms, but there is some evidence to indicate that in the case of parental psychosis, the invulnerability is bought at a price of less intimate object relations. Intellectualization, isolation, and distancing are prominent defense mechanisms. If the individual appears unscathed, it is because his feelings are not involved. He brings to all relationships an almost clinical dispassion that allows him to assess the pros and cons in the way a surgeon studies a wound. Such individuals are able to fashion a niche for themselves that represents an optimal environment for them within generally disturbing circumstances. The analysis of such "invulnerables" is an important research task for psychoanalysis.

Conclusions

A wide variety of theoretical problems relating psychoanalysis to environment have been explored in this presentation. The critical questions that have been raised are as follows: (1) What environment (or what proportion of environment) can psychoanalysis deal with comfortably within the bounds of its current metapsychology? (2) To what extent do the theoretical requirements for object relations, reality testing, and borderline or psychotic functioning entail a significant extension of environment? (3) To what degree does development through the life cycle demand the concomitant notion of an expanding environment? (4) Can the adaptive point of view (the relation between individual and environment) be incorporated into psychoanalytic theory, and does this need a major, a minor, or no revision of psychoanalytic theory? (5) If environment is recognized as an integral part of intrapsychic disorder, what parameters to psychoanalytic treatment will this require?

The reader can judge for himself how close or how distant we are to answering these questions completely. It would appear as if we have been struggling with these questions since the beginning of the psychoanalytic movement and that we will probably continue to struggle with them for some time to come. One thing is fairly clear: the relationship of psychoanalysis to environment has had its ups and downs. Within this historical context, we witnessed the rise and fall of Freud's original environmental theory of neurosis, followed by his apparent preoccupation with purely intrapsychic concerns, although, on the side, he was poaching on the preserves of anthropologists, sociologists, group psychologists, and other environmental scientists. His annunciation of the reality principle and his analysis of the varied functions of the ego brought him constantly to the interface between ego and environment, but his work on environment appeared to be for the most part diversionary and not intimately related to the main channel of his psychoanalytic theory and practice. The rise of child analysis, followed by close, analytically oriented observations of early infant development, brought the mother-baby environment into prominence as a psychoanalytically meaningful area of exploration. It was Winnicott who made a valiant attempt to include this first environment in metapsychology. A further extension into environment took place when Mahler explored the parent-toddler subculture, both observationally and in terms of an extension of psychoanalytic theory. The trio of Hartmann, Erikson, and Rapaport added new and important theoretical facets to a possible future comprehensive psychoanalytic theory of environment, the need for which has been made more pressing by the appearance on the analytic couch of narcissistic and borderline patients, representing failures of early environment. This is about as far as we can go at present, but it may be that continued careful studies on abnormal "developmental environments" (Anthony, 1975) may bring about a breakthrough in our thinking in this area. There is no question about its significance for the future of psychoanalysis, since bad environments appear to be on the increase and are even more intrusive on the developmental process. Psychoanalysts, therefore, need to remind themselves, until it becomes an automatic part of their theory and technique, to think "environmentally," especially if they wish, in their collective efforts, to create what Hartmann always hoped for—a general psychology of human behavior with a psychoanalytic framework. Even a classical psychoanalyst like Glover (1943) could sense the prevailing winds of change in psychoanalysis and the need for a more comprehensive dynamic system:

> No mental event can be described in terms of instinct alone, of ego-structure alone, or of functional mechanism alone. Even together these

three angles [dynamic, structural, economic] of approach are insufficient. Each event should be estimated also in terms of its developmental [genetic] or regressive significance, *and in the last resort should be assessed in relation to environmental factors past and present.* The last of these criteria, namely *the relation of the total ego to its environment, is the most promising of all.* It suggests that the most practical (clinical) criterion of weakness or strength should be in terms of adaptation.

It takes a new kind of psychoanalyst, trained not only in psychoanalysis but also in the more critical sciences of pediatrics and child psychiatry, to look at environment not as a last but a first resort and thus to understand "environmental deficiency diseases" in a new way. It points to the fact, already lamented by Anna Freud (1966), that the significance of environment is a function of age, which is why the child analyst is so much more cognizant of it than the adult analyst.

> The environment is so vitally important at this early stage that one is driven to the unexpected conclusion that schizophrenia is a sort of environmental deficiency disease, since a perfect environment at the start can at least theoretically be expected to enable an infant to make the initial emotional or mental development which predisposes to further emotional development and so to mental health throughout life. An unfavourable environment later on is a different matter, being merely an additional adverse factor in the general aetiology of mental disorder [Winnicott, 1948, p. 162].

References

Anthony, E. J. (1970a), The influence of maternal psychosis on children: Folie à deux. In: *Parenthood: Its Psychology and Psychopathology*, ed. E. J. Anthony & T. Benedek. Boston: Little, Brown.

———— (1970b), The reactions of parents to the oedipal child. In: *Parenthood: Its Psychology and Psychopathology*, ed. E. J. Anthony & T. Benedek. Boston: Little, Brown.

———— (1975), The influence of manic-depressive environment on the developing child. In: *Depression and the Human Existence*, ed. E. J. Anthony & T. Benedek. Boston: Little, Brown.

———— (1979), The group-analytic circle and its ambient network. In: *The Evolution of Group Analysis*, ed. M. Pines. London: Routledge & Kegan Paul.

Benedek, T. (1956), Toward the biology of the depressive constellation. *J. Amer. Psychoanal. Assn.*, 4:389.

Benjamin, J. D. (1966), Discussion of Hartmann's ego psychology and the problem of adaptation. In: *Psychoanalysis—A General Psychology: Essays in*

Honor of Heinz Hartmann, ed. R. M. Loewenstein, L. M. Newman, M. Schur, & A. J. Solnit. New York: International Universities Press.

Bowlby, J. (1969), *Attachment and Loss*, Vol. 1. New York: Basic Books.

Burlingham, D., Goldberger, A., & Lussier, A. (1955), Simultaneous analysis of mother and child. *The Psychoanalytic Study of the Child*, 10:165–186. New York: International Universities Press.

Erikson, E. H. (1950), *Childhood and Society*. Rev. ed. New York: Norton, 1963.

—— (1968), *Identity, Youth and Crisis*. New York: Norton.

Fairbairn, W. R. D. (1944), Endopsychic structure considered in terms of object-relationships. *Internat. J. Psycho-Anal.*, 25:70.

Fraiberg, S. (1969), Libidinal object constancy and mental representation. *The Psychoanalytic Study of the Child*, 24:9–47. New York: International Universities Press.

Freud, A. (1960), Discussion of Dr. John Bowlby's paper. *The Psychoanalytic Study of the Child*, 15:53–62. New York: International Universities Press.

—— (1966), *Normality and Pathology in Childhood*. London: Hogarth Press.

Freud, S. (1887–1902), *The Origins of Psychoanalysis*. New York: Basic Books, 1954.

—— (1896), The aetiology of hysteria. *Standard Edition*, 3:189–221. London: Hogarth Press, 1962.

—— (1905), The fragments of an analysis of a case of hysteria. *Standard Edition*, 7:123–245. London: Hogarth Press, 1953.

—— (1908), "Civilized" sexual morality and modern nervous illness. *Standard Edition*, 9:177–204. London: Hogarth Press, 1959.

—— (1913–1914), Totem and taboo. *Standard Edition*, 13:1–161. London: Hogarth Press, 1955.

—— (1916–1917), Introductory lectures on psycho-analysis. *Standard Edition*, 15/16:320–340. London: Hogarth Press, 1958.

—— (1921), Group psychology and the analysis of the ego. *Standard Edition*, 18:67–143. London: Hogarth Press, 1955.

—— (1923), The infantile genital organization. *Standard Edition*, 19:141–145. London: Hogarth Press, 1961.

—— (1924), Neurosis and psychosis. *Standard Edition*, 19:149–153. London: Hogarth Press, 1961.

—— (1930), Civilization and its discontents. *Standard Edition*, 21:64–145. London: Hogarth Press, 1961.

—— (1939), Moses and monotheism. *Standard Edition*, 23:7–137. London: Hogarth Press, 1964.

Fromm, E. (1947), *Man for Himself*. New York: Rinehart.

Glover, E. (1943), The concept of dissociation. *Internat. J. Psycho-Anal.*, 24:7–13.

—— (1964), *The Technique of Psycho-Analysis*. New York: International Universities Press.

Hartmann, H. (1931–1935), Psychiatric studies of twins. *Jahrbücher für Psychiatrie und Neurologie*, 50/51.

—— (1939), *Ego Psychology and the Problem of Adaptation*. New York: International Universities Press, 1958.

—— (1944), Psychoanalysis and sociology. In: *Psychoanalysis Today*, ed. S. Lorand. New York: International Universities Press.

—— (1950), Psychoanalysis and developmental psychology. *The Psychoanalytic Study of the Child*, 5:7–17. New York: International Universities Press.

————— (1952), The mutual influences in the development of the ego and id. *The Psychoanalytic Study of the Child*, 7:9–30. New York: International Universities Press.

————— (1955), Notes on the theory of sublimation. In: *Essays on Ego Psychology*. New York: International Universities Press, 1964, pp. 215–240.

————— (1956), Notes on the reality principle. In: *Essays on Ego Psychology*. New York: International Universities Press, 1964, pp. 241–267.

————— (1958), Comments on the psychoanalytic theory of the ego. In: *Essays on Ego Psychology*. New York: International Universities Press, 1964, 113–141.

————— (1959), Psychoanalysis as a scientific theory. In: *Essays on Ego Psychology*. New York: International Universities Press, 1964, pp. 329–330.

Horney, K. (1939), *New Ways in Psychoanalysis*. New York: Norton.

Jacobson, E. (1964), *The Self and the Object World*. New York: International Universities Press.

Kardiner, A. (1939), *The Individual and his Society*. New York: Columbia University Press.

Kohut, H. (1966), Forms and transformations of narcissism. *J. Amer. Psychoanal. Assn.*, 14:243–270.

Kris, E. (1950), Notes on the development and on some current problems of psychoanalytic child psychology. *The Psychoanalytic Study of the Child*, 5:24–46. New York: International Universities Press.

————— (1954), Introduction. In: *The Origins of Psychoanalysis*. New York: Basic Books, pp. 3–47.

Kuhn, T. S. (1962), *The Structure of Scientific Revolutions*. Chicago: University of Chicago Press.

Levy-Bruhl, L. (1926), *How Natives Think*. London: George Allen, Unwin.

Lewin, K. (1936), *Principles of Topological Psychology*. New York: McGraw-Hill.

Mahler, M. (1961), On sadness and grief in infancy and childhood: Loss and restoration of the symbiotic love object. *The Psychoanalytic Study of the Child*, 16:332–351. New York: International Universities Press.

————— Pine, F., & Bergman, A. (1975), *The Psychological Birth of the Human Infant*. New York: Basic Books.

Meers, D. R. (1970), Contributions of a ghetto culture to symptom formation. *The Psychoanalytic Study of the Child*, 25:209–230. New York: International Universities Press.

Miller, I. (1975), A critical assessment of the future of psychoanalysis: A view from within. *J. Amer. Psychoanal. Assn.*, 23:139–153.

Modell, A. H. (1968), *Object Love and Reality*. New York: International Universities Press.

Ostow, R. (1977), Autobiographical sources of Freud's social theory: Totem and Taboo, Group Psychology and the Analysis of the Ego, and Moses and Monotheism. *Psychiat. J. Univ. Ottawa*, 2:169.

Piaget, J. (1929), *The Child's Conception of the World*. New York: Harcourt, Brace.

————— (1954), *The Construction of Reality in the Child*. New York: Basic Books.

————— (1971), *Psychology and Epistemology: Towards a Theory of Knowledge*. New York: Grossman.

Rapaport, D. (1947), Dynamic psychology and Kantian epistemology. In: *Collected Papers of David Rapaport*, ed. M. Gill. New York: Basic Books, 1967.

——— (1958), The theory of ego autonomy: A generalization. In: *Collected Papers of David Rapaport*, ed. M. Gill. New York: Basic Books, 1967.

——— (1960), On the psychoanalytic theory of motivation. In: *Collected Papers of David Rapaport*, ed. M. Gill. New York: Basic Books, 1967.

Russell, B. (1959), *The Future of Science*. New York: Philosophical Library.

Sandler, J., & Rosenblatt, B. (1962), The concept of the representational world. *The Psychoanalytic Study of the Child*, 17:128–145. New York: International Universities Press.

Spitz, R. A. (1946), Anaclitic depression. *The Psychoanalytic Study of the Child*, 2:313–342. New York: International Universities Press.

Stone, L. (1961), *The Psychoanalytic Situation*. New York: International Universities Press.

Sullivan, H. S. (1947), *Conception of Modern Psychiatry*. Washington, D.C.: William Alanson White Psychiatric Foundation.

Waelder, R. (1964), Panel discussion. Princeton Meeting of Group for the Advanced Study of Psychoanalysis. Unpublished.

Winnicott, D. W. (1941), The observation of infants in a set situation. *Internat. J. Psycho-Anal.*, 22:229–249.

——— (1948), Paediatrics and psychiatry. In: *Collected Papers: Through Paediatrics to Psycho-Analysis*. London: Tavistock, 1958, pp. 157–173.

——— (1949a), Birth memories, birth trauma, and anxiety. In: *Collected Papers: Through Paediatrics to Psycho-Analysis*. London: Tavistock, 1958, pp. 174–193.

——— (1949b), Mind and its relation to the psyche-soma. In: *Collected Papers: Through Paediatrics to Psycho-Analysis*. London: Tavistock, 1958, pp. 243–254.

——— (1950), Aggression in relation to emotional development. In: *Collected Papers: Through Paediatrics to Psycho-Analysis*. London: Tavistock, 1958, pp. 204–218.

——— (1951), Transitional objects and transitional phenomena. In: *Collected Papers: Through Paediatrics to Psycho-Analysis*. London: Tavistock, 1958, pp. 229–242.

——— (1952), Anxiety associated with insecurity. In: *Collected Papers: Through Paediatrics to Psycho-Analysis*. London: Tavistock, 1958, pp. 97–100.

——— (1954a), The depressive position in normal emotional development. In: *Collected Papers: Through Paediatrics to Psycho-Analysis*. London: Tavistock, 1958, pp. 262–277.

——— (1954b), Metapsychological and clinical aspects of regression within the psycho-analytical set-up. In: *Collected Papers: Through Paediatrics to Psycho-Analysis*. London: Tavistock, 1958, pp. 278–294.

——— (1956), Primary maternal preoccupation. In: *Collected Papers: Through Paediatrics to Psycho-Analysis*. London: Tavistock, 1958, pp. 300–305.

——— (1965), The effect of psychotic parents on the emotional development of the child. In: *The Family and Individual Development*. New York: Barnes and Noble, 1969.

11

Mature and Regressive Determinants of the Keeping of Promises

HERBERT J. SCHLESINGER, Ph.D.

Introduction

My interest in the topic of promising was first aroused by a patient's lifelong pattern of breaking promises and by the feelings of disappointment and frustration that are generated in one to whom such promises are made (Schlesinger, 1978). But, while the breaking of promises tends to capture our attention, broken promises are fortunately not the rule, and the continuity of expectation, anticipation, and fulfillment in our daily lives remains fairly intact. Nor is being broken the only pathology to which promises are subject. I should like to discuss briefly some pathological phenomena at the opposite pole from the breaking of promises, especially promises that must be kept regardless of consequences, even when fulfillment would be maladaptive. I will show that there are forces within the psychic structure that make for the keeping of promises, quite apart from the motives with which the promises are made.

First of all, let me impose a limitation on what I can offer. There are many converging forces that help assure that promises will be kept. To enumerate, there are: (1) social pressures, customs, traditions, common and statute law. (2) There are the counterparts to these social arrangements in individual development that stem from growing up in a context of mutuality and interdependency and that lead to the making of promises when there is a significant counterwish or resistance opposing the promised act. Thus, all the reinforcement of the sense of

311

obligation is added to the wish to keep the promise. (3) There are the infantile magical roots of this developmental process that are entwined in the making and keeping of bonds, as these have been described by Roheim (1945) and others. (4) There is the repetition compulsion, by which term in this context I refer to the tendency to repeat in action what has already been expressed in words. (5) There is the tendency of promises, as representative of the larger class of intentions or interrupted actions, to create a tension system which of itself presses toward discharge. (6) There is the increased vulnerability of such tension systems to subversion by drives, both because of their inherent discharge tendency and because of the particular significance that promises have in ego and superego development. (7) There is also the tendency, in the event of regression, for drives, either directly or through superego channeling, to seize upon the promise and to discharge themselves through its fulfillment.

I am not at all sure that this list of "forces" is complete or, indeed, if all of them are really independent of each other. Perhaps some are merely different points of view toward the same processes. In any case, each of them, however much they may overlap, may add some fresh insight about the total problem. I deal for the most part with only two of them that I hope provide an interesting contrast between the determinants in social and individual psychology.

Upon first considering the matter, we might wonder what pathology could reside in a kept promise. Surely everything that we believe would lead us to conclude that promises are meant to be kept. And yet, a moment's reflection might lead us to recall such clinical commonplaces as the following:

> A parent of a hospitalized psychiatric patient who had seriously wounded himself in an attempt at suicide confessed to the boy's physician that she "knew it wasn't a good idea to give him the gun for his birthday, but what could I do? I promised him he could have it when he was 10."

Or the following:

> A young therapist came to his supervisor in an ethical dilemma. His patient confessed to him, after receiving redoubled assurances that what

a patient says to his therapist is completely confidential, that he had committed a serious crime. Now the therapist was on the spot, burdened both by the secret that he shared and his promise to the patient. He was not even sure if he should tell the supervisor what the patient had told him.

These incidents may remind readers of an event that is still quite fresh in our minds:

> The police chief of Dallas, in spite of all the precautions to thwart any attempt to "get Oswald," chose to move the prisoner from the city jail to the county jail according to a prearranged and preannounced plan and in the presence of numerous newsmen. According to the Associated Press, he said, "If I hadn't promised you people that I would not take Oswald until this morning, we would have taken him during the night. I told you I wouldn't back down on my pledge."

Surely we are free to speculate about the several determinants that led to the literal fulfillment of this pledge and to the overriding of good judgment. But, as in these other instances, the overvaluation of the promise or pledge would remain a problem.

Looking at these incidents, we might be quick to observe that both the parent and the therapist have used the fact that he has made a promise, albeit a foolish one, to bar the further exercise of good judgment. We might be inclined to observe with justified irritation that good parents and good therapists or good chiefs of police don't get themselves into such jams. With a bit more charity, we might be willing to take into account the parent's ambivalent feelings toward the son and the therapist's overidentification with his patient. These dynamic factors did, of course, contribute to each of these episodes. But would we, in pointing to these sources of motivation, have explained how both behaviors came about? Would we have explained, for instance, the peculiar sense of helplessness that both parent and therapist experienced when they found themselves doing what they knew they should not do, almost against their wills?

I hope these examples make plausible my assertion that the mechanism or process of promising, the psychological capacity to make a commitment, can be subverted in the keeping as well as in the breaking. How does the act of promising become the point at which ordinarily repressed forces can erupt? I defer trying to answer this question in order to summarize some thinking about the psychology of making and keeping promises I have presented in detail elsewhere (Schlesinger, 1978).

The Natural History of Promising

The natural history of the capacity to make and keep promises begins in the phase of development that is under the sway of the primary process. At that time, the primary form of promising has mostly to do with omnipotence of thought and resembles only superficially the mature or secondary forms of promising we expect of adults.

It is commonplace to hear statements from children that are couched as promises and which adults even tend to take as promises but which are psychologically not promises at all. Our children learn very early that adults place special value upon statements cast as promises, and they quickly learn to use these verbal formulae, even if they remain ignorant for some time about the total significance that they have for adults. When a child under the threat of loss of love "promises," we tend to accept his token of surrender and allow him back into communion with us. His promise serves its purpose of repairing the breach between the parent and himself. Certainly, the young child who promises to be good has no clear idea what this entails other than to do what mother wants him to at any moment. He can hardly pledge a future of which he has no conception and even less control.

Sharpe (1950) wrote about the cautionary tales we tell our children, which, while couched in the *past* tense, are meant to control the *future* behavior of the child. By analogy, we could call children's promises of this kind "propitiatory tales," for though cast in the *future* tense, they are intended, like an apology, to correct the *past*, to undo a misdemeanor and the resulting alienation of one's parents. Thus, this *primary form* of promising, or propitiatory tale, can be seen as occupying a similar place with respect to secondary narcissism, as the infant's cry had to primary narcissism. Crying, originally an expression of discomfort, comes, through its signal value to the parent, to be the means of relieving discomfort. The cry magically brings back the parent and restores the infant–parent unity. Similarly, the primary "promise" comes to have the magical significance of restoring a somewhat older child to his parents' graces and assuring the continuation of their love for him.

As secondary process replaces primary process in the functioning of the young child, he comes to understand that it is not enough simply to give a promise. Rather, he learns that giving a promise only describes what he must later perform. The agent necessary between a promise and its fulfillment is the promisor himself who binds himself to complete the act his verbal promise has made necessary.

The act of making a promise one intends to fulfill and then does fulfill is one of the highest achievements of secondary process functioning. It requires a well-developed sense of time and of continuity of self over time. There must be the awareness that something stated now may have consequences at a later time, even when the need or other circumstance that prompted the original statement has subsided. There must be the ability to anticipate the future, to foresee the possible situations that may eventuate at the time one commits oneself to redeem one's word. There must, of course, be the capacity to defer action to a later time as well as the ability to remember value received vividly enough to be willing to pay for it at a later time. Or, in the case of a situation of both deferred pleasure and deferred payment, one must be able to invest oneself sufficiently in a future contingency.

Basic to these preconditions, there must be a developed awareness that there are objects apart from oneself and that one exists in a condition of mutual dependency with these objects. Also important, in a related developmental sequence, is that there be a well-developed ability to distinguish between and deal separately with thought and action. The other achievements that mark the growth of relatively autonomous structures for cognition and action are no less important.

The awareness that we live with one another in mutual dependency is reinforced by our shared value system in which such concepts as responsibility, obligation, and honor play important roles. Equally important is that capacity (popularly called "will-power") to act in accordance with one's sense of obligation, in spite of possibly wishing to do otherwise (Piaget, 1962). Making and keeping a promise could well be considered the paradigmatic acts of moral development. We can use promise making and keeping as "windows" through which one can study central aspects of personality development and adult personality functioning.

Why Promises Are Kept

Before we can examine some of the special forces in individual life that press for the fulfillment of certain promises, we must consider, if only in cursory fashion, the more general pressures that make for regularity in this area. We take fulfillment of promises so much for granted that we may fail to realize that promises themselves are but words[1] or symbols, meaningless apart from some act of fulfillment. Tenuous as this foundation may seem, our whole civilization is based upon promises and their sanctity. The checks we are paid with and the currency for which we exchange them are only promissory notes. But, aside from the example of our national treasury, there are a number of sources of pressure to keep promises. Traditions of chivalry, honor, and romantic love idealize the promise, the vow, and the oath and extol scrupulous fulfillment of promises often more highly than life itself. Indeed, in many settings we can say little worse of a person and do little more effectively to place him beyond the pale than to say that he does not keep his word (the paradox that we can also admire, if not openly, those who "can get away with it," deserves separate consideration). Thus, our shared value system, our awareness of social reality, and the consequences of the failure to keep our promises, together with sanctions of custom and social institutions, are potent reinforcers of the sanctity of promises.

---

[1]"Oaths are but words, and words but wind"—Samuel Butler.

Nevertheless, these guarantees of honorable behavior, while quite effective, hardly operate in any absolute fashion. We know that men often are no better than they ought to be and that promises are not always fulfilled. When shared value systems prove insufficient, civilization provides recourse in laws that compel fulfillment of promises or exact punishment for default. But whether we idealize or romanticize the connection between a promise and its fulfillment, take it for granted, or are ever ready to cry "fraud," we expect a promise to be succeeded by redemption. The words imply the act; much of the time we expect to be able to take the word for the act itself.

Often the sanctity of promises in our value system tends to become identified with morality itself. And yet, we have all made observations that undermine any absolute position about the sanctity of promises. For, if a promise is sometimes valued more highly than life itself, it may at other times be valued at less than the breath with which it is spoken.

Even an honorable person will at different times use identical promissory formulae to mean quite different things. And it is highly unlikely that such a person will be misunderstood in each of his or her usages, so prepared are we to take context into account in attributing significance to each other's utterances. There is no need to document the wide variety of implicit, but well-understood, conditions taken for granted in most of our promising behavior—"Yes, of course, I will bring the book tomorrow," with an unspoken, "that is, if I remember it and I am more likely to remember it if, in my estimation, you will really need it tomorrow." In most of our everyday promising behavior, the likelihood of fulfillment is conditioned by tacit (but often mutually understood) reservations in which the dangers, or inconveniences, or embarrassments of nonfulfillment are weighed against the hazards associated with efforts toward fulfillment. This is to say no more than mature promising behavior is subject to the reality-testing function of the ego.

Thus, while solemnly upholding that promises are sacred, we note that paradoxically large segments of our everyday promises are made without any great sense of "moral risk" (Kading, 1960). This absence of "moral risk" is so prevalent that in many interactions a man may not expect to be believed, unless he takes special efforts to signal his sincerity. The signals that he wishes to be taken at face value when his word could, for one reason or another, be discounted by the listener, range from the oath he takes in court through the interjection, "I *really* meant it," or a deliberate reiteration, a fervent handshake, etc. Children, too, soon learn to develop special signals to indicate that they want to be taken seriously ("cross my heart and hope to die") or that they are not to be taken seriously ("cross my fingers"). It is apparent that some element of magic attends these kinds of sealing of bonds (Reik, 1959).

Our language retains many such vestiges of the primal magical meaning of promising which originally were intended not only to compel the hearer's belief but also to guarantee fulfillment. Such expressions as, "I'll be damned if . . . ," which are in the 'if–then" syntax of promising, are, of course, these days not understood as promises. Cultural historians say, however, that they were once deemed to have great force and that the superstitious thought to invoke the devil was tantamount to inviting him to appear. But there was some awareness of the duality of promising even in the earliest times, for a number of reinforcing devices, precursors of "I'll be damned if," were used to make sure that all understood that *this* oath or promise was real. Thus, the oath assumed more force if sworn in blood, on a grave, or in the name of a god or of someone dead or alive whose integrity one honored. To swear in such a way struck listeners with awe for nothing thenceforth could dissuade the swearer from the execution of his intention. He had foresworn control of himself; his pledge would take precedence over all reason (Gaster, 1957). Attenuated gestures, like putting one's hand on the Bible, are the faint residues of ancient and far more heroic practices (Reik, 1959). Our ordinary usage at present is hardly so severe in regard to promising.

Something of the weight given promises and oaths of medieval times can be gained from a glance at English history. Trevelyan (1958), in discussing the reasons for the success of the Norman conquest of England with a relatively small invasion force, notes that William's claim to the throne of England was weak but:

[He had] won the sympathy of continental Christendom by certain arguments which appeal very little to modern minds, though they served conveniently to brand Harold for many centuries as a perjurer–usurper. . . . William had, a couple of years before the death of Edward [the then reigning king], compelled Harold, who had fallen by chance into his hands, to swear on certain relics to be his man and to support his claims to the . . . English throne. The solemn oath and its flagrant breach weighed heavily on the minds of contemporaries, in whose everyday lives and legal proceedings oaths sanctioned by religion played a very much larger part than in our own. The less formal modern mind is more impressed by the fundamental injustice of William's proceedings; he took advantage of an accident to compel his guest, as a condition of safe return home, to swear away his own chances of succession and those of [another more valid claimant] and his country's freedom to decide its own destiny. It is one of the points on which medieval and modern ethics stand honestly at variance [p. 114].

The same text, describing the legal system in England in the century following the Norman landings, tells about:

[T]he barbarous Anglo-Saxon method of trial by 'compurgation,' when a man proved his case by bringing his friends and relations in a sufficient number to swear that they believed his oath. . . . The oaths of these 'compurgators' swearing to a man's innocence or to his character, even if they did not know the facts of the case at issue, held the place which the examination of evidence holds today in criminal justice. It was the oath more than the evidence that was valued [p. 159].

Thus, we see that, in fairly recent times, it did not matter whether the oath was meant, was made in the heat of anger, or was extorted—an oath was an oath, and there could be no mitigating or extenuating circumstances. The concept of justice at this time focused on the *act*—no matter why it was done. The one or the thing that did it must be punished.

The fate of a promise depends on much more than the ostensible (conscious or unconscious) motives for making it. The keeping of a promise may be rationalized in several different ways. For some persons, it is enough that a promise has been made; it is kept as a matter of course; not to do so would be unthinkable.[2] A central characteristic of this attitude is that

---

[2]Along the continuum of such attitudes lie degrees of self-conscious dedication and feelings of solemn obligation. At one pole of this attitude, one cannot be released from a promise, short of fulfillment, even by the person to whom the promise is made.

practical fulfillment of the promise seems not to depend upon any subsequent events. Other promises are kept as if extorted—"If I do not keep it, something bad will happen." Many implicit promises are kept for fear of inner or outer retaliation. Closely linked to this kind is one characterized by fulfillment of the promise, so long as certain expressed or unexpressed conditions are met. For instance, "I will keep the promise if you are good to me, or if you continue to love me, or if I continue to love you." Belonging to this type may be a promise kept in anticipation of some benefit that is to follow.

It is also not uncommon for a promise to be kept for reasons quite apart from those for which it was made. For example, a promise made as an expression of intense emotion, a promise with a large primary element, may become fulfilled for quite extrinsic reasons. A banal instance: we may make a pledge at a charity banquet greater than we can afford because everyone else seems to be doing so. It may later become a point of pride to impoverish ourselves to meet the pledge, or perhaps we may discover that a favorable tax deduction makes the benefaction worthwhile.

A more interesting variety of this phenomenon is common in popular romantic literature. Typically, a young rake gives a "line" of false promises to seduce an innocent girl. Having succeeded in his plan, he proceeds to fall in love with her and insists upon making her an honest woman, redeeming his formerly worthless pledges. Thus, even apparently unmeant promises may become fulfilled, as meant ones are, under the transformations possible through regression when aided by the catalytic action of unconscious guilt.

Case Examples

These digressions may seem a strange way to pursue an argument that began with the implication that a thing said is often as good as done and that promises may fulfill themselves in spite of the wishes of the promisor. But I hope to make my point against the background of our realization that in everyday experience the connection between a promise and its fulfillment is not a simple skein but a complexly woven fabric whose un-even texture reflects influences now from one source and then from another. This fabric of promising is so elastic, so respon-sive to inner reservations and external contingencies, to vari-ables of circumstance and context, that the process ordinarily attending the making of a promise and its subsequent fulfill-ment requires a continual and delicate adjustment and balanc-ing of shifting attitudes and altered realities and attention to the changing significance of one's bond. Fulfilling a promise in a complex life situation is hardly an automatic process.

The very complexity of the interrelationships between promisor and promisee, the multiple influences to which a promise is subject on its uncertain course toward possible ful-fillment, is in itself an expression of what we have come to call cryptically the autonomy of the ego. Put in statistical terms, the greater the complexity of the situation, the more the degrees of freedom; conversely, the simpler the structure, the less free-dom there is in it. This is simply another way of saying that there seems no extrinsic reason why a man should have to do what he says he will do. All the more remarkable, then, to discover those instances in which it seems that, without external compulsion and even against his own wishes, a man must keep his promise, come what may.

> For example, a military guard, while at his post with another sentry, shot and killed his companion, who was also his friend. Investigation showed no obvious motive: There had not been a quarrel or any reason for enmity. But there had been some peculiar precursory events. In the squad of which the murderer and his victim were members, there had developed an unusual amount of mutual teasing about someone getting shot. In a prankish way, the murderer told his victim that he was going to shoot him. A macabre countdown followed, as he reminded his friend that he had only 36 hours to live, then 24, then 8, and so on. When the fateful moment arrived, they were on guard duty together, and the murderer drew his pistol and shot his friend. The murderer could not explain or understand why he uttered the words, nor why this friend was chosen as victim. The words, once spoken, seemed to assume an imperative quality of their own.

I do not mean that we should accept as a complete explana-tion that the soldier did it only because he promised to. Doubt-less an investigation in depth would fill in some of the gaps and explain the sources and vicissitudes of the aggressive motives that culminated in the destructive act. But we would still face the problem of how the spoken word, not even uttered seriously, found its way into action precisely as promised.

I add now some illustrations from the behavior of a patient who avoided making promises as if afraid of just such an eventuality.

> A successful stockbroker had, through years of study and experience, developed what he thought was an excellent system for investing in the market. He was eager to try out his system, using his own funds, but found the greatest difficulty in doing so. He would promise himself to follow his plan to the letter, buying and selling by certain market indicators until he had given the system a fair chance. But, in his attempts to carry out his promise, he found himself inadvertently sabotaging his plan. Rather than waiting until matters developed to the point that his plan envisaged, he found himself second-guessing his plan, impulsively improving on it by buying or selling on hunches, and by doing so he almost invariably lost money. The patient could not explain why he did not give his plan a chance, claiming that he did not realize until after the damage was done that he had effectively undermined it. Analysis linked this peculiar behavior to his behavior in other areas in which he was afraid to be trapped by any plan, commitment, or promise he might make. He permitted himself to make a commitment with only the greatest unease and then frantically tried to extricate himself, to break loose, to prevent himself from being imprisoned by it. This pattern of behavior reflected the fear of loss of his own autonomy or independence which was threatened by any kind of commitment. He struggled against his own entirely self-generated plan, as if, once made, it had acquired a motive force external to him, rather like one of his father's injunctions. Each decision and plan he made had in it the seeds of a potential compulsion, and, in order to protect himself, he had to defeat his own plan before it defeated him.

A promise or plan was more likely to become a trap for the patient, if it was made in anger.

On the golf course he became angry with a foursome that played too close behind his. There were some angry remarks among his friends, and the patient thought it would serve one of the approaching golfers right if he were to pick up his ball and keep it. He was about to swear that he would do it, when he suddenly became anxious and started to talk soothingly both to himself and to his companions. He had suddenly "realized" that, if he did pick up the ball with the intention of keeping it, nothing anyone said or did would make him give it up, even if he had to fight everyone to hold on to it. The patient fantasied the scene and scandal that would result if he, in his position, were caught brawling on a golf course over someone else's golf ball, and the danger was real enough for him to back away before he became the victim of his own intentions.

Promising and Psychopathology

Regression and Magical Thinking

These examples will strike an analyst as familiar in some degree and will no doubt suggest dynamic hypotheses. But it is the mechanisms that shape such behavior, and not the motives that push it, that interest me at the moment. How is it that the act of promising becomes the point through which expressed forces threaten to erupt? And how is it that fulfillment often seems to require either mature reality testing or magical reinforcement, or both?

The fulfilling of any promise (and the style of fulfillment) has as much to do with mediating structures as with initial intentions and even more to do with structures in the instance of promises that "take on a life of their own." The mediating structures and capacities chiefly implicated in promising and in fulfillment of promises seem to me to be much the same as those subverted in obsessive-compulsive thought pathology. I do not mean that promising is intrinsically pathological any more than are doubting, action delaying, and intellectualizing. But all of these acts, promising included, because of their peculiar origin and structure, are particularly vulnerable to intrusion by unconscious motives and thus made to serve neurotic purposes. We are familiar with how doubting or action delaying, cognitive functions essential to reality testing, can become symptoms expressing not the patient's relative autonomy from reality but rather his failure to come to terms with his deepest drives. So with promising; the capacity to make a contract or a commitment that can express the highest purposes of man may also be subverted and become the expression of far more fundamental aspects of his personality. We may see here a specific instance of Freud's general dictum about the close relationship between the superego and the id (Freud, 1923).

The *act* of promising itself has in it some primitive elements; it has regressive as well as progressive features; it contains within its structure the chink through which primary processes and magical thinking can return and with them the destruction of the very hard-won, self-determining capacity—of ego autonomy itself.

We theorize that the development of secondary process out of primary process depends on the occurrence of unavoidable delays in gratification of oral needs. The early involuntary experiences of delay encourage the development of thought, and, as secondary processes become instituted, the capacity for thought permits self-induced and self-regulated delay of impulse and with this the autonomy of the ego from external and internal stimuli. In this way, man becomes something more than a stimulus-response organism. But we should not forget that man is still an animal and that what matters in the end is what a man does and not just what he thinks. So we find that the growth of structure, etc., leads to the development of an autonomous but, by that token, a more effectively *acting* organism in which the elements of delay, thought, choice, and reality testing become modulators, channelizers of acts, *not* preventers of acting.

Through the acquisition of a sense of time and of the ability to predict the outcome of events on the basis of average expectancies and to anticipate consequences, man gains a significant degree of control over his future. Since we depend on perceived regularities to map our behavior, it is only natural that we value order, stability, and predictability in our environment, particularly among the other persons that make up our environments. Perhaps this need for order as a means of controlling the unknowable future may help to explain the high value civilized communities place on law, tradition, customs, and personal commitments to behave in an orderly and predictable manner. Thus, while one of the tasks of early development is to establish autonomy from inner and outer sources of stimulation, one of the tasks of later development is to prepare for the subsequent recommitting of this relative autonomy, this freedom to act. Of course, this description of the development of autonomy and its commitment as a two-phased process is accurate only in a rough sense, comparable in precision with the oversimplified description of psychoanalytic treatment in terms of the development of a transference neurosis and its resolution.

I have underscored this familiar state of affairs as a prelude to reminding you that the connection between word and action has a history of its own and is not to be taken for granted. It is paradoxical that we refer to the making and keeping of promises as an activity of a very high order, perhaps even the crowning achievement of the mature personality, while its essence, the invariable connection of word and action (as well as the temptations that promises put in our way to accept thoughts as actions) is not at all characteristic of secondary process thinking. In fact, the establishment of the reality principle and the attainment of secondary process are based upon the capacity to *separate* thought and action.

The capacity to commit oneself fully and freely and to fulfill one's commitments depends, I believe, upon having achieved a significant degree of secondary autonomy, which state implies that all the apparatus of the secondary process is potentially at the disposal of one's commitment. This capacity has been labeled variously during the brief history of psychoanalytic thinking, but such terms as maturity, genitality, and generativity are conspicuous in the descriptions. Yet, it is a paradox that mature commitment should be the ultimate result of a process of development whose immediate goals, teleologically, are quite in the opposite direction, for we are accustomed to think of the primary process as the state of mind in which thought and act are indistinguishable, in which an action tendency and a completed act, a wish and its fulfillment, are not yet separable. The tasks of early development, mastery of which lead to the acquisition of a sense of reality, consist essentially in establishing these basic discriminations—between self and nonself, between wish and reality, between word and act. Only gradually, as these basic distinctions are achieved, is thinking possible. And the maintenance of the sense of reality and of efficient adaptation is based upon the maintenance of the separateness of the realm of thought and the realm of acts.

But, within this model of the developing ego, what happens when one makes a promise?[3] Do we not, in effect, compromise the separateness of the realms of thought and action that we were at such pains to achieve? When we promise, after all, we forge a link, a "bond" between our words and our deeds. Not knowing what the future will hold, we yet dare to commit a portion of that future by binding ourselves to act in accord with our intention. In this sense, we purport to determine what the future will hold. By speaking in this way, I hope that what I have described is seen as a secondary process version of omnipotence of thought. To the extent that we are serious about our promise and that it is a far-reaching promise, we give up our freedom to base our decisions on our current perception of reality. To that extent, our behavior becomes removed from the influence of reality testing and judgment; secondary process functioning itself, as well as secondary autonomy, becomes impaired. For some patients, at least, the making of a promise is tantamount to contriving and establishing a (possibly) transient compulsive symptom.

"Here I stand—I can do no other," is not just Luther's experience but that of many people who have become the servants of intentions that have gotten away from them. There may be an implied or direct promise or threat involved in a compulsive symptom—the familiar warning behind the compulsive act, "Touch it, or your father will be killed," etc., may be linked to this. The closeness of the formula of promising and the formula of magical thinking can be seen by comparing "I say it and I will do it" and "If I say it, it will happen." These statements, which are, of course, entirely distinguishable at the level of mature secondary process functioning, tend to become

---

[3] I shall confine myself, except where I specify otherwise, to the simplest form of promise which might be defined as an act begun with a declaration of intent which is carried out at a later time. Negative promises to avoid some act or generalized promises to be true to some ideal require some additional consideration.

identical as regression alters the level of functioning toward primary process.

Perhaps I sh uld reiterate once more that I do not mean that promising is tself pathological; as Hartmann has pointed out (1939), the experience of "I must" does not necessarily imply pathology. While theories of mental health usually stress the presence of control by the conscious and preconscious ego, or rationality in general, the normal ego must also be able to yield to "musts." These "musts" Hartmann links to necessary stable automatisms in ego functioning and to higher order "central regulation." The capacity to develop automatisms as well as other forms of "regressive adaptation" (p. 77) is necessary for adaptive functioning. Nevertheless, promising as one of such "detours through the archaic" (p. 78), because it necessarily reunites thought and action (more accurately ideation and motor discharge), creates a point of vulnerability in psychic functioning, a point of lowered resistance through which unconscious impulses may find an easy route to expression. There is also the enhanced possibility that archaic modes of functioning, such as magical thinking in the area of the promise, will reemerge.

Thus, the act of promising tends to reestablish the old functional equivalence between thought and action which the maturing ego worked so hard to differentiate during the establishment of secondary process. In the sense that the conditions of an earlier phase of development replace the accomplishments of a later phase, we can think of promising itself as a regressive act. To call upon the currently fashionable distinction, we can concede that in most instances this turnabout is a "regression in the service of the ego." But whether the promise is "in the service of the ego" or the ego has become the servant of the promise is a distinction of some theoretical and practical importance.

Freud described the phenomenon of a promise that must be kept in his case of the "Rat Man" (1909). This obsessional patient's vow to replay the postal fee to Lieutenant A. is a clear example of this kind. Freud accounts for this phenomenon partly as a regression from action to thought: "Preparatory acts become substituted for the final decision, thinking replaces

acting and, instead of the substitutive act, some thought preliminary to it asserts itself with all the force of compulsion" (p.
244).

To assimilate Freud's example and part of his explanation
to my own frame of reference, one could think of regression[4]
from action to thought or from thought to action interchangeably. At least in the circumscribed area of the neurosis a regression has occurred from secondary to primary process functioning in which thought and action are interchangeable and
psychologically indistinguishable. Under these circumstances, a
thought can well become invested with the "force of compulsion."

The Psychology of Intention

Let me pause for an interim summary. Thus far I have
referred to two sources of pressure in the keeping of promises.
The first was an omnibus factor, including all those forces that
affect mature people acting in a responsible way in a social
context. Shared value systems, reasonable self-interest, obligation, and honor are significant terms in this area—theories of
which are more common in social psychology and sociology
than in psychoanalysis. A second factor was the structure of the
act of promising itself. Because of the reuniting of word and

---

[4]The use of the term *regression* in these several senses encourages confusion. Since man is an actor, the direction of psychological processes from
percept to act is considered progressive (Freud, 1900). When a thought replaces an act subsequent to it in such a chain of events, we deem the process
regression from action to thought. Yet, much of the behavior we describe
clinically as regressive implies, even if indirectly, that higher functions are
replaced by lower ones and that what should only be thought is being acted
upon. In its everyday clinical usage, it is hard to avoid a value connotation to
the term *regressive*, the implication being that there is something "sick" about
it. But to use the term accurately in its proper descriptive sense, one must
divorce it from such connotations. For instance, based on the assumption that
psychological functioning follows the sequence—percept to thought process
to discriminative action, we may term this direction *progressive*. A movement
in the opposite direction would therefore be regressive. This is not to say that
an action that follows a thought will necessarily be adaptive. It might just as
easily be maladaptive. Thus, in terms of our model of the psychic apparatus,
the direction of functioning of a person who after deliberation decides to rob
or murder would have to be called progressive, though his actions might
from most points of view be ill-advised.

act characteristic both of promising and of primary process, a point of low resistance to penetration by unconscious motives is established, resulting in some instances in a compulsive quality to the fulfilling of the promise.

This second factor can be approached from another point of view, for promising can be subsumed both logically and psychologically under the more general heading of intention. A promise is an intentional statement—the first phase of an act whose execution is temporarily suspended. The psychology of such interrupted acts has been intensively studied and may throw some light on the nature of promising.

Freud very early made a contribution to this general area with the observation that certain kinds of memories have a peculiar attribute of endurance, a greater unresolved discharge potential than others. He had already recorded in 1882 that in his dreams occurred only such themes as "were touched upon once in the course of the day and then broken off." This observation was elaborated in *The Interpretation of Dreams* (1900) to include several classes of unsolved and unfinished concerns of the day. This basic process, the striving for expression or realization of unresolved tensions (wishes), whether of mourning (1907), unconscious sense of guilt (1923), or others, has also acquired central importance in our understanding of symptom formation.

The idea that there is a special character to intentional statements was supported from outside the field of psychoanalysis proper. Lewin (1935) evolved a theory and with his students devised ingenious experiments to test hypotheses about such tension systems. The experiments of Zeigarnik (1950) and Rickers-Ovsiankina (referred to by Lewin [1935, p. 242]) are especially important in that they show the tendency of undischarged tensions to linger and to remain effective as "quasi-needs" within the ego organization itself, without necessarily implicating drive tensions. For instance, one experiment showed that, of a long series of simple tasks presented the subject, those were remembered best which the subject had not been allowed to complete. Similarly, other experiments showed that, of a long series of tasks, the subject was most likely to resume spontaneously those tasks which he had been prevented from finishing in the first place. Related experiments showed to what extent fading of the tension system took place and what manner of substitute tasks seemed capable of discharging such tension systems. It is important to note that certain quite superficial experiences of interference with the discharge of presumably quite small amounts of energy result in the establishment of active tension systems which have a predictable fate under certain circumstances. These experiments in the psychology of intention seem to link our well worked-out theory of unconscious motivations to our less well formulated conceptions about deliberate, conscious, and goal-directed actions.

The intentional statement, whether promise, threat, or any other of its forms, has the character of an incomplete task leaving a tension system that will continue to press toward discharge. Such a tension system may pose a special problem for the defense and control capacities of the ego, for it is ever ready to serve as a preconscious "nucleus" available to be infiltrated by some unconscious wish. I believe that the promise acquires this character through its structure—being not only a verbal statement but an anticipator of, or a preparation for, and by that token the inciter of, or beginning phase of an action. A promise is an interrupted act.

It follows that we should not really need to make special efforts to remember a promise as if it were the location of a mislaid object (in the absence of a counterwish to forget it), for the promise itself, like a wish, ought to remind us of its presence. Its undischarged tension system should itself serve as a strong spur to memory. Clearly, promises, like wishes, can be repressed, and also, like them, can return. Each of us has had the experience, I am sure, of having an almost-forgotten promise return to mind. The common experience I believe is that it is accompanied by a rush of feeling with both motor and autonomic components, indicating that it is a far-from-neutral memory that returns. To anticipate a question, I shall add that it is, of course, a matter for fuller consideration to determine how much and what kind of support the memories of unfulfilled promises receive from superego reinforcement. I do hope, however, to establish the relative independence (at least in principle) of these memory-tension systems from id reinforcement. I concede, of course, that all is not "ego," or we would hardly have the opportunity to observe such phenomena in our consulting rooms.

But even the promise that seems to fall into desuetude does not simply cease to exist. On the contrary, I assume that it remains as a tension system, albeit an attenuated one with a peculiar readiness to be revived in full strength at some subsequent time. In this propensity, I would compare it with those seemingly indifferent events that become screen memories for earlier events which through retrospective construction are reinstated as traumata sometime after the fact.[5]

A similar fate may overtake certain promises made to oneself. Let us recall that that part of the "self" to whom we make promises was originally another person who, through introjection and identification, has long since become part of the self. The "self system," while a quite stable affair under many of life's vicissitudes, can under certain conditions become dissociated once again. This phenomenon is most clearly seen in severe depressions when introjects split again into their original components. Some of the severe self-reproaches that are characteristic of this illness may well be based upon promises to the self that have not been kept. It seems likely that old and abandoned "intentions," which when formed had not even the force of a literal promise to the self, or intentions which were allowed to lapse when they no longer seemed convenient or important, may be seized upon and converted retrospectively via displacement and the mechanisms associated with unconscious guilt into broken promises of enormous import. It is as if the superego in depression seizes upon the still faintly cathected memory traces of such unfulfilled promises and abandoned intentions and revives them once again in more than original strength. In the regression associated with depression, the promise forgotten becomes the "promise faithlessly broken" and may be experienced by the ego as if it had been actually made to an outside object.

---

[5]Comparing them with the unfinished tasks that provide the day residue for dreams, the durability of promises suggests that they have considerably more tension associated with them, as well as a more coherent structure.

Some Implications for Treatment

I should like to end by looking at a commonplace of clinical experience, the way in which some patients attempt to solve their oedipal conflicts, from the point of view of promising. How often we explain to a patient the implicit meaning of his behavior in the transference as an unconscious contract he had made with his parent. For instance, "If I am 'good' [that is, a good patient] father will some day give me what I have always wanted." A tenacious resistance is often based upon this formula. The whole analysis—free association, coming on time, paying—comes to be what the patient does for the analyst in the expectation that sooner or later the analyst will redeem a promise to fulfill his deepest wishes that the patient fantasies his parent once promised to make good to him. By living up to what he considers to be his end of the bargain, the patient magically expects to restore, in the person of the analyst, the promising but as yet unredeeming parent-figure. It is perhaps needless to point out how susceptible the analyst may be to acting out his own wishes to be a "good parent" under the pressure of such subtle inducements.

Especially interesting is that this pattern of neurotic solution of an infantile conflict involves, along with the other examples of promising behavior I have mentioned, a subversion of secondary process. Such a neurotic solution to the oedipal conflict is, of course, impossible, unless a considerable degree of psychological maturity has been achieved, for it rests upon the developed capacity for voluntary delay of impulse discharge. What makes the solution neurotic, of course, is that, rather than using the ability to test reality to reject the infantile wish, the patient puts the capacity for delay into the service of magical thinking. The wish is repressed with the implicit hope or expectation that what is impossible now may some day be possible, if certain expiatory or propitiatory conditions are met. Thus, the forbidding parent is construed to have asserted only a conditional prohibition—"You may not have this unless or until you do that." Typically, the effect of such an unconscious exchange of promises is that, rather than renouncing the wish, the patient renounces certain possibilities of realistic gratification in the hope of thus assuring ultimate gratification of the infantile wish sometime in the indefinite future.

In the transference neurosis we see these hopes and promises revivified, and as the patient strives to be "good" in fulfillment of his end of the bargain, the analyst may find himself unwittingly pressed into the mold of the parent. I mention this commonplace phenomenon of psychoanalytic practice here because it is usually referred to in terms of inhibitions or symptoms. From the point of view of ego psychology, we are led to look at the kind of bargains or promissory arrangements that are involved and focus not just on what the patient suffers but on what he hopes to obtain through his suffering. Not the least of the advantages of these promissory arrangements, of course, is that the patient is able to maintain his hold upon tabooed objects and fantasies by displacing or projecting the time of fulfillment into the distant future.

Summary

I have tried to survey some of the factors, rational and social, and nonrational and more deeply psychological, that help guarantee that promises will be fulfilled. Among the more narrowly psychological factors is the peculiar tendency to linger and press toward discharge that promises share with other kinds of interrupted actions. Also, because of its peculiar nature, linking again word and act in order to control a portion of the unknowable future, promising retains overtones of earlier phases of magical thinking and is thus especially vulnerable to penetration and capture by repressed wishes. Thus, to commit oneself, to make promises that, on the one hand, reflect the highest intellectual and moral capacities of humanity, may, on the other hand, also function in a regressive way to serve as a vehicle for the discharge of our deepest drives.

References

Freud, S. (1900), The Interpretation of Dreams. *Standard Edition*, 4:1–338. London: Hogarth Press, 1953.

——— (1907), Mourning and melancholia. *Standard Edition*, 14:243–258. London: Hogarth Press, 1957.

——— (1909), Notes upon a case of obsessional neurosis. *Standard Edition*, 10:151–249. London: Hogarth Press, 1955.

——— (1923), The ego and the id. *Standard Edition*, 19:3–66. London: Hogarth Press, 1961.

Gaster, T. H. (ed. & trans.) (1957), *The Dead Sea Scriptures in English*. Garden City, N.Y.: Doubleday Anchor.

Hartmann, H. (1939), *Ego Psychology and the Problem of Adaptation*. New York: International Universities Press, 1958.

Kading, D. (1960), On promising without moral risk. *Philosoph. Studies*, 11:58–63.

Lewin, K. (1935), *A Dynamic Theory of Personality*, trans. D. Adams & K. Zener. New York: McGraw-Hill.

Piaget, J. (1962), Will and action. *Bull. Menn. Clinic*, 26:138–145.

Reik, T. (1959), *The Compulsion to Confess*. New York: Farrar, Straus & Cudahy.

Roheim, G. (1945), *War, Crime and the Covenant*. Monticello, N.Y.: Medical Journal Press.

Schlesinger, H. J. (1978), Developmental and regressive aspects of the making and breaking of promises. In: *The Human Mind Revisited*, ed. S. Smith. New York: International Universities Press.

Sharpe, E. F. (1950), Cautionary tales. *Collected Papers*. London: Hogarth Press.

Trevelyan, G. M. (1958), *Illustrated History of England*. London: Longman, Green.

Zeigarnik, B. (1950), On finished and unfinished tasks. In: *A Source Book of Gestalt Psychology*, ed. W. D. Ellis. New York: The Humanities Press, pp. 300–314.

12

Psychoanalytic Nosological Considerations

JOHN FROSCH, M.D.

Terminology and Methodology

A nosology fulfills many needs. It enables us to discern similarities and differences between clinical manifestations. It separates and establishes hierarchies. Making a diagnosis accomplishes much more than giving a name to a phenomenon. The latter process is more correctly designated as nomenclature. The concept *diagnosis* encompasses many considerations. Among these are genetic, economic, dynamic, prognostic, and therapeutic implications. A psychoanalytic nosology more specifically should enable us to clarify psychodynamic variations between and among these factors. As such it encompasses etiological variations and specific differences in intra- and interstructural psychological processes. It considers drives and conflicts, as well as object relations and the self. Such a nosology should enable us to focus our psychotherapeutic endeavors more clearly. What is necessary, therefore, is not to dispense with nosologies but rather to clarify our thinking in establishing a nosology.

Any attempt to establish a psychoanalytic nosology, let alone the definition of the concepts in such a nosology, encounters many problems. Not the least of these is the fact that there is by no means any agreement as to the heuristic value of establishing such a nosology, as well as what the frames of reference should be in doing so. Staercke (1920), for instance, felt there was no value in making any differentiation among the various

335

syndromes. Further, there is by no means consistency in the use of terms. Any attempt to evaluate and survey psychoanalytic contributions to the various syndromes founders on both terminological and methodological confusion. This will be seen in the section on neurosis and psychosis, when an attempt is made to delineate what characterizes the psychoses in contrast to the neuroses. As we study the earlier psychoanalytic literature we see that neurosis and psychosis were considered by some as separate entities, whereas by others the terms were used interchangeably. Actually, Freud repeatedly refers to psychotic conditions as neurosis—for instance, in the use of the term "narcissistic neurosis."

As still another example are the many contributions which have ostensibly been made in the area of psychosis, but have dealt primarily with schizophrenia.

In the early psychoanalytic literature it often is difficult to differentiate contributions made about paranoia, paranoid mechanisms, paraphrenia, schizophrenia, etc.; at times these concepts were used interchangeably.

This slipping over from concepts about schizophrenia to psychosis and vice versa is a perennial problem.

Some of the confusion generated in the psychoanalytic literature is due to the fact that terminology has not been used consistently in all areas. An example is the use of the term "narcissistic neurosis" in relation to psychosis. Freud conceptualized the narcissistic neuroses as the counterpart of the transference neuroses, but in the Introductory Lectures (1916–1917) he at times equates the former with psychosis or indicates that they are in some way related. Today the term "narcissistic neurosis" is no longer applied exclusively to the melancholias, as was the earlier practice. In addition, the term has become somewhat debased by the rather broad frame of reference within which the concept of narcissism is used.

The confusion is compounded by the question among psychoanalysts as to whether there is any basic, qualitative difference between neurosis and psychosis, some feeling that it is pointless, in view of the course of the clinical picture, to try to differentiate the two. This is not only a problem in psychoanalysis but represents an ongoing controversy in clinical psychiatry as well, as is illustrated by the controversy regarding the inclusion of psychodynamic concepts in DSM-III. This led for a while to the exclusion of the term "neurosis," on the argument that it could not be clearly defined clinically.[1] The term "psychosis," however, was retained, via a listing of symptoms commonly associated with what is considered a psychotic condition. No attempt was made to define the psychotic process, or the dynamics of psychosis. Ostensibly the classification maintained the diagnosis of various clinical syndromes at a descriptive level, an attempt which it was claimed failed for the concept neurosis.

To help us find our way through these dilemmas, I should like to emphasize some basic methodological considerations. The violation of certain important principles is not infrequent, and leads to unending controversy and confusion. We may examine a phenomenon at three levels: descriptive, dynamic, and genetic. The first step is to describe what we see and to achieve some degree of agreement on this—the descriptive level. We may then direct ourselves to an examination of how the interplay of various forces produces what we see—the dynamic level. Finally we may turn to why it happens, and in just this way. We are now talking of causality and development—the genetic level, which includes not only hereditary and constitutional factors but early developmental factors as well. Psychoanalysis has contributed to all three areas; but it is the latter two, the dynamic and the genetic, that have been the focus of most psychoanalytic contributions. It is important to remember, however, that the dynamic and genetic features allow us better to understand phenomenology and have implications for prognosis and therapy.

Psychoanalysis in its developmental studies has been criticized for lacking a normative frame of reference and taking pathology as its central concept. This, however, is not currently the case, especially with the development of a psychoanalytic ego psychology. Although "ego weakness" has hitherto been easier to define, one can now equally define "ego strength." Several frames of reference are currently available whereby one

---

[1]This was subsequently modified to include the term "neurosis" for several conditions, however, in parentheses.

can define emotional health and emotional illness, or worded otherwise, normal and abnormal, terms which appear to have a pejorative connotation. The concept of normality is of course a highly controversial one. Cultural and social frames of reference are frequently invoked and up to a point are important. However, normality and complete reality adaptation are not identical concepts. The degree of social receptivity to pathology and the extent to which given psychopathology may fit in with a given culture—what has been referred to as sociosyntonic psychopathology—may mask severe psychopathology (Frosch, 1983).

It is clear that frames of reference in addition to the cultural must be evaluated in determining ego strength and ego weakness, emotional health and emotional illness. Among these are the ego's position vis-à-vis the external and the internal environment; the extent to which the individual is functioning up to capacity; the physical and emotional well-being of the individual; the level of the individual's responses to stresses and strains, as well as of habitual modes of mastery; the capacity to permit and reverse regression and dedifferentiation; and, finally, the capacity of the organizing function of the ego to establish a harmonious balance among the various psychic operations. These frames of reference are offered as no more than that, with the full awareness that it is still at times exceedingly difficult to draw a sharp line between emotional health and emotional illness.

Frames of Reference

Rangell (1965), reviewing many arguments both for and against the need for a psychoanalytic nosology, opted for a unified approach to establishing a nosology, one based on detailed study of the function of the three components of the mental apparatus. He proposed an assessment of libidinal aims, ego functions, and superego functions, as well as an evaluation of constitutional and environmental factors.

This is not too dissimilar from Anna Freud's diagnostic developmental profile. In both instances several written paragraphs are required, hardly suitable for the parsimony appropriate to a workable nosology. This drawback was recognized by Rangell, who acknowledged the need for succinct labels for the various conditions. He suggested the following three-part summarizing formula: "Presenting symptoms of—, in a character background of—, and functioning—" (p. 152).

Menninger (1954) chose to view the various conditions as arising out of upsets, under various degrees of stress, of the homeostatic balance and psychic equilibrium established and maintained by the regulatory function of the ego. Glover (1932), addressing himself to the descriptive Schneiderian classification which selects specific symptoms and symptom clusters as a frame of reference, noted that "an end product classification in psychiatry is . . . inadequate and must give way to a more 'functional approach' " (pp. 163–164). In setting up his classification, he used the fate and development of ego-nuclei as his frame of reference: "At the beginning is a cluster formation of ego-nuclei converging on a consecutive series, the elements of which show an increasing degree of organization. The cluster and the first few nuclei that follow, represent the fixation-points of the psychoses; the last organized nuclei represent the fixation-points of the neuroses" (pp. 170–171). He then correlated the various levels of ego nuclei development with the mechanisms of introjection and projection, as well as with reality sense. Out of the interrelation of these factors he developed a classification of mental disorders, quite readily admitting that other frames of reference are equally possible.

It is clear then, that the frames of reference used will have an impact on the nature of a nosology. Since these vary so much, a generally agreed-upon nosology is difficult to achieve. For example with the topographical model of the mind, schizophrenia becomes a prominent focal area. With libido theory and economic factors emphasized, stress is laid on fixation points, on the aims of the sexual instinct, and on object cathexis. The concept of withdrawal and restitution, within the framework of the libido theory, dealt essentially with the patient's relationship with the persons and objects of the world around and within him. In the first instance, that of withdrawal, there is a decathexis; in the second, that of restitution, attempts are made to recathect and to establish contact with the object, attempts which frequently miscarry. It was within this framework that the concept of narcissism was further elaborated. However, the role of object relations, which could evolve from pursuing this line of thought, could equally well be elaborated. The whole area could then be examined within the framework of the dual instinct theory, whereby the role of the death instinct and of aggression, with its impact on self and object, could be studied. By contrast, when the various conditions are viewed within the framework of the structural model of the mind, emphasis is placed on the role of the superego, the ego and its functions, and the level of object relations and self-object differentiation. Object relations theorists and self psychologists focus on the fate of the basic dual relationship of mother and child. All of these frames of reference have had some impact on the nosological categories.

Winnicott (1959), noting the contributions of psychoanalysis to psychiatric classification, pointed out that these are phase-related to developing psychoanalytic thinking, rather along the lines I have presented. He is inclined to agree with Menninger in not establishing definitive and fixed clinical syndromes, as a diagnostic judgment must be made at a specific point in time. The clinical picture, however, may vary at different stages, and the diagnosis may therefore have to be altered. Winnicott's suggestion for a classification depends on what he called the environmental distortion. By "environmental" he refers to the basic child-parent dependency relationship, as well as to any factors that facilitate or traumatize it. In the earliest stages a "double dependency" obtains, whereby the infant is unaware of the very existence of the environment it is dependent on. In another light, this may be viewed as a lack of differentiation between self and nonself. Environmental failure, in which phase-appropriate needs are not met or actual trauma is experienced, will bring in its wake primitive defenses which may lead to psychotic development.

Once there is an awareness of this environment and the mother is recognized as a necessary source of dependence where the environment is deprivatory and there is already the equipment to perceive such deprivation, antisocial tendencies may develop as a reaction. Later, when the individual has developed an Oedipus complex and castration anxiety has created conflict, the individual deals with failure by establishing defenses at a higher level and psychoneurosis or depression may ensue.

In short, Winnicott emphasizes, as an essential frame of reference, the stage and nature of environmental failures to meet the child's dependency.

Classification

In 1976 a committee of the American Psychoanalytic Association compiled statistics of the various clinical conditions treated by psychoanalysts, with varying treatment modalities. A summary of this report has kindly been provided by Dr. Daniel Jaffe, chairman of the committee (see Table 1). It is clear that though neuroses and character disorders account for a high percentage of those treated by psychoanalysis, a considerable number of other conditions are being treated by psychoanalysts, with one modality or another. Most surprising is the high percentage of patients being treated by long-term psychoanalytically oriented therapy.

According to the report, nearly four out of five analyzable patients fall into four main categories: neuroses, character neuroses or disorders, personality disorders, and neurotic reactions. But it is not clear what differentiates these groups more specifically (Table 1).

It struck me, as I made a gross survey of psychoanalytic contributions, that they fall under several headings and subheadings, listed below. These were essentially influenced by prevailing frames of reference, which, however, have repeatedly been revised over the years.

I.   Freud's early concepts revolving around the ideas of trauma and defense
II.   The topographic model

TABLE 1
Patients of Psychoanalysts—Diagnostic Group by Treatment

	Psycho-Analysis (%)	Long-Term Intensive (%)	Long-Term Supportive (%)	Short-Term Therapy (%)	Other Modality (%)	Total: All Modalities (%)
Anxiety	11.3	12.3	4.5	9.0	6.9	9.7
Hysterical	10.5	7.9	4.5	7.3	11.3	8.1
Obsessive-Compulsive	20.0	11.3	3.7	1.8	5.1	9.2
Depressive	10.7	15.7	18.5	20.3	12.9	16.0
Borderline	2.3	4.9	6.0	1.2	1.8	3.3
Narcissistic	6.9	4.3	3.2	3.6	1.1	4.3
Other Neuroses & Neurotic Reactions	8.7	5.6	3.2	5.1	4.1	5.7
Other Character & Personality Disorders	14.3	13.2	14.5	7.5	11.4	12.0
Psychoses	3.8	7.9	24.2	18.8	13.5	12.6
Other Diagnosis	11.5	17.0	17.6	25.2	32.0	19.2
TOTAL	100	100	100	100	100	100
% of all Pts.	21.8	30.6	13.7	26.4	7.4	100

III. The libido theory, with cathectic shifts and fixation points as a frame of reference, and the concepts of withdrawal and restitution

IV. The dual instinct theory and the role of derivatives of the death instinct and aggressive drives

V. The structural model

   A. The position of reality and the object in relation to the various psychic structures (the problem of self/nonself differentiation as well as problems in identity)

   B. The state of the psychic structures

      1. Intersystemic (differentiation or dedifferentiation of psychic structures from each other)

      2. Intrasystemic

         a. State of the ego, id, and superego

         b. Disturbance in ego functions

            i. Defensive

            ii. Primary and secondary autonomous ego functions

VI. Object relations theory

VII. Self psychology

VIII. The defect–defense controversy

It seems to me that most contributions would fall into one or the other area, with emphasis being determined by the theoretical orientation of the contributor. It should be clear that there is by no means a clear delineation in the various phases of psychic development in these contributions. As was pointed out above, there is a great deal of overlap here. For instance, many later contributions on the fate of the object and on self/nonself differentiation were dealt with in earlier contributions within the framework of levels of regression and withdrawal and restitution. It will not be possible to do full justice to many contributions; nonetheless, we will try to relate the contributions to the delineated areas. It is clear that within the space limitations imposed, we will not be able to discuss all the syndromes.

Since we are dealing here with nosological conceptions, we will restrict ourselves to the major clinical categories, with no

extensive discussion of the various subcategories. We will begin
with the neuroses and psychoses.

Neuroses and Psychoses

Since we will discuss these syndromes in greater detail in
the following sections, we will simply emphasize some conclusions reached there.

The clinical manifestations of neurosis and psychosis are
governed by the neurotic and psychotic processes. These processes may eventuate in other clinical manifestations, such as
character and trait disorders, and in idiosyncratic behavioral
manifestations. In delineating the salient features of these processes, I have suggested three frames of reference: the source
of the anxiety, the nature of the defenses, and the presence of
impaired ego states and ego function.

Using these frames of reference, we differentiated between
neurosis and psychosis. The source of the anxiety in neurosis
is at a much higher level in psychic development than in psychosis. The threatening dangers are generally separation, loss of
love, castration, and superego punishment. In psychosis it is
the regressive fear of dissolution and disintegration of self and
reality which is the basic danger. Ergo it becomes a problem in
psychic survival.

The characteristic nature of the defenses, or modes of reaction to the conflict in neurosis, are repression, displacement,
reaction-formation, conversion, etc. These are all in the service
of preserving object contact. In the psychotic, in whom preservation and survival of self are the main frames of reference, we
encounter regressive dedifferentiation, introjection, primitive
projection, fragmentation, projective identification, splitting,
and massive denial.

We turn to the question of whether there are unique distortions and impairments of the ego and its functions that differentiate neurosis from psychosis. It should be pointed out that
in the neurotic process we are dealing with an ego structure
and its functions sufficiently differentiated to cope with the
threatening dangers. The degree of differentiation between

self and nonself facilitates the capacity to maintain contact with reality and the object.

In the psychotic, self/nonself differentiation is not as sharply developed as in psychosis. The psychic structures are not as clearly differentiated from each other. We are dealing with a vulnerable ego whose tenuous boundaries make it difficult to preserve itself as a psychic structure, integrated and differentiated from the other psychic structures and reality. Id-derived fantasies and impulses invade the ego, with ensuing impairment of ego functions, reality testing among them. The ego must keep watch on reality, on the id, and on the superego. It feels itself threatened on all sides, since it is weak to begin with, and has trouble maintaining differentiation and fending off self-dissolution.

We should like to emphasize that the sine qua non for clinical psychosis, in contrast to neurosis, is the loss of the capacity to test reality, and that its retention militates against clinical psychosis even though there may be many other features of the psychotic process present. As has repeatedly been emphasized, defects in the capacity to test reality go hand in hand with disturbances in object relations, with whose development they are inextricably interwoven. It is then obvious that disturbed object relations of a serious nature are equally present in gross clinical psychosis. Although in neurosis there is an impairment of object relations, at no point does this reach the point of distortion of the reality of the object.

It was obviously impossible to do full justice to the many contributions, especially those involving the defect–defense controversy that has invaded the more recent literature. In essence, although defense plays a role in the psychotic process, and may be placed in the service of defect, we are dealing here essentially with defects in psychic development. In neurosis we have conflicts which are dealt with by defenses.

Several contributions are especially critical of the withdrawal-restitution, decathexis, and recathexis frames of reference, to explain the clinical phenomena of psychoses, and suggest that the alterations of ego functions that are seen in psychoses are defenses against the emergence of anxiety. Such defensive alterations affect object relations and contribute to the so-called break with reality.

Historical Development

It is in the early classifications, some features of which persist to this day, however altered by Freud's emendations and additions, and those of subsequent writers, that we find the basis for a psychoanalytic nosology. I have in mind particularly the classical case reports of the early 1900s (e.g., the Wolf Man, the Rat Man, and the Schreber case). In the section on neurosis and psychosis I described some general considerations of these syndromes and sketched the historical background of how psychoanalytic understanding played a role in the evolving nosology. I pointed out how the dominant theoretical frames of reference contributed to the nosology as well as to the understanding of these conditions psychodynamically. I do not intend to offer any detailed discussion of the clinical manifestations of the specific neuroses and psychoses, but simply wish to demonstrate how psychoanalysis played a role in the evolution of the nosology of these syndromes. I will begin with the neuroses.

The Neuroses

It was in the 1880s that Freud's interest in hysteria was engendered and fostered by his work with Charcot at the Salpêtrière. Naturally his interest was directed mainly to somatic manifestations, as this was Charcot's main preoccupation. It was, however, under the stimulation of Breuer's case material, the case of Anna O., and the Dora case (Freud, 1905), that his subsequent interest in hysteria evolved. On the basis of this work, Freud and Breuer enlarged Janet's concept of splitting of consciousness to include what Breuer referred to as hypnoid states—special states of consciousness during which certain ideas emerge.

But the ground-breaking contribution lay in a different direction, namely, in the so-called retention and defense types of hysteria. It is from this latter concept as a jumping off point that Freud evolved his concepts of the role played by defense (repression) in the formation of the neuroses.

Freud's work with Dora (1900, 1905), was used to underline his belief that hysteria is nothing more than a playing out of sexuality. More specifically, infantile sexuality was viewed as including sexual wishes and experiences that subsequently would be rejected. This was in keeping with frames of reference then prevailing. With the development of the dual instinct theory, the structural model, and a psychoanalytic ego psychology, other components were added to the concept of hysteria, including the role of aggression and pregenital complaints.

Despite his early concentration on hysteria, Freud was still left with two main clinical syndromes—hysteria and neurasthenia. The latter included practically everything that hysteria did not. At the time Freud began his studies (1894), anxiety reactions of all types were part of the picture of neurasthenia. By virtue of an evaluation of certain differences in etiological factors, he tended to separate two different clinical syndromes, neurasthenia and anxiety neurosis, although they could be combined if the patient showed all the etiological factors playing a role in the two syndromes.

In both neurasthenia and anxiety neurosis, Freud felt, there was at work a current disturbance in sexual life which acted as a noxious influence. In neurasthenia excessive masturbation and emissions were the common clinical finding, while in anxiety neurosis several sexual problems, having in common the element of abstinence or of incomplete satisfaction, frustrated sexual excitement, or incomplete coitus, were the common factor.

Basically, Freud saw in anxiety neurosis and in neurasthenia somatically generated neuroses, with physiological (chemical) factors playing a role, a view which I believe he held to the end. He referred to both syndromes as "actual neuroses," a category in which he also included hypochondriasis.

Anxiety neurosis, then, is dominated by manifestations of anxiety which were felt to be derived from distorted sexual drives. This view was questioned by many and Freud himself, i.e., in his significant paper (1926), modified his thinking about anxiety, which he then formulated as one of the factors leading

to defense. Both anxiety neurosis and neurasthenia were somatically based and to these he added hypochondriasis, referring to
these as "actual neuroses." "The hypochondriac," wrote Freud
(1914), "withdraws both interest and libido—the latter specially
markedly—from the objects of the external world and concen-
trates both of them upon the organ that is engaging his attention" (p. 83).

Many of the older formulations relating to these early
Freudian categories are no longer accepted as valid. Freud's
concept of neurasthenia as related to excessive masturbation is
not accepted by most analysts, nor is the Freudian description
of anxiety neurosis and neurasthenia as "actual neuroses"—that
is, states caused by the accumulation of undischarged sexual
toxins, in contrast to the psychoneuroses. Nonetheless, there
are some who still adhere to this concept with regard to the
anxiety neuroses. The clinical differentiation based on the "defense neuropsychoses" (1894, 1896) has been considerably
modified. Yet, interestingly enough from a clinical point of
view, many of these designations are maintained, with however
many refinements.

In contrast to these clinical conditions was hysteria. This
Freud believed was psychically determined and belonged to
what he called the psychoneuroses. To these he added anxiety
hysteria and obsessive-compulsive neuroses. In the former,
phobias were the dominant manifestation, the psychodynamics
of which were elaborated in his famous case study of Little
Hans (Freud, 1909). By means of displacement, projection, and
avoidance, the underlying anxiety, generated by sexual or aggressive wishes, was deflected onto other situations.

Regarding the obsessive-compulsive neuroses, in 1896
Freud formulated the concept of the anal character, which
showed the features of obstinacy, frugality, and orderliness.
He postulated that many features of the obsessive-compulsive
disorders, as well as the compulsive character, derived from the
anal-sadistic phase, to which the patient regresses after a failure
to deal with the problem at the phallic-oedipal level.

Freud proceeded to delineate phases in the development
of obsessions and laid the basis for showing how the obsessions

or compulsions, as we ultimately see them, are attempts at defense (i.e., repressions) which, failing, are followed by further attempts at defense. In the obsessional the original idea may be entertained, but the affect is shifted to something else, if not repressed; alternatively, the idea may be repressed and the affect appears, though transmuted. The ideas which appear are distorted in some way—e.g., something present, usually something asexual, is latched onto as the obsession—but in all instances they are derived from the original idea.

Subsequent contributions by psychoanalysts to the understanding of the neuroses were made by Horney (1937), whose frame of reference differed from the more classical psychosexual one. Her contribution to the understanding of the neurotic personality emphasized cultural factors. She believed that the specific cultural conditions under which a person lives determine in the last analysis the particular form of neurotic development. She focused on the basic anxiety generating both conflict and the defenses, which are shared by all neuroses. This anxiety and the fears that occasion it are determined by features characteristic of a given culture, as are the protective devices used to ward them off.

Many views of the nosological categories have been affected by the growing body of data regarding etiological factors. This is especially true of the gradual understanding of preoedipal factors in psychic development. Many clinical conditions have been found to cut across many lines as regards psychic levels of development. Hysteria, for instance, which was initially described as related to unresolved oedipal problems of a specific nature, and to the phallic phase in psychic development, was found to have contributions from much earlier levels of psychic development. Although it is clinically obvious that any condition may cut across many developmental lines, it is important to bear in mind that since psychic development does so as well, there will be contributions from many levels to any given syndrome. But overdetermination does not imply dilution of the organizing role of a particular determining factor. No matter how many elements are contributed by other sources, these are subsumed under a single organizing principle.[2]

---

[2]This principle is also known in physiology. Uchtomsky called it the "Dominate."

With the gradual unfolding of many nosological formulations, anxiety and the measures used to defend against it became a major frame of reference in views of symptom formation. The ego's position vis-à-vis reality and the love object was
yet another. The latter is especially useful in differentiating
neuroses from psychoses. A basic nosological role was assigned
also to the impact of vicissitudes and ultimate fate of infantile
anxieties, drives, fantasies, and experiences.

To reprise Freud's nosological theorizing to this point,
then, he had come to distinguish the actual neuroses (including
neurasthenia, anxiety neurosis, and hypochondriasis) and the
psychoneuroses (including hysteria, anxiety hysteria, and obsessive-compulsive states). We have seen that Freud developed his
nosology gradually, based on his recognition of certain genetic
and dynamic features characterizing these illnesses. As his work
with patients proceeded and his knowledge expanded, he began to find it necessary to widen his nosology or at least to shift
his frames of reference. This occurred in several areas. For
instance, Freud's recognition of various libidinal shifts with regard to levels of object relatedness occasioned an expansion of
the concept of narcissism.

In addition, the concept of defense was progressively
broadened until it became apparent that many defenses were
woven into the warp and woof of the personality. There they
became part of the individual's way of coping with internal and
external stress. Little by little, then, a psychoanalytic characterology evolved, with attention directed to the different clinical
character types and their manifestations in the treatment situation.

As the understanding of the various clinical syndromes
improved, it became clear that some distinction had to be made
between symptom disorders and character disorders. In the
former, specific troublesome symptoms presented themselves
more or less clearly. In the latter, the pathology affected the
total personality and often was reflected in an identifiable lifestyle. It became clear, however, that even the symptom disorders had elements of character pathology, and that in the treatment of character disorders symptoms would become manifest.
The study of characterology broadened the nosological picture

so that clinical entities began to multiply. Among the additions were the neurotic characters, the borderline personalities (or, as I chose to call them, the psychotic characters), the narcissistic characters, and the impulse-ridden characters.

All of this went hand in hand with the development of the structural model of the mind and the development of a psychoanalytic ego psychology. Interest began to focus on the impact of ego defects as well as defenses on various clinical pictures, especially psychotic or borderline patients. With the development of object relations theory and self psychology, emphasis was directed to both borderline and narcissistic characters.

Freud's experiences during therapy had contributed to his nosology, as he began more and more to see the role that transference plays in the treatment of patients. As his interest in the phenomenon grew, he began to consider it one of the most important therapeutic levers. Accordingly he began to classify patients in terms of whether they were able to develop a transference, and to what extent it was able to evolve in the treatment situation. Although this was in a sense a therapy-oriented approach, it nonetheless had its roots in dynamics and genetics, and was related to a theory of personality development in which narcissism occupied a central role. He therefore introduced the distinction between transference neuroses and narcissistic neuroses. In the latter the libido is so wrapped up in the self that the capacity to develop transference is impaired. This is seen for instance in psychosis, especially schizophrenia. Prime instances of the former were seen in hysteria, anxiety hysteria, and obsessive-compulsive states.

Implicit in the concept of transference is that of object relations, the capacity to identify with another person. If this ability is not present, the transference as such is difficult to develop. What we have essentially is indifference. As is always the case, this sharp dividing line is not quite valid clinically, or even theoretically. We know that even psychotics have some capacity for object relations, and that they at times develop a transference. But we know also that the terms "object relation" and "transference" cover a multitude of manifestations and dynamics. The *nature* of the object relation or transference thus begins to take on major nosological significance. For instance, the schizophrenic will often very quickly develop a markedly fervent, wildly irrational transference with all the earmarks of primitiveness suggesting that it is derived from archaic periods of development. It frequently will have magical qualities as well. Although transference neurosis is still used as a nosological term, it reflects a knowledge that these transference neuroses represent one end of a spectrum. Whether this is due to quantitative or qualitative factors, I won't presume to discuss now. Ever present, then, in the developing nosology was the question of the nature of the personality structure of the individual in whom a given illness was seen to reside. This interest evolved into a major component of psychoanalytic nosology—namely, the various categories of character types and disorders, a most fundamental and pivotal aspect of our work.

The Psychoses

Having established that a patient is psychotic (i.e., that the psychotic process is operative), the clinician's task is to establish what type of psychosis is presenting. The principal types are schizophrenia, psychotic affective disorders, and paranoia. I would emphasize that the psychotic process is most likely the core of all psychotic and allied conditions. Variations in the clinical picture depend on the manner in which the various components interrelate. This may vary considerably, depending on many factors, some of which may be constitutional, biological, or developmental. Variations depend also on the extent of defects as well as the type of defenses employed in dealing with basic conflicts. Even when the latter are expressed at higher levels, lurking in the background are fundamental conflicts pertaining, for instance, to fears of disintegration of the self.

The basic features of the psychotic process will be seen more clearly in schizophrenia or in the catastrophic reactions attendant on certain organic brain disorders. Less clearly will they be seen in the psychotic affective disorders or in paranoia, where the conflicts and defenses operate at a more advanced level. Nonetheless, these basic features are in the background of even these conditions, and may under certain circumstances become clearly evident when deeper anxieties and more primitive defenses manifest themselves. All of the psychoses will share certain basic defects, such as decreased reality testing. What follows is an attempt to delineate the more specific features characterizing the different clinical pictures.

Schizophrenias

I should like to turn first to the schizophrenic disorders. As the plural form of this phrase indicates, there are probably many forms of schizophrenia, but here I will confine myself to the basic features which are their common denominator.

We are essentially concerned with nosological considerations insofar as these are influenced by psychoanalytic thinking. In an excellent chapter on schizophrenia, Pao (1979) discusses the psychodynamic aspects of schizophrenia. I will allude to such factors in my discussion. Freud in his attempts at classifying schizophrenia indicated that developmental features must be taken into consideration. The making of a diagnosis must not rely on symptoms (including dementia), for these represent no more than the continuous presence of conflicts the patient cannot resolve, of a maladaptation precipitated out of the interaction between the patient's endowments and the environment.

When Freud stepped onto the psychiatric stage in the 1880s and 1890s, the thinking on the psychoses was dominated by the contributions of Kraepelin and Kahlbaum. Freud's own early contributions in this area were somewhat fragmentary, appearing here and there in his correspondence first with Fliess and subsequently with Ferenczi and Abraham. During this period, Freud's hypothesis of sexual trauma predominated. His early contributions on the neuropsychoses of defense (1894, 1896) reflected his thinking at the time about the neuroses, especially hysteria and the obsessions. His concept of trauma and defense against unbearable ideas and fantasies was his principal frame of reference, the term "defense" being used synonymously with "repression." In fact, this frame of reference was never really abandoned; rather, Freud's thinking on trauma and defense became more refined and sophisticated as his psychoanalytic theory developed.

More and more, the essential concept became that of defense against unbearable (or incompatible) thoughts and affects. The clinical picture was then determined by the fate of the repressed which had returned—in other words, by the nature of the defense, and how it was carried out. By 1911 Freud had formulated the libido theory, in which changes are explained by the shifting of libido rather than by defenses as such. Although Freud did not emphasize the defense concept again until 1926, let us be clear that the shifting of libido is actually defensive in nature. If libido is withdrawn from the outer world because that world is too painful, in the broad sense this is a defensive operation. It was within the framework of libido theory that the concepts of withdrawal and restitution, as well as of narcissism, were developed.

In the Schreber case Freud (1911) attempted to be a little more specific about the nature of the conflict in paranoia. The dual instinct theory, developed around this time, contributed to an understanding of many aspects of depression.

Later, two papers written in 1924 (Freud, 1924a,b) use the structural hypothesis as their frame of reference. They point to psychosis as the outcome of a disturbance in the relation between the ego and the outer world. The conflict and ensuing break with reality Freud associated with painful pressure either from reality or from the id, or from both. Essentially, the difference here between psychosis and neurosis is that in the former the ego gives in to the id, bows to it, and lets itself be pushed around. Of course, this is an oversimplification.

It can be seen, then, that schizophrenia as a syndrome has been understood in keeping with successively adopted frames of reference. Much of the symptomatology of the schizophrenic was related to the concept of withdrawal and restitution and was viewed within the context of the libido theory. The role of aggression was subsequently elaborated to the point where the imbalance between libido and aggression was felt to be one of the basic disturbances in schizophrenia. Hartmann (1953) took a defect in the neutralization of aggression to be one of the focal points in schizophrenia. Bak (1954), using this as a jumping-off point, viewed schizophrenia as an unsuccessful defense against aggressive and destructive drives. Many of the symptoms of schizophrenia were seen to revolve around attempted defenses against aggression, as well as withdrawal, projection, and regression of the ego, sometimes to the point of dedifferentiation.

The relation to objects was impaired by virtue of withdrawal and restitution, the defect in neutralization of aggression, as well as the lack of self/nonself differentiation. There is both a need for support from the object and a fear of getting too close. I have elsewhere discussed the "basic anxiety" in the regressed phase of the psychotic process (Frosch, 1983). This is seen especially in schizophrenia.

As I have suggested, in the early psychoanalytic literature it is often difficult to differentiate contributions on paranoia, paranoid mechanisms, paraphrenia, and schizophrenia. The way these concepts were used interchangeably is well exemplified in a statement by Freud (1911): "we can understand how a clinical picture such as Schreber's can come about and take the name of a paranoid dementia from the fact that in its production of a wish phantasy and of hallucinations, it shows paraphrenic traits, while in its exciting cause, in its use of the mechanism of projection and in its final issue it exhibits a paranoid character" (p. 78).

Freud (1896) refers in his "Further Remarks on the Neuro-Psychoses of Defence" to a case of chronic paranoia, only to question this diagnosis in a footnote added in a later edition, changing it to dementia paranoides. In his earlier paper on the defense neuropsychoses (1894), he interchanges such terms as defense psychosis, defense psychoneurosis, defense neuropsychosis, and neurosis. At times Freud equates neurosis with what Feuchtersleben meant by psychosis, namely, a disease of the mind; at other times, however, he underlines the organic toxic factor in neurosis. As I have noted, Freud repeatedly refers to psychotic conditions with the term "neurosis." He views Schreber's pathology taking neurosis as his basic frame of reference. Equally confusing is his attempt to combine illnesses such as dementia praecox and schizophrenia under the term "paraphrenia," which he uses in connection with both schizophrenia and paranoia.

In these papers Freud locates the conflict structurally, holding that conflict between ego and id reflects psychoneurosis; between superego and ego, narcissistic neurosis; between ego and reality, psychosis. In these discussions of psychosis, Freud focuses on the "break with reality." As I have pointed out elsewhere (Frosch, 1983) in evaluating the role of reality vis-à-vis the psychoses, one must differentiate the relationship with reality, the sense of reality, and the capacity to test reality. All of these are disturbed in schizophrenia, in which problems with reality lead to a withdrawal of libido from the love object in the external world. The detached libido is then invested in the self, leading to grandiose manifestations. Many schizophrenic symptoms evolve from "restitutive" attempts to recover the lost world and lost objects. But these attempts are not successful, recathexis of the object is not achieved. Rather, the "word presentation" of the object is cathected.

It was with the advent of the structural hypothesis that the roles of the ego and the superego were elaborated. Severe ego defects were seen to impair the ability to cope with reality. The defenses initiated by the defective ego are primitive, and its deficient capacity for neutralization plays a significant role in the disruption of many ego functions, including the capacity to relate to the object world. Equally, the archaic and harsh superego, with its potential for externalization, all so characteristic of the regressed aspects of the psychotic process, are in evidence.

Many contributions to the nosology and understanding of schizophrenia were made by the interpersonal school of Sullivan and his followers. A good deal of their early work was done with very sick, hospitalized psychotic patients at Sheppard and Enoch Pratt Hospital, and at Chestnut Lodge. Indeed, the main interest and contribution of the interpersonal school might be described as therapeutic, although it has an underlying theoretical orientation. Sullivan describes many "security operations" designed to deal with the schizophrenic's self-disintegration fears, the terror of possible self-dissolution, which Sullivan refers to as nothingness.

Will (1961) sees the schizophrenic picture as characterized by uncertainty regarding self-identity; misidentification of others; instability of "ego boundaries"; feelings of "depersonalization"; self-disorganization; regression; denial; control by an "influencing machine"; delusions and hallucinations; paranoid phenomena of grandiosity and projection; rage; habit deterioration and withdrawal; and stereotypy and poverty of thinking.

Frieda Fromm-Reichmann (1959) summarized the dynamics of schizophrenia as follows. There is

> narcissistic regression . . . producing withdrawal, the overrating of positive skills and negative powers, difficulty in dealing with hatred and potential violence, and the severe judgment of negative character traits, due to the narcissistic self-conception. Being a severe judge, the narcissistic schizophrenic patient fears his hostile impulses, fleeing into a self-imposed state of psychical and emotional paralysis. The schizophrenic patient fears closeness. . . . The schizophrenic patient also feels the need to be guided; however, his hunger for love and dependence is counteracted by the wish for independence [p. 418].

It might be appropriate to allude to Melanie Klein's concepts regarding schizophrenia. These derive from concepts of early child development. She refers to a very early stage in psychic development characterized by aggressive and sadistic fantasies in relation to the mother. Out of painful rages, the result of oral frustration augmented by the death instinct, there evolve hatred and destructive impulses which are projected onto the mother, who is now viewed as dangerous. These projected bad parts may be reintrojected, leading to feelings of inner persecution. This contributes to the intensity of the hatred directed against other people. This process, to which Klein applies the term "projective identification," is characteristic of what is called the paranoid-schizoid position. The failure to work this through represents a potential which may result, in the adult, in schizophrenia or paranoia.

The paranoid-schizoid position is followed by the depressive position. The fear of destroying the object invokes the possible loss of the good object and the good breast, with consequent guilt, mourning, severe depression, and anxiety. If the hatred and aggression are excessive and stronger than love, the possibility of loss is enhanced. The infant must in some way come to terms with this possibility.

It is thus important that a positive object relationship be established before the real loss of the first object during weaning. There should be an integration of good and bad part objects into the whole mother-object. The infant's coming to terms with this dilemma is the basis for the "depressive position." Klein proposes that the child goes through a depressive episode during this period and that future pathology will ensue if this is not resolved. This is a viewpoint not shared by many. Klein's use of terms implying psychosis in relation to these early stages of psychic development is often criticized. The processes she describes, her critics argue, are variations of self/nonself differentiation consistent with these stages and should not be viewed as manifestations of psychosis. Further, Klein's view that these phenomena are precursors of subsequent psychotic development is also questioned.

The views presented above, though expressed differently, all come down to the same thing. In schizophrenia there is a regression to primary narcissism. The ego has broken down and there is a disintegration of the ego with a disruption in the continuity of the personality. The regression is to a phase in development at which the ego has not begun to be established. This brings in its wake object loss and a break with reality. Within the framework of withdrawal and restitution many of the symptoms reflect the regressive breakdown of the ego and a primitivization of its functions.

Other symptoms reflect the restitutive process and attempts to reverse the regressive process and reach for reality, distorted as this may be. When the dangers which initiated the push toward regression ease, ego and superego push to set up new defenses against the regression, and there is a move toward reality which does not quite succeed. There then ensues an attempt at recathexis, which is short-circuited, bringing in its wake delusions, hallucinations, and language distortion. The idiosyncratic language derives from developmental defects in communication contributed to by defective parental relationships. However this comes about, the representational function of language is lost. Language is also subject to primary process condensation, displacement, and symbolization.

Affective Disorders

When we turn to depression we find, clinically and dynamically, that there is a whole spectrum of conditions. These include reactive depression, neurotic depression, psychotic depression, mourning, grief, and melancholia. Depression may also be manifest in schizophrenia and organic illness. Bibring (1953) tends to cut across all types of depression and proposes common denominators ostensibly encompassing even the psychotic depressions.

In neurotic depression, what is essential is that many features of the neurotic process described above are present. The conflict occurs at a relatively high level and is related to the need for a love object. Instead of the introjection seen in psychotic depression in reaction to object loss, we see a constant reaching out for affection and feeding from the outside to gratify the need for security. In neurotic depression, ambivalence, hatred, and hostility, if present at all, are minimal in contrast to what is seen in psychotic depression. The superego, although involved and producing guilt of some sort, is generally not archaic and harsh, as it is in psychotic depression. As a result of these factors, the person suffering neurotic depression remains object related. Above all, the neurotic depressive retains the capacity to test reality, and may relate to reality quite well, though with diminished capacity.

When we turn to psychotic depression we find that the relation to the object takes on a different dimension. Several factors run like a red thread through the picture. The first of these is loss. Related to this is a feeling of abandonment and a reaction of hatred and anger. There is a feeling of guilt at one's culpability in contributing to this loss, either by having done something to produce it, or by having done nothing to prevent it. Hatred and aggression may have been primary and may have played a role in creating this loss. An attempt is made to deal with the loss by means of a special form of identification. This involves incorporation of the lost object into the self and an intrapsychic playing out of hatred and aggression toward the object and the self. This is facilitated by a regression to oral sadism and narcissism.

I should like now to turn to a detailed examination of these features. The theme of loss of some sort seems to be common to many psychoanalytic contributions on the subject of the affective disorders. Something or someone has been lost. It may be an object in reality, or something in relation to the object—love, a belief, an ideal, approval, etc. Depression may relate to severe frustration and disappointments in marriage, family life, love relationships, sexual prowess, finances, etc. Object loss may be an actual death or a fantasy that the object has died, an actual withdrawal of love or its fancied withdrawal. Any of the above may bring in its wake a marked drop in self-esteem. A physiological loss may bring on the same kind of emptying and sense of depletion. As noted above, one of the most typical forms of dealing with loss characterizing psychotic depression is the introjection of the lost object within the self and their narcissistic identification, wherein the self begins to be treated as though it were the object. There are mixed feelings in this process of internalization. Although incorporation represents a desire to preserve the lost object, it is also an attempt to destroy the hated aspects of the object. This reflects an initial ambivalence. The introjection, because of its sadistic nature, is perceived as a danger and occasions guilt.

All of this represents a special form of regression which has not quite reached the basic fundamental regressive manifestation of the psychotic process described above. There is not that total loss of the object which results in the dedifferentiation so characteristic of schizophrenia.

It is possible to regard these symptoms as attempts at restitution, at repairing the loss and restoring self-esteem. The various reactions of the self—submissiveness, self-accusation, attempts to appease the superego and alleviate guilt—are ultimately ways of achieving self-esteem through restoring and earning the love of the lost object. These strategies fail in depression until it is worked through sufficiently to lead to recovery. However, these reparative attempts may overshoot the mark and in rebellious denial eventuates in mania. Here we have a marked increase in self-esteem. Conscience seems to be abandoned. Conflict between the superego and the ego apparently disappears; the latter has regained dominance and even omnipotence. Hitherto inhibited impulses are now freed and given vent, without fear of punishment by the superego. The manic is not disturbed by self-criticism and has lost his consideration of others. Reaction-formation and denial of underlying depression are operative. In mania a forgiving and loving union, one marked with orality, is established with the superego. Forgiveness is achieved through fusion with the superego

(Rado, 1928). Lewin (1950) sees mania as recapturing subjective feelings of pleasure in nursing and satiation at the breast. The oral component in both depression and mania is illustrated by a patient of mine who when she felt lonely and depressed would get into a warm tub, taking with her a glass of warm milk. As she drank the milk, a feeling of relaxation came on, and a sense of gratification which had many features of elation.

Melanie Klein's concept of a depressive phase in childhood development, if not successfully mastered, may lay the groundwork for future depressions, both neurotic and psychotic. What characterizes this childhood depressive phase is the fear the child has of having lost the mother as a result of his destroying her because of his greed, envy, and jealousy. I have in that earlier discussion indicated the critique of these views.

Although every depressive should be considered a potential suicide, there is no doubt that depressives of certain types are more at risk. There are of course suicides which are not based on depression at all—for instance, the suicide as a symbolic act which may have as its goal not death but eternal life. Seen more often in schizophrenic or other psychotic states, the symbolic suicide is frequently a search for continuity, life, or union with some loved object.

Because suicide is a result that may be reached by many pathways, our understanding of it, and our clinical approach to suicidal ideation and attempts should not be unitary.

The high rate of suicide as a cause of death has led to the belief that this is a recent problem, which is not the case. Friedman (1967), describing a 1910 symposium on suicide held by the Vienna Psychoanalytic Society, appropriately indicated that many of the views expressed at that meeting were in keeping with the then prevailing knowledge, which long antedated Freud's concepts as expressed in his "Mourning and Melancholia" paper and the dual instinct theory, which highlighted the relation between suicide and aggression. It was pointed out that epidemics of suicide among young people had been in existence for almost three centuries. It was pointed out by one observer, a Professor Oppenheim, that "suicide in youth was a social phenomenon which stretched much further back in history than the public grasped" (p. 37). Here I will simply emphasize the role of hatred and hostility in suicide. Although a marked drop in self-esteem may eventuate in suicide, as may factors in the social climate, the presence of hatred in the depression always holds the possibility that this hatred may be turned against the self. At the adolescent suicide conference in 1911, Stekel remarked "No one kills himself who did not want to kill another, or at least wish death to another."

If we turn to the role of such hatred and anger in depressions, Freud's remarks on this phenomenon in melancholia are relevant. Freud (1917) emphasized that thoughts of suicide are murderous impulses against others redirected to oneself. This is especially true in psychotic depression.

Even where sociological factors appear most prominent, the hatred and anger which turns on the self and may eventuate in suicide is emphasized by Hendin.

I have on previous pages discussed the role of loss in depression. In reaction to loss there may be a feeling of abandonment and reaction of hatred and anger to this loss and a feeling of guilt at one's culpability in contributing to this loss. The hatred and aggression may have been primary and played a role in creating this loss. The guilt feeling may be due to either having done something to contribute to this loss or not having done something to prevent it. The potential for turning of the hatred and anger on the self is a great danger in suicide.

Added to these potentials for suicide is a family history of suicide and identification with such situations.

Paranoid Disorders

Several clinical conditions are subsumed under the rubric of paranoid disorders, many of them overlapping and at times difficult to differentiate. Among them are true paranoia, paranoid psychoses, paranoid schizophrenia, paranoid conditions, and paranoid characters. Paranoid delusions are common in all of these, except in the paranoid characters. These delusions may be quite frank and direct or very subtle, highly organized or more diffuse. Some are transient phenomena; others persist and are chronic. Common are strongly held ideas of persecution or megalomania which may be manifested in a wide variety of delusions, mainly persecutory. Others consist of delusions of jealousy, erotomania, litigiousness, or grandiosity, in which the patient holds special ideas of a religious or political nature.

I should like to approach the discussion of the paranoid disorders by seeking to establish a common denominator for them, what might be called the paranoid constellation. Its various components have been identified over the years, with the successive expansion of psychoanalytic frames of reference: the topographical model of the mind, the libido theory, the dual instinct theory, the structural model of the mind, and psychoanalytic ego psychology.

Freud developed his thinking about the paranoid constellation within the framework of the libido theory, within which he proposed an explanation for grandiosity and the role of unconscious homosexuality. Freud felt that grandiosity, viewed by many as the ultimate stage in the development of a delusional system, is in fact a regressive reactivation of the common denominator in all such individuals, an extreme narcissism, with feelings of omnipotence, deriving from the earliest stages of psychic development. What we see as delusional persecutory systems in such individuals are later stages in paranoid development, an attempt at dealing with and resolving basic fears and anxieties. Delusions are reparative efforts at cure, at holding on to reality, which do not quite succeed.

In the paranoid's regression to narcissism there is a stop at the level of homosexuality. This may occur either during withdrawal or during the restitution phase, on the way toward trying to recapture reality. Freud suggested that unconsciously such individuals have not resolved the struggle with their passive homosexuality, but have reached some kind of fragile sublimated balance which enables them to get along. The reactivation and projection of this unconscious homosexuality plays a significant role in the paranoid constellation. Freud emphasized that what is crucial for paranoia is the way this projection is carried out. It is important here to differentiate between unconscious and latent homosexuality (Frosch, 1981). The latter has the potential for becoming overt and has a different significance genetically and dynamically than has unconscious homosexuality, which does not become overt. Unconscious homosexuality does not necessarily eventuate in the paranoid constellation, but it may create a problem in gender identity which may contribute to many clinical manifestations, among them paranoid features.

My own formulation of the paranoid constellation is that unconscious homosexuality is denied, rejected, and projected onto a replica of a significant childhood object. The subject then becomes an unwilling, persecuted, and passive victim. The "persecution" is seen as an anal-sadomasochistic attack, which is felt as degrading and humiliating. Behind this view lie humiliating experiences at the hands of significant same-sex objects from the past, generally a father figure for males and a mother figure for females. These experiences have occurred at crucial stages in psychic development, before sexual identity was established. They were particularly traumatic because they were out of phase with the child's ego and libidinal development at that time and were tied into the child's fantasies. These experiences, then, make passivity humiliating, degrading, and possibly catastrophic. Although there are contributions from many levels of psychic development to the paranoid constellation, it is unconscious homosexuality in this form that is the organizing principle.

However, the presence of the paranoid constellation does not of itself indicate a bona fide paranoid delusion or paranoid psychosis, although it contains the ingredients for such conditions. The paranoid constellation provides the content but not the form in which that content is expressed. This will depend on the nature and variants of the projection, as emphasized by Freud. In addition, in order for a paranoid psychosis to develop, other factors must supplement the paranoid constellation, specifically the components of the psychotic process described above.

Disorders of Impulse Control

Impulsivity is a commonly encountered behavioral manifestation in a variety of psychiatric disorders. However, in the disorders of impulse control, the lack of control over impulses is diagnostic and pathognomonic. For our purposes, we may define impulse as the generally unpremeditated welling-up of a drive toward some action that usually has the qualities of hastiness, lack of deliberation, and impetuosity. Impulses may be sudden and transitory, but in disorders of impulse control the associated tension may manifest itself in a crescendo leading to an explosive expression of the impulse, at times resulting in violent action in disregard of others' safety or even that of the subject (Frosch, 1977).

There are many disorders of impulse control, but they share certain common characteristics which permit their differentiation from allied disorders. These characteristics interweave but will be examined individually.

Ego syntonicity. The impulse and the act which may ensue are consonant with the momentary conscious ego state and aims of the psyche. The impulsive act is therefore not perceived as ego alien at the time of gratification.

Minimal distortion of the original impulse. The impulse is generally expressed in a consonant act: angry impulses result in aggressive assault; sexual impulses result in sexual acts. Although impulsive behavior may be used as a defense and may be distorted, the degree of distortion is not as marked as in classical neurotic symptoms, the compulsive ritual for instance.

Pleasurable component. The impulse has a primary pleasurable and gratifying component at the time of expression.

These three components, ego syntonicity, minimal distortion of the original impulse, and the primary pleasurable component, characterize all impulse disorders and enable one to differentiate them from allied disorders.

To determine the conditions that allow an impulse to come to expression, we must look for some defect, disturbance, or deviation along the line from the appearance of an affect, impulse, drive, wish, or need to a specific type of action. The defect is usually in the important ego function of delay. Interference with the development of this function may lead to the establishment of action patterns which at earlier levels are direct and primitive and at more highly developed levels more distorted. Severe constitutional disruption of development of the delay structure may act as a major determinant in the conversion of fantasy into action. Experiential factors interplay with constitutional factors and play a role in disrupting this development, with consequent manifestations in inappropriate action.

Traumatic occurrences at crucial stages in psychic development play a significant role in determining the mysterious jump from fantasy to action. Such early disturbances may be physiological, psychological, or both. Special coloring of the impulse is lent by specific experiential factors during development. The degree of organization of such action, directly expressed or distorted, sexualized or desexualized, is determined by the nature of the traumatic experience and the stage of psychic development during which it occurs. Oral deprivation or overindulgence may equally play roles in subsequent impairment of the delay factor, which may in turn affect the development of the ego function of anticipation and the potential for illusory gratification, hallucinations, and fantasy. A combination of initial overindulgence and subsequent deprivation may create an imbalance between impulse and control, with impulsive behavior followed by severe superego condemnation (Frosch, 1977).

It is important to differentiate disorders of impulse control from acting out, with which they are frequently confused. Acting out is inappropriate activity which at the very least should not appear in the form or at the time that it does. It results when impulses, wishes, and fantasies which strive for expression are frustrated and cannot work their way through the usual channels of reflective thought, speech, judgment, and goal-directed constructive activity. Acting out has been seen as a substitute action, having within it regressive attempts at resolving problems. It represents the dramatization of a fantasy. Impulse disorder patterns, by contrast, are the substrata or dynamic conditions out of which acting out may develop as a phenomenon. However, a specific economic state of affairs, based on appropriate etiological circumstances, must exist in order for acting out to develop.

The clinical picture of the impulse disorders is characterized either by the expression of symptomatic impulsive acts, or by an overall impulsive quality permeating the personality of the individual. Symptomatic impulsive acts are more or less discrete acts that frequently recur. They may be further categorized as simple impulsive acts, impulsion neuroses, perversions or impulsive sexual disorders, the isolated nonrepetitive explosive act, and intermittent explosive behaviors.

In the impulsion neuroses, the original impulse may be markedly distorted, if the act itself is not distorted, the setting in which it occurs is highly inappropriate and out of phase. Such behavior is seen in kleptomania, pyromania, gambling, and certain addictions, in which the acts in and of themselves (e.g., stealing, the setting of fires) are not so bizarre.

Closely allied to this group and occasionally combined with it (e.g., pyromania and exhibitionism, kleptomania and fetishism) are the perversions or impulsive sexual disorders. The features stand out like symptoms, but the disturbance is more closely allied to the original impulse, which is of a sexual nature.

The fourth syndrome, the isolated nonrepetitive explosive act, also called the catathymic crisis, is characterized by an act of violence which occurs suddenly but has a developmental background of intolerable tension, conscious or unconscious. Such acts may run the gamut from individual or mass murder to fire setting, self-castration, or infanticide.

In the final group the patient manifests intermittent episodes of explosive outbursts, which may be self- or other-directed. I have selected for discussion some of the impulsion neuroses.

Kleptomania. In kleptomania the wish to steal is not distorted, but the setting in which it occurs is highly inappropriate. In contrast to a neurotic symptom, however, there is an impulsive quality to the act and the act in and of itself is not bizarre.

Both the object stolen and the nature of the act may have specific symbolic significance for the patient. The stolen object may be a substitute for pleasures previously denied, and the act itself may be intended to avenge such denials. Common to the act is a feeling of having been deprived—hence the wish to take something forcibly as compensation. It is in a sense an act of revenge for such deprivation, which may have occurred at any psychosexual level, most commonly the oral or phallic. In the latter it may be an attempt to undo or a retaliatory castration.

Pyromania. Pyromania is the irresistible impulse to set fires. Pyromaniacs have an intense fascination in setting the fire and then in watching it. The act may be preceded by a feeling of tension which is released once the fire is set. This may be of a sexual nature accompanied by orgasm, or a feeling of nervousness or anxiety. After setting the fire they will frequently sound the alarm and join in attempts to extinguish the blaze. Alternatively, they may stand apart enjoying their secret knowledge of how the fire started. Sometimes pyromania is a precondition for sexual pleasure and performance, and as such belongs to the perversions. Fire setting may take place during delirious twilight states, or be part of a paranoid religious ritual associated with fire as symbolic of power, something godly and Promethean. There appears, in many cases, a history of persistent bed wetting. In other cases, beds are set on fire, ostensibly by accident, as by smoking in bed. But this has on occasion been clearly associated with a history of bed wetting. Fire mobilizes the sexual feelings through a desire to extinguish the fire by urinating on it. Fire setting also has destructive and vindictive components reflecting a deep-seated sadism.

Gambling. Gambling is an impulsion neurosis which could equally be described under the addictions. To the true addictive gambler, money is only a means for the game. The main thing is the play itself. The condition is characterized dynamically by several features. The gambler views himself as playing against fate. It is, as one patient said, a life-and-death struggle. The gambler is always tempting fate to decide for or against him. Fate is the father, and the gambler is testing whether he will be accepted or rejected. Winning (being accepted) is accompanied by an almost manic feeling of power which ultimately, when the gambler begins losing, gives way to a feeling of rejection, of having been punished by fate. Ultimately he must be ruined, as there is a tremendous need for punishment, viewed as castration, related to a previous sense of guilt. Accompanying all this is an oral quality as well, an ongoing need for supplies and admiration which characterizes the gambler's other activities. Freud viewed gambling as a replacement for masturbation, another form of play with impulsive and addictive features.

The addictions. The addictions are clinically a heterogeneous group. Substance abuse, for instance, may occur in many clinical conditions—in schizophrenia, mania, borderline states, etc. However, the phenomenon of addiction, per se, has unique features which bind addicts together into a single diagnostic category. We find in all of the addictions an insatiable and recurrent craving for substances or activities which induce sensations and states of pleasure or which eliminate unpleasantness and tension.

Substance addictions involve a lifestyle dominated by the addictive substance and by the activities necessary to obtain it and then use it. These will nullify all other interests—sexual, social, occupational, etc. The domination of lifestyle by heroin addiction, for instance, extends to the very injection, which becomes erotized. One addict, asked what happened when her very young children demanded attention while she was taking her fix, said that nothing existed for her, "nothing but that needle and my veins." One addict described the desperate search for an open vein, which drove him to distraction accompanied by violent outbursts.

Many of the major addictive drugs will deaden psychic pain. There are energizing drugs, hallucinogenic drugs, and those which are resorted to in a search for extreme subjective experience or "expanded consciousness." These may often answer a need for stimulation in order to deal with a feeling of emptiness. It should be clear, however, that drugs add nothing that is not already there. People will choose the addictive drug which physiologically and psychologically reinforces trends already present. They tend to mobilize or inhibit energic factors which under normal circumstances are already operative, or potentially so.

Clinically and dynamically, addictions share the three features described above as characteristic of impulse disorders. Addicts, like all impulse-ridden people, cannot tolerate tension, be it derived from anxiety, frustration, loneliness, depression, or any other kind of affect or ego state of a depressing nature. This points to a defect in the stimulus barrier. Truth to tell, many drugs offer a secondary stimulus barrier, guarding against both external and internal stimuli. Given these basic features, we must then determine the factors which eventuate in this specific type of impulse disorder. Addictions have many features in common with the impulse neuroses. Certainly the impulsive and driven craving for a substance is partially defended against, thereby producing distortions in the final expression which meet many needs. We therefore have all the ingredients of the neurotic process: a psychic conflict dealt with by many factors which eventuate in a compromise.

It is doubtful if we can come up with a single profile to cover all forms of addiction. However, there appear to be common denominators grouping some of them. It is probable that abusers of various substances have more similarities with each other than differences, although it is the differences which determine the specific object of their addiction (e.g., heroin or alcohol). Addictions that do not involve drugs (e.g., eating disorders, gambling) probably share more in common with one another than with the other addictions, although certain common denominators are very likely shared by all addictions—e.g., defects in the capacity for delay and a resultant intolerance of frustration and internal tensions. Groups of addictions may also be tied together by what they seek to achieve—e.g., withdrawal, restored ego status, the fulfillment of needs arising from developmental defects.

As regards the psychodynamic factors entering into addiction, there is general agreement that the common denominator in most addictions is a deep oral need for security and self-esteem. Whatever the concatenation of factors that play a role in substance abuse, there is a basic search for the means to achieve feelings which compensate for low self-esteem, depression, loneliness, internal emptiness, and the like. This is a deep and primitive desire that influences all object relations, which are of a passive narcissistic nature. Objects are need-fulfilling, a source of the supplies so necessary for security and self-esteem. The possibility of losing such supplies, and the feeling that one has contributed to this eventuality, plays a role in underlying anxiety, depression, and guilt. The search for these supplies in the course of psychic development assumes more sophisticated manifestations, but basically the core organizing principle in addiction remains this almost indefinable, orally derived tension.

Alcoholism has some additional features as an addiction. The interest in alcohol supplants any true interest in objects, which at times assume a marked homosexual coloration. This may be combined with a love of the bottle, which is nursed and fondled, to fill deep oral passive needs for narcissistic supplies. Coupled with this oral fixation is a marked homosexual conflict at all levels, conscious and unconscious, latent and overt. Alcohol permits the breakthrough of these impulses; it has been said that the superego is soluble in alcohol. Underlying the condition is a powerful castration anxiety that finds its clinical expression in the dismembering motif so commonly seen in alcoholic hallucinosis (Bromberg and Schilder, 1933).

In the alcoholic, problems with love and self-esteem lead to a striving for admiration and appreciation. There is a heightened feeling of the need to be tied to others in mutual love and admiration which may allow the breakthrough of impulses to kiss and embrace them. This behavior stems from an underlying anxiety, a feeling of not quite measuring up, and alcohol may also evoke the opposite compensatory reactions of self-assertiveness, irritability, and aggressiveness. There is in the alcoholic addiction an insatiable demand for evidence of affection and love. The object is nothing but a deliverer of supplies. More than in other addictions, the abused substance—alcohol and the bottle—becomes the love object, as drinking is often substituted for the sexual act itself.

In summary, several basic etiological and dynamic factors are found in alcoholic addiction. There is a partial but strong fixation at oral sadistic levels, and sometimes also at anal sadistic levels involving homosexual conflict. There is a tendency to regress to narcissism, which brings into play the primitive mechanisms seen in ensuing alcoholic psychoses. All of this is colored by a disorder of the superego, which permits the intoxicated alcoholic impulsive expressions only later to inflict severe punishment.

Character Disorders

Psychoanalytic contributions on the concept of character have many features in common, and although some stress certain features over others a generally accepted concept has

emerged. In some contributions the definitions are quite narrow and limited. Reich viewed character as the sum total of an
individual's defenses, in the form of a protective armor against
internal and external dangers. However, it was recognized by
many that character should not be restricted to defense. Character is also reflective of a whole host of conflict-free autonomous functions of the ego. These become part of the typical
and predictable aspects of the individual's armamentarium in
achieving mastery over stressful situations, both internal and
external. They help in achieving security against stress and
strain, as well as in realizing inherent potentials.

These aspects bring in their wake a constellation of relatively stable, ego-syntonic ways of reconciling conflicts between
various parts of the psychic apparatus and of adjusting to the
internal and the external environment. This results in habitual
and predictable behavioral responses which are perceived by
others as typical for a given individual. We depend on character
to be able to predict, anticipate, and identify another person's
behavior.

Deviations may occur in the personality of an individual
which fulfill the conditions for neurosis or symptom development, and these may under certain conditions evolve into a
major character disorder. Alternatively, personality traits may
evolve based on exaggerated defensive activities of the ego such
as passive aggression or marked inhibition in normal activities.
Personality traits may also be derived from oral, anal, or phallic
reaction-formations. These traits may not interfere appreciably
with an individual's functioning, or they may even be adaptive,
although they lend a special cast to this functioning. For instance, the existence of character traits deriving from reaction-
formation to anal drives resulting in parsimony, cleanliness, or
obstinacy may not necessarily result in pathology. An individual
may function quite satisfactorily with these traits, and under
certain circumstances a premium may in fact be put on them.
In order to assess pathology one must first consider the degree
of restriction such traits impose on the individual's functioning
and the price paid internally in consequence of having them.

As regards classification, one may start at the descriptive
level and list character features as they reflect themselves clinically in various forms. Alternatively, one may classify them

based upon certain genetic-dynamic considerations and then try to relate them to clinical manifestations. For instance, Freud (1908, 1931) and Abraham (1921, 1925) based their early classifications on libidinal vicissitudes. Fenichel (1945) distinguished sublimatory and reactive types, depending on whether the instinctual drives achieved discharge of some sort or were defended against by reactive character traits such as phobic avoidance or reaction-formations. Using the structural frame of reference, he classified character traits reactive to the id as oral, anal, urethral, or phallic. Using the superego as a frame of reference, he distinguished moral masochism, lack of guilt, and pathological behavior toward external objects. Kernberg (1976) has proposed a classification based on three levels of instinctual fixation, as well as levels of ego, superego, and object relation. It should be borne in mind, therefore, that although many character traits evolve out of sublimation or reaction-formation vis-à-vis instinctual drives, contributions to the formation of these traits derive from ego and superego development as well as object relations, identifications, and social factors.

In all such instances, traits derivative of psychosexual development are not necessarily pathological; as has been noted, they may even be adaptive. However, under certain circumstances any of these may become so inhibiting of adequate functioning as to merit consideration as character disorders. When these features bring about a character whose life shows a repetitive pattern—highly restricted, inflexible, and stereotyped, but nonetheless more or less ego-syntonic and even in some instances unrecognized by most people though evident to clinicians—we enter the domain of character disorders. Specific instances may be subsumed under the larger category of one of the major disorders, as when an oral character of the dependent and continuously demanding type reaches pathological proportions and is recognized as a neurotic character disorder.

The stage in psychic development at which deviations and distortions are initiated helps to determine the form taken by a character disorder. The earlier in psychic development a deviation occurs, the greater is the potential for psychotic character development; the closer to the oedipal period, the greater is the likelihood of neurotic character development. The structuralization or fixity of pathological defense patterns determines the nature of emerging pathological character development, as do other factors which enter into character development generally. Patterns of this kind are rigid, definitive, once-and-for-all formations.

The development of characterology had a close relationship with the therapy of certain kinds of patients, and also began to influence the focus of therapy. It was with problems arising during therapy in the form of resistance, which took the form of difficulties in association, that also crept into the transference relation, that the focus in therapy shifted. For instance, it was felt by Abraham (1925) that there was a basic narcissism in some character structures who used therapy to feed this narcissism. They took over the treatment and there were difficulties in free association. This had an impact on how the analysis was conducted.

It is necessary, then, to differentiate symptom disorder and character disorder. Both are possible means of compromise formation. Reich viewed the two as clearly integrated and considered symptoms mere exacerbations of character disorders. According to him, some clinical disorders have circumscribed symptoms which others lack, but that in all such symptom disorders there is also an underlying character disorder. Nevertheless, there are features which distinguish the two. Symptoms are ego-dystonic and ego-alien. Symptoms cannot be rationalized. By contrast, character disorders, particularly neurotic character disorders, seem relatively ego-syntonic. Conflict is a constant undercurrent in symptom disorders, and supplies of energy are an ongoing requirement. Once the ego is deformed, however, as in character disorder, there is no longer a need for this expenditure of energy or countercathexis, at least not at this level, except at certain periods. Disruption due to character disorders is part of a longitudinal developmental process and is more diffuse than is disruption occasioned by symptom disorders. The relationship between the two kinds of disorder becomes evident during analysis when characterological defenses begin to weaken and symptoms appear. By and large, the symptom is embedded in a character structure. If a neurotic character decompensates, a symptom neurosis develops; if a psychotic character decompensates, a symptom psychosis.

A word may be added about the repetitive behavior that typifies character disorders. The behavioral pattern during crises or critical events takes on a form which is repetitive. In pathological character disorders the reactions are rigid, stereotyped, repetitive, with limitation on the choice of solution. To many this is reflective of an underlying repetition compulsion derived from many sources, including previous attempts at resolution.

Neurotic Character Disorders

The features that characterize the neurotic process are involved also in the neurotic character disorders. The nature of the conflict, the modes of dealing with it, and the specific ego functions affected are the same. Above all, the capacity to test reality is preserved. The general distinction between symptom disorders and character disorders is applicable to symptom neuroses and character neuroses. In the latter, basic neurotic patterns are experienced as characterological disturbances. As is not the case with symptoms, there is a lack of localization because the neurotic process manifests itself developmentally, longitudinally, rather than as a symptom disorder with a more crystallized, phase-related, and fixated neurotic conflict. An impending neurosis may have been integrated into the personality, and feelings of ego alienness thereby dispelled. Many neurotic aspects are assimilated into the self in the form of a lifestyle. Characterological development out of a neurotic symptom is a containment of the neurotic process, facilitating a kind of adaptation externally which insures survival.

The neurotic character fulfills in its clinical form the characteristic basic features of a character disturbance. There is a lifestyle involving a repetitive pattern that is highly restricted and stereotyped, but that is nonetheless ego-syntonic and unrecognized by the patient. Neurotic characters may betray themselves by fatigue, inhibitions in certain areas or in general, or a somewhat restricted and rigid style of adjustment. The neurotic character lives an active life, frequently punctuated by crises and actions, which often only simulates rational behavior. Many of these patients live out successes and failures in response not to reality but to unconscious tensions related to conflict-derived fantasies. Such stereotyped reactions are most evident at important turning points in their lives. This may bring into sharper focus the disturbed aspects, and may even under certain circumstances bring such people into treatment, though without their having recognized the repetitive nature of their disturbance. They may seek treatment for some degree of suffering, for depression, or to alleviate the feeling that somehow their lives are not fulfilling, that somehow they should have been further along in life than they are. At times, hypochondriacal, phobic, or even paranoid features may be present. Many of these individuals have not found a niche for themselves. They do not know what they want and may be aware of a feeling of unhappiness in new object relations. Because their relations to objects are still influenced by childhood experiences, they may view objects in terms of instinctual conflicts. Current happenings are misunderstood in terms more appropriate to the past. In all of these patients there is a living out of unconscious fantasies in behavior which is not bizarre and which is seemingly understandable in the context of everyday life. In many such situations the professional eye will recognize the patient's role in manipulating events so as to contribute to these need-gratifying situations.

Many distinct syndromes fall within the category of neurotic character disorders, including the compulsive character and the hysterical character. One of the earliest attempts at developing characterological categories was made by psychoanalysts in the framework of the vicissitudes at various levels of psychosexual development. Although, as I have indicated, these are not necessarily pathological and may even be adaptive. However, under certain circumstances they may become disproportionate and may then contribute to pathology in the form of character disorders or even symptom disorders. As noted above, the fate of the instinctual drives may be brought about through direct expression, reaction-formation, or sublimation. The various character types I will describe might more correctly be categorized as character traits than as character disorders, especially those derivative of the classical stages in psychosexual development (the oral, anal, and phallic characterological manifestations).

There is a group of clinical manifestations which may be viewed as personality types or character types that have not reached the point at which they might be considered disorders. Yet they may become so fixed, so inflexible, and so intense—dominating an individual's social, occupational, and interpersonal relations—as to be considered character disorders. To this group belong the dependent, the passive-aggressive, the masochistic, and the avoidant personality, as well as many others. Perhaps most significant is the masochistic personality.

There are a whole group of neurotic characters whose behavior and lifestyle derives from a deep-seated sense of guilt. These individuals try to appease their guilt and rid themselves of it through atonement, self-punishment, and remorse. This may be generally expressed in behavior in situations evoked and manipulated by such individuals. This will result in their suffering in some way. Obviously actively involved in such situations is a severe and highly infantile superego. Associated with this are masochistic needs which are gratified by the suffering. Common in this group are accident-prone individuals, the victims of repeated accidents which appear to happen to them beyond their control. Closely allied to these are the individuals who appear to be the victims of fate and destiny, the so-called *Schicksals Neurose* (fate neurosis). Such individuals unconsciously arrange their lives so that they suffer one severe reversal after another. The "victims" of the destiny neurosis, the sufferers of a malicious fate, are still living out a deep sense of guilt derived from childhood situations; a need for punishment permeates their lifestyle. These features may be expressed clinically in many subtle forms. Freud (1916) described those "wrecked by success," people whose deep sense of guilt and severe superego does not permit them to enjoy any success. They may perform excellently at one level only to stumble and fail when they are advanced.

Another characterological type belonging to this group was described by Freud (1916) as "criminals through a sense of guilt." These are individuals who commit criminal acts because of an unconscious sense of guilt deriving from unconscious fantasies of having committed an even greater criminal act. Among other character neuroses described by Freud (1916) are "the exceptions." These are individuals who feel themselves above the usual moral and social restrictions. Behind this is the feeling that in some way they have suffered in the past from injuries imposed upon them.

Narcissistic Character Disorders

These present a problem in classification. Some believe these are only a variant of neurotic character disorders, whereas others would place them somewhere between the neurotic character disorders and the borderline or psychotic character disorders. The concept of a narcissistic personality type has a long history in psychoanalysis. Freud (1916) described many character types in which narcissistic needs and the self were the main frame of reference. Here he included individuals who have an insatiable need for self-esteem, with an incapacity for satisfaction which leads them to search for it constantly in their relationships with objects. These individuals at the same time remain independent of the external world by simply not caring. Fenichel (1945) summarizes earlier contributions while adding his own elaboration. He says narcissistic persons may, in the narcissistic sentence "I love myself," project the "myself" onto another person and then identify themselves with this person so as to enjoy the feeling of being loved by themselves (pp. 510–511). They strive to induce the object to do what they want. Much of this seems to anticipate Kohut's ideas regarding the mirror transference.

In what follows I will summarize the thinking of Kernberg and Kohut regarding this syndrome, interposing some of my own thoughts. Kohut (1972) views narcissism in libidinal terms, depending on the nature of the instinctual charge. The narcissistic personality arises from fixations on archaic grandiose self-images and on archaic, overestimated, and narcissistically cathected objects. Initially this is part of the development of normal narcissism; it becomes pathological by virtue of fixation. When there is a persistence of archaic self-object relationships, or a breakdown of the cohesive self, we encounter pathology in its various forms, dependent on the nature and degree of the breakdown or fragmentation. At times there occurs a disintegration or fragmentation of higher forms of narcissistic self-object relationships, with a regression to archaic narcissistic positions; then we see a reinstitution of mirror or idealized self-object relationships. The disintegration, which is temporary, may result in a narcissistic personality disorder.

These patients are characterized by a specific vulnerability. Self-esteem is unusually labile. In particular, they are extremely sensitive to failures, disappointments, and slights. In Kohut's clinical experience, those suffering from these disorders manifest an inability to focus on the essential aspects of the condition but may complain secondarily of work inhibition. There may be feelings of emptiness and depression. The anxieties attending the narcissistic character disorders relate basically to an awareness of the vulnerability of the self. The principal source of discomfort, according to Kohut, is an inability to regulate self-esteem. This may result in anxious grandiosity and excitement, on the one hand, or mild embarrassment and self-consciousness, or even severe shame, hypochondria, and depression, on the other. Unlike those suffering from psychoses and borderline states, these patients are not seriously threatened by the possibility of irreversible disintegration of the cohesive self, or of the narcissistically cathected archaic object. In narcissistic personality disorders the breakdown is temporary, and manifestations are autoplastically expressed in such symptoms as depression, anhedonia, lack of joie de vivre, and depression. As Kohut sees it, fundamental to the narcissistic character disorders is that as children those suffering them have experienced a lack of appropriate empathic response from the mother to their emotional developmental needs.

By contrast, Kernberg (1975) feels that pathological drive derivatives, both libidinal and aggressive, as well as the pathological development of structural derivatives of internalized object relations, are the main factors in the development of the narcissistic personality. According to Kernberg, the narcissism of the narcissistic personality is to begin with pathological, and not simply a fixation to archaic "normal" narcissism. The structure of the self is pathological, with intense pregenital conflicts around love and aggression, primarily oral rage and oral aggression. There is a pathological differentiation and integration of ego and superego structures deriving from pathological object relations. Kernberg feels that narcissistic characters suffer from a disturbance of their self-regard, in connection with specific disturbances in their object relationships, which results in a pathological development of narcissism. Behind all of this is a deep oral rage which is projected and may produce paranoid traits. Internalized object relationships are not good ones, and are intense and primitive.

These patients, who unfailingly see themselves as the main focal point in their relations with others, have a constant need to be loved and admired. Although they have an inflated image of themselves, they still need the admiration and tribute of others. Yet they have little empathy for the feelings of these others, whom they frequently envy, deprecate, or treat with contempt if tribute is not forthcoming. Their relations with others, whom they characteristically distrust, are frequently exploitative and parasitic. As noted above, behind this haughty, grandiose, and controlling behavior is a defense against paranoid traits related to a projection of oral rage. There are very intense primitive internalized object relationships of a very frightening kind.

Genetically, Kernberg points out that there is a predominance of chronically cold and narcissistic mother figures. This coupled with inborn intense aggressive drives leads the child to react with oral rage and envy to material frustrations. There is a devaluation of the object and a need to destroy the sources of love and gratification, in order to eliminate the sources of rage and envy. This is accompanied by a defensive withdrawal into the grandiose self.

Borderline Personality: The Psychotic Character

The oft-noted blurring between the narcissistic character disorders and borderline personality disorder is underlined by the fact that narcissistic qualities permeate the latter. But despite many different views regarding the dynamic features in this syndrome, there is a surprising degree of unanimity as regards the clinical picture. The essential feature is instability in a variety of areas, including interpersonal relationships, behavior, mood, and self-image. No single feature is invariably present. Interpersonal relationships are often intense and unstable, with marked shifts of attitude over time, ranging from idealization to devaluation and manipulation. Frequently there is impulsive and unpredictable behavior that is potentially self-damaging. Mood is often unstable, with marked shifts from normal mood to dysphoric moods such as depression, irritability, or anxiety. There may be inappropriate intense anger or frequent losses of temper. These states may shift quickly or last for hours. Profound identity disturbance may be manifested by uncertainty about several issues relating to identity—self-image, gender identity, long-term goals, career choice, values, and loyalties.

To designate this syndrome I have opted for the term *psychotic character disorder*. My feeling is that the term "borderline," by its very vagueness and diffuseness, deprives us of a means to understand this clinical condition dynamically. Dynamic thinking brought to bear on this syndrome enables us to formulate a more coherent frame of reference, which facilitates our understanding of the phenomenology and permits a more rational therapeutic approach. It should be borne in mind that when we speak of the borderline we always mean the borderline to psychosis. The problems and features characteristic of the psychotic process run like a red thread through most of the problems of the psychotic character. The anxiety, the defenses, the disturbed ego states, the specific impairment of ego functions, all so characteristic of the psychotic process, exert an impact on character structure and clinical manifestations. I am speaking here not of clinical psychosis as the common denominator, or as the main frame of reference, but of psychic processes these patients share, processes which play a role in, and underlie, possible psychotic development. These processes are part of total psychic functioning and may eventuate in behavioral manifestations which contaminate the lifestyle, but in ways which of themselves are not necessarily clinically psychotic.

They may eventuate in the clinical manifestations of the borderline, as described above.

Kernberg (1976), although he describes many subsidiary
defenses, focuses on splitting as the main defensive operation
in the borderline. He views splitting as the active process of
keeping apart introjections or identifications of opposite qualities. Because there is a lack of integration of these polarized
introjections and identifications, there results a lack of neutralization, and hence a lack of energy for ego growth. This leads
to ego weakness. Clinically, one may see behavioral expressions
of the different sides of a conflict combined with denial and
lack of concern over such contradictions in behavior. There
may be a selective lack of impulse control, with episodic break-
throughs of primitive impulses. There is a division of objects
into all-good ones and all-bad ones, with abrupt shifts from one
to the other and accompanying reversals of feelings. There may
also be shifts in self-concepts.

If we focus on the clinical features derived from the underlying psychotic process, we will encounter manifestations in addition to those described above. This obviously will have therapeutic implications, including a need to focus on the reality
impairment. These features may include a disorganized and
chaotic lifestyle, body image disturbances, difficulties in separating dream from reality, and intermittent disturbances in
states of consciousness. Despite their presence, however, a tenuous capacity to test reality and a tenuous and impaired reality
constancy are nonetheless retained. The clinical picture of the
psychotic character ranges along a spectrum. There are those
who live teetering constantly and precariously, on the verge
of psychosis, with frequent forays into decompensation; such
psychotic episodes are generally of short duration lasting from
a few minutes to a few hours, days, or weeks.

Character Impulse Disorders: The Impulse-Ridden Character

The character impulse disorders, or impulse-ridden characters, are typified by a diffuseness of the impulse disturbance,
which permeates the personality without attaching itself to a
single kind of impulse. This group strongly resembles the character disorders in structure, and the clinical manifestations are

even more ego-syntonic than those seen in the symptom impulse disorders. In many cases the behavior seems to have an organic base. However, a large group of disorders remains in which organic findings cannot be demonstrated but in which the impulse disturbances nonetheless seem to be woven into the warp and woof of the personality. Patients in this group are usually infantile, immature, and intolerant of tension or anxiety. They tend to react explosively in the face of deprivations. The patient may recognize this and berate himself for his impulsive behavior; frequently he becomes depressed by his actions, at times to the point of attempts at self-destruction. These patients are intolerant of frustration. Whatever they need they must have immediately. They cannot postpone reactions. They generally act instead of thinking. The action may be in direct line with the underlying impulse, or it may be entirely unrelated to an objective or goal, a wild, impulsive flailing out in all directions. Such impulsivity may manifest itself in many spheres, and be reflected in a lifestyle characterized by restlessness and a constant need to be on the go, a running from one activity to another. These patients are rarely able to be by themselves or to concentrate on anything in a sustained fashion. The explosive behavior may be followed by self-reproach, self-castigation, and depression. Impulse-ridden characters are frequently associated with deep-seated anxieties, and depression or loneliness can be elicited by merely scratching the surface. Impulse-ridden characters are "body people," whose modes of communication and tension-relieving techniques consist of action. Their language is frequently not communicative of ideas, but of discharge (as seen in their frequent use of expletives). Nonetheless, impulse-ridden patients can establish object relations and very intense transference relationships.

Many of the features characterizing symptomatic impulse disorders are present as well in the actions of the impulse-ridden character—ego-syntonicity, minimal distortion of the original impulse, and a feeling of pleasure at the time of committing the impulsive act. Just as the ego function of delay is seemingly impaired in impulse disorders, so it is impaired in the impulse-ridden character. The factors contributing to disturbances in the function of delay are similar in both conditions.

Impulsive behavior must again be differentiated from acting out. This has prognostic and therapeutic implications. The impulse disorders, characterized by insufficiency of the control apparatus and the absence of organized fantasy, may call for techniques to support an ego whose basic defect is the lack of capacity for delay. In acting out, substitutive action resulting from a short-circuiting of the ego function of delay at a higher level of development contains within it organized fantasy and may require exploratory therapy utilizing clarification, confrontation, and interpretation. The subtle interweaving of impulse disorder and acting out requires in the earlier stages of treatment an approach more closely allied to that use in the impulse disorders, with a gradual phasing into the exploratory mode used with more classical instances of acting out.

Psychosexual Disorders

Included in the psychosexual disorders are the dysfunctions and the deviations. Psychosexual dysfunctions involve an impairment in potency, which may occur at various stages of the sexual response cycle, and which contributes to subjective dissatisfaction and objective evidence of the impairment. In the male these dysfunctions include premature ejaculation, retarded ejaculation, erectile difficulties, and other conditions. In the female we may encounter frigidities of various types. Persons of either sex may suffer from orgastic impotence.

Psychosexual deviations (which I have discussed above with the disorders of impulse control) are those sexual acts which are obligatory and necessary, and the sole way of achieving sexual gratification. They are the individual's method of choice in sexual activity. They are persistent, stereotypical sexual acts which are ego-syntonic and pleasurable at the time of gratification. Although they are direct expressions of pregenital and polymorphous perverse drives, a component of the latter may be expressed and used as a defense against underlying anxieties related to castration and separation. As such, these acts are ultimately compromise formations, providing an outlet not only for sexual drives but for aggressive ones as well. They are generally characterized by a blurring of sexual differences, with a poor infant-mother demarcation in the background, bringing in its wake gender identity disturbances and impairment of body identity. This makes possible the mutual identification expressed in the fantasies, or by those participating in the perverse activities.

Highly controversial is the inclusion of homosexuality among the deviations. There are a great number of views regarding the genesis and dynamics of homosexuality—or, rather, the homosexualities. The fact that observers have seen different kinds of homosexuals may well account for the variety of views, ranging from the significance of constitutional factors to a variety of developmental fantasies, both male and female. Male homosexuality, more than female homosexuality, appears to have been better understood by these observers. The true homosexual excludes any member of the opposite sex as a true object choice, as lacking certain features longed for as a result of childhood deprivation, real or imagined. The family constellation may contribute in one way or another. The combination of a close-binding, aggressively dominant mother and a distant and passive father has been proposed as a frame of reference for both male and female homosexuality, as has that of a weak and passive mother and an aggressive, hostile, and rejecting father.

Among the many other factors indicated in male homosexuals are castration anxiety, which makes the mother's genitalia, and female genitalia in general, disappointing in a love object. There is a narcissistic overendowment of the penis as the desired organ. Still another factor is an intense attachment to the mother, with both love and envy of the breast. Associated with these is a need to ward off aggression toward members of the same sex. The role of mutual identification in the act may be necessary in both male and female homosexuals, who will thereby fulfill passive and active needs as well as combatting the fear of separation in the interest of survival. One can see the need to study each case individually rather than make generalizations about this perversion.

It is probable that in both the dysfunctions and the deviations there is generally some impairment of orgastic potency. The orgastic experience in the human may assume many forms and degrees. The total orgastic experience is reflected in the release of a mounting sexual tension, with a generalized pleasurable experience. Essential to the understanding of sexual dysfunction and deviations in both sexes is the impairment of orgasm known as orgastic impotence. In this condition the physiological sexual cycle may run its course. Desire and even excitement may be present, and in the male ejaculation may even occur. However, there is a lack of total pleasure and full satisfaction in the orgasm, an inability to let oneself go completely. There is what I would call a lack of ability to permit ego regression in the service of the id.

In orgastic impotence there may be narcissistic gratification in being able to perform, but there is no total sense of real pleasure. A good part of this is related to the lack of full inclusion of the partner, the inability to view the orgasm as a sharing experience. Such individuals are incapable of full love, and the need for self-love and self-esteem may be inordinate. The presence of orgastic impotence will frequently lead individuals to a constant search for repetitive sexual experiences. This has been characterized as the Don Juan syndrome.

A not infrequent lack of orgastic response may be found in some borderline patients, whose tenuous hold on reality may be threatened by the alteration of consciousness which comes with full orgasm. Full orgasm may bring with it a degree of self-nonself dedifferentiation, and a fear of the disintegrative effect of excitement. Equally, the danger of loss of control with the breakthrough of aggressive or other forbidden impulses makes the letting-go of full sexual response a dangerous prospect.

It should be emphasized that evidence of orgastic impotence may be quite subtle and so may not be properly diagnosed. Patients may have difficulty identifying what full orgasm is like, as they may not have experienced it.

Somatic Syndromes

Somatic syndromes range over a wide spectrum. Not all of them fall within the therapeutic scope of psychoanalysis, even where it has been able to offer explanations. Psychoanalytic contributions to the somatic syndromes fall into several areas. There are those which propose to examine the psychological factors contributing to the etiology and development of somatic manifestations. These include factors facilitating the development of somatic illness, the role of symbolization in somatic manifestations, associations with specific personality types, secondary psychological implications, etc. Psychoanalytic contributions have been of significance to many of the syndromes, not only by lending understanding, but having therapeutic implications as well. Still others, though lending understanding, have had little impact on psychoanalytically oriented therapy, such as the organic brain syndromes.

Before proceeding, I would like to comment on the DSM-III use of the concept of somatization to describe patients who may present a wide variety of somatic complaints, of recurrent and chronic duration, which apparently are not caused by physical disorders. This definition of somatization is at variance with the psychoanalytic concept of somatization, which encompasses actual physical and somatic manifestations. Somatization is a typical response on the part of certain patients who speak, so to say, "with their bodies." It is a nonverbal and primitive way of responding to stress and frequently represents a psychotic reaction. Somatization is viewed by some as a variant of Freud's early concept of actual neurosis. Macalpine (1952) considers such manifestations to be rudimentary and partly expressed emotions rather than a defense against conflict. According to her, these patients, like psychotics, suffer from an excess of anxiety from which they cannot defend themselves. This resembles Meng and Stern's concept of organ psychosis (1955).

One of the areas to which psychoanalysis has made many contributions is to the traditional psychosomatic syndromes. Flanders Dunbar (1938) suggested a psychological meaning for many diseases and maintained that different diseases might occur in individuals of different personality types. Alexander (1950) and his associates tried to link specific unresolved unconscious conflicts with specific somatic disorders. They studied bronchial asthma, ulcerative colitis, thyrotoxicosis, essential hypertension, rheumatoid arthritis, neurodermatitis, and peptic ulcers. Alexander saw these disorders as manifestations of blocked emotion which achieved only distorted, inhibited, or partial expression. He felt that these syndromes reflected the activity of the involuntary nervous system in contrast to hysterical conversion symptoms. He formulated certain theoretical frames of reference. Among these were early life factors dealing with unconscious conflicts, and the defense mechanisms used in dealing with these conflicts. Further, precipitating life situations could reactivate these underlying conflicts. He also referred to constitutionally determined organic vulnerabilities and to conflicting impulses that revolve around the need and wish to incorporate, to eliminate, and to retain.

Other contributors have felt that many somatic syndromes were outgrowths of primitive fantasies expressed as pregenital conversions, in contrast to hysterical phallic conversion manifestations. It will be seen that these features characterize neurotic development in general, and that many other factors must play a role in the causation of these syndromes.

A few general theoretical comments on the meaning of the body and the various organs may shed some light on the various somatic syndromes. Essential to all of this is the understanding of body image. This can be traced back to the developmental stage in which one's own body is the goal of object finding. It is a time when the infant is discovering its body, part by part, as the outer world, and still gropes for its hands and feet as though they were foreign objects. The infant's psyche receives stimuli arising from its own body, but acts upon them as if they were produced by outside objects. Schilder (1935) discusses how the body is treated as an outside object during this early stage in development.

Before the development of a unified image and unified self, the state of the psyche is such that parts of the self—the body self and the psychic self—may be projected and extrojected. The body image and the psychic self are ultimately built up by integrating the various autonomous and hitherto disconnected parts of the self. Ultimately out of this should develop a unified and integrated body image, the image one has of what one's body looks like and feels like. It encompasses many features, including affects, the various functions of the body parts, sensations and reactions to stimuli, etc. It also includes the instinctual impact of both libidinal and aggressive drives, the impact of object representations, and the attitude toward one's own body. Kohut's concept of the ultimate formation of a cohesive self has much in common with these processes, which ultimately evolve into a unified body image. In physical illness there may be a proclivity for fragmentation of the body image, which leads to isolated preoccupation with fragmented parts of the self. In this stage the individual parts are disconnected. This applies equally to the breaking down of the unified body image, which re-creates the autonomy of the individual parts and organs of the body.

There are many conditions in which this sense of a unified body image may be impaired, and the individual components may regressively achieve a degree of autonomy which lends itself to somatic manifestations. These may vary from neurotic symbolization to psychotic personification and disengagement and projection of an undesirable part of the self. This is associated with a disruption of the homeostatic balance.

Somatic complaints may be used in several ways. An organ or organ function may lend itself for psychological elaboration because of its possibility for symbolic significance. An organ or series of functions may have some underlying minimal dysfunction or impairment and lend itself for psychological elaboration, especially when it has some special personal significance. Organs which are diseased or have been diseased lend themselves readily to psychological elaboration. Gross organic impairment may be used for the expression of neurotic tendencies, in which case we have what Ferenczi (1916–1917) called pathoneurosis; alternatively, it may lend itself to psychotic elaboration, in which case he calls it pathopsychosis. Related to these are Meng and Stern's organ neuroses and organ psychoses (1955), in which a neurotic conflict or a psychotic conflict is encompassed in physical illness to such an extent that if the physical condition is altered for any reason, a full-blown neurosis or psychosis may eventuate. It is as though in some instances the physical situation has been the defense against these conditions.

In the concepts of pathoneurosis and pathopsychosis Ferenczi posits a psychological imposition on an actual organic illness. Ferenczi suggested the term pathoneurosis where a neurosis is superimposed, and pathopsychosis when a psychosis is superimposed upon the organic illness. Essentially what Ferenczi suggests is the imposition of various psychological reactions on an injured organ. Some of these may assume the form of hysteria, whereby the injured organ takes on a symbolic psychological significance. Others may appear as simple reactions, rather like Freud's actual neuroses, in which the accumulation of libido in a given organ results in tension. Still others may produce pathopsychotic-like rather than pathoneurotic-like reactions, and come under Ferenczi's heading of narcissistic neuroses. Ferenczi is not too clear about all this, but these implications are subsequently developed by Meng (1934) in the concept of the organ neuroses and organ psychoses.

Essentially what is involved in the organ psychoses is that the psychotic process is expressed through the organs. Similarly, in the organ neuroses the expression is via neurotic processes. The organ psychoses are characterized by rather primitive states of psychic development, in which the various organs are treated in terms appropriate to a pre-object stage. Meng views severe ego disturbances as antedating the somatic illness, which masks and represses an underlying psychotic potential. He points out that many of his patients presented features frequently observed in psychoses. The somatic illness was actually substituted for the psychotic one. In other words, the somatic phenomena may serve to ward off psychosis; if they were not present, psychosis would be.

The contributions of psychoanalysis to the organic brain syndromes are essentially to an understanding of the impact of this disorder on the various ego functions. In the organic brain syndrome the ego disturbance may be primarily affected by direct impairment of the brain of a major nature. Serious impairments in cognitive function may result. Alternatively, the insult may produce serious impairment of the ego's relation to the internal and external environment. This would result in an inability to maintain the organizing and integrating function of perception. Further, the ego's reaction to these impairments and defects must be considered, as must the fact that the impaired organ, the brain, which is trying to deal with these manifestations, is itself already affected. There is then a kind of feedback reaction of an impaired organ trying to deal with the consequences of its impairment.

Post-Traumatic Stress Disorders

The post-traumatic stress disorders include a wide range of psychogenic reactions to traumas and their sequelae. It is a nonmorphological emotional disorder which may or may not be complicated by morphological changes in the body. Such traumas may cover a whole host of sudden and unexpected experiences, ranging from military or natural disasters to violent sexual experiences, accidents of various sorts, bombings, fires, explosions, etc. Trauma may equally result from continuous exposure to a stressful experience which cannot be dealt with motorically. The syndromes following military or peacetime traumata do not differ essentially. In the military they have been known by various names—shell shock, battle fatigue, war neurosis, etc.

The symptomatology may be quite varied, depending on the nature of the precipitating experience or actual injury, as well as the personality of the victim. However, certain general manifestations appear to be present in varying degree in all such syndromes. First is an impairment in the ability to control discharge in an organized manner. Second is a blocking or decrease in ego functions. This inhibition of ego functions limits the capacity of the personality for effective, realistic functioning and reflects ʾmotional withdrawal, another condition typical of this syndron. ʾ.

Equally common is anxiety, which may assume many forms. Most common among these is a general lowering of the tolerance threshold to stimuli, manifesting itself in irritability and hyperacusis mounting at times to explosive reactions to rather minor stimuli. There is a marked degree of intolerance to any form of frustration, resulting either in motor discharge or in submissive withdrawal. These emotional reactions interfere with cognitive functioning. Generally, the ability to deal with internal or external stimuli and excitement through reflective thought, fantasy, and other appropriate means is impaired. These reactions are viewed by some as having restitutive aspects. Withdrawal and a quieting down tend to reduce further exposure and at the same time provide a means of collecting oneself to deal with failed mastery. Other restitutive aspects are the attempts at belated discharge seen in many sensorimotor phenomena, the emotional upheaval, and the reexperience of the trauma both in the wakened state and in dreams.

A typical manifestation of post-traumatic stress syndrome are recurrent memories of the traumatic event which intrude into the waking and dream life of the individual. The traumatic experiences become the focus of the individual's emotional life.

According to one of Freud's earliest concepts, what may take place at the end of the trauma is an impairment of the stimulus barrier, so that the ego's capacity to deal with even ordinary stimuli has been impaired. In consequence of the trauma, hitherto existing modes of adaptation fail, and the individual must evolve different ways of adapting, a process which may eventuate in clinical manifestations. The repetition of the traumatic events was viewed by Freud and others as an attempt to achieve a belated mastery through active reproduction of what was experienced passively, in the hope that this time the outcome will be different. This has been viewed by some as an attempt at ultimate desensitization of the experience.

Although Kardiner's concepts (1947) were developed in a study of chronic traumatic war neuroses, he believed that the same considerations could be applied to peacetime post-traumatic stress disorders. The essential basic reaction, he argued, is one of inhibition in various aspects of a hitherto operative adaptation. This inhibition brings about a contraction of the ego, which is now characterized by ineffective executive functioning, withdrawal from reality, and diminished interest in the daily activities of life. This may be accompanied by helplessness, a lack of confidence, and a need to be taken care of. There is an anticipation of danger, which brings in its wake disorganized activity including reactions of irritability, explosive outbursts, and autonomous dysrhythmia.

A number of secondary clinical manifestations may be superimposed on the basic features. Traumatic experiences may be seized upon by some individuals via associative connection as a kind of screen memory for other shattering events in the individual's life. They may be captured by the personality for the purpose of solving residual earlier problems and even for reworking the individual's life problems. Latent neurotic conflicts may be activated because of the disruption of a hitherto stable balance. There may be an increase in previously repressed instinctual forces, leading to increased anxiety that will motivate a need for secondary defense. This will lead to the superimposition on the basic symptomatology of seemingly secondary clinical factors. Old infantile threats and anxieties will be reactivated and associatively connected with the trauma; for instance, the danger of physical injury may reactivate an underlying castration anxiety. In some instances the trauma may mesh with existing sadomasochistic tendencies and hold a mixture of temptation and punishment. Such individuals may deliberately and repeatedly expose themselves to dangerous situations and experience the trauma simply as a punishment. In individuals who feel the punishment is deserved, this may be reinforced by underlying guilt.

A special form of guilt reaction, especially when someone close is killed, is "survivor guilt." Behind this lurks the sense of "Schadenfreude," the sense of elation that it was "somebody else, not me." In accident-prone individuals, the accident may be sought as a symbol of submission and masochistic needs in the service of self-punishment. There is a kind of abandonment to a superior force. In children the vehicle of an accident is viewed as a symbol of unlimited power. All of these reactions may bring in their wake neurotic syndromes superimposed on a basic pathology. But equally one may see psychotic manifestations.

Conclusion

This chapter has described the impact of psychoanalytic thinking on the development of a psychoanalytic nosology, as well as on psychiatric diagnoses. The existing psychoanalytic frames of reference at any given time influenced the developing nosology. These developing frames of reference, as well as how they influenced nosological development, were discussed. The early topographic model of the mind as the frame of reference evolved ultimately to the impact of the development of a psychoanalytic ego psychology, object relations theory, and self psychology.

Clinically, it is at times very difficult to make a clear differentiation in nosology. Very frequently there are shadings-over, combinations, and changes in the picture, so that to say that this and this is a clear case of that and that is often difficult. Freud made this point very clearly. Although he proceeded to distinguish and delineate certain entities, in later years he did not much concern himself with nosology. We cannot, however, ignore nosology altogether. We must familiarize ourselves with presenting symptomatology, of course, but implicit in diagnosis are dynamic and genetic factors. The sharper delineation of a syndrome requires an overall evaluation of the picture and its evolution. Inherent is the question, What is the nature of the personality structure of the individual in which this illness resides? This brings us right up against the question of the character structure of the patient, a most fundamental and essential aspect of our work.

References

Abraham, K. (1921), Contributions to the theory of the anal character. In: *Selected Papers on Psycho-Analysis*. London: Hogarth Press, 1927, pp. 370–392.

———— (1924), The influence of oral erotism on character-formation. In: *Selected Papers on Psycho-Analysis*. London: Hogarth Press, 1927, pp. 393–406.

———— (1925), Character-formation on the genital level of the libido. In: *Selected Papers on Psycho-Analysis*. London: Hogarth Press, 1927, pp. 407–417.

Alexander, F. (1950), *Psychosomatic Medicine: Its Principles and Applications*. New York: Norton.
Bak, R. (1954), The schizophrenic defense against aggression. *Internat. J. Psycho-Anal.*, 35:129–134.
Bibring, E. (1953), The mechanism of depression. In: *Affective Disorders*, ed. L. P. Greenacre. New York: International Universities Press, pp. 13–48.
Bromberg, W., & Schilder, P. (1933), Psychological considerations in alcoholic hallucinations: Castration and dismembering motives. *Internat. J. Psycho-Anal.*, 14:206–240.
Dunbar, F. (1938), *Emotions and Bodily Changes*. New York: Columbia University Press.
Fenichel, O. (1945), *The Psychoanalytic Theory of Neurosis*. New York: Norton.
——— (1941), Psychoanalysis of character. In: *The Collected Papers of Otto Fenichel*, Vol. 2. New York: Norton, 1954, pp. 198–214.
Ferenczi, S. (1916–1917), *Disease or Pathoneurosis: Theory and Technique of Psychoanalysis*. New York: Boni and Liveright, 1927.
Freud, S. (1894), The neuro-psychoses of defence. *Standard Edition*, 3:45–61. London: Hogarth Press, 1962.
——— (1896), Further remarks on the neuro-psychoses of defence. *Standard Edition*, 3:162–185. London: Hogarth Press, 1962.
——— (1900), The interpretation of dreams. *Standard Edition*, 4/5. London: Hogarth Press, 1953.
——— (1905), Fragment of an analysis of a case of hysteria. *Standard Edition*, 7:7–122. London: Hogarth Press, 1953.
——— (1908), Character and anal erotism. *Standard Edition*, 9:169–175. London: Hogarth Press, 1959.
——— (1909), Analysis of a phobia in a five-year-old boy. *Standard Edition*, 9:5–147. London: Hogarth Press, 1955.
——— (1911), Psycho-analytic notes upon an autobiographical account of a case of paranoia. *Standard Edition*, 12:9–79. London: Hogarth Press, 1958.
——— (1914), On narcissism. *Standard Edition*, 14:69–102. London: Hogarth Press, 1957.
——— (1916), Some character-types met with in psycho-analytic work. *Standard Edition*, 14:311–333. London: Hogarth Press, 1957.
——— (1916–1917), Introductory lectures on psycho-analysis. *Standard Edition*, 15/16. London: Hogarth Press, 1963.
——— (1917), Mourning and melancholia. *Standard Edition*, 14:237–258. London: Hogarth Press, 1957.
——— (1924a), The loss of reality in neurosis and psychosis. *Standard Edition*, 19:183–187. London: Hogarth Press, 1961.
——— (1924b), Neurosis and psychosis. *Standard Edition*, 19:149–153. London: Hogarth Press, 1961.
——— (1926), Inhibitions, symptoms, and anxiety. *Standard Edition*, 20:77–174. London: Hogarth Press, 1959.
——— (1931), Libidinal types. *Standard Edition*, 21:217–220. London: Hogarth Press, 1961.
Friedman, P. (1967), *On Suicice*. New York: International Universities Press.
Fromm-Reichmann, F. (1959), *Psychoanalysis and Psychotherapy: Selected Papers*. Chicago: University of Chicago Press.

Frosch, J. (1966), A note on reality constancy. In: *Psychoanalysis—A General Psychology: Essays in Honor of Heinz Hartmann*, ed. R. M. Loewenstein, L. M. Newman, M. Schur, & A. Solnit. New York: International Universities Press, pp. 349–376.

———— (1970), Psychoanalytic considerations of the psychotic character. *J. Amer. Psychoanal. Assn.*, 18:24–50.

———— (1977), The relation between acting out and disorders of impulse control. *Psychiat.*, 30:295–313.

———— (1978), Emotional health and emotional illness. Unpublished paper presented to the New York Psychiatric Society.

———— (1981), The role of unconscious homosexuality in the paranoid constellation. *Psychoanal. Quart.*, 50:587–613.

———— (1983), *The Psychotic Process*. New York: International Universities Press.

Glover, E. (1932), A psychoanalytic approach to the classification of mental disorders. In: *On the Early Development of Mind*. New York: International Universities Press, 1956.

Hartmann, H. (1953), The metapsychology of schizophrenia. *The Psychoanalytic Study of the Child*, 8:177–198. New York: International Universities Press.

Horney, K. (1937), *The Neurotic Personality of Our Time*. New York: Norton.

Kardiner, A. (1947), *The Traumatic Neuroses of War*. London: Hoeber.

Kernberg, O. (1975), *Borderline Conditions and Pathological Narcissism*. New York: Aronson.

———— (1976), Technical considerations in the treatment of borderline personality. *J. Amer. Psychoanal. Assn.*, 24:795–830.

———— (1984), *Severe Personality Disorder*. New Haven: Yale University Press.

Klein, M. (1946), Notes on some schizoid mechanisms. *Internat. J. Psycho-Anal.*, 27:99–110.

Kohut, H. (1971), *The Analysis of the Self*. New York: International Universities Press.

———— (1972), Thoughts on narcissism and narcissistic rage. *The Psychoanalytic Study of the Child*, 27:360–400. New York: Quadrangle.

Lewin, B. D. (1950), *The Psychoanalysis of Elation*. New York: Norton.

Macalpine, I. (1952), Psychosomatic symptom formation. *Lancet*, 1:278–282.

Meng, H. (1934), Problems of the organ psychosis: Psychological treatment of patients with organic disease. *Internat. Z. Psych-Anal.*, 20:439–458.

———— Stern, E. (1955), Organ psychosis. *Psychoanal. Rev.*, 42:428–434.

Menninger, K. (1954), Psychological aspects of the organism under stress: Part I. The homeostatic regulatory function of the ego; Part II. Regulatory devices of the ego under major stress. *J. Amer. Psychoanal. Assn.*, 2:120–151.

Pao, P.-N. (1979), *Schizophrenic Disorders*. New York: International Universities Press.

Rado, S. (1928), The problem of melancholia. *Internat. J. Psycho-Anal.*, 9:420–438.

Rangell, L. (1965), Some comments on psychoanalytic nosology. In: *Drives, Affects, Behavior*, Vol. 2, ed. M. Schur. New York: International Universities Press.

Reich, W. (1928), On character analysis. In: *The Psychoanalytic Reader*, ed. R. Fliess. New York: International Universities Press, 1948, pp. 129–147.

Schilder, P. (1935), *The Image and Appearance of the Human Body*. New York: International Universities Press, 1950.

Staercke, A. (1920), The reversal of the libido sign in delusions of persecution. *Internat. J. Psycho-Anal.*, 1:231–234.

Will, O. (1961), Paranoid development in the concept of self. *Psychiat.*, 24:74–86.

Winnicott, D. W. (1959), Classification: Is there a psychoanalytic contribution to psychiatric classification? In: *The Maturational Processes and The Facilitating Environment*. New York: International Universities Press, 1965, pp. 124–139.

13

Psychoanalytic Perspectives on the Affective Disorders: Neurobiological and Psychosocial Interactions

LOUIS A. GOTTSCHALK, M.D., Ph.D.

Introduction

The Psychoanalyst's Sphere of Observation and the Biological Substrate for the Phenomena Observed

There are many intervening variables involved in the workings of the body that influence emotional expression and affect as they are perceived and understood by the psychoanalyst who is interviewing and observing an individual. Direct observation of affects and their changes and the historical reconstruction of affect and mood in the past by observing current behavior and listening to the content and form of verbal communications, the raw data with which the psychoanalyst deals, provide minimal information with respect to the neurochemical and neurophysiological bases of affect and mood. Modern psychoanalysis recognizes that such basic sciences as neuroanatomy, biochemistry, neurophysiology, psychophysiology, neuropsychopharmacology, psychology, and sociology are necessary to comprehend the underlying bases of the phenomena observed in the intact human individual during the psychoanalytic procedure. The modern psychoanalyst needs to work hard to keep abreast of the continuing developments and enlargements of knowledge in these basic sciences as they bear on an understanding of the phenomena observed in the clinical psychoanalytic setting.

To organize the bulky and complex data germane to my topic, let me first focus on some pertinent definitions and the scope and limitations of our current systems for classifying affective disorders.

Working Definitions of Affects and Moods and Current Classification Systems of Affective Disorders

Affects. Affects are often considered distinct from emotions. Affects denote the subjective and psychological state that can motivate behavior, and emotions include, in addition to a feeling state, the physiological concomitants which accompany this psychological state. Many authors, however, make no precise distinction between affects and emotions, and no differentiation will be made here between these two terms. Affects are usually brief, lasting from minutes to hours, sometimes days. With certain psychiatric disorders, such as psychoneuroses, psychoses, or organic cerebral disorders, affects may become long-lasting.

Moods. Mood refers to affective characteristics which last relatively longer (days to weeks or months) than affects. In the field of psychiatry, manic-depressive reactions or mania or depression separately are referred to as affective disorders. In this chapter, affects or affective states are used in the sense of both short-term and long-term feeling states. Distinctions are made with respect to the duration of these affective states when it appears appropriate to do so.

Classification systems of affective disorders. Before consideration of hereditary, constitutional and environmental factors as they influence affects and the so-called "affective disorders," the validity of current nosological systems must be examined. Evidence for the existence of distinct and useful diagnostic entities varies from one classification system to another.

Grinker, Miller, Sabshin, Nunn, and Nunnally (1961) have espoused a strictly descriptive, phenomenological approach to the analysis of depressive states, an approach which avoids the interpretation of behavior and the inferences resulting from the influence of theory. This classification system confines itself to what can be observed in the patient's behavior and consists of a set of descriptive configurations distinguished by different feeling and behavior patterns; for example, type A is empty and withdrawn, type B is anxious and agitated, type C is hypochondriacal and agitated, and so forth. This typology is somewhat prognostic of response, but it is not in general use, and its predictive capacity has not been tested.

Katz and Hirschfeld (1977), in an excellent review and evaluation of classification systems of depression, indicate that in such strictly empirical classification systems, the assumption has to be made that qualitatively different types exist and that people cannot be ordered simply on a continuum. A thorough analysis of this typological-dimensional controversy in nosology has been made by Jung (1938), and the details are not reviewed here. In the empirical approach to diagnostic classification, a major assumption is that the different types can be discerned on the basis of the *presenting* clinical picture, including characteristic patterns of interpersonal behavior. In most currently accepted systems of classification, however, past history—for example, the number of previous depressive episodes and the course of the depression—are very important in discriminating types. The principal features used in the current systems for distinguishing types of affective disorders are as follows:

Past history

1. previous evidence of depressive or manic episodes
2. occurrence of stressful events in precipitating the episodes
3. normal, neurotic, or depression-prone premorbid personality
4. presence or absence of affective disorders in other family members

Present illness

5. the prominence of depressive or manic affect in the symptom-complex
6. the presence or absence of typical somatic symptoms
7. the presence or absence of psychotic signs
8. the relative severity of the episode

Katz and Hirschfeld (1977) evaluated these and other diagnostic features of the affective disorders, and they offer some useful and provocative conclusions. The *psychotic-neurotic* nosological distinction has its limitations, because multiple meanings exist for both psychotic and neurotic depression and because the distinction may represent a continuum rather than separate categories. The term "endogenous depression," though originally denoting a hereditary proclivity to a disorder (Moebius, 1893), currently refers to a characteristic symptom-complex consisting of early morning awakening, loss of appetite, loss of weight, psychomotor retardation, diurnal mood variation, severe depressed mood, and lack of responsivity to external stimuli. This group of depressive patients has been found to show the greatest differences in response to drug and placebo (Bielski and Friedel, 1976; Raskin and Crook, 1976); to have basically normal premorbid personalities; to be older and more severely ill, with higher scores on almost all symptom variables, such as depressed mood and feelings of hopelessness and worthlessness; and to suffer weight loss and early morning awakening. This nosological classification, hence, appears valid and predictive.

A nosological distinction for research rather than clinical purposes has been proposed by Robins and Guze (1972) and is known as the "primary-secondary" distinction. Primary affective disorders are depressive or manic episodes occurring in patients who have no prior history of psychiatric disorders, with the possible exception of depressive or manic episodes. Secondary affective disorders are seen in patients who have preexisting, diagnosable psychiatric disorders other than a previous primary affective disorder. The purpose of this distinction is to select groups of patients who share common etiologies. Patients with primary affective disorders are predicted to have more affective psychopathological manifestations in their first-degree relatives and to experience fewer symptoms between episodes of affective disorders than do controls. In contrast, patients with secondary affective disorders have a clinical course and intermorbid state resembling those of other patients with their underlying condition; for example, the intermorbid state of a secondary depressive with a preexisting neurotic character disorder is more like that of a character disorder than that of a depressive.

The "unipolar-bipolar" distinction, as elaborated later, is another useful distinction that appears to have some etiological and predictive relevance and usefulness.

All of the above diagnostic systems have been categorical or typological. Some investigators (e.g., Strauss, 1975) have argued that this approach has serious limitations for classifying psychiatric disorders, for though some of these classifications may yield a homogeneous group (e.g., bipolar disorders or primary affective disorders), what should be done with affective disorders not meeting the criteria? A multiaxial approach to diagnosis has therefore been proposed (Strauss, 1975), with the five major axes being (1) symptoms; (2) circumstances associated with the symptoms; (3) previous course and duration of symptoms; (4) quality of personal relations; and (5) caliber of work function. There is a justification for this multiaxial approach, as indicated later in this chapter, for etiological considerations must be accounted for among affective disorders that do not fit into these neat classificatory packages, as well as for those that do. As emphasized later, our lack of ability to measure reliably subtle distinctions that have relevance to etiology, treatment, and outcome limits our understanding of affects and affective disorders. The reader must therefore accept that our current definitions and diagnostic classificatory schemata constitute attempts to organize and make some order of the at times apparent chaos of the phenomenological world, but that our perception of other orderly arrangements among the phenomena under observation may be obscured when we are successful.

The broad scope of our considerations here embrace genetic and constitutional as well as environmental and psychological influences. Psychoanalytic perspectives regarding the etiology and pathogenesis of the affective disorders are usually broadly comprehensive. The therapeutic predilection of psychoanalysts, however, no doubt because of the psychodynamic emphasis of their training and experience, tends to bias psychoanalysts toward a preference for psychosocial rather than biomedical models when trying to modify these disorders. This therapeutic orientation leads psychoanalysts to be more familiar with psychodynamic and psychophysiological mechanisms than with somatopsychic ones.

The Influence of Affect Arousal on Biological Variables and of Psychoactive Drugs on Affects and Their Biological Substrate

Psychological or Behavioral Events Trigger Somatic Biochemical Changes, and Somatic Biochemical Changes Influence Subjective Experience or Behavior

A frequent issue between psychosocially and biomedically oriented scientists is whether psychological or behavioral events trigger biochemical changes in the body or vice versa. Rather than an either/or causal chain, there is convincing evidence that both causal pathways exist and are functional, certainly for short-term and immediate cause-effect relationships and, probably, for more long-lasting and persisting effects. My own work with affects is especially relevant to these short-term cause-effect relationships, and to the question of the relative importance of psychosocial and biomedical factors in the pathogenesis of affective disorders.

In research derived from clinical psychoanalytic theory, my coworkers and I have developed an objective method of measuring the magnitude of psychological states from the content analysis of free-associative speech (Gottschalk and Hambidge, 1955; Gottschalk and Kaplan, 1958; Gottschalk and Gleser, 1969; Gottschalk, 1971, 1976, 1978; Gottschalk Hoigaard, Birch, and Rickels, 1976; Gottschalk and Uliana, 1977). The aspects of natural language and speech we examined were not simply manifest and conscious assertions that one is fearful or angry, but more subtle evidence of the arousal of affects of which the speaker is unaware—that is, preconscious affects, as exemplified by the verbal use of the defense mechanisms of displacement, substitution, projection, denial, and symbolization. These preconscious manifestations of affects, as well as conscious evidences, are what the psychoanalyst listens to and uses in the inferential process of estimating the varying magnitude of the analysand's affects. We demonstrated (Gottschalk and Gleser, 1969; Gottschalk et al., 1976), in numerous construct validation studies using various independent criterion measures (clinical ratings, self-report measures, physiological and biochemical correlates, effects of psychopharmacological agents), that these aspects of speech, as signalized in the content of speech, are significantly related to affect arousal and expression.

Effects of Psychoactive Drugs on Regulation of Neurotransmitters Involved in Cerebral Synaptic Transmission

My colleagues and I examined the effect of various psychoactive pharmacological agents on the content (semantics) and form (syntax) of natural language. One of the major purposes of these investigations was to probe the neurobiological and neurochemical bases of thought and feeling by observing the effects on the mind of these powerful psychoactive drugs.

In this connection, there is evidence that psychoactive drugs exert their effect on the mental processes (affects and cognitions) studied by psychoanalysts through regulating neurotransmitters involved in synaptic transmission in the brain. For example, there is evidence that the benzodiazepenes may exert their tranquilizing and hypnotic effects on mental processes by increasing gamma amino butyric acid (GABA) at nerve synpases (Guidotti, 1977). The phenothiazines block transmission at dopamine synapses located in portions of the limbic forebrain and cortex, and this effect may contribute to their antipsychotic effect (Matthysse, 1964, 1973; Snyder, Taylor, Coyle, and Meyerhoff, 1970; Snyder, Banerjee, Yamamura, and Greenberg, 1974). The tricyclic amines, such as imipramine, block the neuronal uptake of amines into the presynaptic nerve ending (Sigg, Soffer, and Gyermek, 1963; Glowinski and Axelrod, 1966; Baldessarini, 1977). Since uptake is crucial for inactivation of direct sympathomimetic amines, such as norepinephrine, this is sufficient to increase the functional activity of the catecholamines that are synthesized and available to synapses. The monoamine oxidase (MAO) inhibitors block inactivation of direct and indirect pressor amines by the catabolic enzyme, monoamine oxidase, and so potentiate the action of these amines (Sjoqvist, 1965; Stockley, 1973). Amphetamine and related psychomotor stimulants cause the release of dopamine and norepinephrine at synpases in the central nervous system, and this may account for the psychological effects of these drugs (Fuxe and Ungerstedt, 1970).

Some Specific Neuropsychopharmacological Effects of Psychoactive Drugs on Speech Content and Form

In specific studies demonstrating neuropsychopharmacological effects of psychoactive drugs on speech content and form, the minor tranquilizers, chlordiazepoxide (Gleser, Gottschalk, Fox, and Lippert, 1965; Gottschalk and Kaplan, 1972; Gottschalk, Noble, Stolzoff, Bates, Cable, Uliana, Birch, and Fleming, 1973), lorazepam (Gottschalk, Elliott, Bates, and Cable, 1972; Gottschalk, 1977), and the synthetic narcotic, meperidine (Elliott, Gottschalk, and Uliana, 1974), have been shown to significantly reduce anxiety, conscious and preconscious, in speech. The major tranquilizers perphenazine (Gottschalk, Gleser, Springer, Kaplan, Shanan, and Ross, 1960) and thioridazine (Gottschalk, Gleser, Cleghorn, Stone, and Winget, 1970; Gottschalk, Biener, Noble, Birch, Wilbert, and Heiser, 1975) decrease hostility significantly in the speech of schizophrenic patients. And the antidepressant imipramine (Gottschalk, Gleser, Wylie, and Kaplan, 1975) increases hostility and anxiety in nondepressed medical patients.

Some Specific Biological Effects of the Arousal of Affects

My colleagues and I have also done psychophysiological and psychobiochemical studies—not involving pharmacological agents—to determine whether the arousal of various thoughts and feelings can influence neurotransmitter and neuroendocrine activity. It has been possible to demonstrate that, whereas psychoactive drug-induced neurotransmitter changes can significantly influence conscious and preconscious affects, such as anxiety and hostility, the arousal of these affects can, in turn, significantly modify the peripheral biochemical and autonomic concomitants of neurotransmitter function. More specifically, the arousal of anxiety was shown to increase heart rate (Gottschalk, Springer, and Gleser, 1961; Gottschalk, 1974b) and systolic blood pressure (Gottschalk, Gleser, D'Zmura, and Hanenson, 1964), to decrease skin temperature (Gottlieb, Gleser, and Gottschalk, 1967; Gottschalk and Gleser, 1969), and to increase circulating adrenergic substances as adjudged from significant elevations of plasma-free fatty acids in fasting subjects, whether awake (Gottschalk, Cleghorn, Gleser, and Iacono, 1965; Gottschalk, Stone, Gleser, and Iacono, 1969) or asleep and dreaming (Gottschalk, Stone, Gleser, and Iacono, 1966). Also, anxiety scores derived from speech samples were found to be significantly related to serum dopamine beta hydroxylase (Silbergeld, Manderscheid, O'Neil, Lamprecht, and Lorenz, 1975). The arousal of hostility directed outward, as assessed from the content analysis of speech, was observed to increase significantly systolic and diastolic blood pressure (Gottschalk et al., 1964) and plasma triglycerides (Gottschalk et al., 1965; Gottschalk and Gleser, 1969). The arousal of hostility inward was associated with significant positive correlations in average systolic and diastolic blood pressure (Gottschalk et al., 1964).

From such experimental studies there can be no doubt that external events or the evocation of memories of internalized life experiences are capable of significantly modifying biochemical and physiological reflections of peripheral and central nervous system neurochemical activation. On the other hand, the modulation of central nervous system neurotransmitter function via psychoactive drugs can change the magnitude of affects and other psychological states as measured from free-associative speech.

The Biological Substrate of Affects and Affective Disorders

Genetic and Constitutional Individual Differences in the Pathogenesis of Affective Disorders

It is important to realize that genetic factors do not operate in the absence of environmental factors or vice versa. Even after the establishment of a phenotypic characteristic, there is some play in the system for alteration and/or modification, since biological organisms are not fixed. Actually, environmental factors may determine which genes are enhanced or suppressed; in this way, the environment determines effective genotypes because, so far as we know, depressive reactions are not produced either by genetic defects or by life experiences alone. Many factors are considered to be responsible for the pathogenesis of the depressive syndrome. One approach, hence, to weighing the relative effects of genetic or constitutional factors and environmental factors is to hypothesize that the greater the biogenetic factor, the less severe the stimuli necessary from the environment to lead to the depressive syndrome, and the lesser the biogenetic factors, the stronger the environmental stimuli must be. In affective disorders, the biogenetic factor has not been precisely identified in genetic studies but only indirectly assumed by family pedigree studies, studies of monozygotic and dizygotic familial incidence, biochemical alterations, electrophysiological variations, studies of effects of early separation from parents, and so forth.

Several studies have suggested the existence of a significant hereditary and genetic basis for the development of depression. Bipolar affective disorders are those in which there are recurring phases of mania and depression, and unipolar disorders are those in which changes of mood recur in a consistently depressive or manic direction without any occurrence of episodes of opposite polarity. The peak of morbidity for manic-depressive (bipolar) disorder is found between the ages of 20 and 30, whereas the age of risk is between 15 and 60 years of age; after 50 years of age, the risk for morbidity declines. The unipolar depressions, on the other hand, have quite a different morbidity probability; the morbidity before the age of 20 is relatively low, and then it increases and peaks between the ages of 40 and 50.

For centuries it has been known that more women than men develop depressive disorders. In this respect, no single study of psychiatric hospital admissions finds an equal morbidity risk in the two sexes (Slater and Roth, 1969; Fenton, 1977). Differences in treatment-seeking behavior or differences in the ways women respond in a survey have been questioned as satisfactory explanations for higher rates of affective disorders in women (Weissman and Klerman, 1977). Does this suggest a genetic factor at work, or does this implicate the role model by which women are reared? Or does their economic and emotional dependency make them more susceptible to depressive and separation reactions from supporting people? The answer is not clear.

Studies of possible interrelationships between sex, age of onset, and degree of hereditary loading indicate that relatives of early-onset probands have a greater risk for depression than do the relatives of late-onset probands of both sexes. Moreover, a higher incidence of depressive disorders is found among relatives of probands than is found in the general population.

If genetic factors are involved in the affective disorders, then the incidence of these disorders in identical twin pairs should be higher than that in fraternal twin pairs. In the search for pure genetic effects, it has been customary to examine the tendency for both twins to develop a depression (concordance rate) in twins who have been reared apart in order to offset the effects of their common upbringing, for there is evidence that identical twins frequently are raised more uniformly than fraternal twins living within the same family. Price (1968) reviewed the available literature on monozygotic pairs reared apart and showed a concordance in 67 percent, which is similar to the overall concordance rate of 76 percent and significantly greater than the overall concordance rate of 19 percent for dizygotic pairs. No other studies have yet been reported comparing the distribution of affective disorders among the biological and adopted relatives of the index patient, though studies of this kind have been done for schizophrenia (Heston, 1966; Kety, Rosenthal, Wender, and Schulsinger, 1968). Separate studies have obtained concordance rates for monozygotic twins ranging from 50 percent to 100 percent, and for dizygotic twins from 0 to 38.5 percent. A consistently higher monozygotic than dizygotic concordance rate, derived from seven different studies, favors the hypothesis that genetic transmission is involved in the pathogenesis of affective disorders (Rosenthal, 1970; Slater and Cowie, 1971; Tsuang, 1975).

Genetic studies have suggested a possible dominant X-linked transmission for affective disorders (Winokur and Tanna, 1969; Mendlewicz, Fleiss, and Fieve, 1972; Fieve, Mendlewicz, and Fleiss, 1973). In this connection, it has been suggested that the X-linked dominant gene is located on the short arm of the X-chromosome. This is justified by relating familial prevalence of affective disorders to several X-chromosome gene markers, such as color blindness and the red blood cell antigen Xg^a. Criteria for a dominant X-linked transmission would include a 2:1 ratio of afflicted females to males; no father-son transmission; all afflicted sons having afflicted mothers; all daughters of afflicted fathers being afflicted; half the sons and half the daughters of afflicted mothers being afflicted; and a morbidity risk of 50 percent for parents, siblings, and children of probands. Empirical data from family studies, however, do not quite support an X-linked transmission mechanism: A sex ratio of 1.5:1.0 has been obtained for female to male manic probands; one male proband had an affected father; 63 percent of the male probands had affected mothers; the morbidity risk of fathers of female probands was only 23 percent. At our present state of knowledge, genetic studies are incompatible with a strictly X-linked transmission, as these studies indicate the presence of ill father–ill son pairs (Perris, 1973; Von-Greiff, McHugh, and Stokes, 1973; Green, Goetzl, Whybrow, and Jackson, 1973).

Several studies suggest transmission by a single autosomal dominant gene (Slater, 1938; Kallmann, 1950; Stenstedt, 1952; Angst, 1966). On the other hand, polygenes may be another possible mode of transmission (Perris, 1968; Slater and Tsuang, 1968). The present conclusion concerning hereditary factors in depressive disorders seems to be that affective disorders may be either one illness with many modes of transmission or many illnesses, with different modes of transmission corresponding to different kinds of affective disorders.

Although, traditionally, manic-depressive disorder has been considered a single illness, there is accumulating evidence that there are at least two kinds of affective disorders—bipolar and unipolar (Angst, 1966; Perris, 1966; Winokur and Clayton, 1967). Sets of twins have been studied in which at least one had depressive psychosis. Of 83 pairs, 70 percent were concordant; that is, both twins developed a depression. When these 70 percent were studied with regard to type of affective disorder, there was a predominance of concordant twins with a similar form of illness; of these, 81 percent proved concordant for the type of course of the depression. Such twin studies provide support for the hypothesis that bipolar and unipolar depressive psychoses are two genetically separate illnesses.

Although there is accumulating evidence from these twin and adoptee studies that there is a genetic factor in affective disorders, the data are not entirely conclusive. Possible environmental factors may exist, including in utero influences, birth trauma, and differences in early mothering. Also, since not all identical twins also have affective disorders, nongenetic events must also have some important influences. We are beginning to learn to what extent these events can be prenatal, postnatal, psychosocial, and physiological.

Cerebral Electrophysiological Data and Affective Disorders

The brain emits tiny electrical messages in response to sensory stimulations, and these are referred to as "evoked responses" or "evoked potentials." Computer technology provides a simple way of detecting evoked potentials by aggregating and averaging many evoked responses of an individual to a given sensory stimulus, so that an "average evoked response" (AER) can be mathematically derived and visualized. When the sensory stimulus increases, normal subjects tend to have greater amplitude of the AERs. Schizophrenics show decreases in the amplitude of the AERs as sensory stimuli become more intense and, hence, have been classified as *reducers* of the degree of sensory stimulation, or they have reduced AER slopes as compared to normals. (See Figures 1 and 2.)

Buchsbaum and Silverman (1968), Buchsbaum, Goodwin, Murphy, and Borge (1971), Buchsbaum, Landau, Murphy, and Goodwin (1973), Schechter and Buchsbaum (1973), and Buchsbaum (1977) have demonstrated that bipolar affective disorders are associated with augmented AER slopes as compared to normals, and these augmented slopes are seen regardless of the

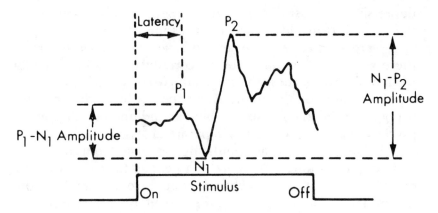

FIGURE 1. Features of the average evoked response (AER). P_1 is the first reliable peak and is often used to measure how long it takes the nervous system to respond to the stimulus—a time called the "latency." The amplitude, P_1 to N_1, is the voltage difference (in microvolts) between the crest at P_1 and the trough at N_1. The amplitude, N_1–P_2, is the following trough to crest.

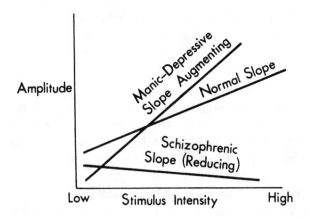

FIGURE 2. Manic-depressive, schizophrenic, and normal amplitude slopes.

manic or depressive phase in which the patient is tested. Studying manic-depression patients before, during, and after lithium therapy has revealed that patients with rather extreme AER augmenting slopes prior to lithium therapy are more likely to improve than those with more normal slopes. That is, individuals with the most abnormal AERs are more likely to improve the most. In addition, patients responding to lithium treatment show changes in AER amplitude slopes toward the normal direction with clinical improvement. That is, as these patients return to more normal behavior, their AERs also become more normal.

Male unipolar depressives can be distinguished from male bipolar affective disorders in that the former have reducing AER slopes and the latter have augmenting slopes. Female unipolar depressives present more of a problem since they, like females with bipolar affective disorders, have augmenting slopes. However, their low amplitude AERs usually distinguish female unipolar depressives from female manic-depressives, who have higher amplitude AERs.

Biogenic Amines and Affective Disorders

Considerable research has been directed toward the relationship between affects or moods and biogenic amine activity, which plays several vital roles in neural transmission and central nervous system functioning. The catecholamines (epinephrine, norepinephrine, and dopamine) and indole amines (serotonin and histamine) have been implicated as having a possible role in the genesis of depression for several reasons (Baldessarini, 1915): (1) Psychoactive drugs used in the treatment of depression increase the level of available amines in the brain; (2) psychoactive drugs known to increase the level of brain amines produce overactivity and alertness in experimental animals and humans; (3) psychoactive drugs (such as reserpine) known to deplete the brain amines produce sedation and inactivity in experimental animals; and (4) psychoactive drugs that deplete the brain amines cause depression in man.

The "catecholamine hypothesis" of affective disorders states that depression is associated with altered availability of one or another of these amines at functionally important receptor sites in the brain, and that mania, conversely, may be associated with an excess of amines.

Two classes of psychoactive drugs, the monoamine oxidase inhibitors and the tricyclics, have been used extensively in the clinical treatment of depressed patients. This area has been reviewed elsewhere in detail (Schildkraut, 1970; Goodwin and Bunney, 1973). While the monoamine oxidase inhibitors decrease the depletion of intracellular norepinephrine, the tricyclics are thought to reduce the reuptake of free norepinephrine from the synaptic clefts (Sigg, Soffer, and Gyermek, 1963; Glowinski and Axelrod, 1966). These antidepressant medications seem especially effective with the so-called "endogenous" depressions. Clinical studies of the excretion of catecholamine metabolites in affective disorders generally show a decrease in depressions and an increase in depressions with clinical improvement.

Although the bulk of research in biogenic amines has been directed toward norepinephrine, there is evidence to support the possibility of a disturbance of serotonin metabolism in some depressed patients (Mendels, 1975). Thus, the hypothesis that changes in catecholamine metabolism are responsible for states of depression or elation is recognized as oversimplified. A number of investigators are proposing that there are several kinds of depressive disorders. Maas (1975), for example, has proposed that one type of depressive disorder is associated with a reduction of norepinephrine without modification of dopamine metabolism and another type of depressive disorder in which the metabolic abnormality involves the serotonin system. There is less than average urinary excretion of tryptamine and lower than normal cerebrospinal levels of 5-hydroxyindoles in the latter kind of depression (Coppen, Eccleston, and Peet, 1974).

The above antidepressant psychoactive drugs cause change in serotonin metabolism as well as in norepinephrine. Also, it has been shown that tryptophan, which is converted by the body into serotonin, relieves depression in some people (Coppen, Shaw, and Farrell, 1963; Pare, 1963; Glassman and Platman, 1969). This suggests that an abnormality of serotonin metabolism may exist in depression. Also, in some depressives the normal breakdown products of serotonin are decreased. Hence, there may be either a reduced amount of serotonin in the body or a decrease in its utilization. Considerable evidence now indicates some deficiency in brain serotonin in people predisposed to manic-depressive illness. The antidepressant action of tryptophan, with or without the administration of a monoamine oxidase inhibitor, does suggest that this abnormality has some causal significance.

Endocrine Factors in Affective Disorders

Sachar (1975) has reviewed the possibility that neuroendocrine regulation might be involved in affective disorders. Such a hypothesis is strengthened by the finding that the neuroendocrine cells, which secrete the hypothalamic-releasing hormones, are themselves regulated by monoaminergic neural tracts. The monoamines involved include those which have been implicated in the chemical-pathological processes of affective disorders: norepinephrine, serotonin, and dopamine. If there is a disturbance in brain monoaminergic functions in affective disorders and it influences neuroendocrine pathways, it could be expected to be reflected in abnormalities of the endocrine system.

A substantial group of depressed patients hypersecrete cortical steroids. Several studies have suggested that this increased adrenocortical activity is more likely to occur in patients who are severely depressed, actively suicidal, very anxious, or psychotically disturbed. This elevation of the cortical steroids also occurs more frequently in unipolar depressive disorders. It is not clear, however, whether this hypersecretion of cortical steroids represents a nonspecific stress response in these patients or whether it is more directly involved in the severe depressive disorder. The increased adrenocortical function may reflect an abnormality in the hypothalamic control of pituitary functions and excess release of adrenocorticotropic hormone (ACTH). The biogenic amines are involved in the regulation of the secretion of the corticotropin-releasing factor (CRF), and it has been suggested that there is a failure in depressed patients to inhibit the mechanism which normally stops the release of CRF. Evidence suggests that noradrenergic neurons are involved in this mechanism. Thus, it may be that the increased adrenocortical activity found in some depressed patients is a reflection of a reduction of activity of noradrenergic neurons which normally inhibit ACTH release. This reduction would result in an increased ACTH secretion and subsequent increased adrenocortical activity. If this explanation were correct, it would support the hypothesis of a norepinephrine deficit in depression.

In adults, growth hormone is secreted in response to falling blood glucose, certain amino acids, and external stress, and during slow-wave sleep. Brain catecholamines with a variety of procedures may inhibit or stimulate growth-hormone responses. Neuroendocrine data are consistent with the concept of a functional depletion of brain norepinephrine in unipolar depressive disorders. A number of reports also indicate diminished growth-hormone responses to insulin-induced hypoglycemia in unipolar-depressed patients, whereas, in bipolar and neurotic depressions, the response to insulin-induced hypoglycemia is normal or enhanced.

Luteinizing hormone is also regulated through secretion of the catecholamines. After gonadectomy or menopause, the secretion of luteinizing hormone and its plasma concentration rises markedly because of the absence of feedback inhibition on brain receptors by circulating estrogens. This postgonadectomy rise in luteinizing hormone can be blocked by brain catecholamine depletors. Studies of unipolar-depressed women indicate that mean plasma luteinizing hormone concentration is significantly reduced in depressed women aged 57 to 60 as compared to normal postmenopausal women. This reduction supports the view of diminished hypothalamic catecholamine activity. It also correlates with the decreased sexual interest characteristic of women with depressive disorders. But these studies need further confirmation, since some studies have shown no change in luteinizing hormone levels.

In any event, these neuroendocrine findings support the viewpoint that there is a somatic component in the severe affective disorders. Whether these changes are induced by the psychosocial state of despair or elation occurring in the affective disorders, or whether these biochemical changes promote the abnormal affects and mood, has never been conclusively established.

Electrolytic Factors in Affective Disorders

Electrolytes have a central role in several critical aspects of neuronal function (Katz, 1966), including involvement in maintaining the normal resting potential of nerves; in carrying the current required for the action potential; in the synthesis, storage, release, and inactivation of neurotransmitters; and in carrying the current responsible for depolarizing postsynaptic membranes. Depression and mania are presumably associated with an alteration in neuronal function. It is therefore conceivable that an abnormality of electrolyte metabolism may be of importance in the development of these conditions.

Several important electrolytes are unevenly distributed within and without the neuron, with a higher concentration of sodium outside the nerve cell and a higher concentration of potassium ions inside. A disturbance in the distribution of intracellular sodium and potassium in depressed and manic patients has been demonstrated. Increased intracellular sodium may be present in patients with psychotic depression, followed by a corresponding decrease in the sodium after clinical recovery (Durrell, 1974). Findings of even greater magnitude have been reported for a group of manic patients. Evidence has suggested that these changes result from a redistribution of the electrolytes within the body and not from a change in the total body concentration of sodium and potassium. Behavioral changes would almost inevitably accompany any sizable shift in electrolyte metabolism, which would probably influence the brain by altering both neuronal excitability and the production, release, and reuptake of monoamines. The finding of a disturbance of sodium distribution in affective disorders has given rise to the hypothesis that there is an unstable hyperexcitability in the central nervous system in depression and, possibly, in mania. This implies that it would require a smaller stimulus than normal to activate neuronal firing. Changes in sodium (and potassium) distribution could arise in several ways. Sodium distribution is affected by such hormones as cortisol, progesterone, aldosterone, and antidiuretic hormone.

Calcium plays an important role in several aspects of neuronal function. It regulates sodium and potassium passage across the cell membrane. During depression, a relative deficiency of calcium may exist at the cell membrane, allowing sodium to pass into the cell in increased amounts, leading to the raised intracellular sodium. With recovery from some depressive reactions, urinary calcium decreases, calcium retention in the body increases, and decreased amounts of sodium pass into the cell. Intracellular sodium thus decreases and returns to normal levels from the previous abnormal high.

Lithium influences sodium pump activity. It may alter neuronal excitability by changing the contribution of electrogenic pump potentials to either the resting membrane potential or the membrane potential following a muscle contraction. Lithium administration has been associated with an increase of sodium concentration in erythrocytes. Patients who improve clinically have increased erythrocyte sodium, but this increase does not occur in patients who show no clinical improvement with lithium (Mendels and Frazer, 1975).

Whether the electrolyte anomalies of depressives have etiological significance is uncertain. These metabolic changes may be secondary to alterations in endocrine function, since steroid hormones significantly influence electrolytes.

Critique of Research on the Biological Substrates of Affects and the Affective Disorders

One issue that has been ignored in genetic studies of identical twins reared apart is the fact that early parental loss has been observed to produce adverse effects in adult life (Deutsch, 1937; Furman, 1964; Wolfenstein, 1969; Fleming, 1972, 1974, 1975), and these adverse effects on personality development cannot usually be corrected unless there is a rapid and congenial substitution for the lost parent. Also, in subhuman animals, prolonged separation of infant rhesus monkeys from their mothers produces depressive reactions (McKinney, Suomi, and Harlow, 1973), but in some species of macaque, such a depressive reaction does not occur when adequate substitute mothering is available (Scott, Stewart, and DeGhett, 1973). Such refined issues as precise age of separation of each twin from the family of origin, whether one or both twins were separated from the parental family, and the quality of the parental surrogates have not been addressed or dealt with in the research design of twin studies by investigators doing genetic studies of mental illness. Merely establishing that twins were reared apart does not prevent important environmental differences conducive to affective disorders from influencing the development of each twin in a biased rather than a random manner.

Williams, Katz, and Shield (1972) concluded, at a conference on the psychobiology of depression, that research in the biochemistry of depression is hampered by the lack of refinement in the measurement of mood and behavior. For example, testing the validity of the catecholamine hypothesis requires more refined analysis and measurement of specific mood and behavioral correlates, such as the "retarded" or "agitated" states of depression presumably closely reflective of central nervous system activity.

Advances in psychobiology and behavioral chemistry require better synchrony of measurement across biology and behavior (Katz and Hirschfeld, 1977). The field of descriptive psychopathology requires innovative expansion beyond the realm of symptoms and symptom-related behavior to include other pertinent aspects of psychological functioning, such as the assessment of the subjective quality of the affective disorders, the social behaviors of the depressed patient, and the physical or expressive manifestations of these states.

The biochemical changes observed in affective disorders may be secondary to emotional stress. Stress may be responsible for overactivity of adrenal cortical hormones, and these may in turn induce a variety of biochemical effects, especially the changes in electrolyte distribution known to be regulated by adrenocortical and pituitary hormones. Since there is internal or external stress involved in both depression and mania, those biological changes in the same direction under both conditions should be examined to determine whether they are induced by stress.

There is evidence for and against the monoamine hypothesis of affective disorders. Supporting the hypothesis, there is evidence of high amine activity in mania and low amine activity in depression, in that there is increased urinary excretion during mania of catecholamines, catecholamine metabolites, and cyclic AMP (the secondary messenger of the adrenergic system) and decreased excretion of these biochemical substances during depression. Also, the levels of 3-methoxy-4-hydroxy-phenylglycol (MHPG), a metabolite of norepinephrine, and homovanillic acid (HVA), a metabolite of dopamine, tend to be increased in the cerebrospinal fluid during mania and to be decreased with depression. Against the hypothesis, some biochemical changes observed in the manic phase are in the same direction as changes occurring during the depressed phase. Cerebrospinal fluid levels of tryptophan and 5-hydroxyindoleacetic acid (5-HIAA, a metabolite of serotonin) tend to be reduced in both phases, and a favorable response to tryptophan administration has been described in both mania and depression. Changes in opposite directions with mania and depression relate to the catecholamines and changes in the same direction to the indoleamines. The suggestion has been made that the direction of mood swings is controlled by the rate of activity of the adrenergic system, whereas the stability of mood is associated with the rate of activity of the serotonergic system (Kety, 1971).

Psychosocial Factors Influencing Affects and Affective Disorders

Interaction of Psychosocial Events and the Biological Substrates Toward Causing Depressive Reactions and Mania

Most psychoanalytic theorists follow the approaches of modern science with respect to the relation of genetic, constitutional, and other biomedical factors and their interplay with environmental factors toward causing pathological depressive reactions and mania. Biomedical factors are considered to play a significant role in the etiology of affective disorders. For genetic or constitutional reasons, some families and the individuals springing from them are considered to be more susceptible to the neurophysiological changes associated with depression or mania in reaction to life circumstances than are other families.

However, though every individual during a lifetime may have brief depressive episodes, just as every individual may experience episodes of anxiety or fear, only certain individuals are considered predisposed to prolonged and somatically involved depressive or manic episodes. The psychosocial experiences that are capable of bringing out the phenotype of affective disorders are partially specific. There are environmental factors associated with child development and parent–child relationships that bring out the worst in one, so to speak, and there are later events during a lifetime which trigger recurring episodes.

An analogy with the process being described here is the hypersensitivity some individuals develop to external allergens. There are genetic and constitutional predispositions to allergic disorders. Some predisposed individuals, never exposed to the pathogenic allergen, may never develop an allergic disorder. Other individuals, so predisposed, may be exposed to the allergen early and be hypersensitive to reexposure episodically through adulthood. Desensitization (various forms of treatment—pharmacological, immunological, and otherwise) may be partially successful in interrupting the pathogenic process.

Initial Psychoanalytic Clinical Formulations on the Psychopathogenesis of Depression and Mania

Psychoanalysts deserve credit for calling the attention of the medical profession and other caretakers of the mentally ill to the psychosocial factors contributing to affective disorders. Freud (1917), Abraham (1911, 1916, 1924), Rado (1928), and Klein (1935, 1940) made pioneering formulations on the psychology of depression. These early psychoanalytic formulations of depression, by their originality and daring, have had tremendous heuristic value in the psychological area of investigation.

The psychodynamic explanations of the depressive states espoused by these psychoanalysts located the central psychopathological process in a pathological sense of guilt. This guilt was derived from a distorted development of the unconscious conscience or superego through internalization of critical and punishing parental attitudes. Fearful of expressing rage or murderous impulses toward loved objects, the depressed individual turned the hostility inward in order to do penance for his guilty anger. This psychodynamic formulation of the underlying basis of affective disorders, like early formulations of the biological substrate, is clearly too simplified, and it does not take into consideration the variety of psychogenetic, psychoeconomic, and psychodynamic mechanisms operative in pathological affective reactions.

What is needed today is a more complex series of statements of such theory and derived hypotheses which better describe and explain the varied clinical psychopathological phenomena associated with the full range of affective disorders.

Contemporary Psychoanalytic Formulations on the Psychopathogenesis of Affective Disorders

The effects of life experiences in predisposing to or triggering affective disorders. Today, just as there have been big strides made in the biomedical understanding of affective disorders over the last fifty years, so there have been various major steps taken in our understanding of how sociocultural influences, family experiences, child rearing practices, child development, and other life experiences predispose and fix the recurrence of affective disorders or increase the susceptibility to these conditions.

Many pathological depressive reactions, particularly those falling into the manic-depressive or endogenous classifications, recur during the course of an individual's life. People subject to such depressions can be regarded as "depression-prone." The fundamental psychologically oriented etiological theory is that the depression-prone individual learns to become depressed early in life. Or, put another way, psychological conditions encountered early in such an individual's life increase the probability that depressive reactions will occur sooner or later, and usually repeatedly.

Following is a composite psychodynamic formulation of the predisposing psychopathogenesis to affective disorders.

1. The depression-prone individual is one who early in life becomes hypersensitive to the threat of interpersonal alienation or decreased emotional support or love from others. He develops an insatiable or inordinate need to be loved and wanted. The conditions which shape this personality makeup are not all

known, but they include either (1) early parental separation, rejection, and loss or (2) a period of early parental overindulgence and a pubertal experience associated with a sense of separation or rejection in that the rest of the human environment, outside the family of origin, does not seem to recognize that the individual is special or extradeserving. The childhood experiences which mold a person to be prone to depression rather than schizophrenia or various psychosomatic conditions are thought by some investigators to be specific and capable of being differentiated. For example, whereas in both affective and schizophrenic disorders there is a hypersensitivity in the individual to a decrease in the quality of human relations, there is a greater tendency in people subject to depressive disorders to blame oneself, and in people prone to the schizophrenic disorders to blame the external environment, human and nonhuman. In this diagnostic formulation, there are, of course, combinations of these tendencies, which are labeled schizoaffective disorders. Other investigators believe that those childhood experiences which predispose to one type of disorder or another are nonspecific and that genetic and constitutional factors have priority in determining which disorder occurs.

2. The above individual, who is inordinately fearful of not being cared for or loved, episodically becomes frustrated that these needs are not met, becomes frustrated and angry as a result, tends to be fearful of alienating others if anger is manifested, and therefore inhibits the outward expression of this hostility. In a state of impasse, under these circumstances, some individuals become adversely critical and angry with themselves, blaming themselves for not being lovable.

3. With each recurring frustration in the interpersonal relations of the depression-prone individual and with the realization of the unlikelihood of obtaining reparations for the separations, rejections, or personal losses suffered, or of recapturing an early childhood paradise that once existed, this depression-prone individual experiences feelings of hopelessness, helplessness, and increasing despair. This chain of events accounts for the psychodynamics of some of the people who develop pathological depressive reactions. But it does not cover the psychodynamic concatenation of all depressive reactions.

*Infrahuman Animal Separation Studies and Their Relevance to
Vulnerability to Affective Disorders*

Many psychoanalysts have tended to ignore separation studies among infrahuman animals as relevant to their investigation, understanding, and treatment of human affective disorders. Inattention to such studies may deprive the therapist of important facts regarding the causal factors and chains of events between psychosocial and neurobiological phenomena that can be demonstrated through these animal studies. Ethical limitations preclude doing these crucial investigations with human beings. Doing these studies fills many gaps in our knowledge of psychosocial and neurobiological interactions leading to affective disorders.

There is considerable evidence that separation from a mother figure, a social group, or familiar surroundings can be followed by strong, unpleasant, and persistent depressive reactions.

Maternal separation studies with dogs. Studies with dogs (Scott, Stewart, and DeGhett, 1973) reveal that two kinds of emotional reactions, depending on the circumstances, may be involved in separation: distress at the absence of familiar objects and fears of strange objects. These emotions are compatible with each other, and the effects are additive.

In these dog studies, the risk of depression has been demonstrated to be modified by genetic differences in susceptibility. There are, indeed, large differences in various breeds as regards reactions to extreme separation techniques (Fuller and Clark, 1966a,b). Also, in subhuman animals, other kinds of symptoms and manifestations can follow separation besides the signs of depression (Fuller and Clark, 1966a,b). However, although variations in the strength and expression of the emotional responses of dogs occur in separation, no exceptions to the response of depression to separation occurred among several hundred young puppies of various breeds that were tested (Scott, Stewart, and DeGhett, 1973).

Maternal separation studies in primates. Research on maternal separation in primates began in the 1960s. Jensen and Tolman (1962) reported the effects of separating pigtail macaque infants from their mothers at the ages of 5 and 7 months for short periods and then reuniting them with their own or another mother. Seay, Hansen, and Harlow (1962) reported the effects of separating rhesus macaque infants from their mothers for longer times. In both of these studies, the separations were highly traumatic for the infants. The behaviors were divided into two categories and labeled "protest" and "despair." Comparisons were made between these infants and the human infants described by Spitz (1945), Bowlby (1960), and Robertson and Robertson (1971).

About the same time Kaufman and Rosenblum (1967) studied the separation reactions of bonnet and pigtail macaque monkeys. Whereas, in the previous studies, the infants had been removed from the mother, Kaufman and Rosenblum removed the mothers from a pen, leaving the infant behind in the social group. They also reported a clear "agitation" phase marked behaviorally by vocalizations of distress, high levels of locomotion, and increased self-orality. The "depressed" stage consisted of decreases in activity, increases in huddling and nonlocomotive behaviors, and a general state of social withdrawal.

The above reaction was typical for pigtail macaque infants, but not for bonnet infants. Bonnet infants did not show the despair stage as did the pigtail infants. This was interpreted as being due to differences in their species-specific social and bonding behavior. Whereas pigtail infants form strong dyadic bonds, bonnets have more substitute caretaking and group mothering. When a bonnet's mother was removed, the infant would form an attachment with other adult females. That was not a natural behavior for the pigtail infants, and they exhibited a much more severe reaction to separation. More recent work has shown that depressive behavior can be induced even in bonnet infants if there is cross rearing and substitute caretaking is not available.

Hinde and Spencer-Booth (1970) were among the first to comment on the high degree of individual variability in the behavior of primate infants, and this issue has proven to be one of the most meaningful in primate studies. Short-term maternal separation, early in development, was found to have long-term

effects some two to three years later, even without any intervening separations. Other research has found that early maternal
separation predipose to a more severe behavioral reaction to
later peer separation.

Neurobiological effects of maternal separation. In addition to
significant behavioral effects, maternal separation occasions
major neurobiological changes. Reite and his associates (Reite,
Stynes, Vaughn, Pauley, and Short, 1976; Reite, Short, Kaufman, Stynes, and Pauley, 1978) have done a series of studies of
pigtail macaque infants undergoing maternal separation. Using
totally implanted multichannel biotelemetry systems, they studied heart rate, body temperature, and sleep physiology of the
infants before, during, and after separation from their mothers. Beginning with the first night of separation both heart rate
and body temperature decreased from baseline levels and the
behavioral patterns became more depressive-like. During reunion, both heart rate and body temperature returned to normal, although some infants had lower heart rate well into the
reunion. The investigators also reported an increased incidence
of cardiac arrythmia and significant sleep changes, including
increased sleep latency, more frequent arousal, less total sleep,
and a disruption of REM sleep.

Rhesus monkey infants in the protest stage following maternal separation have been found to have elevated levels of
serotonin in the hypothalamus and elevated levels of all of the
catecholamine synthesizing enzymes in the adrenal gland
(Breese, Smith, Mueller, Howard, Prange, and Lipton, 1973).
Changes in the levels of serotonin and related neurotransmitters have been found in the hypothalamus of depressed and
suicidal humans (Korpi, Kleinman, Goodman, Phillips, DeLisi,
Linnoila, and Wyatt, 1986).

Levine, Coe, and Smotherman (1978) studied the pituitary-
adrenal response in squirrel monkeys following maternal separation. They found significant elevations in plasma cortisol levels in both mothers and infants following separation, with the
response not being reduced by the presence of familiar animals.
Their data suggest that there is not necessarily always a concordance between the degree of behavioral disturbance shown by
the infant and this index of physiological arousal. That is, the

presence of substitute mothering does not diminish the physiological arousal following acute separation, even though it may modulate the behavioral disturbance. Reestablishment of the original attachment relationship appears to be necessary to reduce the infant's physiological arousal.

Peer–peer separation. The approach to separation studies that was developed by Bowden and McKinney (1972) and by Suomi, Harlow, and Domek (1970) is the peer separation paradigm. The behavioral reaction to peer separation is quite similar to that of maternal separation in terms of the classic protest–despair response. Further, when peer groups are formed and repetitive separations done, the response is obtained with each separation. Not surprisingly, a number of variables can influence the nature of the response, including age, rearing conditions, housing conditions before, during, and after each separation, prior neurobiological status, and treatment with pharmacological agents.

A number of variables can influence the response to peer separation; these have been reviewed by Mineka and Suomi (1978). Developmental variables are important. Two separate studies have found that monkeys reared entirely by peers respond to peer separations more severely than do monkeys reared with their mothers for the first several months of life and then put into peer groups (Suomi, 1976; Kraemer and McKinney, 1979). Some individual variability can be related to neurobiological variables. For example, cerebrospinal fluid norepinephrine appears to be a trait-related marker predicting a more severe response to separations. Animals with lower cerebrospinal fluid norepinephrine respond to separation with more huddling and self-directed behaviors than do animals with higher levels. By contrast, cerebrospinal fluid homovanillic acid and cerebrospinal fluid 5-hydroxyindoleacetic acid are state-related markers that reflect the behavioral response to peer separation (Kraemer, Ebert, Lake, and McKinney, 1984).

Pharmacological agents can also affect the response to peer separation. Imipramine will reverse the reaction to peer separation and prevent reactions to future separations as long as the monkeys are kept on it (Suomi, Seaman, Lewis, and McKinney, 1978). They return to more typical separation behavior when it is withdrawn. Amphetamine modifies the behavioral response to separation in a very similar manner to imipramine, but the overall effects of the two drugs on group social behavior can be distinguished. The dose level of amphetamine that is effective in altering the separation response is also very disruptive to ongoing social behavior in the group situation. This is not true for imipramine. α-Methyl-*para*-tyrosine, which lowers norepinephrine and dopamine, makes the separation response much more severe and does so at doses that have no effect in the group housing situation or in chronically, singly caged animals that are not undergoing the stress of separations. *para*-Chlorophenylalanine, which blocks serotonin synthesis, has no effect (Kraemer and McKinney, 1979). Low doses of alcohol alleviate the peer separation response, whereas high doses make it worse (Kraemer, Lin, Moran, and McKinney, 1980).

According to McKinney (1986),

> depression in humans, however induced, may be associated with some neurobiological changes that are possibly derivative phenomena rather than etiological factors. Nevertheless, preexisting neurobiological changes, whether state or trait related, may have a major impact on the response to drug treatment as well as to social stressors. There needs to be an increased use of research strategies that will permit the study of the combined effects of social stressors and neurobiological functioning [p. 287].

Maternal Separation Studies with Humans

Considerable theoretical and clinical interest among psychoanalytically oriented observers has centered on the adverse effects seen in young children who are separated for various periods of time from the mother (Deutsch, 1919; Bakwin, 1942; Freud and Burlingham, 1944; Spitz, 1945; Spitz and Wolf, 1946; Robertson and Bowlby, 1952; Schaffer and Callender, 1959; Heinicke and Westheimer, 1965). The risk of a depressive reaction in human adults is influenced by previous childhood experiences with separation. According to Heinicke (1973), the risk of depression in later years is increased by the loss of parents in the first fifteen years of life.

The initial response in humans to separation from close kin is usually increased agitation and distress, and this response is thought to be the biological substrate for anxiety. The reaction to prolonged separation is depression and withdrawal, and this reaction has been considered to be the biological substrate of depression (Engel, 1962a,b). These reactions are thought to be protective and adaptive. For example, the response of depression to prolonged separation may be protective and adaptive (Engel, 1962a,b; Kaufman, 1973; Schmale, 1973) in that it prevents the exhaustion that could occur with persistence of distress and agitation, the initial reaction to loss.

Varieties of Depressive Reactions from the Psychodynamic Point of View

Shame depressions. A number of psychological or social factors can precipitate depressive reactions, not only in those who are depression-prone but in all individuals. Depression-prone individuals, however, are more likely to have prolonged depressive or manic reactions to diminishing physical prowess, failing health, or fading beauty, and to repeated failures to reach goals or compete successfully. Such depressions are not the classical "guilt" depressions described by the early psychoanalysts. Rather, these depressions have been called "shame depressions." Shame is an affective response characterized by feelings of inadequacy and inferiority (Piers and Singer, 1953; Lewis, 1971). The lowered self-esteem associated with shame stems from the perception of a reduced amount of recognition from others of achievements in the physical, intellectual, social, or economic spheres of functioning in comparison or competition with others. Guilt is the affective response of self-recrimination, self-criticism, and sense of social condemnation because of unacceptable, principally hostile, impulses. The decreased self-esteem associated with guilt derives from an excessive self-condemnation for having these socially unacceptable impulses or ideas. The decreased performance in the guilty person is based in part on urges to atone and a reluctance to arouse further pangs of conscience. Shame depressions occur frequently in the depressive reactions of older age, and in these instances the depression is based largely on the recognition of dwindling physical resources and mental agility (Busse, Barnes, Silverman, Shy, Thaler, and Frost, 1954; Titchener, Zwerling,

Gottschalk, and Levine, 1958). Guilt depressions tend to follow the real or threatened loss of love objects; hostile and frustrated dependent impulses toward the missing love object are involved.

Schizoid depressions. The life history of another subgroup of depressed patients reveals a premorbid personality that has been typified by a reluctance and avoidance of a continuing, close, intimate, self-revealing relationship with others because of childhood disappointments in the quality and reliability of love available from others. Some of these individuals might fall into a classification of schizoid or paranoid character types or schizoaffective disorders. But a sizable number defy classification into these categories. These individuals prefer superficial interpersonal relationships and have never been psychologically minded; hence, they have been uninterested in the feelings and motives of themselves or others. This subgroup of depressed patients, who have characteristically avoided close and continuing relationships with others, are not likely to be responsive to intensive or even regularly scheduled contact with a psychotherapist (MacLeod and Middelman, 1962). They may respond reasonably well to some antidepressant pharmacotherapy and relatively brief contacts with psychotherapists. This kind of patient is not usually a candidate for psychoanalytic psychotherapy and is not seen by psychoanalysts in their offices, but more likely in public clinics. This chronic depressed individual provides another subtype of person with childhood experiences in which a sense of basic trust in parents and other kin was not experienced and, hence, is not expected from any helping surrogates.

Separation depressions. In adult human beings, prolonged separations from close relatives may precipitate a depression in an individual; according to Paykel (1973) the risk in our society is approximately 10 percent. An association has been established, through well-controlled prospective and retrospective studies, between bereavement and an increased risk of symptoms of morbidity, including depression and mortality. This increased morbidity and mortality appear within a relatively short period following bereavement (MacMahon and Pugh, 1965; Rees and Lutkins, 1967; Stein and Susser, 1969; Parkes and Brown, 1972; Clayton, 1975). The mechanism accounting for a depressive reaction under such circumstances seems to be the stress of separation and loss and the weakening of one's social support system. Brown (1974) conceptualized and developed techniques for measuring life events so that there is little doubt of the causal link between the life event and the onset of illness. The method involves predefining potentially stressful life events, both short- and long-term, obtaining detailed information about the circumstances surrounding the event from the respondent and rating the relative severity of the stress experienced by the respondent from an interview. Using this approach, Brown, Harris, and Peto (1973), in a study involving 115 depressed women and 152 women picked at random from the community, demonstrated that a long-term, markedly distressing event occurred three and a half times more frequently in the group of depressed women (42 percent as compared to 12 percent) prior to the onset of depression.

Stress depressions. Using a Social Readjustment Rating Scale, which consists of 43 life-event items that require change in individual adjustment, Holmes and Masuda (1973) demonstrated that the magnitude of life change is highly significantly related to time of disease onset. Holmes and his collaborators found a strong positive correlation between the magnitude of life crisis and the seriousness of the chronic illness experience. The studies of Holmes and his colleagues demonstrate a wide range of psychiatric, medical, and surgical diseases (including affective disorders) in reaction to these varied life crises.

The Psychodynamic Relationship of Depression and Mania

Mania is psychologically related to depression, according to psychodynamic theory (Cameron, 1942; Lewin, 1950). Mania and hypomania are syndromes in which the underlying psychodynamic is the denial—conscious or unconscious—of the frustration of an expectation or demand which is usually unrealistic in its proportions. The patient attempts to assuage the blow to his self-importance occasioned by such a frustration through self-distraction, keeping busy, trying to avoid paying attention to a deep, oppressive sense of loss, disappointment, hurt pride, and helpless rage. The manic patient is actually overdependent, although he may act confident and occupy the role of a leader. He is self-centered and controlling, and these attitudes are based on needs to be cared for by others. He repeatedly tests others, manipulates them, and involves them in caring for him. He challenges external constraints under the guise of aggressive pseudoindependence (Janowsky, Leff, and Epstein, 1970). There is empirical evidence that pointing out to the manic patient his denial of his loss tends to precipitate a depressive reaction.

Family Communicational Interactions and Psychoses: A Mechanism for the Transmission of Personality Disorders

Parental verbal communication in the pathogenesis of the schizophrenic syndrome. A growing body of research is guided by the hypothesis that when speech characteristics, such as irrelevance, ambiguity, and lack of closure, typify the transactions of parents with their offspring, the likelihood of schizophrenia developing in the children is greatly increased. These communication difficulties are believed taught to the children so that an inadequate sense of reality testing and difficulty in achieving clear or logical thinking are likely to surface when the offspring has to deal with stress. Wynne, Singer, Bartko, and Tookey (1977) have been studying the pathogenesis of the schizophrenic syndrome for many years by examining the characteristics of verbal communication of family members of schizophrenics. They demonstrate that communications and language are significant intermediate variables between predisposing factors in schizophrenia and subsequent schizophrenic manifestations in index offspring. They found that the frequency of communication deviances as scored in individual Rorschach records of parents and their offspring is significantly greater in families with an adolescent or young adult schizophrenic offspring and that this relationship varies directly with severity of disorder in the offspring. Further, although the index offspring, as primary patients, are clinically more disturbed than their parents, they found that the parents have more frequent communication deviances than the patients themselves. Both the index offspring and their siblings have communication deviance scores which are directly related to the severity of clinical disorder in the index offspring. These findings support the view that transactional processes are important as intermediate variables in the development of schizophrenic disorders. This hypothesis may well apply to the pathogenesis of the affective disorders.

Parental communication in the pathogenesis of disordered cognitive processes in affective disorders. Whereas thought disorder in the form of fragmentary and dissonant communication typifies the communication process of schizophrenic patients, a different type of thought disorder typifies affective disorders. No one has systematically pursued research into the extent to which parental verbal communication in families with affective disorders downgrades the self-appraisal of offspring, thus predisposing to affective disorders. Thought disorders manifested by depressed patients are generally considered to be a consequence of basic disturbances in affects or mood.

A cognitive theory of the psychodynamics of depressive disorders is that a primary disturbance in thinking causes the development of the disturbed mood state. Moreover, the affective response is determined by the way an individual structures his experience, and this structuring of experience is a learned phenomenon. Thus, if a person conceives of a situation as unpleasant, he will experience a corresponding affective response. According to this hypothesis, people who develop depression have a cognitive schema concerned with self-depreciation, unwarranted pessimism, and fear of rejection. The thinking remains fixed, and the development of the pattern usually parallels the course of the illness. Such a schema serves as a mediating cognitive structure between the phenomenological world external to the individual and the personality responses.

Primary characteristics of thinking in depressed patients include low self-esteem, ideas of deprivation, self-criticism, self-blame, extremely high standards with respect to duty and responsibilities, and stringent self-commands and injunctions. Underlying all these are a distortion of reality and a systematic bias by the patient against himself. These thought processes of depressive reactions have been classified as follows:

1. *Arbitrary inference*—drawing a conclusion (usually of a personally degrading nature) from a situation that is essentially neutral or impersonal. This is usually done in the absence of evidence to support the conclusion or when the evidence is contrary to the conclusion.
2. *Selective abstraction*—focusing on a detail taken out of context and exaggerated, ignoring other more salient features of the situation, and conceptualizing the whole experience on the basis of this element.
3. *Overgeneralization*—drawing a general conclusion on the basis of a single incident or experience for magnification and minimization—errors in evaluation that are so gross as to constitute distortion.
4. *Personalization*—an inclination to relate external events to oneself when there is no basis for making such a connection.

On the basis of these and other observations, Beck (1972) and others (Ferster, 1974; Lewinsohn, 1974; Seligman, 1974) suggest that depressions may be appropriately considered as a primary disorder of thought, with a resultant disturbance in affect and behavior in harmony with the cognitive distortion, rather than a primary affective disturbance.

Cognitive theory relates depression to goal attainment. According to this theory, depression results when important goals are strongly devalued. The greater the importance of the goal, and the lesser its probability of attainment, the higher is the level of the anxiety. Decreasing the importance of the goal alleviates the anxiety. But since the motivation to act derives largely from the perceived probability of attaining important goals, diminishing the importance of goals lessens motivation. Thus, the reaction to lowered goals is depression, apathy, and withdrawal. In this system agitated depression may be associated with despair of attaining goals originally adhered to. Hope of goal attainment is based on the availability of appropriate actions, patterns, sufficient time, adequate environmental supports, interpersonal and physical. Hopelessness results, then, from the absence of some of these important ingredients of hope. Motivation to respond is largely dependent on an incentive to respond in order to achieve rewards; without it, the patient loses motivation to seek relief.

With this cognitive model to account for depressive disorders, there is a chicken-or-egg problem in deciding whether a disordered affect or a disordered thought comes first. This is probably a false issue, for no learning is likely to result devoid of an affective component. But this so-called "cognitive" approach to formulating the psychopathogenesis of depressions provides a good guideline for psychodynamically oriented family research on the matter.

The diverse findings described above support the hypothesis that adult affective disorders may result from an individual's vulnerability to minimal contemporary stress stemming from separation or other adverse experiences in childhood. In such individuals, as a result of childhood influences, there are an increased vulnerability and predisposition to adult affective reactions precipitated in adulthood by relatively minor life changes rather than by obvious major losses or severe external stress. The former type of affective disorder is likely to be labeled "endogenous," because an external observer, not well informed of the detailed life history of the patient, will not recognize the personal meaning and significance of certain everyday life events for the patient—namely, that these events remind him of loss of love or status or the threat of such. And unfortunately, the patient may not himself understand the psychological triggering mechanisms involved in his "endogenous" affective disorder.

Critique of Research in Psychosocial Factors in Affective Disorders

Problems in adequate testing of psychodynamic hypotheses in affective disorders. A number of problems interfere with adequate testing of psychodynamic and psychosocial considerations in the affective disorders.

1. Psychodynamic concepts are not always directly observable but rather must be inferred entities (for example, "ego strength"), and they may refer either to a dispositional trait (for example, "anxiety-prone") or a current state (for example, "free anxiety"). Untrained observers and researchers using psychodynamic concepts in evaluative research may overlook the necessity for explicit definitions or operational descriptions of what is to be observed, and they may assume that jargon terms

describe an identical universe of characteristics regardless of locale or person (Gottschalk et al., 1976). Hence, interobserver reliability is likely to be poor, even more so when quantitative ratings are requested.

To complicate matters, psychodynamic hypotheses may involve propositions in which chains of psychological variables (which in themselves may be complex) are interrelated. Definitions, conditions, rating scales which pin down the variables in recognizable and descriptive terms are, here again, helpful if not necessary. One cannot go beyond the level of exploratory research, where one may be trying primarily to generate hypotheses or make first approximations, unless the psychodynamic concepts are measured with more rigor and precision. There is evidence (Bellak and Smith, 1956; Gottschalk, Gleser, and Springer, 1963; Knapp, Mushatt, and Nemetz, 1966; Strupp, Chassan, and Ewing, 1966; Gottschalk, 1974a) that complex psychodynamic variables can be used reliably in evaluative research.

2. There is a paucity of psychological measurement instruments capable of providing direct evaluation of many of the relevant psychosocial variables (see, for example, Gottschalk, 1966; Fenton, 1977). To give a few examples, there are not very many standard psychological tests which provide a reliable and valid quantitative estimate of: preconscious separation anxiety, shame versus guilt, preconscious anxiety over being submissive to or dependent on others, inwardly directed hostility or suppressed resentment due to frustrated wishes for support, dependency, and love, and "depression-proneness." Psychological test constructors have not been enthusiastic about developing such measures.

3. The lack of ready-made psychological measuring instruments or tests tailored to assess all potentially relevant psychological factors in psychoanalytically oriented research usually requires that these evaluations be done by the clinical observer. The clinical observer has more breadth, scope, and general perceptiveness than any single measuring device which would help the observer scale or classify items of observations systematically. But the clinical observer's bias and capacity to distort observations in many directions are notorious. Too

many psychodynamic observations are made without arranging to record the data so that other observers can check the observations.

Competing theories of the psychopathogenesis of affective disorders. Two new theories of the psychopathogenesis of depression challenge the primacy of "affect" or "emotions" in this condition and focus on other facets of depression.

Behavior theory focuses on the absence of certain behaviors or events in the lives of depressed people (Ferster, 1974; Lewinsohn, 1974; Seligman, 1974). Depression is seen as a state brought about by the chronic absence of social reinforcement, resulting in a deficit of certain social skills. There results a learned pattern of coping in which there is little or no expectation of reward. Though this viewpoint borrows considerably from psychoanalytic and psychodynamic observations of the origins of affective disorders, it emphasizes the individual's behavior and interactions with other people and the identification of appropriate behavioral reinforcers, both negative and positive.

Cognitive theory, formulated by Beck (1972, 1974), directs attention to a negative cognitive set as the central force in depression, one which precedes the characteristic affect and behavior. Negative ideas and attitudes, about the world and the value of the self, control and shape the perceptual and affective life of the depressed individual. Beck's approach to affective disorders is clearly influenced by psychodynamic and psychoanalytic perspectives, but his emphasis on the patient's negative ego ideal and self-appraisal strongly suggests a therapeutic approach to influencing the disordered affect.

Conclusions

Upon reviewing the compelling biomedical characteristics associated with affective disorders, a reader might initially wonder how psychosocial factors could play a role in these affective disorders. However, the cause-effect relationship of biomedical to psychosocial manifestations has also not been clearly pinpointed. Such an issue, though ambiguous, leads the clinician and even the scientist to favor the simplest explanation and rationale proposed as underlying any phenomenon. This principle of parsimony has tended to prevail with respect to the understanding of biomedical and psychosocial factors in the causation of affective disorders. The simplest theory has been favored and has been that one or the other category of factors is solely responsible for a disorder. The opposite point of view says that some combination of these kinds of factors is involved—that is, that some kind of interaction between neurobiological and psychosocial factors accounts for the phenomena associated with the affective disorders. The preference for a theoretical model should be based on thoroughly considered answers to these questions: (1) What model validly explains the most phenomenological data? (2) Does the model permit one to predict outcome, with or without therapeutic intervention?

In contrast to an interactional theoretical model involving both psychosocial events and biological substrates in the pathogenesis of the affective disorders, there is a noninteractional etiological model which holds that these phenomena do not mutually influence each other. This view holds that affective disorders occur periodically, monitored by some unknown biological mechanism and an internal time clock that dictates the onset, duration, termination, and mood (depression or mania) of the affective disorder. Further, it claims that biological factors entirely regulate emotions and moods and that the psychological experiences of the affective disorders are secondary to involuntary biological changes in the human organism, and only in this limited sense does an interaction occur. But according to this model, no psychodynamic events lead to the biological concomitants of the affective disorders.

Though this noninteractive theoretical model has been customarily a stronghold for the biologically oriented psychiatrist or psychologist, some psychoanalysts espouse this position. For example, Pollock (1977) has hypothesized, after studying patients who are manic-depressives and are concomitantly being treated with lithium to control their mania, that it may be possible for patients to have two independent coexisting disorders, each having its own independent course and etiology, though possibly capable of influencing one another. He points out that an individual may have two or more different physical diseases at the same time, or a physical disorder and an unrelated mental-emotional one. Contrary to psychosomatic and holistic approaches, he suggests that patients may have more than one condition with mental-emotional manifestations that have distinctly separate causes. He proposes, for example, that a lithium-controlled manic patient could develop a manageable transference neurosis and be successfully treated psychoanalytically for a depression or an obsessive-compulsive neurosis. He has had some actual experience along this line, which should contribute to our theoretical understanding of the affective disorders when he is prepared to publish his findings.

Rather than regarding genetic and constitutional factors as being involved in an opposing hypothesis, it would be more reasonable to regard the vulnerability to have an affective disorder to be increased by both experiential and genetic factors. In writing of the psychopathology of the psychoses in general, Zubin (1977) has classified these two etiological models as "biological" and "ecological." He points out that each of these approaches has contributed to the deeper understanding of, and better intervention into, mental disorders, but none has captured the entire field single-handed. He lends support to the position emphasized here with respect to the pathogenesis of the affective disorders—namely, that interaction between these two approaches is fruitful. He espouses also the position put forward here that individuals subject to affective disorders are vulnerable individuals who, when exposed to more stressful life experiences than their threshold can tolerate, develop an episode of illness. The components of this increased vulnerability need to be thoroughly explored, described, and measured. The more that these steps have been achieved, the better the nature and degree of the interactions between these pathogenic components can be specified.

We must conclude that it is likely that there are multiple pathways in the pathogenesis of affective disorders and that various etiological mechanisms are operating, including early adverse life experiences, successive accumulation of adverse life experiences, immediate losses capable of evoking biological reactions of anxiety and the neurophysiological concomitants of such, and the more delayed reaction of depression-withdrawal with the various neurophysiological concomitants that have been observed with depression and mania.

I have provided evidence—both neurobiological and psychodynamic—that there are many different types of depressions. Since there is also a demonstrative variable response of the affective disorders to psychoactive drug treatment (Klerman, 1973), this too provides additional strong support for the theory that there are multiple subgroups in the depressions, each of which may have a different pathophysiological mechanism.

References

Abraham, K. (1911), Notes on the psycho-analytical investigation and treatment of manic-depressive insanity and allied conditions. In: *Selected Papers on Psycho-Analysis*. London: Hogarth Press, 1927, pp. 137–156.
———— (1916), The first pregenital stage of the libido. In: *Selected Papers on Psycho-Analysis*. London: Hogarth Press, 1927, pp. 248–279.
———— (1924), A short study of the development of the libido, viewed in the light of mental disorders. In: *Selected Papers on Psycho-Analysis*. London: Hogarth Press, 1927, pp. 418–501.
Angst, J. (1966). Zur atiologic und nosologic endogener depressiven psychosen [On etiological and nosologic endogenous depressive psychoses]. *Monographien aus dem Gesamtgebiete der Neurologie une Psychiatrie*, 112. Berlin: Springer.
Bakwin, H. (1942), Loneliness in infants. *Amer. J. Dis. Childhood*, 63:30–40.
Baldessarini, R. J. (1915), An overview of the basis for amine hypothesis in affective illness. In: *The Psychobiology of Depression*, ed. J. Mendels. New York: Spectrum Publications, 1975, pp. 69–83.
———— (1977), *Chemotherapy in Psychiatry*. Cambridge, Mass.: Harvard University Press.
Beck, A. T. (1972), *Depression: Causes and Treatment*. Philadelphia: University of Pennsylvania Press.
———— (1974), The development of depression: A cognitive model. In: *Psychology of Depression: Contemporary Theory and Research*, ed. R. Friedman & M. Katz. Washington, D.C.: Winston-Wiley, pp. 3–27.
Bellak, L., & Smith, M. B. (1956), An experimental exploration of the psychoanalytic process. *Psychoanal. Quart.*, 25:385–414.
Bielski, R. J., & Friedel, R. O. (1976), Prediction of tricyclic antidepressant response: A critical review. *Arch. Gen. Psychiat.*, 33:1479–1489.
Bowden, D. M., & McKinney, W. T. (1972), Behavioral effects of peer separation, isolation and reunion on adolescent male rhesus monkeys. *Devel. Psychobiol.*, 5:353–362.

Bowlby, J. (1960), Grief and mourning in infancy and early childhood. *The Psychoanalytic Study of the Child*, 15:9–52. New York: International Universities Press.

Breese, G. P., Smith, R. D., Mueller, R. A., Howard, J. L., Prange, A. J., & Lipson, M. A. (1973), Induction of adrenal catecholamine synthesizing enzymes following mother-infant separation. *Nature: New Biology*, 246:94–96.

Brown, G. W. (1974), Meaning, measurement, and stress of life events. In: *Stressful Life Events: Their Nature and Effects*, ed. B. S. Dohrenwend & B. F. Dohrenwend. New York: Wiley, pp. 217–243.

——— Harris, T. O., & Peto, J. (1973), Life events and psychiatric disorders: Part 2. Nature of causal link. *Psychological Med.*, 3:159–176.

Buchsbaum, M. (1977), Average evoked response augmenting/reducing in schizophrenia and affective disorders. In: *The Biology of the Major Psychosis: A Comparative Analysis*, ed. D. X. Freedman. New York: Raven Press.

——— Goodwin, F., Murphy, D., & Borge, G. (1971), AER in affective disorders. *Amer. J. Psychiat.*, 128:19–25.

——— Landau, S., Murphy, D., & Goodwin, F. (1973), Average evoked response in bipolar and unipolar affective disorders: Relationship to sex, age of onset, and monoamine oxidase. *Biological Psychiat.*, 7:199–212.

——— Silverman, J. (1968), Stimulus intensity control and the cortical evoked response. *Psychosom. Med.*, 30:12–22.

Busse, E. W., Barnes, R. H., Silverman, A. J., Shy, G. M., Thaler, M., & Frost, L. L. (1954), Studies of the process of aging factors that influence the psyche of elderly persons. *Amer. J. Psychiat.*, 110:897–903.

Cameron, N. (1942), The place of mania among the depressions from a biological standpoint. *J. Psychol.*, 14:181–195.

Clayton, R. (1975), The effect of living alone on bereavement symptoms. *Amer. J. Psychiat.*, 132:133–137.

Coppen, A., Eccleston, E. G., & Peet, M. (1974), Total and free tryptophan concentration in plasma of depressive patients. *Lancet*, 2:60–63.

——— Shaw, D. M., & Farrell, J. P. (1963), Potentiation of the antidepressive effect of a monoamine-oxidase inhibitor by tryptophan. *Lancet*, 1:79–81.

Deutsch, H. (1919), A two-year-old boy's first love comes to grief. In: *Dynamic Psychopathology of Childhood*, ed. L. Jessner & E. Pavenstedt. New York: Grune & Stratton, 1959, pp. 1–5.

——— (1937), Absence of grief. *Psychoanal. Quart.*, 6:12–22.

Durrell, J. (1974), Lithium salts and affective disorders. In: *Factors in Depression*, ed. N. S. Kline. New York: Raven Press.

Elliott, H. W., Gottschalk, L. A., & Uliana, R. L. (1974), Relationship of plasma meperidine levels to changes in anxiety and hostility. *Comprehen. Psychiat.*, 15:249–254.

Engel, G. L. (1962a), Anxiety and depression—withdrawal: The primary affects of unpleasure. *Internat. J. Psycho-Anal.*, 43:89–97.

——— (1962b), *Psychological Development in Health and Disease*. Philadelphia: Saunders.

Fenton, F. R. (1977), Epidemiology of affective disorders: A selective review. In: *Assessment of Depressive Disorders in Different Cultures*, ed. N. Sartorius, A. Jablensky, W. Gulbinat, G. Ernberg, & F. Fenton. Geneva, Switzerland: World Health Organization, pp. 48–70.

Ferster, C. B. (1974), Behavioral approaches to depression. In: *The Psychology of Depression: Contemporary Theory and Research*, ed. R. J. Friedman & M. M. Katz. Washington, D.C.: Winston.

Fieve, R. R., Mendlewicz, J., & Fleiss, J. L. (1973), Manic-depressive illness: Linkage with the Xg^2 blood group. *Amer. J. Psychiat.*, 130:1355–1359.

Fleming, J. (1972), Early object deprivation and transference phenomena: The working alliance. *Psychoanal. Quart.*, 41:23–49.

——— (1974), The problem of diagnosis in parent loss cases. *Contemp. Psychoanal.*, 10:439–451.

——— (1975), Some observations on object constancy in the psychoanalysis of adults. *J. Amer. Psychoanal. Assn.*, 23:743–759.

Freud, A., & Burlingham, D. (1944), *Infants without Families*. New York: International Universities Press.

Freud, S. (1917), Mourning and melancholia. In: *Collected Papers*, Vol. 4. London: Hogarth Press, 1925, pp. 152–170.

Fuller, J. L., & Clark, L. D. (1962a), Effects of rearing with specific stimuli upon post-isolation behavior in dogs. *J. Compar. & Physiol. Psychol.*, 61:258–263.

——— ——— (1962b), Genetic and treatment factors modifying the post-isolation syndrome in dogs. *J. Compar. & Physiol. Psychol.*, 61:251–257.

Furman, R. A. (1964), Death and the young child: Some preliminary considerations. *The Psychoanalytic Study of the Child*, 19:321–333. New York: International Universities Press.

Fuxe, K., & Ungerstedt, U. (1970), Histochemical, biochemical, and functional studies on central monoamine neurons after acute and chronic amphetamine administration. In: *Amphetamine and Related Compounds*, ed. E. Costa & S. Garattini. New York: Raven Press, pp. 257–288.

Glassman, H. H., & Platman, S. R. (1969), Potentiation of monoamine oxidase inhibitor by tryptophan. *J. Psychiat. Res.*, 7:83–88.

Gleser, G. C., Gottschalk, L. A., Fox, R., & Lippert, W. (1965), Immediate changes in affect with chlordiazepoxide in juvenile delinquent boys. *Arch. Gen. Psychiat.*, 13:291–295.

Glowinski, J., & Axelrod, J. (1966), Effects of drugs on the disposition of H^3-norepinephrine in the rat brain. *Pharmacol. Reviews*, 18:775–785.

Goodwin, F. K., & Bunney, W. E., Jr. (1973), Psychobiological aspects of stress and affective illness. In: *Separation and Depression: Clinical and Research Aspects*, ed. J. P. Scott & E. C. Senay. Washington, D.C.: American Association for the Advancement of Science.

Gottlieb, A., Gleser, G. C., & Gottschalk, L. A. (1967), Verbal and physiological responses to hypnotic suggestion of attitudes. *Psychosom. Med.*, 29:172–183.

Gottschalk, L. A. (1966), Depressions: Psychodynamic considerations. In: *Pharmacotherapy of Depression*, ed. J. O. Cole & J. R. Wittenborn. Springfield, Ill.: Charles C Thomas.

——— (1971), Some psychoanalytic research into the communication of meaning through language: The quality and magnitude of psychological states. *Brit. J. Med. Psychol.*, 44:131–148.

——— (1974a), The psychoanalytic study of hand-mouth approximations. In: *Psychoanal. & Contemp. Sci.*, 3. New York: International Universities Press, pp. 261–295.

—— (1974b), Self-induced visual imagery, affect arousal, and autonomic correlates. *Psychosomatics*, 15:166–169.

—— (1976), Children's speech as a source of data toward the measurement of psychological states. *J. Youth & Adolesc.*, 5:11–36.

—— (1977), Effects of certain benzodiazepine derivatives on the disorganization of thought as manifested in speech. *Current Therapeutic Research*, 21:192–206.

—— ed. (1978), *The Content Analysis of Verbal Behavior: Further Studies*. New York: Spectrum Publications.

—— Biener, R., Noble, E. P., Birch, H., Wilbert, D. E., & Heiser, J. (1975), Thioridazine plasma levels and clinical response. *Comprehen. Psychiat.*, 16:323–337.

—— Cleghorn, J. M., Gleser, G. C., & Iacono, J. (1965), Studies of relationships of emotions to plasma lipids. *Psychosom. Med.*, 27:102–111.

—— Elliott, H. W., Bates, D. E., & Cable, C. G. (1972), Content analysis of speech samples to determine effect of lorazepam on anxiety. *Clin. Pharmacol. & Therapeut.*, 13:323–328.

——Gleser, G. C. (1969), *The Measurement of Psychological States through the Content Analysis of Verbal Behavior*. Berkeley: University of California Press.

—— —— Cleghorn, J. M., Stone, W. N., & Winget, C. N. (1970), Prediction of changes in discontinuation and administration of phenothiazines in chronic schizophrenic patients: Language as a predictor and measure of change in schizophrenia. *Comprehen. Psychiat.*, 11:123–140.

—— —— D'Zmura, T., & Hanenson, I. B. (1964), Some psychophysiological relationships in hypertensive women. *Psychosom. Med.*, 26:210–217.

—— —— Springer, K. J. (1963), Three hostility scales applicable to verbal samples. *Arch. Gen. Psychiat.*, 9:254–279.

—— —— —— Kaplan, S. M., Shanon, J., & Ross, W. D. (1960), Effects of perphenazine on verbal behavior patterns. *Arch. Gen. Psychiat.*, 2:632–639.

—— —— Wylie, H. W., Jr., & Kaplan, S. M. (1975), Effects of imipramine on anxiety levels derived from verbal communications. *Psychopharmacologia*, 7:303–310.

—— Hambidge, G., Jr. (1955), Verbal behavior analysis: A systematic approach to the problem of quantifying psychological processes. *J. Proj. Tech.*, 19:387–409.

—— Hoigaard, J., Birch, H., & Rickels, K. (1976), The measurement of psychological states: Relationship between Gottschalk-Gleser content analysis scores and Hamilton Anxiety Rating scale scores, Physician Questionnaire Rating scale scores, and Hopkins Symptom Checklist scores. In: *Pharmacokinetics, Psychoactive Drug Blood Levels, and Clinical Response*, ed. L. A. Gottschalk & S. Merlis. New York: Spectrum Publications, pp. 61–113.

—— Kaplan, S. (1958), A quantitative method of estimating variations in intensity of a psychologic conflict or state. *Arch. Neurol. Psychiat.*, 79:688–696.

—— —— (1972), Chlordiazepoxide plasma levels and clinical response. *Comprehen. Psychiat.*, 13:519–527.

—— Noble, E. P., Stolzoff, G. E., Bates, D. E., Cable, C. G., Uliana, R. L., Birch, H., & Fleming, E. W. (1973), Relationships of chlordiazepoxide blood levels to psychological and biochemical responses. In: *Benzodiazepenes*, ed. S. Garattini, E. Mussini, & L. O. Randall. New York: Raven Press, pp. 257–283.

———— Springer, K. J., & Gleser, G. C. (1961), Experiments with a method of assessing the variations in intensity of certain psychological states occurring during two psychotherapeutic interviews. In: *Comparative Psycholinguistic Analysis of Two Psychotherapeutic Interviews*, ed. L. A. Gottschalk. New York: International Universities Press.

———— Stone, W. N., Gleser, G. C., & Iacono, J. (1966), Anxiety levels in dreams: Relation to changes in plasma free fatty acids. *Science*, 153:654–657.

———— ———— ———— ———— (1969), Anxiety and plasma free fatty acids. *Life Sciences*, 8:61–68.

———— Uliana, R. L. (1977), Further studies on the relationship of non-verbal to verbal behavior: Effect of lip caressing on shame, hostility, and other variables as expressed in the content of speech. In: *Communicative Structures and Psychic Structures*, ed. N. Freeman & S. Grand. New York: Plenum, pp. 311–330.

Green, R., Goetzl, U., Whybrow, P., & Jackson, R. (1973), X-linked transmission of manic depressive illness. *JAMA*, 223:1289.

Grinker, R. R., Sr., Miller, J., Sabshin, M., Nunn, R. J., & Nunnally, J. C. (1961), *The Phenomena of Depressions*. New York: Hoeber, pp. 1–249.

Guidotti, A. (1977), Synaptic mechanisms in the action of benzodiazepines. In: *Psychopharmacology: A Generation of Progress*, ed. M. A. Lipton, A. DiMascio, & K. Killam. New York: Raven Press, pp. 1349–1358.

Heinicke, C. M. (1973), Parental deprivation in early childhood. In: *Separation and Depression: Clinical and Research Aspects*, ed. J. P. Scott & E. C. Senay. Washington, D.C.: American Association for the Advancement of Science, pp. 141–160.

———— Westheimer, I. J. (1965), *Brief Separations*. New York: International Universities Press.

Heston, L. L. (1966), Psychiatric disorders in foster home reared children of schizophrenic mothers. *Brit. J. Psychiat.*, 112:819–825.

Hinde, R. A., & Spencer-Booth, Y. (1970), Individual differences in the responses of rhesus monkeys to a period of separation from their mothers. *J. Child Psychol. & Psychiat.*, 11:159–176.

Holmes, T. H., & Masuda, M. (1973), Life change and illness susceptibility. In: *Separation and Depression: Clinical and Research Aspects*, ed. J. P. Scott & E. C. Senay. Washington, D.C.: American Association for the Advancement of Science, pp. 161–186.

Janowsky, D. J., Leff, M., & Epstein, R. S. (1970), Playing the manic game. *Arch. Gen. Psychiat.*, 22:252–261.

Jensen, G. D., & Tolman, C. W. (1962), Mother-infant relationship in the monkey. Macaca nemestrina: The effect of brief separation and mother-infant specificity. *J. Comp. Physiol. Psychol.*, 55:131–136.

Jung, C. G. (1938), *Psychological Types*. New York: Harcourt, Brace.

Kallmann, F. J. (1950), The genetics of psychoses: An analysis of 1,232 twin index families. *Congres Internationale de Psychiatrie: Rapports VI. Psychiatrie Social*. Paris, pp. 1–27.

Katz, B. (1966), *Nerve, Muscle, and Synapse*. New York: McGraw-Hill.

Katz, M. M., & Hirschfeld, R. M. A. (1977), The phenomenology and classification of depression. In: *Psychopharmacology: A Generation of Progress*, ed. M. A. Lipton, A. DiMascio, & K. K. Killam. New York: Raven Press, pp. 1185–1195.

Kaufman, I. C. (1973), Mother-infant separation in monkeys. In: *Separation and Depression: Clinical and Research Aspects*, ed. J. P. Scott & E. C. Senay. Washington, D.C.: American Association for the Advancement of Science, pp. 33–52.

—— Rosenblum, L. A. (1967), The reaction to separation in infant monkeys: Anaclitic depression and conservation-withdrawal. *Psychosom. Med.*, 29:648–675.

Kety, S. (1971), Brain amines and affective disorders. In: *Brain Chemistry and Mental Disease*, ed. B. T. Ho & W. M. McIsaac. New York: Plenum, pp. 237–244.

—— Rosenthal, D., Wender, P. H., & Schulsinger, F. (1968), The types and prevalence of mental illness in the biological and adoptive families of adopted schizophrenics. In: *The Transmission of Schizophrenia*, ed. D. Rosenthal & S. Kety. Oxford: Pergamon, pp. 345–362.

Klein, M. (1935), A contribution to the psychogenesis of manic-depressive states. In: *Contributions to Psycho-Analysis: 1921–1945*. London: Hogarth Press, 1948, pp. 262–289.

—— (1940), Mourning and its relation to manic-depressive states. In: *Contributions to Psycho-Analysis: 1921–1945*. London: Hogarth Press, 1948, pp. 344–369.

Klerman, G. L. (1973), Pharmacological aspects of depression. In: *Separation and Depression: Clinial and Research Aspects*, ed. J. P. Scott & E. C. Senay. Washington, D.C.: American Association for the Advancement of Science, pp. 215–222.

Knapp, P. H., Mushatt, C., & Nemetz, S. J. (1966), Collection and utilization of data in a psychoanalytic psychosomatic study. In: *Methods of Research in Psychotherapy*, ed. L. A. Gottschalk & A. H. Auerbach. New York: Appleton-Century-Crofts, pp. 401–422.

Korpi, E. R., Kleinman, J. E., Goodman, S. I., Phillips, S. E., DeLisi, L. E., Linnoila, M, & Wyatt, R. J. (1986), Serotonin and 5-hydroxyindoleacetic acid in brains of suicide victims. *Arch. Gen. Psychiat.*, 43:594–603.

Kraemer, G. W., Ebert, M. H., Lake, R. C., & McKinney, W. T. (1984), Cerebrospinal fluid measures of neurotransmitter changes associated with pharmacological alteration of the despair response to social separation in rhesus monkey. *Psychiatry Research*, 11:303–315.

—— Lin, D. H., Moran, E. C., & McKinney, W. T. (1980), Effects of alcohol on the despair response to peer separation in rhesus monkeys. *Psychopharmacol.*, 73:307–310.

—— McKinney, W. T. (1979), Interactions of pharmacological agents which alter biogenic amine metabolism and depression: An analysis of contributing factors within a primate model of depression. *J. Affect. Disord.*, 1:33–54.

Levine, S., Coe, C. L., & Smotherman, W. P. (1978), Prolonged cortisol elevation in the infant squirrel monkey after reunion with mother. *Physiol. Behav.*, 20:7–10.

Lewin, B. (1950), *The Psychoanalysis of Elation*. New York: Norton.

Lewinsohn, P. M. (1974), A behavioral approach of depression. In: *The Psychology of Depression: Contemporary Theory and Research*, ed. R. J. Friedman & M. M. Katz. Washington, D.C.: Winston, pp. 157–178.

Lewis, H. B. (1971), *Shame and Guilt in Neurosis*. New York: International Universities Press.

Maas, J. W. (1975), Biogenic amines and depression. *Arch. Gen. Psychiat.*, 32:1357–1365.

MacLeod, J. A., & Middelman, F. (1962), Wednesday afternoon clinic: A supportive care program. *Arch. Gen. Psychiat.*, 6:56–65.

MacMahon, B., & Pugh, T. F. (1965), Suicide in the widowed. *Amer. J. Epidemiol.*, 81:23–31.

Matthysse, S. (1964), Schizophrenia: Relationship to dopamine transmission, motor control and feature extraction. In: *The Neurosciences: Third Annual Study Program*, ed. F. Schmitt & F. G. Worden. Cambridge: MIT Press, pp. 733–737.

———— (1973), Antipsychotic drug actions: A clue to the neuropathology of schizophrenia. *Federation Proceedings*, 32:200–205.

McKinney, W. T. (1986), Primate separation studies. *Psychiatric Annals*, 16:281–287.

———— Suomi, S. J., & Harlow, H. F. (1973), New models of separation and depression in Rhesus monkeys. In: *Separation and Depression: Clinical and Research Aspects*, ed. J. P. Scott & E. C. Senay. Washington, D.C.: American Association for the Advancement of Science, pp. 53–66.

Mendels, J., ed. (1975), *The Psychobiology of Depression*. New York: Spectrum Publications.

———— Frazer, A. (1975), Lithium distribution in depressed patients: Implications for an alteration in cell membrane function in depression. In: *The Psychobiology of Depression*, ed. J. Mendels. New York: Spectrum Publications, pp. 91–116.

Mendlewicz, J., Fleiss, J., & Fieve, R. (1972), Evidence for X-linkage in the transmission of manic-depressive illness. *JAMA*, 222:1624–1627.

Mineka, S., & Suomi, S. J. (1978), Social separation in monkeys. *Psychological Bull.*, 85:1376–1400.

Moebius, P. J. (1893), *Abriss der Lehre der Nervenkrankheiten* [Digest of the Science of Nervous Diseases]. Leipzig: Abel.

Pare, C. M. D. (1963), Potentiation of monoamine-oxidase inhibitors by tryptophan. *Lancet*, 2:527–528.

Parkes, C. M., & Brown, R. J. (1972), Health after bereavement: A controlled study of young Boston widows and widowers. *Psychosom. Med.*, 34:449–461.

Paykel, E. S. (1973), Life events and acute depression. In: *Separation and Depression: Clinical and Research Aspects*, ed. J. P. Scott & E. C. Senay. Washington, D.C.: American Association for the Advancement of Science, pp. 215–236.

Perris, C. (1966), A study of bipolar (manic-depressive) and unipolar recurrent depressive psychoses. *Acta Psychiatrica Scandinavica*, 42(Suppl. 194).

———— (1968), Genetic transmission of depressive psychoses. *Acta Psychiatry Supplemental*, 203:45–52.

———— (1973), The genetics of affective disorders: In: *Biological Psychiatry*, ed. M. Mendels. New York: Wiley, pp. 385–415.

Piers, G., & Singer, M. D. (1953), *Shame and Guilt.* Springfield, Ill.: Charles C Thomas.

Pollock, G. H. (1977), Foreword. In: *Manic Depressive Illness,* ed. E. A. Wolpert. New York: International Universities Press.

Price, J. S. (1968), The genetics of depressive behavior. In: *Recent Developments in Affective Disorders,* ed. A. Coppen & A. Walk. *Brit. J. Psychiat.,* Special Publication No. 2. Ashford: Headley, Ashley, and Kent, pp. 37–54.

Rado, S. (1928), The problem of melancholia. *Internat. J. Psycho-Anal.,* 9:420–438.

Raskin, A., & Crook, T. H. (1976), The endogenous-neurotic distinction as a predictor of response to antidepressant drugs. *Psychological Med.,* 6:59–70.

Rees, W. D., & Lutkins, S. G. (1967), Mortality of bereavement. *Brit. Med. J.,* 4:13–16.

Reite, M., Short, R., Kaufman, J. C., Stynes, A. J., & Pauley, J. D. (1978), Heart rate and body temperature in separated monkey infants. *Biol. Psychiat.,* 13:91–105.

———— Seiler, C., & Pauley, J. D. (1981), Attachment, loss and depression. *J. Child Psychol. & Psychiat.,* 22:141–169.

——— Stynes, A. J., Vaughn, L., Pauley, J. D., & Short, R. A. (1976), Sleep in infant monkeys: Normal values and behavioral correlates. *Physiol. Behav.,* 16:245–251.

Robertson, J., & Bowlby, J. (1952), Responses of young children to separation from their mothers. *Courrier du Centre Internationale de l'Enfance,* 2:131–142.

——— Robertson, J. (1971), Young children in brief separation. *The Psychoanalytic Study of the Child,* 26:264–315. New York: Quadrangle.

Robins, E., & Guze, S. B. (1972), Classification of affective disorders: The primary-secondary, the endogenous-reactive, and the neurotic-psychotic concepts. In: *Recent Advances in the Psychobiology of the Depressive Illnesses,* ed. T. A. Wiliams, M. M. Katz, & J. A. Shields, Jr. DHEW Publication No. (HSM) 70–9053. Washington, D.C.: U.S. Government Printing Office, pp. 283–293.

Rosenthal, D. (1970), *Genetic Theory and Abnormal Behavior.* New York: McGraw-Hill, pp. 201–221.

Sachar, E. J. (1975), A neuroendocrine strategy in the psychobiological study of depressive illness. In: *The Psychobiology of Depression,* ed. J. Mendels. New York: Spectrum Publications, pp. 123–132.

Schaffer, H. R., & Callender, W. M. (1959), Psychologic effects of hospitalization in infancy. *Pediatrics,* 24:528–539.

Schechter, G., & Buchsbaum, M. (1973), The effects of attention, stimulus, intensity, and individual differences on the average evoked response. *Psychophysiol.,* 10:392–400.

Schildkraut, J. J. (1970), *Neuropsychopharmacology and the Affective Disorders.* Boston: Little, Brown.

Schmale, A. H. (1973), Adaptive role of depression in health and disease. In: *Separation and Depression: Clinical and Research Aspects,* ed. J. P. Scott & E. C. Senay. Washington, D.C.: American Association for the Advancement of Science, pp. 187–214.

Scott, J. P., Stewart, J. M., & DeGhett, V. J. (1973), Separation in infant dogs. Emotional response and motivational consequences. In: *Separation and*

448   LOUIS A. GOTTSCHALK

Depression: Clinical and Research Aspects, ed. J. P. Scott & E. C. Senay. Washington, D.C.: American Association for the Advancement of Science, pp. 3–32.

Seay, B., Hansen, E., & Harlow, H. F. (1962), Mother-infant separation in monkeys. *J. Child Psychol. & Psychiat.*, 3:123–132.

Seligman, M. E. P. (1974), Depression and learned helplessness. In: *The Psychology of Depression: Contemporary Theory and Research*, ed. R. J. Friedman & M. M. Katz. Washington, D.C.: Winston, pp. 83–126.

Sigg, E. B., Soffer, L., & Gyermek, L. (1963), Influences of imipramine and related psychoactive agents on the effect of 5-hydroxytryptamine and catecholamines on the cat nictitating membrane. *J. Pharmacol. & Experimental Therapeutics*, 142:13–20.

Silbergeld, S., Manderscheid, R. W., O'Neil, P. H., Lamprecht, F., & Lorenz, K. Y. (1975), Changes in serum dopamine-beta-hydroxylase activity during group psychotherapy. *Psychosom. Med.*, 37:352–367.

Sjoqvist, F. (1965), Interaction between monoamine oxidase (MAO) inhibitors and other substances. *Proc. Roy. Soc. Med.*, 58:967–978.

Slater, E. (1938), Zur erbpathologie des manisch-depressiven Irrescins: Die Eltern und Kinder von Manisch-Depressiven [On the pathologic inheritance of manic depressives: The parents and children of manic-depressives]. *Zeitschrift fur die Gesamte Neurologie und Psychiatrie*, 163:1–47.

—— Cowie, V. (1971), *Genetics of Mental Disorders*. London: Oxford University Press.

—— Roth, M., eds. (1969), *Moyer-Gross Clinical Psychiatry*. London: Bailliere, Tindall & Cassell.

—— Tsuang, M. T. (1968), Abnormality on paternal and maternal sides: Observations in schizophrenia and manic-depression. *J. Med. Genet.*, 5:197–199.

Snyder, S. H., Banerjee, S. P., Yamamura, H. I., & Greenberg, D. (1974), Drugs, neurotransmitters and schizophrenia. *Science*, 184:1243–1253.

—— Taylor, K. M., Coyle, J. T., & Meyerhoff, J. L. (1970), The role of brain dopamine in behavioral regulation and actions of psychotropic drugs. *Amer. J. Psychiat.*, 127:199–207.

Spitz, R. A. (1945), Hospitalism: An inquiry into the genesis of psychiatric conditions in early childhood. *The Psychoanalytic Study of the Child*, 1:53–74. New York: International Universities Press.

—— Wolf, K. M. (1946), Anaclitic depression: An inquiry into the genesis of psychiatric conditions in early childhood, II. *The Psychoanalytic Study of the Child*, 2:313–342. New York: International Universities Press.

Stein, A., & Susser, M. (1969), Widowhood and mental illness. *Brit. J. Prevention & Social Med.*, 23:106–110.

Stenstedt, A. (1952), A study in manic-depressive psychosis: Clinical, social, and genetic investigators. *Acta Psychiatrica Scandinavica Supplement*, 79.

Stockley, I. H. (1973), Monoamine oxidase inhibitors. I. Interactions with sympathomimetic amines. *Pharmacol. J.*, 210:590–594.

Strauss, J. (1975), A comprehensive approach to psychiatric diagnosis. *Amer. J. Psychiat.*, 132:1193–1196.

Strupp, H. H., Chassan, J. B., & Ewing, J. A. (1966), Towards the longitudinal study of the psychotherapeutic process: Problems of methodology and quantification. In: *Methods of Research in Psychotherapy*, ed. L. A. Gottschalk & A. H. Auerbach. New York: Appleton-Century-Crofts, pp. 361–400.

Suomi, S. J. (1976), Factors affecting responses to social separation in rhesus monkeys. In: *Animal Models in Human Psychobiology*, ed. G. Serban & A. Kling. New York: Plenum, pp. 9–26.

—— Harlow, H. F., & Domek, C. J. (1970), Effect of repetitive infant-infant separation of young monkeys. *J. Abnorm. Psychol.*, 76:161–172.

—— Seaman, S. F., Lewis, J. K., et al. (1978), Effects of imipramine treatment of separation induced social disorders in rhesus monkeys. *Arch. Gen. Psychiat.*, 35:321–325.

Titchener, J., Zwerling, I., Gottschalk, L. A., & Levin, M. (1958), Psychologic reactions of aged to surgery. *Arch. Neurol. & Psychiat.*, 79:63–73.

Tsuang, M. T. (1975), Genetics of affective disorder. In: *The Psychobiology of Depression*, ed. J. Mendels. New York: Spectrum Publications, pp. 85–100.

Von-Greiff, H., McHugh, P. R., & Stokes, P. (1973), The familial history in sixteen males with bipolar manic depressive disorder. Paper presented at the Sixty-third Annual Meeting of the American Psychopathological Association, New York City.

Weissman, M. M. & Klerman, G. L. (1977), Sex differences and the epidemiology of depression. *Arch. Gen. Psychiat.*, 34:98–111.

Williams, T. A., Katz, M. M., & Shield, J. A., Jr., eds. (1972), *Recent Advances in the Psychobiology of the Depressive Illnesses*. DHEW Publication No. (HSM) 70–9053. Washington, D.C.: U.S. Government Printing Office.

Winokur, G., & Clayton, P. (1967), Family history studies: II. Two types of affective disorders separated according to genetic and clinical factors. In: *Recent Advances in Biological Psychiatry*, ed. J. Wortes, Vol. 9. New York: Plenum, pp. 35–50.

—— Tanna, V. L. (1969), Possible role of X-linked dominant factor in manic depressive disease. *Dis. Nerv. Sys.*, 30:89–93.

Wolfenstien, M. (1969), Loss, rage, and repetition. *The Psychoanalytic Study of the Child*, 21:93–123. New York: International Universities Press.

Wynne, L. C., Singer, M. T., Bartko, J. J., & Tookey, M. L. (1977), Schizophrenics and their families: Recent research on parental communication. In: *Developments in Psychiatric Research*, ed. J. E. Tanner. Sevenoaks, Kent: Hodder & Stoughton.

Zubin, J. (1977), An overview of the psychopathology of psychoses: Past, present, and future of the biometric approach. In: *Research on Disorders of the Mind: Progress and Prospects*. DHEW, Alcohol, Drug Abuse, and Mental Health Administration, NIMH DHEW Publ. (ADM) 77-362. Washington, D.C.: U.S. Government Printing Office, pp. 29–33.

14

From Metapsychology to Pathopsychophysiology: Toward an Etiological Understanding of Major Affective Disorders

EDWARD A. WOLPERT, M.D., Ph.D.

Berger, writing in *Science* in 1978, summarized the staggering cost of major affective illness when he reported that while 600,000 Americans with bipolar depressive illness and 1.5 million Americans with unipolar depressive illness are treated yearly, at least 4.5–7.5 million depressed people do not receive the treatment they need. While most depressed patients appear identical when seen cross-sectionally—psychomotor retardation or agitation, thoughts of despair, slowing of thought processes and physiological functions—longitudinally they differ greatly from each other in frequency, length, depth, and patterning of episodes. Some patients have psychoses accompanying their depressions; some do not. Some have depressions only; some have manias as well. Some have one episode of illness; some have recurring episodes, the patterning of which is quite variable.

In the manic state the patient has vastly increased energy available which drives physiological as well as psychological functions. In such a state of hyperarousal, the patient is hypersexual, his ideation is speeded up, actions are quickened, vital functions are increased, and dream time and total sleep are decreased (Hartmann, 1968); indeed, in the extreme case, the physiological speeding up is dangerous to the patient's life: hyperpyrexia and cardiovascular racing and collapse make

451

acute manic excitement a medical emergency. In the depressed state, the reverse is true. Energy is decreased, and both physiological and psychological functions are slowed; ideation is slowed, sometimes to muteness, and sexuality is decreased; sleep time and dream time may be increased (Hartmann, 1968) by shortened REM latency (Thase, Frank, and Kupfer, 1985), and activity is limited; and vital functions are normal or slower than normal. In the phase intervening between mania and depression, psychological and physiological functions are within normal limits. These observations, almost self-evident to the clinician, have recently been experimentally confirmed for motoric activity. Self-contained monitoring devices placed on the wrists of 26 euthymic patients, 24 depressed patients, and 12 manic patients, showed increased wrist activity throughout the day in manic patients, and decreased activity in depressives. Nocturnal wrist activity, much diminished for all groups, was still greatest for manics (Wolff, Putnam, and Post, 1985). Such nocturnal wrist activity probably represents a motor accompaniment of dreaming (Wolpert, 1960).

The best way, then, to make the diagnosis of manic-depressive illness is to demonstrate the existence of three clearly differentiated psychophysiological states alternating with each other. Such a finding indicates a bipolar recurrent affective state, as contrasted to the more usual monopolar (usually depressed) recurrent affective state, which is itself characterized by two clearly differentiated psychophysiological states (Leonhard, Korff, and Schulz, 1962). It is important to recognize that there are degrees of bipolar affective disorder; some patients show mild swings ("cyclothymic personality"), while others show extreme ones ("manic-depressive psychosis").

The ubiquitous nature of major depressive illness is celebrated in medical and artistic literature throughout the ages. In Imperial Rome, Soranus wrote of a senator's daughter who was "languishing." Taking her pulse, which he found to be weak and hard to obtain, he noted it bound and speed on the approach of her father's charioteer. The physician believed the girl's state of "languishing" would soon be fatal, as the charioteer was a slave and hence could never marry her.

Earlier still is a story dating from 1800 B.C. or earlier of an Akkadian merchant who fell ill with a depression. This account, rendered into English by Edith Ritter and J. V. Kinnier Wilson, merits close study. Not only is it the earliest case report of depressive illness in Western medicine, but its explication provides insights into problems in the current treatment of depression and demonstrates that over the past several millennia, despite recent advances in our knowledge, little has changed. The case report is written as if it is an abstract description of a group of cases, but I am assured it is an individual case report.

> If an *awilum* [man] has had a (long) spell of misfortune—and he does not know how it came upon him—so that he has continually suffered losses and deprivation (including) losses of barley and silver and losses of slaves and slave-girls, and there have been cases of oxen, horses, sheep, dogs and pigs, and even (other) *awilu* (in his household) dying off altogether; if he has frequent nervous breakdowns, and from constantly giving orders with no (one) complying, calling with no (one) answering, and striving to achieve his desires while having (at the same time) to look after his household, he shakes with fear in his bedroom and his limbs have become "loose" to an extreme degree; if he is filled with anger against god and king; if his limbs often hang limp, and he is sometimes so frightened that he cannot sleep by day or night and constantly sees disturbing dreams; if he has an (ataxic) "looseness" in his limbs (from) not having enough food and drink; and if (in speech) he forgets the word which he is trying to say; then, as for that *awilum*, the anger of (his) god and goddess is upon him.
>
> (Since) his god and goddess are angry with him, if that *awilum* should (subsequently) become ill with qat mumili, sudimmerakku, qat ameluti or murus himmate, the iniquities of father and mother, brother and sister, of clan, kith and kin, will have taken hold of him [pp. 25–26].

In the case at hand the magical healer (Asipu) fabricated elaborate male and female figurines outfitted with the appropriate clothes and equipment for a journey; endowed with human qualities, the figurines then were substituted for the patient and buried in the earth. The Asipu then conversed with the gods through the figurines on behalf of the patient. This was only one part of the treatment that might be rendered to a patient. In the Babylonian system of medicine and that which preceded it in Sumer and Akkad there were two complementary professions: the Asipu, or magical expert, and the Asu, or physician. The former was learned, having spent eight years learning cuneiform writing in a school for scribes. He sat cross-legged and discoursed with his patient with the magical figurines between them. He was allowed to take only those patients he felt he could help. In many respects the Asipu is the ancestor of the modern psychotherapist. The Asu, or physician, by contrast, was not learned, could not read or write cuneiform script, could refuse no patients, and treated his patients with medications, purgation, and bindings (Ritter, 1965). Some might cynically say the two types of practitioner differ little from their modern counterparts.

The parallel between the Babylonian system and current Western practice is indeed striking. Today we sometimes find a division of treatment into two functions: the giving of medication by a physician and the talking over of problems by a psychotherapist, who may come from a different professional hierarchy. A dynamic formulation of Babylonian magical therapy might be that the figurines are a concrete representation (displacement) of parental imagos; the superego or ego ideal (a god or gods) is placated by concretely burying these images, as if to encourage the patient to resolve the childhood neuroses relating to these imagos. A modern patient began to lay wreaths of flowers spelling "peace" on his mother's grave when told that for his depression to resolve he would have to make peace with his dead mother. Concrete thought processes are not the exclusive province of early man.

While Babylonian psychiatry may be interpreted retrospectively as having recognized that tension between the patient's ego and internalized parental imagos is involved in the genesis of depression, speculation concerning the specific etiology of depressive illness was not recorded until much later. In what follows, a brief survey of currently competing theories of the etiology of depressive illness will be given. A mechanism will then be proposed that might be supraordinate to these theories.

Phenomenology at the Turn of the Century

In 1921, some 3600 years after the treatment of the Akkadian merchant was completed—its result lost to history—Emil

Kraepelin summarized his forty years of experience with manic-depressive illness in his psychiatric clinic in Munich. Kraepelin had originally divided affective disorder into a great number of subvarieties according to the predominance of various symptoms, but as he observed his patients over a long span of time he noted that the various subvarieties seemed to replace each other in a kaleidoscopic manner. He came to the conclusion that these subvarieties of disorder were varying surface manifestations of one underlying affective disorder, "manic-depressive" illness, which had a tendency to spontaneous remission not seen in the organic dementias (syphilitic in origin in most of his cases) or in dementia praecox. This unitary view of affective illness has been challenged by many, and today this unitary "manic-depressive" illness has been fragmented into a unipolar variety consisting of major depression, whether recurrent or occurring but once, and a bipolar variety comprising episodes of both mania and depression. Milder forms of depression are called dysthymic disorder.

Kraepelin, following his Akkadian predecessor, noted that while certain critical life events (birth, marriage, illness, death, etc.) might sometimes seem to be temporally related to the onset of affective episodes, other episodes seem to originate with no obvious precipitant in the outside world. He therefore asserted that the illness was due to "inner structural change." But, despite many experimental attempts to determine these physiological-anatomical changes, at the end of his life the hypothesized structural change remained elusive.

Psychodynamic and Structural Explanations

Karl Abraham (1911) accepted Kraepelin's assertion that all affective disorders were one and presented a psychodynamic formulation of manic-depressive illness that denied Kraepelin's physiological-anatomical concept of inner structural change, replacing it with a psychodynamic concept. In Abraham's view, episodes of affective disease were precipitated by the loss of a libidinal object and occurred because the patient had suffered psychological fixation during the oral sadistic period of development. This fixation made it impossible for the patient, whose character was obsessive-compulsive, to deal with current traumatic events; he then regressed but, unlike the typical obsessive-compulsive, abandoned his object.

Freud (1917) was not so sure that all affective disorders were one. "Melancholia," he wrote, "whose definition fluctuates even in descriptive psychiatry, takes on various clinical forms the grouping together of which into a single unity does not seem to be established with certainty; and some of these forms suggest somatic rather than psychogenic affections" (p. 243). Again:

> The most remarkable characteristic of melancholia, and the one in need most of explanation is the tendency to change round into mania—a state which is the opposite of it in its symptoms. As we know, this does not happen to every melancholic. Some cases run their course in periodic relapses during the intervals between which signs of mania may be entirely absent or only very slight. Others show the regular alternation of melancholic and manic phases which has led to the hypothesis of a circular insanity [p. 253].

Nevertheless, Freud explained melancholia as a response to the loss of the object, with attendant impoverishment of the ego, and mania as the resolution of this loss, with an attendant release of previously bound energy.

Freud (1921) elaborated on the mechanism involved in mania, describing a psychogenic and a spontaneous type of cyclical illness. In the psychogenic type, the loss of an object precipitates a melancholia in which the object is set up inside the ego by identification and is condemned by the ego ideal; if ego and ego ideal fuse because of a "rebellion of the ego," then a mania supervenes. In the spontaneous type of cyclical illness, by contrast, "external precipitating causes do not seem to play any decisive part; as regards internal motives, nothing more, or nothing less is to be found in these patients than in all others. It has consequently become the custom to consider these cases as not being psychogenic" (p. 132). Freud, speculating on the origin of these spontaneous oscillations of mood, suggested the hypothesis that the ego reacts in an automatic way with a change in mood if the ego ideal is too strict. He had no concrete evidence to support such a hypothesis and stated that these mood oscillations may be due to other causes.

In 1923 Freud elaborated his most far-reaching view of manic-depressive illness, stating that in melancholia "the excessively strong super-ego which has obtained a hold upon consciousness rages against the ego with merciless violence. . . . What is now holding sway in the super-ego is, as it were, a pure culture of the death instinct, and in fact it often enough succeeds in driving the ego into death, if the latter does not fend off its tyrant in time by the change round into mania" (p. 53).

Abraham (1924) accepted Freud's emendation to his previous work and listed five etiological factors, which together were necessary to cause the occurrence of a melancholic depression: (1) a constitutional accentuation of oral erotism; (2) a special fixation of the libido at the oral level (these were considered necessary, predisposing factors for the development of the illness); (3) a severe injury to infantile narcissism; (4) occurrence of the injury before oedipal wishes were overcome; and (5) a repetition of primary disappointments later in life. In addition, Abraham tentatively explained manias that arise without antecedent depression. "In 'pure' mania, which is frequently of periodic occurrence, the patient seems to me to be shaking off that primal parathymia [a feeling of hopelessness the child has when his oedipal wishes are thwarted] without having had any attack of melancholia [in the present] in the clinical sense" (p. 475).

Thus by 1924 psychoanalytic thinking had conceptualized the affective episodes of manic-depressive illness into two types—spontaneous and psychogenic. In spontaneous episodes a change in psychic structure periodically occurs for unknown reasons; this leads to the same psychological symptoms as are found in psychogenic episodes. In the latter an object loss is followed by identification with the object and its incorporation into the ego. The superego, reproaching the incorporated object, is responsible for the generalized impoverishment of the ego manifested in melancholic symptomatology. By unknown mechanisms the ego can overcome the superego (or fuse with it), and the previously bound energy is released in the typical symptoms of a mania. Constitutional and developmental factors are postulated that would predispose the individual to develop the illness. Presumably a complementary series would hold so that in some cases the constitutional factors—and in other cases the developmental—would predominate in the genesis of the disease. Hints exist that the spontaneous form of the illness is linked to somatic or physiological factors. Psychotherapy would be directed toward helping the patient deal with vulnerability to object loss in the psychogenic episode.

In Fenichel's encyclopedic discussion of psychopathogenesis (1945), the structural-dynamic viewpoint is pushed to the extreme, emphasizing the connection of each pathological state (including manic-depressive illness) with specific failure at a given point in psychosexual development. While this formulation is neat, it is not confirmed in practice, for the clinician easily recognizes bipolar patients with a variety of character disorders. Some patients are oral, pregenital characters, some are anal, and others are genital. In sum, there is no clinical typology specific to bipolar illness, as postulated by Fenichel.

Economic Considerations

By the time Freud wrote of two specific subvarieties of affective disorder he had spent years elaborating an economic theory to explain certain clinical observations. This theory, that of the "actual neurosis," has not been accorded the importance due it. Its explication may begin to provide the organic basis Freud wished for his psychological theory (see Freud [1895]).

In 1896 Freud differentiated between the simple neuroses (the direct effects of sexual noxae) and the neuropsychoses of defense (the consequences of memory traces of the sexual noxae). Two years later he coined the term "actual neuroses." These were considered the mental consequences of past sexual noxae (Freud, 1898).

In a paper on visual disturbance Freud (1910) stated:

> Psycho-analysts never forget that the mental is based on the organic, although their work can only carry them as far as this basis and not

beyond it. . . . Generally speaking, the neurotic disturbances of vision stand in the same relation to the psychogenic ones as the 'actual neuroses' do to psycho-neuroses: psychogenic visual disturbances can no doubt hardly ever appear without neurotic ones, but the latter can appear without the former. These neurotic symptoms are unfortunately little appreciated and understood even today; for they are not directly accessible to psycho-analysis and other methods of research have left the standpoint of sexuality out of account [pp. 217–218].

Freud (1912) soon added hypochondria to his list of the actual neuroses and pointed out that at the center of each psychoneurotic symptom was a "small fragment of undischarged excitation connected with coitus which emerges as an anxiety symptom or provides the nucleus for the formation of hysteroid symptoms" (p. 248). Thus, by 1912 the actual neuroses had taken on a physiological cast—the "sexual noxae" of the 1890s became the "undischarged excitation connected with coitus." In 1914 Freud related each of the actual neuroses to a psychological illness—hypochondria is related to paraphrenia (schizophrenia) as neurasthenia is to obsessive neurosis and anxiety neurosis to hysteria. Each psychological illness has at its core a physiological state that achieves psychological representation as a symptom.

In the *Introductory Lectures* Freud (1916–1917) discussed the actual neuroses in the most complete exposition he was ever to give. The actual neurotic symptoms have no psychical meaning but "are also themselves entirely somatic processes" (p. 387). Further, the actual neuroses, "in the details of their symptoms and also in their characteristic of influencing every organ system and every function, exhibit an unmistakable resemblance to the pathological states which arise from the chronic influence of external toxic substances and from a sudden withdrawal of them—to intoxications and conditions of abstinence" (p. 388). But what these toxins might be, "the vehicle of all the stimulant effects of the libido," we do not know (pp. 388–389). "The theoretical structure of psycho-analysis that we have created is in truth a superstructure, which will one day have to be set upon its organic foundation. But we are still ignorant of this" (p. 389).

Thus, Freud conceptualizes the actual neuroses as illnesses of a physiological nature caused by toxinlike substances released by a damming up of excitation or the sudden withdrawal of such damming up. After the creation of the tripartite structural theory and the signal anxiety theory, Freud (1925) stated that he continued to maintain his original view of the actual neuroses despite the changes in details the new theories would necessitate. In 1926 he described the psychoneuroses as being caused by a psychical danger in the id activating the ego's danger signal and the actual neuroses as caused by a somatic danger in the id causing an automatic physiological reaction.

Fenichel (1945) discusses the actual neuroses under the subtitle "Actual neuroses; Symptoms of unspecific inhibitions," pointing out that "any defensive mechanism using a countercathexis necessarily creates a certain impoverishment of the personality" (p. 185). Some of the symptoms noted are inhibitions, a direct and automatic experience of the state of being dammed up; other symptoms represent floods of uncontrolled excitement and involuntary emergency discharge.

Thus, the actual neuroses present symptoms appearing in the psychic sphere caused by either a lack or an excess of physiological factors leading to symptoms of poverty or overabundance of psychological functioning. The symptoms in such an illness do not have a primary psychogenic meaning, since they are the result of inhibitions or excess of discharge. While it is true that the symptoms may secondarily become invested with a psychogenic meaning, such investment is quite rare.

Manic-depressive illness may be considered the actual neurosis par excellence: it is an illness characterized by periodic excesses and retardations in function in the psychic sphere as a consequence of physiological changes in the nervous system. Manic symptomatology results when the psyche is acted on by a sudden burst of increased "physiological energy"; depressive symptomatology results when there is a decrease in the "physiological energy" that is available. The content of the illness, oral in nature, so well described by Abraham and all who followed him, depends on the relation of the overabundance or lack of physiological energy available to the psychological process.

Benedek (1956) feels that the origin of the depressive constellation lies in the psychophysiological state of nursing.

In the spontaneous cyclic episode described by Freud, the cycles of behavior depend on a basic fault in the physiological affective system being triggered off internally, while in the psychogenic type they depend on external loss reactions triggering the same mechanism. If adequate biochemical treatment can be devised, the internally triggered attacks cease to exist, but the externally triggered attacks must be handled by a different mode of treatment. This is exactly what seems to have occurred with the chemical treatment of manic-depressive and unipolar illness (Schou, 1968; Davis, 1976); adequate chemical treatment seems to abort spontaneous episodes, and psychotherapy teaches the patient to handle losses in a way that sidesteps the fault in the physiological affective system. Some manic patients are treated successfully with lithium carbonate alone; others need psychotherapeutic intervention as well. In unipolar illness, antidepressants, or sometimes lithium, aborts spontaneous episodes.

Intrafamilial and Developmental Considerations

Other thinkers have viewed the major depressions from the point of view of intrafamilial social considerations, on the one hand, and from developmental considerations, on the other.

Fromm-Reichmann's group at Chestnut Lodge (Cohen, Baker, Cohen, Fromm-Reichmann, and Weigart, 1954) studied the intrapsychic status and interpersonal relationships of twelve middle- to upper-class manic-depressive patients in intensive psychotherapy and concluded that a specific interpersonal configuration was associated with the illness. The marital pair, comprising one warm but inadequate parent and one cold but quite able parent, expected extraordinary success from the child-to-become-manic. The entire family group was considered a minority within its social, economic, and geographic milieu. This hypothesis, based on intensive interview techniques and translated into scale behavior by Gibson, Cohen, and Cohen

(1959), was found to differentiate manic-depressive and schizo-phrenic patients in a large public hospital, a finding that supports the validity of the original study.

Arieti (1959) gave a similar social formulation, which differs only in detail. For him, the future manic patient was traumatized in childhood by a sudden change from a giving, duty-bound mother to a mother giving less and expecting a great deal from the child. The result is resentment on the part of the child, who cannot form normal parental introjects. Such a child incorporates other objects in the environment and, having no stable parental introject, is particularly vulnerable to losses.

More recently Ping-Ni Pao (1968, 1971), also writing from Chestnut Lodge, has discussed the developmental aspects of mania, taking as his starting point the work of Margaret Mahler. Pao views elation to be a normal response to either the joy of reunion with a temporarily lost object or to pleasure at a successful work performance. Mania, by contrast, is considered a pathological defense against object loss. In these views psychotherapy is crucial in controlling the affective disorder, and pharmacotherapy ignored as a significant contributor.

The theoretical positions described up to now, with the exception of that of Kraepelin, would in Akkad call for the intervention of the Asipu, the magical healer. Now it is time to turn our attention to the work that in Akkad would be the province of the Asu, the physician.

Recent Research Findings

Chemical Treatment

It was by serendipity that Cade (1949) in Australia discovered empirically the use of lithium salts in manic-depressive illness. The somewhat later observation that drugs in the mono-amine oxidase inhibitor group could ameliorate severe depressions was to some degree offset by the occurrence of dangerous side effects if patients unwittingly ate foods containing tyramine. The discovery in the fifties and sixties of the tricyclic antidepressants and then the quartenary cyclic antidepressants became a tremendous incentive to biochemical research; the clinical fact that treatment with antidepressants decreased the length-of-stay statistics for most types of depression was undisputed. Much evidence suggests that chemical prophylaxis of patients with recurrent depression, either unipolar or bipolar (the narrower type of manic-depressive illness), may radically change the natural history of these entities (Davis, 1976).

Chemical theorists (Schildkraut, 1965; Bunney, Goodwin, and Murphy, 1972) suggested that depression was related to functional deficiency of neurotransmitters (catecholamines) at central adrenergic receptor sites, while the reverse, a functional excess of neurotransmitters, led to mania. Work by a number of researchers indicates that there may be two chemical subgroups of depression, one based on a deficiency in serotonin metabolism, the other on a deficiency of noradrenaline metabolism. Janowsky, El-Yousel, Davis, and Sekerice (1972) have advanced the hypothesis that the presence of mania or depression depends on the relation between the levels of cholinergic and adrenergic neurotransmitter activity. Other theories involve the sensitization of receptor end points and the inhibition of such sensitization (Richelson and El-Fakahany, 1980). The overall neurotransmitter theory, however, regardless of its specification, asserts that depression is the result of a slowing of central nervous impulse, whereas mania is the result of its speeding up (Thase, Frank, and Kupfer, 1985). It is important to note parenthetically that the chemical mediation of the synaptic jump by the impulse is the modern counterpart of Freud's hypothetical "toxin-like substances" released by the "damming up of excitation" or the "sudden withdrawal" of such damming up. Thus the organic or physiological basis Freud sought for his metapsychology is fast at hand.

Biological Clocks: Circadian Rhythms

Engelmann (1973) observed that the period of time that a petal of the flower Kalanchoe remained open lengthened as the concentration of lithium ion in a LiCl watering solution increased. This pioneer work has since been extended to humans (Johnsson, Engelmann, Pflug, and Klemke, 1980, 1982), suggesting that lithium works by lengthening the periodicity of a hypothesized biological clock. Support for this hypothesis comes from a remarkable series of observations in which severe depression is temporarily reversed by a variety of nonchemical, nonpsychotherapeutic, physical measures that have in common only one property—the ability to phase advance the sleep cycle.

A vast body of knowledge, summarized by Kleitman (1963) and furthered by Moore-Ede, Sulzman, and Fuller (1982) and by Wehr and Goodwin (1983), indicates that many psychological and physiological functions vary according to a twenty-four-hour diurnal cycle, and that these functions may be organized into two distinct patterns. In X the variable studied is organized about the sleep-wakefulness cycle, while in Y the variable studied is organized about the body temperature cycle. In each of the situations to be discussed the sleep cycle is phase advanced by physical methods, and this leads to a relief of depression.

Vogel, Traub, and Ben-Horin (1968) noted REM deprivation to have an antidepressant effect, and Pflug and Tolle (1971) described an antidepressant effect of one night's total sleep deprivation. The effect of both procedures is to phase advance the sleep cycle. Wehr, Wirz-Justice, Goodwin, Duncan, and Gillin (1979), noting spontaneous improvement in mood in depressed manic-depressives when awakening time spontaneously advanced, were able to temporarily improve mood in depressed patients by phase advancing sleep by having the patient go to sleep and arise six hours earlier than usual. Pflug (1984) advocates one night per week of sleep deprivation for all hospitalized depressives to facilitate the action of antidepressants. Kielholz, Terzans, Gatspar, and Adams (1982) go so far as to recommend the use of sleep deprivation as an adjunct to the treatment of seriously depressed patients who are refractory to a highly experimental intravenous infusion of a combination of serotonin and nonadrenaline uptake blocking agents.

Kripke, Mullaney, Atkinson, and Wolf (1978) review the evidence suggesting that two distinct circadian rhythms exist in humans, and that these rhythms, produced by two different oscillators, the X oscillator connected with the sleep-wakefulness cycle and the Y oscillator connected to the body temperature cycle, are capable of desynchronizing from each other and from the environment. Experimental shifts in the time of sleep cause dysphoric mood and poor performance, producing symptoms with some resemblance to retarded depressions; derangements of circadian rhythms cause a characteristic early wakening and shortened REM sleep latency, mimicking sleep patterns thought specific to primary depression. Kripke presents the hypothesis that manic-depressive illness is a disorder of the biological clock in which the circadian oscillators uncouple and free run fast in normal environments. Since lithium slows circadian rhythms, it counteracts the illness whenever the rhythms run fast. Interestingly, lithium nonresponders turn out in Kripke's work to be patients whose body temperature curve is slower than that seen in responders.

Biological Clocks: Infradian Rhythms

In a somewhat different vein, patients with seasonal affective disorder (depression in the fall, hypomania or mania in the spring) have recently been studied, and the findings are most intriguing. Lewy, Kern, Rosenthal, and Wehr (1983) report a patient with seasonal mood cycle of mild degree (depression beginning in July, lasting about 29 weeks; hypomania beginning in January or February, lasting 22 weeks) treated in December 1980 with fluorescent light mimicking his spring photoperiod. This treatment after 4 days led to a remission in depression not expected for 13 more weeks. Rosenthal, Sack, Gillin, Goodwin, Lewy, Davenport, Mueller, Newsome, and Wehr (1984) extended this work to a total of eleven patients and confirmed Lewy's findings. Bick (1986) reports on four patients with major episodes of illness that follow a seasonal pattern. This suggests that in some patients with seasonal affective disorder light intensity/duration factors may be involved in the genesis of the disorder, operating through the interesting anatomical afferent pathway of retinohypothalamic tract to the suprachiasmatic nucleus, now postulated to be the X or weak oscillator (Moore and Eichler, 1976; Schwartz and Gainer, 1981). An anatomical basis for the Y oscillator has yet to be identified.

Eastwood, Whitton, Kramer, and Peter (1985) report a fourteen-month long study of normals and affectively disordered patients in which mood, anxiety, and energy level were subjectively rated on a nine-point scale and length of sleep measured by clock. Thirty-four controls and 30 patients completed the study. The majority of the subjects demonstrated clear seasonal cycles, with the affective disordered patients demonstrating a greater amplitude in their periodicities. The authors conclude that "this makes affective disorder akin to hypertension and diabetes, wherein a physiological variable shades into a pathological variant" (p. 298).

Genetics

While work on the somatic genetics of affective disorder suggests several different inheritance patterns, one sex linked, another autosomal dominant, the majority of affective patients have no clearly demonstrable genetic loading. Ostrow and others (Ostrow, Pandey, Davis, Chang, and Tosteson, 1977; Pandey, Davis, and Ostrow, 1977; Pandey, Ostrow, Haas, Dorus, Casper, and Davis, 1977; Ostrow, Pandey, Davis, Hurt, and Tosteson, 1978; Shaughnessy, Greene, Pandey, and Dorus, 1985) have described cell membrane abnormalities under genetic control. Work establishing the genetics of circadian rhythm abnormalities has yet to appear, but such work is expected.

Prodromal Symptom States: The Switch

It has often been noted anecdotally by clinicians that episodes of mania are ushered in by prodromal symptoms that for a given individual may be said to be pathognomonic of the episode. According to Lange (1928),

> there are manic depressive patients who become confused and hallucinated for a day, and only on the next day display a well defined mania. Occasionally, during this time, the patients seem to have undergone a rich experience strongly reminiscent of an oneiroid subjective state but fugitive in character. Manifestations such as these take place in sleepless or dreamy nocturnal episodes and they may be repeated on several nights in succession [translated in Lewin, 1950, p. 139].

Levitan (1973) reported two dreams in which a dangerous situation was replaced by a magical solution accompanied by hilarity. In each case a hypomanic episode resulted. In a study of manic patients (Wolpert and Mueller, 1969; Wolpert, 1975), a colleague and I noted several patients who were normothymic or depressed who had dreams in which external authority figures (police, government authorities, university authorities) were overwhelmed either by the patient in disguise or by id elements in disguise (e.g., as barbarians or rioters). A manic episode followed each of these dreams.

Many behaviorally oriented clinicians and experimenters have been interested in the "switch process"—the sudden change from mania or normal to depression or from depression to normal or mania (Bunney, Goodwin, and Murphy, 1972; Paschalis, Pavlou, and Papdimitriou, 1980). The "switch" referred to seems identical either to the prodromal symptom state described above or to its final moments.

In a panel moderated by Bunney (1977), a number of workers reviewed their research approach to the understanding of the switch process. They conceptualize manic-depressive illness as a disorder of the kinetics of bodily functions in which, as Wehr stated, there is "an underlying process that is continuous over time, where change occurs daily, and where remission as well as relapse are expressions of the illness" (p. 321). The disturbance itself is in a mania an acceleration of, and in depression a deceleration of, "motor activity, mean temperature rhythm (that is, whether faster or slower than 1 cycle/24 hours) and noradrenergic activity" (p. 323). The acceleration at the switch into mania is more pronounced than the deceleration at the switch into depression.

Hartmann (1968) in his longitudinal study of the EEGs of manic-depressives observed one very depressed patient switch into a manic episode during sleep. Seeing this, he began to collect cases of the switch into mania and noted that all such switches occurred during sleep. Unfortunately, dreams were not available. Bunney (1978) has discussed at length the various drugs reported to produce these switches, but his interpretation is denied by Lewis and Winokur (1982), who report a similar spontaneous incidence of switches in manic-depressive patients not treated with drugs.

While the majority of switches are observed to occur at night, at times the prodromal state is a state of pansensory hyperarousal during the day (Wolpert, 1977). In work with lithium carbonate in the treatment of manic-depressive illness (Wolpert and Mueller, 1969; Mueller and Wolpert, 1974; Wolpert, 1975, 1977), Mueller and I have noted that if a patient can by introspection identify the mental accompaniments of the "switch"—that is, report either dreams or waking hyperacute sensations indicating a prodromal symptom state—the illness is easily controlled by lithium, the dosage of which is simply increased when a change of motility threatens.

In one of our lithium-treated manic-depressive patients the first indication of incipient mania is a typical nocturnal dream experience in which swirling vortices of multicolored lights are accompanied by equilibratory and somesthetic sensations without any ideational content or story line. If the lithium dose is not then increased, this patient will within a day develop racing thoughts and a high degree of distractibility; sleep the second night will be much decreased in total length and will be accompanied by an exaggeration of the previous night's dream experience. The second day is a frank manic episode. However, if lithium is increased as soon as the initial dream is reported, no episode of mania ensues. This use of prodromal symptoms to alert the clinician to impending mania was first suggested by Jacobson (1965), before the general availability of lithium carbonate in the United States, and so was not immediately researched.

It does not seem to do violence to the facts to interpret these dream patterns or other prodromal experiences as being the psychological result of physiological changes in the affective structure—that is, the psychological correlate of the "switch." Somehow there occurs a physiological change in which energy becomes hyperavailable to the nervous system and is discharged psychologically either by the symbolic representation of an overthrow of a psychological controlling structure or by a pure sensory experience of extreme intensity. If these phenomena are untreated once they appear the whole train of manic symptomatology follows, and a manic episode supervenes. This, then, is the spontaneous manic episode described by Freud.

Rapid Cycling

In some cases patients seem to have a tremendously great number of switches, as if the mechanism were faulty; the resulting mixture of mania and depression is both destructive to personal life and chaotic in effect, making treatment most difficult.

Prior to the introduction of lithium and antidepressant treatment of affective disorders, a few cases of "periodic catatonia" were described in the German and Scandinavian literature (Gjessing, 1938; Gjessing and Gjessing, 1961). Clinical descriptions emphasized abruptly appearing and disappearing periods of catatonic excitement and/or stupor, with no significant thought disorder other than what is secondary to the affective state. At times the patients appeared to have developed this syndrome either spontaneously or after a head injury (Jenner, Gjessing, Cox, Davies-Jones, Hullin, and Hanna, 1967), and in such patients lithium carbonate was often quite effective (Hanna, Jenner, Pearson, Sampson, and Thompson, 1972). The descriptions of these patients make them appear to have primary affective illness.

By the mid-seventies Dunner and Fieve had recognized a type of manic-depressive patient not likely to have a good outcome with prophylactic lithium carbonate treatment. These were patients who had four or more affective episodes per year and had been treated with antidepressants. Dunner and Fieve (1974) recommended continued use of lithium, supplemented by antipsychotic medications during the manias, and called these patients "rapid cyclers." Rapid cycling is by now known to be a most difficult clinical state to control.

Since this initial work a large body of data has been accumulated indicating that rapid cycling, although not unknown in the era before lithium and antidepressants, has markedly increased since their introduction (Bunney, 1978; Wolpert, Goldberg, and Harrow, 1990).

Indeed, the possible induction of rapid cycling by these agents is a very real risk to the patient; a prospective follow-up study indicates that cycling of mood in the same illness episode is the only factor known to correlate with a higher risk of suicidal outcome in bipolar patients (Fawcett and Scheftner, 1985).

Oppenheim (1982) carefully distinguishes between the spontaneous form of rapid cycling and the drug-induced form. The pharmacotherapy of affective disorders is conceptualized "as bringing about and holding in remission symptoms of an underlying illness with its own inherent cyclicity" (p. 940). This hypothesis suggests that the point in the cycle where rapid cycling begins determines the appropriate treatment. Withdrawing the offending drug may leave the patient depressed, euthymic, manic, or continuing to rapid cycle. Oppenheim suggests that the appropriate treatment is to withdraw the antidepressant once the patient switches out of depression, and to use lithium for any residual hypomanic, manic, or cycling state.

Roy-Byrne, Joffe, Uhde, and Post (1984) summarize more completely the literature on rapid cycling, and state that "the most plausible theory of the aetiopathology of rapid-cycling illness implicates changes in the intrinsic periodicity of specific circadian pacemakers" (p. 545). To support their hypothesis they cite the following facts: (1) tricyclic antidepressants both shorten the intrinsic pacemaker and induce rapid cycling; (2) a change from the normal 24-hour sleep–wakefulness cycle to a 48-hour cycle is associated with a switch into a hypomanic state; and (3) total sleep deprivation results in a switch of affective state from depressed to hypomanic. Reviewing the treatment options, they agree with Oppenheim in recommending the withdrawal of any drug thought to play a causative role; they then suggest the use of Li_2Co_3 or carbamazepine (Tegretol) with thyroid, clorgyline, and neuroleptics kept in reserve.

The phenomenon of rapid cycling, a pathological variation in normal circadian rhythms, can thus best be understood as a dysfunction of circadian pacemakers. Chemical treatment and sometimes electroshock treatment (Berman and Wolpert, 1987), physical measures such as sleep deprivation, dream deprivation, or crossing seven time zones by jet (Wehr and Goodwin, 1983), have the ability to reset the circadian pacemaker, thereby normalizing circadian rhythms and ending the pathological state.

Combined Psychological and Pharmacological Treatment of
Affective Disorders

The author (1988) has previously reviewed experimental attempts to evaluate the efficacy of the treatment of depression by psychological and/or pharmacological means. Most studies reviewed were brief, consisting of small numbers of relatively mildly depressed outpatients assigned randomly (in the ideal case) to drug alone, psychotherapy alone, combination drug-psychotherapy or placebo conditions. The type of psychotherapy was sometimes exactly described (interpersonal therapy of Klerman, Weissman, Rounsaville, and Chevron, 1984; cognitive therapy of Beck, 1967), and the drugs were clearly defined. The results suggested a relative equivalence of treatments and all treatment conditions superior to placebo. Similar evaluation of the treatment of major affective disorders was unavailable.

More recently two analytic papers have appeared describing the combined treatment of individual manic-depressive patients by psychoanalysis and lithium. Galatzer-Levy (1988) reports on one patient of three he analyzed. Loeb and Loeb (1987) report on three of seven patients treated. The two reports, presumably dealing with the same clinical phenomena, could not be more dissimilar. In Galatzer-Levy's analyses the use of lithium never emerged as a central issue for either the analyst or patient. Indeed he goes so far as to state that "this finding leads me to doubt the central role of orality and regression to the oral phase discussed by analytic investigators, starting with Abraham" (p. 88); Loeb and Loeb, on the other hand, describe "a predictable relation between our manic depressive patients' blood lithium levels and particular changes in their conscious and unconscious mental processes . . . predictively related to specific changes in these patients' overt manic symptomatology. . . . Each of our patients' manic episodes was heralded by a marked increase in unconscious or conscious phallic sexual thoughts, feelings, and behavior . . ." (p. 877).

In their divergent analyses of their clinical material, Galatzer-Levy and Loeb and Loeb agree in asserting that their hypothesized metapsychological formulation holds for all manic-depressives, but disagree on the nature of the formulation.

For Galatzer-Levy the central pathology is an arrest in ego development "manifest in the absence of the capacity to dream, to fantasize and to talk of their psychological situation." Treatment succeeds "through the reactivation of the processes that were interrupted by the unavailability of appropriate self-objects in the second year of life . . . [by] being accurately empathized with by the analyst and analyzing failures in the analyst's self object functions . . ." (p. 101). Lithium is only incidental and serves to protect the treatment from disruption.

Loeb and Loeb contend, on the other hand, that "a *primary* increase in our patients' phallic instinctual drives *secondarily* overwhelmed the capacity of their egos to defend against these drives, and that this, in turn, resulted in the development of our patient's overt manic symptoms." Their treatment seeks to make the patient "consciously aware both of their previously unconscious phallic sexual thoughts and impulses, and of their defenses against them" so the inappropriate impulses can be counteracted with increased doses of lithium "to avoid overt manic episodes" (p. 877).

In the first formulation manic-depressive illness is a specific form of psychic defect in biologically vulnerable individuals that can be rectified through learning; in the second formulation it is an increase in specific instinctual drive (energy) that cannot be controlled without increasing a biologically active antagonist.

To complicate the matter we have had in analysis a patient whom we felt periodically experienced increases in instinctual drives, sometimes oral, sometimes anal, sometimes phallic, sometimes genital, occasioned at times by loss experiences, at times by nothing we could imagine. Such a patient suggests that our current formulations, in that they seek the chimera of the Abraham–Fenichel nosology—one disease process for one set of antecedent conditions—are too narrowly taken.

Conclusion

Having surveyed various attempts to account for depression, one of the earliest recorded of man's emotional afflictions, what can we safely conclude? Is depression a social, interpersonal, intrapsychic, neurophysiological, or biochemical phenomenon? Clearly a supraordinate theory must account for all the phenomena described, regardless of their origin. Fortunately we seem to be on the threshold of just such a formulation.

Wever (1979) presents a critical set of observations that may provide a beginning for organizing these disparate findings into an understandable and coherent whole. His work indicates that social and psychological cues, as well as environmental and physical conditions, can desynchronize the two independent oscillators (X and Y) and thereby set a depression or a mania in motion. Thus, cues of a purely physical nature (changes in light or darkness), cues of a purely social nature (changes in approval from others), cues of a purely psychological nature (changes in self-regard), and cues of a biochemical nature (changes in speed of transmission of nerve impulses) all may lead to oscillator desynchronization and hence to depression in a susceptible individual. This susceptibility may itself be determined by hereditary, psychogenic, or interpersonal factors, or by a combination of these.

We seem to be on the threshold of delineating a mechanism with an organic physiological substrate to explain how divergent causes from different levels of abstraction can lead to a single result: depression. We are now in a position to understand why affective illness does not occur in only one psychological typology or at fixation at only one level of psychosexual development, and why depressive patients may differ so greatly physiologically. In this view, any factor able to cause oscillator desynchronization will lead to a depressive or a manic episode, and different individuals are vulnerable on different levels of analysis.

Treatment of the illness, in this view, requires the physician to find a psychological, physical, or physiological method of resetting the circadian oscillator (the pacemaker) so that resynchronization can occur and symptoms terminate.

Although such a view is not shared by all (for a dissenting view, see Thase, Frank, and Kupfer, 1985), we do seem to be on the path of a truly multifactorial pathopsychophysiology of depression in which a vast variety of divergent causes can lead through a common physiological mechanism—oscillator desynchronization—to the same result. The modern psychiatrist must now integrate the functions of both the Asu and the Asipu of ancient Akkad into one person. The psychotherapist of the depressed patient must also be the physician; otherwise we will incorrectly use psychological methods in attempting to treat disorders originating at the cellular level, err in using biochemical methods in treating vulnerability to psychological loss, and fail to recognize a case in which both methods are necessary for proper treatment.

References

Abraham, K. (1911), Notes on the psycho-analytical investigation and treatment of manic-depressive insanity and allied conditions. In: *Selected Papers on Psycho-Analysis.* London: Hogarth Press, 1927, pp. 137–156.
——— (1924), A short study of the development of the libido, viewed in the light of mental disorders. In: *Selected Papers on Psycho-Analysis.* London: Hogarth Press, 1927, pp. 418–501.
Arieti, S. (1959), Manic-depressive psychosis. In: *American Handbook of Psychiatry,* ed. S. Arieti. Vol. 1. New York: Basic Books, pp. 419–490.
Beck, A. T. (1967), *Depression: Causes and Treatment.* Philadelphia: University of Pennsylvania Press.
Benedek, T. (1956), Toward the biology of the depressive constellation. *J. Amer. Psychoanal. Assn.,* 4:389–427.
Berger, P. A. (1978), Medical treatment of mental illness. *Science,* 200:974–982.
Berman, E., & Wolpert, E. A. (1987), Single Case Study. Intractable manic-depressive psychosis with rapid cycling in an 18-year-old woman successfully treated with electroconvulsive therapy. *J. Nerv. Ment. Dis.,* 175:236–239.
Bick, P. A. (1986), Seasonal major affective disorder. *Amer. J. Psychiat.,* 143:90–91.
Bunney, W. E., Jr. (1977), Panel report: The switch process in manic depressive psychosis. *Ann. Intern. Med.,* 87:319–335.
——— (1978), Psychopharmacology of the switch process in affective illness. In: *Psychopharmacology: A Generation of Progress,* ed. M. A. Lipton, A. DiMascio, & K. F. Killam. New York: Raven Press, pp. 1249–1259.
——— Davis, J. M. (1965), Norepinephrine in depressed reactions. *Arch. Gen. Psychiat.,* 13:483–494.
——— Goodwin, F. K., & Murphy, D. L. (1972), The "switch process" in manic depressive illness: III. Theoretical implications. *Arch. Gen. Psychiat.,* 27:312–317.
Cade, J. J. F. (1949), Lithium salts in the treatment of psychotic excitement. *Med. J. Austral.,* 36:319–352.

Cohen, M. B., Baker, G., Cohen, R. A., Fromm-Reichmann, F., & Weigart, E. V. (1954), An intensive study of twelve cases of manic depressive psychosis. *Psychiat.*, 17:103–137.

Davis, J. M. (1976), Overview: Maintenance therapy in psychiatry II: Affective disorders. *Amer. J. Psychiat.*, 133:1–13.

Dunner, D. L., & Fieve, R. R. (1974), Clinical factors in lithium carbonate prophylaxis failure. *Arch. Gen. Psychiat.*, 30:229–233.

Eastwood, M. R., Whitton, J. L., Kramer, P. M., & Peter, A. M. (1985), Infradian rhythms: A comparison of affective disorders and normal persons. *Arch. Gen. Psychiat.*, 42:295–299.

Englemann, W. A. (1973), Slowing down of circadian rhythms by lithium ions. *Zietschrift fur Naturforschung*, 28(c):733–736.

Fawcett, J., & Scheftner, W. A. (1985), Bipolar disorders and suicidal outcome. Abstract presented at American Psychiatric Association Annual Meeting, Dallas, Texas, May.

—— —— Clark, W., Hedeker, D., Gibbons, R., & Coryell, W. (1987), Clinical predictors of suicide in patients with major affective disorders: A controlled prospective study. *Amer. J. Psychiat.*, 144:35–40.

Fenichel, O. (1945), *The Psychoanalytic Theory of Neurosis.* New York: Norton.

Freud, S. (1895), Project for a scientific psychology. *Standard Edition,* 1:283–397. London: Hogarth Press, 1966.

—— (1896), Further remarks on the neuro-psychoses of defense. *Standard Edition,* 3:159–185. London: Hogarth Press, 1962.

—— (1898), Sexuality in the etiology of the neuroses. *Standard Edition,* 3:261–285. London: Hogarth Press, 1962.

—— (1910), The psycho-analytic view of psychogenic disturbance of vision. *Standard Edition,* 11:209–218. London: Hogarth Press, 1957.

—— (1910), "Wild" psycho-analysis. *Standard Edition,* 11:220–227. London: Hogarth Press, 1957.

—— (1912), Contributions to a discussion on masturbation. *Standard Edition,* 12:241–254. London: Hogarth Press, 1958.

—— (1914), On narcissism: An introduction. *Standard Edition,* 14:69–102. London: Hogarth Press, 1957.

—— (1916–1917), Introductory lectures on psycho-analysis. *Standard Edition,* 15–16. London: Hogarth Press, 1963.

—— (1917), Mourning and melancholia. *Standard Edition,* 14:243–258. London: Hogarth Press, 1957.

—— (1921), Group psychology and the analysis of the ego. *Standard Edition,* 18:69–143. London: Hogarth Press, 1955.

—— (1923), The ego and the id. *Standard Edition,* 19:12–66. London: Hogarth Press, 1961.

—— (1925), An autobiographical study. *Standard Edition,* 20:3–74. London: Hogarth Press, 1959.

—— (1926), Inhibitions, symptoms and anxiety. *Standard Edition,* 20:77–174. London: Hogarth Press, 1959.

Galatzer-Levy, R. M. (1988), Manic-depressive illness: Analytic experiences and a hypothesis. In: *Function in Self and Progress in Self Psychology, Vol. 3,* ed. A. Goldberg. New York: International Universities Press, pp. 87–102.

Gibson, R. W., Cohen, M. D., & Cohen, R. A. (1959), On the dynamics of the manic depressive personality. *Amer. J. Psychiat.*, 115:1101–1107.

Gjessing, R. (1938), Disturbances of somatic functions in catatonia with a periodic course and their compensation. *J. Ment. Sci.*, 84:608–615.

————— Gjessing, L. (1961), Some main trends in the clinical aspects of periodic catatonia. *Acta Psychiatr. Scand.*, 37:1–13.

Hanna, S. M., Jenner, F. A., Pearson, I. B., Sampson, G. A., & Thompson, E. A. (1972), The therapeutic effect of lithium carbonate on a patient with a forty-eight hour periodic psychosis. *Brit. J. Psychiat.*, 121:271–280.

Hartmann, E. (1968), Longitudinal studies of sleep and dream patterns in manic-depressive patients. *Arch. Gen. Psychiat.*, 19:312–329.

Jacobson, J. (1965), The hypomanic alert: A program designed for greater therapeutic control. *Amer. J. Psychiat.*, 122:295–299.

Janowsky, D., El-Yousel, M., Davis, J. M., & Sekerice, H. J. (1972), A cholinergic-adrenergic hypothesis of mania and depression. *Lancet*, 2:632–635.

Jenner, F. A., Gjessing, L. R., Cox, J. R., Davies-Jones, A., Hullin, R. P., & Hanna, S. M. (1967), A manic depressive psychotic with a persistent forty-eight hour cycle. *Brit. J. Psychiat.*, 113:895–910.

Johnsson, A., Engelmann, W., Pflug, B., & Klemke, W. (1980), Influence of lithium ions on human circadian rhythms. *Zeitschrift für Naturforchung*, 35(c):503–507.

————— ————— ————— ————— (1982), Period lengthening of circadian rhythms in humans by lithium carbonate: A prophylactic for depressive disorders. *Internat. J. Chronobiol.*, 8:129–147.

Kielholz, P., Terzans, S., Gatspar, M., & Adams, C. (1982), Combined antidepressive infusion therapy. *Directions in Psychiatry*, 2(16):1–8.

Kleitman, N. (1963), *Sleep and Wakefulness*. Chicago: University of Chicago Press.

Klerman, G. L., Weissman, M. M., Rounsaville, B. J., & Chevron, E. S. (1984), *Interpersonal Psychotherapy of Depression*. New York: Basic Books.

Kraepelin, E. (1921), *Manic Depressive Insanity and Paranoia*. London: Livingstone.

Kripke, D. F., Mullaney, D. J., Atkinson, M., & Wolf, S. (1978), Circadian rhythm disorders in manic-depressives. *Biol. Psychiat.*, 13:335–351.

Lange, J. (1928), Die endogenen and reaktiven Germutserkrank Heiten und die manish-depressive Konstitution: II. In: *Handbuch Der Geisteskrank Heiten* (VI spez Teil 2), ed. O. Bumke. Berlin: Springer.

Leonhard, K., Korff, I., & Shulz, H. (1962), Die Tempermente in den Famielien der monopolaren und bipolaren phasichen Psychosen. *Psychiat. Neurol.*, 143:416–434.

Levitan, H. (1973), Dreams preceding hypomania. *Internat. J. Psychoanal. Psychother.*, 1:50–61.

Lewin, B. D. (1950), *The Psychoanalysis of Elation*. New York: Norton.

Lewis, J. L., & Winokur, G. (1982), The induction of mania: A natural history study with controls. *Arch. Gen. Psychiat.*, 39:303–306.

Lewy, A. J., Kern, A. A., Rosenthal, N. D., & Wehr, T. (1982), Bright artificial light treatment of a manic-depressive patient with a seasonal mood cycle. *Amer. J. Psychiat.*, 139:1496–1498.

Loeb, F. F., Jr., & Loeb, L. R. (1987), Psychoanalytic observations on the effect of lithium on manic attacks. *J. Amer. Psychoanal. Assn.*, 35:877–902.

Moore, R. Y., & Eichler, V. R. (1976), Central neural mechanisms in diurnal rhythm regulation and neuroendocrine responses to light. *Psychoneuroendocrinol.*, 1:265–279.

Moore-Ede, M., Sulzman, C., & Fuller, C. (1982), *The Clocks That Time Us.* Cambridge: Harvard University Press.

Mueller, P., & Wolpert, E. A. (1974), Lithium carbonate in the treatment of manic depressive disorders: A follow-up study. *Ill. Med. J.*, 145:505–511.

Oppenheim, G. (1982), Drug-induced rapid cycling: Possible outcomes and management. *Amer. J. Psychiat.*, 139:939–941.

Ostrow, D. G., Pandey, G. N., Davis, J. M., Chang, S., & Tosteson, D. C. (1977), Clinical study of lithium transport: A defect of phloretin-sensitive lithium transport in bipolar illness. *Sci. Proc. Amer. Psychiat. Soc.*, 130:152–153.

———— ———— ———— Hurt, S. W., & Tosteson, D. C. (1978), A heritable disorder of lithium transport in the red blood cells of a subpopulation of manic patients. *Amer. J. Psychiat.*, 135:1070–1078.

Pandey, G. N., Davis, J. M., & Ostrow, D. G. (1977), Lithium transport in red blood cells of manic-depressive patients. *Clin. & Pharmaceut. Therapeut.*, 21:113–114.

———— Ostrow, D. G., Haas, M., Dorus, E., Casper, R. C., & Davis, J. M. (1977), Abnormal lithium and sodium transport in erythrocytes of a manic patient and some members of his family. *Proc. Nat. Acad. Sci.*, 74:3607–3611.

Pao, P.-N. (1968), On manic depressive psychosis: A study of the transition of states. *J. Amer. Psychoanal. Assn.*, 16:809–832.

———— (1971), Elation, hypomania, and mania. *J. Amer. Psychoanal. Assn.*, 19:787–798.

Paschalis, C., Pavlou, A., & Papadimitriou, A. (1980), A stepped up forty-eight hour manic depressive cycle. *Brit. J. Psychiat.*, 137:332–336.

Pflug, B. (1984), Sleep deprivation in the treatment of depression. *Directions in Psychiatry*, 4:1–8.

———— Tolle, R. (1971), Disturbance of the 24 hour rhythm in endogenous depression and the treatment of endogenous depression by sleep deprivation. *Internat. Pharmacopsychiat.*, 6:187–196.

Richelson, E., & El-Fakahany, E. (1980), Changes in the sensitivity of receptors for neurotransmitters and the actions of some psychotherapeutic drugs. *Mayo Clin. Proc.*, 57:576–582.

Ritter, E. (1965), Magical expert (= Asipu) and Physician (= Asu): Notes on two complementary professions in Babylonian medicine. In: *Studies in Honor of Benno Landsberger on His Seventy-Fifth Birthday*. Chicago: University of Chicago Press, pp. 299–321.

———— Kinnier Wilson, J. V. (1980), Prescription for an anxiety state: A Study of Bam 234. *J. Anatolian Studies*, 30:23–30.

Rosenthal, N. E., Sack, D. A., Gillin, J. C., Lewy, A. J., Goodwin, F. K., Davenport, Y., Mueller, D. S., Newsome, D. A., & Wehr, T. R. (1984), Seasonal affective disorder: A description of the syndrome and preliminary findings with light therapy. *Arch. Gen. Psychiat.*, 41:72–80.

Roy-Byrne, P. P., Joffe, R. T., Uhde, T. W., & Post, R. M. (1984), Approaches to the evaluation and treatment of rapid cycling affective illness. *Brit. J. Psychiat.*, 145:543–550.

Schildkraut, J. J. (1965), The catecholamine hypothesis of affective disorders: A review of supporting evidence. *Amer. J. Psychiat.*, 122:509–522.

Schou, M. (1968), Special review of lithium in psychiatric therapy and prophylaxis. *J. Psychiat. Res.*, 6:67–95.

Schwartz, W. J., & Gainer, H. (1981), Localization of the biological clock in the brain. *JAMA*, 246:681.

Shaughnessy, R., Greene, S. C., Pandey, G. N., & Dorus, F. (1985), Red cell lithium transport and affective disorders in a multigeneration pedigree: Evidence for genetic transmission of affective disorders. *Biol. Psychiat.*, 20:451–460.

Thase, A. D., Frank, E., & Kupfer, D. J. (1985), Biological processes in major depression. In: *Handbook of Depression. Treatment Assessment and Research.* Homewood, IL: Dorsey Press, pp. 816–913.

Vogel, G. W., Traub, A. C., & Ben-Horin, P. (1968), REM deprivation: II. The effects of depressed patients. *Arch. Gen. Psychiat.*, 18:301–311.

Wehr, T. A., & Goodwin, F. K. (1983), *Circadian Rhythms in Psychiatry.* Pacific Grove, Calif.: Boxwood Press.

——— Wirz-Justice, A., Goodwin, F. K., Duncan, W., & Gillin, J. C. (1979), Phase advance of the circadian sleep-wake cycle as an antidepressant. *Science*, 206:710–713.

Wever, R. (1979), *The Circadian System of Man.* New York: Springer Verlag.

Wolff, E. A., Putnam, F. W., & Post, R. M. (1985), Motor activity and affective illness: The relationship of amplitude and temporal distribution to changes in affective state. *Arch. Gen. Psychiat.*, 42:288–294.

Wolpert, E. A. (1960), Studies in psychophysiology of dreams: II. An electromyographic study of dreaming. *Arch. Gen. Psychiat.*, 3:602–607.

——— (1975), Manic depressive illness as an actual neurosis. In: *Depression and Human Existence*, ed. E. J. Anthony & T. Benedek. Boston: Little, Brown, pp. 199–221.

——— (1977), Nontoxic hyperlithemia in impending mania. *Amer. J. Psychiat.*, 134:580–582.

——— (1980), On the nature of manic depressive illness. In: *The Course of Life: Psychoanalytic Contributions Towards Understanding Personality Development: Vol. III. Adulthood and the Aging Process*, ed. S. I. Greenspan & G. Pollock. Washington, D.C.: NIMH, pp. 443–452.

——— (1988), Combined therapies for depression and mania. In: *Depression and Mania*, ed. A. Georgotas & R. Cancro. New York: Elsevier, pp. 538–548.

——— Goldberg, J., & Harrow, M. (1990), Rapid cycling in bipolar and unipolar affective disorders. *Amer. J. Psychiat.*, 147:6, 425–728.

——— Mueller, P. (1969), Lithium carbonate in the treatment of manic-depressive disorders. *Arch. Gen. Psychiat.*, 21:155–159.

15

The Contribution of the Concept of Self Representation/Object Representation Differentiation to the Understanding of the Schizophrenias

CLARENCE G. SCHULZ, M.D.

This chapter presents a developmental model to facilitate the understanding of clinical phenomena in psychotic patients, with particular reference to failure of self representation/object representation differentiation. In addition to delineating clinical symptoms and signs as derivatives of the failure of differentiation of self and object, I discuss some treatment implications and the research potential for utilizing these concepts. A simple example graphically illustrates fusion: two patients were at the drinking fountain; the first patient leaned over drinking water, while the second patient stood by swallowing.

The earliest reference to fusion is by Tausk (1933) when, in discussing a symptom in schizophrenia, he presented the concept "loss of ego boundaries." As a result of the loss of ego boundaries, the patient thought others could read his mind, know his thoughts, and had no sense of a separate, private psychical boundary.

Federn, presenting formulations that were in contrast to those of Freud, thought psychosis was not due to an enrichment of ego cathexis at the expense of object libido, but rather was due to an impoverishment of ego cathexis. Referring to schizophrenias, Federn (1952) states: "The disease begins with an impairment of ego cathexis; the ego boundary, in particular, can no longer be held cathected to its normal extent" (p. 211).

Jacobson's (1954) metapsychological description is clear:

The baby's wish for oneness with the mother, founded on fantasies of oral incorporation of the love object, will easily bring about refusions between self- and love-object image whenever the child experiences gratifications, physical contact, and closeness with the mother. Evidently, such experiences of merging with the love object are always connected with a temporary weakening of the function of perception—i.e., of the awakening sense of reality—and with a return to the earlier, undifferentiated state [p. 242].

In the same article Jacobson acknowledges Hartmann's contribution to the term *self-representations*. "In a previous paper on depression I introduced for the better metapsychological understanding of such preoedipal, primitive identifications the term 'self-representations,' which Hartmann had also suggested. This term—analogous to the term object-representations—refers to our mental concept of the self; i.e., to the unconscious and preconscious images of our body self and of our own personality" (p. 242).

Mahler's (1968) work on individuation and differentiation is fundamental to understanding the concepts to be presented. In describing the pathological outcome she said: "In consequence, the intrapsychic representational world contained no clear boundaries between self and object—the boundaries between ego and id remained deficient and so did the boundaries and connections between the intersystemic parts of the ego" (p. 26).

In a subsequent work (1971), she elaborated various phases and subphases in human development that are pertinent to self representation/object representation differentiation. "Disturbances during the rapprochement subphase are likely to reappear in much more definite and individually different forms during the final phase of that process in which a unified self representation should become demarcated from a blended and integrated object representation" (p. 413).

Finally, Kernberg (1970, p. 810) has described self–object fusion as the distinctive aspect to differentiate psychosis from the borderline states. In Kernberg's descriptions, borderline patients and psychotic patients might both show regressive phenomena and primitive defenses such as splitting, denial, and projection, but the characteristic difference is in the degree of self–object differentiation and fusion. While I am not in complete agreement in that I think many severe borderlines show marked defects in differentiation, nonetheless, he does underscore the importance of fusion in severe psychopathology.

While presenting a model of psychopathology, we must be clear in our understanding that we are not necessarily talking about the *etiology* of schizophrenia. We are concerned with possible dynamic factors which could account for some of the symptoms and signs as well as provide a framework of conceptualizing treatment intervention. Constitutional biogenetic factors as well as family dynamic factors of importance in etiology, are perhaps interacting in some way that eventuates in schizophrenic disorders. Again we might be dealing with schizophrenias of varying etiology and composition that show some superficial similarities in terms of the commonality of symptoms. The developmental model is here being presented for its practical value in providing a road map of the clinical territory in order to help us find our way. A model, although scientifically unproven, may still be useful.

Schematic Outline of Development to the Point of Self Representation Differentiation from Object Representation

The following outline is in no sense comprehensive but is purposely simplified in order to provide a schema for applying developmental concepts to the phenomenology of signs and symptoms in schizophrenia.

To begin with, the biological separation of the infant organism from the mother occurs with the cutting of the cord and the infant's ability to obtain oxygen under its own power. The comparable psychological individuation is not achieved until about three years later.

It is postulated that during the first three months of life the infant has no psychological awareness of there being a difference between inside and outside or self and other. Instead,

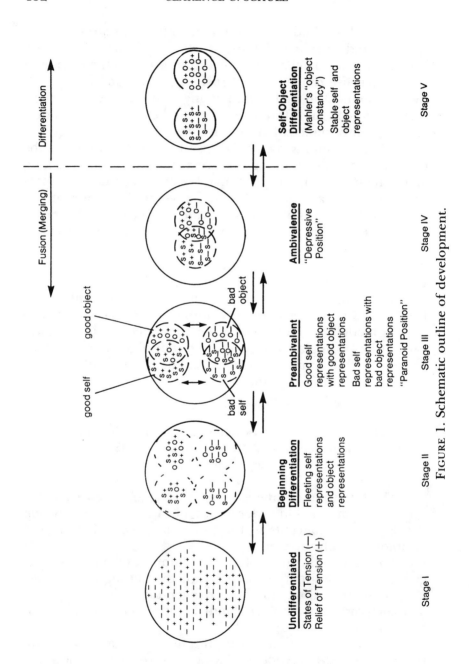

FIGURE 1. Schematic outline of development.

there are various states of tension and relief from tension occurring within the infant's experience. There occur dysequili-
bria as needs occur and a return to equilibrium when needs are
satisfied. During these first three months it is as though the
infant is at one with the surroundings. This is schematized in
Stage I of Figure 1. Stage I has a circle that is to represent the
scope of the infant's psychological being. This is an intrapsychic
model illustrating experiences of tension and relief. As Burnham, Gladstone, and Gibson (1969, p. 17) quote William James
(1890), "it is a blooming, buzzing confusion." The pluses in
this experience represent the "good," gratifying, and satisfying
experience, and the minuses indicate the "bad," dysjunctive
tensions of the experience.

With neurological maturation and with the experience of
frustration and gratification, glimpses of a sense of separateness
of self from other begin to develop after the first three months.
There is still a tendency toward an undifferentiated state, but
this is interrupted with periods of tension and need which are
then satisfied; the separation of inside and outside begins to
take place, contributing to the beginning delineation of something outside of self. The positive, gratifying, and satisfying self
experiences tend to be connected with a sense of a positive,
loving, and tension-reducing object. Similarly, the dysjunctive,
frustrating, and nongratifying experiences of tension experienced in the self tend to be related to a comparably negative
object. This shift from a diffuse nonobject world to the beginning glimpses of the formation of differentiation of self from
object is illustrated in Stage II of Figure 1.

In this Stage II, clusters of S+ reflect the good feelings of
self, and clusters of O+ represent the early need-satisfying
representations of the object within the psychological experience. Similarly, the clusters of S− equal the negative experiences of self, and the clusters of O− represent the negative
associated object experience.

Stage III represents the progression from a stage of merging a positive, integrated self and object experience to a somewhat unstable sense of self beginning to differentiate from an
object. The relationship of the positive sense of self representation with the positive experience of an object representation

and a comparable negative sense of self with a negative object representation occurs. It is to be emphasized that these experiences of separateness move back and forth from a sense of merging to a sense of fleeting differentiation. There are no clear-cut boundaries of self and other, and probably there is nothing that can be defined as reality testing at this point. All experiences would seem to revolve around the infant as the center of its universe, in terms of its perception of this experience. There would be the tendency to relate everything that one experiences as connected with oneself. Feelings of omnipotence associated with successful gratification would alternate with an opposite sense of total helplessness, associated with a sense of impotence and frustration. This concept has important clinical relevance.

There is a possibility for terminological confusion with Mahler's concepts in the way I present this model. She uses *differentiation* as an early subphase, while I will be using this term to convey the final achievement of self representation/ object representation differentiation. In addition, she uses the term *object constancy* to refer to her final subphase at 25 months. I will also speak of object constancy as having been completed by about 33 months, but conceive of the beginning of object constancy as coinciding with the "stranger anxiety" occurring usually at about 8 months. Fraiberg (1969) provides an excellent summary of the conceptual terminology and development in her article "Libidinal Object Constancy and Mental Representation."

An important feature of this period from 3 to 6 months is the inability to integrate the positive sense of self with the negative self and the comparable lack of integration of the positively perceived object with the negative object. It is as though these are two separate experiences of self and two separate representations of the object. This opposition is represented in the figure by divergent arrows. The lack of integration of positive and negative constitutes "splitting." It becomes the prototype for a subsequent defense mechanism prominent in both paranoid schizophrenic phenomena and in borderline patients. Along with this splitting occurs the tendency toward projection of the negative aspects of oneself onto the object as a way of ridding the self of negative aggressive percepts. For conceptual clarity, I suggest that when speaking of development we use the term *preambivalence* and then reserve the term *splitting* for the defensive measure that utilizes the mechanisms of the preambivalent phase of normal development.

Rapaport (1951), following Freud's concept, postulated that the earliest thought occurred in the form of hallucination in the absence of or as a result of delay in gratification. Thus, if the infant experiences hunger and the nipple is not forthcoming during this period of delay, the infant will "hallucinate" the nipple. Thus, hallucinations become an early form of thinking related to lack of object gratification. As an extension of this, one can see that delusions would be related to the lack of reality testing and the sense of egocentricity that would accompany early thinking phenomena.

At about the age of 6 months, the infant, again through the process of further maturation and development, experiences the ability to integrate positive and negative attitudes toward the object and thus experiences both good and bad feelings toward one object. The infant is also able to integrate both good and bad feelings toward the self into one self. At this point, the infant becomes ambivalent instead of splitting and has achieved what Klein has referred to as the "depressive position" (1955, p. 21). At the point of integrating good and bad, the infant is capable of experiencing depression rather than fragmentation in response to the loss of an object. Again, this is not achieved once and for all, but there is a shift back and forth between integration and splitting (preambivalence) as represented in Stage IV. Schafer (1973, p. 158), in order to define terms more precisely and avoid the vagueness of "self," proposes the terms *representational differentiation* and *representational cohesion*. One can see the immediate relationship between the latter term and Kohut's (1971) "cohesive self." In addition to splitting appearing as a separation of good and bad, such as occurs by thinking of one parent as good and another as bad, I expanded the concept of splitting to include all-or-none phenomena or an approach in the form of extreme attitudes (Schulz, 1980). Hartmann (1953) emphasized the importance of the impairment of neutralization as a fundamental feature of the ego disorder in schizophrenia. Splitting is accompanied by a projection or riddance of intolerable aggressive aspects of the self. Facilitating integration of opposite attitudes, as well as specific "good" and "bad" aspects of self and object to bring about representational cohesion, must be connected with ego functions of neutralization. Ego defense or countercathexis must assist in the deaggressivization and delibidinization to facilitate integration.

Lampl-de Groot (1963) provides possible maternal participation with the child that might prevent representational differentiation:

> In schizophrenic patients we often observe representations of parts of their own bodies as being separate from other parts, as well as a fusion of the boundaries between the self and the object-world. In other words, there is a kernel of confusion between self-representations and object-representations, and the need to be "one" with the mother cannot be adequately dealt with. A mother, who, clinging to the child, is unable to let him develop his own personality . . . will promote the arrest of the child's ego-development at this point. A very disturbed mother, confused, egocentric, distracted, or rapidly changing from love to hate, does not provide the child with a stable image to incorporate. As a consequence, the development of delineated object-representations will be defective. The confusion between self and object influences the function of reality-testing. A number of other ego-functions may be drawn into this pathological process as well. The development of motor-actions is dependent upon bodily sensations, including passively experienced movements. A disturbed, unloving mother is unable to hold and to carry around her baby with loving attention. . . . This can lead to a lack of satisfaction in the motor sphere, resulting in a poor development of motility in the child [pp. 7–8].

Since differentiation and integration proceed hand in hand (Searles, 1959), one can see that the development of secondary process thinking is an important feature in understanding schizophrenic symptoms and signs. For example, with the failure to develop sublimations and high levels of defenses, the patient is more apt to be dealing with the primitive defenses mentioned above (denial, projection, and splitting) and to be exhibiting phenomena that relate to unneutralized aggression. Consequently, one sees impulsivity and an inability to delay sometimes culminating in expressions of violence or a catatonic paralysis which prevents almost all action.

In Stage IV, the diagram depicts the integration of good and bad self into one sense of self (represented by $S+$ and $S-$) as almost differentiated from a good and bad object representation integrated into one object (represented by $O+$ and $O-$). Subsequently, further movements back and forth with the fusion or merging of self with object lead to the eventual differentiation of self from object.

In this final Stage V, it is to be noted that there are firm boundaries surrounding the sense of self and object to indicate their relative permanent establishment, as opposed to the dashed and dotted lines of earlier senses of self showing their tendency toward instability. That is not to say that the self and object are incapable of becoming fused, but fusion takes place more in "the service of the ego," and in any case such fusion would be quite transient, with a very firm sense of identity and separateness being retained. This is achieved at about the period of 33 months of life and represents the completion of the psychological birth of the infant from the mother.

It is postulated that in patients vulnerable to schizophrenia and psychotic experience there is no clear-cut establishment of a self representation as distinct from an object representation. Furthermore, a vulnerability to the experience of fusion of self representation with object representation occurs as there is an approach of intimacy or closeness in the psychological experience with the object. This, then, presents the schizophrenic patient with the "need–fear dilemma," as described by Burnham et al. (1969). It is as though the person needs an object and cannot be separate or unattached and at the same time is threatened with the fear of engulfment or merging due to the lack of differentiation. As one patient put it, "I have the urge to merge." This observation brings up the question of why the infant can merge and fuse, while adult psychotic patients, by contrast, experience aversion to fusion. It must be that, in the latter, development has proceeded far enough to establish a beginning, although fragile, sense of self-identity which is then threatened via fusion. In other words, much of what we see as the symptomatology of schizophrenia can be explained on the basis of this model. Either the person attempts to prevent the fusion that might occur or fails to maintain a sense of identity or separateness of self when threatened by the loss of boundaries.

Let us see how these concepts can be applied clinically in understanding how a patient might use afferent body stimuli to establish a sense of self-identity. It is to be remembered that Freud (1923, p. 27) spoke of the first ego (self) as a body ego (body self); that is, the infant first knows itself through the experience of its body. Hence, we help to define ourselves by stimuli that impinge upon our somatic organism. If I awaken in the morning, I know that I exist by feeling my joints and muscles, touching the bedcovers, or seeing light, or by some peripheral stimulus input. In a comparable way, schizophrenic patients who are threatened with a loss of their sense of self might attempt to define a body boundary through some stimulus input, such as head banging, scratching, staring in the mirror at themselves for long periods of time, overeating or undereating to feel their stomach sensations, shouting to hear themselves, smoking to produce cough or bronchitis, cutting or burning themselves, scratching themselves, picking at their skin, jiggling their feet or appendages, hugging themselves, taking hot and cold showers. Through these or a variety of other peripheral stimuli they attempt to define themselves as separate. It is noteworthy that this occurs particularly at a time when the person is threatened in the form of the loss of self through closeness resulting from the merging of self and object representation.

In a comparable way, the schizophrenic patient's "negativism" serves as a way of self-definition. We know that the child's use of no is important in enhancing self-definition during normal development. Here the patient seems compulsively, "willfully," and methodically to take an oppositional stance to whatever the therapist or others adopt as a position. It does not matter what the nature of the particular battleground is; whether it is over the refusal of medications, having an interview, conforming to the regulations of the unit, or "cooperating with psychotherapy," the form is one of oppositional distance-producing self-definition. If this negativism can engender anger or a comparable kind of counteropposition in the staff, it will further enhance the production of a type of temporary definition and differentiation that must substitute for the lack of a more fundamental sense of differentiation.

Splitting as a defense does not necessarily mean that the patient is "fixated" prior to 6 months. Splitting is a primitve type of defense that occurs, especially along with denial and projection, as a way of dealing with hostile, aggressive, negative feelings and attributing these to an external source. One can readily see how projection is more apt to occur when there tend to be fusion and lack of differentiation resulting in a readiness to attribute to the object aspects that belong to the self. Masterson (1976) and Mahler, Pine, and Bergman (1975) specifically locate the developmental difficulties of the borderline patient during the rapprochement subphase occurring between 15 and 25 months.

Another important feature of this developmental schema is the beginning of object constancy. Somewhere around 6 to 8 months, following the integration of positive and negative attitudes into one ambivalent object, the infant moves on to establish more clearly the representation of the mother as herself—separate from other objects. Prior to this, in early infancy, the infant can be handed from one person to another without too much distress, as long as the infant is not becoming hungry or is not made anxious in some way by the person caring for the infant. However, with the beginning of the recognition of the mother as separate from others, there is a distinct change described as "stranger anxiety." With the appearance of this phenomenon, handing the infant over to someone who is an unfamiliar object immediately elicits cries of distress from the infant. Also, at this time the infant does not want to have its mother out of its sight and tends to become upset if the mother leaves the room. However, at a somewhat later stage, the infant begins to be able to hold the memory or image of the mother within its experience so that the mother can be in the next room running the vacuum cleaner without upsetting the infant. Gradually, the infant is able to retain a sense of the mother in the absence of the actual mother, and this development of object constancy is probably complete along with the final mature differentiation of its self representation from the object representation at about 33 months. This has implications for disruption and discontinuity in relationships for the schizophrenic patient. If we go back to the period of development before ambivalence, the comparable level for the patient would indicate an inability to experience depression on separation from another person. Instead, the patient seems to show confusion, disorganization, or paranoid projection. As improvement takes place, the patient shows depression in his response to interruption. This is consistent with the so-called "postpsychotic depression."

Clinically this shift manifests itself as a paranoid patient becomes depressed instead of appearing confused, disorganized, or paranoid when the therapist is absent or goes on vacation. Continuing with this developmental schema, one sees that patients are sometimes unable to carry forth an image of the therapist outside of the actual session. Patients who have this tenuous sense of objectification of the therapist might resort to calling their therapists at various times between sessions to verify appointments or might have an auditory hallucination of the therapist's voice when the patient is lonely. Later on a patient will be able not only to hold the therapist's image within recall but, even in the absence of the therapist, be able to carry on a fantasy session with a clear-cut anticipation of the therapist's attitudes and responses to various issues which would occur in such a fantasied interview.

Our topic centers on self–object differentiation, but I do not want to propose that as the explanation for everything. Other parallel, developmental aspects occurring at the same time must be emphasized. For example, the development of narcissistic aspects of the self representations in the infant would be an important feature. The importance of ego and superego identification in the maintenance of self representations as well as other aspects of personality must be included. Another feature would be the integration and differentiation that go on within the structural development of personality. The differentiation of id, ego, and superego and the integration of the ego with its functions are fundamental. Here the capacity to shift from primary process thinking to secondary process thinking is important but too complex to be gone into at this time, except to say that we need to be cognizant of the differences between primary and secondary process in giving a more comprehensive view of psychotic phenomena. The role of anxiety is crucial. One can think of the schizophrenic patient as being ill-equipped to deal with the relatively overwhelming amount of anxiety encountered in the gratification of his needs. Here the patient is unable to utilize the ordinary defensive management of anxiety and attempts the use of a variety of measures of primitive defenses or then more advanced defenses; then comes the failure of defense along with disintegration, a return to earlier levels, and the infusion of primary-process experience, such as one ordinarily experiences only in one's dreams. However, we must also keep in mind that the patient can and does show continued but variable preservation of competent functions. This is important in the treatment approach that attempts to address itself both to the patient's capabilities as well as his disabilities. I think it might be a mistake at this time in our knowledge from clinical observation and theoretical construction to attribute specificity to one or another feature among those mentioned as having specific importance or priority in the psychodynamics of schizophrenia. In the next section, I elucidate clinical phenomena that seem particularly related to the failure of self and object differentiation.

Clinical Signs and Symptom Manifestations Related to Fusion

I have given some examples relating to issues of self-stimulation in order to obtain body–self definition, as well as the role of negativism in an attempt at differentiation. While negativism has often been emphasized from the vantage of avoiding fusion, it is rarely recognized as a form of relatedness. The negativistic patient does not simply ignore the other person; he retains a relationship that will insure prevention of fusion. I have elsewhere referred to this as "warmth by friction" (Schulz and Kilgalen, 1969). Vulnerability to separation anxiety due to the lack of object constancy has already been mentioned. These patients show regressive responses of confusion, disorganization, or paranoid orientation instead of affective experiences of grief, anger, or sadness in response to separation from another. In fact, one of the hallmarks of improvement with the psychotic patient is a progression from the disorganized or paranoid response to the experience of affective reaction to separation or loss.

I now give examples from additional categories of phenomena representing fusion and also mention the polar opposite of differentiation in order to provide a contrasting perspective. When considering examples in these various categories, we must keep in mind that it is not the single occurrence of a phenomenon that is diagnostic but, rather, the total pattern of these responses that often appear in combination.

Impaired Ability to See Oneself as Separate from Surroundings

The patient may feel as though his thoughts are controlled by forces outside of himself. He may also feel that people imitate his movements or that he in turn influences the actions of others. Ordinary environmental stimuli become personalized with delusions of reference, or outside events have a direct message or connection with the patient's activities or thoughts. The patient becomes attentive to and preoccupied with noticing extraneous events. He may take cues from sounds, such as airplanes flying overhead, and conclude that he should initiate or cease a certain action. These patients often experience the television or newspaper as referring directly to them or think that a song on the radio is being played specifically for them. When groups of people at some distance are talking or laughing, the patient interprets this as referring to himself. The opposite end of this fusion attitude is the capacity to see oneself as separate from the surroundings.

Overreaction to Loss of Body Parts

Quite regressed patients may ingest their feces, urine, and hair in order not to let go of what has been part of their bodies. They may also in a similar way save menstrual pads, refuse to have their fingernails trimmed, or even refuse to provide samples of blood for laboratory examination. Patients not reflecting fusion simply accept the loss as a natural function.

Gender Identity Confusion

There may be marked confusion about whether one is male or female or whether the voice or certain parts of the body are of the opposite sex. These patients make frequent slips of the tongue and mix the gender pronouns. A female patient may be afraid to get close to men or be attracted to a man, because she may then become a man. A differentiated opposite attitude is a stable sense of gender identity, accompanied by the ability to identify with aspects of the opposite sex.

Patient's Experience Believed to Be the Experience of the Other Person

Here there is a lack of feeling of body or mental privacy. The patient may show delusions of mind reading or thought transmission or experience his thoughts being broadcast. One patient was unable to tell whether or not she affected the television set by causing a change of the scene when she entered the room. The patient is reluctant to reveal secrets and thoughts as a way of keeping some separateness from the therapist. Such patients may be silent out of the belief that the therapist can read the patient's mind in the first place, and it is superfluous to speak out one's thoughts. The polar opposite representing differentiation is a sense of privacy of body and mental experience. One recognizes that one's feelings or attitudes might be revealed through facial or body gestures, which are different from reading one's mind.

Pretransference Projective Phenomena

Here the patient often is involved in intense prejudicial attitudes with marked projection evident immediately upon meeting the therapist or any new person. These are aspects of oneself that are projected onto the other, rather than a higher level transference attitude which comes later in the developmental scheme representing the phenomena of differentiation. This often accounts for patients who are psychotic, abruptly terminating an interview after only a few seconds.

Inability to Have Close or Emotionally Intensive Relationships or Has Many Superficial Relationships

These people are unable to engage in any emotional attachment or commitment to one person out of the fear of engulfment and fusion. It may often be experienced as a sense of surrender or being controlled by the other person. We see repeated sequences of approach and retreat in relationships, particularly within the therapeutic setting. The opposite pole representing differentiation is the capacity for durable intimate relationships which are highly valued.

Misidentification of Self or Others

Such patients may have delusional attitudes, feeling that others are in disguise or masquerading or being represented by doubles, as well as misidentifying themselves as being someone other than who they actually are. Sometimes these patients object to being categorized as a member of the group, since they feel they will be lost within the group. The opposite pole is a clear conception of oneself and others with a fairly consistent and durable sense of identity.

Agreement, Consensus, or Closeness with the Therapist Associated with Engulfment, a Fear of Being Swallowed Up, or a Negativistic Reaction

One sees here the sequence of movement toward the therapist, which may be as mild as an understanding of the patient's communication on the part of the therapist leading to anxiety about fusion and counterreactions of negativism, paranoid behavior, or withdrawal. The opposite is the ability to allow such closeness with the therapist leading to an enhancement of the sense of self-identity.

Patient Oversensitive to Intrusive Aspects of the Therapeutic Situation

Here the patient may actually physically avoid meeting with the therapist or be involved with intense and prolonged secretiveness in relation to the therapist. The opposite end, reflecting differentiation, is the ready ability to disclose one's thoughts and feelings, even though experiencing anxiety and guilt or shame.

Inability to Agree or Disagree with the Therapist in a Discriminatory Way

The patient threatened by fusion may disagree with everything the therapist says or show excessive compliance. There is an absence of listening, weighing, and deciding things independently on their merits. The patient may even show imitations of the therapist's movements in an automatic compliance. The opposite is the ability to be autonomous about expressing one's opinions to the therapist and to others, and also the ability to listen in a discriminatory way.

Patient Confuses Role with That of the Therapist

Here the patient may begin to interview the therapist or ask questions in the manner of the therapist, or he may sit in the therapist's chair in the office. The differentiated patient can collaborate with the therapist and retain a clear delineation of roles.

Countertransference Fusion of Patient and Therapist

Searles (1976) placed a great deal of emphasis on the countertransference fusion aspect of the treatment experience with these patients. This is often difficult to detect, but symbiotic phenomena on the part of the therapist show as slips of the tongue that mix up the patient and the doctor or affects that become vaguely and diffusely referable to either party when discussing the treatment situation. An example given by one resident in supervision was her experience of having seen a quite regressed patient and, upon termination of this session, was looking through her mail. When going down the list alphabetically to find her name in the communication from her medical school, she looked under the letter of the patient's name rather than her own. Another therapist, while speaking with a patient who had gone to law school, asked the patient if a certain event happened when he was in medical school. The opposite representation of differentiation is the absence of symbiotic countertransference, although the therapist still has feelings about the patient.

Accentuation of the Great Gulf of Inequality Between Therapist and Patient

Here the patient repeatedly and almost constantly emphasizes the difference in gender, religion, value system, intelligence, competence, approach to treatment, and medications, especially as the two parties experience closeness in the relationship or as the patient becomes aware of some similarities that may exist between the two of them. Movements toward differentiation represent a closer approximation of the patient and therapist status, which leads to enhancement of feelings of the patient's self-esteem.

The above groupings are ways of coming to understand the phenomenology of schizophrenia as these derive from issues around fusion or the attempt to maintain a sense of differentiation, of self representation from object representation. They become useful ways of approaching treatment and also for research methodology, as discussed below.

Treatment Implications

The application of the above concepts to treatment can be found in detail in a previous publication (Schulz, 1975). One important value of the concept of understanding treatment from the framework of development is the provision of a common frame of reference for the various members of the treatment team. Not only in individual psychotherapy are these formulations relevant, but more importantly they provide nursing staff, teachers, activities therapists, and others involved in the treatment effort a frame of reference that can lead to an integrated approach to treatment, whereby each discipline can be working in a synergistic fashion. Each aspect of the treatment team can make its own individual contribution and at the same time avoid working at cross-purposes. I give only a brief clinical example from my previously mentioned paper (1975). It illustrates how self–object differentiation concepts can be utilized in the therapy of a patient and how this intervention by the psychotherapist can also be understood by the nursing personnel.

I would like to illustrate the importance of communication through the example of a severely ill schizophrenic young man who, over the course of our individual therapy sessions, repeatedly requested a decrease in his medication dosage. Eventually, we were able to see that he introduced this complaint whenever he felt that the two of us were getting closer, either through my understanding him or his feeling more trust in me. He reported a parallel situation that occurred during a visit by his mother. They had gotten along unusually well during this visit and were having lunch together. She began to complain when he started using his fingers to eat his salad. Reexamining the sequence, we could clearly see how the use of his fingers was a way of annoying her and recreating distance between them. His sense of separateness had been threatened by the convivial closeness of the immediately preceding events. In another session the patient reported a comparable interchange with the charge nurse on his hall. He spoke of how she had urged him to clean up his room, but he thought it was clean enough. When I offered to go with him at the conclusion of the session so we could evaluate this together, he laughed and declined, saying that he would clean it up. He then described how the charge nurse had come to his room and had a quite meaningful discussion with him. During the course of their talk, she requested that he take a shower, generally pay more attention to his appearance and, again, that he straighten up his room. He did take the shower, combed his hair and put on a clean shirt, but by drawing the line at cleaning his room he was reinstating a differentiation of himself from the nurse. Our discussion of this interaction enabled him to straighten up his room. However, I took it one step further by meeting with the nurse and explaining to her the reasons for his failure to carry out her suggestion initially. We discussed the dynamics of his need to maintain some sense of differentiation and to avoid being overpowered or swallowed up by the other person through this negativistic type of approach. I connected for her the examples of his complaint about the tranquilizer, the salad incident with his mother, and his not cleaning up his room. While this vignette illustrates several points, the one I am emphasizing here is the importance of coordinating the entire treatment approach by sharing with the rest of the treatment staff the insights gained in the psychotherapeutic session [pp. 48–49].

The concepts derived from developmental theory of self–object fusion and differentiation have already played an important role in the understanding and treatment of negativistic patients. Often these patients have been regarded as "unsuitable for," "unavailable to," or "not yet ready for" a dynamic psychotherapy approach. Those clinicians used to working with neurotic patients have been unable to establish a similar "therapeutic alliance" with the disturbed or negativistic patient. However, if one keeps in mind the threat to the patient's self identity, one can allow optimal distance and at the same time help the patient observe the defensive functioning of his behavior at those times when fusion is about to occur.

References

Burnham, D., Gladstone, A., & Gibson, R. (1969), *Schizophrenia and the Need–Fear Dilemma*. New York: International Universities Press.

Federn, P. (1952), *Ego Psychology and the Psychoses*. New York: Basic Books.

Fraiberg, S. (1969), Libidinal object constancy and mental representation. *The Psychoanalytic Study of the Child*, 24:9–47. New York: International Universities Press.

Freud, S. (1923), The ego and the id. *Standard Edition*, 19:12–66. London: Hogarth Press, 1961.

Hartmann, H. (1953), Contribution to the metapsychology of schizophrenia. In: *Essays on Ego Psychology*. New York: International Universities Press, 1964.

Jacobson, E. (1954), Contribution to the metapsychology of psychotic identification. *J. Amer. Psychoanal. Assn.*, 2:239–261.

James, W. (1890), *The Principles of Psychology*. New York: Dover.

Kernberg, O. (1970), A psychoanalytic classification of character pathology. *J. Amer. Psychoanal. Assn.*, 18(4):800–822.

Klein, M. (1955), The psycho-analytic play technique: Its history and significance. In: *New Directions in Psychoanalysis*, ed. M. Klein, P. Heimann, & R. Money-Kyrk. New York: Basic Books.

Kohut, H. (1971), *The Analysis of the Self*. New York: International Universities Press.

Lampl-de Groot, J. (1963), Symptom formation and character formation. *Internat. J. Psycho-Anal.*, 44 (Part1):342–343.

Mahler, M. (1968), *On Human Symbiosis and the Vicissitudes of Individuation*, Vol. 1. New York: International Universities Press.

——— (1971), A study of the separation–individuation process. *The Psychoanalytic Study of the Child*, 26:403–424. New York: Quadrangle.

——— Pine, F., & Bergman, A. (1975), *The Psychological Birth of the Human Infant*. New York: Basic Books.

Masterson, J. (1976), *Psychotherapy of the Borderline Adult*. New York: Bruner/Mazel.

Rapaport, D. (1951), The autonomy of the ego. *Bull. Menn. Clinic*, 15:113–123.

Schafer, R. (1973), The experience of separation-individuation in infancy and its reverberations through the course of life. 2. Adolescence and maturity. *J. Amer. Psychoanal. Assn.*, 21(1):157–159.

Schulz, C. (1975), An individualized psychotherapeutic approach with the schizophrenic patient. *Schizo. Bull.*, 13:46–69.

———— (1980), All or none phenomena in the psychotherapy of severe disorders. In: *The Psychotherapy of Schizophrenia*, ed. J. S. Strauss, M. Bowers, T. W. Downey, F. Fleck, F. Jackson, & I. Levine. New York: Plenum, pp. 181–189.

———— (1976), Presentation of a clinical scale to assess self-object differentiation in psychotic patients. In: *Schizophrenia 75*, ed. J. Jorstad & E. Ugelstad. Norway: Lie & Co., pp. 387–396.

———— & Kilgalen, R. (1969), *Case Studies in Schizophrenia*. New York: Basic Books.

Searles, H. (1959), Integration and differentiation in schizophrenia: An overall view. *Brit. J. Med. Psychol.*, 32:261–281.

———— (1976), Psychoanalytic therapy with schizophrenic patients in a private-practice context. *Contemp. Psychoanal.*, 12(4):387–406.

Tausk, V. (1933), On the origin of the "Influencing Machine" in schizophrenia. *Psychoanal. Quart.*, 2:519–556.

16

The Narcissistic Character and Disturbances in the Holding Environment

ARNOLD H. MODELL, M.D.

When one attempts to describe a particular character type, one is immediately confronted with the limitations of the concept of character itself. The nosological entities implied in such terms as "borderline states," "narcissistic characters," and the more classical "transference neuroses" are not of course absolutely demarcated from each other; one must allow for transitional forms where assignment to one category or the other may not be possible. Yet in spite of this limitation we believe it possible for the clinician to establish such diagnostic differentiations with a fair degree of consistency. However, when the attempt is made to communicate these differential diagnoses to one's colleagues, the use of these terms tends to be idiosyncratic.

For this reason I wish to describe as carefully as I can what I mean by a narcissistic character. This designation may or may not coincide with the patient group defined as such by Kohut (1971, 1977), but I suspect that there are at least some overlapping similarities.

Psychoanalysts since Freud have used what can be called an operational method of establishing a diagnosis; that is, the applicable nosological categories are determined by means of the transference. Therefore a definitive diagnosis may not be established initially; it must await the unfolding of the analytic process. For example, Kohut has defined the syndrome of the narcissistic character by means of a particular transference formation based for the most part on a need for the affirmation of the self by the other (the mirror transference) or an externalization onto the other of grandiose and omnipotent aspects of the self (the idealizing transference). These selfobject transferences are rather uniform, in contrast to the almost infinitely variable content of the transference neurosis. This uniformity suggests that we are observing the re-creation of a developmental process. However, in addition to these aspects of the transference described by Kohut there is another obvious characteristic of the transference that I believe can be used for diagnostic purposes.

I am referring to the analyst's perception that the patient is in a state of nonrelatedness. Here the observer's own emotional response may be used as a diagnostic instrument: one perceives that there are not two people in the consulting room—the patient acts as if the therapist is not there or, as if he or she is not there. The patient is turned off emotionally and does not use affects to communicate. When the analyst is continually in the presence of someone who does not seem interested in him or acts as if he is not there, he may experience this as an affront to his own narcissism and may accordingly become bored and sleepy. Although this may be defensive, it is a very human response to the patient's state of nonrelatedness and can be put to good use for diagnostic purposes.

The Cocoon

This state of nonrelatedness that the analyst perceives has, of course, its counterpart in the patient's endopsychic perception. The patient experiences a feeling of being cut off from the human environment—a sense of not really being in the world. As we shall describe more fully, this endopsychic perception is supported by an illusion of omnipotent self-sufficiency. I have used the metaphor of a cocoon to describe this, for a cocoon is a created environment that provides the potential for further growth and, more pointedly, must be attached to something that will serve as a future source of nourishment. Despite the attachment, the cocoon is insulated and walled off from its environment—there is no *apparent* interchange (Modell, 1968, 1975, 1976, 1985). In our patients this illusion of self-sufficiency is paradoxically accompanied by a profound dependency. Yet they are walled off so that nothing enters and nothing leaves; they are not able to give freely or receive affection, nor are they able to communicate or accept what is communicated. Some of my patients have, in describing themselves, used this metaphor of the cocoon. Others have felt themselves to be in a plastic bubble or mummy case, or behind a sheet of glass. The bell jar is no doubt another variant. They experience an illusion of self-sufficiency, whereby there is no necessity to relate to others. As one penetrates further, one learns that the sense of self-sufficiency is coupled to a magical illusion that they occupy a protected sphere removed from the dangers of the world—that is, removed from death and misfortune. In this sense they are "not really in the world."

This illusion of omnipotent self-sufficiency is buttressed by specific grandiose fantasies. One patient with moderate artistic ability believed himself to be an undiscovered Rembrandt; another identified himself with Jesus Christ; still another firmly believed that he was the most intelligent person in his profession. In many instances, as we shall see, these fantasies are reinforced by mothers who have an exaggerated and equally grandiose view of their children's capacities.

Psychoanalysts believe that the sense of unrelatedness is a leading clue to the diagnosis of the narcissistic character. We must acknowledge, however, that it is possible to be misled. Some patients appear to be relating to us who in fact are not, and after some time we begin to discern that the affects that are communicated are not in fact genuine; rather, they are based on a need to comply, to provide the analyst whatever is expected. I am not suggesting that this compliance is consciously manipulative; the patient, too, is cut off from awareness of his genuine feelings. Anger may be feigned, and the patient's tears do not move us. Indeed we may discover that an entire phase of what we had presumed to be genuine transference affects proves to be false. What I am describing here corresponds, I believe, to Winnicott's concept of the false self (1965).

In some patients, feelings are used to artificially counteract the fear of deadness of the self. For example, patients may induce a seemingly never ending series of environmental crises whose function one eventually learns is to create a surfeit of affects to reassure themselves that they are not psychically "dead."

Noncommunication and the Fear of Merging

The cocoon—the state of nonrelatedness—can be understood in another context as a defense against communication. Some patients fill the hour with talk—talk from which the affective charge is removed so that the analyst feels as if he is drowning in a sea of words. Others appear to communicate, but one senses that this talk is not going anywhere. On closer examination, one observes that sentences are often broken off in the middle and that if one responds to the patient's communication, the subject is switched to another area, sometimes rather subtly.

We all know that a love relationship is promoted through the sharing of oneself, that is, the sharing of what is ordinarily kept hidden. This sharing of secrets promotes and strengthens an object tie. The corollary is that the nonsharing of one's inner life will defend and protect against the closeness of an object tie. One can observe regularly that, in this patient group, a close love relationship is sensed as dangerous, for it threatens the integrity of the self. They fear a loss of their autonomy, that they will be "swallowed up," dominated, and controlled. Behind the fear of being swallowed up we believe there is a regressive wish to merge with the other, to surrender the self to someone who will hold them and protect them from the dangers of the outside world. The fight for their autonomy is more acute because they sense their wish to surrender. Our patients believe (with some justification) that one's inner life is the *only* thing that cannot be controlled by others. The autonomy of the self is in this respect preserved by feelings which must be kept secret and hidden. If such feelings are exposed, our patients report, there is the danger that their sense of self may be shattered.

One woman described feeling as if her sense of self were an egg: to share her feelings would be to crack herself open, and the precious yolk would run out and be lost. What I am describing is the well-known phenomenon of narcissistic vulnerability.

In addition to the fear of being controlled, there is also the fear of being humiliated. This again may be the consequence of an actual earlier experience with unempathic parents who were insensitive to the child's inner life. The experience is akin to casting one's pearls before swine—the failure of an empathic response threatens the existence of the sense of self. Kohut (1971, 1977) has stressed this observation, and I have placed the need for positive mirroring in the context of affective communication (Modell, 1985).

The Analytic Setting as a "Holding Environment"

The psychoanalyst is in a certain sense analogous to a naturalist observer, an ethologist who sits behind a blind day after day, for months on end, recording what he observes. But unlike the ethologist, who can observe his animals with a minimum of involvement, the analyst is a participant observer. For example, the analyst makes use of his own affective response to the patient's state of nonrelatedness as a diagnostic instrument (Modell, 1975). This means, I believe, that the perception (or nonperception) of affects is the primary source of psychoanalytic data. Accordingly, the affects of the transference are the primary field of observation.

The concept of transference, as originally described by Freud (1912), referred to the artificial neurosis, induced by the psychoanalytic procedure itself, in which specific elements of the patient's earlier childhood neurosis are externalized and transferred to the analyst. But there is a different type of transference repetition that is largely a post-Freudian observation and perhaps for this reason is not widely accepted or recognized. This is the observation that the analyst's work with the patient—that is, the actuality of the analytic setting and the analytic procedure—forms the basis of an object relationship which, in a manner similar to the transference neurosis, may

artificially re-create the disturbances of earlier object relationships. This point of view was suggested by the work of Spitz
(1956), Loewald (1960), Balint (1968), Zetzel (1970), and Gitelson (1973), among others. The view that the analytic setting
is an object relationship is expressed perhaps most vividly in
Winnicott's evocative term, the "holding environment" (1965).
This term is not limited to the *actual* holding of the infant or
child, as it includes the *symbolic* holding that occurs with the
mother's use of empathy. Winnicott perceived that the holding
environment could be taken as a metaphor for certain aspects
of the psychoanalytic situation. In this extended definition, the
"holding" referred to the caretaking function of both parents
in relation to the older child as well as the infant. The holding
environment provides an illusion of safety and protection, an
illusion that depends on the bonds of affective communication
between parent and child. The holding further suggests not
only protection from the dangers of the external world but
also from internal dangers, through the setting of limits, as
exemplified by the parent who holds a child in the throes of a
temper tantrum. Further, the holding environment provides a
potential gratification of the patient's wish to merge.

I am not suggesting, and there is considerable confusion
concerning this point, that the patient actually regresses in the
analytic setting back to the age of, say, 2 or 3. Instead I am
suggesting a symbolic or metaphorical equivalent. For example,
the mystical oceanic experience of merging with the universe
and abandoning the sense of self is a repetition of a very early
mother–child experience before the sense of separateness has
been firmly established (Mahler, 1968). Despite the origin of
this experience in early development, it is a common feature in
many religions. It would be foolish to suggest that the religious
adult who experiences merging has in fact regressed to the
first years of life. The oceanic experience is testimony that the
experience of merging can persist into adult life with no necessary pathological implications. There are many ways in which
the analytic setting symbolically re-creates the holding environment. First there is the analyst's intuitive understanding, his
empathy. As Winnicott (1965) put it, "The analyst is holding
the patient and this often takes the form of conveying in words

at the appropriate moment something that shows that the analyst knows and understands the deepest anxiety that is being experienced or waiting to be experienced" (p. 240). The analyst's empathy is then understood as part of the holding environment.

Consideration of the analytic setting as a holding environment is part of a larger theory of the therapeutic action of psychoanalysis in which the analytic setting and the analyst's activity symbolically re-creates elements of developmental conflict (Modell, 1985). Conflicts concerning merging and separateness can be symbolically re-created and thus reexperienced in small doses. If we understand the psychoanalytic setting as a symbolic recapitulation of early mother-child and parent-child relationships, we know that mothers cannot omnipotently meet the child's needs. This relative failure promotes the sense of autonomy and separateness. At times when the child must take responsibility for communicating, it cannot rely only on its mother's empathic understanding. If the mother has met the infant's need without the infant's having had to indicate it, it would be as if the infant were still merged with the mother and she with the infant. "In this way," Winnicott (1965) says, "the mother, by being a seemingly good mother, does something worse than castrate the infant. The latter is left with two alternatives: either being in a permanent state of regression and of being merged with the mother, or else staging a total rejection of the mother, even of the seemingly good mother" (p. 51).

I have found that it is necessary, after a period of suitable preparation, gradually to confront the patient with the need to exert some efforts on their own behalf. I have discovered that in some instances it may be necessary to tell patients that analysis is possible only through the medium of affects, and affective communication is something the analyst cannot do for the patient. At suitable times patients need also to be reminded that they have some responsibility for the actual work of the analysis; that is, the analyst cannot do it for them omnipotently. These confrontations are made, of course, without any moral implications and are stated as simple matters of fact. In these developmental struggles the analyst may be used by the patient as a surrogate of the reality principle. The timing of these confrontations is of the utmost importance. What I am describing, of course, is the transition from a state of fusion or merging to a state involving two persons; this developmental struggle is essential for the patient's establishment of what is inside and what is outside, and contributes to their growing individuation.

I am proposing that the analytic setting provides a new beginning and a new outcome to a developmental disturbance. Again, I must emphasize that I am referring not to a literal recapitulation but to a symbolic capitulation. I have described the details of this phase of analysis elsewhere (Modell, 1976) and will limit myself here to two observations: (1) this process of establishing separateness is accompanied by rage; and (2) when this phase is successfully traversed, the entire climate of the analysis and the analytic relationship is perceived to have changed. Instead of the sense of absence and nonrelatedness there is now a feeling that affects are genuine and communicated—there are now two people present, both engaged in the work of the analysis. The patient reports a greater sense of separateness, with some relief despite the storminess of this phase of the analysis.

Allow me to summarize what I have observed to be the core of the psychopathology in the narcissistic character. The state of illusory self-sufficiency that I have called the cocoon is paradoxically accompanied by its very opposite, that is, a sense of fusion and merging with the analyst (see Khan, 1974). I have pictured this visually to myself as a sphere within a sphere. There is the sphere of the cocoon—the illusory self-sufficiency—held within the larger sphere of the analytic holding environment. The cocoon is supported by an illusory grandiose sense of self that is fragile and easily disrupted. The major analytic work occurs around the process of individuation and the development of a true sense of autonomy. That is to say, the illusory protection of the analytic setting as a holding environment and the fantasy that the patient is fused or merged to the analyst become a focus of the analysis and are then disrupted by means of the natural disillusionment that occurs when wishes come into conflict with an immovable reality. In some instances this naturally occurring process must be reinforced by the analyst's confrontation (see Kernberg, 1974).

When there is a sense of two separate participants, transference interpretations become effective in terms of their ostensible content (see Modell, 1985). This entire process, I believe, recapitulates the oscillation that occurs in mother–child interactions, an oscillation in which empathy (that is, the illusion of omnipotent understanding supporting the sense of being merged) is counterbalanced by the need to communicate in order to be understood, a need that promotes individuation.

As noted above, this unfolding of the analytic process with narcissistic patients can be used as a nosological marker to distinguish these patients from "classical" cases. In the initial phase of the analysis, a phase which may extend for one or more years, the analytic setting functions as a holding environment and provides a new and different object relationship from that experienced by the patient in childhood. But empathy and intuitive understanding, as we have seen, may reinforce a regressive trend, and it is necessary for the analyst to traverse the very difficult middle period that promotes individuation and a sense of separateness. Problems of separateness and individuation are of course universal and appear in every psychoanalysis, but in the narcissistic character these problems take center stage.

Developmental History

The reconstruction of patients' early developmental history requires of us a greater degree of inference than is necessary for our immediate experience of the transference. Patients' memories of their early relationships are of necessity distorted. However, once we have known them over many years and can understand their defensive need to distort their early history, it is possible to form some estimate of their parents' characters and the quality of their interaction with the patient. I recognize that the validity of historical reconstructions made by means of the analytic method has been the subject of recent debate. Some (e.g., Spence, 1982) assert that it is impossible to accept as *historical* truth anything our patients tell us or, for that matter, anything we are able to reconstruct; all we can observe, they argue, is *narrative* truth. This assertion, in my opinion, is a gross over-statement. In the analyses I have conducted with narcissistic personalities, a certain configuration tends to emerge. Most characteristically, one parent is emotionally absent or distant, while the other is overinvolved with the patient to the point of intrusion. These intrusions, as I shall describe, imply a lack of sensitivity or respect for the child's need for autonomy and separateness. In some cases, states of emotional absence and intense intrusiveness may alternate in the same parent.

One patient's mother was constantly "all over him." She had an exaggerated view of his talent and intellect, thinking him capable of becoming a Rhodes Scholar, although he possessed a very ordinary intelligence. She undressed in front of him until he entered puberty, as if he were not a separate person and it did not matter. His father, though aloof, distant, and uncommunicative, was covertly seductive during the patient's latency years, often leaving pornographic material where his son could find it. In another case this pattern was reversed. For days the mother would be emotionally unavailable, being withdrawn and practically speechless, while the father was extremely intrusive. He was physically so, taking his son into his bed, and in other ways did not accept the patient's separateness. He imposed his own unfulfilled grandiose wishes on the boy, literally expecting that he would hold high political office and controlling his life accordingly. In yet another case, the parents did not recognize or respect the patient's bodily autonomy. The mother toilet trained the patient by inserting rectal suppositories from the age of 6 months whenever they were thought to be needed. During the patient's latency years her father bathed her, often rubbing the inside of her vagina to the point of pain. Her body was not her private property.

The human holding environment, I believe, is a protective environment both real and illusory. It is a real protection in the sense that significant information is conveyed from parent to child through the medium of affects. If the parents are in a state of affective unrelatedness, they cannot be relied on to provide this information. Some of our patients were able to observe in early childhood that their mothers were "off." One patient who was intellectually precocious observed at the age of

2 or 3 that his mother was mad, although this fact was not acknowledged by others. In other instances, patients observed their mothers to be flighty, fatuous, and silly. The parents' faulty judgment, coupled with an incapacity to communicate, means that the child cannot depend on the parents as a protective holding environment.

I have hypothesized, along with Khan (1974), that this relative failure of the human holding environment results in a precocious maturation. It is as if the child is saying to himself, "I cannot rely on my mother's judgment; therefore I have to be a better mother to myself." This self-mothering takes the form of fantasies of omnipotent self-sufficiency which underlie the psychic cocoon described above. This sense of self, based as it is on omnipotence, is fragile and vulnerable and easily disrupted. It represents a precocious separation from the mother, a separation that is not a true separation, as it is accompanied by a continued yearning to merge which is recapitulated in the transference.

How is this different from the borderline case? If we return for a moment to the use of the analyst's perception of affects as a method of diagnosis, the sense of boredom and sleepiness that one experiences with the narcissistic character stands in marked contrast to the therapist's countertransference in the presence of a borderline patient. In the latter situation, the analyst not infrequently experiences intense affects. The analyst may experience anxiety, depression, guilt, or rage and may at first believe that these affects have their origin within himself. Later he learns that in some as yet poorly understood fashion he is reacting to affects that have their origin within the patient. The analyst may react to these affects even though they remain outside the patient's awareness. This process has long been recognized by Kleinian analysts, who have given it the name of projective identification.

These observations suggest certain structural differences between borderline and narcissistic patients. The narcissistic patient seems to have achieved precocious closure vis-à-vis the environment, while the borderline seems to remain an open system. Anna Freud (1959) used the concept of an open system to refer to a state of connectedness between the child and the environment prior to the internalization of psychic structure. By contrast, the narcissistic patient may have achieved a precocious but fragile closure. Narcissistic patients act as if they need nothing from others and hence do not communicate their affects, in contrast to borderlines, who at times convey an intense affect hunger and seek a state of connectedness. In the one case we may remain bored, sleepy, and indifferent, while in the other we respond with intense affects that we sense the patient has placed in us. I believe, along with Winnicott (1965), that the borderline state may result from a failure of the maternal environment in the first or second year of life and that this relative failure of an object relationship results in the miscarriage of the normal process of identification, a failure to take something in, leading to a relative absence of structuralization. The environmental disturbances in the borderline case may be relatively massive as compared to the more subtle disturbances in the holding environment that are experienced by the narcissistic character.

I do not wish to imply, however, that there is a simple one-to-one correspondence or linear relationship between environmental trauma and the formation of character. It is quite possible for similar traumatic events to have quite different outcomes in character formation, and genetic factors as yet unrecognized may contribute to differences in temperament, especially the capacity to bear psychic pain. I can only report that in all the cases I have treated who can be thought of as narcissistic personalities, a disturbance in the parental holding environment has been in evidence; this suggests that a disturbance of this sort may be a necessary though perhaps not sufficient precondition for this type of character formation.

Some Observations Concerning Psychotherapy

The observations presented here come almost entirely from patients treated in psychoanalysis. Although I have also treated such patients in psychotherapy and believe that significant gains can be made using that modality, psychoanalysis remains the treatment of choice if the patient is sufficiently motivated and it is otherwise feasible. While it is important not to blur the distinctions between psychotherapy and psychoanalysis, the following general observations concerning treatment apply equally to both.

I have described how the holding environment, which is based on a fantasy of the analyst's omnipotence, gradually gives way to a stage of disillusionment and conflict with reality which may require the use of confrontation. This phase of the treatment promotes individuation and results in a greater sense of separateness. But this middle phase must be preceded by a long period in which the therapist accepts the patient's nonrelatedness. During this period the therapist also conveys an understanding of the defensive nature of the patient's noncommunication. If confrontation is necessary, its proper timing is essential. Although the optimal timing of a confrontation cannot be given by a general rule, there comes a time when the patient is ready to move forward, and there is also a time when the therapist's tolerance of the continued state of nonrelatedness becomes strained. It is quite possible that the patient will unconsciously provide, through manipulation of the therapist's countertransference, a signal that he is ready to move forward.

The phenomenology regarding the communication or noncommunication of affects takes a variety of forms. One position may be described as a comfortable state of nonrelatedness, analogous to the position of a child playing comfortably in the assurance that the mother is in the next room. It is a state of absence in the protective presence of another person; communication is not necessary if there is a belief that a magical contiguity exists between patient and therapist.

Another position is perhaps the very opposite: there is an intense wish to communicate, but the patient's cut off and unable to do so. One patient described a dream in which he is drowning in a swimming pool while his mother stands there on the edge and does nothing. The greatest danger was of imprisonment within the cocoon of self-sufficiency; there was a desperate desire to communicate, but an inability to do so. In a third position the anxiety stems not from the inability to communicate but from a fear of intrusion—a fear that the sharing of affects will fracture and destroy the self. Here the patient suffers not so much from imprisonment as from the fear that his fortress will be breached.

These fundamental dilemmas concerning relatedness lead to corresponding dilemmas for technique. If the patient desperately wishes to communicate but is unable to do so, the therapist's passivity may be experienced as an abandonment, as in the dream in which the patient's mother stands by and watches him drown. Alternatively, if the patient's predominant fear is that of intrusion, the therapist's activity will be experienced as threatening the very existence of the self. It is at these times that interpretation itself is experienced as a danger. It can be understood that these patients require us to use all of our empathic and intuitive skills to assess which position predominates at any given time in the treatment. Because of this nearly insoluble dilemma, many of the patient's defensive maneuvers will be directed toward regulation of the optimal distance and closeness. I shall return to this point.

Another issue the therapist must face is that of the negative therapeutic reaction—the observation that every step forward is accompanied by a step backward. We usually understand such a reaction as an indication of the power of unconscious guilt. In earlier papers (Modell, 1965, 1971) I described what can be called separation guilt—that is, the guilt that accompanies the process of individuation, based in part on the fantasy that to have something for oneself means that someone else in the nuclear family will be deprived. With some patients there is a clear belief that to become a separate person will injure the mother or actually lead to her death.

In the narcissistic character the negative effects of a "good hour" may be understood in relation to the need to regulate distance. The conflict concerning the communication of affects has been understood in part as a reflection of extreme narcissistic vulnerability—the belief that the sense of self is dependent on the response of others. If one expresses and shares love, the other has the power to absolutely fracture and devastate one's sense of self. In such patients the fear of expressing positive feelings, loving feelings, far outweighs the fear of their rage and negativity. This means that after a "good hour," one in which there is a sense of relatedness and working together, there is frequently—in some instances, invariably—a "bad hour." This negativity of course takes different forms. The patient may retreat into the cocoon or may act out in various ways known to be obnoxious to the therapist. Indeed, obnoxiousness as a character trait may in certain instances be understood in this context. But whatever form the negativity takes, it has as its purpose the regulation of distance. The therapist must understand this process, for otherwise he may be defeated and discouraged. He must learn to expect this to-and-fro movement in the therapy as a matter of course, and its function must be communicated to the patient.

A Sociological Note

Whether the ecology of the neuroses, variations in the incidence of character types, is linked to specific cultural changes is a problem for the historian and sociologist. The clinician, although he cannot prove the truth of his impressions, can offer an opinion on these matters. Among psychoanalysts there is considerable difference of opinion regarding the source of our current interest in narcissistic personalities. Is it the consequence of certain advances in the theory of narcissism, which have simply allowed us to identify more individuals in what remains a stable population, or of certain tendencies in contemporary culture that contribute to an actual increase in their numbers. As for myself, I favor the latter hypothesis. The narcissistic character seems gradually to be displacing the so-called classical case, which now has become something of a rarity, as the psychopathological type most characteristic of our time (for similar opinions, see Green, 1975; Kohut, 1977).

There is here an apparent paradox: if the etiology of the narcissistic character is understood as a response to disturbances in the parental holding environment, how can we assert that the increase in frequency of narcissistic disorders reflects a historical or cultural process? The psychoanalyst's field of vision is such that he does not directly observe sociological or historical processes. We must admit that we can only speculate about the interconnection between the development of the individual in a changing culture. I have discussed these issues in greater detail elsewhere (Modell, 1985).

Although the relation between character change and society remains obscure, the problem was noted in a remarkably prescient book published almost three decades ago; I refer to *The Lonely Crowd* (Riesman, Glazer, and Denney, 1950), which described a shift in the American character (although the problem is not limited to the United States) from inner-directedness to other-directedness. Their description of the latter is remarkably similar to what we observe in the narcissistic character, whose personality organization is based on compliance and inauthenticity. We must admit that we do not know the pathways of interconnection between the development of the individual and a culture in which such personality defenses are eminently adaptive.

References

Balint, M. (1968), *The Basic Fault*. London: Tavistock.

Freud, A. (1959), Lecture to the Los Angeles Psychoanalytic Society. Rep. H. Tausend. *Bull. Phila. Assn. Psychoanal.*, 9:111–112.

Freud, S. (1912), The dynamics of transference. *Standard Edition*, 12:99–108. London: Hogarth Press, 1958.

Gitelson, M. (1973), On the curative factors in the first phase of analysis. In: *Psychoanalysis: Science and Profession*. New York: International Universities Press, pp. 311–341.

Green, A. (1975), The analyst, symbolization and absence in the analytic setting. *Internat. J. Psycho-Anal.*, 51:1–22.

Kernberg, O. (1974), Further contributions to the treatment of narcissistic personalities. *Internat. J. Psycho-Anal.*, 55:215–240.

Khan, M. (1974), *The Privacy of the Self*. New York: International Universities Press.

Kohut, H. (1971), *The Analysis of the Self*. New York: International Universities Press.

——— (1977), *The Restoration of the Self*. New York: International Universities Press.

Loewald, H. (1960), On the therapeutic action of psychoanalysis. *Internat. J. Psycho-Anal.*, 41:16–33.

Mahler, M. (1968), *On Human Symbiosis and the Vicissitudes of Individuation*. New York: International Universities Press.

Modell, A. (1965), On having the right to a life. *Internat. J. Psycho-Anal.*, 46:323–331.

——— (1968), *Object Love and Reality*. New York: International Universities Press.
——— (1971), The origin of certain forms of pre-oedipal guilt and the implications for a psychoanalytic theory of affects. *Internat. J. Psycho-Anal.*, 52:337–346.
——— (1975), A narcissistic defense against affects and the illusion of self-sufficiency. *Internat. J. Psycho-Anal.*, 56:275–282.
——— (1976), The "holding environment" and the therapeutic action of psychoanalysis. *J. Amer. Psychoanal. Assn.*, 24:285–307.
——— (1985), *Psychoanalysis in a New Context*. New York: International Universities Press.
Riesman, D., Glazer, N., & Denney, R. (1950), *The Lonely Crowd*. New York: Doubleday Anchor.
Spence, D. (1982), *Narrative Truth and Historical Truth*. New York: Norton.
Spitz, R. (1956), Countertransference. *J. Amer. Psychoanal. Assn.*, 4:256–265.
Winnicott, D. W. (1965), *The Maturational Processes and the Facilitating Environment*. New York: International Universities Press.
Zetzel, E. (1970), The concept of transference. In: *The Capacity for Emotional Growth*. New York: International Universities Press, pp. 168–181.

Name Index

519

Subject Index

531